CALL ME
DAVE

Also by Michael Ashcroft

Pay Me Forty Quid and I'll Tell You:
The 2015 Election Campaign Through the
Eyes of the Voters (2015)

Special Ops Heroes (2014)

Heroes of the Skies (2012)

George Cross Heroes (2010)

Minority Verdict: The Conservative Party,
the Voters, and the 2010 Election (2010)

Special Forces Heroes (2008)

Victoria Cross Heroes (2006)

Dirty Politics, Dirty Times (2005)

Smell the Coffee: A Wake-Up Call for
the Conservative Party (2005)

www.lordashcroft.com
www.lordashcroftpolls.com
www.lordashcroftmedals.com
@LordAshcroft

Also by Isabel Oakeshott

Farmageddon (with Philip Lymbery, 2014)

Inside Out (with Peter Watt, 2010)

CALL ME
DAVE

THE UNAUTHORISED BIOGRAPHY OF
DAVID CAMERON

MICHAEL ASHCROFT *&*
ISABEL OAKESHOTT

Biteback Publishing

This new edition published in Great Britain in 2016 by
Biteback Publishing Ltd
Westminster Tower
3 Albert Embankment
London SE1 7SP

ISBN 978-1-78590-022-8

10 9 8 7 6 5 4 3 2 1

A CIP catalogue record for this book is available from the British Library.

Set in Sabon by Adrian McLaughlin

Printed and bound in Great Britain by
CPI Group (UK) Ltd, Croydon CR0 4YY

CONTENTS

Preface to the Second Edition

by Michael Ashcroft

When I began work on this biography with Isabel Oakeshott early in 2014, many thought it likely that voters would remove our subject from Downing Street in little more than a year. By the time *Call Me Dave* was published the following September, David Cameron had been re-elected as Prime Minister with an overall majority. At that point, by contrast, few expected that his premiership would be over just nine months later. This updated edition, then, is not just an opportunity to record the story of the referendum that led to his downfall, but an unforeseen chance to reflect on his whole leadership of the Conservative Party and the country.

As I set out in the first edition of this book, my relationship with Cameron has not been easy. We first met in 2005, when he was running for leadership of the party and I was on the board. He impressed me, as he did when we met again that year, shortly after his victory. He had read *Smell the Coffee*, my analysis of the Tories' third consecutive general election defeat, and was determined to act on my two main conclusions: that the party needed to be more focused and disciplined in the way it used its campaign resources, and that it had to grasp how it had come to be seen by voters who ought to have been its supporters. He asked me to help implement these lessons by becoming deputy chairman of the party with responsibility for its private research and its campaign in target seats. I was delighted to accept.

After some wrangling over where my team and I would be based – I had wanted us to work from my Cowley Street office – we moved into Conservative Campaign Headquarters at 30 Millbank, where we remained until the 2010 election. Cameron and I talked regularly during this time, and it was during one of these discussions that I believe we agreed the type of role that I would play were he to become Prime Minister. I made a full, contemporaneous note of our conversation. My tense relationship with Cameron since 2010 dates back to that time, because it transpired that we each had, shall we say, a different understanding of what we had agreed.

A few days after arriving at No. 10, he telephoned to thank me for the work I had done. In a very tight election, our operation in the target constituencies had delivered seats that would not have been won on a uniform swing, so we could take some credit for helping to make the Conservatives the biggest party in the new parliament. I thanked him in turn, and asked what my next role would be.

'Ah, it's difficult,' he replied awkwardly. 'We probably need to have another conversation.' A few days later, after lunch at Chequers, he told me that Nick Clegg, leader of the Liberal Democrats and Deputy Prime Minister in the coalition government, had vetoed any position for me. After Clegg stepped down in 2015, we checked this version of events with his office. Clegg said he had no recollection of having barred any Conservative appointments. I was left with the feeling that Cameron had broken his promise to me, and anyone wondering why we have not been close since then need look no further for an explanation.

Even so, I am proud of the two assignments I completed at Cameron's request during his time in government: a strategic review of Britain's sovereign military bases in Cyprus, and the *Veterans' Transition Review*, which examined the provision for those leaving the forces and returning to civilian life. In both cases my recommendations were accepted and I am glad to have been able to make a contribution in these important fields.

Moreover, I want to be clear that my motivation for writing this book is not about settling scores, however sorry I was about what happened. When we began the project, the only biography of the Prime Minister, by Francis Elliott and James Hanning, had been written in 2007. It seemed time to produce a new one. I was anxious that the book should be objective, and I asked Isabel Oakeshott, then political editor of the *Sunday Times*, to co-author the work. Although Cameron discouraged his friends and colleagues (and indeed Isabel herself) from getting involved, I am pleased to say that a number of individuals close to him have helped, though some understandably on condition of anonymity. As has been the case with the extensive political polling I have published since 2010 – in which I regularly pointed out that Cameron remained his party's biggest asset – I hope readers will agree we have achieved our aim of being balanced and fair.

As for his legacy, it seems inevitable from our current standpoint that Cameron will be remembered as the Prime Minister who took Britain out of the European Union. Since I supported this outcome, it would be churlish for me to complain about it. Still, as some of his critics have since observed, the referendum itself was a symptom of his style of government: doing what was needed to get through the immediate crisis, and banking on his own ability to cope with the next one when it arose. Until then, it had worked. If his fate was inevitable once the Brexit result was clear, it can at least be said that he embraced it. He knew the game was up and did the right thing quickly, which is not something you can say about every politician every day.

Overall, Cameron was too lacking in vision; too exclusive in his leadership style; and achieved too little in foreign policy terms, to go down as a great Prime Minister. He may bitterly regret the way his premiership ended, but he has much of which to be proud. He formed the first coalition government of modern times and made a success of it. His government put the economy back on its feet after a disastrous financial crisis and a deep recession. He achieved an overall majority against the odds, and against historical precedent. Overcoming the electoral (if not material) disadvantage of his background, he became a Prime Minister people liked and were comfortable with. For the longer term, he understood the predicament in which the Conservative Party found itself and put it back in a position in which it could win elections.

Out of office before the age of fifty, his contribution to public life may not be over yet.

Michael Ashcroft
July 2016

ACKNOWLEDGEMENTS

Several hundred people kindly agreed to be interviewed for this book, many of whom asked not to be named. Accordingly we cannot identify everyone we would like to thank, but without the very many individuals who gave background interviews, *Call Me Dave* would not have been possible.

A number of figures who are happy to be associated with the project made an exceptional contribution, for which we are enormously grateful. Among those who were particularly generous with time, information and advice are: Andrew Cooper, the Conservative peer and former Downing Street director of strategy; Daniel Finkelstein, the Conservative peer and *Times* journalist; James O'Shaughnessy, the Conservative peer and former director of policy at Downing Street; Guy Black, the Conservative peer and former Conservative Party director of communications; Andrew Mitchell, the Tory MP and former Cabinet minister; Iain Duncan Smith, Secretary of State for Work and Pensions; Don Porter, the former chairman of the National Conservative Convention; Peter Cruddas, the former Tory Party treasurer; Graham Brady, chairman of the 1922 Committee; Henry Macrory, former head of press to David Cameron; and the journalist Bruce Anderson.

Contributions from former Chief of the Defence Staff, General Sir David Richards; Mayor of London Boris Johnson; former Carlton boss Michael Green; former Tory Party leader Michael Howard; former chair of the BBC Trust Chris Patten; former Chancellor Norman Lamont; veteran MP Sir Nicholas Soames; journalist James Delingpole; David Cameron's godfather Ben Glazebrook; BBC journalist Chris Berthoud; Conservative peer Michael Ancram; and former Director-General of the BBC Greg Dyke were also particularly appreciated.

Tom Gardner, our researcher, provided excellent briefing notes and editorial support including assistance with interviews and some drafting. Laura Hughes, now on the political team at the *Telegraph*, was an outstanding reporter for the project, tirelessly tracking down and charming sources, as well as enthusiastically transcribing endless interview recordings. Nick Mutch acted as researcher for the paperback edition and was a fantastic asset. The meticulous and indefatigable investigative journalist Margaret Crick turned up much valuable material and was a source of wise counsel. The political journalist Michael Crick offered important practical advice at the outset of this project, which was carefully noted and heeded. The journalist Will Stewart and his excellent team in Moscow connected us with current Kremlin and former KGB sources; while the French political journalist Charles Jaigu, of *Le Figaro*, dug deep into his contacts book to provide material from Paris. Nigel Rosser offered journalistic advice, ideas, moral support and an extremely critical eye. Jane Sherwood did picture research, and Witney-based photographer Barry Clack took great trouble to find unpublished images from his archive. Thanks also to the formidable Angela Entwistle and her team at Cowley Street, and Iain Dale and his team at Biteback.

Dan Ritterband; Guto Harri; Sir Henry Keswick; Harry Mount; Tim Allan; Adrian Hilton; Abdullah Rehman; Stanley Johnson; Sir Robert Balchin; Matthew Oakeshott; Matthew Elliott; Sean Kemp; Derek Laud; Christine Carder; Baroness Anne Jenkin; Alex Deane; Liz Leffman; Liz Reason; Mike Heenan; Danny Kruger; Ian Birrell; Linda and Francis Whetstone; Maxwell Beaverbrook; Sir Paul Stephenson; Garry Poulson; Marcus Warren; James Deen; Philip Basset; Steve Rathbone; Martin Popplewell; Ivan Massow; Ivo Daalder; Brendan Chilton; Ted Bromund; Dan Hannan; Tim Chatwin; Jack Grimston; James McGrath; Peter Riddell and Dominic Cummings all made valuable contributions.

Many MPs and former MPs assisted. They include Tory MPs Mark Field, Sir Alan Duncan, Boris Johnson, Liam Fox, Cheryl Gillan, Desmond Swayne, Conor Burns, Jacob Rees-Mogg, Adam Holloway, David Davis, Owen Paterson, John Redwood, Greg Clark, Kwasi Kwarteng and Bill Cash; and former Tory MPs Tim Yeo, Andrew Mackay, Andrew Robathan, Patrick Mercer, Ann Widdecombe and Greg Barker, and the former Labour MPs Denis MacShane, David Kidney and Shaun Woodward.

ACKNOWLEDGEMENTS

This list is far from exhaustive – many others helped the project in one way or another, and we are grateful to them all.

Finally, we should acknowledge Francis Elliott and James Hanning, whose own biography of Cameron, first published in 2007, was the starting point for our research. Their book made our job harder because it is so good.

PART ONE –
TO THE MANOR BORN

I

CHIPPING SNORTON

'Politicians are just like anyone else that gets promoted: we worry
deeply about being found out as too unimaginative, too idle or just
too stupid to do the job we've just been given.'

– David Cameron, 25 March 2004

New Year's Eve, 2008

In the grounds of a honeycomb-coloured Cotswold farm, thudding music
from a giant marquee reverberated into the night. Blacked-out Range
Rovers, the vehicle of choice for west Oxfordshire's wealthy, spread across
a field like a row of small tanks, unremarkable next to the sleek limousines
and sports cars with their personalised number plates. Under black skies,
shadowy figures pulled on cigarettes – chauffeurs, collars turned up against
the cold, braced for a long night.

The setting was a property in Sarsden, epicentre of the infamous Chipping
Norton set. Inside the marquee, more than 500 of the richest and most
powerful people in Britain were seeing in the New Year in style. The
Moroccan-themed tent was festooned with floor cushions. Beautiful people
draped over pouffes sipped drinks by flickering lamp light.

It was the annual New Year bash for 'the set', one of society's hottest
tickets, a party so exclusive and impenetrable by paparazzi that guests
conditioned to restraining themselves at social occasions for fear of
capture on camera were able to relax. They could be confident that whatever
happened in the marquee would stay in the marquee, for nobody in this
gilded circle risks ostracism by breaking the omerta that governs
social gatherings.

The guest list was hand-picked and tightly controlled by the stars of the set: TV personality Jeremy Clarkson; former Blur bassist turned gentleman farmer Alex James and his wife Claire Neate; racehorse trainer Charlie Brooks and his glamorous sister Annabel, and the Queen Bee of them all: Rebekah Wade. Flame-haired protégée of Rupert Murdoch; friend of prime ministers; partner of Chipping Norton racehorse trainer and Old Etonian Charlie Brooks; and editor of *The Sun*, she was one of the most powerful and best-connected women in the land. Every potential invitee required the approval of all – a process designed to ensure nobody inappropriate slipped through the net.

Among the guests that night was David Cameron, then Leader of the Opposition, and his wife Samantha, who live a mile or two away in the hamlet of Dean, a cluster of pretty villages above a shady dell. There too were shadow Chancellor George Osborne and his wife Frances; Andy Coulson, former *News of the World* editor; Lord Black, former director of communications to Michael Howard; and Mark Bolland, former aide to the Prince of Wales. Other famous faces included television presenter Alan Yentob, and Mark Thompson, director-general of the BBC.

By the time Matthew Freud and his then wife Elisabeth Murdoch swept in, the party was in full swing – loud, boozy and perhaps not entirely free of class-A drugs. Who knows who might have brought such substances onto the premises (or turned a blind eye if they were in circulation)? Certainly not the hosts – but, fairly or unfairly, social gatherings among the upper echelons of society in this part of west Oxfordshire have acquired a reputation for featuring narcotics. So much so that some affectionately dub Chipping Norton 'Chipping Snorton'.

As the clock approached midnight, guests in varying condition trooped out of the marquee for a spectacular firework display. Many seemed euphoric, including Mrs Cameron. In the small hours of the morning on 1 January, she was giving it her all on the dancefloor; dragging on a cigarette; her husband nowhere to be seen.

Not everybody was happy, however. A newspaper executive well used to scenes of excess recalls being shocked at the concentration of power and money.

'It was incredible to see all these people letting their hair down. But something felt wrong. There were just too many people in too many powerful positions too close to each other. I remember saying to the person I was with, "This will end in tears." It wasn't right.'

Emerging from the loos later that evening, the former newsman, a working-class boy made good, bumped into Cameron.

'You're not one of us, are you?' the Leader of the Opposition quipped cheerfully. The guest was left wondering whether the remark was a reference to his politics, his social status, or both.

It is at such exclusive social occasions, in his constituency in Witney, that David Cameron can really be himself. In manor houses, converted barns, farmhouses and stately homes belonging to friends, the Prime Minister could kick off his shoes and let his guard down, safe in the knowledge that anyone with a long lens would first have to find him (no mean feat in an area replete with muddy farm tracks and unmarked country lanes) and then run the gauntlet of security cameras and electric gates.

Details of these parties rarely leak. Members of the gilded circle generally have a strong interest in keeping their mouths shut about the fascinating personal relationships between key players; their lavish lifestyles; and what they get up to behind closed doors. Theirs is a world of helicopters, domestic staff, summers in St Tropez and fine food from Daylesford, the organic farm shop owned by Lady Carole Bamford, wife of billionaire industrialist and Cameron supporter Sir Anthony Bamford. The Camerons would dip in and out, knowing the political damage too close an association could cause.

A first-hand account of a private Conservative Party fundraiser held at the Georgian stately home of Cameron's millionaire friend and neighbour Lord Chadlington, for example, makes unedifying reading. It took place a stone's throw from Cameron's own house in the tiny hamlet of Dean.

According to one dismayed attendee:

> There was a huge marquee full of ladies with big hair and even bigger jewellery. The entertainment for the evening was Dave in conversation with Jeremy Clarkson, who seemed to be smashed off his face. There was a lot of drink around. David was loving the whole laddishness of it. He was really, really playing up. Clarkson's opening line to Dave was, 'Come on; let's face it, no one in this tent could

care less about comprehensive schools. What they want to know is why organic milk is so expensive at Daylesford?' David tried to bluster his way out of it, but Clarkson just went on, saying things like, 'Seriously, Dave, everyone sends their kids to private schools...'

There are other embarrassing snippets. One member of the set has told how the Prime Minister became so inebriated at one late-night party that he lost his mobile phone.

'He was wandering around drunk, asking if anyone had seen it. I couldn't believe it,' she recalled.

When she feels as if she is in safe company, Samantha herself can be extraordinarily indiscreet, once regaling guests at a private party with a colourful account of how she and Cameron became so intoxicated on holiday in Morocco that they vomited.

Such was the character of the Prime Minister: an Old Etonian 'toff' most at ease among the super-wealthy after his own apparently effortless climb to the top. Political opponents were eager to exploit and propagate the image, portraying him as hopelessly privileged and out of touch. It is a stereotype he painstakingly avoided reinforcing in public (he was so anxious to avoid being seen in tails that he toyed with the idea of wearing normal work clothes to the wedding of Prince William and Kate Middleton), but appears to live up to behind closed doors. The events in Sarsden and at the home of Lord Chadlington are just a soupçon of life in the Chipping Norton set.

But if this is the 'real' David Cameron, a man at home with some very wealthy and louche characters, it is only a small part of the picture.

His may have been a tale of privilege, but his rise to the premiership was the result of some remarkable qualities, not least an unflinching self-belief, endless optimism and a rare political ability to attract – or at least not repel – many of those who would not normally vote Tory. Unlike Tony Blair, with his zealous interventionism driven by religious conviction, and Gordon Brown, with his black moods and roaring temper, Cameron remains a well-balanced character, which makes him harder to write about but lay at the heart of his electoral success.

He is the political product of the hopes and ambitions of others, too: exceptionally talented and ambitious friends and relatives who invested in him and helped propel him to the top. His bid for the premiership came as he was coping with not one but two personal traumas: a desperately disabled son and the personal difficulties of a close family member. With remarkable resilience and optimism, he made it to the top anyway, becoming the first leader of a coalition since the Second World War. Not only did he make the coalition last, he then defied all expectations and historical precedent to lead his party to victory in the 2015 general election. Had he failed – as pollsters and pundits predicted – he would have been the Prime Minister who never won an election. Instead, he was a winner, delivering the first Conservative majority since 1992.

Amid the shock and euphoria among Tory supporters, a new narrative quickly sprang up among his critics: that his remarkable career was the result of remarkable luck. This uncharitable interpretation characterised Cameron as the accidental beneficiary of a succession of political and economic events, in particular in Scotland, that he did little or nothing to control.

Can anyone really be this fortunate?

The alternative explanation for his achievements is that he made his own luck – just as he was the architect of his own eventual misfortune.

In fact, Cameron's rise to power began with the machinations of a small group of highly intelligent individuals who were determined to restore the fortunes of the Conservative Party in the face of Tony Blair's mighty Labour machine – and they identified Cameron as the most appropriate vehicle for their purpose.

His ascent reached its zenith in the early hours of 8 May 2015, when, seat by seat, up and down the country, the Conservative Party trounced the opposition. That general election result redefined him as a winner.

His nadir came little over a year later, when, around 3 a.m. on 24 June 2016, he was told he had lost the EU referendum He would announce his resignation hours later.

This is his life story thus far.

2

TWO SILVER SPOONS

*Cabinet minister: 'You were born with a silver spoon in your
mouth.'*
Cameron: 'No, I was born with two.'

By his own admission, David Cameron had an extremely comfortable
start in life. In a sign of the privilege to which he would become accus-
tomed, he made his entrance on 9 October 1966 not in an NHS hospital
– though there were plenty nearby – but in the London Clinic, off Harley
Street, a private hospital favoured by the royal family.

In the late 1960s, when it was customary for mothers and their newborns
to spend a week or longer in hospital, giving birth privately was a luxury
only the richest young couples could afford. A Cabinet colleague who once
teased that Cameron was born with a silver spoon in his mouth was amused
when he responded: 'No, I was born with two.'

His parents' wealth was both inherited and self-made. Though the
Camerons are not blue bloods, there are titles and big houses in the background, as well as the strong sense of public duty characteristic of solid
British families. Members of Samantha Cameron's much grander family wince
when they hear the Camerons described as 'upper class', but they are hardly
bourgeois: the Prime Minister is a fifth cousin (twice removed) of the Queen.[1]

His childhood home was in Peasemore, a village near Newbury in the
Berkshire Downs. His father Ian and mother Mary moved there when he was
a baby, after deciding they wanted to bring up their family in the countryside.

With his arrival they now had three children (a fourth would arrive in

1   Debrett's.

1971), and exchanged their grand house in Kensington (worth £5 million in 2015) for a lovely rectory.

In a sign of the strength of the family unit, several Camerons still live in the village today: Cameron's older brother Alex, now a successful QC, who lives at the Old Rectory with his wife Sarah and is chairman of Peasemore Parish Council; Mary, who lives in a smaller adjoining property; and, remarkably, Cameron's old nanny, Gwen Hoare, who also looked after Mary when she was little. Now in her mid-nineties, Gwen is a stalwart of the community, and only recently gave up delivering the parish newsletter. On her 90th birthday, her most successful young charge invited her to Chequers.

Once upon a time, Peasemore had a primary school and post office, but the school closed in the 1950s and the post office is long gone. Today, the population is just 300 and the village struggles to rustle up a cricket team. Though it is pretty enough, compared with the golden stone villages in Cameron's Cotswold constituency it is an unremarkable little place, where characterless red-brick new-builds sit alongside more attractive period properties. The thunder of the A34 never feels far away.

Hidden from public view behind high walls, Cameron's childhood home is a Grade II listed building with extensive grounds, including a tennis court and swimming pool, which would be ceremonially opened for summer every 1 May. There is also an elaborate pagoda, built by Cameron's father, which his friends called 'Ian's erection'.

Inside, the house is comfortable (though not ostentatiously plush – one visitor remembers the odd broken table) and furnished with decent antiques. Some were auctioned off in 2006, fetching a huge sum. Two eighteenth-century French paintings alone went for more than £1 million.

Cameron's upbringing there was quintessentially English, full of fresh air, croquet and homemade cakes. One childhood friend who came from less well-off stock and spent many happy summers lounging by the pool with him and his siblings was mesmerised by the old-fashioned wholesomeness of it all.

> To me it was like a fairy tale; like living in an Enid Blyton book. His mother would come out to the pool with jugs of homemade lemonade and freshly made cakes. It was just idyllic, the house was absolutely gorgeous, and they were very privileged – but very nice.

The pool was a focal point of the kids' life. We just hung out there… Dave was a very good swimmer and I remember him diving.

We spent time in the kitchen and of course there was an Aga and all that posh stuff. We played board games and cards by the pool. I don't remember watching TV; it wasn't that kind of era. We amused ourselves; I remember going on walks in the countryside and cycling, and going to the local shop for sweets.

The Old Rectory was always strewn with newspapers: the *Sporting Life* and the *Financial Times* were Ian's favourites, though he also liked *The Times*, and took *The Guardian* for its racing coverage.[2] In the living room was a glass-fronted – and very well-stocked – drinks cabinet, a source of temptation for Cameron and his friends as teenagers.

'I do remember we snuck some booze out of the cabinet one night,' says the friend. 'We nicked half a bottle of wine and drank it.' It was relatively innocent fun: they were too well brought up to binge.

To childhood friends, Ian and Mary seemed kind but a little remote. They recall Cameron and his siblings greeting their father rather formally and deferentially when he came home from work.

'I got the sense there was respect,' says one who used to play with Cameron as a child.

When Ian came home from work, everybody said, 'Hello, Daddy.' There was no talking back; I think Dave respected both his parents. Mary was quite frightening to me because she was so grand and proper. She was always impeccably dressed. She was quite abrupt with children; I don't know if she was particularly warm. She always seemed to be doing her own thing, she was very involved in the local church, and she was always involved with stuff in the village. They were all close, but I never saw any signs of affection, hugging and kissing and that kind of stuff.

Cameron was close to both parents but worshipped his father, whom he has described as a 'wonderful eccentric' and 'huge hero figure' in his life. Born with deformed legs, Ian was an extraordinary character: full of energy and

---

2   Harry Mount interview for the *Sunday Times Magazine*, 5 April 2015.

mischief, with a well-developed taste for the finer things in life. Cameron's godfather, Ben Glazebrook, who was one of Ian's oldest friends, says:

> I think Ian was the most extrovert person that I have ever known in my whole life. You know he was born with those stumpy legs? Well, he wouldn't mind unscrewing a leg in front of everybody. There was no point in averting your eyes, because it was so natural somehow. Once, we were driving through Holland and he took his leg off and put it on the table.
>
> We went to the Maldives a lot, and Ian and Mary wanted to go to the Maldives, so Ian said, 'Give us a few tips?'
>
> I said, 'Well, look, it's an Islamic island, so don't take in any booze, because they will just confiscate it.'
>
> He said, 'Well, we might have a bit of a problem there: I always take a spare leg on holiday. It looks like a magnum of champagne under the security photographs. It's the same sort of shape.'

Home life followed a strict routine. Glazebrook says that there was 'never really any mucking about'.

'They would have to turn up for lunch at one o'clock, otherwise they got torn off a strip. You just had to obey the rules. You could call it a conventional upbringing,' he recalls.

While Ian commuted to his London office by train from Didcot, a trek that involved leaving the house at 7 a.m., Mary was largely based at home, though she was constantly busy with good works. The four siblings – Alex, Tania (two years older than Cameron) and Clare, who was born in 1971 – got on well. As very young children, they went to a private 'pre-prep' school, called Greenwood, in Newbury, to which they were driven every day by a rota of local mothers.[3] When they came home, they were given supper by Gwen.

Gwen's brother Bert, who at ninety-two is two years her junior, confirms what an important figure she has been for several generations of the family.

'She brought up the Camerons,' he says simply.

Ian would arrive home from work around 7 p.m. and, as the children grew up, the whole family would all sit down together to eat.

---

3   Francis Elliott and James Hanning, *Cameron: Practically a Conservative* (Fourth Estate, 2012), p. 10.

'There was lots of chat about the world', including some politics, Cameron has said of these family dinners, though neither parent was particularly party political.[4] Cameron himself was never short of words.

'He always had something to say, even when he was five or six,' his mother has recalled. 'We used to go on holiday with another family, and they used to say, "Can't you shut David up?"'[5]

Everyone in the village knew and liked the family. During school holidays, the children would roam the woods and fields with their Jack Russell dogs and get involved in whatever was going on in the village.

Jenny Mascall, who lives on a neighbouring farm and has known the family since Cameron was a toddler, says:

> They always joined in all the village things like the fête. My memo-
> ries are of Cameron in fancy dress aged about two…David's father
> was on the parish council for years and years. When the children
> were home [from boarding school] they went to church every week-
> end. His dad was an absolutely charming man. His disability didn't
> stop him from weeding the churchyard and helping out.

Though neither parent was particularly pushy, school reports were taken seriously, particularly by Ian ('He used to sit us down and read them,' Cameron has recalled) and there was an expectation that they would go to university. Ian himself had not, which he considered a 'terrible mistake'. Instead, he had done an accountancy course, which he hated. It gave rise to one of three rules he set for his children. They were: that nothing in life is ever completely fair; that they should not marry until they were at least twenty-six; and that they should never become chartered accountants.[6]

Animals played a significant part in their lives: Cameron learned to ride when he was little, and Mary kept bantams. Ian would take the children to the races, and encouraged Cameron to learn to shoot. According to Mascall, the family also kept a few sheep.

There were plenty of foreign holidays, even when the children were very young. They would typically go to the seaside in Brittany, where they would

---

4   Harry Mount interview, op. cit.
5   *Trevor McDonald Meets David Cameron*, ITV 1, 14 March 2010.
6   Harry Mount interview, op. cit.

stay in a hotel, sometimes hooking up with grand friends like the Benyons, who lived a few miles from Peasemore in a stately home. These were old-fashioned beach breaks, with picnics and 'lots of messing about in the sand'.[7]

From an early age, Cameron learned the value of public duty. While Gwen looked after the children, Mary sat as a Justice of the Peace in Newbury, where she developed a reputation for being tough.

'I used to come home, to almost warn the children about the perils of doing the wrong thing, and he learned quite a lot from that,' she has said, adding that she 'wasn't always successful'.[8]

When she wasn't in court or with the children, she was likely to be doing charitable or community work. Garry Poulson, the former Mayor of Newbury, says that over the years, she gave her time to numerous local causes, including acting as a volunteer driver for the disabled.

> The first proper time I met her it was the 25th anniversary of our charity [the Downland Volunteer Group]. At that point she was Deputy Lieutenant of the County, so she was representing the Queen at the special service we had. I remember her warmth and generosity – she gave me a very generous cheque from her own purse. She was ordinary and approachable, doing the right thing in the community and not making a fuss about it. Being involved as a volunteer driver, in a village car scheme, you meet all sorts of people from all sorts of backgrounds. You've got to be a very accepting person to do that. She remains involved with many charities, including one for children with learning difficulties called Swings and Smiles.

The Tory MP Nicholas Soames, who is a family friend, describes the Camerons as 'very, very good people', with a strong sense of civic duty.

'They really do their whack, always did. Everyone who knows his mother loves her. I know so many people who are absolutely devoted to her, and so many people who were absolutely devoted to Ian.'

Another family friend agrees, saying:

> Mary comes from a family of real doers. I remember sitting at some

---

7   Private information.
8   *Trevor McDonald Meets David Cameron.*

lunch, just after David became leader, and one old, rather detached MP was saying, 'I don't think he really understands the kind of life that exists in rural Britain, about parish councils, life in rural England, and the importance of the church, village life, and voluntary organisations.' It was absolute bollocks – he's been brought up in that environment all his life. There's not a voluntary organisation in any part of the constituency where Mary Cameron and, in his lifetime, Ian aren't involved. They really do get that.

So, where did the money come from? The swimming pool at the rectory is said to have been the result of a big win at the bookies: Ian loved the races, and knew his stuff. Every year, he and Mary would throw a big party to celebrate Ascot with another family, the Pilkingtons. However, the supply of what Cameron calls 'the folding stuff' was not contingent on racing successes. There was 'old' money on both the paternal and maternal sides of the family, as well as his father's considerable income as a stockbroker.

Born in London in 1932, Ian came from a long line of successful bankers and financiers on his father's side and MPs and barristers on his mother's. Sir Ewen Cameron, David's paternal great-great-grandfather, was London head of the Hong Kong and Shanghai Banking Corporation and helped the Rothschilds sell war bonds during the Russo-Japanese war. David's paternal great-grandfather, Ewen Allan Cameron, was a senior partner in the stockbrokers Panmure Gordon. His grandfather Donald, also a Panmure Gordon partner, left the equivalent of nearly £1 million. Donald had married into the Levita family, one of whom – another of David Cameron's great-great-grandfathers – was Emile, a German-born Jewish financier who was the director of the Chartered Bank of India, Australia and China, which became Standard Chartered Bank. He sent his sons to Eton, starting a family tradition.

Ian's disability was severe. He had no heels and his feet were twisted, one with only three toes, the other with four. As a child, he underwent various operations, but doctors were never able to straighten his legs. At the time, such a disability was quite a stigma. His parents decided not to have any more children, leaving Ian as an only child.

From a young age, he learned how to entertain himself. 'You had to be inventive to keep yourself amused,' Cameron has said of his father's childhood. 'He loved fantasy and he loved reading *The Hobbit*. I always claim that I watch *Game of Thrones* because Dad would have loved it. It's my excuse. He would have loved that whole mixture of intrigue, power, sex.'[9]

Ian's father left his mother when Ian was young, a development that left her struggling for cash. It meant Ian started work younger than many of his contemporaries. He was very proud to be able to help his mother out, including buying her car. As a result of his disability, he was unnaturally short for his build, reaching only 5 foot 8 inches,[10] and needed prostheses, but he never let it hold him back, carving out a highly successful career as a banker and, like his father and grandfather before him, a partner in Panmure Gordon. He was for some time the chairman of White's, the oldest and grandest gentlemen's club in London.

Friends remember a 'remarkable man' who was 'immensely brave'.

Soames says: 'He was a very accomplished man. He struggled through this terrible disability and never complained. He was immensely stoic.'

Ironically, given the political sensitivities surrounding tax avoidance today, Ian's area of expertise was offshore investment funds.[11] He set up business in 1979, shortly after it became legal to take large sums of money out of the UK to avoid tax. He proved very skilled at it, so much so that he rose to the top of a string of asset management firms, including a Jersey-based company and a firm registered in Panama. He also had shares in a firm based in Geneva. In 2007, the *Sunday Times Rich List* estimated his worth at £10 million.[12]

Mary Cameron's family is equally well-heeled and has substantial property assets. The Prime Minister's maternal great-great-great-grandfather, William Mount, was a wealthy MP whose son, known as WG, became a barrister and MP for Newbury, as well as the proprietor of Wasing, a grand house in Berkshire on a 660-acre estate. WG's son (who became a baronet) was also an MP, and WG's grandson, 'WM', who was to become David Cameron's grandfather, was High Sheriff of Berkshire. All the boys in the family were sent to Eton.

---

9   Harry Mount interview, op. cit.
10   *Trevor McDonald Meets David Cameron*.
11   *The Guardian*, 20 April 2012.
12   When he died in September 2010, Ian left an estate valued at £2.74 million. (Philip Beresford, *Sunday Times Rich List*, 2007.) The discrepancy was until recently a mystery, although given that his will only detailed UK assets, it seemed highly likely that he had placed some of his money offshore. A Channel 4 investigation in April 2015 confirmed what many had long suspected: he left assets in Jersey (http://www.channel4.com/news/cameron-david-ian-jersey-tax-haven-conservatives).

One of three daughters of WM and his wife, Mary was born in 1934 and grew up in an old-fashioned, church-going environment. Her cousin Ferdinand Mount, a former adviser to the Thatcher government, has described the family as 'straight-laced' and imbued with *noblesse oblige.*

By the time Mary married Ian in 1962, some of the Wasing estate had been sold off. In the 1990s, the rest passed to her sister Lady Cecilia (Cylla) Dugdale. Nowadays, the beautiful eighteenth-century parkland is held in a family trust. It can be hired for weddings, meetings and sporting events, and is used as a film location.

Lady Cylla's husband, Sir William Dugdale, 2nd Baronet, who died in November 2014, was among other things chairman of Aston Villa Football Club, and used to take David and Alex to watch matches. They would do it in style, sitting in VIP seats and visiting the dressing room afterwards.[13] Dugdale's family seat, the 485-year-old Blyth Hall near Birmingham, also provided his nephews with extensive woodlands and fields where they could shoot rabbits, which they both enjoyed. It was one of two large houses on the Warwickshire estate.

Cameron's childhood could hardly have been better designed to produce a happy, secure and well-balanced character. He had total stability and appeared to want for nothing, either emotionally or materially. It was, in his own words, 'straightforward' and 'uncomplicated', 'very happy, very close'.[14] It was also a world to which only a tiny proportion of the population can relate.

'He is a real, proper Englishman, who would love to defend what he sees as the real England, but his real England is different to almost everyone else's,' says a childhood friend.

His only real worry seems to have been competing with his big brother, which he saw as a significant challenge. He says he struggled to carve out his own identity and feared he was 'set on a track' to live in Alex's shadow.

'Everything I did I felt he had already done,' he has said. 'You think that you are doing everything the same, only three years later...that was

---

13   *Daily Mail*, 17 November 2014.
14   David Cameron and Dylan Jones, *Cameron on Cameron: Conversations with Dylan Jones* (Fourth Estate, 2012), pp. 37, 40.

something I used to worry about quite a lot, that I was never going to break out of my brother's shadow.'[15]

Nowhere would he feel this more acutely than at school. His formal education began in an institution that was a throwback to a bygone world, a place of chilly dormitories, corporal punishment and Latin verbs. The creature comforts of the Old Rectory would seem very far away.

---

15   Ibid., p. 37.

3
ANGELS' COFFINS

'Good health, sir!'
  – Cameron, aged eleven, raising a glass of Dom Pérignon

Cameron was shipped off to boarding school before he turned eight.
There was no 'need' for him to be sent away – his parents lived only
a few miles down the road. It was simply the done thing in the circles in
which they moved.

The prep school Ian and Mary chose was a small but grand institution
called Heatherdown, whose business was providing an old-fashioned education to young sons of the establishment. By the time Cameron arrived, his
older brother had been there for three years, and was already as big a shot
as a little person can be in a small place.

Founded in 1908, Heatherdown catered for fewer than 100 boys at any
one time, but what it lacked in size, it more than made up for in social exclu-
sivity. According to one account of Cameron's time there, among the parents
of his contemporaries were 'eight honourables, four sirs, two captains, two
doctors, two majors, two princesses, two marchionesses, one viscount, one
brigadier, one commodore, one earl, one lord, and one Queen (*the* Queen)'.[16]
Cameron's classmates included the grandson of oil billionaire John Paul Getty,
thanks to whom he would later enjoy an extraordinary holiday in America;
and Prince Edward, whose older brother Andrew was also educated there.

The main building was a Victorian mansion with bay windows set in
landscaped gardens on a 30-acre estate. At the back was a separate property
called Heatherlea for the youngest boys. On the roof was a dovecote which
housed a flight of fantail pigeons belonging to the headmaster, James Edwards.

---

16   Francis Elliott and James Hanning, p. 20.

By the early 1970s, Edwards, a former navy man, had been at the school for almost a decade.[17] Educated at Radley and Magdalen College, Oxford, he was married to a chain-smoking divorcée called Barbara whose first husband had been a Russian prince. According to Christine Carder, who was school matron when Cameron and Alex were there: 'Barbara always came down to her little kitchen off the school dining room and cooked her breakfast in her dressing gown, then went upstairs to her bedroom. She constantly had a cigarette hanging from her mouth. She and the headmaster used to smoke in front of the boys.'

On the first day of term, Ian and Mary drove Cameron and Alex to the school, where they were ushered into the headmaster's house for the 'new boys' tea party'.

A former teacher recalls:

> It was held in the Edwards' drawing room in their private quarters and there were sandwiches and so on. It was a very nice tea, done by the school, not Barbara. It was a social – a chance for teachers to meet the new parents and for the parents to discuss with us any worries they might have. It was a way of reassuring the mothers. If the boy had an elder brother at the school, he'd be invited. Then the new boys would be taken to Heatherlea.

A former housemother at the school recalls that many new parents 'were more worked up than the boys' as the moment for goodbye loomed.

'Afterwards, we would walk over to Heatherlea and they'd find their beds and unpack – always a lot of packing and unpacking!' she says.

Boys slept in cold dormitories with bare wooden floorboards. They brought travel rugs from home for their beds, and were allowed a favourite teddy.

Days followed a rigid routine, starting at 7 a.m. sharp, when boys would be woken for ablutions. According to one report, the headmaster himself would help rouse the children, fortified by a glass of whisky and water, with a pipe clamped between his teeth.[18] By 7.40 a.m., boys would be washed and dressed, ready for Scripture before breakfast at 8 a.m. Meals were taken in

17   *Bracknell News*, 23 May 1968.
18   *Daily Mail*, 15 May 2010.

a refectory at long wooden tables with faux-marble tops. The oak-panelled walls were decorated with shields honouring school heads, sports captains and other distinguished pupils. After breakfast, pupils trooped off to the loos, where they were made to recite Latin verbs or other rote. This arcane daily ritual was rigidly enforced, with each boy required to tick his name off a list pinned to the cubicle after his visit. Then lessons would begin, interspersed with breaks.

'They used to have milk and biscuits in the morning, and another drink in the afternoon, and sometimes those long iced buns. If they had chocolate icing they were called devils' coffins and if they had white icing they were called angels' coffins,' Carder says.

Twice a week, if they had been good, boys would be allowed to take two sweets from a tin that was passed around after lunch. To supplement these scant treats, they would sneak contraband into their dormitories. Carder recalls finding 'doughnuts under mattresses, maybe forgotten or left because they didn't have time for a midnight feast', while Nick Cunningham, who shared a dormitory with Cameron, remembers 'stashing a few sweets' under a loose floorboard by the future Prime Minister's bed.

After supper, there were prayers in the chapel, led by the headmaster, followed by prep, baths and bed. Younger boys would be read a story by Matron before lights out at 7.30 p.m.

Every day, Carder, a qualified nurse, would issue Mrs Edwards with a report on pupils who were unwell.

'We were very careful about that sort of thing,' Carder remembers. 'She was always concerned about children's health. I used to go and give her my daily report and she would still be sitting in bed reading the newspaper. I very rarely rang parents if anything was wrong – she would do that herself.'

Edwards seems to have been an eccentric but amiable figure. In an interview with a reporter who visited the school ahead of Prince Andrew's arrival in 1968, he said that the 'main object' at the school was for pupils to be happy.

'The fewer rules you can do with, the better…You can get so much more out of children if they are happy,' he said. He claimed pupils were rarely homesick, telling the newspaper that he thought the separation was 'harder for the parents than for the boys'.

Evidently he impressed the reporter, who gushed about his professional qualities in the report she filed for the *Bracknell News*.

A relaxed, almost casual manner masks the firm purpose of the Schoolmaster, and it is evident that he has that all-too-rare capacity for making pleasurable the acquisition of knowledge. This modern 'Mr Chips', whose interests range from croquet to mountain walking in his native North Wales, from cricket and golf, history and Latin to Fantail pigeons, is able to communicate to young minds a full enjoyment in the world around them, which after all, is the true essence of education.

Like other prep schools at the time, Heatherdown was run by a handful of long-serving senior staff, assisted by a shifting cast of younger masters, sometimes not long out of school themselves. Geared to Common Entrance requirements, the curriculum included French, Latin, Scripture and general science, as well as Greek and ancient history.

Sport was cricket, tennis, soccer and rugby, and a few boys took up golf. The uniform included a red-and-black blazer and a grey suit on Sundays.

As the younger sibling of an older pupil, the future Prime Minister was known as 'Cameron Minor', shortened to 'Cameron Mi'; while his brother – remembered by former teachers as the more extrovert and popular of the two – was known as 'Cameron Ma'.

According to former teacher Christopher Bromley-Martin, Cameron Mi was 'tidy' and 'a sort of miniature example of what he is now'.

'He hasn't changed in appearance at all, really, except in an obvious sort of way. He is quite unmistakable,' he says.[19]

Carder remembers both him and his parents with affection.

I remember him being a cheerful, happy little guy, lovely nature. His parents were both delightful. His mother was charming. She was very easy to talk to. She obviously cared an awful lot about her children. In prep schools in those days, the nannies did more for the children than the mummies, but I only ever spoke to the mother about things. His brother was an absolutely delightful child, outgoing, lovely sense of humour, and David was very like him, though perhaps a little quieter.

---

19   *Daily Telegraph*, 13 May 2010.

Cameron did well academically, though he was not regarded by teachers as exceptional. In an unusual system, Heatherdown promoted children through the ranks according to performance rather than age, meaning that the most gifted boys could leapfrog their peers. The future Prime Minister was clever enough to be pushed up a year.

One of his teachers recalls:

> It was quite possible for a boy to go steaming up the school much faster than another boy who came at the same time, but who had less intellectual capacity. Each individual was promoted on merit and capacity. We used to have a meeting at the end of every term to discuss who should go up from form 3B to 3A, from 5 to 6, and so on. Obviously we took account of intellectual capacity, but also readiness – whether the child would be rather swamped by being in the wrong age group. We tried to create a balance between the two considerations. David went up fairly rapidly.

However, he was not thought bright enough to sit the 'murderous' exam for a scholarship to Eton. The standard of this paper was set between that of O level and A level – making it a huge stretch for boys of eleven or twelve.

According to the teacher:

> It was to test the intellectual character of a boy – not only how much he knew but…how he was going to cope when his back was against the wall, what his promise was…I used to teach for it and it was really testing. David was not up to that. He was a very sound, solid, reliable Common Entrance candidate, definitely in the top category there.

The same source describes Cameron as an 'adequate' sportsman, whose best game was cricket. Rugby was never his thing but, as he grew up, he became an accomplished tennis player.

At weekends, Heatherdown boys were allowed to roam the grounds wearing green boiler suits. Cameron's best friend at the school, Simon Andreae, now a television producer, has told how they 'built camps in the woods, staged elaborate battles with toy soldiers, and shot air rifles'. He recalled other adventures, some nocturnal, such as 'creeping out of our dormitory windows to go midnight swimming in the school pool, which was freezing'. He has claimed the boys would also have 'trysts' with girls from Heathfield, a nearby girls' school, in a graveyard that lay between the two establishments.

On occasional Sundays, they were allowed home. After such 'exeats', the Queen would personally escort her young sons back to school, where she would be received by Edwards and his wife. A former teacher recalls the lengths to which the headmaster went to protect the young royals. 'It was a very private school. James Edwards shunned publicity. When we had the two princes in the school, he was an absolute past master at keeping the school out of the limelight.'

A highlight of the school calendar was the annual play, watched by proud parents, including the Queen. Chris Black, the teacher who produced the shows in Cameron's day, kept various mementoes, including a photograph of a nine-year-old Cameron on stage, playing 'Harold Rabbit' in a 1975 production of *Toad of Toad Hall*, as well as a programme signed by all the young actors.

Looking back, Black says:

> I recall there being more than the usual nervous excitement before that evening's performance ... because we were all aware that Her Majesty would be in the front row ... Queen Elizabeth was merely there in the capacity of a supportive parent, enjoying watching her youngest son, Prince Edward, playing the role of 'Mole'. However, to me, as a young schoolmaster recently arrived from South Africa ... it was an unnerving experience. My stress level was not helped by the fact that I had composed a musical score for the production which required me to sit out front and provide the musical accompaniment, not only for the young actors up on stage, but also for the whole audience to stand after the finale and join together in the traditional singing of the national anthem. Playing 'God Save the Queen' while the person in question looked on from just a few feet away was a truly surreal moment![20]

Black says that Cameron 'spoke his few lines with complete composure'

20   *The Witness*, 12 September 2013.

and came close to securing the lead role in the play two years later, J. M. Barrie's *The Boy David*.

> My casting notes from that production reveal that the final selection for the coveted part of 'David' came down to a closely run contest between just two contenders, the much younger David Cameron and the somewhat more experienced Simon Andreae. I still recall agonising over my final decision, which eventually went in favour of Andreae. However, knowing how bitterly disappointed David Cameron would be and not wanting to dent his confidence and enthusiasm, I decided to create an additional role that was not part of [the] original script. And so David Cameron was made the play's narrator. Dressed in a flowing white shirt and cummerbund, he stepped up to the lectern, which had been discreetly scaled down to match his ten-year-old stature, and, with total poise and confidence, introduced each new scene with a passage from the Old Testament.

At a time when air travel and foreign holidays were beyond the reach of most ordinary people, pupils at Heatherdown enjoyed ski trips and African safaris. Every year, the headmaster would take a party of boys to Switzerland, Austria or the French Alps, accompanied by one or two younger masters to keep them in order. Black recalls taking Cameron's brother and three of his classmates on a three-week trip to Natal, in South Africa, in the summer of 1975.

> We used Cowan House prep school as our base, from where we explored the Drakensberg and surrounding area, before setting off on a 'safari' to Zululand – an adventure which to this day they still recall with excitement.
>
> I came to know the Cameron family well during those years. I found them extremely well balanced and down-to-earth, and Ian and Mary were always the most helpful and supportive of parents. The family seemed totally unaffected by the fact that their two sons just happened to have ended up in the same school as members of the royal family.[21]

---

21   *Scotland on Sunday*, 9 May 2010.

At the age of eleven, Cameron was treated to a trip that must have put all previous and subsequent school holidays in the shade. It kicked off by Concorde, spanned several American states, and included a helicopter flight.

He was one of four boys invited on the all-expenses-paid jaunt to celebrate the birthday of their classmate Peter Getty. Accompanied by Rhidian Llewellyn, who was just ten years older than the boys and was a young master at the school, they spent four days in Washington, sightseeing by air-conditioned convertible, dining in fine restaurants and generally larking about, before flying on to New York, where they stayed in a luxury hotel and explored the Empire State Building and World Trade Center.

Llewellyn, who had been a pupil at Heatherdown, recalls: 'I was eighteen and had to vaguely try and control this group of five ten- and eleven-year-old boys! Fortunately the Getty boy had a French nanny, so between us we just about coped with them.'

In an interview published in 2007, Llewellyn described how, aboard Concorde, the youngsters tucked into caviar, salmon and beef bordelaise. He 'turned round to check that all was well and that his charges were more or less behaving themselves [and] was met with the sight, a few rows behind, of David Cameron, eleven years old, cheerily raising a glass of Dom Pérignon '69 and exclaiming, "Good health, sir!"'[22]

After New York, the boys went to Disneyworld in Florida and the Kennedy Space Center at Cape Canaveral, before heading to Las Vegas, where it was too hot for sightseeing. Instead, they hung around the hotel swimming pool and played the slot machines. The tour concluded with three days at the Grand Canyon and a trip to Hollywood, followed by a week of rest and relaxation at the Getty family home at Pacific Heights, overlooking San Francisco's Golden Gates.[23]

Most people could only dream of such experiences, but there were few luxuries at Heatherdown. The environment was tough. These were the days of corporal punishment, as Cameron Mi learned to his cost. In the interview with the *Bracknell News* reporter, Edwards admitted he was 'not wholly opposed' to administering the odd thwack, though he claimed it happened rarely, and said he never used a cane.[24] His tool of choice appears to have been a hairbrush, the sting

22   Francis Elliott and James Hanning, p. 23.

23   Ibid., p. 24.

24   *Bracknell News*, op. cit.

of which Cameron experienced 'a couple of times' for various misdemeanours,[25] including once stealing strawberries from Mrs Edwards's garden.

Speaking about such punishments, Llewellyn says: 'The worst thing about it was that it was never done on the spot. It was scheduled for after breakfast the following morning. I was a pupil at the same time as Prince Andrew, and he was beaten regularly. But then he was fairly bumptious.'[26] Daniel Wiggin, another former pupil, has spoken of being beaten simply for 'taking my teddy for a walk in the corridor after lights out'.[27]

Far darker forces may have been at work. One of Cameron's former masters was recently exposed as a paedophile. Andrew Sadler, who appears in a formal photograph with Cameron at Heatherdown, was a French teacher. (It is not known whether any former pupils have ever complained about his behaviour.) Long after he left the school, he was identified by police as a key player in an international paedophile network. He was convicted and served time behind bars for a string of serious sexual offences against young boys.[28]

Though there are no reports of abuse having taken place at Heatherdown, some former staff feel, in retrospect, that aspects of the regime were unduly harsh for very young children.

'Things have changed so much,' Carder reflects.

> In those days, corporal punishment wasn't frowned upon, and the parents were always in agreement. The view was that if there had been a misdemeanour, it was their fault and they deserved to be punished for it. When I became a mother, I realised I was probably quite hard, quite tough, on children who were really quite small. The thought of sending my own child away to school was horrendous.

After the royals left, Heatherdown fell out of fashion. The roll declined, and the school slipped into obscurity. Eventually, in the early 1980s, it closed. The site was sold; everything inside – beds, tables, chairs, photographs and other memorabilia – was auctioned off, and the buildings eventually razed.

By then, Cameron was at Eton, on an altogether bigger stage.

25 *Mail on Sunday*, 8 April 2007.
26 Ibid.
27 *Daily Mail*, 15 May 2010.
28 Mail Online, 7 November 2014.

4
POP CONTEST

'The sole Monégasque is so delicious.'

– Cameron, aged fourteen

A year into Cameron's premiership, Eton held a party to mark the 200th anniversary of its elite sixth-form club, Pop. All 725 former pupils invited to the jamboree had been singled out at school as something special. After assembling in the college chapel, the former 'Poppers' belted out 'Jerusalem' before heading to a marquee and starting on the champagne. A shambolic attempt to take a group photo from a high window was met, according to one there, with 'benign tolerance' as the atmosphere became increasingly merry.

Where was Dave?

As Boris Johnson, one of Pop's most distinguished former members, could not resist pointing out, the Prime Minister was not there, because he did not make it into Pop. (Membership was equivalent to celebrity status at Eton, and was the dream of every boy at the school.)

Surveying the ranks of rich and famous at the party, Chris Berthoud, a former Popper who is now a BBC executive,[29] found himself pondering the significance of the school society. Did an individual, he wondered, need 'special DNA' to be in Pop? Why didn't Cameron get in?

The PM's association with Eton has repeatedly been exploited by political opponents keen to present him as out of touch. Unlike Johnson, who also attended the school but is proud of his exclusive education, the Prime Minister has sometimes seemed embarrassed by his alma mater – so much so that when the school asked him for a signed photograph a few years

---

29   Head of Digital Impact.

ago, to display alongside that of other prime ministers in the Eton College Museum, they were initially turned down.

'It was sort of ridiculous,' says an alumnus who went on to advise Cameron in opposition. 'There are any number of Old Etonian politicians who'd have given them signed photographs, but here was the Leader of the Opposition and they said they were having terrible trouble persuading him.'[30]

No wonder some masters have been looking forward to the day he leaves office. Proud as the school is to have produced its nineteenth Prime Minister, privately, some teachers have been known to reflect gloomily that he has brought only negative publicity.[31]

Yet Cameron's Eton years are fundamental to his story. The education he received and the connections he made were instrumental in his ascent and have coloured his entire political career. Moreover, a number of the friendships he made proved lifelong, providing him with a remarkably stable and loyal social base.

Today, Eton is well integrated with the local community, with links to state schools in Slough, Hounslow and Windsor. When Cameron arrived in 1979 as a nervous twelve-year-old, however, it was a parallel universe of medieval cloisters and coat tails in which centuries of tradition dictated almost every aspect of the school day. Save for occasional forays into Windsor to window-shop and buy magazines and sweets, there was little reason for boys to mingle with – or be troubled by – the world outside. It was a surreal stage on which to play out one's teenage years.

Founded in 1440 by King Henry VI as a charity school to provide free education to seventy poor boys, Eton gradually morphed into a school for the privileged few. In Cameron's day, 'the whole ethos was your success story',[32] and boys took it for granted that they would do well in life.

Marcus Warren, who was in the same year as the future Prime Minister, said:

> It sounds arrogant, and I don't think arrogance is necessarily a quality you should attribute to all Etonians, but there was an assumption that in later life one would probably be in a position of some authority or privilege. One would be more fortunate than others...That

---

30   Private information.

31   Private information.

32   Chris Berthoud.

just seemed to be the way things were. You didn't see a lot of questioning going on around that…With hindsight, there was a sort of sense of entitlement. Here we were in this extraordinary school, a fantastic privilege and fortune, at a time when Britain had just come out of the 1970s. It had been a really bruising time for the country, and there were changes afoot. There was a sort of low-intensity revolution underway, with miners' strikes and mass unemployment. It seemed to pass us by.

Indeed, Cameron had not been at Eton for long before he was telling people he would be Prime Minister one day. A friend who used to hang out with him in Peasemore during school holidays recalls:

You know when you are a kid you just tend to talk about crap? We would always say, 'What do you want to do?' Cameron would reply, literally from the age of fourteen, 'I am going to be Prime Minister.' Normally you would take the piss if somebody said that, but with him, you didn't – he said it with such conviction. It's just such a weird thing for a fourteen-year-old to say. It was obvious that he really meant it.

This was just teenage banter, of course. There is no evidence that Cameron was particularly interested in politics or that he planned a career in public life from a young age. However, he clearly assumed he had a big future ahead of him, a notion the Eton environment encouraged.

Throughout the school, there was intense pressure to perform. It was ruthlessly academic.

'You could no longer get in because your dad had been there. Academic standards had risen a lot. People were definitely being steered towards Oxford. There weren't a lot of Hooray Henry stupids,' Warren says.

The headmaster was a distinguished Scot named Eric Anderson, who had previously taught Tony Blair at Fettes and Prince Charles at Gordonstoun. He has described Cameron as 'clever' and 'nice', saying that he was an 'excellent House captain' who 'showed leadership qualities early on'.

As a new boy, Cameron's integration was significantly eased by the presence of his brother Alex, who had by then been at the school for three years and was extremely popular. This was a mixed blessing. As at Heatherdown, where it was Alex who made the bigger impression, the future Prime Minister initially struggled to compete with his effortlessly charming and extrovert sibling, who was, former pupils say, 'someone people adored immediately'.[33]

Alex Cameron also had a taste for practical jokes. James Deen, another of Cameron's peers, recalls him returning to Eton aged twenty or twenty-one and locking everyone in the chapel. 'He was caught and had to go to his old housemaster,' he says. 'Alex was more of a prankster and Dave was just your normal well-behaved little brother.'

Arriving for his first term, Cameron was enrolled in 'JF' House, where he found himself among fifty boys, including Alex, ranging in age from the most junior year (known as F block) to sixth form, known as B and A blocks. In JF (named after housemaster John Faulkner), he had his own room, a luxury that gave him some privacy. His year group was the last to be subjected to so-called 'fagging', an arcane tradition in which twelve- and thirteen-year-olds were forced to carry out menial tasks for sixth-form boys. Curiously, there is no record of Cameron suffering this indignity, perhaps thanks to the protection of Alex. He was eventually to become House Captain, a notable though not outstanding achievement (it was a competition between ten).

At Heatherdown, Cameron had done well academically but was not one of the highest flyers. At Eton, his respectable but unremarkable track record continued. Unlike Johnson (two years his senior), he was not among the elite group of gifted Etonians known as King's scholars, whose academic prowess earns a 10 per cent discount on the annual fee, and exclusive accommodation in a section of the school known as College. Nor was he in a second tier of scholars, who did not live in College but were considered gifted. Indeed, when Cameron and Johnson became political rivals three decades later, the fiercely competitive Johnson (who, according to friends, still considers he has the superior brain) liked to tease the Prime Minister about his failure to become a 'KS'. He once sent him a cheeky text message suggesting that if he needed any help with a policy, he could call on a long list of fellow Old Etonians who had made the grade. (Cameron's riposte is unknown, but he may have countered that he went on to achieve a First at Oxford, whereas the London mayor scored an Upper Second.)

---

33   Chris Berthoud.

Boys were continuously ranked via internal exams known as 'Trials', establishing a clear academic hierarchy. There was no hiding place for those who were struggling: the results were read out publicly in the school theatre, starting at the bottom.

Someone who has kept copies of the old league tables says Cameron ranked in the 'low 100s…not in the middle, but slightly above the middle'.

Contemporaries feel this was broadly reflective of his ability, at least until he was sixteen. One who followed him to university says:

> At Oxford, I was amazed when people would come up to me and say, 'You went to Eton, so you must know David. He's really clever.' I thought…What?! He clearly absolutely shone at Oxford, but I think most people at school with him would have been surprised that he was academically top notch. That was not the impression he created.

William Buckland, who had the same sixth-form history teacher as Cameron, the late Michael Kidson, is more generous.

'In our history class, my impression was that Kidson felt that four kids stood out: the two King's scholars and two others, one of whom was Cameron. When difficult things were being discussed, Kidson would generally turn to one of those four,' he says.

Kidson was a charismatic figure whose lively lessons made a lasting impression.

Buckland recalls:

> We mostly studied nineteenth-century British history, particularly the empire and various related conflicts and political history – Peel, Gladstone, Disraeli, Palmerston etc. Kidson was an inspirational teacher who acted many of the major events himself. I vividly remember him playing out the imperial reactions of British politicians towards rebellious upstarts in places like Egypt and Sudan. I seem to recall that Cameron sat in the front row on the left. So Kidson was performing only a few feet from the nose of someone who was later to exhibit similar reactions, towards Libya, Islamic State, and when he voted in favour of attack on Iraq in 2003.

This may be fanciful, but Cameron certainly appreciated the lessons. When his old master died in 2015, he sent a tribute to be read out at his memorial service.

'He was an inspirational teacher who made you feel you were in the room with the people he taught you about. He was so passionate about Gladstone that when he read the last few pages of [Philip] Magnus's great biography aloud in class, he started to cry,' Cameron said.[34]

Kidson was less gushing about his famous former pupil.

In later life he liked to tell people that Cameron's success at A level was 'among the most inexplicable events in modern history'.[35]

Another teacher to whom the Prime Minister owes lasting gratitude is Jeff Branch, who was his tutor in 1982. Adrian McGlynn, who was also in Branch's group, recalls:

> Mr Branch, whose nickname was Twiggy, was an accomplished English teacher and very artistic. It was the first time I had really come into contact with David, and we had the whole academic year in that tutor group – about six of us, I think.
>
> Twiggy was very keen that we had some experience of public speaking. One term, he set each of us weekly tasks of research and presentation. He would give us a topic that we had to present to the group in a five-minute speech the following week. Research to be conducted in the school's amazing libraries – this all before the internet, of course – and then we had to stand up and speak in front of our peers. Naturally, at first we were all hesitant and simply read out a written essay on what we had discovered. But then Mr Branch asked us to present on things that interested us…and without reading from notes. Really scary. But I have this memory of David doing something with amazing fluency and articulacy on, I think, Raphael. Whenever I see him now stand up and pull the trick of speaking without script or notes, I think back to the Mr Branch tutorial group of '82.

One of Cameron's favourite subjects was art. McGlynn recalls him taking it extremely seriously.

---

34   *Daily Telegraph*, 3 July 2015.
35   *Last Word*, Radio 4, 9 August 2015.

of marriage proposals received that leap year. The rules had to be clarified to underline that each proposition had to come from a different girl, 'thus excluding Dave Cameron's two calls from the same lovesick princess'.

He was now old enough to frequent the school bar, Tap, where boys had a limited allocation of beer. In a habit that he would not shake for decades, he also began having the odd sneaky cigarette behind the cricket pavilions, a transgression that carried the risk of being 'gated' (confined to the boarding house during social events). By this time, corporal punishment at Eton was rare. Minor disciplinary breaches were treated with detentions or Latin lines, known as 'Georgics'. Those who were late for lessons were forced to get up very early to sign a so-called 'Tardy book' at the school office, a punishment imposed for a week.

More serious offences could mean immediate ejection from the school. Cameron's year group had the ignominious distinction of a record number of expulsions – a fate the Prime Minister himself narrowly escaped after he was 'busted' for taking cannabis.

The episode, which took place just a few weeks before he was due to sit his O levels, was sufficiently serious for police to be called in. Seven boys were thrown out of the school on the day the scandal broke, and the investigation snowballed, with many others, Cameron included, hauled before teachers. The affair exposed a significantly more widespread drug problem than the school authorities had anticipated. When it came to light after Cameron's rise to the Conservative Party leadership, it prompted a media furore, but friends say he was only a bit player.

'I always thought he was an unwilling participant,' says James Deen.

> He was very like me in that I never did anything wrong in five years. All his friends were quite naughty, drank, smoked…probably did things they didn't have a fucking clue about. But he was quite goody-goody. There were some 'characters' in his House, and willing or not, he became part of it. It's a very typical thing at Eton, that if someone is caught doing something, unfortunately everybody in that year and that House suffers because of it.

Among those expelled was Max Wigram (who now runs an art gallery on

New Bond Street in London), who seems to have been a dazzling figure at Eton. His sudden departure was a shock to pupils.

'He was a very intelligent non-conformist – fifteen going on twenty-five. He was hanging out with supermodels at the age of fourteen, when the rest of us didn't even know what a pigtail was,' Deen recalls.

Looking back, Berthoud dismisses the drugs scandal as

> all just bravado, the equivalent of sneaking behind the bike sheds for a fag…I remember the expulsions thing as being 'Oh my God, wow.' They were the subversive heroes, in as much as Eton had a counterculture. Max was a bit of a sporting hero, immensely good-looking and charismatic, and rebellious towards the teachers, and then he was expelled. I remember I was very shocked by that. I thought in a way that we were all untouchable.

On school trips, boys were given more leeway. A 1984 edition of *The Chronicle* records a junket to Rome one Easter that was packed with riotous antics, including a kerfuffle with the Carabinieri.

The article records:

> It was Franz Calice and Fred Collin who really gave proceedings a bang when they purchased a couple of remarkably lifelike toy Colt 45s, which made a satisfactorily loud noise. Within hours the shop was cleared out and the entire party was armed and firing at any unattractive Italian that moved. Unfortunately the entertainment was brought to a close when the local police became a little excited and told us to put them away.

Halfway through the expedition, Cameron sprained his ankle 'when dancing overenthusiastic reels to the dulcet tones of his old friend Ben Weatherall's bagpipes' while trying to raise a few *lire* for beers that night. The incident limited his sightseeing somewhat, but the paper records that he 'made up for it in other departments', presumably involving one or more Italian girls. Parents may have been reassured to learn that the lads were at least on their best behaviour when they were taken to the British ambassador's residence, where two of the boys performed a piano recital while another of the group, one Andrew Morgan-Williams, 'engaged the ambassador in polite, genteel, cocktail conversation'.

Cameron's closest friends at Eton included 'Toppo' Todhunter, Simon Andreae (whose twin Giles also became a close friend at Oxford), James Learmond, James Fergusson, Tom Goff and Ben Weatherall, who remain in close contact with the Prime Minister and fiercely loyal to their friend. (Todhunter and Goff were joint best men at his wedding.)

It is testament to Cameron that few Old Etonians have anything seriously disobliging to say about their old classmate. Some thought him a little arrogant and charmless, but his worst social offence seems to have been to stick to a small clique, a habit that remained.

According to one former classmate:

> My reading of it is that he actually wasn't that popular. I knew him well enough to share classes and speak to him every now and then. He didn't make friends easily and seemed to cling on to very close friends, who were mainly in his [boarding] house. From my perspective, that looked to me like he was very cliquey and slightly arrogant. It definitely did strike me that he was noticeably less sociable, easy-going and friendly than a lot of people. He defiantly stuck to a very small group of people, much more than anybody else. Looking back, thirty years later, I sort of read that as maybe he was slightly insecure, possibly even a bit shy.

Former teachers generally recall him as cheerful, confident and well mannered. Yet it is clear he was not a massive figure at the school. James Wallis, who was in several of the same 'divs' (Eton slang for classes) as Cameron, says:

> Others from our year did stand out – Nick Rowe [now an actor]; James Wood [now a successful writer and literary critic]; Giles Andreae; and of course Boris, who despite being two years above us was known to pretty much everyone in the school. Then there was Josh Astor [an adopted member of Samantha Cameron's family], who left early under a drug-related cloud, dated Jade Jagger, and did hard time for coke dealing. The last I heard of

him was a one-paragraph story in *The Independent* sometime in the 1990s, headlined something like 'Naked Man on Hotel Roof "High on Crack"'.[38]

It was clear even then that these people were going to make some kind of impression on society, even if it was a skidmark. But David Cameron…nothing. When he first appeared as an MP, I mentioned my non-memories of him to another OE friend from our year and they couldn't remember him either.

Others are more complimentary. Philip Bassett, an Eton and Oxford University contemporary, said:

> I liked the guy enormously. He was a friend. He was a fabulous guy, a really nice guy. I went to my first ever ball with him when I was fourteen. It was the Feathers' Ball, which is something a lot of thirteen- and fourteen-year-olds go to. There were three of us going, organised through a friend of ours – me, him and Max Wigram. It was a formative experience because we didn't have any partners then. We were rather scared fourteen-year-old boys! He always handled himself well. He wasn't a guffawing drunk.

James Deen, who was in all the same classes as Cameron all the way through school, says, 'I think he played a very straight bat. He was a very nice person at the periphery of a group of quite naughty boys. He was what you'd call a very decent Englishman.'

The suggestion that Cameron was not as popular as he would have liked is borne out by his failure to make it into 'Pop'. At the time, boys were elected to the society by their peers. For many, acquiring the credentials to be selected was a major preoccupation.

In an article for the school magazine in 2011, Berthoud reflected on what an obsession it could be:

> As we progress up the Blocks in school, we all wonder, at some stage, are we Pop material? Are we bright enough, sporty enough,

---

38   The original *Independent* article has proved hard to trace; the incident was recorded in the *Daily Record* of 13 May 1999.

popular, respected, noticed? Is our hair interesting enough, do we smell nice, can we make people laugh? Have we joined enough societies, do we play the right instruments, can we act? How many existing members of Pop can we count as our friends? What is the magic formula to step into sponge-bag trousers and a mildly racy waist-coat?

Berthoud says modestly that he himself 'felt a bit of a fraud' in Pop, having no great claim to sporting or academic prowess.

> I certainly wasn't chosen for my anticipated abilities of keeping law and order at the school. When it came down to it, I was lucky – I knew quite a few in Pop, I hadn't been naughty enough to have a blemished record, and I think I had ... the ability to listen.

It seems Cameron simply did not bother to network – and paid the price. While he was gregarious at school, he did not reach out beyond his immediate social set. Perhaps his knockback in this early popularity contest made him more determined to shine in later life, though it would be a mistake to read too much into it. In his article for the school magazine, written after he attended the 2011 reunion, Berthoud says:

> I looked around the tables and tables of OEs. There – a man who was in Pop in 1941. Going very strong. That guy – one of the most successful hedge fund managers in the country. That one – a property tycoon. A clutch of celebrities. Yet also among us – engineers, architects, photographers, some unemployed – even a few journalists. Did anything link these people?

His conclusion is not.

> There was nothing to distinguish these guys as Poppers. Time had really levelled us. In spite of the privilege, we were getting old, just like the rest of the population. We faced strife, difficulty, problems in our lives. Being in Pop was not a golden ticket to wealth and happiness. Pop people are not in any sense god-like.

On other fronts, Cameron was ticking most of the right boxes for holding high office. He was smart, well rounded and self-assured. In a character trait he would later display as Prime Minister, he had a tendency to coast, but when it really mattered he pulled out the stops and could be brilliant.

Nonetheless, he did not appear to be anything special, especially when compared with Johnson.

Buckland, who has observed both of their careers, says:

> By Eton standards...Cameron was 'good second-rate' in terms of talent. Furthermore, there is a world of difference between the merely very capable, such as Cameron, and the brilliant, verging on genius, such as Johnson. The latter can, and often do, make their own way in the world, whereas the former have to compromise, rely on others, work hard, and so on. When I read some time ago that Cameron did well academically at Oxford, I wasn't surprised. The top fifty kids in our Eton year group were all capable of that, if they applied the necessary level of effort.

Of course, a good brain is not the only prerequisite for success in politics. Cameron's next step – a gap year – would give him a taste of life at Westminster, as well as adventures in far-flung places.

5
I SPY

'I was not that young man who fed David Cameron with caviar.
Though if I had been that man, I would not admit it.'
— General Yuri Kobaladze, former KGB spy

Cameron was lounging on a beach after a 6,000-mile odyssey across Siberia when he had one of the strangest encounters of his life.

It was 1985, and the liberating breeze of glasnost had yet to sweep across Mikhail Gorbachev's Russia, thawing the icy grip of the Cold War.

The repressive Soviet empire was still a place of hammer-and-sickle totalitarianism, where KGB eyes were everywhere and informants lurked on street corners.

Cameron has never spoken publicly about the train journey from Japan to Moscow on the Trans-Siberian Express (unlike David Bowie, who did the same trip twelve years earlier and has described it as 'a glimpse into another world').

However, he has talked about a strange incident afterwards when he and an old school friend, Anthony Griffith, were in Crimea. As they sunbathed on a beach in Yalta reserved for foreign tourists, they were surprised to be approached by two Russians rather older than themselves who spoke perfect English. The men were normally dressed, extremely friendly and clearly well off, and proceeded to engage them in conversation, before inviting them for lunch and dinner. Over caviar and sturgeon, Cameron and Griffith found themselves being 'interrogated in a very friendly way about life in England and politics'. Surprised, they became guarded, and turned down an offer to meet their new friends again the following evening. The identity of the Russians was a mystery – as it remains, tantalising so. Cameron himself has speculated that they were KGB spies looking to recruit him. However, a fresh investigation has now cast a different light on what happened – suggesting that while the men were indeed KGB agents, their motives were different.

The Soviet trip was the third element of Cameron's gap year. Before embarking on his Siberian travels, he'd taken up two enviable internships. Cameron's parents had been happy to call on relatives in high places to pique their son's interest in politics while he was at Eton. Now they used their extensive social and professional network to set him up with two prestigious job placements shortly after he left school: one in the House of Commons; the other working for a billionaire in the Far East. They were the sort of internships most school leavers can only dream of, and they fell into Cameron's lap.

The first came about because his godfather, Tim Rathbone, was a Tory MP. Rathbone was a pro-European, described by Cameron himself as 'a very nice guy but a bit of a wet'.[39] The MP set him to work investigating the poor provision of nursery education and the failure of government drugs policy. This research seems to have caught his imagination: he showed an unusual interest in drugs policy when he entered politics himself.

The second placement was in the Hong Kong offices of Jardine Matheson, a highly successful trading conglomerate whose origins traced back to Imperial China. It was run by an old friend of Cameron's father, Sir Henry Keswick, who was delighted to help out by offering Cameron a role as a so-called 'ship jumper'.

Keswick recalls:

> He worked for us for six months. His father was our broker and very good friends with everybody. David was what they call a ship jumper, which is actually a rather nice job. When the ships come into Hong Kong, somebody has to go out to the launch with the customs and immigration and the port authorities, and organise to take off the cargo. You have to be ready night and day, so you are quite busy. It's a proper job, and he did it very well. We liked him very much.

---

39   David Cameron and Dylan Jones, p. 42. Rathbone was later expelled from the Conservatives for backing a breakaway pro-European party, having become a serial parliamentary rebel.

The crews he dealt with spoke to each other in pidgin English. Cameron has recalled how he found himself trying to translate Mandarin pidgin English into Cantonese pidgin English.[40]

Keswick was so impressed by Cameron's general performance that he offered him a place on Jardine Matheson's graduate training scheme after he finished at Oxford. He remembers Cameron politely declining, saying he wanted to go into politics.

Instead of flying home from Hong Kong, Cameron decided on a much more adventurous route home by land and sea. His first stop was Japan, from where he took a ferry to the bleak Soviet port of Nakhodka, then the stepping-off point for the Trans-Siberian Railway. (Its eastern terminus, Vladivostok, headquarters of the Soviet Pacific Fleet, was closed to foreigners at the time.)

For an eighteen-year-old fresh out of Eton, the Trans-Siberian Express must have been unforgettable. Those familiar with the experience in those days talk of primitive toilets and dreadful, monotonous food; the feeling of being snooped on; looking out of grubby windows at endless birch trees. They talk of seeing conscripts going to work in their units, unsmiling train attendants bearing samovars of tea, stunning Siberian women, and the boredom of an eight-day journey through wasteland. They remember brief stops at some of the remotest stations in the world, with babushkas selling smoked fish, pickled vegetables and fur hats to passengers on the platform. Some itineraries included overnight stops in bleak hotels, devoid of basics like bath plugs. For many Westerners, the sheer culture shock of that first gulp of the USSR was monumental.

The experience of Communist Russia affected Cameron deeply.

He has said of the visit:

> It was just remarkable. You had people following you everywhere and you had to have passes to go here, there and everywhere. It was such a controlled existence…That split between East and West was one of the things that definitely got me interested in politics and in particular Conservative politics; that whole issue of

---

40   Interview in Woodstock Town Hall between David Cameron and Godfrey
      Howard, author of *The Macmillan Good English Handbook*, 13 October
      2006.

the individual versus the state, that whole thing, that was what
fired me up.[41]

However, attempting to get to the bottom of what happened to him once
he arrived in Crimea is no easy task, not least because the Russian authorities are so twitchy. The incident first came to light in 2006 when Cameron
appeared on BBC Radio 4's *Desert Island Discs*. During the programme
he talked about the encounter on the beach, speculating that the men were
KGB agents. He revealed that MI5 showed considerable interest in his trip
to Russia when he later applied for security clearance to become a special
adviser at the Treasury. He said he discussed the encounter with Vernon
Bogdanor, his politics tutor at Oxford, who also interpreted it as an attempt
by the KGB to recruit him. He repeated the claim after he became Prime
Minister, mentioning it during a speech at Moscow State University on an
official trip to Russia in 2011. Afterwards, Dmitry Medvedev, now Prime
Minister, was asked by journalists if he thought Cameron would have made a
good KGB agent. The British Prime Minister immediately interjected, saying,
'No.' In good humour, Medvedev disagreed. 'I am sure that David would
have been a very good KGB agent, but then, he would never have become
Prime Minister of Great Britain,' he replied.

Evidently the exchange unsettled the Kremlin. It has emerged that spy
chiefs were ordered to get to the bottom of it. According to a highly placed
secret service source in Russia: 'Checks were made and the definite conclusion
was that there was no attempt to recruit him. Nothing like that happened,
it wasn't true.'

So anxious was the Kremlin to quash the story that shortly before this book
was published, in July 2015, a rambling article appeared in *Komsomolskaya
Pravda*, a pet newspaper of the regime, suggesting that the two men who
approached Cameron and his friend were notorious local gays and that
Cameron's Russia trip was in fact sponsored by MI6.[42] As we shall see, this
does not stack up.

We retraced Cameron's journey across Russia, tracking down various
retired officials involved in foreign tourism at the time. We also spoke to
several KGB veterans and Russian intelligence experts. Our research suggests

---

41   David Cameron and Dylan Jones, pp. 33–4.
42   http://www.kp.ru/daily/26413.3/3286488.

Cameron attracted attention from the Soviet authorities long before he reached Crimea, not least because of his high-level family connections.

As a British teenager a few months out of Eton, with connections to both the Conservative Party and the royal family (his godmother, Fiona Aird, was a lady-in-waiting to Princess Margaret, and her husband, Sir Alastair Aird, was at the time Comptroller of the Queen Mother's Household), travelling alone across Russia 'the wrong way' from the Pacific coast to Moscow, he was always going to stand out. It is likely he came under special scrutiny from the moment he applied for his visa.

The Russian intelligence expert and author Gennady Sokolov has examined Cameron's trip across Siberia at this time and spoken to his contacts among Cold War KGB spies.

'Let's look at the facts here, starting with his background,' he says.

> Of course, no one could know about his future career then, but there were some interesting elements about him which might have begun to show up after he made his booking and provided information for his visa application for what was a most unusual trip. Being an Etonian on his way to Oxford University was one factor, but other aspects about him too might have shown on checks.

Sokolov lists Ian Cameron's work for Panmure Gordon, a company that dealt with the foreign debt of various countries, and his position as chairman of White's, as well as the Camerons' proximity to the Tory establishment and links with the royal family.

'A close family friend and neighbour of the Cameron family was Sir Brian McGrath, who, in 1985, the year of David's trip, was private secretary and treasurer to Prince Philip. So this was a very well-connected young man,' he says.

How much of this would Russian intelligence agents have known, though?

KGB veteran Igor Prelin – a colonel who coached a young spy named Vladimir Putin in the dark arts of espionage – said that even before the age of super-fast computers 'we had a good system of databases and a simple check of the name could have brought amazing results'.

In the long history of spying between the Soviet Union and Britain, 1985 was a remarkable year. Shortly before Cameron arrived in the USSR, Oleg

Gordievsky, Moscow's senior spy in London, was abruptly recalled amid suspicions that he was an MI6 double agent – as indeed he was. He was drugged and subjected to ruthless interrogation. He managed to alert the British that he was in danger, and a plot was hatched to smuggle him out of Russia to Finland in the boot of a diplomatic car in July 1985, giving Britain one of its greatest espionage triumphs of the entire Cold War.

Against a backdrop of deep political mistrust, foreign travellers to the USSR were issued with a number of blunt warnings by their embassies, echoed in guidebooks. It is likely that Cameron had a copy of Fodor's *Soviet Union*, which cautioned travellers not to compare Russian standards with those in the West. 'Beware of agents provocateurs. Avoid sexual entanglements,' it counselled.

We tracked down the Russian official who oversaw Cameron's arrival. As head of 'Intourist-Nakhodka' – the local government tourist office – Gennady Eslikov was responsible for all travellers who entered the Soviet Union from Japan during this period. He explained how the process worked.

'All tourists, even if they came as individuals rather than on a group tour, were accompanied by our translators. This was the system. It was easier for us to control foreigners.'

Travellers arrived by ferry: either the *Felix Dzerzhinsky*, named after the cruel founder of the Soviet secret service following the Bolshevik revolution – or one of three smaller vessels. The circuitous journey took fifty-four hours and would have been Cameron's first taste of Soviet Communism.

Eslikov says:

> The crew of these ships included musicians, who gave two concerts during the journey. All the waitresses and chambermaids were selected according to their ability to sing or dance traditional Russian songs. Some talented girls were selected. They did their jobs during the day, and performed with the musicians in the evening. Why were they interested in such work? They were paid in hard currency and could use it to buy foreign goods in Yokohama.

They had another function too: to monitor new arrivals to the USSR on behalf of the KGB.

Entering the Soviet Union at Nakhodka was a cumbersome and bureaucratic process. 'The sea port was built by Japanese prisoners of war in the

1950s,' Eslikov says. 'It was wooden and cramped, with insufficient space for customs and border guards. With several hundred people disembarking, the paperwork went very slowly, and the train to Khabarovsk, where tourists joined the Trans-Siberian train, often left later than scheduled.' Bags were routinely opened and searched by unsmiling officers, who were ordered to seize any pornography or religious literature, as well as anything deemed to be spying or printing equipment. All supplies of foreign cigarettes or liquor in quantities that might be used for black market trading were also confiscated.

The shepherding and controlling of tourist groups began at once. Though it was only a three-minute walk, travellers were usually bussed from the port to the modest railway station. The aim was to shield them from the squalor they might observe, and from the risk of being robbed.

'The fact is we lived much poorer [lives] than our foreign visitors, but we did not want them to see the poverty, to avoid giving them facts for counter-propaganda,' Eslikov says.

For the 547-mile overnight run to Khabarovsk, Cameron is thought to have joined one of the plushest trains then in service in Russia. 'It was quite exotic, made before the Second World War in Germany,' according to Eslikov. It would have swiftly dispelled the idea that the USSR was classless.

'Usually, the train had eight or nine wagons, two of them superior class, and the rest first class. The schedule was connected to the timing of the ships.'

The unusually luxurious sleeping berths on this special green and cream-coloured train, with its air conditioning, comfortable couches, bronze handles and even shower cabins, were almost exclusively occupied by foreigners. It left at 8 p.m., after which passengers would have dinner and then settle down for the night.

According to Fodor's guidebook:

> The next morning, lady attendants call passengers with tea from the samovar, typical Russian tea in a glass, while breakfast is taken in the diner, the Ussuri River may be seen on the left of the train, with wild forest and hill country on the other. In the forests are the last Siberian tigers.'

Russian Intourist guides who accompanied the train were taught to be vigilant and report anything untoward to the KGB.

Some individuals would come under 'intense scrutiny'.

'It was noticed that one Japanese tourist woke up at about 4 a.m. and tried to take pictures through the window. It turned out that his target was military airfields which were hidden by trees and earth walls,' Eslikov recalls.

The secret services often worked through interpreters and guides accompanying tourists. According to Eslikov, 'They could ask, for example, to talk to tourists in order to know their mood; their impressions; their views. Just to try to understand them.'

According to another former worker on the route, Cameron would have stood out because of his age. Intourist translator Natalia Shevarkova, who worked in Nakhodka, says it was very rare to see British tourists travelling east to west. Most were much older than Cameron and came from Australia and New Zealand.

Generally, foreigners on the actual Trans-Siberian trains, from Khabarovsk to Moscow, were physically segregated from locals in tourist wagons. However, there were occasional opportunities to meet and interact with Soviet travellers, for example, in the restaurant car or wandering around the train.

'We helped with the translations. Russians told about themselves, about their families, children, told their stories. Some had relatives that moved abroad or participated in the World War Two...They exchanged souvenirs, books, postcards, badges,' Shevarkova says.

When he finally arrived in Moscow, Cameron met up with Griffith, an old friend from Eton. It is not known what the other Old Etonian, son of a well-connected Welsh farmer and landowner, was doing in Russia, but the pair travelled to Leningrad and then by plane to Simferopol, the capital of Crimea, and on to Yalta. On the southern coastline of the Crimean peninsula, Yalta was the Soviet Union's premier summer playground. Dubbed the Russian Riviera, it had a subtropical climate and pebbly beaches beneath a craggy mountain ridge thick with pine and juniper forests.

In Yalta, as on the Trans-Siberian journey, the extent of snooping on foreigners in 1985 was prodigious. The resort was seen as the tourism jewel of the USSR, and had two main hotels for foreigners, including Western diplomats. There were small KGB offices on the premises.

A guide and interpreter who worked there the year Cameron visited says: 'Diplomats were closely watched, but so too were other foreigners who were perceived as being of interest. I was told that bugging hotel rooms, and listening to phone calls, was easy for them, and not uncommon.'

Another guide explains: 'The old men on the external doors of the hotel, checking hotel cards to ensure only guests got inside, were KGB pensioners. The floor ladies in the hotel were by and large the wives of KGB officers.'

Stationed on each floor of the Soviet hotel, these female staff were a peculiarity of the Communist era. Having checked in at reception, guests would be issued with a hotel card, which they would exchange with the floor lady for a key. The women might also sell bottled water and small snacks and would watch guests with a hawk's eye, especially foreigners, who stayed in slightly better-quality rooms on separate floors from Soviet guests.

Today, security in Yalta is also vigilant, following the political upheaval linked to Russian annexation, though at the larger hotels, there is still scope for revelry. Some offer 'erotic shows' and spa treatments and massages. The restaurants serve wide-ranging international cuisine. Back in 1985, things were more restrained. In a section on 'Nightlife', Fodor's guide would have told Cameron: 'By and large, there is no such thing in the Soviet Union, no nightclubs or bars, though there is often singing while you eat in restaurants and hotels.'

However, there were plenty of beachside cafés and some better restaurants where it could be very difficult to get a table. This does not seem to have been a problem for the two men who took a shine to Cameron and Griffith on the beach and invited them to lunch and dinner. They claimed to work at one of the local hotels.

Griffith has told how they were plied with large quantities of vodka and 'may have been a little intoxicated when they began hitting us with questions. It all seemed rather strange.'

After a while the Old Etonians began feeling uneasy. The men appeared to be encouraging them to criticise Britain and the Thatcher regime. It seems to have been Cameron who began wondering how the pair could afford such extravagant food and drink if they only had fairly menial jobs. 'How can he afford to pay for this lunch on his meagre salary?' he is said to have whispered, before taking the lead in opting not to meet the Russians for a second night.[43]

---

43   *Sunday Telegraph*, 18 September 2011. There was a subsequent apology for misquotation in the article, which has been removed from the *Telegraph* website. Extensive efforts were made to get Griffith to identify inaccuracies, to no avail.

Our research among those familiar with both main hotels in Yalta at the time – the art deco tsarist-era Oreanda, much later visited by Tony Blair (whose grinning picture hangs on a wall of the hotel along with such luminaries as Dominique Strauss-Kahn), and the gargantuan concrete monster the Yalta Intourist – suggests Cameron was right to be wary. The men did not work at either of the hotels.

However, nor were they from the local KGB office. We tracked down the former head of the KGB office in Yalta at the time, who spoke to us on strict condition of anonymity.

'I can assure you that this was not an operation by Yalta KGB,' he declared. 'None of my former colleagues can recall two young British men. If we'd had a plan to take them for dinner, then invite them to a second dinner, and they got scared and left, this would have been remembered.'

He believes the approach may have come from KGB headquarters in Moscow or the Far East.

> This moment was on Yalta beach but these KGB men from another region were not obliged to inform us in Yalta about their work here, not even about their visit. We can only guess what this other KGB needed them for. Maybe it was an attempted long shot, like the Cambridge Five story, just because they were two Eton students.

This view is echoed by another Yalta source with a sharp memory of this period.

> If they were indeed KGB officers, ordered to find more about these two Old Etonians on their Soviet adventure, then it would appear they were sent from Moscow, and were not the local agents. The descriptions given of these men do not fit those who worked here at the time.

He pointed out that buying caviar and sturgeon in the mid-1980s, in large quantities, was exceptional. While they are well-known Russian delicacies, and were available to the masses in Soviet times, in 1985 such largesse would have been expensive. We can conclude that the men either had a large expense account or considerable sway with the restaurant. KGB agents might have both.

Sokolov suggests that so far from attempting to recruit Cameron and his friend, the KGB may have feared the Old Etonians were actually MI6 assets.

'Cameron's trip echoed an earlier adventure by another Eton and Oxford man half a century before. That man was Duncan Sandys, and he went on to be a Conservative politician and, indeed, the Minister for Defence of the United Kingdom,' Sokolov says.

> He was accompanied by Christopher Fuller, the son of a former MP. There were other such 'tourist' trips too, over the years, and the KGB came to believe that the British secret services used these visits as intelligence-gathering operations and/or to test out the ability and suitability of young men who might later be recruited as agents. How well did they notice things? Could they talk to the Russians they met without arousing suspicions? The belief was that on such trips there was sometimes a minder posing as an older tourist, who was indeed a career spy, in the same group, watching and assessing.

It sounds far-fetched – after all, Cameron was only eighteen – but at the time, the Russians were convinced young travellers were used in this way. It was an era in which foreign intelligence services struggled to engineer access to the Soviet Union, and young tourists were a potential vehicle for information gathering.

The suggestion in *Pravda* that the approach was homosexual – a consideration that also occurred to Cameron and Griffith – was rubbished by our sources. Gay sex was illegal in Russia at the time, and the men would have been taking an extraordinary risk. Furthermore, it seems unlikely they would have attempted to engage their targets in hostile political questioning.

'It doesn't make sense,' says a former Yalta tourist guide.

> If these men wanted to get them into bed, why did they annoy them so much by leading them into a political discussion that made the young Brits so uneasy? The other point is that for two Soviet citizens to openly try and pick up these foreigners on the beach with a sexual motive – knowing that these foreigners could have been closely watched by the KGB – would mean that the two men were extremely powerful and had very high-level protection indeed.

Pravda's claim that the two Russians were also 'fartsovschiki' – small-time black market traders who would sometimes approach Western tourists to trade things like jeans, T-shirts and electronic goods – has attracted equal scepticism from those in the know. Such individuals might have been hoping to make useful business contacts through Cameron and Griffith, but the explanation does not fit with the heavy political conversation or expensive entertaining.

'The black marketeer idea is nonsense,' says the former head of the KGB in Yalta. 'I never met a black marketeer the age of the older man. They were all youngsters. And they were keen to make money, not to waste it on dinners with unknown people, even foreigners.'

So if the pair were KGB officers from Moscow, what did they hope to achieve?

Igor Prelin believes it may simply have been a fishing exercise.

'I can believe it was a generous meeting, with good food – we always knew how to please our guests. I would not necessarily call it "recruiting", but it might have been a meeting aimed at making friends.' He agrees that Cameron may have aroused interest as he applied to enter Russia, or on the Trans-Siberian, or perhaps because of some contacts the pair had in Moscow. He adds that it could have been the KGB just ticking boxes: agents were encouraged to file reports, however trivial.

Retired General Yuri Kobaladze was regarded as one of the ablest KGB spies of his generation during his seven years working undercover in Britain. Posing as a Soviet radio journalist, he targeted mainly Labour and trade union figures, winning a reputation for being able to drink Fleet Street's finest hacks under the table. He is unsure how to interpret what happened.

He says cryptically:

> One needs to be very cautious here, since we are talking about the country's Prime Minister. I can tell you one thing for sure – I was not that young man who fed David Cameron with caviar. Though, I can tell you another: if I had been that man, I would not admit it.

The most compelling explanation is that Cameron and his friend were being used by the KGB as part of a routine training exercise. This theory was advanced by another retired spy with vast Cold War experience. He reviewed all available information about the case and talked to former colleagues. He asked to meet in a small, unfashionable café, a mile and a half north of the Kremlin. He arrived ten minutes early, sat unobtrusively in a corner, and ordered black tea. He spoke clearly and fluently, saying he had little time.

'No one will ever provide documents to show you what happened here, but I have a strong hunch, though you cannot take this as any kind of official confirmation,' he said.

It is very possibly right that this was a meeting with serving agents, as these two suspected at the time, but I think the reason is rather different to what has been suggested. I am pretty certain there was no thought of recruitment. Let's be logical. These boys were straight out of school, and theirs was hardly an academy that produced ardent Communists, though maybe there were the occasional exceptions. The direction of their life was not set yet. They were in this gap year, which by its name implies these lads have not yet found themselves, nor their path.

What happened here, to my mind, was that Yasenevo [the area of Moscow where the KGB's foreign intelligence directorate was sited; now the headquarters of the SVR espionage agency] became aware that these two Etonians were taking their vacations in the Soviet Union, and this offered the chance for a couple of agents to meet and converse with real-life well-educated young Brits. I would think the agents in question were people who might be later posted abroad, very possibly to Britain, but who – because of our system – had very little experience of communicating with educated British people. Nowadays tens of thousands of young Russians go to London each year to language school; they mix freely, travel widely, so this is hardly an issue. But then it was different. The agents were, to my mind, seeking to learn about what these people believed, their interests, their way of speaking, what they liked, what annoyed them. Trying to get a hook on the British.

In fact, it wasn't so unusual. Our agents might be deployed as Foreign Ministry interpreters for socialist politicians coming to the Soviet Union, say Labour MPs or trade unionists, or journalists or businessmen. It was like a training exercise, trying to understand better the people you would later be working amongst. Some could later turn into contacts, perhaps, but with two such young guys, no.

He laughed and took a final sip of tea. 'Now then, if we had known how high Cameron would rise, we might have tried harder.'

There is a final curious twist to the tale. Just before this book went to press, we were alerted to an old article buried in a Russian weekly newspaper, *Argumenti Nedeli*. It was published in 2011, shortly after Cameron's comments at Moscow State University, and went unnoticed by Western media. The author of the article, a reporter called Alexander Kondrashov, claimed to have tracked down one of the two men who wined and dined Cameron and Griffith. He identified the individual as Igor Kuznetsov, a former KGB colonel.

The reporter met the retired spy, who gave him a highly colourful account of his supposed encounter with the future Prime Minister, claiming that it was indeed a recruitment attempt, and involved a 'swallow' – a busty female agent – in whom the two Englishmen showed no interest. Kuznetsov further claimed that during the evening, Cameron asked his new Russian friends for drugs.

'I remember David was so surprised when for the dinner with black caviar we paid just ten roubles per person, fifty roubles altogether,' he told the reporter.

> At first there were only men. And after the fifth glass of wine a girl of fantastic beauty joined us. Her operational nickname was Oksa – just a short version of her real name. She was the best 'swallow' of the Yalta KGB office. We drank a lot that day. The black caviar was very much appreciated by the young aristocrats [*sic*]. And provocative Oksana with her large breasts did not attract them. The nineteen-year-old boys were more interested in a slim figure called Valery, a local Intourist interpreter who was in the KGB.

Asked how the evening ended, the retired KGB officer told the reporter: 'Oksana was the first to leave – she felt offended with the lack of male attention. Then we carried deadly drunk Griffith to his room. David Cameron kept going, but asked us to find some "grass" for him or maybe even something stronger. We promised to do it next day.'

He claimed KGB bosses refused to let him supply any narcotics, and decided to abandon any recruitment attempt. 'In London, it is said, the Soviet resident considered Cameron to have no prospects. Young man, likes drugs, he won't go too far in his career…As we see now, the resident of Soviet intelligence made a serious mistake.'

Our attempts to substantiate this tantalising tale drew a blank. We could not find any record of an Igor Kuznetsov in the KGB in Yalta at that time. Then again, he may have used a different name back then. He died two years ago, perhaps carrying the key to what really happened in Yalta to his grave.

6

THE FLAM CLUB

'We were probably the last of an era. We drank champagne...'
– James Delingpole

Safely back from his adventures in Russia, Cameron headed up to Oxford to begin his degree. At university, he was in no hurry to join any of the many political clubs, but he did become a member of an obscure secret society whose activities were of the illicit recreational variety.

Now and again, members of the club would meet in an upstairs bedroom in Christ Church, where they could be found sprawled on the floor smoking dope. Naturally, the door was shut, but anyone walking past might have caught a whiff of the sweet musky smell of drugs and heard laughter and music coming from within.

Whiling away the hours riffing about this and that while dragging on joints were three exceptionally bright young men: James Fergusson, who was to become a distinguished writer; James Delingpole, who was to become a high-profile right-wing journalist; and the future Prime Minister.

The setting was Delingpole's room in Peckwater Quad, one of the finest quadrangles in one of the finest, if not *the* finest, colleges in Oxford. More likely than not, the trio would be listening to the 1970s rock band Supertramp and bantering inconsequentially about their love lives while getting stoned. They even gave themselves a name: 'The Flam Club'.

'My drug of choice was weed, and I smoked weed with Dave because James's drug of choice was also weed,' says Delingpole.

> So he and James would come round to my room and the three of us would listen to Supertramp albums. I wasn't in one of the grand

shared rooms in Peckwater Quad – I had a room on the top floor, and we would all sit on the floor and smoke dope, and we would call ourselves the Flam Club. A flam is a succession of drum beats close together, designed to create a richly satisfying noise, and Supertramp use them quite a lot.

The origins of the Flam Club lay in the friendship between Delingpole and Fergusson, who were both studying English. Fergusson had been at Eton with Cameron, as a result of which the three became friends, though they were very different personalities.

Delingpole remembers:

James had just come back from Guatemala and El Salvador and he was wearing those hippy threads and had long hair and he'd strum his guitar. Dave and I used to tease him for being a fucking hippy. We'd tell him to go get a haircut. Dave was much more obviously Old Etonian than James – he had a much fruitier accent. He had that assured accent of the upper classes, and was always well presented; very conventional. He would be wearing a cricket sweater.

While Cameron was still at Eton, Christ Church had featured heavily as a location in Granada TV's adaptation of the Evelyn Waugh classic *Brideshead Revisted*, which explores the relationship between the unsophisticated undergraduate Charles Ryder and a dazzling aristocratic student called Lord Sebastian Flyte and his family. The series made a huge impact. While the novel was set in the 1920s, some who watched it in the early 1980s and became Oxford students themselves were so struck by it that they appear to have wanted to make life imitate art.

According to Delingpole:

Dave arrived a year after me. When I arrived, *Brideshead Revisited* had just been on TV. There was a division at Oxford between those of us who wanted to live the Brideshead lifestyle – to ape it – and the people wearing donkey jackets who were in support of the miners. The atmosphere among those of us who wanted to live the Brideshead life was really quite pleasant. There were cocktail

parties in the Masters' Garden…and we could all play at being
Sebastian Flyte.

A 1987 issue of the student newspaper *Cherwell* reported that Oxford
'remains obsessed with the eccentricities of public school privilege and the
Brideshead Sloane clone set. Students here seem to have avoided all the more
radical manifestations of alternative culture, as if 1977 took the ring road
to avoid passing through the dreaming spires…'

Christ Church has produced thirteen British prime ministers, as many as
all other Oxford colleges combined, but Cameron is not among them. Before
leaving Eton, apparently on the advice of Eton masters, he had applied to a
less famous college, Brasenose. In the early 1980s it was generally considered to be a 'sports' college, rather than an academic one. However, it had
begun to acquire a good reputation for PPE, and for economics in particular. Cameron gave a sufficiently impressive performance to be awarded an
exhibition, a form of partial scholarship, despite being caught bluffing in
the interview.[44] Along with four other Old Etonians from his year, he took
up his place in autumn 1985.

Arriving in college, he was eager to make friends with people like himself.
A contemporary who had a room across the corridor from his recalls:

> I met David on the very first day. He asked where I had come from,
> and I didn't realise he actually meant which school I had been to, so
> I said, 'Luton', as that was where I was living at the time. He then
> gave me a big smile and exclaimed, 'But I'm from Eton too! Have
> we never met?' He had misheard. It was funny. When I repeated that
> I was from Luton he looked at me in disbelief. Luton was a bit of a
> dump, and he had probably never met anyone from a place like that.[45]

Cameron's political coming-of-age coincided almost exactly with Margaret
Thatcher's eleven years in office: by the time he arrived at Oxford, Thatcher
was comfortably into her second term. Arthur Scargill and the National
Union of Mineworkers had agreed to return to work seven months earlier,

---

44   About how much philosophy he had read; Francis Elliott and James Hanning,
     p. 45.
45   Private information.

ending a year of brutal confrontation between the government and the NUM. As with much of the Thatcher government's programme, the episode was divisive, but Cameron was always clear which side he was on. 'If you grew up under Thatcher,' he reflected later, 'you either thought she was doing the wrong thing or she was doing the right thing and I thought she was doing the right thing.'[46] He took a similar view of the Wapping unions dispute, which began during his second term in Oxford. 'I thought it was bizarre, these people at university who refused to take *The Times* because of the Wapping dispute,' he has said[47] of the row between print workers and Rupert Murdoch's News International. For him, advancing economic progress and eradicating outdated practices was paramount. 'I was never in any doubt about the print unions; it was always very clear-cut to me.'

It was a period of bitter ideological battles: protectionism versus free trade; privatisation versus nationalisation and trade union power versus consumer power. Cameron has said that these arguments were 'uppermost' in his mind during this period.[48] If so, he was insufficiently exercised to play an active part in the debate. While the Oxford Union is not formally a party political institution, and membership does not require allegiance to any party – it is simply a debating society – it is an ideal platform for students who aspire to a career in politics. Running for office in the Union, or the Oxford University Conservative Association, or a college, was an obvious opportunity to practise for future electioneering. Yet Cameron was not interested.

It would be wrong to suggest he didn't enjoy a hearty intellectual debate. Steve Rathbone, who was at Brasenose with him, says he showed a clear interest in the key issues of the day and seemed 'quietly confident he had formed a sensible position on things'. However, he preferred to chew things over in the bar.

> Our college was a place of feisty debate in the JCR. There were some very witty people. David Cameron was very much one of those. In those days you would have the very po-faced lot known as the Left Caucus; they really were po-faced beyond measure. They would earnestly trot in and want to talk about the weighty issues of the

---

46   David Cameron and Dylan Jones, p. 34.
47   Ibid., p. 35.
48   Ibid, p. 79.

> day. Then there was quite a raw group of people who wanted to
> have a good time and not lament what was happening elsewhere.
> David was very good – he was part of the group that was able to
> have a good laugh and puncture pomposity with wit.

Some were so struck by his repartee that they speculated that he was destined for a political career. Rathbone remembers: 'I said, "He'll be in the Cabinet one day." It was his brain power; his ability to communicate quite complex ideas very clearly; his self-confidence – there was a very strong vein of that going through him.'

Yet all this was informal. His most proactive political intervention seems to have been throwing a party in his college room to celebrate Thatcher's 1987 election triumph.[49] His failure to participate in student politics has been a source of puzzlement, especially as it was such a lively scene.

A cursory glance at the pages of Oxford's student press at the time reveals just how febrile the political atmosphere was among students of this era. Street protests were regular occurrences, and 'no platform' controversies surrounding the invitation of far-right guests to speak at the Oxford Union were frequent and often fiercely contested. Contemporaries who went on to have stellar political careers were getting stuck in.

Fellow PPE-er Ed Balls, who had joined the Labour Party at sixteen, was so keen that he joined all three of the Labour, Conservative and SDP Societies when he arrived at Oxford, apparently because he wanted to see as many visiting speakers as possible.[50]

Jeremy Hunt, who went on to become Culture Secretary and Health Secretary under Cameron, was President of the Oxford University Conservative Association (OUCA). Surprisingly, for a politician who now has a reputation for well-mannered diplomacy, he was a divisive figure. The *Cherwell* described him variously as a 'failed hack'; a 'self-styled over-achiever' and finally, in a particularly bilious piece taking aim at his 'dadsie' for purportedly securing him a post with a Hong Kong financial house, 'the king of yuppies…Jeremy "Merchant wanker" Hunt'.

Meanwhile Michael Gove, later to become Cameron's Education Secretary, was so outspoken when he arrived at Oxford that he was anointed 'Pushy

---

49   Francis Elliott and James Hanning, p. 68.
50   Guy Adams, *The Independent*, 5 July 2006.

Fresher of the Year' by the *Cherwell* (an honour also bestowed on the future BBC political editor Nick Robinson). His name crops up in numerous back issues, where he is described as 'the best debater in the Union'. There are references to his 'lilting Aberdeen tones and impeccable Young Fogey dress sense', as well as a claim that he concealed 'rabidly reactionary political views under a Jane Austen cleric-like exterior'. Gove also achieved notoriety for an alleged five-in-a-bed 'romp' with fellow Oxford Union members and for his role in a bitter love triangle.

As for Boris Johnson, he was President of the Union in 1986, having already made his mark running unsuccessfully for the post a year earlier.

Delingpole says: '*Everyone* knew who Boris was. Boris had, in that Churchillian way, made up his mind who he was going to be by that time, while most of us were still experimenting with our personalities. Boris was already fully formed.'

Many other future MPs who were at Oxford during this period made their mark in student politics: David Miliband (who led a campaign to boycott Barclays Bank and hassled the university authorities to build more student accommodation); Ed Vaizey (described variously as a 'pompous, round-bellied windbag' and an 'inflatable bore' with a 'Friar Tuck girth' by *Cherwell*) who set his sights, unsuccessfully, on the Union presidency and was active in the OUCA; and Jacob Rees-Mogg, another winner of *Cherwell*'s 'Pushiest Fresher' award and later an OUCA president. Yet there is no mention of Cameron in back copies of these student publications.

It was global issues that most exercised his Oxford contemporaries. By the mid-1980s, the anti-apartheid movement was reaching its zenith on British campuses, and Oxford students were at the forefront of the international divestment campaign. Four colleges – although not Brasenose – closed their Barclays bank accounts early in 1986 and urged the entire university to do the same. Palestine, too, was a cause célèbre: in Cameron's last year the First Intifada broke out in the Occupied Territories, capturing the imagination of student journalists and activists throughout the university and prompting calls for student solidarity with the Palestinians. Gay rights, Women's Lib and AIDS awareness campaigning were also zeitgeist concerns for large numbers of students of this generation.

An exhaustive search of the university archives reveals no record of Cameron speaking out on these issues, though he did join a committee to organise his college May Ball. This marked the beginning of an important friendship – the chairman was Andrew Feldman, who has been described as Cameron's 'oldest political friend' – but it was hardly evidence of a burning desire to set the world to rights.

A consequence of his avoidance of student politics is that primary source evidence of his early political thinking is thin on the ground. We are left with the recollections of his former tutors and Oxford contemporaries. Peter Sinclair, his former economics tutor, recalls him taking a 'more pro-market' view than many of his contemporaries.

'He was rather keener than the others on the logic of what the market would lead to and slightly less concerned with the wrinkles that could justify a different view…His views were on the whole a bit more to the right than most of the others,' Sinclair has said.[51]

Cameron's philosophy don, John Foster, has said he 'didn't lose sleep over philosophical problems, about the ultimate nature of things', an observation now made by a number of sources commenting on his political thinking as party leader ('You don't get many levels down the argument with him,' says one who knows him.) Steve Rathbone, president of Brasenose JCR in Cameron's day, has said his politics were 'very much centrist Tory', adding that he had no time for 'Monday Club types'.[52]

However, he did support the right of a Monday Club representative to speak at Brasenose, adopting the same freedom of speech principle in relation to an appearance by Sinn Féin leader Gerry Adams, a view he apparently changed having listened to the speech.[53]

Why, after securing a stint in the Commons during his gap year and apparently declaring aged fourteen that he would one day be Prime Minister, did he not get more involved? Perhaps he simply thought that there would be plenty of time for all that in later life. After all, his father, who had been incredibly proud when Cameron won his place at Oxford, had always encouraged him to strike a healthy work–life balance.

'He thought you could work and enjoy yourself…You should have some time to think and make friends,' Cameron has said.[54]

51 Francis Elliott and James Hanning, p. 71.
52 The Monday Club was a right-wing Conservative group disaffiliated from the party in 2001 because of its policies relating to race and ethnic minorities.
53 Francis Elliott and James Hanning, p. 70.
54 Harry Mount interview, op. cit.

It is certainly not that Cameron was lazy. Having set his sights on a First, he worked hard. Delingpole has described the Oxford University experience as 'a bit like a war – long periods of blissful inactivity and then intense moments of overnight essay crises when you'd take your Pro Plus and your coffee, because otherwise you'd get your arse kicked by your tutor', adding that there was 'room in our lives for the occasional spliff…particularly in the summer term'. Yet Cameron was well organised and conscientious. Fergusson remembers being 'impressed and slightly alarmed' by his intense focus. 'I was keen on my subject, but nothing like as keen as he was. He knew exactly what he wanted, which was to be the top-dog student and to get a First. That was it without a doubt. He loved it, he was passionate about it.'[55] In recognition of his talent and commitment, his tutors upgraded his exhibition to a full scholarship.[56] He also chose the more difficult path to obtaining a top-class degree, opting to continue with all three elements of the PPE course after his first year, rather than dropping one subject and sitting extra papers in the others, as he was entitled to do. His former tutor Vernon Bogdanor, whose distinguished reputation apparently attracted Cameron to Brasenose, has said he was among the brightest 5 per cent of students he has ever taught. He has suggested that Cameron made such an impressive contribution in tutorials that he may have helped lift the grades of less able students in his group. Peter Sinclair has also described him as an 'outstanding student', saying he was diplomatic and charming in response to those who disagreed with his point of view and would thank his tutors after sessions.[57]

Delingpole thinks Cameron simply didn't feel the need to play the student politics game.

> It comes back to this thing of it being the Thatcher era – we'd won the battle! If we were at Oxford now, I think we'd be talking seriously about the way that government has got too big; the way that our freedoms have been taken away; about political correctness. Of course, there was political correctness, but nothing like there is now. It was a different era. I'd say our era had more in common

---

55   Francis Elliott and James Hanning, p. 56.
56   Ibid., p. 57.
57   Ibid., p. 56.

with the period written about in *Children of the Sun* – the 1930s of
Evelyn Waugh and Brian Howard – than it does with the Oxford of
today. We were probably the last of an era. We drank champagne...

Sinclair has suggested that the relaxed atmosphere at Brasenose may also
have been a deterrent. He has described how

people would just sit around and drink coffee, chatting and just
loving it. It was a contented, cheerful, unstressed place. When [Cam-
eron] arrived, people in the year above would have said, 'Don't
bother with the Union, they're horrible hacks, knifing each other,
publicity-seeking creeps.' That's the line he would have heard from
everybody in Brasenose, so he might have thought, 'Right, that
sounds good advice.'[58]

Steve Rathbone agrees. 'He probably groaned a bit at the clichéd stuff
that would have been going on at the Oxford Union and the Conservative
Society. I think he probably wanted to have a good time and not become too
earnest too quickly.'

Cameron himself has said his happiest memories of university were
'drinking and chatting'. Asked what obsessed him at the time, he replied:
'Mainly girfriends!'

Clean cut, supremely self-assured, and good-looking, with 'slightly floppy
hair', he did not want for female attention. Rathbone says he would dress
'in a way that reflected that he was fairly well heeled. He would have been
considered to be well dressed, but by no means a dandy.'

By all accounts he was a hit with women, enjoying nights on the pull (a
recreation he apparently called 'wooding') at a club called Playpen, run by
some friends. The venue had a reputation as a meat market.

A contemporary whose room was across the corridor from his in college
recalls 'a conveyor belt of pretty girls coming in and out of his room'.

'Living next to him, I was quite jealous. Most people were, I imagine. I
think he slept with all the good-looking girls from college,' he recalls.

However, his romantic encounters were not all brief. At Oxford, he had
two serious girlfriends, Catherine Snow whom he dated in his first term,

58   Ibid., p. 71.

and Francesca Ferguson, a tall, half-German history student, with whom he had a long and committed affair. The daughter of a diplomat, she was far from the typical Sloane who fell at Cameron's feet. She has said that she 'didn't really feel part of his very English world', and 'didn't go skiing with everyone else, or stay in the same house in France as they all did'. She was bored by many of the people she met on the social circuit and felt Cameron was different. For his part, he was 'mad about Fran' and happily took up an invitation to stay with her and her family in Kenya, finding a holiday job 'shifting crates' to save money for the trip. Fran's parents apparently found him delightful, and were impressed when he discreetly left a thank-you note and tip for the Kenyan lady who cleaned his room.[59]

Cameron was not only well mannered, he was also kind, perhaps unusually so for someone at what is typically a self-absorbed age. Giles Andreae, who developed Hodgkin's disease in their last year at Oxford, has given a touching account of how Cameron helped care for him, even though they were in the middle of finals. Andreae was diagnosed late and his condition was life-threatening. Cameron used to drive him to Peasemore to recuperate after bouts of chemotherapy which would leave him very weak.

'Dave used to take me down in his car, tuck me up in bed, and give me some videos,' he has recalled. Andreae would stay in Peasemore for several days, watched over by Cameron's mother, while Cameron himself returned to Oxford to sit his exams.

Another Brasenose contemporary witnessed a similar act of compassion.

> In the summer of 1986, we let a fire extinguisher off through the letterbox of the *Cherwell* offices. Two of my co-conspirators were hauled before the college dean. One guy, Mark Mitchell, was hit with disciplinary action. Just after he was sentenced, he was moping around in New Quad at Brasenose. Dave came up to him and asked him what was up. To cheer him up, he offered to take him to his house in the countryside, where he had a lovely time, lounging by the pool and being fed cookies and milkshakes.

Not everybody was enchanted. To some, Cameron was an arrogant social climber.

59   Ibid., p. 65.

He was a regular guy, who would be in the Brasenose JCR drinking pints. But at the same time, there would be something in him that meant he could at any time just cut you, for not being quite the thing…Dave would have 'cocktail eyes' – so if you were at a drinks party, he'd give you the time of day, but if somebody more interesting came along, he'd soon be off.

The observation comes from someone who liked him anyway.

Before Cameron went up to Oxford, his godfather Tim Rathbone urged him to have fun. It was a piece of advice he took to heart. Later, he would defend what he called a 'normal university experience', but some of his behaviour would return to haunt him, particularly his involvement with the notorious Bullingdon Club.

Founded in 1780, the club began life as a hunting and cricket society (the badge still shows a cricket bat, stumps and a man on horseback) but gradually descended into a riotous drinking club for a highly select band of the super-rich. The bespoke uniform, of navy tailcoats, mustard-coloured waistcoats and sky-blue bow ties, could run to thousands of pounds, putting membership beyond the reach of ordinary students.

No other aspect of Cameron's life before he became an MP has played so beautifully into the hands of his political opponents, or proven such an ongoing source of embarrassment, as his fateful decision to join the 'Buller'. It may be an old story, but throughout his leadership various theatrical and cinematic representations ensured it never went away. Strangely, the highest-profile of these, a movie called *The Riot Club* which went on main release in cinemas across the UK in autumn 2014, was produced by Cameron's close friend Pete Czernin, with whom he was at Eton, and with whom he shared a flat when he was in his twenties. How Czernin could have imagined the film, a graphic and shocking tale of a debauched Buller gathering in an Oxfordshire pub, would do anything other than a disservice to his old friend is a mystery.

The worst damage was done by a photograph showing Cameron posing with fellow members of the society. The excruciating image of him in full 'Buller' regalia, which first emerged in 2006, kiboshed his early attempts to portray himself as a different kind of Conservative, conveying the message that he was hopelessly over-privileged and out of touch with ordinary people. So inconvenient was the image, that when the company that owned the original, Gillman & Soame, suddenly withdrew all copyright, rumours swirled that they had been paid off.

The photograph was originally uncovered by investigative journalist Margaret Crick, when she visited the office of Gillman & Soame asking to see any Oxford society or club photographs from Cameron's period. A picture assistant produced the image, taken in 1986 or 1987. It is thought the picture had previously hung in the nearby university outfitters, Ede & Ravenscroft, which supplies Bullingdon uniforms, which was why it was framed. Crick, who was helping Francis Elliott and James Hanning research their early biography of Cameron at the time, told them about the image, and permission was secured to reproduce it in their book. The agreement was that it would be credited to a 'private collection'. It is not known how much money changed hands.

The publication of the picture triggered a furore and copyright permission was abruptly withdrawn. Fleet Street picture desks and TV stations were issued with warnings. Simultaneously, Gillman & Soame withdrew its entire archive, stretching back decades, from media use. Whether the blanket ban was a way of justifying the removal of the controversial Bullingdon photo or whether it was genuine company policy following some kind of review is a matter of debate.

Gillman & Soame went bankrupt in 2001, reappearing as Gillman & Soame UK in 2002. The company's chequered financial history fuelled speculation that the directors may have accepted a lump sum in 2007 to withdraw their archive. Such a windfall would presumably have been welcome. For one thing, the company would have made a small fortune if it had carried on charging thousands of pounds for use of the picture. Rumours swirled that either Lord Chadlington – a wealthy PR man, Cotswold neighbour of Cameron and one of his earliest backers – or the party's former treasurer, the multimillionaire Michael Spencer, might have made a sizeable donation to the photographers to compensate them for such a loss. Both men vigorously deny it. It appears Gillman & Soame simply decided its reputation would suffer long-term damage if it developed a track record of releasing embarrassing pictures of students after they became public figures.

A spokeswoman for the company told us they felt it was not 'good business practice to release images to the media of photographs that were meant for private individuals; something that could affect our relationships with our main customers such as schools and colleges'. She added that the picture of Cameron was published before the new policy kicked in. 'We have never been offered money, or indeed accepted money, to withdraw this photograph. We understand that it might seem an interesting story to suggest otherwise, but the truth is much more mundane,' she said.

After Gillman & Soame slapped their ban on the Buller picture, television channels found ingenious ways to give viewers a flavour. Margaret Crick's former husband Michael, then a journalist on *Newsnight*, commissioned an Oxford artist called Rona to paint a replica. In any case, the original picture kept resurfacing. When a new Bullingdon photo emerged on the eve of the 2015 election, showing Cameron right in the middle of the group shot, nobody bothered trying to suppress it.

How much significance should be attached to Cameron's decision to join the Bullingdon Club? One Tory colleague, no fan, thinks the answer is 'considerable'. The MP concerned was himself once asked to join the club but attended just one gathering before walking out in disgust. 'What it basically involved was getting drunk and standing on restaurant tables shouting about "fucking plebs". It was all about despising poor people.' He questioned whether youthful exuberance is sufficient excuse.

Delingpole admits he 'rather wanted' to be in the Bullingdon, recalling how his hopes of admission were momentarily raised when members of the society arrived at the flat he shared with Ewen Fergusson (no relation to James) to perform the traditional recruitment ritual of trashing a prospective candidate's room.

> Depending how much they liked you, they'd either trash it majorly or minorly. But they'd come to trash the room not of James Delingpole, but of Ewen Fergusson, who was one of my housemates...
>
> Looking back, a) I didn't have enough money to be in the Bullingdon, and b) I wouldn't have actually enjoyed the sort of things they did, because I'm not very good at drinking heinous quantities and behaving really, really badly. It's weird now, because I'm actually slightly appalled to think that being in the Bullingdon was something I ever wanted to do. Actually it's about mindless destruction, and conspicuous excess, and the rather ugly side of upper-class life.

> It's interesting that Dave was a member…Imagine if you were run-
> ning a restaurant and were on the receiving end of these nasty little
> twenty-somethings doing horrible things? It's actually loathsome.
> I don't think this is me editorialising after the event and trying to
> justify, or make excuses, for my failure to have been admitted – it's
> just the process of maturity.

In Cameron's defence, there is no evidence that he personally damaged any property or hurt or offended others. Like so much else about his life, his participation appears to have been measured.

David Worth, an American postgraduate student at Oxford who was in the club at the same time as Cameron, recalls how his first outing with fellow Bullers involved taking a boat to Cliveden House, a former stately home in Berkshire converted into a magnificent luxury hotel. According to the hotel's website, its history is 'speckled with unapologetic debauchery'.[60]

As they floated along the Thames, quaffing champagne, Worth recalls the future Prime Minister spouting quotes from Churchill.

'There was a surreal Brideshead Regurgitated quality to the evening,' he told the journalist Catherine Mayer in 2008.

> I remember David quoting Winston Churchill extensively by memory
> – Churchill was a bit of a lush, so they were quotes about drink-
> ing – and he was very funny. A few people leaned over the side of
> the boat occasionally because if you've drunk two bottles of cham-
> pagne in an hour, your stomach is going to get queasy. I don't know
> if David had only sipped a bit, but he was articulate and lucid, and
> I always remember him like that – the centre of attention.[61]

Boris Johnson, a fellow 'Buller', brushes it all off as the legacy of a public school education at an elite school that encouraged elite societies (Pop) involving 'wearing fancy bits'.

---

60 It is said to be where John Profumo met Christine Keeler. http://www.
    clivedenhouse.co.uk/hotel/profumo-affair.aspx.
61 *Time* magazine: http://content.time.com/time/world/
    article/0,8599,1840461,00.html.

As he puts it:

> You're an undergraduate, you haven't got a clue what's going on; you have these people invade your room in the middle of the night. They watch you drink some utterly ghastly thing; you feel a sense of prickly horror and embarrassment every time, [but] you go along with it because you think it must be vaguely traditional.

For all the showing off and male bonding, Johnson claims – rather unconvincingly – that being in the Buller was 'thoroughly dull', primarily because it was 'all male'.

'You wake up in the morning with that terrible hungover sense of shame, accentuated by the feeling that you could have had much more fun if you'd just taken your girlfriend out to dinner. I mean, what was the bloody point?'

Andreae claims Cameron preferred playing pool to hanging out with the 'Buller'.

'What we tended to do at the end of the day was basically go to the pub and shoot pool. We weren't all dressing up in tails and prancing around drinking champagne by any means. And he's very good at pool.'[62]

Steve Rathbone, who arrived at Oxford from a grammar school in North Yorkshire, is even more generous.

'I don't think anyone would have realised just how toxic these societies would be for them in the future. If you've come from Eton, you walk effortlessly into that sort of thing and you don't think much about it,' he says.

In any case, the Bullingdon was not necessarily the forum for Cameron's worst excesses. It has emerged that he was also involved in another notorious Oxford dining society, the Piers Gaveston, whose gatherings were the scene of more shocking student behaviour. During the course of our research, a distinguished contemporary of Cameron's at Oxford claimed the future Prime Minister once took part in an outrageous initiation ceremony at a Piers Gaveston event involving a dead pig. His extraordinary suggestion is that Cameron put his penis in the animal's mouth.

The source – himself an MP – first made the allegation out of the blue at a business dinner in June 2014. Though it was a private conversation,

---

62   *Trevor McDonald Meets David Cameron.*

he was sitting at a table of eight people, meaning he could have been over-heard. Sotto voce, he claimed to have seen photographic evidence.

Our initial assumption was that it was a joke. It was therefore a surprise when, some weeks later, the MP repeated the allegation. He stuck to his story. Some months later, he repeated the allegation a third time, providing a little more detail. He claimed the hog's head was resting on the lap of a Piers Gaveston society member while Cameron performed the bizarre act. He gave dimensions of the alleged photograph and provided the name of the individual he says has the image. This person failed to respond to our approaches.

Perhaps it is a case of mistaken identity. Yet it is an elaborate story for an otherwise credible figure to invent. Furthermore, there are a number of accounts of pigs' heads at debauched parties in Cameron's day. The late Count Gottfried von Bismarck, an Oxford contemporary of Cameron who became notorious after Olivia Channon, the daughter of a Tory government minister, died of a heroin overdose in his Christ Church bedroom, was an enthusiastic member of the Piers Gaveston Society and reportedly threw various dinner parties featuring pigs' heads. The Piers Gaveston, named after the lover of Edward II, specialises in bizarre rituals and sexual excess. Its gatherings, typically held amid great secrecy in country houses, were described in a 2014 article in society magazine *Tatler* as 'basically a very well-organised orgy'.

As his university years drew to a close, events in the wider world were drawing many of Cameron's contemporaries to a career in the City. On 27 October 1986, the 'Big Bang' blew open the nepotistic guild of the City of London. It would no longer be dominated by small institutions that had been around for ever. De-regulation attached booster rockets to the British economy, with the big privatisations of the late '80s – British Gas in 1986, British Airways in 1987 – opening a plethora of money-making opportunities.

For many of Cameron's peers, a career in finance was now the only game in town. The *Cherwell* lampooned 'yuppie' students for 'scrambling for summer jobs in London with ludicrously named companies like Kleinwort Gusset Buttocks & Co.', while the student magazine *Isis* reported disap-provingly that the university seemed 'obsessed' with 'yuppiedom, just as England in general is'.

'Oxford is already churning out quite enough mammonistic, moronic clones designed to communicate with VDUs rather than real people, eager to join the new breed of city brokers and merchant bankers, and seems set fair to produce thousands more in future.'

With his father's connections, and the fall-back option of a place on Jardine Matheson's graduate training scheme, it would have been a natural next step for Cameron. Yet it did not appeal.

It was not that he was committed to a specific alternative. As his finals loomed, he didn't know what he wanted to do. He had interviews with *The Economist* and various management consultancies, but nothing came of it.

'I didn't have a career plan,' he has said.[63]

Then an advert in the university careers department caught his eye.

'Conservative Research Department: bright graduates needed', it said.

'I thought, that looks interesting,' Cameron would later recall.[64] Of course, getting into what was then an elite part of the Conservative machine would be highly competitive.

Luckily he had friends in high places who were happy to help. For the third time in his young life, somebody had a quiet word with somebody, and his path was smoothed.

---

63   David Cameron and Dylan Jones, p. 42.
64   Harry Mount interview, op. cit.

PART TWO –
YOUNG MAN ABOUT TOWN

7

PETER'S PINK BOUDOIR

'Effortlessly superior.'

– Derek Laud, on Cameron at twenty-one

Barry Nicholas, the Principal of Brasenose, did not expect Cameron to excel in his finals. On the day the future Prime Minister's exam results were announced, he raised his eyes in surprise.

'Did you expect Cameron to do so well?' he asked one of Cameron's tutors. He thought the sociable PPE-ist had been too busy having a good time to fulfil his potential.

'Absolutely,' his colleague replied. He had seen something special in Cameron and was not surprised when he was awarded a good First.

'He has a very high intellect, and an impressive ability to learn and reflect. There's a quiet confidence about him,' he said. He then predicted that Cameron would be 'very successful' in both his professional and personal life. He was not wrong: by autumn, his former student had sauntered into a plum job in an elite department of the Conservative Party.

Exactly who helped Cameron get this job and how is a matter of debate. Until now, attention has focused on a mysterious phone call, purporting to be from the royal household. However, he may also have been helped by a second source.

The anonymous phone call went through to Alistair Cooke, now Lord Lexden, then deputy director of the Research Department, shortly before Cameron's first interview. The caller, who had a grand voice, told Cooke to stand by for someone special.

'I understand that you are about to see David Cameron. I've tried everything I can to dissuade him from wasting his time on politics, but I have failed. I am ringing to tell you that you are about to meet a truly remarkable young man,' he said, and hung up.

Much has been made of this incident since it first came to light some years ago. Naturally, Cameron's political opponents seized on it as evidence that he owed the job that set him on a path to the premiership to his connections. Yet the caller has never been identified, and the impact of the intervention is debatable. While the Camerons had various royal links, the obvious potential suspects – Captain Sir Alastair Aird, then Comptroller to the Queen Mother; and Sir Brian McGrath, a family friend who worked as a private secretary to Prince Philip – have vehemently (and convincingly) denied it was them. It is possible that it was simply a hoax.

Either way, Cameron already had an exceptionally helpful contact in the highest echelons of the party: his cousin Ferdinand Mount, who had helped him with his piece for the Eton school magazine. According to a well-placed insider, Mount invited Cameron to lunch as an undergraduate and persuaded him to apply for the Research Department.

'Ferdy Mount invited Cameron to Downing Street while David was still at Oxford and encouraged him to apply. I think Mount was a referee. Game, set and match,' the source claims.

Mount says he did not play any role in Cameron's appointment, though he admits he would have been 'delighted' to put in a word for his cousin. By the time Cameron graduated, Mount had left government, though of course he still knew all the right people. That it was received wisdom in the Research Department that Cameron had had a 'leg up' may have been a case of colleagues putting two and two together and getting five.

In any case, with good looks, a first-class degree from Oxford, and a pleasant manner, he was just the type they liked and could doubtless have got there under his own steam. Numerous sources testify to his ability, saying that he outshone many of his colleagues from the start. Cooke has described him as 'one of the very best of all the young people' he ever interviewed, while another contemporary, Derek Laud, who was a Tory special adviser at the time, remembers him as 'effortlessly superior, because he knew he was good'.

Having been offered a role as a researcher with a starting salary of £10,000 a year, Cameron arranged a flat share in London with his old school friend Pete Czernin, an heir to the Howard de Walden fortune. The pair established themselves in a pleasant apartment on Harrington Gardens in south

Kensington, a smart address they would have struggled to afford were it not for Czernin's wealth.

Over the next five years, Cameron gained invaluable experience in several different roles, rising rapidly through the ranks from junior researcher to special adviser to two of the most powerful figures in Margaret Thatcher and John Major's administrations: Norman Lamont as Chancellor and then Michael Howard as Home Secretary. As his job evolved, it gave him experience of election campaigning, both at local and national level, and a taste of Downing Street, when he was drafted in to help Major in the vital business of preparing for the gladiatorial contest of Prime Minister's Questions. Perhaps most importantly, this period saw him forge relationships with a number of figures who would become lifelong friends and be pivotal to his future career.

In the 1980s and 1990s, the Conservative Research Department (CRD) was a prestigious place to work, and attracted the brightest young minds.

'It was such an elite and important place. It had an aura and reputation that was really something. It was a big deal,' remembers one of Cameron's colleagues there.

Arriving at Central Office on Smith Square, a stone's throw from the Houses of Parliament, Cameron was surprised to discover it was run by what one colleague has described as 'a coterie of homosexuals'. This played to his advantage: not only was he handsome, he was also entirely comfortable surrounded by gay men, an attitude not shared by all his male colleagues.

Laud says: 'This coterie of homosexuals did all the preferring. In that sense, David has always been on the liberal wing of the party, so that was not horrific for him, whereas it was a bit more difficult for quite a few others, who could easily have been rivals for David.'

Soon after Cameron joined, one of the gay men, Sir Peter Morrison, then deputy chairman of the party, ordered a complete redecoration of the offices in taste that prompted much politically incorrect tittering.

'He moved everyone around, and had the whole place done up in pink and blue. We used to call the place "Peter's Pink Boudoir",' says one of Cameron's former colleagues.

Cameron's career with the party began in September 1988, an exciting time in British politics. Though Thatcher had recently won a third election, the gloss was fast fading. Her personal approval ratings were healthy, especially compared to her Labour opponent, Neil Kinnock, but cracks in her leadership were deepening. The economic boom of the late 1980s was in full flow, but Thatcher and her Chancellor, Nigel Lawson, clashed over policy, not least on the crucial issue of the day: British membership of the Exchange Rate Mechanism (ERM), the predecessor to the Euro. Though dividing lines on the ERM – a proxy for the wider argument over Britain's place in Europe – had been staked out in the early 1980s, the issue was now coming to a head. By autumn, Thatcher had ruled out full British membership until well into the 1990s, delivering her infamous 'Bruges Speech' to the College of Europe just a few days before Cameron started work.

High politics of this kind were peripheral to Cameron's early work in CRD. On his first day, he discovered 'an ordered sort of chaos'.

'Papers on the floor, rather than in files. Lunches that went on for considerably longer than would seem appropriate today. Deadlines met, only just,' he has recalled.[65]

He was not averse to disappearing for a long lunch himself. He would sometimes dine with Laud, at the fashionable and expensive Le Caprice, round the corner from the Ritz, or at White's, his father's private members' club. On one occasion, the pair bumped into Jeffrey Archer at Le Caprice, who feigned astonishment at their presence, as Laud recalls.

> He looked down his nose at us, and said, 'Oh, workers! Workers! How can the workers afford to come here?' Then he marched on. Cameron just laughed, whereas I was very offended. He was always better at getting on with people older than himself, a character trait that has served him well.

Cameron's first brief was Trade and Industry, Energy and Privatisation, which was livelier than it sounded, because of the controversial programme of privatisations underway. Cameron's instructions from Cooke were clear: to produce quick, accurate briefing notes for MPs and ministers and suggest lines of attack and defence.

'All your drafts for briefing papers and speeches must be written with absolute clarity; they must be set properly in the context of Mrs Thatcher's evolving programme of reform; they must give accurate sources for all

---

65   Alistair Cooke (ed.), *Tory Policy-Making: The Conservative Research Department, 1929–2009* (Conservative Research Department, 2009), p. 95.

references; and they must draw out the weak points in the opposition's policies,' he told Cameron, adding that 'jargon' was 'absolutely forbidden'.[66]

One of the best aspects of the job was that at the tender age of twenty-one, a CRD staffer could find himself or herself briefing the most senior people in the party.

'When you heard your material being used by a minister on television or in the Chamber of the House of Commons, it was extremely rewarding,' Cameron has recalled.[67] Laud remembers happy times after work in Cameron's flat, watching news programmes to see if ministers would use the lines they had scripted.

'We would sit there and say, "He's going to say this now!", which was fun. For Cameron, it was all about the tactics and the mechanics, whereas I would sometimes get very cross about the principle of an argument.'

The well-connected Laud, who had been working for the party since the early 1980s, became a useful ally.

'I spent a lot of time introducing him to the Tory high command – we had dinners with people like Michael Portillo,' Laud says.

> He was always nervous in the company of those who were considered very clever, like Portillo, and was very quiet – so much so that afterwards, some of them would forget they'd met him. I remember one dinner with Peter Lilley [then a rising star]. David came prepared, and made three points. Everyone there was desperately trying to impress.

Inside CRD, Cameron quickly made an impact. His former line manager, Guy Black, now Lord Black of Brentwood, who headed the Political Section in 1988, recalls:

> There wouldn't have been more than twelve or thirteen desks at that stage, so everybody knew each other pretty well. Some desk officers were more likely to succeed than others. It was pretty clear from day one that here was a first-class intellect, but also, a very political mind.

---

66   Ibid., p. 96.
67   Ibid.

Though he was only twenty-one, colleagues began talking of him as a future Prime Minister, though, as a former CRD colleague puts it, in an office packed with high flyers, this simply meant he was 'a bit better than the others'.

> It was the kind of thing people said about that place. It wasn't just about him. It was a function of CRD that people who were in it went on to be, if not prime ministers, certainly members of the Cabinet. It was definitely seen as a route to the top. There was almost an assumption that if you wanted to, you would become an MP and probably a minister, if not a Cabinet minister.

Cameron's peers were indeed a talented, ambitious bunch. Several would later be instrumental to his future success. Ed Llewellyn, a fellow Old Etonian and Oxford graduate (although, unlike Cameron, he'd studied modern languages) was one such figure. He'd arrived at CRD one year earlier, and the two men soon grew close: in time, Llewellyn would become one of Cameron's closest political advisers and eventually his Downing Street Chief of Staff. After leaving CRD, he went on to work in Hong Kong with the last British governor, Chris Patten – a noted Tory 'wet', whose relationship with Cameron's old colleague is so close that Patten describes him as a 'sort of honorary godson'.[68]

Following hot on Cameron's heels straight from Oxford to Smith Square was Ed Vaizey, another future political ally and friend, who would go on to spend two years in the department before leaving to train as a barrister and eventually winning a seat in Parliament and a ministerial job in Cameron's government. The son of illustrious intellectual stock, the young Vaizey had done a voluntary spell at CRD during his gap year, and had made a name for himself at Oxford as an outspoken and controversial Union and OUCA 'hack'.

Also on the CRD payroll at the time was Rachel Whetstone, a young woman who was as highly strung as she was clever. Educated at Benenden and Bristol University, she came from a distinguished right-wing family: her mother Linda is today a trustee of the Institute of Economic Affairs, a crucible for libertarianism founded by Rachel's grandfather, Sir Antony Fisher. When the young Rachel – reputedly then known as 'the Witch' by Cameron and

---

68   Private information.

friends[69] – started out in the Research Department in 1989, she was seen as something of a Thatcherite firebrand, but became somewhat more moderate after being headhunted as a special adviser for Virginia Bottomley, a young and attractive Tory MP on the party's left flank. Her political connections would later prove crucial to Cameron's ascent to the top of the party.

But the most significant new recruit from the perspective of Cameron's future political career was the charismatic Steve Hilton. Once memorably described as a 'pint-sized Rasputin', he would become one of Cameron's closest and most influential political allies.

Like many of the team at this time, Hilton too was a recent Oxford graduate – and, like Cameron, read PPE – but his background was unusual: his parents were Hungarian immigrants (not refugees, as has been widely and incorrectly reported),[70] and his biological father abandoned the family when Hilton was only five. He grew up in a different world to Cameron, but he did benefit from a private education, having won a scholarship to Christ's Hospital in Sussex.[71] After graduating from Oxford, he did a stint for a small insurance firm in Brighton, processing claims from the Great Storm of 1987, but after volunteering for the Tory Party he was parachuted into Smith Square within months. There, he gained a reputation for being a 'sharp-suited, sharp-witted' prodigy, and something of a 'Jack-the-lad' character.[72] He was rapidly promoted: first to the office of Peter Lilley (then the Trade Secretary), and later on secondment with the advertising agency Saatchi & Saatchi, where he was made chief liaison between the party and the agency during the 1992 election campaign. Maurice Saatchi thought so highly of the 22-year-old that he hired him after the election. The Tory peer would later say, 'No one reminds me as much of me when young as Steve.'[73]

Many years later, Hilton, along with Whetstone and Vaizey, would play a key role in Cameron's campaign for the party leadership.

In such company, it took exceptional energy, commitment and flair to stand out. Yet, according to Black, Cameron was 'very much the star' of his intake.

69 Matthew d'Ancona, *In It Together: The Inside Story of the Coalition Government* (Viking, 2013), p. 30.
70 Francis Elliott and James Hanning, p. 79.
71 An independent school where children from less wealthy families have nearly all their fees paid by a charitable trust.
72 *The Times*, 1 May 1992.
73 Giles Hattersley, *Sunday Times*, 26 March 2006.

One of the jobs I did was to brief ministers for programmes like *Question Time*, *Any Questions?* and so on. If there was a big economic story, Cameron would have had to give me the information to go and do the briefing. The material from him was always streets ahead of anything from anyone else on the economic brief.

From the party's point of view, the best briefing papers would set out relevant facts, suggest political points, and identify potential areas of vulnerability and attack. Black says Cameron was superb at this work, adding that his enthusiasm and affability gave him an 'almost puppy-like quality'.

Here was somebody who wanted to get on; make a name for himself. He was all over the place all the time, making friends and making contacts. I got on exceptionally well with him. If I look back at my appointments diaries, I saw a great deal of him around that time. He played a full part in the life of the Research Department.

Another peer who testifies to the quality of Cameron's work at this time is Lord Beaverbrook, who was soon to become party treasurer.

'He was helping with speechwriting for various people, and did some speeches for me. They were very good. Luckily, I was sensible enough to acknowledge his work. I used to send him a bottle of champagne from time to time,' he says.

What Cameron's job lacked in terms of pay, it more than made up for in intellectual stimulation and opportunities to work with great characters, like Ian Gow, one of Thatcher's closest aides.[74] Cameron remembers helping him prepare for a debate on the 'new opportunities for mankind' after the fall of the Berlin Wall.

'After it was over, he rewarded me with the ultimate accolade: two of his famous White Lady cocktails in the Pugin Room of the House of Commons,' he has recalled.

CRD also offered travel opportunities. In Cameron's case, it was something controversial: an all-expenses-paid eight-day trip to South Africa in

74   A year later, in July 1990, Gow, who had resigned from Thatcher's government, was murdered by the IRA. Cameron has described him as 'a great man and outstanding patriot'.

1989, at a time when it was a pariah state. The country was at a crossroads: the apartheid regime was in its death throes as international isolation and domestic unrest threatened full-blown political, economic and social collapse. As we have seen, three years earlier, in 1986, a young David Miliband had led a divestment campaign in Oxford against Barclays' involvement in South Africa, while across the Atlantic the United States Congress defied Reagan's presidential veto and forced the passage of a comprehensive anti-apartheid act, imposing sanctions and travel restrictions on the regime and calling for the release of Nelson Mandela and other political prisoners. At the time of Cameron's trip, Nelson Mandela was still behind bars. The expedition was organised by Laud, who was by then working for a company called Strategy Network International, a London-based lobbying firm linked to a group of mining companies and rumoured to be a puppet of the South African government in Pretoria.[75] The firm's clients included the South African Chamber of Mines, for whom the export of vast quantities of cheap South African coal was being hampered by economic sanctions. All-expenses-paid tours of the country – including comfortable stays in luxury hotels in Johannesburg and Cape Town – were intended to convince sympathetic Conservatives that international sanctions were counter-productive and economically reckless.

Looking back, Cameron's acceptance of Laud's offer does not reflect well. The international campaign against apartheid was just reaching its climax and white rule was unravelling. Choosing to visit the country under the auspices of a firm battling against the very movement that would shortly declare victory seems ill judged today.

In fairness, though civil servants and special advisers were strongly advised against such trips, the Tory Party was officially opposed to the sanctions agenda. So while Cameron's decision to go has been criticised, it was consistent with the party line.

Romantic opportunities were another perk of the job. One contemporary describes Central Office at that time as 'an absolute bonking shop', an environment in which Cameron thrived.

'All the girls fancied him,' according to one account.[76]

Andrew Mitchell, former International Development Secretary, recalls Cameron joking, years later, about his romantic success at Smith Square, which

---

75 *The Independent*, 26 October 1994.
76 Francis Elliott and James Hanning, p. 83.

he modestly attributed to a shortage of competition because so many of his colleagues were gay. His most significant conquest was a beautiful blonde called Laura Adshead who seemed destined for a stellar political career. Their relationship is one of the quirkier features of his time at Central Office, as she is now in a nunnery. These days she is known as Sister John Mary and lives at the Abbey of Regina Laudis in a little town called (appropriately) Bethlehem, in Connecticut, USA. The abbey is famous for its Prioress, Mother Dolores Hart, a former Hollywood actress who once starred in movies with Elvis Presley.

Now in her late forties, Adshead was educated at Cheltenham Ladies' College and Christ Church, Oxford. Though her path crossed with Cameron's at university, it was not until they were both working at Central Office that they became close. They dated for over a year. When Cameron called it off, she was so upset she reportedly had to be given a period of compassionate leave from work. She later left London for America, where a hard-partying lifestyle spiralled into drink and drug addiction, before she entered the nunnery. Some years ago she appeared in a film about the abbey, *God Is the Bigger Elvis*, during which she spoke openly about her struggles, revealing she still attends Alcoholics Anonymous ('people are surprised to see a nun at the meeting').

'This place doesn't solve my problems magically,' she said. 'It's amazing that we do have this idea that there's a group of people called nuns who are floating around happily, because why would that be so? We're just human beings.'

Cameron himself quickly moved on.

As at Eton and Oxford, he was not universally admired. One contemporary in the Research Department describes him as 'intolerably arrogant'.

Even his godfather Tim Rathbone seems to have thought him rather bumptious. According to a contemporary:

> I remember we'd finished lunch once and went back to the Commons, and I bumped straight into Tim Rathbone.
>
> I said, 'I've just had lunch with Cameron.'
>
> And he said: 'Senior or minor?'
>
> I said, 'Minor.'
>
> He said: 'Oh, those Camerons. They do get on my nerves sometimes. They spend their whole time telling you how clever they are.'

It's a family trait. I think they do quite like being clever. I remember thinking that Ian was quite pleased to be clever. A very, very nice man, but cleverness was important to him.

There are claims that Cameron could be unpleasant about people behind their backs and that as he rose through the ranks, he was less kind to those junior to him than he might have been. But others contradict this. 'He was terrific to work for,' says one more junior member of the Research Department at the time. 'When he gave you a job to do, he was clear about what he needed and made a point of thanking you afterwards, which was by no means the case with everyone.'

In summer 1989, he had his first taste of electioneering, when a Labour MP with a safe seat in Vauxhall, south London, resigned to take up a job in academia. Cameron was asked to be point man and researcher to the Tory candidate in the subsequent by-election.

The poll coincided with the European elections that June and took place against a febrile political backdrop. Under Kinnock's stewardship, the Labour Party was rediscovering its mojo, while Tory fortunes were ebbing in tandem with the economy. When the by-election was called, Labour was five points ahead, and went all out to present it as a national mid-term referendum on a decade of Thatcherism. A nervous Central Office responded by mounting a 'Don't let Labour in by the back door' campaign.

Though the Tory candidate Michael Keegan did more than go through the motions, the seat was always going to be a no-hoper. The departing Labour MP had a majority of over 9,000, a figure that was hardly likely to fall, given the climate.

Yet the contest gave Cameron invaluable first-hand experience of the way relatively minor issues and incidents can escalate out of all proportion in the hysterical atmosphere that accompanies some by-elections. Vauxhall had it all: a bitter race row over the selection of the Labour candidate Kate Hoey, accusations of a smear campaign, and talk of libel suits. Years later, Cameron's experience of just how bitter and dirty local campaigns can become would stand him in good stead. Keegan has praised his contribution to his campaign, describing his briefings and advice as 'very professional, very considered and meticulous in detail'.[77]

---

77   Ibid., p. 82.

That autumn, Guy Black was offered a new job as special adviser to the then Energy Secretary John Wakeham, creating a vacancy for head of the Political Section. He immediately suggested Cameron.

'There wasn't a single question about who should do it, because he was the most accomplished figure within the Research Department at that moment,' Black says now.

Cameron took up the post immediately after party conference in autumn 1989. By now, storm clouds were gathering over Thatcher's administration. The infamous 'poll tax' had been introduced in Scotland in April that year, and popular unrest was gathering pace. At Westminster, rows over the value of sterling, interest rates and Europe rumbled on. Thatcher herself was becoming isolated, particularly from the two men who had been most influential in her governments throughout the 1980s, Howe and Lawson. When Lawson resigned after six years at the helm of the British economy, the news sent shockwaves through Whitehall, Westminster and the money markets. By February 1990, Labour was seventeen points ahead in the polls.[78]

This was a time when Tory MPs desperately needed Central Office to grip the party and mount a vigorous defence against Kinnock's onslaught. Yet complacency had crept in. The leadership had been slow to recognise the scale of the threat, allowing Central Office to plod along as if the party could expect to be in government for ever.

One staffer who left a job in the private sector to work for the party machine at that time was appalled by the apathy.

'I couldn't believe how unprofessional it was. I was really struck by how bumbling they were,' she says.

The arrival of Andrew Lansley, a former civil servant, as director of CRD injected some energy. The budget was beefed up, and the troops were ordered to start laying into Labour on the economy, trade unions, the NHS and Europe. Cameron was at the heart of the new propaganda machine.

The political columnist Bruce Anderson recalls Cameron relishing going on the offensive, rapidly becoming 'the best sniper' in the Research Department.

> I began to hear Cameron's name mentioned as an up-and-coming man. Everyone just said he was the best. He was efficient, he wrote well, and had excellent political judgement. He was tireless.

78   *Sunday Times*, 25 February 1990.

> I remember at the beginning of the 1992 election, I said to him, 'I'll try not to bother you and I will ring you once a day.' After about two days, I was ringing him every hour.

As head of the political section, Cameron told people he was 'in charge of stories' that he could dole out to favoured journalistic contacts.[79] It was a powerful position that allowed him to start building a fan base in the lobby. The odd newspaper diary item started to appear, tipping him for greater things.

Yet there was little that Lansley, Cameron or anyone else at Central Office could do to shore up Thatcher's position. On 1 November 1990, Howe followed Lawson and quit. Two weeks later he excoriated the Prime Minister and her Europe policy on the floor of the House of Commons. The next day, after months of speculation, Michael Heseltine, the charismatic former Defence Secretary who had dramatically resigned from the Cabinet in 1986 over the Westland affair, announced he would stand for the leadership. On 22 November 1990, Thatcher resigned. For Cameron, Hilton and co., it was a devastating moment. Yet there was no time to look back: a new Prime Minister would be installed within a week.

---

79   Francis Elliott and James Hanning, p. 96.

8

BRAT PACK

'He rarely expressed any strong views.'

– Derek Laud, on Cameron

In the immediate aftermath of Thatcher's resignation, Central Office went into lockdown. Staffers were under strict instruction to remain neutral in the leadership contest and were banned from helping candidates during office hours.

However, the rule did not prevent them visiting the contenders in a strictly observational capacity, or volunteering for campaign teams at the weekend.

Holed up just off Smith Square in the Gayfere Street home of Alan Duncan (soon to become an MP), John Major's campaign team was cheered to receive a visit from Ed Vaizey.

'Sorry I can't do anything to help now, but I just wanted to let you know I'm supporting you,' he told them cheerfully, adding that he would make himself available that weekend. A number of other Central Office staff dropped by, including Cameron and Llewellyn, who turned up together. Like Vaizey, they offered warm words of support and made noises about pitching in as soon as they could.

That weekend, Vaizey turned up at Major's campaign headquarters as promised, but there was no show from Cameron or Llewellyn. Long after it was all over, Major's supporters discovered that the pair had delivered the exact same warm words of support to Michael Heseltine and Douglas Hurd, leaving all three contenders under the happy illusion that they enjoyed the support of two of the party's bright Young Turks. Smart, fly, or both? Admirers will see the episode as the mark of an astute political operator ready to work with anyone who could further his aims. Detractors will interpret it as evidence of a lack of principle and a willingness to deliberately mislead others for his own ends. Both sides would probably agree that it showed nous and a hunger for advancement by whatever means.

When Major won, Cameron's hedged bet paid off. Under the new regime, his career flourished. Having developed a reputation for his media and communication skills, he was invited to help prepare the new premier for Prime Minister's Questions. It was an incredible opportunity. Aged just twenty-four, he now had one-to-one access to Major twice a week, allowing him to develop a rapport with the premier and gain an insight into his political thinking as well as the inner workings of Downing Street.

A fellow member of the PMQs prep team at the time recalls:

> At around 7 a.m., we'd go through all the papers with a big black
> felt tip, ringing all the stories that might come up, and then devising
> the most difficult questions he might face and preparing answers.
> We did that for about a year or so. We were quite successful.

Though it did not lead to a bigger promotion to political secretary, a role some say Cameron coveted, it did raise his profile, prompting a handful of diary items suggesting he was responsible for improving Major's performances. In any case, the looming general election presented new opportunities on an even bigger stage. While there was little chance that Major would call an early election – the poll tax was too toxic, and it would take time to formulate an alternative – Central Office had to be ready for any eventuality. Cameron was now handed serious responsibility: compiling chapters in Alistair Cooke's official campaign guide, an important dossier of facts, figures, policy details, briefing on opponents' positions, and 'lines to take' designed to ensure uniformity of message. (The guide was always an unusual shape: long and narrow, reputedly so that it would fit in the pocket of the candidate's hunting jacket.)

The party geared up for the election under a new chairman, Chris Patten, and a new director of communications, a 32-year-old former BBC producer named Shaun Woodward. Advertisers Saatchi & Saatchi were re-engaged, and Steve Hilton was charged with liaising with the ad men. The role meant he was often out of the office, a situation not entirely unwelcomed by some of his superiors, who found him a bit 'all over the place'.

'He was frightfully nice, but I always thought he was a bit flaky. He had these airy-fairy qualities. [Whereas] David was confident and cheerful and came up with the bacon. He was very obviously a young MP-to-be,' says one of their former managers.

Another contemporary says Hilton 'always came in late', was 'completely wacky' and 'lacked good manners'.

In terms of personality, Cameron and Hilton could hardly have been more different, but they made a good team. Together with Llewellyn, Vaizey and Whetstone, they formed a tight clique. The press began referring to them as 'the Brat Pack'. They started hanging out together in the evenings and at weekends, sometimes at the Old Rectory in Peasemore, or at the country home of the parents of another CRD staffer, William Wellesley, in the Weald. If the house party was in Peasemore, Cameron would set off from London on the Friday night to prepare for the arrival of his guests the following day. The weekend would be a mix of country walks, fine food and wine, and politics.

Derek Laud, who was at some of these get-togethers, recalls Cameron being an excellent host.

> He was very boyish, always smoking a cigarette like people did when they were fourteen or fifteen, when they were learning to smoke; always making rings with it. Always in a woolly jumper, and forever picking up the dogs. He is a very good cook and loves a decent claret – we all did. There was always a bit of competition as to who could produce the best vintage, because William Wellesley is a great wine snob, so there was always a great rivalry between the Weald and the South Downs, as to who could produce the best wines.

Occasionally, one of the guests would present a 'paper' on a topical political issue, such as privatisation, and everybody would chew it over. The debate could be long and heated – especially after a few drinks. Remarkably, Laud, who was close to Cameron for more than a decade, does not recall him ever giving a view on any issue discussed.

'He has rarely expressed any strong views in his life,' he says.

Instead, Laud says Cameron would focus on how the party should position itself.

'What he was very good at doing was talking about the mechanics of something, rather than the principle,' he recalls.

Some found the Brat Pack's youth and chutzpah threatening – Hilton was not even old enough to have voted in a general election. Portillo and Heseltine were among those reportedly uneasy at the combination of their inexperience and increasing influence with the party leadership.[80] Yet Patten, who had taken over as Tory chairman, found the young bloods life-enhancing.

'They were a bit indulged but I don't think [they were] ever bumptious,' he says.

In a sign of his growing status, on 3 March 1992, Cameron oversaw a top-secret exercise to test the party machine's readiness for the election.[81] Staff assembled at 32 Smith Square at 5 a.m., where they were put through their paces, combing through newspapers, monitoring TV and radio bulletins for useful stories and information, and preparing mock briefing notes for Major. They also practised preparing a policy launch. The event was a success. Impressed, Patten asked Cameron to be Major's point man at Central Office, and gave him responsibility for briefing the Prime Minister before morning press conferences. It was another coup for Cameron, but the stakes were higher than ever. In the heat of an election campaign, there would be no hiding from mistakes.

Long marchers in the Tory Party remember 1992 as a particularly bloody campaign. Back in January 1991, Patten had warned Major that 'the cupboard was bare' on planning, money and policy.[82] Many commentators felt the party lacked a 'big idea' or a sense of direction. The brutal manner of Thatcher's departure also left open sores and a parliamentary party in constant danger of turning in on itself. Central Office found itself fighting a war on two fronts: against Kinnock; and against those within the Tory Party whose disillusion and indiscipline threatened to undermine the campaign.

One senior figure recalls:

> There were so many sides: the people who thought Thatcher should
> still be there; the people who thought Heseltine was the great missed

---

80   Ibid., p. 105.

81   Ibid., p. 98.

82   Tim Bale, *The Conservative Party: From Thatcher to Cameron* (Polity Press, 2011), p. 38.

chance; the pro-Patten people; the anti-Patten people. Trying to
hold the whole thing together was very difficult. There was a lot
of blame flying around.

Tensions between No. 10 and Central Office – both responsible for the
manifesto and for day-to-day organisation – were a persistent feature of
the campaign. A former Central Office staffer has shuddering memories of
screaming matches between Sarah Hogg, head of Major's Policy Unit, and
various Central Officers, including Lansley. At the height of the campaign,
Cameron had a close shave when Major received an inadequate briefing
ahead of a media appearance, leaving him floundering. An insider recalls
Hogg hitting the roof. Though Cameron was nominally responsible, he
seems to have escaped the flak.

He came closer to being burned during the infamous 'War of Jennifer's
Ear', an episode that has entered political folklore. It began with a Labour
Party political broadcast about an unnamed girl who urgently needed a
simple operation to restore her hearing but had been forced to wait months
by the NHS. When both her parents and her GP weighed in, all with dif-
fering views on who and what was to blame for the delay to surgery, the
controversy escalated into a firestorm that dominated the media for days.

For a while, the Tories had the moral high ground, after the doctor, whose
letter to the Labour Party had prompted the broadcast, retracted his initial
suggestion that the government was at fault. However, the party found itself
on the back foot when a junior Central Office staffer leaked the girl's identity.

'It was one of those awful episodes...I remember we had to do a very
fast job in assembling a reasonable case,' Patten recalls.

Having developed a reputation as an accomplished media handler,
Cameron played a key role in orchestrating the fightback. It involved securing written testimony from Jennifer's GP exonerating the party from blame
over the delay to her operation.

Everything was going to plan, until Cameron, alighting on a draft copy
of the crucial press release, started rejigging the doctor's testimony to make
it more fluent – a move that could have been disastrous had the GP noticed
and objected.

According to Elliott and Hanning, John Wakeham, the Energy Secretary,
who was standing in for Patten while the party chairman was trying to save

his seat, was apoplectic, laying into Cameron in front of colleagues.[83] In Cameron's defence, Wakeham has said he was only 'reorganising' the statement, as opposed to the much more serious offence of embellishing quotes.

If the episode dented Cameron's confidence, he didn't show it. One journalist was shocked by the way he threw his weight around on the campaign trail.

'I remember seeing this very young guy shouting at the Prime Minister, and thinking, "Who the hell is that?" I couldn't believe the way he was speaking to him.'

A former colleague – no fan of Cameron – seconds this, but with grudging admiration.

'That swagger, that self-confidence, was always there, but in the heat of the campaign, it was quite useful,' he says. Others say 'everyone' bossed Major around.

Against the odds, the Tories won handsomely, securing more votes than any party in British political history. Only the idiosyncrasies of constituency boundaries prevented a massive Commons majority. 'The uncelebrated success of the 1992 Conservative election campaign', wrote Major in his memoirs, 'was winning in a recession, against the shadow of the poll tax, and with barely a mention of Europe.'

Cameron's reward would be another promotion.

83   Francis Elliott and James Hanning, p. 104.

9
P45

'People's personalities changed in front of me.'
                              – Cameron, on Black Wednesday

Watching Cameron on the campaign trail, Chancellor Norman Lamont had been impressed.

'He is one to watch,' Lamont thought.

So when Downing Street suggested Cameron might move to the Treasury after the election to become a special adviser, Lamont readily agreed. The only thing that bothered him was Cameron's youth, but he had seen that the young aide was no political novice.

He recalls:

> I came across him in the 1992 campaign when he was briefing Major and me, and other people. He was just quite outstanding; very quick. A lot of people brought you problems; he brought you one solution. He had a very positive attitude. If you wanted to adopt a line on something, he would come up with arguments for it. He wouldn't say, 'You can't do this; you can't do that.' He would say, 'Yes, you can do it, this way.'

Cameron's new role was a tremendous opportunity. With a reputation for employing the finest minds in Whitehall, the Treasury guaranteed intellectual stimulation for those in senior roles and was a fast track to the most coveted positions across the administration. He would have no job security – special advisers are both personal and political appointees whose destinies are tied to the Secretary of State they support – but would benefit from a ringside seat at the most exciting day-to-day business in government. Assuming he did not mess up, he could also expect the pick of lucrative jobs in the private sector if fate handed him a P45.

Arriving at the department in May 1992, he found that he was one of two special advisers working for Lamont. In an arrangement that is still common in Whitehall today, one dealt with media and communications while the other focused on policy. The policy adviser, Dr Bill Robinson, was much more experienced, but was immediately impressed by his new colleague. 'He is extraordinarily smooth and able, but very young,' Robinson wrote in his diary.[84]

The Permanent Secretary was Terence Burns, now a life peer. (Many years later, as Prime Minister, Cameron would turn to Burns for informal advice on the economy.) Lamont's private secretary was Jeremy Heywood, who would go on to become the most powerful civil servant in Whitehall when Cameron was Prime Minister.

Bruce Anderson recalls Cameron being 'in awe' of Heywood, whose intellectual exertions seemed to eat up more calories than he cared to consume.

'His shirt collars had plenty of room. People thought he lived off coffee and cigarettes. He'd get stopped at airports, because he looked like a druggy. [David] thought he was massively clever, the cleverest guy he'd ever met,' Anderson says.

During the Blair and Brown years, special advisers (spads) could be extremely powerful figures, exerting almost as much influence behind the scenes as their masters.[85] In Cameron's day, the role was more limited. It was primarily political and presentational, writing speeches, liaising with journalists and providing advice ahead of media appearances.

In Central Office, he had been able to sail close to the wind in his dealings with reporters without serious danger of capsizing, but in the Treasury, he soon learned to be more careful. Former colleagues recall that he was sometimes reprimanded by the mild-mannered Burns for overstepping the mark. On one occasion, for example, he casually provided Anderson with highly sensitive public borrowing figures, a serious breach of protocol. Anderson recalls:

---

84   Ibid., p. 111.
85   For example, Gordon Brown's spad, Damian McBride.

> I went in to see him with a notebook. There was talk of the public sector borrowing requirement, which everyone was saying was between £35 billion and £37 billion. David actually told me it was £36 billion. I printed this in the next day's *Times* and David said he was terrified all day that there would be a leak inquiry.

He got away with it.

'I think people just thought I'd split the difference,' Anderson says.

The indiscretion could have cost Cameron dear, but it was of no significance compared to what was around the corner: an unprecedented economic catastrophe that would cost the country billions and dog the Conservative Party for many years to come.

While Cameron's personal responsibility for events leading up to and surrounding Black Wednesday is negligible, there is no denying his presence in the background. His appearance in a photograph of Lamont on the fateful day that Britain crashed out of the Exchange Rate Mechanism (he can be seen standing behind the embattled Chancellor as he announced Britain's exit) is an unfortunate visual reminder of his association with the event.

The scene for the disaster had been set in late 1990, when, after years of internal squabbling, Major – then Chancellor – finally persuaded Thatcher to take Britain into the ERM. Two years later, when Major himself was Prime Minister, the government suffered the ignominy of a humiliating forced exit, as sterling went into freefall overnight and the Bank of England blew £3.3 billion desperately trying to shore up its value. This was the dramatic event that came to be known as 'Black Wednesday' in British political folklore, and it dealt Major's administration a reputational blow from which it never recovered. 'I've got a large bucket of shit lying on my desk,' the editor of *The Sun* memorably told Major at the end of the day's turmoil. 'And tomorrow morning I'm going to pour it all over your head.'[86]

Even for seasoned politicians it was traumatic. There have been suggestions that John Major 'suffered a sort of nervous breakdown' that day.[87] For a young man in his first job in a government department, it must have been profoundly shocking.

---

86   Tim Bale, p. 44.
87   Francis Elliott and James Hanning, p. 121.

'It was the most turbulent time I'd ever seen in government, like being on a roller-coaster in full view of everyone in the country,' Cameron has said.

> I was surrounded by the most intense people I'd ever seen. People's personalities changed in front of me and then I realised what it meant to be in politics. It was then that I realised that you have to put everything into it, because if you don't it's going to consume you anyway.[88]

For those interested in the minutiae, Elliott and Hanning offer a more detailed account of Black Wednesday and its aftermath, setting out exactly where Cameron was and what he was doing as the crisis evolved from summer 1992 to the denouement. It contributes to the historical record but tells us little of significance about Cameron himself, except that when the chips were down, he had cojones and a sense of humour. At one point he presented his boss with an enormous cigar, telling him that by the time he had smoked it, all his troubles would be over.[89] Fortunately, Lamont saw the funny side.

'I thought it was very endearing, although I've often said I'm thinking of sending it back to him with the same note,' the former Chancellor says now.

The reason we do not learn more is that Cameron's role was minimal and tangential. Significantly, nobody who has since attacked him for being 'there on Black Wednesday' has identified any aspect of the crisis that was specifically his fault. While he had real influence over Lamont's communications with voters and the media, he had no say on decision making. Burns confirms that policy discussions were between ministers and officials, with little to no input from spads. Though they would be present in such meetings, by and large, they would not intervene.

Lamont himself, who remains fond of Cameron, insists his young adviser had no role whatsoever in what happened.

> First of all, membership of the ERM was a settled policy. He was never involved in those decisions. It was all to do with technicalities about interest rates [and] intervention in the market...these were not arguments that were presented to the public. These were

---

88   David Cameron and Dylan Jones, p. 20.
89   Francis Elliott and James Hanning, p. 119.

highly technical decisions made by a tiny group of people. I didn't involve other ministers. I was on my own. Not even Michael Portillo, who was the Chief Secretary [to the Treasury] – not even he played any part in it.

Yet Cameron did help Lamont formulate his public response to Black Wednesday, Derek Laud recalls:

He rang me from the Treasury on Black Wednesday – I was on a train. He said, 'I need your help.' I was positioned well with the Tory right; they were the people he needed to win over – people who were most vexatious about the Exchange Rate Mechanism. I spent my weekend doing what I could for him – doing what he couldn't do, which was reaching MPs, who would pick up the phone and speak to me.

Despite everything at stake, Laud says Cameron did not seem in the slightest agitated.

'Not at all. We had a long chat. But the thing about David is that he's very optimistic. Very! Black Wednesday is just an example.'

After surviving the immediate crisis, Lamont had to get through party conference in Brighton three weeks later. Already under intense pressure, the Chancellor needed to give the speech of his life. He arrived in Brighton in a black mood, with his long-suffering advisers apparently bearing the brunt. In his diary, Robinson recalls being summoned to Lamont's hotel room in the Brighton Grand, where he found his boss in a foul temper.

He has a splendid room in one of the turrets, lots of windows, unusual shape. But the mood is vile. Too late to bed, too much to drink, bed too small and hard. Rosemary [Lamont's wife] is looking pretty pinched and strained as well and [Lamont] has a plaster on his neck where I had noticed an incipient boil. He glares at us [and] asks David if he has cleared the CPC speech with Charles Powell, mutters something about not being able to work with these people. David goes off to do a press release.[90]

---

90   Ibid., p. 124.

The draft speech was repeatedly knocked back by a jittery No. 10, forcing Cameron and Lamont to make multiple changes.[91] When the Chancellor finally delivered the speech, the autocue failed, leaving him struggling to read Cameron's carefully crafted words. Lamont recalls that on the one occasion he 'had to be word-perfect' he could hardly see a thing.

> It was a very good speech actually, but there was a huge problem with the autocue – the light was shining right through it. I don't need autocues, but everyone insisted I have one. I could have spoken just from notes, but I had to be word-perfect…The trouble was, I couldn't read it. It hadn't been like that in the rehearsal. The speech bombed.

It is impossible to imagine a Cabinet minister involved in a crisis on this scale today surviving anything like as long as Lamont. Under the remorseless spotlight of a 24-hour news cycle and the relentless pressure of social media, he fwould almost certainly have been ousted within days. Though the media was a different beast in 1992, it was no less hungry for blood, and Cameron deserves some credit for helping his boss cling on for a full eight months after Black Wednesday. At one particularly low point, *The Sun* presented his face to readers in the form of a cut-out-and-keep dartboard.

As Lamont's media handler, Cameron's achievement was all the greater given Lamont's propensity to dig himself deeper into a hole. Flippant, ill-timed comments made about singing in the bath and not regretting anything hardly helped his cause. (Cameron would later deny he had anything to do with Lamont's notorious '*Je ne regrette rien*' remark. 'I am far too young to remember Edith Piaf,' he sniffed.)

The best Cameron could do was limit the damage, but the writing was on the wall.

When Major finally sacked the Chancellor in May, Cameron was also out of a job.

Years later, he would tell the former Chancellor that what he most enjoyed about his time at the Treasury was the quality of intellectual debate. Observing ferociously clever mandarins dissecting proposed policy was incredibly energising. Yet it was the trauma of the ERM crisis that probably did most

---

91   Ibid., p. 125.

to equip him for his future career. He still winces when old TV footage of Lamont emerging from the Treasury on Black Wednesday is replayed ('far too often for my liking', he has said). He looks fresh-faced and slightly apprehensive in these photos. But the experience taught him several lessons. Being in the eye of the storm that calamitous day shaped his views on the perils of joining the euro.

> I learned something. You can argue forever about whether sterling's parity was fixed too high (it was, but that made no difference to the end result) or whether a realignment within the exchange rate mechanism was on offer (it wasn't). In my view these questions are entirely irrelevant to the debate about the euro, which means fixing your exchange rate forever. Our experience in the ERM proved one incontrovertible fact – if you fix your exchange rate, or join a single currency, you give up the ability to set your own interest rates to suit your own domestic circumstances.[92]

More importantly, Black Wednesday put every other political drama he experienced into perspective. Long before he became an MP, he knew what it was like to be at the epicentre of a political earthquake. He saw how it was for politicians to wrestle with events beyond their control. He learned how careers and markets can rise or fall on a politician's choice of words. He learned how it feels when the press bay for blood.

As Prime Minister, Cameron would acquire a reputation for preternatural calm in the face of difficult events. Mostly, the skill would prove a huge asset, but it would also prompt accusations of a tendency to let important matters come close to getting out of hand before gripping them properly.

When the skies fell in on Black Wednesday, nobody resigned and the government did not collapse. From this, did Cameron learn that politicians can survive even the greatest mistake? Perhaps it is a clue as to why, as Prime Minister, he slept so soundly. Alas, this lesson would not apply to him.

---

92   *Guardian* blog, 8 July 2002.

10

SUMMER LOVING

'It just became the right thing to do. I fell in love with her.'
                                                              – Cameron

On a balmy Friday evening in May 1992, a long convoy of trucks, bat-tered buses, caravans and camper vans picked its way through the Malvern Hills in search of a party. It was bank holiday weekend, and hun-dreds of new age travellers, gypsies and students were gathering for the annual free festival in Avon and Somerset.

When they arrived at the usual spot, however, they were turned back by police, who dug trenches to prevent them setting up camp. Instead, they were directed over the county border to a little place called Castlemorton.

Soon, Castlemorton Common was a sea of revellers and tents, with thou-sands more flocking to the site after hearing about it on television news bulletins. By nightfall, more than 20,000 people had gathered on the out-skirts of the tiny Worcestershire village, a figure that would almost double over the long weekend.

With deafening sound systems pumping out incessant beats, and class-A drugs circulating as freely as cannabis, Castlemorton became the scene of a vast, lawless rave. For 100 hours, locals were subjected to non-stop ear-splitting acid house music. A distraught villager told a local newspaper that the 'hypnotic continuous pounding beat' was 'driving people in the front line into a frenzy'. So desperate did locals become that at one point, eight villagers armed with shotguns threatened to 'put a ring of fire' round the place. An eyewitness told of police attempting to drive through the crowd and being forced to abandon their vehicle. Within minutes, a dreadlocked traveller was selling acid off the bonnet.

What happened in Castlemorton horrified Middle England. It was the most extreme of hundreds of illegal raves that took place in fields and disused warehouses in the late 1980s and early 1990s, and prompted the government to embark on a moral and legal crusade against the 'rave' trend. In his second and last job as a special adviser, David Cameron found himself at the heart of this battle. It would not be dull.

Lamont's departure from No. 11 had almost marked the end of Cameron's career as a special adviser. Though he had hoped to stay at the Treasury – spads occasionally outlast their secretaries of state – it was always a long shot. Very briefly, it looked as if he might have to find a job in the private sector. Though disappointed, he was philosophical: at the Treasury, he had been earning around £26,000 a year, a healthy enough salary but far less than he could command in the City. He was now in the process of buying his own flat in Notting Hill and, in his own words, 'money was a concern'. If he had to leave government, he told himself, there would be some compensations. On the day he lost his job, he sloped off for a boozy lunch with Derek Laud.

Laud recalls: 'He rang me up and said "I've just been fired." I said, "Ah, do you need to be fortified?" We went for lunch and he took me through the whole story.'

If Cameron was anxious about his next move (and there is no evidence he was), he need not have worried. While he dined with Laud, allies were already hitting the phones on his behalf. Once again, his path was being smoothed.

According to Laud, 'It was amazing, because by the time we'd finished lunch, William Astor, Alexander Hesketh [both House of Lords whips] and various others were on the phone to sort out his future career! This was nothing. David didn't have to do a thing!'

Laud thinks that Max Hastings, the impeccably connected editor of the *Telegraph*, was among those who weighed in on Cameron's behalf, though Hastings denies he was involved. In any case, Michael Howard, who had just been appointed Home Secretary, says he received a call from Ken Clarke, the new Chancellor, pressing Cameron's case.

> Ken phoned me, very soon, maybe the day after the reshuffle, and said, 'I'm bringing in my own special adviser, but there's this chap David Cameron there – do you know anyone who would take him?' I said I would take him like a shot. He was obviously extremely

able and he was engaging, easy to get on with, had a pleasant manner. What more do you want?

For Cameron, it was an opportunity to work in another major Whitehall department, with a Secretary of State on the rise. Though he did not stay with Howard long, the bond they formed was crucial to Cameron's later political ascent. He also gained first-hand experience of pushing through legislation in the face of bitter opposition. Furthermore, his new role gave him an insight into the personality and political tactics of a figure who would become the Conservative Party's nemesis, a Labour MP who went on to win three successive elections: Tony Blair.

Arriving at the Home Office, Howard had received depressing advice from mandarins.

He recalls: 'The first presentation the civil service gave me, they showed me this inexorable rise in crime for the last fifty years, and they said, the first thing you must understand, Home Secretary, is that there's nothing you can do about it. Your job is to manage public expectations.'

It was a counsel of despair the new Home Secretary refused to accept. Instead of giving up before he began, he embarked on a sweeping programme of radical criminal justice reforms, designed to burnish the Conservatives' reputation as the party of law and order.

'I set about changing the whole thing as far as I could,' he recalls.

> I wanted to deter people from committing crimes, and I wanted to make it easier for the police to catch them if they did. I wanted to make it easier for them to be convicted if they were caught, and I wanted them to be properly punished if they were convicted. So that was a comprehensive agenda, which required a huge amount of work.

In the months that followed, Cameron was intimately involved in the formation of a raft of tabloid-friendly proposals, resulting in one of the most notorious pieces of legislation since Thatcher's 'poll tax' four years earlier: the 1994 Criminal Justice Bill. While hugely popular with the right-wing media, it upset an unusually diverse group: judges, ecologists, lawyers, ravers, squatters, bishops, gypsies, peers and trade unionists. Some 35,000 people took to the streets to demonstrate against it.[93] Aspects of the legislation may also have been uncomfortable for Cameron himself, specifically a proposal to increase the maximum fine for possession of cannabis from £500 to £2,500. As we have seen, he had not been averse to occasional recreational drug use.

The Bill also contained a crackdown on raves in the wake of Castlemorton. It infuriated students. Though Cameron himself has never been known to attend a rave (in 2009, the Tory Party leadership categorically denied that grainy video footage showing a lookalike moshing at a music festival in the '90s was him), he was now dating a bohemian art student named Samantha Sheffield who loved to let her hair down at such events.[94] Blue blooded, beautiful and much cooler than he could ever hope to be, she was an incredible catch. Cameron says they first met when she was a teenager at a party in Peasemore thrown by his sister Clare. The two girls had been close friends since they were young, though they went to different schools – Clare was at St Mary's Calne, while Samantha attended a school called St Helen and St Katharine in Abingdon. It seems he didn't make much impression, as she can't remember meeting him on that occasion. It was not until she was twenty-one, when Clare invited Samantha to join a family holiday in Italy to mark Ian and Mary Cameron's 30th wedding anniversary and Ian's 60th birthday, that their relationship took off.

It was the last week in August 1992, and it was no ordinary summer break: the holiday party comprised more than two dozen of Ian and Mary's family and friends, half in their twenties, the rest middle-aged. Between them, Clare, Tania and David (Alex was busy) brought nine of their own friends, while Ian and Mary invited six couples.

'That's when it all started,' Cameron has said of his romance with Samantha, hinting that while the age gap (only four and a half years, but both were young) was an initial worry, he swiftly got over it. 'I just began being more and more certain about it…It just became the right thing to do. I fell in love with her.'[95] According to a detailed account of the holiday, the party block-booked part of a resort in southern Tuscany, where the younger

93   *The Independent*, 11 October 1994.
94   Francis Elliott and James Hanning, p. 159.
95   David Cameron and Dylan Jones, p. 206.

crowd seem to have spent most of the time lounging by the pool sipping cocktails mixed by a waiter called Giovanni.[96] As they whiled away the hours sunbathing, eating and drinking, Cameron could not take his eyes off Samantha. Tall and willowy, with long, glossy hair, she was stunning. From Cameron's point of view, it was love at first sight.[97]

Watching with amusement, Pete Czernin and Dom Loehnis, another Oxford friend, knew their old friend was smitten when they spotted the pair playing tennis. By all accounts, Samantha is a lousy player, while Cameron is accomplished and extremely competitive, and hates playing with anyone worse. 'She struggled heroically and he took pains not to humiliate her,' according to an account.[98]

By the end of the trip, they were an item. In the months and years that followed, they managed to make the relationship work despite very different lifestyles. While he lived in a swanky flat in London and worked at the heart of government, she was an art student in Bristol living in downmarket student digs. When he stayed with her, he would have to 'shove coins into a payphone' if he needed to talk to the boss. Having no particular interest in politics, she was underwhelmed by his political connections, once apparently light-heartedly instructing him to tell Norman Lamont to 'fuck off'.[99]

To some friends, they seemed an odd match. Bruce Anderson remembers meeting Samantha for the first time on a deer-stalking expedition soon after they started dating. The special adviser's new girlfriend was not what he had expected.

'Sam didn't make much of an impression on me, but she did have a stonking cold – it might even have been mild flu. I thought she was really quiet. I thought David was keen, and I was surprised.'

However, another member of Cameron's social set, who joined the young couple on another group holiday to Tuscany, was impressed. On this occasion, the party comprised various high-flying Oxbridge friends of Cameron who holidayed together several times in the 1990s. Veterans of the trips include Ed Vaizey; Michael Gove and his then girlfriend Simone Finn (who went on to become a Cabinet Office aide in the coalition); Chris Lockwood (who

---

96   Francis Elliott and James Hanning, p. 139.
97   *Total Politics*, 20 May 2013.
98   Francis Elliott and James Hanning, p. 139.
99   Ibid., p. 131.

would work for Cameron in No. 10); the journalists Matthew d'Ancona and Robert Hardman; Jane Hardman (no relative, who later married Alan Parker, founder of the Brunswick PR group); documentary maker Marcus Kiggell; and Lizzie Noel (who would become a coalition education adviser).

Most were older and more intellectual than Samantha, but according to one member of the group, she more than held her own.

> Samantha was new to me. She was younger and at Bristol. I was expecting a sort of hippy chick but in fact we spent a lot of time talking about literature and she rather impressed me. I certainly had more conversations with her than I did with Dave, who was definitely very self-possessed and leader of the group. Dave had his tail up – he was clearly delighted to be with Samantha.

It helped that she was excellent at bridge, an activity Cameron enjoyed and which seems to have dominated most of the holiday.

'They played bridge every day, which was an incredible yawn for someone who didn't. I felt it wasn't really something you did on a villa holiday – it was a bit stuffy. Afternoons, after lunch or siesta or whatever, they would go off and play bridge till dinner, Samantha included,' the friend recalls.

Though Cameron had organised the trip and the daily routine followed the pattern he preferred, the friend says Samantha was 'not in the least the little woman with him on that holiday'.

The source adds: 'I'm not saying she could take or leave Dave, but it was definitely a partnership. She didn't feel, "Oh gosh, how wonderful he's chosen me!"'

While Cameron knew he had found 'the one', there would be no rushing to the altar.

'It took me a couple of years to persuade her to marry me,' he has said.[100]

What he had in his favour was a BMW (albeit a battered one), an important-sounding job, and the wherewithal to take her out for fancy dinners (their first date was at the upmarket restaurant Kensington Place). She claims he was her first boyfriend with such credentials, which is surprising, given the circles in which she moved. Her network included Jade Jagger, who was Clare's best friend and lived up to rock-star stereotypes when she was expelled

---

from St Mary's at sixteen after being accused of sneaking out of school to meet Josh Astor, a distant relative of Samantha's who was himself kicked out of Eton over drugs and later spent time in prison for handling cocaine.[101]

Back at the Home Office, Michael Howard was emerging from the storm over the Criminal Justice Bill with new status as the darling of the Tory right. With the help of Cameron and his fellow spad Patrick Rock (memorably described by Derek Lewis – head of the Prison Service and Howard's *bête noire* – as being 'somewhere to the right of Attila the Hun'),[102] the Home Secretary was skilfully playing the media. His famous 27-point programme – introduced at the 1993 autumn conference and containing the controversial 'Prison works' slogan – was a populist masterstroke that delighted the party faithful while upending the liberal assumptions of the six previous Conservative Home Secretaries since 1979, from Willie Whitelaw to Ken Clarke.

The abduction and murder of the toddler James Bulger by two ten-year-old boys in February 1993 had prompted a moral panic and sharpened public appetite for further law and order reforms. Howard's problem was that he now had to compete with the ambitious and telegenic Tony Blair as shadow Home Secretary. Worse, Howard's opposite number was relentless in his determination to show that a Labour government would be 'tough on crime, tough on the causes of crime'.

For young special advisers in both parties, observing Howard and Blair slugging it out was fascinating. The brightest and best Labour and Tory aides were not too tribal to socialise, conducting what Elliott and Hanning describe as a 'political flirtation', both for fun and to enhance their careers.

Blair's adviser Tim Allan (who went on to found the PR firm Portland) became quite friendly with Cameron and his circle at this time, and was sometimes invited to dinner parties as what he describes as a 'sort of comedy Labour person'. He quickly overcame his initial reservations about Cameron.

> The first time I met him, I thought, 'Oh God, he's exactly the kind of bloke I avoided at university.' He seemed like a complete Tory toff, and I just thought, 'Oh gosh, he looks absolutely awful.' I then did get to speak to him a few times and thought he was quite funny

101 Francis Elliott and James Hanning, p. 136.
102 Michael Crick, *In Search of Michael Howard* (Simon & Schuster, 2005), p. 274.

and quite sort of raffish and naughty and a bit of a laugh. He was very clever but funny and very good on policy detail. I was very ambitious and working constantly on policy issues – prison numbers, that sort of thing. We were both across the detail and both insanely ambitious. Even though we were trying to do things from a different angle.

Allan remembers, with admiration, Cameron obsessing over Labour's tactics.

I think it's often the case that the best politicians in opposition are the ones who obsess about the government, and the best ones in government are the ones who obsess about the opposition. Cameron always wanted to know what was going on; who was up, who was down, and what the programme was.

Cameron's stint in the Home Office offers very little insight into his own views on crime and rehabilitation. As we have seen, he rarely if ever expressed an opinion on the principle of a policy or approach, even in relaxed company. In any case, he was not being paid to articulate or push his own agenda. Michael Howard has said that his two spads occasionally persuaded him to approach an issue differently, but gives the impression that this was unusual.

Patrick Rock has said he can't remember any instances of Cameron raising any serious concerns about 'the general drift of policy'.[103]

After a year at the Home Office, Cameron was tiring of the job. The hours were long, the pace gruelling, and the pay modest relative to what he could earn elsewhere. From the start, he had been frank with Howard about his real ambition.

'He always said he was going to become a Member of Parliament,' Howard says.

The scale of the challenge for any Tory MP entering Parliament at the next election was clear. The party was heading for near-certain defeat. Labour's character assassination of Major, typified by the specious claim that he tucked his shirt into his pants, was well underway. His 'Back to Basics' campaign – a call to traditional Tory values launched in October 1993 – would soon unravel in a succession of sex scandals involving his ministers. Worst of all

103   Francis Elliott and James Hanning, p. 160.

was the sudden death of the Labour Party leader John Smith, on 12 May 1994, a tragedy that created a vacancy for Blair. Trooping off to the Two Chairmen pub near the Home Office, Rock and Cameron glumly concurred that the transition from Smith to the dynamic and charismatic shadow Home Secretary meant the Tories were 'fucked'.[104]

However, Cameron was undeterred. Before leaving the Home Office, he submitted an application to join the party's official list of approved potential parliamentary candidates. Given his credentials – five years working for the party and for government ministers in a variety of roles, with an unblemished record – the selection process was a formality. The next step was finding a seat, a far more difficult and competitive business.

In the meantime, he began putting out feelers for a new job. He did not have to try hard: Samantha's well-connected mother Annabel was only too happy to help. A single phone call from the formidable businesswoman was all it took to set her future son-in-law on a lucrative new path.

---

104   Ibid., p. 158.

11

Bunter

'I paid for my love of politics with a pay cut before I had even started.'

– Cameron

The lodge on the wind-lashed peninsula of Rubha nan Crann is the perfect hideaway for those seeking total tranquillity. Tucked away on the east coast of the Hebridean isle of Jura, the whitewashed bothy is by a sandy beach overlooking Tarbert Bay, some twelve miles north of the island's only village of note. Telecommunications are intermittent, and those staying at the property are unlikely to come across another soul, save for boatmen who occasionally bring supplies.

The lodge is the holiday home of Cameron's mother-in-law Annabel and her husband William Astor. Even with a fair wind, the journey from Glasgow takes four hours, involving a spectacular drive through the Trossachs to the Mull of Kintyre, followed by a two-hour ferry crossing to the neighbouring island of Islay; another ferry trip across the Sound of Islay to Jura and finally a long drive to the lodge. Annabel loves entertaining close friends and family at the retreat, where days take on a familiar routine, starting with a slap-up breakfast, followed by a bracing day on the moors, a hot bath and a hearty dinner of venison and other Scottish delicacies from the mainland.

Cameron himself has been going there since the 1990s, when he first got together with Samantha. He has never minded cold water, and loves to swim in Tarbert Bay or spend an afternoon fishing for sea trout or mackerel. Before the potential political backlash outweighed the pleasure, he used to stalk on Jura too, returning from the hard slog across the peaks happy but soaked through. A friend who accompanied him on such expeditions before he became an MP recalls:

> You go up with a ghillie and just follow him. It's so exciting. You go at a slow pace, but the ghillie never stops, and you just have to keep going. If you don't, the ghillie won't wait. It rains, and rains, and never stops, so that absolutely everything is wet. David came back absolutely scarlet. He's very fair-skinned, and he came back looking absolutely ridiculous. It was embarrassing, but he'd stuck with it. There was a certain grit, a toughness there.

Among the guests Annabel regularly invited to Jura in the 1990s was a charismatic self-made multi-millionaire named Michael Green, who found a neat solution to the challenge presented by the remote location: he would arrive by helicopter. He considered the place 'paradise', and went year after year. Often, there would be no electricity and evenings would be spent in front of a peat fire, chatting in the soft glow of an oil lamp or reading by candlelight.

During these magical holidays, Green and Annabel got to know each other well. He respected her business nous and considered her an exceptional judge of character. Their friendship, cemented when Green was at the height of his powers in the media industry and Annabel was poised to launch her own hugely successful company, was directly responsible for the next stage in Cameron's career.

By now he was committed to becoming an MP and was actively looking for a winnable seat. He was conscious that local Tory selection panels tend to prefer candidates with experience outside Westminster, and he knew he could earn far more in the private sector than at the Home Office. It was at this point that his future mother-in-law stepped in.

Cameron had proposed to Samantha, rather awkwardly, while they were relaxing one evening in his flat. Though he had hoped the moment would be romantic, he never quite found the right time, and eventually asked for her hand in marriage as they sat on the sofa watching the Martin Scorsese crime movie *Mean Streets*.[105] Around the same time, he sold his flat on Lansdowne Crescent, swapping it for a bigger place in north Kensington, which he bought with the help of his father and some money he inherited

---

105   *Daily Telegraph*, 27 April 2015.

from a great-aunt. This property, at 3 Finstock Road, would be their first marital home.

Now they were engaged, it seemed natural to Annabel to use her contacts to help her future son-in-law's career. Knowing he wanted to leave the Home Office, she called Green to enquire whether he knew of any suitable openings.

It was mid-1994, and her old friend ran the large and controversial media company Carlton Communications. In a business as big as his – it had some 13,000 employees – openings for talented young people, especially those with personal links to the boss, could always be found. Green listened carefully to what Annabel had to say.

'Get him in to see me,' he replied.

Having left school at seventeen with just four O levels, Green had initially gone into business with his brother, setting up a printing and photo processing company, which expanded into video and television. After a number of acquisitions, the firm was listed on the London Stock Exchange in the early 1980s, making him a multi-millionaire. At first, the company made adverts, rock videos and corporate films, but Green's vision was to acquire a broadcasting station. In the late 1980s, the market dramatically opened up and Carlton became a terrestrial broadcasting company.

As it happened, he was looking for a senior communications executive. It was a high-profile and sensitive role for which it was particularly important to find the right person. With Carlton Communications under attack from industry rivals, customers and the press, the new recruit would need the skill and resilience to engage in a war of attrition with the media. More importantly, they would need the right personality to work with Green himself. As far as the media boss was concerned, someone who came with a personal recommendation from Annabel would leapfrog any other candidate. Cameron's lack of experience in the industry would, he felt, be an advantage.

Green remembers:

> He knew something about television and about media, but [as for a] public company – how it was constructed, what we needed in terms of investor relations, PR, corporate affairs and so on – that was not a skill base he had. And I found that very attractive, because

CALL ME DAVE

> he would come at it from a fresh angle. I liked his brightness; he
> was fresh; he had energy; he could listen; he could take it in; and
> he wasn't tainted by the usual investor relations background.

At interview, Cameron did not disappoint. There was just one problem: his determination to go into politics, about which he was upfront. For Green, totally consumed by the business, it was nearly a deal breaker.

He says: 'I was focused on Carlton, and I wanted people dedicated and ambitious for the rest of their careers. Why would I want him thinking about another career? But David said very early on, "I'm interested in politics." He was absolutely consistent.'

Green offered Cameron a post on the corporate affairs team, on a pay package that compared extremely favourably to his Whitehall earnings. (Former colleagues believe he would have started on a salary of around £80,000, a considerable sum for a young man in his twenties in the 1990s.) Though the job did not initially come with a big title, a paragraph announcing the appointment in *PR Week* hinted at its status, noting: 'It is believed he will act as PA to chairman Michael Green.'

According to Cameron, there was one proviso: he should promise not to stand for a seat at the next election. The Prime Minister has claimed that when he refused to give such an undertaking, Green initially withdrew the job offer, but then relented, reverting with a slightly less favourable deal.

'I paid for my love of politics with a pay cut before I had even started,' he has said.[106]

Green says he has no recollection of this, and that in any case he was quietly confident his new recruit would not look back.

So, in September 1994, Cameron took up his only significant job outside politics, a role which gave him valuable new experience. In the seven years that followed, he would learn about the functioning of a listed company, from share prices to investor relations to dealing with a hostile media and the technicalities of accounting and broker circulars. In his new job he was under almost constant pressure, both internally, from Green, and from outside the organisation, which was under remorseless scrutiny. Working closely with Green, a fiery character, he also learned how to handle a highly demanding and mercurial boss, experience that would equip him to deal

106   David Cameron and Dylan Jones, p. 72.

with complicated and difficult characters in his political career and which almost certainly contributed directly to his remarkable unflappability as a party leader. Those who worked closely for Green in his heyday testify that while he was an inspirational figure and the experience was never dull, it took stamina, fortitude and sangfroid to deal with his demands and volcanic temper. A number of his employees simply could not take the pressure. That Green and Cameron still hold each other in high esteem and remain friends today shows the aplomb with which the future Prime Minister handled this extraordinary character.

Cameron joined Carlton at an exciting time. Its share price was soaring but it was under constant fire. The company had benefited from Thatcher's massive shake-up of ITV's franchise system in the late 1980s. The reforms, prompted by a furore over the documentary *Death on the Rock* about the SAS shooting of three Provisional IRA terrorists on Gibraltar (the film questioned the government's version of events), gave an advantage to companies with big wallets. It was a commercial environment in which Carlton was well placed to prosper, but the company's output was controversial.

A prominent business journalist who followed its fortunes throughout the 1990s recalls:

> In the early 1990s, ITV franchises were basically a licence to print money. Thames had had really quality output, but Carlton was just cheap crap. All the luvvies hated it, so they got a lot of bad press, from papers like *The Guardian*. The culture of the company became very, very defensive.

A few months before Cameron took up his new job, Carlton was castigated by the Independent Television Commission (ITC) for providing an array of 'unimpressive and very disappointing' programmes for the ITV network, which were 'neither distinctive nor of noticeable high quality'. The company's output included *The Good Sex Guide*, which prompted two written warnings from the ITC for breaching taste and decency. During his time as Carlton's top PR man, Cameron was called on to defend the dumping of *News at Ten* to make way for a revival of *Mr and Mrs* with Julian Clary; make the case for adverts targeted at children; defend the broadcast of salacious material uncomfortably close to the watershed; and, in the words of *Times* financial editor Patrick Hosking, 'explain how Carlton had come to screen a one-hour programme, conceived, sponsored and entirely funded by British Telecom'.[107]

In its worst debacle – a PR disaster Cameron was forced to handle – Carlton produced a documentary purporting to reveal a drug-smuggling route from Colombia to Britain.

It emerged that the show was riddled with fabrications and fake footage and Carlton was fined £2 million. According to a snippet in the *Guardian* media diary at the time, when faced with the allegations,

> Cameron initially refused to take or return phone calls from *The Guardian*'s media correspondent four days in a row. Eventually he seems to have inadvertently picked up his own phone. After the *Guardian* reporter introduced herself, she was confronted with the amazing sound of someone who sounded a lot like David Cameron maintaining that he was called 'John Smith' and just happened to be walking past the phone.[108]

Carlton's offices were initially in Mayfair and subsequently Knightsbridge, overlooking Hyde Park. In the Knightsbridge office, Cameron's desk was in a suite on the fifth floor with the corporate development, strategy and PR team, one level below Green. To keep staff on their toes, Green liked to keep the temperature low. Former employees claim he 'believed that you worked harder if it was cold'. He would wander round the building in his socks, smoking a cigar. From a screen in his office, he kept an eye on Carlton's fluctuating share price, storming downstairs to remonstrate with employees if he didn't like what he saw. Sometimes he would lash out at business contacts, leaving Cameron to smooth ruffled feathers.

A former Carlton colleague recalls:

> David was incredibly genial, and pretty tough. His job was effectively to manage Michael's relations with investors in the City. It was not easy. The reality was that Michael would talk out of turn, upset people greatly, and it was David's job to phone them up the next day, and say, 'Well, what Michael actually meant to say was…'

107 Ibid., p. 21.
108 Francis Elliott and James Hanning, p. 193.

It was an extraordinary place to work, because in a way it was completely free of politics. There was Michael at the top, who could give bollockings to anyone, which had the effect of flattening the hierarchy. There was a great esprit de corps among people who worked there, and tea and sympathy for any recipient of the last bollocking. You had to go through a kind of test, which involved a series of terrible bollockings. Once you'd passed that test, you were one of his boys. Then he became incredibly loyal, and he would advance your cause.

The former colleague, who held a senior position at the company, offers a personal insight into what it was like to be at the sharp end of Green's temper. Recalling a typical outburst, he says:

The bollocking I particularly remember was rather typical of Michael's style. He came down to the fifth floor, which was open plan, went up to my boss's desk, and said: 'Why do we still employ this guy?' I was three yards away! Everything went silent while I had to listen to my boss's rather feeble defence of me. Then he [Green] just walked away. The point that I decided I'd had enough was when we had a food channel, and I had to sell an interest in it to Sainsbury's, and it was taking a bit of time. It was after the dotcom bust. He phoned me up and said, 'Why haven't you fucking closed this deal? You couldn't even fucking close a door!' and he put the phone down. I kind of thought, life is too short for that. But it was pretty typical of his management style.

At least with Green, what you saw was what you got. Those who were able to roll with the punches speak of him with affection.

'He's a warm person, Michael, not a kind of fake, plastic person, so I think most people who survived that initial battering felt quite warm towards him,' says the same source.

Green himself is frank about his management style. Of Cameron, he says:

We worked well together because he didn't get flustered. He stood up to me, which was important, and yes, I was aggressive, and I got angry about the press, because that's what chairmen do – angry about your share price, angry about people not understanding us. David was very straight. He understood it. He understood what we wanted to do; what I wanted to do.

Cameron's colleagues included a competent and curvaceous woman called Edwina Paine, who adored him and had the ear of the boss. She took Cameron under her wing, frequently coming to his aid when Green was in one of his moods.

'Edwina was the only person in the whole company who could tell Michael to fuck off. And she got on well with David. She was a bit of a secret weapon for Dave,' according to the former employee.

Green concurs that Paine frequently 'picked up the pieces' when Cameron was under pressure.

'Edwina was a star. She knew what she had to do, but she also knew what he had to do. She would be constantly telling him…"David, you've not spoken to Technicolor!" or, "You've forgotten this, or that!" she was brilliant.' (She would later donate £10,000 to his Tory leadership campaign.)

Those who observed Cameron's relationship with Green at close quarters could not help admiring the way he handled his boss.

'The hairdryer treatment from Michael Green didn't seem to worry him at all,' says a colleague. 'He would fight his corner, and be quite equipped to argue back.'

Bruce Anderson recalls Green haranguing Cameron early one Sunday morning, when he might reasonably have considered himself off duty. Cameron took it in his stride.

> He rang him up at quarter to eight in the morning, and said, 'You haven't read all the papers yet, have you?' David calmly said he hadn't…I remember [another time] David writing a speech. Michael picked it up and said: 'This is crap!' David said: 'Put it down! It's not finished yet. It's not ready for you to see.'

As well as heading Carlton, Green was chairman of ITN. During Cameron's first year in the job, Green repeatedly clashed with ITN's then chief executive,

David Gordon. A senior figure who was caught between the two men admired the way Cameron managed the relationship.

'Michael hired David Gordon on the recommendation of others, without really knowing him,' he recalls.

> Within weeks, both men realised they had made a terrible mistake and hated each other. During the mad period when both were in power, Michael would come to see me without Gordon knowing, and so would Cameron. One day, Gordon, who was in the office next door, saw Cameron in my office, and stormed in, shouting at him and calling Green, in his absence, everything under the sun. What struck me was the elegant way Cameron handled the whole thing. Knowing that Gordon outranked him, he didn't give him a mouthful back but nor did he defer to him. He didn't wind Gordon up further by defending Green, but nor did he accept any criticism of his boss. I was impressed.

Since Carlton was a multinational business, relations with Europe were a running theme. Cameron's time at the company offers a glimpse into his perspective on the EU.

Green says that on Europe the two 'disagreed', describing himself as 'much more pro-European' than his former PR man.

> We worked in Europe, we had companies in Europe; we traded in Europe. Half our sales were overseas, so I was terribly interested as a businessman that we had Europe as our context. When we did business with Disney or Paramount, we didn't do business with them in the UK, we did business in Europe. So I felt very strongly pro-European, and he was certainly aware of that.

Green is sketchy on specifics, but former colleagues echo his recollection that Cameron was Eurosceptic.

A former colleague who shared an office with Cameron recalls him riffing about the EU in largely disobliging terms.

'I can't remember his exact words, but his basic view was that Europe was a kind of stitch-up between the French and the Germans. I think his view was that we shouldn't really be part of the EU, though I don't know if he quite said this,' he says.

As he earned Green's trust, Cameron was asked to take on more responsibility, often accompanying the boss on business trips to America. Green would fly first class, but had no compunction in relegating Cameron to cattle.

On one occasion, he asked Cameron to stand in for him at a major presentation in America.

> I was exhausted. I just said, 'Come on, you know it better than I do – you can probably do it better than me! So we went into the meeting and he presented as the chairman and chief executive…He was very good at it. He was fun and we would laugh afterwards.

Did Cameron ever let his hair down on such trips? Green says not.

> If you're asking, when we were in New York, and it was 1 a.m., and I was thinking about going clubbing, was David about to go to The Box with me, the answer is no. David would go to bed. There's not another side of David that I was unaware of. He took work seriously, he took politics seriously, and he took Samantha very seriously, very wisely!

A former colleague testifies that while there was 'a fair bit of shagging' at Carlton, Cameron 'did none of it'. Nor, he says, was there any culture of recreational drug taking among those who worked there.

'I think Michael would have been incredibly intolerant of that. It was completely drug free,' says the source.

During this period, Samantha's own career, in retail, was going from strength to strength. However, Green paints an endearing picture of her coming to collect Cameron when he was working late.

> I can still see Samantha downstairs, at 25 Knightsbridge, waiting [for him]. I would be leaving, and I would say, 'He's just finishing. Go up and sit with him!' And she would say, 'No, no, I'll sit here,' and she would sit so amazingly [patiently], in reception, and David was on the fourth or fifth floor, and he would always be later than

he should have been. He was working really hard. And they were an amazing couple. This would be seven or eight at night! She would often pick him up; she'd drive him about. He wouldn't have his keys; or they'd be going somewhere…they were a popular couple.

In less than two years at Carlton, Cameron rose through the ranks in the PR department to become director of corporate affairs, a high-profile role that became increasingly difficult and stressful as Carlton battled for supremacy in a cut-throat market. The 1990s marked the start of the long struggle between terrestrial broadcasters and satellite operators for power and audience share, pitting Carlton against Rupert Murdoch's BSkyB. Competition between the companies that made up ITV was also intensifying, with increasing consolidation via takeovers and mergers. At the same time, new digital broadcasting technology was emerging, prompting a race to develop new viewing systems and secure franchises to exploit the new platform. Questions of media ownership and permissible market share were heated and political. Cameron's job became particularly fraught when Carlton launched a controversial new service called ONdigital, a terrestrial multi-channel service and a precursor to Freeview. Its slogan was 'Plug and Play', but it was beset by technical hitches, and the slogan was soon lampooned as 'Plug and Pray'.

An insider recalls:

> There was a lot of grumbling from shareholders about how much this was costing to set up. Carlton was also going head to head with Sky. When ONdigital was set up, there were three shareholders – Carlton, Granada and Sky. Then the regulator stepped in and said Sky couldn't get involved because they wanted more competition. So ITV and Granada bought Sky out, which ratcheted up costs. This thing was going to be loss making for a while and the shareholders didn't like that.

For Carlton's PR department in general and Cameron in particular, the job became an exhausting firefight. For a period, he was chronically overworked. When Green insisted that he hire help, his first call was to Rachel Whetstone, who agreed to come on board. These days, Green describes Whetstone as 'formidable'. Her role at Carlton must have toughened her up, for, according to former colleagues, Green frequently reduced her to tears.

'She would get the brunt of it if things weren't going well,' says one. 'Instead of talking to David, Michael would make her the first port of call for the onslaught.'

During his time at Carlton, Cameron was good to other old friends. When Lord Beaverbrook, for whom he had written the odd speech at Central Office, tentatively asked whether it might be possible for his daughter to do some work experience at Carlton, Cameron was quick to arrange it. He had not forgotten that Beaverbrook used to reward him with a bottle of champagne when he did well.

Cameron's role brought him into direct and daily contact with financial journalists, a number of whom were already prominent and influential, and would become more so in the years that followed. This is important, because at least two of those individuals – Jeff Randall, formerly of the *Sunday Times*, BBC, *Daily Telegraph* and Sky News; and Ian King, former business editor of *The Sun*, and now the face of Sky's business coverage – crossed swords with him in episodes they have neither forgotten nor entirely forgiven. Cameron's behaviour made a deeply negative impression.

In King's case, the dispute was prompted by a negative piece he ran about Carlton in the business section of the *Mail on Sunday* in the late 1990s. The article was based on conversations with three of the company's top ten shareholders, who were uneasy about the way the company was being run, and concerned by Green's dominance.[109]

As is standard journalistic practice, King called Cameron for a response before running the piece. Cameron's reaction was to rubbish the claims. Confident in his sources, King ran the story anyway. That might have been the end of it, had Cameron not, in King's words, gone 'completely off the dial' after the story appeared. In a bizarre and confrontational move, the future Prime Minister penned a 'vile' letter to King's boss, accusing the journalist of bias, and hinting he should be sacked. King was stunned to discover a copy of the letter waiting for him on his desk when he arrived at work the following day.

A meticulous record keeper, he still has a copy of the missive. Many years

---

109 At around 5 per cent, his personal stake in Carlton was unusually large for a FTSE 100 company.

later, on the eve of the final vote in the Tory leadership contest, he dished up his revenge, penning a blistering column for *The Sun* in which he described Cameron as a 'mendacious creep':

> I was unfortunate enough to have dealings with Cameron during the 1990s when he was PR man for Carlton, the world's worst television company.
>
> And a poisonous, slippery individual he was, too.
>
> Back then, Cameron was far from the smoothie he pretends to be now. He was a smarmy bully who regularly threatened journalists who dared to write anything negative about Carlton – which was nearly all of us. He loved humiliating people, including a colleague at ITV, who he would abuse publicly as 'Bunter' just because the poor bloke was a few pounds overweight.
>
> A recent *Sun* interview with Cameron generously called him a former Carlton 'executive'. No, he wasn't. He was a mouthpiece for that company's charmless chairman, Michael Green…
>
> We desperately need a strong opposition to this wretched government. But Tory Party members must be on whatever Cameron is alleged to have smoked if they think this mendacious creep will provide it.

The identity of the unfortunate individual Cameron nicknamed 'Bunter' (after the fictional overweight schoolboy Billy Bunter) remains a mystery, but such name calling was not entirely out of character. A number of those who disliked Cameron at Eton and Conservative HQ and gave 'background only' interviews for this book noted a propensity to be unkind about people behind their backs.

Cameron's dispute with Randall took place in late 1999, when the journalist got wind of a possible merger between two of the three major ITV companies, Carlton, Granada and United News and Media. It was a potentially sensational scoop, but it was unprintable without some signal from one or both parties that it was true.

It is easy to imagine Cameron's horror when Randall put the story to him. The proposed merger was highly market sensitive and by no means a done deal. Any leak could jeopardise the entire plan. Randall would never have expected confirmation, even off the record, but he would have known how to interpret a carefully formulated corporate response that stopped short of a denial. For his part, Cameron could have deployed any number of tactics to avoid actively 'standing the story up' while maintaining his integrity. Instead, he went to great lengths to deter the journalist from writing the story, even though it was true. In Randall's words, the PR man 'put up so much verbal tracer that you started to lose your own guidance system. He put me right off it.'[110] When the merger was announced a few weeks later, the business journalist was apoplectic.

'I wouldn't trust him with my daughter's pocket money,' he fumed later.

How much significance should be attached to Cameron's behaviour in relation to Randall and King? At the very least, he showed poor judgement, making two very powerful enemies quite unnecessarily. It is interesting that, at the time, he purportedly dismissed Randall as 'a person of no consequence',[111] a risky assessment to make of any national newspaper or television journalist. Cameron should have known that figures like King and Randall would have many influential contacts and would probably be in the business for a while, rising to increasingly powerful editorial positions. His decision to write to King's superior was hasty, short-sighted and inflammatory, and was a very unusual response from a PR man.

Furthermore, Randall and King are not the only journalists to have gone on record attacking his approach. Chris Blackhurst, who went on to become editor of the *Independent* newspaper, took an equally dim view of him at Carlton, describing him in 2007 as 'aggressive, sharp-tongued, often condescending and patronising, but when awkward questions were put to him, frequently obstructive and unhelpful…If anyone had told me at the time that he might become premier, I would have told them to seek help.'

With the passage of time, Blackhurst's assessment is more generous: that Cameron did a fairly good job for an often impossible boss.

> Green was very sensitive and tetchy, and would ring journalists up and literally rant at them. His language was blue. Classically, you'd then get a call from Cameron, apologising for Michael. He'd say things like: 'You have to understand, Michael is just very passionate

---

110   Francis Elliott and James Hanning, p. 197.
111   Ibid.

about the company; he takes it very personally,' and so on. Cameron was charming, smooth, urbane. At that time, it was pretty much open season on Carlton, and Cameron did the job quite well.

If Cameron routinely behaved as badly as he did in Randall and King's case, he would not have survived in most PR companies let alone prospered. Green points out that his PR man dealt with big-name journalists all day, every day, for many years, often under very difficult circumstances. In his view, to have fallen out irreparably with only two (at least only two who have spoken out) is a fair record.

> There were thirty journalists who every day woke up and talked about media. Every day they wanted a story. So if you think about how many journalists David dealt with, to only have had two [be angry] – that's impressive. Jeff Randall says David misled him. Well, he didn't. David did his job. And he behaved absolutely correctly at a very sensitive time about a merger or takeover. I believe that David knew that his job and his reputation was everything. David had an incredibly difficult job, where there were a million stories that we didn't want out, and he had to tread very carefully on how he handled it. He was asked lots of [share] price-sensitive questions by journalists who couldn't wait to break the story, which would be very inappropriate for a public company. There's a conflict almost every day in terms of what a journalist wants to hear and what he was able to tell them.

Yet it is hard to avoid the conclusion that Cameron was given more leeway than most PR executives for making enemies in the press. Green had come to trust him implicitly, and with Carlton constantly receiving a battering, the pair may both have felt it was them 'against the world'.

12

SNOW QUEEN

'I was overcome with such very happy emotions.'

– Cameron

On a disappointingly wet day, two affluent families and around eighty friends congregated at St Augustine of Canterbury for a traditional white wedding. It was a Saturday in June 1996 and, as far as the rector conducting the ceremony was concerned, there was nothing particularly unusual about the day, save for the plain-clothes security officers hovering at the back of the church. They had parked in his garden, in the Oxford-shire village of East Hendred, to keep an eye on the Home Secretary, who was among the guests.

Had he known he was marrying the future Prime Minister, the Reverend Ernest Adley would not have done anything differently. He says David Cameron, twenty-nine, and Samantha Sheffield, twenty-five, were like any other bride and groom, happy and in love, and for all their evident money and connections (the former Chancellor was also in the congregation), they were given no special treatment.

As he would with any couple he was marrying, Revd Adley had taken time to get to know them before the big day. In the run-up to the wedding, they met three times at his house, first to talk through practicalities, second for a deeper discussion about the meaning of Christian marriage, and third to rehearse the ceremony. He remembers the couple sitting happily on the sofa in his front room, drinking tea and patting his dog. He recalls feeling very confident that they both understood the importance of the vows they were preparing to take. He liked the fact that they did not want anything flashy.

The wedding of David and Samantha was a delightful occasion. They were a pleasant couple and so easy to get on with. What marked that wedding out was the happiness of it, which came through loud and clear. My wife said that she was sitting in the choir and she could see David and he was looking very quiet and happy. Like all bridegrooms, he was going to be a bit nervous, but it didn't show.

Since they were not officially local, Cameron and his fiancée needed special dispensation to marry at St Augustine's. They chose the church because it was near where Annabel lived with her second husband, Samantha's step-father Viscount William Astor. Revd Adley was able to swing it for them, as he would on occasion for other couples, on the basis that Samantha still had a room at her parents' home. The marriage certificate lists her address as Ginge Manor while Cameron lists his childhood home, the Old Rectory at Peasemore.

Cameron's stag party took place in a marquee in Lambourn near Peasemore. After an afternoon at the races, the stags, a mix of old school friends (including 'Toppo' Todhunter, James Fergusson and Tom Goff) and Cameron's political and journalistic friends (Robert Hardman, Steve Hilton, Michael Gove and Ed Vaizey, among others) let their hair down in style at a black-tie dinner. The drinking and revelry went on late into the night.

Bruce Anderson, who was at the party, recalls:

> It was near the Goffs' [house close to Peasemore]. Everyone was billeted with the Camerons or the Goffs, so that nobody had to drive. It wasn't riotous, but it went on till the late hours. It was very jolly, but there weren't any strippers. I remember being called upon to make an impromptu speech at about three in the morning.

Thus Samantha Sheffield, who described herself for the official record as an 'artist and designer', became Mrs Cameron, after a romance that had started four years earlier. During the ceremony, both shed tears of joy.

'This lovely Oxfordshire girl sang a beautiful piece of music, and we were right up in the nave, sitting down, and it was just a very beautiful moment and I felt very emotional,' Cameron recalled a decade later.

I was overcome with such very happy emotions. There I was, marrying Samantha, this wonderful, beautiful girl who I'd fallen in
love with, and there were all my family, all my friends, this lovely
church, and this beautiful singing. I tend to cry when I'm happy,
and I did then. And then Samantha started crying, and she's very
cleverly arranged the pictures of the wedding in our bathroom to
make them look as though she started crying first![112]

The ceremony was followed by an evening of well-mannered revelry.
According to an excerpt from the *Times* diary column, 'Lamont proved to
be the hit of the evening when he abandoned his low-slung frame to the lilting
beat of a folk reggae band. Fellow dancers could only stand back in awe.'[113]

Cameron's choice of bride is fascinating, not least because their personalities are so different. On the face of it, she is highly improbable material for
the spouse of a Tory politician. She sports a tattoo on her ankle, used to be
a 'Goth', and likes to holiday in Ibiza for the sunshine and clubbing scene.
Her extended family is full of colourful and racy characters, from her father,
a traditional Tory toff, to her exotic cross-dressing half-brother Robert,[114]
who works at the auctioneer Christie's – not to mention various relatives
with a druggie past. (Her sister Emily was kicked out of school after cannabis was found in her dormitory during a police raid.)[115] As an art student
she could be found hanging out playing snooker with a thief and alleged
small-time drug dealer in downtrodden pubs, and had no interest in politics.
All that was long ago, but she never entirely shook off her rebellious streak.
This was never more apparent than when, aged forty-three, she became the
first prime ministerial spouse in history to stage an event that could credibly
be described as a 'rave' at Chequers, hiring a Radio 1 DJ known as 'Sarah
HB' (for 'Hard Bitch') to spin discs. These days, she shares food, fashion
and travel tips on Pinterest and uses a smartphone app called Shazam to
identify obscure dance tracks, while her radio station of choice remains the
indie rock outlet 6 Music.[116]

All this makes her a most unlikely fit with the über-conventional son of

112 David Cameron and Dylan Jones, p. 205.
113 *The Times*, 3 June 1996.
114 Mail Online, 28 March 2014.
115 Mail Online, 29 August 2010.
116 Interview in *You* magazine, 5 April 2015.

a Home Counties stockbroker and a magistrate, yet the relationship more than works. One very close personal friend describes the marriage as 'the strongest' she knows. It has survived not only the intense pressure of what Cherie Blair called 'life in the goldfish bowl' in Downing Street but also the appalling tragedy of the death of a child. Rumours that Samantha was at one point having an affair with a member of her security detail are entirely unfounded. Quite how this gossip began circulating is a mystery (it came up on a number of occasions during our research), but it would be totally out of character. Friends say it would never happen, because the marriage is solid as a rock. In any case, a bodyguard would not be her type.

'She's far too much of a snob,' snorts one confidante indignantly. 'A grungy musician who interested her, maybe, if she wasn't so happy with David; but a policeman? No way!'

As for Cameron, he says openly that Samantha is far and away the best thing that has happened to him and that his family is 'the most important thing' in his life.[117] Even those with little else good to say about the Prime Minister did not question his commitment to her or the children.

So who is she?

On her marriage certificate, Samantha listed her father Reggie's occupation as 'farmer', a description that is laughable in its modesty, as was Cameron's characterisation of her property assets as a 'field in Scunthorpe'.[118] The truth is that her family is stupendously rich, and Sir Reginald Sheffield does not spend his time pootling around in a tractor or herding sheep. He is the eighth holder of a baronetcy that dates back to 1755, and in his own words, lives off 'unearned income garnished by the occasional planning consent'. His property portfolio, which includes 3,000 acres of arable land, and a £5 million stately home near York called Sutton Park, is worth upwards of £20m.[119] One of his cousins, Davina, was an early girlfriend of Prince Charles, while another was a lady-in-waiting to the Queen's late sister, Princess Margaret.[120] Friends describe him as an 'absolutely delightful character from the Tory old school' who loves traditional country pursuits, particularly riding and fishing.

---

117   David Cameron and Dylan Jones, p. 193.
118   Ginny Dougary, *The Times*, 16 May 2009.
119   Philip Beresford, *Sunday Times Rich List*. In 2007, Beresford put the
         Camerons' combined wealth at £30 million. The rather loose calculation took
         into account their respective families' wealth.
120   Simon Heffer, *Sunday Telegraph*, 10 December 2005.

'He's not a sharp dresser, lots of Wellington boots and mud. People recognise him because he invariably wears a bow tie. This is old money, frayed at the edges, all inherited furniture,' his former local MP Michael Brown has said.[121]

The Sheffield family seat is Normanby Hall, a large Regency mansion in 300 acres of beautiful parkland open to the public. In 1964, the family leased the house and grounds for ninety-nine years to what was then Scunthorpe Borough Council.[122] Samantha's half-brother Robert helps run the estate company, and members of the family still stay in a flat there at the weekends, exercising their dogs in the woods, although their main residence is Thealby Hall, another impressive property with formal gardens twenty minutes' walk away. Like all grand families, they also have somewhere in London: a place in a smart block of flats in Bayswater. It was bought for £1,415,000 in 2011.

Both of Samantha's grandmothers are colourful figures. In a connection that she has never revealed, she shares her paternal grandmother, Nancie Sheffield, with the famous interior designer Cath Kidston. Indeed, Samantha and Cath bear a remarkable physical resemblance. They both have the same high cheekbones, long legs and glossy hair, and each inherited an entrepreneurial streak. Both have had highly successful careers in interior design and retail.

Born in 1906, Nancie married a dashing Royal Naval officer called Glen Kidston at the age of nineteen. The couple had an exotic honeymoon in Ceylon and a baby son named Archie soon followed. A record-breaking aviator and motor-racing driver, Kidston was one of the 'Bentley Boys' of the 1920s, famous for day-long parties and romantic dalliances. His lovers included Barbara Cartland and the Duchess of Argyll. He survived several brushes with death, including one as a submariner. In 1929 he was the sole survivor of a civilian plane crash, battling through a mile of woodland at night to get help, with his clothes still smoking from the fire. He competed in many motor races, including Monte Carlo and the Isle of Man TT, and owned the first Bugatti in the UK, before winning the famous Le Mans race in 1930, driving a Bentley. A year later he made a record-breaking flight from England to Cape Town in six and a half days, apparently to show how the mail service could be speeded up. It was at this point that his luck finally ran

---

121   *The Independent*, 10 October 2009.
122   http://www.normanbyhall.co.uk/house-grounds/the-house-family.

out: the plane he had borrowed broke up in mid-air during a dust storm in South Africa, and he and his companion were killed.

Nancie did not remain a widow long: six months after her husband's death, she became engaged to Reginald Sheffield, the son of a former Tory MP. A Scottish newspaper that carried the announcement featured a picture of her taken by a society photographer. Like her future granddaughters Samantha Cameron and Cath Kidston, she was an elegant brunette with almond-shaped eyes. The couple married quietly in London. It was a happy union which produced four children, the youngest of whom was Samantha's father, Reginald.

Samantha's maternal grandmother, Pandora Clifford, was equally exotic. A renowned beauty, she caused a scandal when, aged just seventeen, she became pregnant by an older man. Her paramour, Timothy Jones, was a handsome and suave Old Etonian who had lost a leg in the Second World War after stepping on a landmine. He did the decent thing and married her, but the wedding, 'on a dark day in January', was a 'hurriedly arranged, poorly attended affair'. The bride, two months pregnant with Samantha's mother Annabel, wore black.[123] Though money was tight, the marriage, which also produced a son, Alexander, lasted until Annabel was twelve.[124]

At twenty-one, Annabel married Reggie Sheffield junior, giving birth to Samantha in 1971. Samantha's sister Emily came along two years later. The couple split up in the 1970s, after he had an affair with Annabel's friend Victoria, but the break-up was amicable. In a confusing twist, Annabel went on to marry William Astor, her stepfather's nephew, who inherited his title in 1972. They set up home in Oxfordshire and have now been together for thirty-nine years.

Today, the Astor and Sheffield families are thoroughly intertwined and on excellent terms.

Bruce Anderson says:

> Reggie and Annabel have a very happy divorce. Most divorces leave
> scars, but Reggie and William are really good friends. They often
> have Christmases together with all the extended family. The wives

---

123 Francis Elliott and James Hanning, p. 132.
124 In 1961, Pandora re-married, to Michael Astor, son of the 2nd Viscount Astor.

get on. David says Victoria's main recreations are fishing, her dogs, and Virginia tobacco. She's a very good fisherwoman.

So close is the bond between Reggie and William, that according to Anderson, they sometimes jest that they don't know whose children are whose.

> William and Reggie regularly have lunch, and joke, 'Is Emily one of yours or mine? If she's one of yours, then why is she asking me for a bigger allowance?' All the children get on as if they were the same [family]. It's unusual, because everybody is happy. The kids are very loud, like teenagers. If you want to make a point, you need to get it in in the first half of the sentence.

Until the age of sixteen, Samantha went to a private girls' school in Oxfordshire called St Helen and St Katharine. She was not particularly academic, and cheerfully admits she was in the bottom set for maths, though she did better at English. But she was creative and went to Marlborough for sixth form on an art scholarship. Her contemporaries remember her as being rather quiet.

'I remember she used to walk between classes with her arms tightly crossed over her text books. She was fairly low-profile. I guess it was quite intimidating being a girl in what was then a boys' school,' says one.

Another former pupil described her as a 'pretty good sport' and has vague recollections of 'getting her on stage in her underwear'.

After Marlborough, she completed an art foundation course at Camberwell College of Art before heading to Bristol to study fine art. At the time it was one of the best fine art courses in the country, with strong links to St Ives, where pupils would spend the summer painting. Bristol also had a lively street art and music scene and was close to Glastonbury, ideal for a young woman who loved clubbing. Somehow she acquired the nickname 'Snowy' or 'Snow Queen'.[125]

Though there is no proof that she took recreational drugs, a number of those who know her have privately suggested that this was the case, not only at university but in later years. Either way, it did not affect her studies:

---

125   http://www.newstatesman.com/uk-politics/2008/01/labour-minister-westminster.

teachers remember her as an excellent student. Part of her course involved a term overseas, a particularly formative experience.

Her former fine art tutor, Paul Gough, recalls:

> Samantha went to one of our twinned art schools in Berlin. Being a student in Germany would have been an amazing experience – the art schools in Berlin are not quite what we are used to here. They are very old-fashioned; the studio would be run by a professor and they would have had to work in a 'disciple' arrangement. The overseas experience in the middle of second year was an important part of growing up and Samantha would have gained hugely from it. They had to be fairly self-motivated – these were pre-email days and you would have to be trusted to be independent. Not fall to pieces.

He has never forgotten one of her pieces of work, a six-foot-high image of a loo entitled 'The Philosopher's Throne'.

'I can still see it now,' he says.

> She had a postcard made of it in her final show, a large painting of a box room in one of the houses she lived in. It was a big pile of furniture, and in the middle there is a toilet. She used complementary colours – orange through to grey – and I remember talking about this painting and generally advising and encouraging.

In what he describes as a very strong cohort of students that year, Samantha stood out.

'She had a very sublime use of outline and a sense of ownership of that space. She stood out in that group, despite the fact there were thirty or so of them all trying to be individual. They were quite competitive with one another, but also quite supportive.'

Throughout her twenties, Samantha consistently downplayed her wealth, class and connections. In Bristol she made a point of slumming it, hanging out with a DJ and small-time criminal[126] named Tricky in the backstreets of Montpelier and St Pauls. These were rough parts of the city, typically avoided by the student population. She and Tricky – real name Adrian Thaws – used

---

126   By his own admission; see Francis Elliott and James Hanning, p. 137.

to play snooker in dodgy pubs. He had no idea of her background, and thought she was 'quiet, polite and humble'.

When she started dating Cameron, she continued to suggest her father was simply a 'farmer'. A friend recalls her making a clumsy attempt to bond with a working-class Labour spin doctor on the basis that they both came from the north.

> It was at a dinner party. She and I were among other guests including Derek Draper, who came from Lancashire, and he made much of this. Sam said, rather sweetly, 'My parents live just outside Sheffield.' Of course they live in this fantastic stately home. I remember being a bit gobsmacked that she would introduce the fact that she came from the same area, knowing myself that she came from this incredibly wealthy family, and I had no doubt that Derek Draper didn't. I felt it was a bit too salt of the earth.

With so much family money, she might easily have eschewed a career after art school: she quickly realised it was hard to make a living from painting. Yet she always stood on her own two feet. As a teenager, she had occasionally helped out at the exclusive Bond Street stationery boutique Smythson, where her mother was a design consultant. After art school, it became a full-time job. Over time, she rose to become the firm's creative director, on a six-figure salary. Meanwhile Annabel runs the luxury furniture and home accessories company Oka, a £20 million-a-year business she set up in 1999. Her personal stake has been valued at around £30 million. Cath Kidston's business is a global enterprise valued at over £70 million. Few families have produced such a successful trio of businesswomen.

Exactly what cool, bohemian Samantha saw in crashingly conventional 'Dave' is a question that still exercises some political observers. When the couple started dating, he was fond of wearing red braces and smoking cigars, while she was more likely to be wearing a velvet jacket, gold hoop earrings, and smoking a roll-up cigarette.

One Tory MP who moved in the same social circles when they were younger said: 'Those sisters were very cool, very moneyed, very hip. Everybody talked about them. They were rich girls with titles and palaces who adopted Estuary accents. Dave did very well to get her.'

Part of the answer may lie with Annabel, who was extremely ambitious for her girls. One source who was at Marlborough with Samantha and Emily speculates that in marrying Cameron, Samantha was finally doing what her mother had long hoped for and expected of her: settling down with a clever, ambitious young man from a wealthy family, who, if not quite her social equal, was connected to the highest levels of the political establishment, and was on the fast track to a big Westminster career.

'Marrying Dave was very much the kind of thing Annabel would have wanted for her daughter,' he says.

At the same time, Cameron was good-looking, self-assured, and made Samantha laugh. She has said his sense of humour was the primary attraction when they first met. Though she could not possibly have known how far he would climb, he ticked all the conventional boxes as a good potential husband and father, even if he was, in the eyes of some of her cooler friends, a little 'square'.

The fact that she is not a political anorak would prove an asset: she helps keep him real.

Anderson recalls a conversation over dinner with the couple, when Cameron first became an MP, during which she refused to be patronised about her lack of political expertise.

It was in Witney, and Sam said at the dinner table that she was fed up with William Hague's fascist rhetoric. David and I said: 'What fascist rhetoric?' She said, 'All this talk of One Nation.' We laughed and explained the genesis of One Nation, Disraeli and so on; that it was usually a left-wing Tory slogan. Sam said, not at all abashed, 'Well, I may not have been educated at Oxford, but I know as much about politics as most people and it means nothing to me.' I suddenly thought she was dead right [about] a lot of the language politicians use.

Cameron himself has described her as 'unconventional and challenging', suggesting she keeps him on his toes. Away from the cameras, she is not

averse to telling him to stop being 'boring' when he gets too intense.[127]
He has said she stops him 'being too straight down the line'.[128]

Family life in No. 10 was not always easy. When they first moved into
the Downing Street flat, the fusty environment was a shock. They spent the
full £30,000 taxpayer-funded allowance available to refurbish the property,
and thousands more installing a state-of-the-art kitchen in an attempt to
make the place more modern and homely.

To add to the pressure, there is no great love lost between Samantha and
George Osborne's wife Frances, her next-door neighbour in Downing Street.
Perhaps it is no surprise: the two women have very different personalities.
Unlike Samantha, who has a stylist and special adviser, and designers falling
over themselves to lend her beautiful outfits for official functions, Frances
has no taxpayer-funded support, a disparity she is said to feel keenly. There
is no outward hostility between them, but the relationship is not warm. Such
tensions cannot make living above the 'shop' any easier.

For all the uniqueness of their situation, Cameron depicts their marriage
as similar to those of millions of other ordinary working parents: juggling
childcare, bickering about minor stuff, relaxing at the end of a long day with
a glass of wine and a DVD boxset.

'I'd say the most common thing we row about is arrangements. Why have
you organised this? Well, because it's time we did that…Well, you didn't
ask me etc. The normal stuff that married couples row about,' he has said.
'Normally we row over the things that need to get done. Why haven't you
fixed the car? Why haven't you done this or that? And that could be me
saying that to her, or the other way round. It's very even.[129]

Their marriage is central to understanding the way Cameron approaches
his job. His commitment to their relationship and family unit accounts
for his determination to spend 'quality time' with her and his children
whatever else is going on in the world. In practice, this means regularly
finishing work at a reasonable time, setting aside 'date nights' and taking
frequent family holidays. He talks about 'Sam's rules', under which they
must have 'plenty of time together, plenty of time with the children', and,

---

127 Private information.
128 David Cameron and Dylan Jones, p. 51.
129 Ibid., p. 206.

twice a week, he must be home from work early enough for the children's supper and bath time.[130]

It led to criticism while he was in Downing Street that he was too relaxed about his job, but if he wanted to keep her happy – and give their family life any normality – he almost certainly had no choice. Friends say that behind closed doors, she calls the shots.

'I've no doubt at all that she wears the trousers,' says a friend who has known them both since their twenties. 'If she said "Jump!" he'd say, "How high?" I wouldn't mess with Sam. Not that she's bossy or bad-tempered, but she definitely knows her own mind.'

---

130   Ibid., p. 204.

13

BREAKTHROUGH

'I must have won.'

– Cameron, 2000

Michael Green had thought Cameron would be so dazzled by the money-making opportunities at Carlton that he would soon forget his ambition to become an MP. He was wrong. Much as he enjoyed corporate life, Green's PR man remained determined to find a parliamentary seat – a process that would prove lengthy and frustrating.

Given his credentials, he might have expected to be parachuted into a winnable seat. After all, the party leadership could, and occasionally did, fast-track exceptional individuals. But his battle to become an MP was long and arduous.

It was not for want of talent. His initial appearance before the party assessment board had been a resounding success.

A former party official who sat on the panel describes his performance as 'brilliant'.

> I was his assessor when he came forward … In the group stuff, you could see he was a natural leader, very good at persuading the others. I did quite a few of these [assessments] over the years, and he was by far the most outstanding of them all. Afterwards, I said to him, 'You're brilliant. You're going to pass, and when you're Prime Minister, I expect you not to forget me.

Unfortunately, a succession of local party associations proved more resistant to his charms. His tilt at Ashford, at the end of 1994, got off to a bad start at a drinks party for candidates and their spouses when Samantha wore a skirt with a revealing split. Apparently it was considered too daring, and after somebody had a quiet word, she felt obliged to borrow a safety pin.[131] The competition was stiff – among his rivals were Damian Green and Theresa May – and Cameron arrived late. The seat went to Green. Cameron also flunked applications for Reading and Epsom in 1995. Finally, in January 1996, his fortunes changed when he applied for a seat in Stafford. This time, he came through with 'flying colours' – despite a kerfuffle when Samantha tripped over as she accompanied him up some steps to make his speech.[132]

Mike Heenan, the chairman of the local party at the time, recalls: 'He was by far the best speaker we've had. And he was very clearly, back then, somebody to watch. You could see that he'd got tremendous abilities.'

Cameron's application form highlighted his experience at the Treasury and Home Office, and his close relationships with his former bosses Lamont and Howard. The panel was impressed.

'Obviously we knew that he worked with Norman Lamont and had been there on Black Wednesday and all that sort of thing. I've seen quite a few candidates, but he was very tuned in to the political world, and to political contacts, compared to quite a few other people,' Heenan recalls.

The constituency was new. A boundary review had sliced off a chunk of the original seat, eating into the Tory vote. Notionally, the new patch retained a healthy Conservative majority, but the incumbent MP, Bill Cash, was uneasy. He recalls:

> I'd taken the majority up from 3,000 in the 1984 by-election, to I think around 13,000, but when the boundaries changed the seat was significantly different. If I was asked, 'Was it going to be won in '97?' I would have been very doubtful. Historically the seat is a very interesting one – I think it was one of the first seats in the 1880s to go to what was effectively the new Labour movement. Basically it has got a very strong, traditional Labour core. When the rural areas are attached to it, the rural people of Staffordshire invariably vote Conservative. They are the absolute centre of gravity of the heart of England, Conservative vote.

131 Francis Elliott and James Hanning, p. 171.
132 *Trevor McDonald Meets David Cameron.*

But these rural areas had gone, apportioned to a new seat called Stone, where Cash decided his prospects were better. What remained was a predominantly urban belt. Perhaps Cameron felt the size of Cash's majority meant he could win it even without the rural sections of the seat. The number of applicants for the Tory candidacy – there were some 350 – certainly suggests the seat was still regarded as an attractive prospect.

Yet the portents for the Tory Party nationally were bleak.

Despite a formidable economic recovery, the Labour leader Tony Blair had propelled Labour to its highest ever poll share, while Major's personal rating had dropped to an all-time low for any Prime Minister.[133] Few doubted a Labour victory at the next general election. By the time of Cameron's selection, the opposition had managed to sustain an average lead of thirty points for nearly eighteen months.

Against this backdrop, Cameron knew there was no room for complacency, even in a seat he expected to win. He and Samantha rented a farmhouse in a village outside Stafford, and would spend weekends canvassing and networking.

Heenan remembers:

> At the time, the great success was the economy. From a difficult situation on Black Wednesday, the management of the economy had been very good indeed, so we had a good tale to tell. That was our main pitch. We did a lot of work, going round different factories and businesses, meeting people, meeting employees. We ran a very thorough campaign in that respect. I think that coming from London, David found it quite an eye-opener, learning about a north Midlands seat. It's a very different environment to London, and I think he learned a great deal.

Cameron is fond of recounting a jokey exchange with Heenan while they were out on the stump.

Nicholas Soames, to whom he has told the story, says:

> During the campaign, the chairman of the association said to him, 'David, I've got a question to ask you. If you're standing on the edge of a cliff, and you have, with their toes facing out over the

133 Peter Riddell, *The Times*, 26 August 1994.

edge of the cliff, a Labour and a Liberal Democrat Member of Parliament, who do you push over the edge of the cliff first?' And David said, 'Uh, well, I imagine Liberal.' And the chairman said, 'David, it's always Labour. Business before pleasure!' He often tells that story himself.

As the election drew closer, friends and family offered their services. Among the big hitters Cameron persuaded to come to the constituency were Michael Howard and Michael Heseltine.

Heenan says:

> He brought a whole load of helpers from London, which was very positive. They joined members of the association and we were delighted to have them. There were some notable names among them. It was a very good campaign. Samantha was very support-ive. She came up every weekend. She was very much part and parcel of the campaign.

Local activists recall her diligently trooping around the town with a paint pot and ladder, ensuring all the placards on lamp-posts were an appropriate shade of blue. Though her style sometimes raised eyebrows (she was appar-ently banned from smoking roll-ups at the local party headquarters), she was well liked and her contribution gratefully received.

'I well remember her pasting about 300 poster boards,' Heenan says.

Combining the contest with his high-pressure job at Carlton must have been exhausting, but Green gave Cameron some leeway as well as reassur-ances that his job would be kept open if he failed to win the seat. Yet as far as the Labour candidate, David Kidney, could see, Cameron did not anticipate having to take up Green's offer.

> My impression is that he thought he'd been selected for a safe Tory seat and this was the start of his parliamentary career. To me, he was what I'd say he is now – very strong on the PR side, rather than the politics side. Smart, always well turned out, spoke extremely well in general terms about policies. Took part in hustings meet-ings with me and the other candidates in several different venues.

Kidney has never forgotten one particular hustings, which was dominated by a debate over local education funding.

> It was an evening meeting kicking off at around 7.30 p.m. and at the start time for the event, I was there; the Liberal Democrat candidate was there; but there was no David Cameron. Actually, we started without him. After about a quarter of an hour, he rushed in, all flustered, made his apologies, and joined in the meeting. The reason that I still smile at this is because the next morning, my news release to the local media, which was carried, was that David Cameron had 'played truant from school meeting'. It went down very, very well. When David did get elected four years later, he and I bumped into each other in Parliament, and he remembered that headline about the truancy.

While some parliamentary candidates spend years cultivating a seat, Cameron's selection to Stafford came late in the electoral cycle, forcing him to play catch-up on what mattered to the community. Kidney cannot recall him campaigning on local issues. Instead, he focused on the economy and Europe, a running theme in that election because of the Referendum Party. Heenan recalls Cameron broadly toeing the party line, arguing for continuing EU membership but against the rise of a federal European state. This is not the whole story. In the run-up to the election, Cameron was among 200 Tory candidates who made it clear they opposed monetary union, putting them out of step with Major, who had not at this stage ruled out such a move.

In his book *The Conservative Party: From Thatcher to Cameron*, Professor Tim Bale says there were 'powerful incentives' for Tory candidates to rebel on this issue, specifically the hope that taking a strong Eurosceptic stance might discourage UK Referendum Party candidates from fielding a candidate in the constituency. If this was Cameron's objective in going out on a limb, it was in vain: the Referendum Party did run in Stafford, threatening to further eat into the Tory vote.

Nonetheless, as election day approached, Cameron's camp felt they might scrape through. Heenan felt his candidate was exceptional and could buck the national swing to New Labour.

I actually had a bet with him. I said, 'If you get to Downing Street, you must treat me to dinner one evening.' He seemed to be going places. It was obvious – the political connections he had, plus his ability. He wrote quite a lot of our election material, and it was superb quality. It was quite clear that he had tremendous political nous.

Cameron spent election day criss-crossing the constituency meeting party activists before heading to the count. When the polls closed, the signs were ominous.

Heenan recalls:

It was a very depressing thing. I remember driving in to the count. I wasn't with David at the time, but the radio was on, and we could hear what was happening and it was very disheartening. Stafford declared around 2 a.m., but we could see by about two-thirds of the way through that we were struggling to win.

Looking at the increasingly disconsolate Tory camp, Kidney recalls feeling sorry for his rival.

It was all a bit sad actually because obviously, we all get there very excited, and all the rosettes are all there in view, but as the night went on, and it looked like the Conservatives were going to lose, the local supporters started to drift away. By the end of the evening, Cameron looked rather friendless, and someone from my team sort of cosied up to him and kept him company until the announcement of the results.

In the end, Kidney won the seat with a 12.6 per cent swing to Labour, securing over 4,000 more votes than Cameron. The former Labour MP, who lost the seat to the Tories in 2010, says: 'I think Cameron was, to the end, a bit surprised. I still think he thought he'd been parachuted in to win the seat and go to Parliament. To learn that wasn't going to happen was quite disappointing for him.'

Cameron would later describe the count as 'the worst torture in the world'.[134] Putting a brave face on it after the results were declared, he gave a gracious and upbeat speech. His tone reflected the civility of the campaign, which had been fought on policy, not personality, leaving no rancour between the candidates.

Though the loss of the seat was a blow to the party, in the post mortem, no blame was attached to Cameron.

Heenan says:

> After the vote we had that awful discussion that one has between a constituency chairman and a defeated candidate. We both agreed that there was nothing much more we could have done campaign-wise. I think we ran a very good campaign. Indeed, it was congratulated and held up by the West Midlands Conservatives as being a model campaign. So we had no regrets.

Cameron never forgot his bet with Heenan. Some thirteen years later, he would invite the constituency chairman to his Downing Street flat for a celebratory drink, just as he promised.

Following his defeat, Cameron returned to Carlton with renewed determination to find a winnable seat. The background to his eventual success is an important part of his story.

An attempt to secure the selection for Wealden in Sussex, in 2000, had been another blow. This time, he had valuable local contacts and knowledge: Rachel Whetstone's parents were leading figures in the local association. Perhaps the connection gave him a false sense of security, because, when it came to the crunch, according to Rachel's father Francis, he gave dull, monosyllabic answers to questions and failed to engage with the panellists. Whetstone feared the worst when Cameron missed an open goal, a trick question from the panel about whether he'd prefer to work in the Home Office or Foreign Office. The correct answer was, of course, that he was only interested in being MP for Wealden, but Cameron flunked it by taking it at face value.

After an initial round of questions, candidates were asked to leave the room while the first ballot took place. As Cameron sauntered out, he was

---

134   Reg Little interview, *Oxford Times*, 28 June 2001.

overheard saying to Samantha: 'That was one of the most boring evenings I've been to in years. The other two [candidates] are awful. I must have won.'

Samantha, who was wearing a set of pearls she had hastily borrowed from the Whetstones, was better at reading the runes.

'I wouldn't be too certain, if I were you,' she replied.

She was right: he was discarded at the first ballot.

Looking back, Linda Whetstone thinks Cameron 'misjudged' the situation. She says he appeared too detached and ambitious for that particular constituency, which 'tends to look for a great constituency MP first and high flyer second'.

By now, Cameron had really done the rounds on the selection circuit, a process that had been costly, time-consuming and dispiriting. His breakthrough came in extraordinary circumstances and in a constituency very different to Stafford.

Ten miles from Oxford, on the edge of the Cotswolds, Witney is a thriving market town where the historic streets are lined with upmarket boutiques, and a large branch of Waitrose does a booming trade. In good times, unemployment figures hover just above 1 per cent, among the lowest in Britain. Lying on the River Windrush, it has a thirteenth-century church, an eighteenth-century town hall and a medieval square, as well as all the usual leisure facilities of a busy, affluent place. It has been voted among the best places to live in Britain.

Lovely as it is, however, the town is low on the list of attractions in the wider constituency, which is a luscious, honeypot slice of rural England, peppered with golden stone villages which seem almost too good to be true. The rolling countryside is all hedgerows, grazing herds and winding country roads with handsome detached period properties round every corner. Two towns vie for the status of jewel in the constituency crown: Burford and Woodstock, the latter home to Blenheim Palace, a World Heritage Site and the birthplace of Winston Churchill.

The seat had been Douglas Hurd's since the early 1980s (and before, when the boundaries were different). His retirement in 1995 opened up one of the most prized Tory berths in the country.

Step forward Shaun Woodward, Cameron's old Central Office colleague, who won the selection for 1997 by just one vote. Some 400 people turned up to vote at the final stage of the contest. Throughout the process, Woodward had deflected attention from his views on Europe, which were in marked contrast to the predominant Euroscepticism in Witney. When he became an MP, however, he could no longer hide his Europhilia, setting him on collision course with the local party.

He recalls:

> Witney is an extraordinarily beautiful constituency, some of the most spectacular countryside in the south of England. But from the start it was fraught. Anti-Europeanism was very strong in the constituency, and for somebody who came from a very pro-European point of view, that was very hard. As soon as I got elected, there was a leadership contest. I was on the side of Stephen Dorrell, who was a friend of mine, and then Ken Clarke – and William [Hague] won the leadership. So it was a rough ride from day one. When William arranged that ballot on a new position for the party in Europe, I was vehemently against. I had an association with some very strong anti-European minded people, so from the beginning, the horns were locked, and it just got worse.

From that moment, he believes Witney Conservatives marked him down as a 'lefty liberal'. His discomfort was exacerbated because he was genuinely local, having moved to a palatial property in the undulating countryside outside Chipping Norton after marrying the supermarket heiress Camilla Sainsbury. Their children were at school in the area and they had close personal connections with a number of senior Tory figures in the constituency. Increasingly, Woodward felt the chill of their disapproval.

In July 1998, he caused further ructions by supporting a parliamentary motion tabled by Labour MP Ann Keen to lower the age of consent for homosexuals from eighteen to sixteen, a policy with scant support among Tories. Matters came to a head a year later over Labour's plans to repeal Section 28, the notorious piece of legislation that banned the 'promotion' of homosexuality in schools. Having been involved in setting up ChildLine, Woodward, by now London spokesman for the party, was painfully aware of the impact of homophobia on young people and categorically refused to toe the line.

He remembers: 'It got me into a lot of difficulty in my constituency.

Really what the association wanted was one of them. I think they were pretty convinced by the time this row took place that I wasn't one of them.'

Just after 6.30 p.m. on 2 December, having been issued with an ultimatum by whips, Woodward was summarily sacked. Both in the Commons and in Witney, his relationship with the Tory Party was now at breaking point. On Saturday 18 December 1999, he dramatically announced he was crossing the floor to Labour.

It is hard to overstate the outrage his defection triggered among Tories. Hague vented his fury in an open letter, demanding he stand down from Witney and call a by-election.

'If you were a man of honour, who valued his constituents as much as you say you do, you would resign your seat now, fight a by-election and give them the opportunity to judge who it is that represents their views and their instincts more accurately,' Hague thundered, accusing Woodward of betraying loyal party members, not out of integrity or principle, but for his own 'careerist reasons'.

Woodward's refusal to relinquish the seat left 'true blue' Witney with a Labour MP for eighteen months, a source of huge local upset and resentment. The embarrassment was all the more acute because the Woodwards had close personal ties with Lord Chadlington, the president of West Oxfordshire Conservative Association, and his wife Lucy, both of whom were devastated.

It was against this bitter backdrop that Chadlington and his colleagues began searching for a replacement for Woodward for the 2001 contest. Bruised local Tories needed a Eurosceptic of impeccable political pedigree whose loyalty to the party was beyond question. The denizens of Chadlington and Chipping Norton, the nucleus of Conservatism in Witney and the setting for its social gatherings, needed to find, in Woodward's words, 'someone who was one of them', and they were in no mood to take chances.

Now Cameron entered the scene. Here was an attractive, well-spoken Old Etonian who told them exactly what they wanted to hear. In west Oxfordshire, awash as it is with privilege and money, he was able to deploy what one old university friend calls his 'silky country house skills' in a way that did not resonate in Stafford. His traditional public school and Oxford education, his self-assurance and charm, as well as his connections at the highest level in the party, made him the perfect fit. That he grew up in the countryside but was also an urbane Londoner was the icing on the cake, for the upper echelons of Witney society are dominated by successful people who spend three or four days a week in the city. It helped that his key rival in the selection contest was Andrew Mitchell, who had lost his Nottinghamshire seat in Blair's landslide. Unlike Cameron, Mitchell was not a 'clean skin' and came with baggage, including the unwelcome attention of a Thatcherite splinter group called Conservative Way Forward, which monitored the political credentials of prospective parliamentary candidates and could make life difficult for those not judged to be 'sound'.[135]

In a technique he would later employ with devastating success in the party leadership contest, Cameron sealed his victory at the selection by eschewing a lectern and speaking to the panel without notes, standing directly in front of them. They loved it. He was now within a whisker of becoming a Member of Parliament.

When the election was called on 8 May 2001, he took to the campaign trail brimming with self-confidence and enthusiasm. He did nothing to hide his sense of superiority over candidates from other parties. From the pages of a personal blog on *The Guardian*'s website – a convenient new platform he'd recently acquired to raise his profile – he heckled his opponents, referring to one as a 'rock-crushing bore' and another, borrowing a description by a journalist, as a 'human–hamster cross'. Their 'sheer dreadfulness', he said, gave him the edge at hustings:

'They did not understand the difference between bilateral and multilateral debt, waffled on asylum and talked for so long that the congregation was kept on their backsides for two hours even though half of their questions were left unanswered,' he puffed, after one church meeting.[136]

If he comes across rather full of himself, he was never complacent: according to observers, including Lord Chadlington (who offered him and Samantha the use of a cottage on his estate which would later become his constituency home), Cameron was industrious and energetic throughout the campaign. He came up from London every weekend, and even took part in a charity bike ride that meant visiting every single village in the constituency. In one blog entry he recalled embarking on a day's canvassing at the crack of dawn – handing a 'dazed commuter' a leaflet at a train station while quipping,

---

135 Simon Walters, *Tory Wars: The Conservatives in Crisis* (Politico's Publishing, 2001), pp. 143–5.
136 *Guardian* blog, 29 May 2001.

'The early bird catches the worm.' (Although he admitted this line backfired: 'Her response was sharp: "If you call me a worm I won't vote for you."')[137]

Friends and family also pitched in. An amusing early blog post recalls how a 'horse-trading friend' – almost certainly Tom Goff – 'galloped down from Newmarket' for a day on the streets of Witney and proved a questionable asset.

> It seemed to be going swimmingly…until we reached The Lamb in Cassington at the end of a long, hard canvass. 'You don't recognise me, do you?' asked the barmaid. 'You burst into my bathroom and asked me how I was going to vote while I was bathing the kids.' I crossed my legs and prayed: 'Please don't say: I didn't recognise you with your clothes on.' In vain.[138]

Scarred by his experience in Stafford, Cameron remained on edge right until the final result.

'As the ballot boxes empty all you see are votes for the other candidates. No matter how many times your election agent tells you: "It's going to be okay", you sweat, chew gum, smoke, fidget, and generally drive your campaign team up the wall.'[139]

In the event, victory came easily. As one of the safest Tory seats, Witney was never going to be a re-run of Stafford. Cameron's majority of nearly 8,000 was respectable, and he had increased the Tory share of the vote. After a struggle that had begun in 1994 when he first started casting around for a seat, he was finally on his way to the green benches.

---

137 *Guardian* blog, 15 May 2001.
138 *Guardian* blog, 29 May 2001.
139 *Guardian* blog, 11 June 2001.

PART THREE –
GREASY POLE

14

THE BEST CHAIR

'I've broken my duck, lost my virginity, put my first toe on the greasy pole.'

– Cameron

From the cleaners to the Prime Minister, everyone at Westminster has their place, but the hierarchy is complex and some are further up the food chain than their titles suggest.

That David Cameron had no intention of settling for the lowly status of the average new MP was apparent from the outset, from the way he swept along corridors, a retinue of staff trailing in his wake, to his body language in meetings with more senior figures.

Between 2001 to 2005, he moved effortlessly through the ranks in the Commons, taking on a variety of increasingly important roles. The manner in which he rose mirrored his trajectory at Conservative Central Office a decade earlier. Within four years he would be ready to stand for the party leadership.

For most new MPs, starting work at Westminster is a huge culture shock. The labyrinthine corridors (almost two miles of passages; a hundred staircases); the arcane language and endless unwritten rules (not all chairs are for sitting on; and some coat pegs are for swords); the strange 'men in tights' who look like extras from a pantomime; the bored-looking policemen with machine guns slung over their chests; all make for an extraordinary and challenging working environment.

For Cameron, however, it was not too daunting. Though he still managed to get lost on his first day, accidentally wandering into one of the vast industrial kitchens where armies of white-uniformed chefs prepare meals for more than 9,000 pass-holders a day, he knew plenty of people; had a decent grasp of parliamentary procedure, and had contacts in the press lobby. He even had a secretary, Pippa Way, whom he 'inherited' from the outgoing MP David Faber. While he waited for the authorities to find him a permanent office, he perched happily enough in the corner of her room. 'He was a very easy person to be around,' she remembers fondly. 'We got on very well. He was delightful.'

He had shown he meant business when, just ten hours after his general election victory, he agreed to open a new primary school hall in a suburb of Witney. He joked that he had already broken a political record: 'the shortest time between poll and plaque'.[140]

From his first week in the job, letters from constituents began pouring in. Woodward had left him various files stuffed with documents and correspondence, and invitations from businesses, charities, pressure groups and publishers were already stacking up on his makeshift desk. In all the confusion, he managed to miss his first Queen's Speech, having misjudged how long it took to get from one end of the parliamentary estate to the other.

'Nobody explains that if you sit in the Commons and wait for Black Rod to appear, by the time you get to the Lords to hear the Queen, you cannot see or hear a thing,' he lamented.[141]

As he attempted to grip all these demands, he was mulling a serious question: who to support in the forthcoming party leadership contest. Hague had resigned immediately after conceding defeat at the election, having fallen nearly 100 seats short of his target. He had gained just one seat. By the time the new parliamentary session began, jostling to replace him was well underway.

Initially, the choice appeared to be between the 'modernising' Portillo and the Europhile Ken Clarke. Few pundits expected much from Michael Ancram, who was seen as a rather grey 'continuity candidate', or David Davis, the thrusting backbencher popular with many on the party's right. (A putative bid by Ann Widdecombe, the shadow Home Secretary, never got off the ground.)

Cameron's instinct was to jump on board what he called the 'Spanish armada' – a reference to Portillo's Spanish heritage – having worked with him in the Treasury. However, he wanted to keep his options open. In a

---

140   Reg Little interview, op. cit.
141   Ibid.

typical display of cool self-assurance, he played hard to get with Portillo's people, telling a local newspaper reporter that he had used his 'brief moment of power' to alter the timing of a meeting they had arranged with him.[142] It is hard to imagine the average newly elected backbencher pulling such a stunt. In a sign of how comfortable and well established he already felt at Westminster, according to Elliott and Hanning, he even fleetingly considered running for the leadership himself, reportedly remarking to a confidant: 'It's too early for me to stand, isn't it? Yes, of course it is.'[143]

If true, this may give a misleading impression of his hunger and drive for the top job – when the time came a few years later, it would take others to push him forward – but the fact that it even crossed his mind indicates his extraordinary self-confidence at this stage.

In the meantime, he nonchalantly told anyone who asked that he would vote for the candidate who was most polite about his rivals.

'My real obsession, as an ex-Conservative Central Office goody-goody, is that all the leadership contenders should praise each other. After all, they may all end up serving in the shadow Cabinet,' he said, perhaps aware that it sounded a bit pompous.[144]

A more pressing concern was his maiden speech. Dropping in to the Chamber to hear how others did it, he was struck by the high standard of interventions by other young MPs, not only in relation to maiden speeches, but also in other debates. He was particularly taken with Labour MP David Lammy's response to the Queen's Speech. It was lively and entertaining and kept everybody awake – a considerable feat during such parliamentary set pieces.

'It made me realise that old buffers talking about "holding the House" really do mean something,' Cameron mused.[145]

In the event, his own maiden speech on 28 June 2001, during a debate on parliamentary procedure, was a run-of-the-mill affair. Cameron stuck closely to the traditional formula, focusing heavily on his constituency and its various attributes and challenges. His genuine delight in representing such an aesthetically pleasing area shone through, as he listed its loveliest towns

---

142 Ibid.
143 Francis Elliott and James Hanning, p. 208.
144 Ibid.
145 *Guardian* blog, 21 June 2001.

and villages and urged colleagues to visit. He also used the opportunity to take a stand for hunting, making crystal clear his position on an issue that would dominate Blair's second term in office.

'There is a long tradition of hunting in west Oxfordshire…I will always stand up for the freedom of people in the countryside to take part in country sports,' he declared.

Reading the speech today, some fourteen years after it was delivered, something else stands out: his words about Shaun Woodward. After acknowledging that it was 'traditional' for MPs to pay tribute to their immediate predecessors, he had a dig at Woodward's wealth, making a joke about his use of domestic staff and the size of his home.

'We are, in fact, quite close neighbours. On a clear day from the hill behind my cottage, I can almost see some of the glittering spires of his great house,' he said.

It is strange that Cameron, whose parents were millionaires and whose parents-in-law own several stately homes between them, should have taken aim at Woodward in this way. The cheap joke may have prompted a few titters, but it struck a discordant note. Having made his official entrée to Parliament, Cameron lost no time getting his feet under the table, accepting a place on the Home Affairs Select Committee. This gave him a foothold on the shadow home affairs team led by Oliver Letwin. Though he was technically the most junior figure, he literally refused to take a back seat.

A colleague recalls:

> It was very interesting to see that little team in operation. I remember the first meeting to which David came. It was held in Oliver's very poky Commons office. There were various armchairs and seats round the side, and everybody crammed in. Young researchers like me who were wet behind the ears would stand at the back. There was one very nice armchair just in front of Oliver's desk. Up until that point it had always been Oliver's seat, because it was right in the middle and he would have everyone else around him. At David's very first meeting, he came in and sat himself down on that very chair. He just popped himself down! I remember Oliver, from that point onwards, having to sit on a small chair nearby. Here was a guy who had just been elected, but who was extremely confident in

himself and his abilities. He just sauntered into the best seat in the room. I was very struck by that. Parliament works on a very hierarchical system. What was also interesting was that he was clearly a cut above the other MPs on the team. They were from the older intake – leftovers from Major's time as PM. He was high-quality compared to them. It was a generational shift.

Inevitably, Cameron's supreme self-confidence raised hackles. Patrick Mercer, who became a Tory MP at the same and would later become a bitter opponent, was among those who did not like the cut of his jib.

Mercer recalls:

When I arrived at Westminster, people would say to me that I must meet this wonderful young man called David Cameron. But I was not impressed. The first time I met him he was speed-marching along a committee corridor, with a great swallowtail of kids. He got hold of some boy and gave him a real bollocking for something. It was a piece of work that hadn't been done properly or hadn't been presented in the way that he wanted. I really didn't know who he was, but I thought to myself at the time, 'I wouldn't talk to a dog like that.' It immediately put my back up and from then on I started to notice him.

Yet by all accounts he was polite in the company of his seniors and respectful towards party etiquette.

Conor Burns, a Tory councillor who later became the MP for Bournemouth West, remembers meeting him at an intimate reception in Thatcher's office on Prince's Gate in Kensington and being struck by Cameron's deference and sense of propriety.

In those days I smoked, and so did he. I didn't really know who he was. I was talking to him and went to light up. He said, 'You can't smoke in here!' I said, 'Well, there's an ashtray on her desk; what do you think that's for?' So I leaned across and said, 'Margaret, is it okay to smoke?' She said, 'Of course it is, dear.' And only after I'd lit up did he light up.

With summer recess approaching and the party leadership contest gathering pace, Cameron finally came out for Portillo – only to see his man knocked out in the second round of the contest, squeezed out by Clarke and a dark-horse candidate: Iain Duncan Smith. MPs had narrowed the contest down to these two, and ballot papers were sent out to party members to make the final decision.

For Cameron, Portillo's failure was a significant blow. He had nailed his colours to the wrong mast, a move that could seriously jeopardise his political career. He trooped along to Portillo's post-match drinks in downcast mood, reflecting that the Conservative Party had not been ready for such a progressive figure.

'In many ways it is a view I share,' he mused.

> Michael is a great man, and it would have been one hell of a ride, perhaps even ending in triumph. Why didn't enough 'colleagues' want to make the trip? I remember Chris Patten asking me in Hong Kong, circa 1995, who should be next leader of the Conservative Party. 'Michael Portillo,' I replied. He looked at me quizzically and said: 'I am not sure we are ready for a Spanish Prime Minister.' Rich, really, for a Europhile. But in a strange way, he turned out to be right.[146]

In a place replete with oversized egos, it is easy to overstate the impression Cameron made on colleagues during these early years. Many were too preoccupied with their own careers and constituents to distinguish him from the pack of young MPs on both sides of the House striving to stand out.

Yet he steadily built his profile, seizing every opportunity to get himself on the airwaves. With some self-deprecation, he admitted, just six months into the job, that he had become a 'media tart'. So desperate was he to be invited on to TV and radio shows that he would hoodwink producers into thinking his views were more radical and interesting than they were – only to tone them down the minute the microphone was switched on.

Explaining his modus operandi in his *Guardian* blog, he wrote:

> Most producers only seem to want Conservatives if they are foaming at the mouth and likely to reinforce the proposition that the

---

146   *Guardian* blog, 18 July 2001.

party is somewhere to the right of Oswald Mosley…So when the BBC's *Crimewatch* producer rang me up to ask my views on 'Should women be sent to prison for the same crimes as men?' I was ready for her. The ensuing rant must have sounded like a cross between Alf Garnet [*sic*] and Germaine Greer, but it certainly did the trick. Several hours later, I was 'in makeup' together with assorted victims of crime, police officers looking forward to their first television appearance and a variety of stolen pets, including a cockatoo. Well, that's show business for you.

Once on, I took a slightly different tack and seemed to be in broad agreement with the director of the Prison Reform Trust. OK, so it wasn't great television, but I was on it and able to make my point. To rephrase the old adage, it's not the winning that counts, it's the taking part.[147]

Laying bare the extent of his preoccupation with publicity, he admitted in the same blog that he had spent 'a large portion' of the preceding week 'negotiating with, preparing for and appearing on radio and television programmes'.

'It all started on Friday with my debut on Radio 4's *Any Questions?*, moved slightly downmarket to a Tuesday morning walk-on part for BBC1's *Crimewatch* and ended with the distinctly tabloid *Richard and Judy Show* on Channel 4,' he recounted.

For most backbenchers, such exposure would be a triumph, but for Cameron, it was not enough.

'Early signs are that my bid for national recognition has been a complete failure. Combine the audience of all three shows and we are probably talking five million listeners and viewers,' he wrote. Reading it, you can almost hear him sigh. Perhaps recalling the huge audiences Carlton's most popular shows could draw, he considered a few million listeners small fry.

After his long, hard slog to win Witney and exhausting introduction to life as an MP, Cameron felt he and Samantha deserved a particularly good summer break. At great expense, he organised a spectacular Kenyan safari with a big

147   *Guardian* blog, 6 December 2001.

group of friends including Dom and Tif Loehnis. The plan was to ride into the Masai Mara to look at game from horseback; a ten-day camping trip that promised amazing close encounters with wildlife. At US$500 a night per head, it was to be a once-in-a-lifetime experience.

They were all good riders, Cameron himself having learned as a boy, but deep in the African bush, unpredictable things happen. And so it was that on day six of the trip, on a particularly hot afternoon, the holiday nearly ended in disaster, when the party came face to face with a lioness. Tristan Voorspuy, the tour guide from Offbeat Safaris who accompanied Cameron and his friends into the bush, has never forgotten the terrifying drama.

He recalls:

It was a year with very long grass. I always use the story as an example, because you don't find long grass like that in the Mara any more, because the herds of cattle have increased so much. It was after the longest day we'd had – we had ridden about 35 miles. It was a very hot day and I was only a second [assistant] guide back then. I was always at the back to check on the people behind. The main guide was always in the front. It was a big group, there were about twelve of them, I think. We were very close to camp – it must have been close to 5 or 6 p.m. and we were only maybe a mile away and I was gagging for a cigarette. We had run out of cigarettes at the back, and I decided to go up to the front and ask the chief guide, Mark, for one.

So I trotted forward and we were both lighting up at the same time, and suddenly I heard a stampede behind us. I turned around and I saw both girls – it was Tif and somebody else – charging through the long grass with a lioness behind them. These two girls were completely out of control on their horses. Funnily enough Tif was riding a little pony called Runaway, because that little horse had run away and been mauled by lions before – she had all sort of scars on her. This little pony was not having anything from this lioness and was charging through the grass with the lioness behind her. These two girls bumped into each other and Tif fell off. Obviously Mark and I reacted immediately: we turned around and we headed towards this lioness to intercept her, because when Tif fell off she stood up and started running, the lioness charging after her. Mark and I intercepted this lioness. Then the lioness saw us galloping towards her and sort of crouched, because she didn't know what was going on. We managed to fend her off and she stopped the charge, but Tif was still on the ground, in shock. We formed a circle around her but she was in so much shock she couldn't get back on the horse. Now all we wanted to do was get the hell out of there and all she was doing was crying and not really reacting. Then one of the guys in the group said: 'She's coming back!' and he meant the lioness – this time with another! Now there were two big cats crawling through the long grass and coming towards us. We stood our ground in front of the lionesses – usually we have a whip or something to crack to intimidate them a bit but these lionesses seemed to mean it. Eventually they jumped back into the bush. I think that's when Tif came to her senses and got back on the horse. So we got her on the horse and galloped off.

Seeing his wife in mortal danger, an alarmed Loehnis had rounded on the chief guide, accusing him of dropping his guard. In a very tense atmosphere, Voorspuy recalls Cameron being the diplomat.

David and Samantha were trying to support Tif. It's a funny situation when people are in shock like that. I think Dom was having a go at Mark, because Dom was very nervous, and Mark was trying to console Tif – Dominic wasn't liking this. It was a very tense situation and David was trying to keep everything in order. We eventually got to camp and it ended up being quite a boozy night, because after so much adrenalin you have to somehow relax. When Tif fell she had cut her leg, but we only found out when we got to camp.

The incident – the most dramatic lion charge the guides have experienced in a lifetime working in the bush – brought the horseback safari to a juddering halt. The party decided to continue in the relative safety of a 4x4, but there was to be a second frightening incident.

The guide recalls:

Everyone was relaxing from the whole stress of the events and we found this herd of elephants. Tif was in my car on the roof, taking pictures of these lovely big elephants, and we turned the engine off. They were all around the engine and really close – one big elephant cow stood right in front of the Land Rover, while the rest of the herd moved off. I had a local Masai in the car, and the elephant got a bit closer. One of the girls ran out of film, and her camera started rewinding. The elephant got surprised by the sound, turned around and looked at us and shook her ears, intimidating us. I could see the Masai guide getting really nervous. He looked down and said: 'Start the engine! We have to go!' I thought that if the Masai was scared, then I was scared! So I started the engine and when I did, the elephant got a bit of a surprise, jumped, and then started charging towards us. I was in reverse gear, going I don't know where, with the elephant charging towards us from the front and the two girls on the top of the roof, bouncing around and diving into the Land Rover for cover. This was the day after the lion incident!

Cameron, who was in another vehicle some hundred metres ahead, was not caught up in the second drama. Voorspuy recalls that everyone on the trip, which took place in an area of the Masai Mara called Olare, was 'fun and easy'. Despite two uncomfortably close shaves, he says they all had a lovely time. Later, he and his fellow guide took a 4x4 back to the spot where the lionesses had sprung to investigate and discovered that she had been protecting cubs.

'The grass had been so long that we couldn't see them,' he says.

The chief guide Mark Lawrence remembers Cameron as a 'decent chap' and says Samantha was 'very sweet', though both guides had a keener memory of Loehnis.

Back in Britain that autumn, the Tory leadership contest was entering its final phase. Head-to-head with Ken Clarke in a ballot of all party members, Iain Duncan Smith, long considered the outsider, came into his own. As far as the grassroots were concerned, a Eurosceptic 'headbanger' was preferable to Europhile Clarke despite his supposed voter appeal. Over 60 per cent of activists plumped for the former army man. Shortly after his victory, Cameron was surprised and delighted to receive a phone call from the whips, offering him a junior post on the opposition front bench. It would have been a remarkably quick ascent, particularly given that he had supported Portillo. Sadly, it turned out to be a mix-up: within minutes, the chap called back, embarrassed and apologetic, saying he'd confused Cameron with someone else. Out and about in Witney that weekend, doing his duty as a local MP, Cameron ruefully related the story to a constituent who wished him better luck next time.

Duncan Smith's leadership was dominated by two big themes: the build-up to the Iraq War and his own battle to survive. Cameron was caught up in both.

Having won the leadership contest the day after the 11 September attacks in America, the new Tory leader had promised to support Blair, who in turn had pledged to stand 'shoulder to shoulder' with George W. Bush. It quickly became clear that this meant war.

For Cameron, as for the majority of MPs, the invasion of Afghanistan posed no difficulty. 'I am an instinctive hawk about these things,' he said at the time.[148] Yet he wrestled with his conscience over the invasion of Iraq, writing, during the long build-up to war in summer 2002, that in this instance he had 'distinctly dove-ish tendencies'.[149] He feared Blair would 'move heaven and earth' to avoid a Commons vote before sending troops, not least because the Labour backbenches were a 'veritable dovecote', and he struggled to see the logic in putting boots on the ground.

'The question no one seems able to answer is the following: even if we believe that President Saddam now has lethal weapons, wouldn't an invasion make him more likely to use them, as he would be left with no way out?' he wrote in his blog.

Six months later, having listened carefully to the arguments, he remained uncomfortable with the prospect of military action and hoped there might be a way out.

'All our political lives we have been nurtured on the theory of deterrence. We were talking about it and fighting for it when Blair and Straw were still

---

148   *Guardian* blog, 15 August 2002.
149   Ibid.

members of the CND. Now we are being asked to swap deterrence with something new called pre-emptive war,' he wrote.[150]

> Most of us would also like something else to be done before [the] threat [of war] becomes a reality. More time for the inspectors. Another resolution with a final, final warning. One more heave from the international community. A delegation from the Arab League to visit Saddam and tell him the game is up. Whatever.[151]

Back in Witney, his mailbag was full of letters from constituents hostile to war. He continued to agonise, knowing that opposing the invasion would please many local voters as well as 'provide a self-righteous glow in the short term'.

Gareth Epps, the Liberal Democrats' prospective parliamentary candidate in Witney, remembers his unease at a public meeting in the run-up to the invasion.

> I was heavily involved in the peace movement. We held a public meeting, and quite strikingly, a load of servicemen's families came over and explained how concerned they were. Cameron actually sat on the platform at the top table and listened and empathised. I thought at one point he was going to wobble, in terms of commitment to the party whip over Iraq. It appeared to be genuine. He was genuinely sympathetic and persuaded by their arguments.

By mid-March, against a deafening drum beat to war, Cameron had reluctantly come to a decision. He felt the US–UK alliance at the heart of NATO – what he described as 'the key to peace in the post-war world' – would be 'shaken, if not broken' if Britain did not back Bush. Warning of the grave potential consequences of a 'no' vote in the Commons, he wrote:

> In terms of the UK, we would have let down our strongest ally and friend. In terms of the US, any chance of the administration following a multilateralist approach in the future would be virtually at an end.

---

150 *Guardian* blog, 18 February 2003.
151 *Guardian* blog, 17 March 2003.

> In Iraq, Saddam would celebrate a great victory. He would have
> completed his aim of dividing those who stood against him...Finally,
> the UN and the concept of international law would suffer. Instead
> of talking about world order, we would face world disorder.[152]

His conclusion was that there was 'no alternative' but to back Blair and pray
that it was all over quickly. Sitting in the Chamber listening to the Prime
Minister make a final, impassioned appeal for support from the House, he
could not help but be impressed.

'Blair himself has been masterful,' he wrote, after a day of high drama in
the Commons. 'It pains me to say so, but it's true. The speech in the great
debate was a parliamentary triumph and it would be churlish to deny it. I've
even sent copies to constituents writing to me about the war.'[153]

Cameron rightly predicted that the conflict would be long and unpopular and prove Blair's undoing. He also foresaw that Conservatives would
someday be 'tainted' by their support for the operation. He deserves some
credit for anticipating these consequences, though many commentators were
saying the same at the time.

Indeed, his stance on Iraq was ultimately very middle-of-the-road. He
admitted he was in awe of Blair's powers of persuasion and consistently
followed the government line, repeatedly backing its motions and opposing
all rebel amendments. Only a tiny handful of Tory MPs, most notably Ken
Clarke, did otherwise. Like Blair, Cameron was – and remained – essentially
an interventionist, believing in the need to step in to protect civilians under
threat from despotic rulers and promote Western values abroad. Like Blair, he
placed significant emphasis on multilateralism and the role of international
institutions like the UN and NATO. Yet compared to his closest political
allies at this early stage in his career – George Osborne, Michael Gove and
Ed Vaizey – he was cautious. While he was weighing up the pros and cons of
invasion, Osborne was hailing the 'excellent neoconservative case' for action
against Iraq and calling himself a 'signed-up, card-carrying Bush fan'.[154] For
his part, Michael Howard later said he would have gone to war even if he
had known there were 'no weapons of mass destruction' and even if the case

---

152 Ibid.
153 *Guardian* blog, 1 April 2003.
154 *The Spectator*, 28 February 2004.

for war was 'not clear cut'.[155] Duncan Smith went even further than Blair in talking up the missile threat from Saddam.[156]

In summer 2003, Cameron took to his blog to announce, with excitement, that he had been given his first shadow ministerial post.

'In House of Commons terms, I've broken my duck, lost my virginity, put my first toe on the greasy pole...I was summoned to Iain Duncan Smith's office and offered a job – as shadow Deputy Leader of the House,' he enthused.[157]

It was not the most exciting of briefs, being mostly about parliamentary procedure, but it was empowering, giving him the inside track on various issues that mattered to colleagues. It also supplied his first opportunity to appear at the despatch box. Standing in for his boss, Eric Forth, at the weekly session of Business Questions, an uncharacteristically nervous Cameron put a series of questions to Leader of the House Peter Hain.

He described the experience as 'terrifying' – not least because veteran Labour MP Dennis Skinner, the so-called Beast of Bolsover, heckled him throughout.

Recounting the experience, he wrote that his column had nearly been his 'downfall' during the debate.

> Referring to an article on the front page of the *Guardian* newspaper, I declared my interest – 'I too am a Guardian columnist.' Dennis Skinner...back from a heart bypass operation and in flying form, shouted across the floor: 'Eh? Bloody 'ell, whatever next.'
>
> My mouth opened and closed like an ornamental Koi Carp. Unprepared for this impromptu sledging I tried to mumble something about the shadow leader being away, but said 'deputy' instead. Dennis shouted: ''E wants the top job already.' Oh dear.[158]

However, parliamentary sketch-writers, for whom Business Questions is a weekly fixture, were impressed. The *Daily Mail*'s Quentin Letts described it as 'the best parliamentary debut' he had seen, while Bruce Anderson, writing

---

155   *The Guardian*, 3 May 2005.
156   Tim Bale, p. 172.
157   *Guardian* blog, 11 July 2003.
158   Ibid.

for *The Spectator*, enthused that Cameron had a rare combination of qualities that would, in time, make him a 'candidate for the highest office of all'.[159]

A week later, the Commons would empty for the long summer recess. Cameron couldn't wait to escape; not just his airless office (London was in the grip of a heatwave) but the pressure-cooker atmosphere in the party caused by ructions over Duncan Smith. The new leader's tenure had been troubled almost from the start. By summer 2003 he had already faced down one attempt to depose him, in November the previous year, triggered by a misguided decision to slap a three-line whip against a government plan to allow gay and unmarried couples to adopt children. His popularity with activists, the logistics of organising a successful defenestration, and fears among MPs that members might crown yet another ineffective leader saved his neck for a full year, but the rumblings never went away. Throughout 2003 the media was awash with rumours of a Howard coup. When MPs returned from their sun loungers, the unrest grew worse. The 2003 October party conference was billed as a 'do-or-die' affair for the leader. Few expected him to last the year. A row over the use of taxpayers' money to employ his wife Betsy (what came to be called 'Betsygate') further undermined his position. His notorious 'Quiet Man' speech, during which he promised to 'turn up the volume', won standing ovations and eight minutes of applause at the end, but few were convinced.[160]

By contrast, Howard pulled a star turn. He now looked like party leader in all but name. As his allies began canvassing colleagues, party grandees and donors openly appealed to MPs to finish the job.

IDS's plight was not an issue Cameron could ignore. For around a year he had been helping the leader prepare for PMQs (along with two fellow stars of the 2001 intake, Boris Johnson and George Osborne), a challenge with which he was familiar, having done the same for Major. It meant he witnessed the leader's struggles at close quarters and put him in an awkward position.

While others, including the chief whip David Maclean, broke ranks, telling Duncan Smith to step down, Cameron wavered. His heart told him to be loyal; his head told him the game was up. On 29 October, the day after forty-one MPs finally wrote to the chairman of the 1922 Committee, Michael

---

159   *Daily Mail*, 11 July 2003; *The Spectator*, 26 July 2003.
160   Tim Bale, p. 187.

Spicer, demanding a no-confidence vote, Cameron had a private word with his boss after the usual Wednesday morning briefing.[161] According to Duncan Smith, his young colleague spoke frankly, urging him to go without a fight in order to prevent a divisive ballot, but he also hedged his bets, promising to back the leader if he wanted to put it to the vote.

'I want this vote,' Duncan Smith replied. 'We need some kind of closure after all this infighting.'

Preparing for what he knew could be his last ever Prime Minister's Questions as party leader, he was full of gallows humour.

'I cannot remember seeing him more relaxed or on better form,' Cameron later recalled.

> Jokes about what might or might not happen peppered our discussions about the best questions to ask Tony Blair at noon. The appearance of Boris Johnson in a new suit (already crumpled, of course) produced howls about a potential leadership bid. Iain even did a more than passable impersonation of David Brent from his favourite TV show, *The Office*.
>
> Once our business was done I spent ten minutes trying to persuade Iain not to go ahead with the confidence vote. I thought it would split the party, both in the Commons and the country. But he was determined: the Conservative Party had to decide whether to unite behind him or start again.[162]

The confidence vote proved terminal, but the bloodletting had been restorative. Blogging a week after the final denouement, Cameron reflected:

> He was right, I was wrong. The vote was…not only necessary for the party, it was also necessary for Iain. How could he resign without knowing whether he had the backing of colleagues or not?…I backed him, but the die was already cast…For the way he graciously stepped down and called for unity with no recriminations, no one deserves…credit more than Iain Duncan Smith.[163]

161   Tim Bale, p. 192.
162   *Guardian* blog, 3 November 2003.
163   Ibid.

Cameron's reaction to the leadership crisis is slightly ambiguous: privately, he encouraged Duncan Smith to resign without fuss, but he was not disloyal. His relationship with Howard was such that he was highly likely to benefit personally from regime change, but he was unwilling to stab his boss in the back. Perhaps he was wary of upsetting Witney grandees, who expected unwavering loyalty to the leader in the wake of the Woodward affair.[164] In any case he has no track record of treachery. On the contrary, during his own leadership, his dealings with colleagues have suggested a fixation with loyalty which sometimes distorts his judgement. In this instance, it seems likely that a sense of propriety overrode self-interest.

Howard's coronation took place against a backdrop of mounting anticipation of the Hutton Report, the findings of a judge-led inquiry into the circumstances surrounding the death of UN weapons inspector David Kelly that summer. In the run-up to Christmas, there was widespread media speculation that both Blair and his former spin doctor Alastair Campbell would be heavily criticised over the treatment of the scientist and over the bitter row with the BBC prompted by Andrew Gilligan's claims that Downing Street 'sexed-up' intelligence material designed to highlight the threat posed by Saddam Hussein. For the Conservatives, it was an exciting time: a damning report could end Blair's premiership and disgrace the Labour Party, possibly even paving the way for Tory victory in 2005.

Surveying the political landscape after Duncan Smith's departure, Howard was in no doubt what was at stake.

Guy Black, who was by then director of communications for the party, recalls:

> Howard had one shot at No. 10, and the one thing that could have changed the whole course of that election was the Hutton Inquiry. This could have been the big opportunity. He had always taken the view that it was going to be the major political issue for the first few months of 2004. It would shape politics one way or another up to the election.

To the new leader's dismay, nobody at Central Office had been doing any groundwork ahead of the report's expected publication in January. Nor had

---

164   Francis Elliott and James Hanning, p. 230.

anyone on the Tory side followed the inquiry in detail. It threatened to be a serious wasted opportunity. What was needed was someone smart to crawl all over the evidence to identify potential ammunition against Labour. Both Howard and Black felt Cameron was the man for the job.

Black says:

> There was a panic, a real panic. We were starting the operation from scratch. David was the obvious person to do it, because he was one of the brightest and cleverest of the MPs around; highly political and could digest a large amount of work in a short time. He was given a team of researchers to help and they did have to scramble.

Cameron spent much of that Christmas poring over transcripts of the evidence sessions, trying to identify Blair's vulnerabilities. Initially he was enthusiastic and relished the challenge. He came to hate it. Perhaps he had a sixth sense that Hutton would not prove Blair's undoing. Yet he continued to base all his preparations on an assumption that the Prime Minister would be castigated. It would prove a very grave error. When the long-awaited report finally arrived, it was the Tories who were left reeling. Leaked to *The Sun* on the eve of publication, it sensationally cleared the Prime Minister and Ministry of Defence while lambasting the BBC.

As opposition leader, Howard was allowed to read the report a few hours before it was officially published, on 28 January 2004. He took Cameron with him. Having set 'an absurdly early alarm clock', the pair wrapped up warm and trudged to the Cabinet Office at 5.55 a.m. En route, Howard felt sick with foreboding. He rang Black from his car.

'What should I say to the cameras when I go in?' he asked wretchedly.

'Don't say a word. Nothing until you've read the report,' Black advised.

On arrival at the Cabinet Office, where Cameron had expected to be ushered into 'a dank room with one table, two stools and a pencil', they were shown into a smart office with comfortable chairs, a fully functioning computer and 'enough stationary [*sic*] to re-supply Rymans'.[165]

'I should have known something was up,' Cameron wrote later.

---

165 *Guardian* blog, 3 February 2004.

Instead of the standard Whitehall biscuits there were croissants, bacon sandwiches and sausage rolls…Knowing what was in the report the sensitive souls in the Cabinet Office were clearly expecting us to chow down on a big breakfast, make long chains out of all the paper clips they had provided and play battleships on their computer. Perhaps we should have done.[166]

The findings were as unhelpful as *The Sun* had suggested. Cameron was rueful. He reflected miserably:

I spent months trying to become a Hutton expert. I read thousands of pages of evidence. I digested the Campbell diaries. I cross-checked the Hoon testimonies. I even tried to read the scribbled notes in the margins of memos posted up on the Hutton Inquiry website…[and it] turned out to be a Chinese meal of an inquiry: half an hour later and everyone wanted another one.

After digesting the detail, they returned ashen-faced to the shadow Cabinet room in the Commons.

'This is a complete stitch-up,' Howard said grimly. 'What are we going to do?'

If Cameron – the individual most on top of the detail – had any helpful suggestions, nobody can remember them. Though he was definitely at the meeting, Black doesn't recall him playing an active part in the painful discussions that day. They all felt blindsided.

Black says now:

It's bizarre when you look back on it, but of all the different scenarios that had been planned for, for all the different sets of notes, and lines to take that had been prepared, with endless permutations and scenarios, nobody had planned for Blair's exoneration. Had they done so, there would at least have been discussions about whether to reject the findings of the report.

But there was no time to consider the potential ramifications of such a step. In any case, as a former lawyer, Howard was instinctively opposed to

166   Ibid.

rejecting the conclusions of a highly respected judge. He says now that he felt he would have been ridiculed if he had gone for such a drastic response.

'I just didn't think it was an option...It was extremely difficult,' he says.

The Hutton Report marked a turning point in Blair's fortunes, removing the immediate threat to his premiership and ushering in a period of stability for the Labour Party. It allowed the party to re-group and gave the Prime Minister a licence to appeal to voters for a third term. Would better preparation for Hutton's exoneration of the government have made any difference to the Tories in the medium or long term? It is very doubtful. Either way, Black absolves Cameron of blame, saying the failure was 'collective'.

'We had not war-gamed,' he says simply.

There is, however, an important postscript. During our research, we discovered that Cameron *was* warned about the report's conclusions. At a private dinner party before Christmas, a lawyer with insider knowledge of the inquiry tipped him off.

'There was all this stuff in the media at the time saying that Blair was going to be found guilty,' the lawyer told us.

> Because of where I worked, I happened to know that everybody who was going to get a rough ride from Hutton had been sent formal letters, allowing them to challenge the findings. Blair had not received such a letter. It was therefore inconceivable that Hutton was going to find heavily against Blair, because of due process. At that time, it was not widely known who had received these letters. I told Cameron that Blair would not be criticised. I warned him that they should back off Blair, or they'd end up with egg on their faces.

Yet Cameron failed to make contingency plans. Why?

'There are two possibilities,' the lawyer says now. 'One: he thought, "Who the hell is this person?" The other possibility is that he just doesn't listen.'

The Old Rectory at Peasemore, where Cameron grew up. Today it is occupied by his brother Alex and Alex's family, while their mother Mary lives next door.

Cameron aged ten, in a play at his very old-fashioned prep school, Heatherdown. He was narrator in the production of *The Boy David*. It was the second-best part.

Playing Harold Rabbit in *Toad of Toad Hall*, another play at Heatherdown, in 1975. Pictured on the left, he was nine. The part of 'Mole' was played by an eleven-year-old Prince Edward. The Queen came to watch.

LEFT: Cameron embraces his younger sister Clare after her wedding to Jeremy Fawcus in 2010. Their childhood nanny, Gwen Hoare, who is now in her nineties, can just be seen between them.

RIGHT: Cameron's beloved parents Ian and Mary in April 2010. Ian, who was born with deformed legs but never let his disability get in his way, died a few months after his son became Prime Minister.

ABOVE: Cameron's gregarious older brother Alex, now a QC. As a child, Cameron felt overshadowed by his popular sibling.

RIGHT: Cameron's older sister Tania, at Clare Cameron's wedding in 2010. He has described Tania as 'the family leftie'.

Cameron's late uncle Sir William Dugdale, a former chairman of Aston Villa Football Club. As a boy, Cameron would watch the team play from the luxury of a VIP box. In the heat of the 2015 election campaign, the Tory leader momentarily forgot the name of his favourite club.

As a new boy at Eton in 1980 (third from right, front row). Cameron settled in quickly, but stuck to a tight clique of friends.

In the rugby team in his final year at Eton, 1984 (front row, second from left). Rugby was not his thing, but he became very good at tennis.

ABOVE: Ferdinand 'Ferdy' Mount, Mary Cameron's first cousin, who was head of Downing Street's Policy Unit from 1982 to 1983. As a sixth former, Cameron pitched up at Mount's office to interview him for the Eton school magazine.

Brasenose College, Oxford, which had a particularly good reputation for PPE in Cameron's day. He came away with a good First, rather to the surprise of the Principal, the late Barry Nicholas, who feared he spent too much time partying.

That picture of Cameron in the Bullingdon Club. A fellow Buller remembers him holding court at one of their rambunctious gatherings, quaffing champagne and quoting Winston Churchill.

RIGHT: In Bullingdon Club attire, at a university ball in 1987. Good-looking, funny and supremely self-confident, Cameron was not short of female admirers.

In his penultimate year at Brasenose College, Oxford, 1987. Others lark around, but the future Prime Minister (fourth from the left at the back) looks straight down the camera lens.

Horsing around with his Oxford friend James Delingpole and Delingpole's brother Dick, in Devon. 'We were twenty, so we were probably pissed,' Delingpole says now.

Messing about with Rachel Whetstone in Scotland when they were both in their twenties. They met at the Conservative Research Department (CRD) in 1988 and became lifelong friends.

Cameron's old friend Derek Laud. They met at the Conservative Research Department in the late 1980s, where the well-connected Laud proved a useful ally. He thinks Cameron has been 'lucky, lucky, lucky'.

Samantha Cameron modelling for a friend. Recently married, she told the stylist she didn't want to look too raunchy, because her husband was a rising star in the Conservative Party.

LEFT: In love and engaged to be married in 1995. He was a crashingly conventional Tory boy; she was an arty hippy chick.

BELOW: Cameron's mother-in-law Annabel Astor, with her second husband Viscount Astor. A formidable businesswoman, she helped Cameron get his first (and only significant) job in the private sector.

RIGHT: Cameron with his old boss Norman Lamont. He was the former Chancellor's special adviser. The pair survived Black Wednesday together.

With former Prime Minister John Major. An ambitious young Cameron used to brief him for Prime Minister's Questions, but the relationship seems never to have been warm.

Out on the stump for local elections in Witney in 2008. Apparently Cameron privately called this his *Reservoir Dogs* picture, jokingly referring to the ladies as his 'bitches'.

Cameron looking slightly nervous as he heads out with the Heythrop Hunt on Boxing Day 2004. It is the first picture of him on horseback to have entered the public domain. The hunting ban was about to come in.

ABOVE: Reading a children's story at his local church in Chadlington, west Oxfordshire. To his left is Lord Chadlington, a neighbour and local party grandee. In recent years, he has become something of a father figure to Cameron.

BELOW LEFT: The redoubtable Sir Nicholas Soames, grandson of Winston Churchill and a lifelong friend of the Camerons. He was one of the earliest supporters of Cameron's party leadership bid in 2005.

BELOW RIGHT: Boys on bikes: Cameron and George Osborne cycling to work in 2006. Cameron had been party leader for less than a year. So close was his relationship with Osborne that it would effectively become a dual premiership.

15

IVAN

'The world stops, the clock stops, everything stops.'
— Cameron, on the death of his first son

For a few blissful days after the birth of David and Samantha Cameron's first child, nobody realised anything was wrong.

The baby was delivered by Caesarean section on Monday 8 April 2002 because he was breech, but he looked perfect, and mother and baby were discharged from Queen Charlotte's Hospital in London after a few days. They called him Ivan, and took him to Ginge Manor, where Annabel was on hand to help.

Joy at the newborn's arrival soon gave way to concern. Like most new parents, the Camerons were inexperienced and did not know what to expect, but by day five or six, something didn't seem right. The baby seemed to be making unusual movements. A midwife who made a routine post-natal visit the following day was reassuring.

'All new mums worry,' she said.

But in the days that followed, there were more disturbing signs. Ivan's hand would sometimes jerk open and spasm. He was also exceptionally sleepy and was losing weight. Cameron has described how he and Samantha 'got more and more concerned'. Eventually they took him to a local GP, who thought he might be suffering from a kidney malfunction.[167] He sent them to Accident and Emergency at the John Radcliffe Hospital in Oxford. There, in front of doctors, Ivan had his first major seizure. It was becoming apparent that there was something seriously wrong.

---

167   Francis Elliott and James Hanning, p. 232.

Over the next forty-eight hours, the newborn underwent a battery of tests. The diagnosis, which took some days, was devastating: Ivan Cameron had a profoundly disabling neurological disorder called Ohtahara syndrome. In a side room, a doctor gently explained the shattering prognosis. His life expectancy was limited, though it was hard to put a time frame on it. He would never walk or talk.

'It's your worst nightmare,' Samantha has said. 'They did a whole load of tests, you go into the office with the doctor and they push the box of tissues towards you and you feel like you're in an episode of *Casualty*.'[168] They had him christened at the earliest opportunity.

The months that followed were deeply traumatic. While friends celebrated the arrival of their own healthy babies, the Camerons' lives had changed fo ever. There would be no joyful first steps, no first word. It was, in Samantha's words, 'tough, lonely, and isolating'.

'You're living in a completely different world to your friends who've had babies at the same time. You're suddenly in this weird world of doctors and social services. You know your child is never going to meet the normal milestones,' she has said.[169]

As the couple struggled to absorb the full implications of Ivan's condition, their closest friends rallied. A tearful Rachel Whetstone broke the news to those who hadn't already been told, including Michael Howard, offering herself as a point of contact for those seeking updates. During this period, she and Steve Hilton, who were now dating, spent a great deal of time with the Camerons, giving practical and emotional support.

It is impossible to overstate the importance of Ivan to Cameron's life story. Before his arrival, Cameron had known little real suffering. Blessed with a loving family, a fine mind, an interesting job, good health, good looks and a beautiful and accomplished wife, hitherto he had enjoyed every advantage in life. He was thriving at Westminster, lived in a desirable north Kensington flat, and had a fabulous social network, including a tight-knit group of exceptionally close friends. He had no reason to doubt that the road ahead would be anything other than a continuation of the path he'd already travelled: a smooth and satisfying route to more happiness and success. Suddenly the young MP was the father of a child so profoundly

168 Geordie Greig interview for *You* magazine, *Mail on Sunday*, 5 April 2015.
169 Ibid.

disabled he would need 24-hour care for life. The ramifications – emotional, practical, professional, financial – were so wide-ranging and enormous that they were almost impossible to take in. In Cameron's own words, the shock hit him 'like a freight train'. His charmed life would never be the same again.

Yet in their darkest hour, the Camerons proved remarkably resilient. While many marriages collapse under the strain of raising a disabled child, friends say they were determined not to let their new circumstances ruin their lives.

'They just decided they were going to have a very happy family life, come what may. I think they were just very, very good to each other in that period,' according to a source.[170]

Samantha, who describes herself as a 'New Testament Christian', says that they 'could have been angry with God', but decided that they had been 'given' Ivan to look after and had to do the best job they could.[171]

Cameron himself has recalled a sort of epiphany a few days after Ivan's diagnosis, when he realised he and Samantha were 'going to get through this'.

'If we can't do a good job and look after him, then we have failed,' he thought to himself.[172]

In the months and years that followed, he lived up to that private pledge. Friends were impressed and deeply moved by the way the couple 'just dealt with it'.[173]

'I thought they behaved amazingly. You can't imagine discovering that with your first child. Gradually you discover that they are never going to be in any way normal. They both just dealt with it. I think that shows incredible strength of character,' says a family friend.

Managing Ivan's condition was an intensive process, which became more complicated as he grew. There were endless medications to administer – as many as twenty different drugs a day – and regular emergencies relating to infections, seizures and fluctuations in his blood pressure. The exact nature of his treatment was constantly in flux. Soon after his first birthday, he had a tube inserted into his stomach to make administering food and drugs easier. It helped, but the delicate daily routine of sleeps, feeds, medications and therapeutic exercises could be thrown into chaos at any moment if he had

170   Francis Elliott and James Hanning, p. 235.
171   Geordie Greig interview, op. cit.
172   Francis Elliott and James Hanning, p. 233.
173   Private information.

one of his terrible seizures or caught an infection that required hospitalisation. Pneumonia was a frequent problem.

At first, the Camerons tried to cope on their own, but the stress, sleep deprivation and sheer relentlessness of the demands of caring for a very sick child pushed them to the brink. By the end of the first year, they were, in Samantha's words, 'shattered and pretty much at breaking point'. Doctors encouraged them to get help. Luckily they could afford it, so they started hiring night nurses to give them some sleep. Cameron says they knew their own limitations and decided not to be martyrs.

'The parents of disabled children are not necessarily angels,' he said.

> They didn't ask for this to happen. And you mustn't pretend to be an angel if you're not, because if you do I think you'll exhaust yourself or your marriage will break down or your other kids will suffer. You have to try and be who you are. I'm not an angel and neither is Samantha. We're good parents, and we do our best, but we need lots of help, we need lots of breaks…I think it's important to have that and to try and keep your life together.[174]

Evidence of their determination to maintain some sort of normality in their lives came within a few days of Ivan's birth, when Cameron returned to work. Less than a week after the diagnosis, he was blogging for *The Guardian*. Giving no hint of the turmoil at home, he fired off a long diatribe on the shortcomings of Brown's Budget. In the weeks that followed, he threw himself into the job.

An ardent royalist, he cut himself no slack over the celebrations for the Queen's Golden Jubilee in June, during which MPs were in particularly high demand in their constituencies. He stuffed his head through faux medieval stocks, threw balls at coconut shies, judged maypole-dancing competitions, belted out 'Land of Hope and Glory' and 'Rule Britannia' at concerts organised by the local Tory branch, and sang 'The White Cliffs of Dover'. Perhaps it was a welcome distraction from the domestic heartache. When the festivities finally wound down he admitted he was 'knackered'.

> It's difficult to be sure which event tipped me over the edge…Was it handing out 100 jubilee mugs and pens to primary school children

---

174 David Cameron and Dylan Jones, p. 198.

in Witney? Crowning the May Day King and Queen in Bladon? Or launching jubilee celebrations in Wootton, where in place of a 21-gun salute, the good burghers rushed to the top of the church tower and fired their shotguns?[175]

Yet he kept up the pace: according to a breathless account in his Guardian blog, that same month he travelled from Witney to Oxford on the back of a vintage Enfield 500 to mark the motorcycle industry's 'ride to work day'; had an Indian head massage on the pavement outside the Co-op in Carterton to promote adult education; had his picture taken shaking hands with a skeleton to support people with osteoporosis and held a cup of Fairtrade coffee in support of Colombian farmers.[176]

Samantha, too, was keen to return to the office. Three and a half months after Ivan was born, she was back at Smythson two days a week. After five months, she was doing nine-day fortnights.

Yet the couple in no sense 'contracted out' Ivan's care. Though they had a rota of carers as well as practical help from Cameron's parents and Samantha's half-sisters Flora and Alice, they were both extremely hands-on, sharing the load at weekends and when Ivan needed to be rushed to hospital during the night. Cameron himself spent countless nights dossing down on makeshift beds on wards, somehow finding the energy to haul himself back to the Commons the following morning. In one particularly distressing six-month period, his son was hospitalised sixteen times, often after the severe epileptic seizures associated with his condition. Cameron found these fits 'agony' to watch, feeling utterly helpless as his son jerked and screamed and there was nothing he could do to ease the suffering. Cheryl Gillan, MP for Chesham and Amersham, recalls Cameron becoming very distressed during a conversation about epilepsy.

'He was almost in tears about having to inject his son when he was fitting. There was a huge level of humanity there, you could just see how deeply it was affecting him. Really this enormous level of compassion,' she says.

That autumn, Cameron went to Bournemouth for his fourteenth consecutive Tory Party conference. At first, the seaside gathering was a refreshing change of scene, especially as organisers had decided not to hold important business until after lunch.

---

175 *Guardian* blog, 5 June 2002.
176 *Guardian* blog, 20 June 2002.

Cameron was delighted by the new regime.

'Painful morning sessions nursing a hangover and listening to overlong speeches are a thing of the past…It leaves delegates free to wander along the beach, lie in bed or go shopping at Marks and Spencer's. It's only Tuesday morning and I've already done all three,' he enthused in his *Guardian* blog. His immediate concern at that point was a small party he was organising for the twenty or so delegates from his constituency. 'I have battled with the quandary – do I match my predecessor Shaun Woodward's lavish hospitality with champagne, canapés and a butler, or is it warm beer and crisps in the ante-room of my B&B? Clearly, Woodward-like tendencies would only arouse suspicion, so warm beer it is,' he said.[177]

Then he received a frantic call from Samantha: Ivan was back in hospital. He dropped everything and rushed straight to Great Ormond Street. Though he tried to keep up with events at the seaside, he found little enthusiasm for the BBC's party conference coverage among Ivan's fellow little patients on the ward.

'My powers of political persuasion proved utterly useless against sophisticated children aged ten and under,' he lamented. He resigned himself to *The Lion King, Power Rangers* and *Teletubbies*.[178]

Exactly a year later, Cameron again had to abandon party conference when Ivan, by then eighteen months old, was admitted to St Mary's Paddington with yet another complication. This time, they had their own room, complete with a wobbly TV.

There was an upside: Cameron mused that there were aspects of party conference he was happy to miss.

> No difficult conversations with journalists hungry for a story, or delegates worried about our poll ratings. No lobbying. No hangovers. No Blackpool-style, cholesterol-packed, heart-stopping breakfasts. Instead I might actually watch some debates and learn about our policies…I can watch as much coverage as the BBC provides. The nurses watch me with strange fascination. I am expecting a visit from the psychiatric team at any moment.[179]

---

177 *Guardian* blog, 8 October 2002.
178 *Guardian* blog, 9 October 2003.
179 Ibid.

From an early stage, the Camerons had decided not to torture themselves searching for miracle cures. They accepted the medical consensus: that Ivan's disability was so severe he would always be wheelchair-bound. Rather than attempting to prolong his uncertain lifespan, they focused on his quality of life, learning by trial and error, and the smile that would light up his face, what made him happy. It was a frustrating process – Samantha has recalled taking him to the zoo only to find he slept through the whole experience – but it was worth it when something worked.

He liked being in swimming pools – a kindly neighbour in Dean who has a private pool would keep it heated for him – and enjoyed feeling the wind on his face and looking at animals.

Bruce Anderson recalls:

> They made him as happy as could be. He liked gurgling at pigs. There were pigs in a neighbouring farm at Dean, which belonged to a wonderful farmer, a splendid country character who had only been to London twice. He would let his animals graze on the side of the road and was completely chaotic. They would take Ivan to see his pigs.

Cameron would also take his son to a family service at the local church, during which Ivan would sit on his knee. In the evenings, the pair would take a bath together, Cameron gently lifting the little boy in and out of the water without the aid of a hoist, not least because his son was 'lovely to pick up and cuddle'. He would joke with friends that Health and Safety types would have a heart attack if they knew.[180]

Though the strain was enormous, the Camerons found caring for Ivan hugely rewarding, particularly when they discovered something he found stimulating. He would turn to them and beam, which delighted everyone. His smile was slightly crooked, and sometimes accompanied by a little moan. It never failed to make Cameron, in his own words, 'both happy and immensely proud of him'.[181]

With some financial support from their parents, the Camerons could afford as much professional help as they needed. As Ivan became bigger,

---

180 David Cameron and Dylan Jones, p. 195–6.
181 *Daily Telegraph*, 22 May 2004.

they converted their north Kensington home to create a bedroom and bathroom for him on the ground floor, with a hoist and pulley system as well as facilities for a specialist nurse. Every morning, at 7.30 a.m., the nurse would bring him upstairs and hand him to Cameron, who would take over what they called his morning routine. It involved multiple face creams and massages, brushing Ivan's teeth and hair, dressing him for the day, and manoeuvring him into his wheelchair. In order not to upset his son by suddenly putting a toothbrush into his mouth, Cameron would – on expert advice – gently and repeatedly tap Ivan's forehead as a signal that intrusive ablutions were coming. He became adept at multi-tasking. A longstanding friend and fellow MP who spent a weekend at Dean when Cameron was party leader recalls him effortlessly switching between work and childcare while relaxing at home.

> One Sunday morning that I was there, they put a rug out in the garden. We were all sitting out there reading the papers and drinking cups of coffee. David was reading the paper while doing Ivan's exercises. Then he got an important call. He'd say, 'I have to take this call,' and he'd get up and come back. Suddenly he'd be very much in Leader of the Opposition mode with a large party funder on the phone; then he'd put down the phone to deal with Ivan; and then switch to reading something which interested him.

One person who could truly relate to their experience was newspaper journalist Ian Birrell, who has a profoundly disabled daughter who was aged eight when Ivan was born. By chance, Birrell, who was deputy editor of the *Independent* at the time, had arranged a working lunch with Cameron shortly after Ivan's birth. Instead of talking politics, the young MP and the journalist ended up having an intimate conversation about disability and parenting.
Birrell recalls:

> We had a very moving, quite deep discussion. We talked in incredible depth about it all. I suspect he may not have had anyone in such a similar position to talk to. I just remember talking about what it was like; the impact on your life and how you handle it. When you have a child like that, you basically go through a very deep

depression, actually a form of grieving. It's recognised as a form of grief. So I guess I was talking about that. He was remarkably upbeat.

Birrell remembers being 'very, very struck' by the sense that Cameron was different to most Conservatives he had met.

He seemed very comfortable in the modern world, which I found refreshing and unusual. We just got on really well. I really liked him as a person. I also liked him as a politician, and obviously we had this immediate bond that we could talk about. The truth is that nobody else understands the pressures on you and your family – what it's really like for you emotionally.

They became close friends as well as colleagues (Birrell worked as one of Cameron's speechwriters in the run-up to the 2010 election). As well as understanding, Birrell was able to provide practical advice on how to harness the help of social services and find the right special school. This proved a bitter battle: initially, educational psychologists were insistent that Ivan should go to a mainstream nursery.

'It was political correctness gone mad,' Samantha has said.

It simply wasn't the right thing [for him] and was really upsetting as a parent. Ivan had a feeding tube, very bad epilepsy. He couldn't sit up. He couldn't communicate at all. He needed to be somewhere more sensory and stimulating, with people who knew how to look after him.[182]

Eventually they got him a place at a school in Hammersmith for children with severe learning disabilities. It proved a godsend. Here he received plenty of one-to-one attention and specialist help.

Securing local authority funding for respite and day care involved reams of bureaucracy and literally dozens of assessments. Birrell says that for parents of disabled children, navigating the system is 'one of the many things that make your head explode'. Inevitably, Cameron began to use his power and influence as an MP to highlight the shortcomings of services for disabled

182   Geordie Greig interview, op. cit.

children, and to campaign for reform. In January 2004, a few months before Ivan turned two, the MP for Witney was overjoyed when he successfully pushed through an amendment to Labour's new child trust fund scheme, removing the cap on tax-efficient savings for disabled children.

Under the measure he called 'Cameron's Law', parents would also be allowed to withdraw money from the fund to pay for specialist care and equipment before the child reached the age of eighteen.

'I've done it. I've changed something,' Cameron reported proudly. 'Whatever else happens from this day onwards my parliamentary career will have some meaning. My obituary – short, dull, and largely unread – will have at least one significant paragraph.'

Explaining how it would make a difference, he said:

> Families with disabled children face massive extra costs in terms of childcare, specialist equipment and support. Bath hoists, stair lifts, wheelchairs, special cars – the list is endless. While the NHS and social services help with some of these things, many are means tested and the waiting lists can be horrendous. It's a well-worn joke among these parents that the new standing frame, wheelchair or buggy turns up just as little Johnny has grown out of it.[183]

This triumph coincided with a much bigger cause for celebration: the birth of the Camerons' second child, a girl named Nancy. Her safe arrival was a huge relief. Doctors were never sure whether or not Ivan's condition was genetic, meaning there was no guarantee other children would not be affected. The Camerons were told that if the problem was genetic, the chance of it recurring was as high as one in four; if not, the chance was one in several thousand. Overall, experts put the risk at around one in twenty.[184] The Camerons had been alarmed to hear of another couple to whom it had happened twice. In the event, Nancy was healthy, as was the Camerons' third child, Arthur Elwen, who arrived in February 2006, and their fourth, Florence, born in August 2010.

The years ahead would be extremely challenging on the domestic front, with each new child adding to the chaos as well as the joy. Life with three

183 *Guardian* blog, 19 January 2004.
184 Francis Elliott and James Hanning, p. 237.

very young children, one profoundly disabled, was exhausting, complicated, and hugely resource intensive. Family holidays would involve a van full of Ivan's special kit.

'It's very difficult to look after all three,' Cameron explained.

> I sometimes take all three to the park, and it's really quite touch and go, because you've got to be with Ivan because he can have a spasm or a seizure at any moment. So if one of your children decides to strangle a cat in the corner of the playground – not that the Cameron children make a habit of it, I hasten to add – it's very difficult to stop them doing it. You do often need two people.[185]

Cameron started talking publicly about Ivan's condition soon after his son's first birthday. Just how much he should say was a question he and Samantha discussed at length. It was an issue that Gordon Brown and his wife Sarah also faced, as the parents of a young son with cystic fibrosis. Brown chose never to be photographed with his son nor to talk about his condition publicly. By contrast, Cameron was keen to be open about what they were going through, while trying to maintain a reasonable balance between public and private.[186] Once he became Leader of the Opposition the issue became considerably more loaded. One of his closest advisers says:

> There was always an acceptance that it had to be done sensitively and should not be overdone. Sam was the regulator of that. But he completely rejected the [Gordon] Brown characterisation about using your children as props. He felt being a family man was an important part of who he was, and in modern politics you had to be willing to show voters who you are, otherwise you shouldn't put yourself forward. He always seemed very at ease with those issues to me.

The Camerons had never known how long Ivan would live. When he became unwell at home in London on the night of 24 February 2009, shortly before his seventh birthday, it did not seem critical. They had taken him to hospital

---

185   David Cameron and Dylan Jones, p. 197.
186   Ibid., p. 195.

countless times before. There was nothing to suggest that this would be the last.

Describing the terrible events that followed, Cameron has said:

> What happened at the end was that he had this very distended stomach and it got worse and worse that evening and that night. We were watching out all the time and seeing what we could do. We had so many dramas with Ivan in his life. And then we took him to the hospital. We thought. 'Well this isn't right, and it looks like it's getting worse.' So we took him to the hospital and, and, he died. I mean it was very, very quick. I think we had always worried about the severity of his epilepsy and that it might be what took him away from us, but it wasn't. It was a breakdown of his digestion and his organs. It was totally unexpected and very sudden.

Samantha says simply, 'We had built our entire lives around him. Suddenly he's not there any more.'[187] A heartbreaking statement released by the Camerons three days after Ivan's death laid bare their grief.

> We always knew Ivan wouldn't live forever, but we didn't expect to lose him so young and so suddenly. He leaves a hole in our life so big that words can't describe it. Bed time, bath time, meal time – nothing will feel the same again. We console ourselves knowing that he won't suffer any more, that his end was quick, and that he is in a better place. But we all just miss him so desperately.
>
> When we were first told the extent of Ivan's disability I thought that we would suffer having to care for him but at least he would benefit from our care. Now as I look back I see that it was all the other way round. It was only him that ever really suffered and it was us – Sam, me, Nancy and Elwen – who gained more than I ever believed possible from having and loving such a wonderfully special and beautiful boy.

A close aide remembers the shock among colleagues.

---

187 Geordie Greig interview, op. cit.

When Ivan was alive we were all terribly conscious of the sort of sadness about the whole thing, and how much David adored him. He was absolutely devoted to him. There was nothing to indicate that he was about to die. I remember the whole office was absolutely shell-shocked. There were people in tears; everyone was heartbroken really.

Letters of condolence flooded in. Among the many thousands they received was a particularly warm and moving note from Gordon Brown, who could relate to their devastation, having himself lost a baby daughter, Jennifer Jane.

Ivan was laid to rest after a private funeral in Chadlington, the nearest village to Dean. His old friend Giles Andreae has described the service as 'extraordinary'.

It was incredibly moving and emotive...I just remember David looking back halfway through the service and seeing all his friends and welling up in tears. He [Ivan] meant so much to them and I think he taught them a great deal about compassion and patience and the joy of family.[188]

Cameron returned to work a fortnight later. It was too soon.

A friend says:

He accepts he came back too quickly and hadn't fully recovered. There was this misconception that it would be a relief, but it was the death of a child and that's the most upsetting thing a parent ever has [to deal with]. When he went back to work, he was under huge pressure; under the microscope; everyone wanted to talk to him. It was just a really tough time for him. Sam obviously struggled as well.

The truth was that Cameron was reassessing his whole life – including whether he wanted to continue in politics.

He later recalled:

---

188   *Trevor McDonald Meets David Cameron.*

After Ivan died I did stop and think, you know, is this what I want
to do?…It makes you think about everything, you know…it's a
moment when the world stops, the clock stops, everything stops,
you go back to your family, you spend a lot of time just talking
and thinking and reflecting on everything that's happened and
then working out how do we start putting one foot back in front
of another again.

But put his best foot forward he did: feeling clearer than ever that he had
chosen the right path.[189]

Had it not been for Ivan, it is quite possible Cameron would never have
risen to the top in politics. His life had simply been too straightforward,
too charmed, to enable him to connect with many voters. A generation ago
that might not have mattered, but modern voters crave leaders who have
experienced – and survived – some turmoil or hardship.

A number of those who know and admire the Prime Minister argue that
Ivan changed him for the better.

A former aide says:

I remember talking about this with Lord Chadlington. He said
Cameron had had everything given to him in his life. What changed
him was the birth of Ivan. Having a son who wasn't perfect, wasn't
normal, really affected him and changed him for the better. I agree
with that thesis. My impression of Cameron before Ivan was that
he was a snobby little snot.

Another former colleague believes he 'became a different human being'
thanks to his son.

He became aware that with all the advantages he'd had in life, there
are things you can't change. I think it did give him a different perspective. The first impression you had of him as a 24-year-old was,
'Oh my God, what a frightful, braying Tory.' I think he became
much less of a frightful, braying Tory over the years.

189   Ibid.

Thanks to Ivan, Cameron could credibly claim to understand and care about the NHS, having had extensive first-hand experience of both its marvels and shortcomings. This has always been crucial to his pitch to voters. His disabled son taught him about the very toughest, and most rewarding, aspects of parenting. It may seem heartless to weigh up the extent to which this was a political advantage, yet historians should be dispassionate. There were also downsides. As a backbencher, Cameron had less time than many other MPs to socialise with colleagues in the bars and restaurants of Westminster. This was much more important than it sounds. While other new backbenchers were forming lasting bonds and alliances, he would frequently have to leave work early to tend to Ivan.

It may well have been a factor in his failure to build a wide network of friends and supporters in the parliamentary party. This would have serious long-term consequences. Though, naturally and rightly, Cameron would never see it in such terms, his domestic situation therefore put him at a competitive disadvantage. He never used it as an excuse.

An aide recalls:

> I remember him saying once that he'd had a really tough PMQs, because he'd spent all morning with Ivan in hospital. They'd suddenly found this experimental treatment they wanted to try on him and they wanted to do it straight away. Sam was in New York, so Cameron had to go in with him. He'd done no prep at all for PMQs, and he'd been slagged off.

Did Ivan also make Cameron bolder? Birrell says being the parent of a desperately disabled child puts everything else in perspective, making it easier to take risks.

'Say you're a complete disaster; you're laughed at; your career is over. Obviously you care, but it's not the end of the world – you've suffered far worse. It gives you a certain confidence to do things you might not otherwise have. You just say fuck it.'

16

TALLY-HO

'Shut up, you pompous prat.'
        – Cameron, to veteran Labour MP Gerald Kaufman

Every year, in the lull between Christmas and New Year, the Heythrop Hunt meets a few miles from Cameron's constituency cottage. They assemble at Cornbury Park, a stately home which provides a spectacular backdrop for the horses and hounds. Staff from the big house distribute sausage rolls and mince pies to spectators while the huntsmen sip hot toddies and their magnificent mounts paw impatiently at the gravel, snorting little white clouds into the chill winter air.

The estate belongs to friends of the Prime Minister, and many of his social set are involved in the annual meet. Over Christmas 2014, the property was let to Elisabeth Murdoch, whose presence ensured the Chipping Norton set turned out in force. Among those who gathered to see the horses off was Charlie Brooks, husband of Rebekah; Prince William's friend Hugh van Cutsem and his wife Rose; and Elisabeth herself, astride a stunning bay and flanked by her socialite friend Emily Oppenheimer, who also rode out.

Watching them thunder off over the fields in pursuit of a scent is unforgettable, but one person who could not enjoy it was Cameron himself. Since becoming Prime Minister, he has avoided being seen at hunts, let alone being photographed on horseback. Given the associations of equestrianism with class and privilege, he believes it is simply too toxic. Yet he is an avid supporter of hunting, and does what he can to help hunts and huntsmen behind the scenes.

From the moment he became an MP, he was crystal clear about his position on what has long been a deeply divisive and emotive issue. Labour had promised a free vote on banning hunting with hounds in its 1997 election manifesto, but a Private Member's Bill introduced during Blair's first term ran out of time. The issue dragged on through most of Blair's second term, with numerous failed attempts to push through revised proposals before a workable Bill was finally put to the vote. In a sign of the strength of feeling in the countryside, some 250,000 demonstrators marched on Parliament Square to protest at the proposed ban, blaring hunting horns and blowing whistles as they snaked their way past Downing Street. As the Bill reached its closing stages in the Commons, there were extraordinary scenes both inside and outside Parliament.

Cameron found the issue so infuriating he struggled to control himself during parliamentary debates.

'I have spent all week in a state of complete fury,' he admitted, after sitting through hours of speeches on the issue in the Commons.

> Like a man possessed with an advanced case of Tourette syndrome, I have been shouting at traffic and assailing my fellow men (and women). What has brought on this demented state? The hunting debate…Sitting in Parliament involves hours of listening to opinions with which you profoundly disagree. I am usually able to do this without shouting, but as soon as I hear Labour Members calling for hunting to be banned, I completely lose it.
>
> When John McFall [MP for Dumbarton] gets to his feet I shout, 'Go back to Scotland, you've already banned it.'
>
> Interrupting Gerald Kaufman during one of his lengthy and over-precise questions to the minister, I heard myself baying: 'Shut up, you pompous prat.'
>
> I even found myself barracking our very own Ann Widdecombe [an opponent of hunting]. As she spoke eloquently about hounds pursuing foxes, I kept interrupting: 'Yes, but what about your cats?'
>
> It was pathetic. And not even particularly amusing.[190]

Widdecombe certainly did not find it funny. She recalls:

> I remember when I made my speech against hunting, and Kate Hoey

---

190   *Guardian* blog, 22 March 2002.

[a pro-hunting Labour MP] was on the other side, some Conservative backbencher yelled out: 'Come over here, Kate! Join us!' And
Cameron shouted: 'And you can have Widdecombe!' I thought,
'That's not the way you talk about senior backbenchers. That's
not the way you do it.

In standing up for the sport, Cameron was defending not only a way of life
in the countryside, but also what he considered an important part of Britain's
cultural heritage. He genuinely loves rural life and wants to protect its tradi-
tions – the backdrop to his environmental push in the early leadership years.
(Many years later, he would be accused of abandoning the green agenda,
but his environmentalism is more about conservation and stewardship than
climate change treaties and carbon emission targets.)

It was a world he grew up with and understood; he is good with animals.

'He can scratch a pig's back so effectively that the creature sighs. This I
saw with my own eyes,' reported an interviewer who accompanied him on
a walk to a farm near Dean.[191] (He told the same journalist that he could
'castrate a ram with a pair of pliers'.)

His mother is said to have hunted with the Vine and Craven Hunt, and
Samantha's family is also very keen. It's in their blood: Samantha's grandmother Nancie was an accomplished horsewoman who survived a serious
riding accident when her mount fell on her. When Cameron was in his
twenties and thirties, many of his friends were regulars on the hunting
circuit. Some even took part in the more unusual sport of deer hunting on
horseback. In 2003, his old university friend James Delingpole joined a meet
of the Devon and Somerset Staghounds, alongside Steve Hilton and Dom
Loehnis's brother Al.

Delingpole recalls:

I was at a party thrown by Lord Saatchi, and I got talking to a
group of people including Rachel Whetstone. She was waxing lyr-
ical about stag hunting. I said, 'Wow, I'd love to do that!'

And she said, 'Why don't you?'

I said, 'Well, I can't ride very well, and I've never been hunting.'

She said, 'Don't worry, it's easy.'

---

191   Lesley White, *Sunday Times Magazine*, 22 April 2007.

So I had riding lessons and got fit, and went down to this big country house on Exmoor, which had been hired by some Germans who go hunting regularly. It was an extraordinarily diverse party, including [the late] Rose Gray [of the River Café], whose daughter was at the time married to the son of these Germans who hunted regularly, and Steve Hilton was there. Steve was a mad-keen stag hunter, whereas I was very nervous. We got talking the night before, and I said, 'Will you stay around to hold my hand?' and he said, 'I'm frightfully sorry, but I'm so into it, I want to be right at the front.' So that was fine, and I was looked after by one of Dave's Eton contemporaries, Al Loehnis.

Delingpole says he and Loehnis enhanced the natural high from hunting with other substances.

'I remember him bringing this great big skunk spliff, which we smoked on horseback in the middle of the hunt.'

Cameron himself was not present on this occasion, and his personal involvement in hunting has been exaggerated by critics who have an interest in making it a political embarrassment. In January 2003, he went out with the Heythrop Hunt, after which he wrote a piece for *The Guardian* which strongly implied that it was his first time.

To show my solidarity with the hunts in my constituency over the government's illiberal and bossy hunting Bill, I climbed on board a horse and went out for a day with the Heythrop Hunt.

Nothing had prepared me for the sheer terror of a day's hunting. I battled in vain to control my powerful steed and careered through trees and bushes completely out of control.

Trying to hover at the back of the field, I ended up at the front as a fox broke cover from behind. A fifteen-minute gallop along narrow paths in a forest followed, during which I thought death (for me at least) would be a release. The fox escaped. Having survived two and a half hours without being unseated, I dismounted and collapsed in a sweating heap on the ground. My horse had hardly broken a sweat.[192]

---

192 *Guardian* blog, 7 January 2003.

That this was Cameron's first hunt is surprising, given his background. Bruce Anderson says he used to joke that the 'terrible thing about the hunting Bill is that only two people are affected by it: Prince Charles and me' – suggesting it was a regular hobby. Yet a Tory MP who has been riding with him on a number of occasions over the years thinks he had genuinely done little to no hunting as an adult before this outing with the Heythrop.

'It's not impossible he hadn't been before. Maybe he's a bit like me – I hunted as a child on ponies, but not extensively, and I wasn't from a hunting family. Then I had a gap of fifteen years before I went again. That's probably more like it.'

Publicly, Cameron has admitted to hunting about ten times in total, including with the Old Berks Hunt, of which his stepfather-in-law, William Astor, is a former master. Guy Avis, his next-door neighbour in Dean, is honorary secretary of the Heythrop, and says Cameron has the use of a mount stabled at Ginge.

Journalists have long sought a picture of him riding, to no avail, prompting suspicions that someone with Cameron's best interests at heart might have paid to take any such images off the market. After extensive enquiries, however, we finally uncovered a photograph of the future Prime Minister preparing to set off for a day's sport. It was taken at the final gathering of the Heythrop Hunt before the ban came into effect, a few days after Christmas in 2004. Cameron can be seen on a fine bay mount, looking a little nervous, as horses assembled in the square in Chipping Norton.

Perhaps his anxiety was linked to the physical challenge ahead: those who have seen him hunting say he is not fit enough to do it well. A member of the Heythrop Hunt recalls him struggling to keep pace when he joined them.

> He only came for a short while because he's too unfit, and so he'd be knackered. The horses that William [Astor] would have brought would have been fit hunters, and they are quite strong. He wasn't up to it. He's not a hunter. He came to ride twice at most.

Addressing the question of cruelty, Cameron has argued that hunting is no more, and often less, cruel than shooting foxes. He was moved by letters from members of the Heythrop who told him they were animal lovers. The kennel master told him:

> We are not cruel people, quite the opposite. We have ... animal wel-
> fare at the heart of everything we do. With animals you have the
> heartache as well as the good times and we just cannot contem-
> plate life without our hounds, horses and all that goes with them.
> Please do your best.

He was persuaded, writing in his *Guardian* blog that the fox population
had to be controlled.

> I have shot foxes with a farmer friend in Norfolk (in an area where
> there are no hunts) and even for a good shot, it is literally a hit and
> miss (or hit and wound) affair. At least with hunting, the fox either
> dies or escapes unharmed.
>
> Set against the cruelty of factory farming or coarse fishing, hunting
> hardly registers. So while I might listen to a lecture about the cru-
> elty of the chase from a vegan wearing plastic shoes, the calls to ban
> hunting from the meat-eating, leather-wearing, angling-enthusiast
> class warriors on the Labour benches make my blood boil.[193]

The hunting ban finally came into force in 2005, after the government used
the Parliament Act to push the Bill into law. So far from dying out, however,
the sport is booming, mostly in the form of trail hunting, in which hounds
pursue an artificially laid scent. The new sport is designed to generate a chase
as similar to a traditional fox hunt as possible, using trails that are laid in
a way that mirrors the movement of hunted live quarry. However, it is little
secret that 'accidents' often happen, meaning hounds ferret out real foxes,
which are pursued in the same way as they have been for hundreds of years.

The Heythrop has been involved in a number of court cases relating to
such mishaps. While Cameron was Leader of the Opposition, his friend Julian
Barnfield, a professional huntsman with the Heythrop, which rides out up
to four days a week during the season, was charged with various offences
of hunting a fox, relating to alleged incidents in 2007, 2008 and 2009. The
charges were subsequently dropped, though, several years later, Barnfield
had another run-in with the law, in a celebrated prosecution brought, at
huge expense, by the RSPCA.

193   Ibid.

We discovered that Cameron intervened in the initial case, writing to the Attorney General on behalf of his constituent in June 2008.

Some years later, Chris Edgell, a former detective constable involved in the case, attempted to obtain a copy of Cameron's letter using the Freedom of Information Act, but his application was rejected on the grounds that it 'contained personal data of third parties...and disclosure would breach the fair processing principle as to disclose personal and confidential information would be unfair to third parties'.

Cameron's constituency office also refused to provide Edgell with a copy of the correspondence on the basis that it followed 'a private meeting between a constituent and his Member of Parliament – in this case, Mr Cameron'.

Did the police and CPS go easy on Barnfield under pressure from the Leader of the Opposition? It is more than possible. Edgell, who remains angry that the case was dropped, says:

> I have learned from CPS and police sources that Mr Cameron's letter to the Attorney General was sent on to CPS headquarters, who sent it on to Thames Valley CPS, who then sent it to Gloucester CPS, who then sent it on to the Complex Case Unit at Bristol, where barrister Kerry Barker dealt with it. Eventually the charges were dropped.
>
> I saw the letter. It said something along the lines of 'Is this really a productive use of police time?' The hunters have a very powerful ally in David Cameron.

Cameron's attitude to hunting tells us something bigger about his political outlook. His defence of the pursuit went beyond simply protecting his 'own people'. It was part of a broader political philosophy which rejected anything that smacked of the 'nanny state'. He has always described himself as a 'liberal Conservative', a woolly term which means different things to different people, but is partially characterised by a laissez-faire attitude to how people choose to live their lives, in so far as their choices do not harm others. He viewed the proposed ban as an affront to individual freedom.

For Delingpole, Cameron's personal decision to eschew hunting altogether following the ban, as well as his failure to deliver a pledge in the 2010 coalition agreement to hold a free vote in the Commons on repealing the Hunting Act, reflects poorly on his character. It is one of a number of issues that once made Cameron furious but which he no longer fought for once he was in power.

'The stag hunt was probably one of the best things I've ever done,' Delingpole reflects.

> It was awesome. You're living totally in the moment for four or five hours, with this intense sensory experience rushing at you. The idea that Dave should have to renounce that...Well, what it says is that he's an arch-pragmatist, and also, somebody who, when push comes to shove, does not fight for the things that are worth fighting for. In the run-up to 2010, all the hunts did a lot of work for Dave and for the Conservatives. Hunts are the backbone of the countryside; they have a very good organisational structure. And they feel very betrayed.

However, as Cameron has pointed out regretfully in conversations with friends, 'law makers can't be law breakers'. In any case, hunts were under no illusions about the prospects of winning a vote to repeal the ban under the coalition or a Tory government with a majority of twelve. They are content to bide their time.

A less controversial equestrian interest for Cameron is racing, a love of which he inherited from his father. For Cameron senior, the Sport of Kings was more than just a hobby: it was a lifelong passion. His career as an owner spanned five decades, during which he invested in a number of top-class horses. An early success was a share in a horse named Isle of Skye, which won the Festival Trophy Handicap Chase at the Cheltenham Festival in 1960. In 1996, Ian, who was also a successful breeder, owned a horse called Emerging Market, which won the Wokingham Stakes at Royal Ascot. Interestingly, long before his son started dating Samantha, Ian co-owned a horse with her father Reggie Sheffield.

An Eton contemporary thinks Cameron belonged to some form of betting syndicate at school, made possible because all those involved were 'fucking loaded'.

'He was part of the whole racing scene at Eton. He was in a group of schoolboy bookmakers who were big into horse racing and went to Ascot to bet,' the fellow Old Etonian says.

Living in Peasemore, the Camerons were conveniently located for Newbury racecourse, where the children were regulars. Ian Cameron was a familiar figure on the course, and would sometimes be invited to watch the day's sport from the royal box, as a guest of the directors of the course. He also liked to take his children to Epsom.

Cameron still loves the races. A former Tory aide recalls him breaking off from filming a complex and expensive party political broadcast in his garden to dash inside to watch the Grand National:

> It was all going quite well; there were loads of people around, we were going big on it, we had the Saatchi guy involved...We would be in the middle of recording, we'd just be nailing it, and then Cameron would suddenly disappear, saying, 'Sorry, chaps, the Grand's on.' The sound guy was this south London lad, who couldn't understand why they kept having to stop filming.

On occasion, Ian's involvement in racing threatened to be a political embarrassment to his son. In 2008, he had a share in a horse named Mountain Pride, which had a real prospect of winning the Derby. According to Bruce Anderson, Cameron was terrified it would.

'David was thinking, "What a nightmare! Imagine the public reaction!" He said it would have been a huge embarrassment...toff, toff, toff.' Fortunately for the Tory leader, the horse did not live up to expectations.

Though he was careful to avoid being photographed with a gun, Cameron is also an accomplished shot and loves stalking in Scotland, another activity he felt obliged to give up when he became Prime Minister. Bruce Anderson says his father encouraged him from a young age. In his teens, Cameron would go to Perthshire with Toppo Todhunter and his parents, who used to hire a hunting lodge. As a boy, he would also go shooting in Scotland with his father's old friend Sir Henry Keswick.

Anderson testifies to Cameron's skills with a rifle, saying that he can 'do lefts and rights'.

> We had a wonderful [stalking expedition] once where there were beasts on the skyline and he shot one and killed it. As it died, there was a rattle of antlers; then he shot another one, because they

[the other stags] didn't scatter. It was extraordinary. He's got some magic – normally they run.

Life after Downing Street will doubtless involve horses and guns once again.

17

LINES TO TAKE

'If you take cocaine with others, all of you are bound together forever.'

– Media figure who has partied with Cameron

To make a mark, a new backbencher must find a subject and make it their territory, taking every opportunity to highlight the issue in the media and in parliamentary debates. Cameron's choice was unusual and controversial: drugs. If his intention was to draw attention to himself, it worked, but as hungry for airtime as he was, on this occasion, he cared as much about achieving change as he did about generating noise.

His opportunity to get his teeth into an issue he really cared about arose through his role on the Home Affairs Select Committee. As luck would have it, the chairman announced plans to investigate government drugs policy, a subject Cameron described as a 'no-go area for most politicians' but which, for personal reasons, was close to his heart.

Writing for *The Guardian* during parliamentary recess in August 2001, he spoke of his 'delight' at the chance to get involved, suggesting a number of fact-finding missions.

The committee's report could be 'interesting and controversial', he mused. They discussed a possible field trip to Amsterdam, a suggestion he thought 'rather old hat'. He had better ideas: 'Why not Ibiza to look at ecstasy use? Or Portugal where they are pioneering an entirely new approach to dealing with heroin addiction? I suppose in the interests of balance we could pop over to Saudi Arabia to check out the really tough approach.'

Hinting at his own instincts on the subject, he took aim at Home Secretary David Blunkett, labelling him 'deeply illiberal', and teasingly suggesting it would be unwise for the committee to examine the hardline approach to drugs in the Middle East, in case it gave the minister ideas. Cameron's own view was that 'state bans on anything' were generally to be avoided if possible.

'The option of decriminalisation is actually in the terms of reference,' he enthused.[194]

He wanted to look at heroin addiction, or scope for changing cannabis regulation. On both counts, he had a personal interest.

As we have seen, at university he had enjoyed the occasional spliff with Delingpole and Fergusson, which had done him no apparent harm. He felt the law was unduly harsh.

But it is his attitude to harder drugs, in particular heroin, that is more interesting, and hints at his private heartache over a close relative who became addicted to class-A substances.

The identity of the individual concerned is an open secret at Westminster, but while their troubles are part of Cameron's life story, it is unnecessary to refer to them by name. Suffice to say that the relative, whom we shall call X, was for a period of years in the grip of crippling and life-threatening drug addiction, which involved at least one extensive period of residential rehabilitation at a South African clinic. Among snippets of information that came our way about X's life was a report that, while Cameron was a young MP, X's partner was a drugs mule, who collapsed and died in an Argentinian airport when bags of narcotics burst in his stomach. This proved impossible to verify without undue intrusion, but it hints at how dangerous and chaotic X's life became.

It is unclear when X's problems began, and we decided not to investigate the detail, on the grounds that X is not a public figure and is entitled to privacy. To have pursued it would have caused significant upset to the Cameron family, who have moved on. X has recovered, is married, and has a good job.

Yet X's condition was a matter of great heartache for Cameron when he was a young MP, and explains why, soon after entering Parliament, he was prepared to stick his neck out on the extremely divisive and difficult issue of drug regulation and control. The trauma he and his family experienced as they battled to help a loved one overcome addiction undoubtedly coloured his perspective on the law, equipping him to comment on its shortcomings, and on the extent to which the needs of addicts are being met.

194   *Guardian* blog, 2 August 2001.

'Friends and people close to me have had their lives ruined by drug abuse, and I want us to tackle this problem properly,' he admitted after the select committee inquiry had finished.

In a sign of how much he cared about the issue, he became patron of a drugs rehabilitation charity in his constituency called the Ley Community, which specialises in helping heroin addicts. Twice a year, the charity would hold 'graduation' ceremonies for recovered addicts, during which they would tell their stories. When he attended one of these ceremonies in 2006, Cameron became extremely emotional, and was photographed wiping away tears.

Paul Goodman, who was chief executive of the charity at the time, recalls:

> Hearing people talking about their journey...attaining what they thought was unattainable – holding down a job, having a relation-ship, paying the rent and so on, was a very powerful experience and he was very moved by it. We invited him to say a few words after-wards in his role as patron. He'd just been elected leader and said that in the past few months he'd had to sit through many speeches by world figures and none had moved him to the extent of what he'd heard that evening.

Goodman says Cameron never went into detail about X, but staff at the Ley Community were aware that somebody close to him had drug issues.

Taking a stand, Cameron called for various reforms that were extremely unpopular with his party. He annoyed a number of colleagues at Westminster, raised eyebrows in his constituency, and risked opening a can of worms about his own personal drug use. It would return to haunt him.

The Home Affairs Select Committee took evidence from a wide range of expert witnesses. Cameron also spent considerable time investigating drugs policy in his own constituency. Part of his research involved sitting at the back of a secondary school class while they were visited by a group of former addicts who explained, in graphic detail, the risks of dabbling with drugs. He told colleagues the experience was 'incredibly powerful':

> The students were gripped by what they were told. These ex-addicts described how their experimentation with drugs had led them down a dreadful path to losing their homes and friends, breaking up from

their families, prison, and the collapse of their lives. They had credibility and their programme had power. They were not 'men in suits'.[195]

He also spent time talking to Oxford police officers responsible for drug treatment and testing programmes. As the select committee inquiry continued, his personal inclination towards relaxing the law in relation to some substances, as well as his conviction that a new approach towards heroin addiction was urgently required, became increasingly apparent. In particular, he favoured the introduction of so-called 'shooting galleries', where addicts could inject in a controlled environment.

He argued:

> When I first heard about the concept of safe injecting rooms, I hated it. I thought the concept of the state providing a room for someone to inject something into their veins awful, but I listened to the arguments...People who live in inner-city areas whose children have to step over drug paraphernalia in the streets and on housing estates deserve a break from heroin use in their communities...Safe injecting rooms at least get heroin users to a place where they can be contacted by the treatment agencies so that the work of trying to get them off drugs can start.[196]

Having branded Blunkett illiberal, he was taken aback when, in evidence to the committee, the Home Secretary suddenly indicated that he was considering reclassifying cannabis from class B to class C, taking the wind out of the committee's sails. Cameron's reaction suggests he wanted to go further: during the hearing, he described the move as 'sensible' but 'feeble', and questioned why the Home Secretary wasn't 'addressing the real problem' of cannabis being a 'black market drug, such as heroin and cocaine'. He seemed to be drawn to the idea of wholesale decriminalisation of cannabis, saying during a later evidence session that he would be disappointed 'if radical options were not at least looked at'.

The committee's eventual report, published in May 2002, did not go as far as he would have liked, but was controversial nonetheless. Recommendations

195　Hansard, 5 December 2002.
196　Ibid.

included downgrading ecstasy from class A to class B, and a trial of shooting galleries. In an unusual step that illustrated the sensitivity of the subject, one Conservative member of the committee, Angela Watkinson, disowned the report.

Cameron suffered an immediate backlash. When he agreed to give an interview to a local radio station, the presenter introduced him derisively as 'a Conservative MP who thinks that heroin addicts should be given prescriptions for ecstasy'.

'That was a tough one; it was difficult to explain my way out of it,' Cameron said later.

Yet he stuck to his guns, defending the report in an article for the *Daily Mail*, in which he argued that police should concentrate on tackling hard drug use.

'Drugs policy in this country has been an abject failure…It is no good preaching to young people, or telling them that all drugs are just the same. They won't listen. Ranking ecstasy alongside heroin simply makes no sense,' he wrote.[197]

Later that year, a fortnight or so before the House of Commons rose for Christmas, he returned to the theme, angering Tory whips with a speech that was way out of line with party policy. In a virtuoso ten-minute performance, he spoke passionately about the rising death toll from drug abuse, making the case for a catalogue of reforms. He appealed for a compassionate approach from the government, calling on ministers 'not to return to retribution and war on drugs'.

'That has been tried, and we all know that it does not work,' he declared.

During his speech, he issued repeated heartfelt pleas to the government to 'be brave' and act fast.

'We have to realise that every day that an addict spends out on the streets funding their habit is a time of crime, of ill health, and possibly death.'[198]

Listening open-mouthed as he called for sympathy for sections of society many regarded with disdain, Cameron's colleagues were appalled – not least because he had failed to tell anyone in advance.

According to a senior colleague who has never forgotten the episode, the whips were 'incandescent'.

---

197   'Forget it, Blunkett – we can never win a "war on drugs"', *Daily Mail*, 23 May 2002.

198   Hansard, 5 December 2002.

The same colleague, who later served in Cameron's Cabinet, recalls:

> With complete and utter self-assurance, he just cruised into this ten-minute speech, which effectively denounced official Conservative policy on drugs, with all the Labour Members looking on. It was a very impressive performance, but it was noteworthy that it broke the rules. If you are going to disagree, there are certain ways that you do that. We allowed a lot of latitude to backbenchers in opposition. It wasn't a big deal, but was quite striking. This is my one memory of him as a young backbencher, standing up and delivering an absolutely emphatic speech about drug reclassification, and cannabis not being damaging. Total self-assurance, and, as I say, no regard for anybody else before he did it.

Called upon by the whips to defend his actions, Cameron was probably too discreet to mention X. But X's situation goes a long way to explaining why he threw caution to the wind. He really cared, describing the select committee inquiry as 'by far the most interesting thing I have done in the year and a half I have been in Parliament'.

Did Cameron himself use hard drugs? The question has been hotly debated. At university, there is no evidence he had anything other than an occasional joint. Delingpole says that even if Cameron had fancied something stronger, class-A drugs were hard to find.

> I'd have been doing class-A if they were available – they just weren't around. There was a tremendous stink in my first year when Olivia Channon died after taking heroin and champagne and that was all very sad. I remember a BBC crew coming round to Oxford and interviewing my friend, asking if Oxford had a drugs problem. He said, 'Of course there is! We can't get hold of them for love nor money.' And I think that was a fair assessment.

What about later, in his twenties and early thirties? In the absence of a photograph of Cameron snorting cocaine, there is no proof. But we have spoken to one member of his social circle who recalls it being in open circulation at a dinner party at the Camerons' home. This guest did not see either Cameron or Samantha take the drug, but the fact that those present should have felt comfortable doing so under their roof suggests it was not an unfamiliar scene.

Further evidence is second-hand and falls into the category of 'hearsay'. Ed Miliband's former spin doctor Tom Baldwin, who was notorious for his own cocaine habit when he was a journalist, has privately told several sources that he has personally seen Cameron taking cocaine. We have spoken to two individuals, neither of whom has an agenda to discredit the Prime Minister, who have had such a conversation with the spin doctor. Asked about it now, Baldwin refuses to comment.

The reality is that those who have taken cocaine in each other's company have an interest in protecting each other: they all have something to lose.

A source familiar with the unwritten rules of the game says:

> If you take cocaine with others, all of you are bound together forever. You all have the power to bring each other down. And so there is a culture of secrecy. In a way it is pernicious – it is corrupting. Because everyone involved protects each other. The only option is silence.

It is Cameron's own response to the question that is most revealing. Pressed on whether he has taken class-A drugs at any time, an issue that has never quite gone away, he has repeatedly refused to deny it. He has, however, denied snorting cocaine since becoming a parliamentarian.[199] The fact that he has given a definitive response to the question about cocaine use since becoming an MP, but has failed to offer the same assurance about cocaine use before he entered Parliament, is a strong indication of the state of affairs. Voters are left to draw their own conclusions.

Many people probably feel it does not matter either way. According to the official Crime Survey for England and Wales 2012–13, one in three adults – around fifteen million people – have taken drugs at some point in their lives; three million have done so in the past year. While cannabis is the most common recreational drug, an estimated five million adults have taken class-A drugs. If Cameron took class-A drugs, some might consider

199 http://conservativehome.blogs.com/toryleadership/2005/10/david_cameron_d.html.

it does not reflect entirely badly on him, suggesting he is not too uptight to experiment, and was not too ambitious to take any risks. Using carefully chosen words, he has sought to turn the question to his advantage, saying – without further elaboration – that he had a 'normal university experience'.

For an older generation, however, his behaviour – albeit a long time ago – is likely to meet with disapproval. It suggests that he has been willing to flout the law. It may suggest a degree of self-indulgence.

Given how passionately he felt about the issue as a young MP, it is interesting that when, as Prime Minister, Cameron was in a position to implement the sweeping reforms he had wanted in 2002, he chose not to do so. In his latter years as Leader of the Opposition, and as Prime Minister, he has rarely mentioned drug policy.

By the time he became Prime Minister, X had long since recovered, and the issue was no longer close to home. Indeed, when a Home Office report on drugs policy recommended relaxing the law, he rejected the findings outright, coming full circle from his position in 2004.[200]

'I don't believe in decriminalising drugs that are illegal today,' he said. 'I'm a parent with three children; I don't want to send out a message that somehow taking these drugs is OK or safe.'

His family's private drugs trauma is now history. For Cameron, the caravan has moved on.

---

200   Home Office/Norman Baker, 'New psychoactive substances review: report of the expert panel', September 2014.

18

BISTRO BOYS

'Is it going to stick, this dreadful label?'

– Cameron

By now, Cameron was making a name for himself, as was another young MP who lived in the same fashionable part of town: George Osborne.

Under Michael Howard, both were given shadow ministerial roles, and their profiles soared.[201] Both were working the TV and radio studios, and it was paying off. The Westminster village began to talk of them as future leadership material.

Boris Johnson's father Stanley, who hoped to become an MP in the 2005 election, remembers joking about the two young Turks at a gala dinner for party supporters in Newton Abbot.

'Who is the Blair and who is the Brown?' he asked.

The audience laughed knowingly.

'We all wonder if there is some kind of "Granita pact",' Johnson continued, alluding to the gentlemen's agreement between Blair and Brown. 'All I can tell you, ladies and gentlemen, is that the Cameroons are coming!'

As Howard's golden boys, the pair had been elevated to VIP status on the Conservative social circuit. Cameron was guest of honour at the dinner. He had been an MP for just four years but he already knew how to work a room. As the event got underway, the then 65-year-old Johnson remembers the 38-year-old counselling him on the importance of 'gladhanding'.

---

201   Osborne was made shadow Chief Secretary to the Treasury, while Cameron was made deputy party chairman, then frontbench spokesman for Local Government Finance, before being promoted to head of policy coordination. Earlier, under Iain Duncan Smith, he had been made shadow deputy leader of the House of Commons.

'You can't just sit at the top table,' Cameron advised. 'You've got to get out there; work the tables.'

Johnson was happy to take his advice: he knew Cameron was one to watch. That he referred to the 'Cameroons' rather than the 'Osbornites' suggests that he, for one, considered Cameron to be the Blair to Osborne's Brown – though, at this stage, no one was quite sure if this was the right way round.

Regardless, the 'Blair and Brown' tag was fast gaining traction. As early as October 2003, a small item had appeared in *Scotland on Sunday* making the first public reference to the two as the 'Blair and Brown' of the rising generation of Tories.[202] This was echoed by Michael Portillo in a piece for *The Guardian* the following month:

'Perhaps,' he wrote, 'just as Labour produced Blair and Brown in 1994, in an ideal world the Conservative Party would now produce two bright young things, unsullied by having held office in a previous administration. We have George Osborne and David Cameron, but they aren't ready.'[203]

Unlike Blair and Brown, however, Cameron and Osborne were close personal friends. In years to come, under the most intense pressure, their relationship would prove rock solid. Their strikingly similar backgrounds meant this had come naturally. Osborne's schooling was marginally less grand (he attended St Paul's, a private day school in west London), but his family origins were undoubtedly on a par: Osborne's father is a baronet, and the family tree is littered with politicians, magistrates, lawyers and sheriffs.[204] Christened Gideon (later, as an insecure teenager, he changed it by deed poll), he too had a very privileged childhood, though the circles in which he and his parents moved were different to Cameron's Shire Tory set.

As a child, the future Chancellor enjoyed relaxing in the idyllic pastures of The Vinnicks, a house in a village just a few miles from Peasemore. He then followed Cameron to Oxford, where he studied history. Like Cameron, he joined the Bullingdon Club and kept clear of student politics (although he did edit the student magazine, *Isis*). From Oxford, he too joined CRD, where he was 'almost a mini-me of Cameron' – their similarity in manner and build attracting the attention of colleagues who had stayed long enough

---

202   John McTernan, *Scotland on Sunday*, 5 October 2003.

203   'Ruthless and right', Michael Portillo, *The Guardian*, 2 November 2003.

204   Janan Ganesh, *George Osborne: The Austerity Chancellor* (Biteback Publishing, 2014), p. 2.

to have worked with both. (Cameron was working for Howard by the time Osborne, four year his junior, joined Central Office.)[205]

But while the Cameron clan clung to rural respectability, Osborne's family was more urbane. His parents settled into the glamorous and cosmopolitan world of 1960s Chelsea, his father establishing a fashionable wallpaper business on King's Road. They wore their social liberalism like a badge of honour, passing these instincts on to their son, who as a politician would display notably few hang-ups on moral or cultural questions. (As Chancellor, he once left colleagues open-mouthed when, behind closed doors, he launched an impassioned defence of the current abortion time limit. 'I did not come into politics to stop a woman's right to choose,' he exclaimed.)[206]

By the time he entered Parliament in 2001 – the same year as Cameron – Osborne was a hard-edged politician with the air of one who had seen it all before. His path through the thickets of backroom Tory politics in the 1990s was strewn with disappointment and frustration: the Conservatives had been out of office for almost the entirety of his political life and he had witnessed back-to-back Labour landslides up close. As speechwriter to a beleaguered William Hague from 1997 until Hague's resignation of the party leadership in 2001, he was chained to an operation that alternated between slapstick and disaster. It left him with a hunger for power that has marked him ever since, and pushed him down the 'modernisation' road several years before Cameron decided to follow in his footsteps.

Between 2001 and 2004, Cameron and Osborne started to spend more and more time in each other's company, working together for both Iain Duncan Smith and Michael Howard. They also began socialising, taking advantage of the proximity of their homes in west London and a shared bicycle route back from the Commons. When the Camerons' first daughter Nancy came along in 2004, Osborne became her godfather.

It didn't take long for fellow Tories, jealous of their closeness to the party leadership, to start backstabbing. In July 2004, the first of what would be

205 Ibid., p. 7.
206 In many ways Osborne has more in common with the former Liberal Democrat leader Nick Clegg, who is also a relatively wealthy London day-school boy raised in a relaxed metropolitan milieu.

a string of poisonous commentaries concerning the duo and the emerging group of 'Cameroons' surrounding them began appearing in the press.

'This is what we call the Notting Hill set,' the controversial right-wing MP Derek Conway told journalists. 'They sit around in these curious little bistros in parts of London, drink themselves silly and wish they were doing what the rest of us are getting on with.'[207]

To old-school Tories, Steve Hilton – who had recently returned to London and the Conservative parish following years of drifting around the outside – seemed a particularly objectionable figure. One who worked with him says: 'He was slovenly. He came in late, was completely wacky, and was totally and utterly unreliable. The next thing I know, he's Saatchi's favourite boy to be the whizz-kid advertising genius of the twenty-first century…'

Conway wasn't the originator of the 'Notting Hill set' tag (that award goes to Peter Oborne, writing in *The Spectator* a month previously), but the venom in his words caused a stir. 'He said we met in *bistros*,' says one of Cameron's friends scathingly, as if the very idea were an insult. Civilised dinners at home were more their style.

Cameron too tried to discredit the briefings, disputing that he even lived in Notting Hill. 'I live half the week in Oxfordshire and half the week in…I don't know what you call it. North Kensington? Certainly not Notting Hill. An estate agent might call it Notting Hill…Is it going to stick, this dreadful label?'[208]

But despite these protestations there was little the group could do to shake off the sobriquet. They might not all have lived in W11, but they were certainly a recognisable social group, and sufficiently well-heeled to be able to enjoy a comfortable Notting Hill lifestyle.

The set included Ed Vaizey and Nick Boles, one of the founders of an influential modernising think tank, Policy Exchange. Gove, also a Policy Exchange founder, was another key member. Described mischievously as a 'comfortably upholstered commentator' by Cameron in his *Guardian* blog, the *Times* journalist planned to stand for a seat in the next election – having been under pressure from friends including Cameron to do so for some time.

'You can do something that I have been pressing on you for years,' Cameron urged his friend via his blog.

---

207 'Who are the Notting Hill Tories?', Charlie Methven, *Daily Telegraph*, 28 July 2004.
208 *Daily Telegraph*, 2 October 2004.

Give up the journalist's expense account and cast aside ambitions of editing *The Thunderer*. Gird up your loins and prepare for late nights sitting on uncomfortable green benches.

Instead of dashing off 700 words at your PC that will flow effortlessly into the op-ed page of *The Times*, you may have to wait seven hours to make a ten-minute speech that few newspapers will ever report. In short, Michael, become a Tory MP.[209]

It was a fluid circle of friends, with plenty of fringe players, including George Bridges – another Old Etonian and a former political secretary to Major – and Kate Fall, a friend of Cameron's since Oxford. Yet the most important members were Hilton and his on/off girlfriend (and future wife), Rachel Whetstone. Known for her sharp tongue, she was a divisive figure. A friend of the group recalls:

She raises the temperature unnecessarily. I heard from one youngster that they'd gone to see Michael [Howard] and before he could say anything she said, 'Michael, shut the fuck up.' When she apologised for being bad-tempered, he said, 'That's what I pay you for.' One who worked with her closely on a Conservative campaign recalls her ringing him up at all hours: 'I thought Rachel was a bitch from hell. She had a big job to do but dealing with her personally was horrific. She'd phone me up at 4 a.m., screaming her lungs out because she couldn't get her computer to work. I was like, 'Argh! I don't know anything about computers!'[210]

In summer 2004, just when the 'Notting Hill set' was beginning to excite the media, Whetstone had a bitter fallout with Cameron and his wife. The immediate trigger for the row was a salacious piece of gossip in the *Daily Mail* diary, which reported that Whetstone had 'formed a close friendship with a married older man who is a well-connected Tory grandee'.

The gentleman in question, it soon transpired, was none other than William Astor, Samantha's stepfather. Cameron, who had been in the dark about the relationship, was furious. It was a humiliation for his friend Hilton and

---

209   *Guardian* blog, 15 October 2002.
210   Private information.

deeply upsetting for his wife, not to mention his mother-in-law. According to a friend, he told Whetstone that he would never talk to her again, although the rift eventually healed.[211]

Astor 'got the hots for Rachel', Bruce Anderson says. 'The initiative came from William. But I don't think Sam will forgive Rachel in a hurry. As I said to David, "It takes two to tango." To which he replied, "Yes, but you can't sack your stepfather."'

The 'Notting Hill set' did not begin as a political grouping. At first, it was about hanging out in London and holidaying together. As far back as the summer of 1991, Hilton and Cameron had rented a car and spent a happy ten days driving around the Italian countryside, staying in an old farmhouse and visiting some of Cameron's friends in Tuscany – including an ex-girlfriend. A few years later, the two men – this time accompanied by their respective girlfriends, Rachel and Samantha – visited Hilton's family in Hungary for the Easter holiday. The four of them stayed in Budapest for a few days before travelling south to the town of Szeged to meet Hilton's grandmother. Later, as the group widened, there were further trips, including horse-riding holidays to Syria, Lebanon and Jordan.[212]

There was always political chitchat, but it was not yet a major feature of their social occasions. In their late twenties and early thirties, however, the exchange of ideas became more serious. As the Conservatives headed for a third successive election defeat, and the group matured, there was a dawning realisation that they might be in a position to change things. It was only at this relatively late point, in 2004, that the 'set' became a political force.

'At first, we were just kids, really,' says one of the group.

> In the earlier days, when we were at CRD, we were young and junior and would talk about office stuff, and the [1992 election] campaign, and whatever Labour were doing and what we thought we should do. But we were not at the level that we were able to implement anything. We never really had any delusions about that. As time went on we talked about it more, and the next thing was,

---

211   Francis Elliott and James Hanning, p. 265.
212   Nicholas Watt, *The Guardian*, 28 July 2004.

when we started to see each other more at weekends, we'd talk more about *ideas*. About social responsibility and the role of business in society, and about how it's not just about cutting the size of the state. That was when the Conservatives were going slightly off the rails and we were talking about that. But it was not yet at an 'operational' level.

Later on, we thought, well, actually, there is not just an opportunity but a responsibility to develop an alternative argument. Without anyone actually saying it, there was a dawning realisation that we were the leadership generation that was coming. No one actually said that, nobody actually talked about it; but the fact that Dave was an MP and George was an MP…it was obvious. We talked more about ideas, political themes and philosophy, and how to operationalise that.

As we have seen, exclusive dinners discussing elevated philosophical concerns did not do much to endear them to those outside the charmed circle. 'There was a lot of jealousy towards David and George, right from the word go,' a fellow MP of the 2001 intake admits. 'They were demonstratively good. For someone like me, who hadn't been on the political circuit before coming into Parliament, it seemed obvious that George and David were ahead of everyone else. They conformed to my idea of what a party leader would be.'[213]

For some, the 'set' is evidence of a deep-rooted cliqueyness in Cameron's character. He went from the Bullingdon Club to the Brat Pack – also known as the 'Smith Square set' – straight into the 'Notting Hill set' and, later, the 'Chipping Norton set'. He is nothing if not clubbable.

One of the 'Notting Hill set' says:

> From A to Z, then till now, Dave has managed to keep his friends close – people I holidayed with back in the 1990s are either working for him directly or working for him in some way or other. In some ways it's a credit to his early friendships; in another way it's cliquey.[214]

---

213 Private information.
214 Private information.

What is more, those in these groups have tended to come from a very similar background. Almost all the 'Notting Hill set' were privately educated and went to Oxford (with the exception of Whetstone, who was at Bristol), and almost all came through CRD (with the exception of Gove and Boles). They were bound together by a realisation that the party would have to change to win again and a belief that they were the people to make it happen. In time, they would identify Cameron as their best vehicle.

19

AWOL

'We are at the start of a long, painful slog.'

– Cameron

'Where is that posh cunt?' spluttered Lynton Crosby, scanning the room for any sign of Cameron.

The 2005 general election was imminent and the MP for Witney was nowhere to be seen.

As his star soared under Howard, Cameron had been asked to write the manifesto, propelling him to the heart of the party machine. He became closer than ever to the leader, laying the foundation for his own bid for the top job. He also began forging a professional relationship with Crosby, the Australian election strategist drafted in to run the campaign. Yet in the final weeks of the 2005 campaign, he made a strategic decision to absent himself. As nerves frayed before polling day, the man dubbed 'the Wizard of Oz' made no secret of his frustration with Cameron's sudden disappearance from Central Office.[215]

Yet the rapport they established before he vanished was important. Later, the controversial election strategist would play a key role in Cameron's own leadership of the party, helping deliver successive Conservative victories in the London Mayoral elections in 2008 and 2012. He would also mastermind the Conservatives' triumphant general election campaign in 2015.

Howard's leadership had ushered in a period of stability and optimism in the parliamentary party.

'A Tory revival is underway,' Cameron enthused in his blog in November

---

215   Central Office had recently become the Conservative Campaign Headquarters (CCHQ).

CALL ME DAVE

2003. Howard had made him deputy chairman of the party, a position which meant he had to start minding his words.

'That's it, I'm afraid,' he wrote.

> No more indiscretions about life on the green benches in the House of Commons or piercing insights into Tory feuds. Forget the candid assessments of our electoral prospects or vivid descriptions of my latest rebellion. As the new deputy chairman of the Conservative Party – oh yes, that's me – this column will have to be re-designated as a Tory Party propaganda sheet. From now on, it shall be called Pravda.[216]

He took it in good part when a colleague pointed out that the party always had 'lots' of deputy chairs.

His new role involved examining how to make the party more electable, a question he and the so-called Notting Hill set had been wrestling with for years.

'We are at the start of a long, painful slog,' he predicted, rattling off a list of challenges for the party before polling day.

Just a few months into his deliberations, however, he was taken off the task.

'I was summoned to [Howard's] office and sat alone for a few brief moments with the great man,' he wrote in his blog.

> After some pleasantries, he uttered the fatal words. 'David, I would like you to take on responsibility for local government finance.' I have to admit that my first reaction was: 'But I thought we were friends?' There are only about three Members of Parliament who actually understand the council tax and the associated complex web of 'formula spending shares' and 'standard spending assessments'…My expertise extends about as far as paying the damned thing and not much further.[217]

With a sinking heart, Cameron immersed himself in the Byzantine world of council grants and funding. Characteristically, in a few days he had it figured

216 *Guardian* blog, 17 November 2003.
217 *Guardian* blog, 25 March 2004.

out, concluding that the job was in fact 'incredibly simple'. He decided that all he had to do was 'blame the government' for council tax rises; 'trash' the Liberal Democrats' proposal for a new local income tax; and come up with a better system.

In any case, he didn't have to trouble himself with it for long.

In summer 2004, Howard gave him a fresh challenge: co-ordinating the party's election manifesto. Based in a tiny office on the Yellow Submarine corridor at party headquarters (so called because of its porthole-like windows), where his official title was 'head of policy and co-ordination', he would be intimately involved in devising the party's pitch to voters. While he did the big thinking, James McGrath, a party official who went on to become Boris Johnson's senior campaign strategist, was charged with ensuring there would be no presentational blunders. Few at CCHQ had forgotten the horror of the 2001 manifesto launch in Wales, when Hague's wife Ffion glanced at the document in the helicopter en route to the big press conference and realised the wrong version of the language had been used.

Lynton Crosby had arrived at CCHQ that autumn, charged with putting together a minimalist campaign based on crime and immigration. He came with a formidable reputation. Born into a conservative Methodist family in rural South Australia, he had been instrumental in delivering successive election victories for Australian Liberal leader John Howard. However, he was not without political baggage. In an episode that became known as the Children Overboard affair, he was suspected of ruthlessly exploiting public angst about illegal immigrants by suggesting that boat people seeking asylum had deliberately thrown their children into the sea as a blackmail ploy. The claims, in 2001, sparked an outcry, but John Howard, who promised to take a hard line on immigration, was re-elected with an increased majority.

In London, Crosby's plan was to encapsulate the Tory pitch in just eleven words: 'More police, cleaner hospitals, lower taxes, school discipline, controlled immigration, accountability.' The idea was for Howard to present the six policy areas as the 'simple longings' of the British people.

Not everyone at CCHQ was happy. Guy Black, Cameron's old boss at the Conservative Research Department and later Howard's press secretary, felt that the manifesto was too thin and worried that a four-week campaign based on repeating the same five commitments would soon run aground. Among those who sided with Black were George Bridges, then head of the Research Department, and Osborne, who was by then shadow Chief Secretary to the Treasury, reporting to Oliver Letwin. Underwhelmed by Letwin's presentational skills, Crosby had tasked Osborne with being 'the face and voice' of Tory Treasury policy during the campaign.

As they wrestled over messaging, Black also worried that they had nothing to say on Iraq.

> From summer 2004, I was saying to Howard and Crosby that whatever they wanted to do with the manifesto, the actual campaign would come down to Iraq, because it was going to be an Iraq War campaign. I was saying to them that if we had nothing to say on Iraq, we would be squeezed out of the game, and it would become a campaign between Labour and the Liberal Democrats. And to an extent that is what did happen towards the last week of the campaign, because of the Attorney General's leaked advice.[218] The media wanted to concentrate on Iraq, not cleaner hospitals.

It was a painful and protracted debate, in which Cameron was remarkable for his absence. Having been intimately involved in producing the manifesto, during the crucial final weeks of the campaign, he suddenly deserted.

An insider recalls: 'Cameron went AWOL. It was very noticeable. Osborne was still hanging around CCHQ, but there was no sign of Cameron at all. I actually remember Lynton, in a meeting, exploding – as Lynton does sometimes – about where Cameron was. He called him a "posh cunt". Cameron had no excuse.'

In fact he *did* have an excuse, claiming that he was required back in Witney. He enlisted Whetstone, now Howard's chief of staff, to put it about that he needed to nurture the seat. Colleagues were unconvinced.

The insider says: 'I think it was a deliberate strategy on his part. He'd decided we were going to get smacked at the election and wanted to distance himself.'

Another senior figure involved in the campaign concurs that Cameron was 'playing a quite careful game'.

---

218 Shortly before polling day, the top-secret advice of the then Attorney General, Lord Goldsmith, to Blair – prior to the Iraq invasion – was leaked to the press. It revealed that Blair had been told in a confidential minute less than two weeks before the war that British participation in the American-led invasion of Iraq could be declared illegal.

'Rachel had been telling people that because it was his first election defending Witney, he had to spend all his time there. But he had a huge majority! Michael never really questioned it much, but Lynton was much more, you know, "Where is he?"' he says.

The Tory campaign proved highly divisive. Billboards about immigration featuring the slogan 'Are you thinking what we're thinking?' were decried as racist, while a battery of policy announcements on prisoners, asylum seekers and gypsies backfired. In election diaries for *The Guardian* in 2005, Nick Clegg labelled Crosby a 'Rottweiler' and accused him of a 'savagely populist' campaign.

'No issue is safe from Howard's tireless attempt to attract attention, create a stir, and sprinkle fear and loathing in the public debate,' he wrote.[219]

In this febrile atmosphere, Cameron seems to have made a dangerous move. Having established a safe distance from party headquarters, he appears to have briefed *Telegraph* columnist Rachel Sylvester that he and Osborne were 'embarrassed' by Howard's focus on immigration. In an article published just ten days before the election, the journalist claimed two 'bright young things who are talked of as a future Prime Minister and Chancellor' were uncomfortable about the strategy. She quoted 'one member of the so-called Notting Hill group' as suggesting that there were 'more important things' to talk about.

Her treacherous source told her: 'It's about tone and emphasis rather than content of policy – but, in an election, tone and emphasis are everything. After the election we'll be wanting to do a complete makeover.'

Describing Cameron and Osborne as 'the acceptable faces of the Conservative Party', Sylvester gushed that they were 'young, clean cut, eloquent and clever…the media stars of the Tory campaign'. She predicted that they would soon wash their hands of it.

Black recalls the article prompting 'a hell of an inquest'.

'The story was huge for a day or two. The irony was that Howard hadn't been talking about immigration much, but it was one of the eleven words. It did cause terrible waves.'

A furious Whetstone was determined to smoke out the source. An insider recalls 'lots of phone calls between CCHQ and Witney, trying to get to the root of what was going on. Of course, it was all fiercely denied.'

219   Nick Clegg, *The Guardian*, 24 March 2005.

Whetstone, who initially suspected someone else, was dismayed to find the evidence pointed firmly at Cameron. It was no surprise when the investigation was 'quietly shelved'. Loyal as she was to Howard, she was not about to sell out her old friend.

When the 2005 campaign did indeed end in defeat, Cameron's quiet decision to absent himself looked well judged. Self-serving it may have been, but he had set his sights on bigger things.

PART FOUR –
TAKEOVER

20

EXTRAVAGANZA

'We couldn't believe how easy it was to take over the party.'
– George Osborne

In the historic surroundings of an exclusive private members' club, an American showman was giving a virtuoso performance. Before him sat twenty-eight men and women watching intently while he played a succession of video clips. They registered their reactions to the footage, using handheld electronic devices. The results were displayed on a monitor in the form of an electronic worm, which wriggled up and down according to whether the viewers liked what they heard.

For the most part, the worm quivered languidly, occasionally flat-lining when the audience was bored. Then the showman unveiled his *pièce de resistance* – a video clip of a smooth-looking young man with an optimistic air – and suddenly the worm perked up.

With the air of a magician who had just produced a beautiful white rabbit, the maestro breathlessly declared:

'I've never seen a turnabout like this!…We may have seen history being made.'

The date was 3 October 2005, and the video segments were of candidates in the race to become the next leader of the Conservative Party. In the Churchill Room of the Carlton Club – dubbed 'the establishment's establishment' – Frank Luntz, political pollster and self-styled 'public opinion guru' was conducting a focus group to gauge who would be most popular with ordinary voters. The experiment was being filmed for BBC *Newsnight*. The name of the youthful MP attracting so much excitement was David Cameron.

Luntz claimed the verdict of his focus group was unanimous.

'Average voters, those who would consider voting Conservative, have spoken clearly and as one. In fact, if the Labour Party's watching tonight, they're probably nervous…If these people were any indication, David Cameron was exactly what swing voters are looking for in a Conservative Party leader,' he said.

Cameron's team was ecstatic, rushing out triumphant press releases to print and broadcast media and distributing copies of Luntz's polling to every MP. In their haste, they overlooked copyright rules, running into trouble with BBC lawyers. They also breached parliamentary regulations by using an internal mailing system at Westminster to circulate footage, earning a rap over the knuckles from Commons authorities. Luckily, nobody found out.

The frenzy of activity paid off. Literally overnight, the young MP for Witney surged from rank outsider in the leadership contest to frontrunner.

As far as the BBC was concerned, Luntz was an impartial observer conducting an objective exercise. He did not declare any interest.

But all was not as it seemed.

Tentative discussions about a possible Cameron leadership had begun in 2004, when he had been an MP for three years. However, the idea did not come from the man himself. It was first mooted by MPs who wanted to stop someone else inheriting the crown: the controversial shadow Home Secretary David Davis.

For some time, it had been clear that the former SAS man would be the one to beat. He certainly had a compelling back story, having grown up on a council estate as the son of a single mother. Among acolytes, he inspired almost fanatical loyalty. However, he had as many detractors as friends. Pugnacious, arrogant and impatient, over the years he had alienated many in the parliamentary party. Those who dreaded the prospect of him as party leader began searching for an alternative. It was against this backdrop that conversations about a potential Cameron leadership bid began.

Greg Barker, a debonair Tory whip with a safe seat in East Sussex, recalls sitting down with fellow whip David Ruffley in summer 2004 and assessing the likely allegiances of every Tory to figure out whether the MP for Witney would stand a chance.

'We went through a list of names and I thought we could do it,' he recalls.

That autumn, Cameron spent a weekend at Barker's home, during which Barker sounded him out.

'He did a very unconvincing "I don't know if I'm ready" kind of thing. I wasn't bold enough to push it, but then we started having kitchen suppers in Notting Hill, talking about policy, and I was absolutely clear why we should do it,' Barker recalls.

It was not until just before the 2005 election that Cameron sat down with Hilton and Osborne to discuss the question seriously. Having privately concluded that the party was heading for a third successive election defeat, the three friends wanted to be ready for the fallout.

'It was a very extended conversation,' according to a source familiar with the discussion.

> It was interesting, because George was being touted as a potential leader as well, and the press was behind him. He was shadow Chancellor and in that sense more senior than Dave. But there was a very clear view that it was Dave who should run for the leadership. So yeah, that was the moment that the plan got explicit.

Around this time, Bruce Anderson remembers Cameron seeking his advice.

> We were in Dean and we'd had quite a lot of claret for lunch. I think we had been drinking a magnum. We left some of it for tea, and went for a walk. He asked me: 'Should I run?' I said: 'Yes, I think you should.' He said: 'It will mean changes. There won't be many long, relaxed Sunday lunches.' I said, 'Well, you've got what it needs and you can do it.' I think he'd made up his mind. Sam encouraged him. She said: 'If this party is going to recover, it more or less needs you. If we are going to stick around, then we've got to make it all work, and you can do that.'

It was not just Cameron's coterie who thought he might be the answer to the party's travails. He had also caught the eye of a number of senior backbenchers, including Nicholas Soames.

'I was thinking about the future of the party, which I have been worrying about since I became an MP. I'm quite clear David [had] a determination to try to put his generation in charge, which is what was needed,' he says. He recalls being drawn to the energy of the Notting Hill set.

> I was complete baggage – the sort of stuff you chuck up in the balcony and pretend isn't there, because I am way outside their age group. But I was very attracted to what they were doing, and their drive and determination. They had a sort of fervour to them. It wasn't a religious fervour, but a fervour of everyone sticking together, which was essential.

The 2005 general election was the failure the Notting Hill set predicted. At Cameron's own count in Witney, one observer was left in no doubt that he had set his sights on the leadership. Liz Leffman, the Liberal Democrat candidate in the constituency, recalls:

> We were sitting in the bar watching the results come in on television. He had his team on one side, and we were sitting in the corner on the other. At the time, the Lib Dems had what was called a 'decapitation policy', which was about targeting shadow Cabinet members, and one of them was David Davis. Most of the time, when the results came in and the Tories won or held on to seats, everybody was cheering and jumping around. My husband gave me a nudge at one point because the results were coming in for David Davis, and you could see the intensity on David Cameron's face. It was palpable. He was watching really closely to see what happened, because it was a marginal seat. And when David Davis won, all Cameron's chums were going, 'Yay! Hurrah!' and Cameron just sat there looking very thoughtful. My husband said to me, 'He's going to go for the leadership.' It was absolutely clear to me from that moment that he had the leadership in his sights.

How hungry he was for it was another question. Throughout Cameron's life, others had helped manoeuvre him into good jobs. With the exception of his long quest to find a safe parliamentary seat, he was not used to having to try very hard for good things to come his way. Now, once again, energetic figures with their own interest in pushing him up the greasy pole were ready to assist. The first, and perhaps most important, of those who helped smooth his path was his old boss, Michael Howard.

Having led the party to defeat on 5 May, Howard was keen to step down immediately. What happened next was crucial to Cameron's ascent. Casting aside his own desire to quit straight away, the outgoing party leader – no fan of David Davis – set about maximising the chances of a successful campaign by someone else by staying in post for a further six months. Encouraged by Rachel Whetstone, he declared that he would remain opposition leader until autumn. It denied the shadow Home Secretary a swift coronation.

Howard admits the timing of his departure was governed by a 'wider agenda'. Publicly, he will only say that he wanted to spare the party from making another mistake.

> When I took over, I was the third leader of the Conservative Party in three years. The one thing I wanted to avoid was a quick decision and then things not turning out brilliantly, and people turning around six months later and saying, 'If only we hadn't rushed into this.'

Privately, however, he was hoping that either Osborne or Cameron would fill his shoes and he knew they needed time to get their act together. Of the two, his preference was for Osborne. Though he liked and respected Cameron, he told a number of confidants he thought the younger man was the one to watch, a view that may have been reinforced when Cameron declined the offer of the shadow chancellorship in his post-election reshuffle. Instead, Cameron asked for the shadow education brief.

A senior party figure says: 'I think at that point Howard may have thought Cameron did not have the killer instinct. Howard was very, sort of, "I think Osborne is the man for the future."'

However, at just thirty-three, Osborne felt he was too young and lacked sufficient experience outside politics to stand. A former Tory aide overheard him say he thought Cameron had better credentials.

> Osborne had had a good election. He had been a good media performer and had come out of it well. But it was always clear it was going to be Cameron first. There was never any tension [between

them] in that way. Osborne said to Cameron, in my hearing, at one point, 'Look, you've got the Carlton thing; you've got that space I don't have.'

During this period, the aide recalls Osborne, Cameron and Hilton being 'in and out of each other's offices all the time'. Hilton, who had been working as a special adviser to Maurice Saatchi while the latter was party chairman under Howard, had failed to find a parliamentary seat, but remained very much in circulation.

'They would be chewing over the issues of the day and how the party was positioning itself, talking about how things would play out, this way or that,' the source recalls.

Why did Cameron turn down the shadow chancellorship? He probably felt that it did not present much political opportunity. After all, the economy was robust and Brown had seen off six shadow Chancellors in eight years. He may also have calculated that the post would hold him back, having observed Blair work his way to the top of the Labour Party via roles that were less demanding than the shadow chancellorship.[220]

He was also genuinely interested in the education portfolio, as a result of his long battle to secure suitable special needs services for Ivan. Alex Deane, a former Tory staffer who worked for him for six months when he was shadow Education Secretary, recalls how quickly and seriously he took to the brief.

'When DC arrived, he could have just used it as a placeholder, and spent all his time pushing for the leadership. He didn't do that. He threw himself into it.'

Deane was an experienced hand on the shadow education team, having worked for the previous incumbent, Tim Collins. A sharp operator himself, he says he was quickly outpaced by his new boss.

Within about three weeks, he left me for dead! People talk sometimes about him being lazy, but I just don't recognise that description at all from the man I spent six close months working with. I saw somebody who immediately had the facts and figures at his fingertips. He would turn up to meetings and demand to know how many

220 Francis Elliott and James Hanning, p. 276.

people worked in the department for education, or how many people were doing this or that. Clearly that was the sort of thing he would have known if he was doing my role so, within a few days, I made sure I knew it. It was also clear that once it went into his head, he never lost it. He mastered the brief, and wanted to change the team, in ways he didn't have to – because it was clear things were going to change either way, come the leadership election – but he wanted to make something of it. He cared about it.

Thanks to the way Howard had arranged his departure, nominations for the leadership would not formally open until autumn, but the Davis machine was already cranking up. In the weeks immediately after the election, his acolytes deployed a combination of menace and charm to galvanise support. Many MPs who were not natural Davis fans assumed he was unbeatable and reluctantly fell into line.

One MP says: 'They were bullying people into signing up. I knew a lot of people who didn't want to vote for him but were pressurised into it. They couldn't see anybody else getting anywhere and they thought it was the least worst option. They were not natural allies of David Davis.' By contrast, Cameron was still weighing up his options. Publicly, he refused to confirm or deny that he was standing, but he did nothing to discourage speculation.

The Berkshire MP Richard Benyon, a childhood friend, bumped into him in the division lobby shortly after the general election and quizzed him about his intentions.

'Are you going to go for it?' Benyon asked.

Cameron was non-committal, but airily invited Benyon to his office for a 'chat' with colleagues. At the appointed time, Benyon couldn't find the venue, and was amused to bump into Boris Johnson looking equally lost.

'Are we going to the same place?' asked Benyon sheepishly.

'Secret squirrel meeting? Yes,' came the reply. The pair eventually located Cameron's office, where they found a handful of other MPs, including Nicholas Soames, Michael Gove, Greg Barker, Hugo Swire, John Greenway (who would later jump ship) and Andrew Robathan.

Perched on the end of his desk, Cameron gave a few words about 'shaking up the party', and more or less left it at that.

Robathan recalls: 'My memory of that meeting was that it was a preliminary sounding out, to see who was going to be there, and who really believed he could win. It was quite a mixed bag of colleagues.'

If Cameron were to go for it, his campaign would need money. From an early stage, it was evident that this would not be a problem. His old university friend Andrew Feldman, who had big business connections, had been putting out feelers to wealthy potential backers. The response was encouraging. Among those keen to offer support was Lord Harris, a carpet tycoon who had invited Cameron to his house in Eton Square to try to persuade him to stand. Worth some £250 million, the peer would later provide helicopter rides plus a healthy £90,000 to Cameron's campaign. Lord Chadlington, Cameron's landlord and neighbour in Dean, chipped in £10,000, as did his old colleague from Carlton, Edwina Paine. At least thirty-nine other individuals would eventually contribute significant sums.[221]

On 29 June, Cameron delivered a speech to the Policy Exchange think tank, setting out his vision for the party's future. It went way beyond his brief as shadow Education Secretary and was widely interpreted as confirmation that he would run. Yet he had still not committed himself.

The speech was a broad-brush affair that ticked many traditional right-wing boxes, attacking excess taxation and regulation, the 'unmistakable coarsening and vulgarising of national life', the expansion of the state, and deficiencies in state education. In music to the ears of grassroots Conservatives, he also proselytised about marriage, calling for tax breaks for married couples. Though he described himself as a 'moderniser', framing the speech in terms of what a 'real moderniser' meant for the party, there was little meat on the bone. Indeed, he played down his plans for radical reform.

'You never get anywhere by trashing your own brand,' he said.

Listening to the speech, Andrew Cooper, a former senior figure at Central Office who had gone on to found the polling firm Populus and was to become Cameron's director of strategy at No. 10, recalls feeling dispirited.

'It was very safe and unchallenging, very conventional. As a result it wasn't really sparking any enthusiasm. Davis looked like he was unstoppable,' he says.

James O'Shaughnessy, then a researcher for Policy Exchange (he would eventually become Cameron's director of policy in No. 10), is blunter.

---

221   *Daily Mail*, 24 November 2011; *The Guardian*, 2 June 2006.

The speech was really crap! It was so disappointing. My feeling was sort of, hang on a minute, you're meant to be our great hope? It was meant to be a leadership speech, what he stood for and so on, but it wasn't obvious, having listened to it, what he wanted. It wasn't a call to arms. At Policy Exchange, we had lots of interesting stuff about Conservative means and progressive ends – helping people get on better in life through markets, but with a social mission – but that stuff just didn't seem to be reflected.

The measured tone reflected Cameron's own uncertainty about his pitch. At this stage he was far from the radical 'moderniser' he would later appear. Indeed, the idea that Cameron always wanted to overhaul the party is a popular misconception. For years, he lagged behind some in his own social circle in terms of conviction that the party needed fundamental reform.

As far as Cooper was concerned, few of this set in the late 1990s and early 2000s, least of all Cameron himself, truly grasped the scale of the problem facing the party. He found their dinner-table discussions in this early period frustrating.

He recalls:

I was being quite grumpy with everyone. I didn't understand why people didn't get it. I was very unreasonable, demanding that they all get the totality of how bad I thought it was; and he didn't, so I didn't take him particularly seriously. I think in the discussions we had and the dinners and things, the frustration was whether people were willing to accept that some of the ways we were seen by voters [were] true, instead of just a perception problem. There was a tendency to think that John Major was weak and hopeless, and the MPs were behaving terribly; and once that was past, that this younger, fresher generation coming through would be enough of a change on its own.

One evening in the early 2000s, the usual crowd met for dinner at Soho House, where they had a heated debate. For Cooper, who came to admire Cameron later, the attitude of the young MP and several of his friends in that discussion encapsulated the problem.

He remembers:

> It was an argument about tax cuts. And it was a discussion about what sort of tax cut the Tories could offer that would be 'the modern tax cut' that would win over voters. As they saw it, the Tory Party is the party of tax cuts or it's the party of nothing. My argument was, that's a completely delusional view; because with voters, [we were] associated with putting up people's taxes when we promised not to, and introducing a massive, definitively unpopular tax [the poll tax] under Thatcher – so it's not how people see us! Secondly, all the evidence is, at the moment, that all that voters are concerned about is whether we believe in public services and if so what's the Conservative approach to those? To bang on about tax cuts is just as bad as banging on about Europe.

He recalls that most of those present at the dinner, including Osborne, Hilton and Whetstone, disagreed. Gove and Boles were more sympathetic.

The Tories' third successive defeat in 2005 made the case for change in the Conservative Party inescapable. The party's predicament was set out unambiguously in *Smell the Coffee*, a comprehensive analysis of the Tories' brand problem based on detailed polling.[222] Voters thought the Conservatives were out of touch, did not understand or care about ordinary people, and were even less likely than other parties to keep their promises. This meant the Tories needed to do more than come up with new policies: even the most attractive proposals would not impress voters who mistrusted the party's motivations and doubted its ability to deliver. Inevitably, *whoever* won the leadership contest would have to do some 'modernising'. Even though Davis was widely characterised as a 'status quo' candidate, the shadow Home Secretary also ran on a ticket of 'modern Conservatism'. Indeed, many months before Cameron claimed the agenda as his own, senior party figures were working on plans to rebrand the party, having discovered its image, not its policies, was deterring voters. Led by Francis Maude, this work began immediately after the election defeat in 2005, and involved devising proposals that could be adopted by whoever won.

In terms of modernisation, the difference between Cameron and Davis

---

222   Michael A. Ashcroft, *Smell the Coffee: A Wake-Up Call for the Conservative Party* (Politico's Media, 2005).

was largely – though not wholly – cosmetic: Cameron would later make a virtue of championing reform, while Davis did not seek to represent himself as a total break from the past. It helped that Cameron was a relatively newly elected MP, and not yet forty. Perhaps he felt this was enough. To the frustration of those who wanted to change more, faster, the Cameroons were prone to see themselves as the personification of modernisation. As Hilton was fond of saying privately, 'Dave *is* the change.'

Cameron was still keeping his options open – not least because winning over the parliamentary party was proving such an uphill struggle. Some MPs who liked the look of him felt he was simply too inexperienced.

Greg Clark, the MP for Tunbridge Wells, recalls:

> I knew he was a serious contender and I went to see him in his office before I announced my decision to support David Davis. It was a nice, friendly conversation. I said, 'Having worked for three Leaders of the Opposition…I know just what a tough job it is, and how much gets thrown at you; how the storms come, and you'll be tossed around.' David had only been in Parliament for four years, and I thought that when even someone as experienced as William Hague ended up being quite badly buffeted by the storms, he didn't quite have enough experience to withstand that buffeting. Whereas Davis was a longstanding MP and frontbencher; pretty tough.

Clark assured Cameron his decision to support Davis was not personal.

Cameron replied that he was confident he could take the heat.

'I think I would be able to stand up for my views and principles, and wouldn't be blown off course, and I hope that I'll be able to show that over time,' he told Clark.

At this stage, few on Cameron's side believed victory was possible. Among activists who feared Davis would lead the party into the abyss, there was mounting concern. One recalls a panic-stricken discussion over dinner at Benyon's stately home in Berkshire.

> Everyone thought Davis was going to win. I remember going to Richard's huge pile in Newbury – the only time in my life where they actually passed the port around! – with a bunch of modernising

types. Nick Boles and Greg Barker were there. There was an argument around the table about how we were going to protect the modernising agenda if DD won. Richard Benyon, who was on Cameron's campaign, was saying, 'You haven't seen the best of us yet. There's more to come!'

The following week, one of Cameron's supporters lunched with Osborne and lamented that his campaign – such as it was – was going nowhere. The shadow Chancellor concurred. It was at this point, according to the well-placed source, that those around Cameron decided that his best chance of winning was to big himself up as the 'modernising' candidate.

'George said that he and Gove had been discussing this and what they were trying to persuade Cameron was that whether he liked it or not, he was the modernising candidate, just because he was the young, fresh, different one,' according to the supporter.

Fearing it would all be over before it had begun, shortly before recess, Osborne and Gove confronted their candidate.

'They said, look, this campaign is going to fade and die. We need to do something. We need to reframe you as the bold, exciting, modernising one, because that's the natural role you have in this field,' according to the insider.

As the Commons emptied for summer recess, Davis still looked invincible.

Andrew Mitchell, his campaign chief, remembers: 'We were absolutely on top. DD was the crown prince; the heir apparent. Cameron and Osborne were just young MPs.' With embarrassment, he recalls briefing journalists that the young Turks needed time to mature.

> I remember saying to *The Times* that I had recently been given a present of a bottle of Chateau Latour. I told them I put it in my cellar to keep it there for many years, because it was a bit young in the bottle. I said, 'In a few years, it will be absolutely magnificent, and I give the same advice to George and David.' It was a joke, but it all appeared in the paper.

Keen to bolster his credentials, Cameron replied by embarking on a hunt for big-name supporters to lend his campaign legitimacy. One key name on his list was John Major. He asked for the endorsement of his old boss, but it never came. The former Prime Minister has remained curiously tight-lipped about his opinion of his successor, claiming he has no particular memories of Cameron from their period working together in 1992. Given how much contact they had, this is hard to believe, and suggests that there is little warmth between them. (Indeed, while Cameron was Prime Minister, Major was at times distinctly unhelpful towards his former adviser. In the run-up to the 2015 election, for example, he suggested Cameron's campaign 'lacked passion'. He threw himself at the Prime Minister's service during the EU referendum campaign, however, becoming an outspoken advocate for remaining in the EU, and a fierce critic of the Brexit camp.)

Yet despite their comfortable position, Mitchell warned Davis and his supporters against complacency.

He recalls:

> On the last Tuesday of term in July, there was a big meeting in Davis's office, down the shadow Cabinet corridor. We invited fifty MPs who had pledged their support. I got up on a chair, and said, 'Let's hope you all have a jolly good recess, but don't forget, we're in a real bat-tle here. Remember, the favourite never wins in the Tory Party! I got hooted at by colleagues. Then we all went off for the holidays.

As Davis sauntered back to Yorkshire, having told Mitchell he needed to take the whole of August off, Cameron's camp were preparing to transform their man into a winner.

That summer, Cameron took not one but two holidays. Neither was exotic, but it is interesting that, as he prepared to run for the second most powerful political job in the land, from a position well behind the favourite, he felt able to go away. Luckily for him, others were working hard on his behalf.

His first break was to his in-laws' place on Jura; the second to Devon (where Samantha had a time-share), where he was joined by Hilton. They spent some of the holiday working on a policy speech, but were hampered by the poor mobile signal. When they needed to send an email, they would trudge up a nearby hill and put a laptop on top of a bail of straw, at which level it was just about possible to get enough reception.

By now, Hilton was giving it his all, and was frustrated by the lack of media interest in the earnest policy proposals on social responsibility and quality of life he was cooking up with Cameron. But while Hilton was putting heart and soul into it, Cameron's drive was less apparent. Bruce Anderson was among those who were unimpressed, telling his old friend bluntly that he thought his efforts were lacklustre.

'It won't start until September,' Cameron shrugged.

Anderson says now – with some admiration – that his friend simply 'has a slow pulse and doesn't panic'.

Over the summer, relations between the Cameron and Davis camps were surprisingly cordial. Mitchell and Osborne, who like each other, were in regular contact by text message. In late summer, Mitchell mischievously invited Osborne and a bunch of Cameroons and their wives to a 'riotous' dinner party at his country house in Nottinghamshire, where there was much jovial banter about defections.

'I remember it was very late; wine had been consumed, and one of the wives shouted at me: "You're one of us! Why aren't you supporting David Cameron?" At this point, Cameron's team could have fitted into a taxi. We had a great time.'

Never off duty, Osborne took a sneaky look at Mitchell's visitor's book, gleaning valuable information about his rival's campaign and its personnel. Afterwards, Cameron was glad to receive a text from Osborne reassuring him nobody had crossed sides.

Cameron was still in a position where he could pull out of the contest without huge loss of face: he had yet to announce he was standing. Some claim that towards the end of the summer recess, he toyed with throwing in the towel. This is emphatically denied by Hilton, but Mitchell is adamant that at least one such discussion took place.

'The Cameroons definitely had a meeting where Cameron said, "Shall we just throw in our lot with Davis?" I don't know where it was; I don't think it was in London, but there was definitely a meeting. They were quite close to packing it in,' he says.

Over breakfast in early September, Robathan, who was keeping a tally of supporters, persuaded the shadow Education Secretary that there was still all to play for.

He recalls:

David said to me, 'Everyone tells me I'm not going to win.' I sat
down with him with a list of 195 names. I went through them, and
I said, 'You've got 100 votes there.' He asked how I knew. I replied,
'Because they don't want to vote for anyone else.' So I think that
was quite an encouragement. Sam Cameron said to me, when I met
her, 'Oh, you're the person who keeps telling David he can win. He
comes back and says, "Everyone says I'm going to lose except for
Andrew Robathan."'

Robathan's encouragement seems to have galvanised the candidate. Just as
Cameron had promised Anderson, in September, his embryonic campaign
began acquiring structure and pace. Office space was rented in Greycoat Place
near party headquarters and a team was put in place – which included Kate
Fall, as well as George Eustice and Gabby Bertin, both of whom resigned from
the party's press office to throw their weight behind him. Dan Ritterband, a
young ex-Saatchi & Saatchi executive, was drafted in to handle marketing.
Ritterband recalls a youthful buzz in the office.

It was a really good environment. I liked them. I thought, 'If we can
really modernise the party to be about quality of life, equal marriage, ambition, and all those things, then that's the kind of party
I can sign up to!

Steve [Hilton] was the energy, the ideas, the passion, while George
was the steadying, tactical hand. It was a good balance.

On 29 September 2005, Cameron finally committed himself, publicly
announcing his intention to run. In addition to Davis, he would be up
against former chancellor Ken Clarke, still a popular figure in the wider party,
and the ambitious Scottish right-winger Liam Fox, who had a considerable
following among Thatcherites.

Cameron's official launch was staged just a couple of hours after Davis's
took place. The 'back to back' timing was deliberately designed by Cameron's
camp to present the contest as a two-horse race. Neither Clarke nor Fox bothered with a formal launch: the former simply declared it was 'Time to Win';
while the latter, targeting Eurosceptic right-wingers, unveiled plans to pull the
party out of a centre-right but federalist group in the European Parliament.

Davis's launch was in a fusty oak-panelled room in the Institution of Civil Engineers, just off Parliament Square. Mitchell admits they didn't put much thought into it.

'I just wanted somewhere that was big enough and free. We were top dog at that point,' he recalls. With the benefit of hindsight, he acknowledges it was 'very wooden and traditional'.

'It was rooted in the past, to build on the Thatcher inheritance. We were trying to convey traditional Tory values.'

In a particularly damaging comment, one newspaper columnist wrote of 'leery-eyed whips' hovering at the back of the room.

By contrast, Cameron's team pulled out all the stops. Conscious that it was make or break, Ritterband and Hilton left nothing to chance. They lavished resources on the visuals, using mood lighting and a contemporary set. In place of the usual lukewarm tea and digestive biscuits, journalists trooping over from Davis's launch were offered strawberry smoothies and chocolate brownies. Feldman, who had casually agreed to foot the bill, was apparently dismayed to find himself forking out some £20,000.[223]

'We just wanted to do it differently,' Ritterband recalls. 'Having come from a commercial background, I knew those little touches make a difference. The message was, "There's a new boy in town." The mood was infectious.'

Despite the attention to detail, the attitude among journalists arriving for the launch was dismissive.

'They were like weary parents indulging a small child's fantasy,' says one.

Ninety minutes later, the atmosphere was transformed. Cameron had wowed by speaking without notes, on a theme of 'modern, compassionate Conservatism'. He further impressed hard-bitten hacks by devoting a full hour to a question-and-answer session. It was a watershed. On the television news bulletins that night, both BBC's political editor Nick Robinson and his ITV counterpart Tom Bradby enthused about the dramatic shake-up in the contest.

The excitement spread quickly. Canvassing chairmen of constituency party branches in the days that followed, Ritterband detected an extraordinary shift.

> I remember doing the ring-round of Association chairmen to get an
> idea of numbers [who supported Cameron] and work out where

---

223 Private information.

we were going to take him on tour. We did it plenty of times. We set up a spreadsheet, and if they were dithering, we'd get Dave to call them. There was real positivity.

For the first time, Davis's team began to feel nervous. In a major error of judgement, they responded by turning the thumbscrews on waverers. Rumours swirled of threats and intimidation. MPs who had planned to back him began switching to the other side.

One of Cameron's organisers says:

> A lot of them had been pressurised into supporting Davis, but they backed away. Davis is a twat of the first order, very idle, and when they were presented with an alternative, they saw it was a better way forward. A lot of voting for Cameron was in many ways a vote against Davis.

The format of the leadership contest gave the party's 250,000 or so members the final say. As a former party chairman, Davis could have developed a powerful support base. Instead, he had developed a reputation for 'talking down' at people. By contrast, Cameron went out of his way to charm.

A former Tory staffer says: 'There are always two sides to people. Cameron, in my view, made sure "Bad Cameron" was only seen by a minority of people, whereas "Good Cameron" was seen by most people. DD was the opposite – basically a minority of people saw "Good DD".'

By now, Cameron had a significant secret supporter: the party machine.

A former Central Office source says: 'CCHQ was supposed to be completely neutral, but it wasn't. There was a widespread feeling that we should skip a generation. We had to be very careful not to let this be known, but everybody was rooting for David in a big way.'

The next big test would be party conference.

The annual seaside jamboree, which kicked off on 3 October, was a three-day-long beauty parade for the leadership candidates. The first ballot of MPs was just a fortnight away. Mitchell had instructed his candidate to spend summer preparing a killer speech.

DD was supposed to go off and think brilliant thoughts for his speech. I said to him, 'Listen, you've got to come up with a speech about why you want to become PM.' He said, 'Yes, yes, yes, but I've got to take August off. I'm knackered.' Well, he never really got round to doing it.

Alarmed, Mitchell set about assembling a team to write the speech for him.

'I thought, if he's not going to write it himself, we'll get the best speech makers in the party to do it,' he recalls.

So I got Damian Green, David Willetts, Paul Goodman, Nick Herbert and Iain Dale involved, all of whom are very good. I thought if I asked them nicely to produce the speech of the year, they'd do it. Of course, if I'd thought it through, I'd have realised you can't write a speech by committee, particularly with a bunch of prima donnas who all have serious ideas. It was a massive failure. Conference arrived and we had no proper speech.

To show some pizzazz, the Davis camp had chartered a helicopter to whisk him to Blackpool in style. They set off from Battersea as if they were preparing to take power. However, Mitchell recalls feeling uneasy.

'I remember looking down at the English countryside from the helicopter, worrying about the speech,' he says.

To compound the situation, Davis's conference diary was stuffed with engagements. It was another mistake.

'Everyone wanted a bit of Davis, so we agreed back in the summer that we should do all these meetings,' Mitchell laments. 'We thought he was the king, about to be crowned. So he arrived with no speech, and a fucking massive programme, and he was on the back foot. There wasn't even any time to rehearse.'

On the opening night of party conference, BBC2's *Newsnight* carried out what it admitted was a 'totally unscientific' straw poll of delegates in Blackpool's Winter Gardens, handing out different-coloured wristbands to supporters of the rival leadership candidates. When Davis appeared in the lobby, flanked by his henchmen, a reporter was unable to interest him in one of his own wristbands. He swept past imperiously. By contrast,

Cameron stopped to joke with the *Newsnight* crew, appearing to enjoy the encounter.

Newsnight dropped its real bombshell later in the programme, when it carried the feature with Luntz, in which focus group participants appeared to be wowed by Cameron. The film concluded with one woman gushing: 'I think David Cameron has actually reinvented politics for me.'

The poll had a spectacular impact. In an article for *The Observer* head-lined 'How a celebrity pollster created Cameron', Nick Cohen would later describe it as a 'decisive factor' in the leadership contest.

'Cameron came from nowhere because *Newsnight* commissioned a focus group...that appeared to prove that the young politician could become extraordinarily popular and the Conservatives believed him,' he wrote, after Cameron won.[224]

It has now emerged that Luntz had strong links with several members of Cameron's campaign team, raising serious questions about the impartiality of the *Newsnight* piece.

Ironically, it would all be long forgotten were it not for Luntz himself. In late June 2012, he was invited to No. 10 to give a private presentation on 'words that work' to a number of staffers. During an informal discussion afterwards, he was asked about the *Newsnight* poll. To the astonishment of one present, he declared, in terms, that he had deliberately presented the findings to show Cameron in a positive light. According to our source, he also suggested that he had been paid for his work, not by *Newsnight*, but by a wealthy Cameron supporter. This has been impossible to substantiate, and today Luntz emphati-cally denies it. Our source, a well-known and respected Westminster figure who has no axe to grind with Luntz, remains adamant that this is what he heard. Furthermore, early in our research for this book, a former member of Cameron's campaign appeared to substantiate the suggestion that Luntz had been paid for his help, saying a Tory donor brought him to the UK to 'help' Cameron's campaign. The source later retracted the claim, which could not be verified independently. Luntz insists no money changed hands.

What is not disputed is that Luntz was at Oxford at the same time as both Johnson and Gove – two of Cameron's earliest supporters – and knew them both well. After they all graduated, Luntz brought the pair over to America to take part in various debates. (He also knew Ed Llewellyn – Cameron's

224 *The Observer*, 10 December 2006.

old friend from the CRD and his future chief of staff – who he says lived across the street from him in Oxford.)

A source involved in Cameron's campaign claims he 'came over as a kind of friend' during the leadership contest, though the specific pull was the opportunity to appear on *Newsnight*. Luntz claims he was less well known then, and it was a chance to raise his profile.

Had *Newsnight* been aware that Luntz was so close to members of Cameron's campaign team, they might have thought twice about running the piece. A number of sources on Cameron's team concede that Luntz was able to skew the results, less by sleight of hand than by putting his own gloss on the responses from participants. This was not intrinsically dishonest – any bias may even have been subconscious on Luntz's part. Of course, *Newsnight* producers, blissfully ignorant of any connection between Luntz and the Cameron camp, may have played their part, in the way the film was edited and cut. After all, exciting results made for a better story.

'I think it's fair to say that in any kind of polling or research, you can mould things slightly to the way you want. Frank was just so overly excited about the way he described Cameron, that it came off very good for us,' the source admits, adding: 'We believed the polling, because we believed in our candidate. But timing wise, it was extraordinarily helpful.'

The media buzz created by the poll took Cameron's team by surprise. According to the source:

> We genuinely never thought it would have such an impact. We were pumping out a link to the show, and the BBC told us we had to take it down, as it was copyright. We sent out a load of DVDs and that was a copyright infringement too, so they stopped us. And we got into trouble because we used the internal mail of the parliamentary system to send it to every MP. We got away with that.

In America, Luntz is a controversial figure. The pollster's handling of a focus group for Fox News in August 2015, carried out during the first Republican presidential debate, infuriated billionaire businessman and presidential hopeful Donald Trump, who publicly accused him of picking 'anti-Trump panels' and described his focus groups as a 'total joke'. Lashing out at Luntz on Twitter, Trump declared that the self-styled public opinion guru's polls were 'rigged' and that his company had 'run out of $' in 2011.[225]

Luntz hit back, accusing Trump of resorting to 'fuck you' politics[226] and insisting that his only interest has been accurately assessing the presidential race. He remains a regular contributor on the Fox News channel. It is not the first dispute over his polling, however. In 1997, he was criticised by the American Association for Public Opinion Research, an organisation of which he was not a member, for refusing to release poll data to support some of his results. Three years later, he was censured by the National Council on Public Polls for allegedly misrepresenting the results of focus groups he had conducted during the 2000 Republican Convention.

One of Cameron's coterie says that Luntz had long been keen to work with the Conservatives. Speaking about the *Newsnight* poll, this second source says: 'Looking back at it, the way Frank represented it was that it was a much more clear-cut and overwhelming vote for Cameron than actually happened.'

In his *Observer* piece, Nick Cohen described Luntz as a 'mediocre propagandist', writing:

> British pollsters tell me that Luntz's work for *Newsnight* shouldn't have been allowed to influence a parish council election, never mind the future of a great party. If you can't follow their case against him, their overall explanation is easy to grasp: a well-run focus group could never fill fifteen minutes of airtime. It would be too boring. To begin with, standard focus groups have six to eight members, but a handful of people isn't an impressive sight on television, so *Newsnight* had Luntz meet twenty-eight voters.

All that can be said for sure is that the *Newsnight* poll that worked such wonders for Cameron was murkier than Luntz had viewers believe.

225 @realDonaldTrump: '@John832TheTruth: @FrankLuntz your focus groups are rigged and your company ran out of $ in 2011. KEEP SPEAKING THE TRUTH! TRUMP 2016!♡'

226 http://www.politico.com/story/2015/08/fox-luntz-blasted-trump-donald-koch-seminar-121466.html.

Fired up by his *Newsnight* coup, the following day, Cameron gave the speech of his life.

'I hadn't written anything until that weekend, and I remember a whole bunch of us went out to lunch – Danny Finkelstein, George, a few others – and talked about what I should do, and then I went home with Steve and we wrote the speech together,' Cameron recalled. It was penned in Hilton's poky hotel room, which had the misfortune of being located above the kitchen and had a radiator that would not turn off. In its sweaty confines, Cameron geared himself up for his make-or-break moment. Just as he had done to win his seat in Witney, he ditched the lectern and delivered it all from memory. 'It was a big roll of the dice,' he later admitted.[227]

Wearing a brand-new suit designed by the fashionable tailor Timothy Everest (hastily purchased by Samantha from Blackpool's M&S), he sauntered around the stage, addressing the audience with ease. His pitch was unremittingly optimistic, exuding what the Tories desperately needed: hope. It prompted a standing ovation. A beaming Samantha, heavily pregnant, joined him on stage. He was photographed tenderly patting her stomach, while whispering in her ear. 'I love you' were the words reported in the press the following day. Samantha later confessed that the exchange was rather less romantic: 'Am I sweating too much?'[228]

For his part, Davis gave a respectable, workmanlike performance. It was not enough.

As the applause died down, political editors rushed back to the media room to consider their verdict. In less than a minute, they had agreed the 'line': Cameron's performance had been spectacular while Davis's had flopped.

'From that moment onwards, we were fucked. We were managing failure,' Mitchell recalls.

> Straight after the speeches, I went to find Trevor Kavanagh [the then political editor of *The Sun*], and he was very pro-Cameron. What he said was that he'd decided he was going to go with Cameron. He was trying to find reasons to justify it. From that time on, we were on the back foot.

227 David Cameron and Dylan Jones, p. 84.
228 Francis Elliott and James Hanning, p. 296.

It got worse. The next morning, the Cameroons had put a note under everyone's door in the hotel. Brilliant! It was Hilton's idea. As I headed to the station to catch the train, a very pretty, lovely girl came up, wearing a Cameron sweatshirt, and said to me, with a big smile: 'Would you like one of these leaflets?' I said: 'Thanks very much' and took the leaflet off her. I knew we had been outclassed.

Back in London, Davis's team held a council of war without their candidate.

'There was a bit of black humour, but it was pretty tense,' Mitchell recalls. 'Davis had gone back to Yorkshire. The next day, stuff from our meeting leaked. We knew then that we were in big trouble, because successful teams don't leak. There was finger-pointing going on, and things were starting to splinter. Some of our supporters started to flake away.'

The final weeks of the campaign were not all plain sailing for Cameron. During this critical period, he came under intense pressure to come clean about his personal use of recreational drugs. He was first ambushed on the subject at a fringe meeting at conference on the same day as his big speech. Asked whether he had taken drugs at Oxford, he replied blandly that he had had a 'normal university experience'.

'There were things that I did then that I don't think I should talk about now that I'm a politician,' he said dismissively.

It was a 'non-denial' and journalists scented blood. Under further inquisition during the rest of the campaign, he stuck doggedly to the line. The truth, as we have seen, is that he took soft drugs at school and at university, and he has never denied taking cocaine in his twenties. Perhaps he simply calculated that nobody could prove it, and he was right.

On 6 December 2005, Cameron became the twenty-first leader of the Tory Party, after securing more than double the number of votes from party members as David Davis.

The speed and relative ease with which the Notting Hill set co-opted the Conservative Party took even its lead figures by surprise.

'We couldn't believe how easy it was to take over the party,' Osborne privately remarked later.

Was Cameron his own creation, or was he manufactured by a powerful cabal, rooted in Notting Hill but with tentacles well beyond W11, who saw him as their best prospect of seizing power? According to one of his Eton contemporaries, Tory grandees were making contingency plans for a long stretch in the political wilderness as much as a decade earlier.

The source says:

> In the mid-1990s, the Tory Party was exhausted, divided and rudderless after a decade and a half of rule. I remember discussing this with an ex-Tory minister at an Eton dinner. This individual said to me that a suitably qualified Old Etonian could take the party and lead it back to power over a decade or so. He encouraged me personally to undertake this and offered assistance. I told a few other Etonians of my vintage of this opportunity (not Cameron), but they and I did nothing. Cameron went on to do exactly that.

The source hypothesises that Tory grandees had long been 'out looking for talent', and that rather than being 'self-made', Cameron was 'manufactured' to fit the bill. He would not be the first. Alec Douglas-Home, who succeeded Harold Macmillan as Tory leader in 1963, was also an Old Etonian 'moderniser' who rose to prominence rapidly and seemingly from nowhere, aided by a chummy world of gentlemen's clubs and private smoking rooms. Thatcher, on the other hand, made her way up the ranks slowly, with little expectation and even fewer allies.

Tantalising as it is to imagine a shadowy group of Old Etonians carving up the future leadership of the country, much as they had more than forty years earlier, this probably tells us more about the sense of entitlement among the school's alumni than it does about how Cameron came to power. Yet, right from the start, he was just one of a cast of characters in his own show.

Though he was ambitious enough and he was confident he had what it took for the top job, he was never desperate for it. According to one who knew him intimately in his twenties and thirties, he never expected to become Prime Minister, nor expressed any particular desire to do so – though he thought he would reach the Cabinet.

Others projected their drive and ambition on to him, and he was happy to be a vehicle for their ideas. It took Hilton's energy and zeal to get him onto the pitch, and Osborne's tactics to open the goal. He hit the back of the net, but only because of these two brilliant players. What he presented as his unique selling point – his eagerness to 'modernise' the party – was neither unique nor his.

Beyond the efforts of the Notting Hill set, and of Hilton and Osborne in particular, mighty forces were at work, seeking somebody who could make the Conservatives electable again. Their agendas differed widely, and their efforts did not coalesce until the final few weeks and days. From the outgoing party leader to the sympathetic pollster to the journalists who just wanted a good story about the triumph of the underdog, they propelled Cameron to power. Now he had to prove he meant business.

21

COSMETICS

'Two old fogeys…and me!'

– Cameron

Trussed up against the Arctic chill in a pair of black salopettes, Cameron surveyed the pristine frozen wilderness through his reflective shades.

'Take off the glasses. You look a bit *Eurotrash*!' his spin doctor instructed.

The newly elected Leader of the Opposition laughed and removed the offending eyewear, smoothing his hair. Squinting into the dazzling white light, he adopted a different pose.

'Got your money shot yet?' he quipped, grinning at the photographer.

It was April 2006 and Cameron was on a glacier on a remote Norwegian archipelago, three hours by sled ride from the nearest civilisation. The primary purpose of the trip was to observe the impact of climate change on the Svalbard icecaps, but of equal importance was the image he projected to voters and Conservative Party members still adapting to the arrival of a fresh face on the political centre stage.

Accompanied by an expert from the Worldwide Fund for Nature, he had arrived in the region by private jet, having first offset the estimated carbon emissions. Just one photographer and one television crew were invited to accompany him. Their footage would be beamed around the world.

The young snapper, Andrew Parsons, knew the new Tory leader well. In what would prove the shrewdest move of his career, he had stuck with Cameron during the earliest days of the leadership contest when everyone else thought he was a no-hoper. They had spent hours on the road travelling to constituency hustings in a beat-up Ford Mondeo, the candidate sustaining himself between engagements with cheap sandwiches from petrol stations and the occasional drag on a cigarette. Now they trusted each other enough for Cameron to agree to risky photo stunts, safe in the knowledge that if the pictures were a disaster they would never see the light of day.

'Let's try something with the dogs,' Parsons suggested, gesturing towards a pack of huskies waiting to tow them across the ice.

'OK,' Cameron replied gamely, and began rounding up the animals.

Half an hour and much flying fur later, the photographer was getting nowhere. The dogs simply refused to sit still.

'Get down on your haunches and just bloody hold on to them!' Parsons yelled, trying to make himself heard over the barking.

Cameron crouched down, gripped one of the animals by the collar and beamed into the lens. Finally, Parsons had his 'money shot'.

Thus was created the most iconic photographic image of David Cameron. Though the media gave Hilton the credit for stage-managing the shot, the picture that appeared on the front page of every newspaper the following day was entirely unplanned.

The expedition that became known as 'the husky trip' symbolised the dramatic change underway in the Tory Party. Traditionally, it had had little truck with touchy-feely issues like the environment. Indeed, the party harboured many climate change sceptics. Now Cameron was applying for planning permission for solar panels and a wind turbine on his own roof and asking people to 'vote blue, go green'. In truth, he was a recent convert to the cause. Liz Leffman, the Lib Dem candidate in Witney in 2005, remembers him being asked about the environment during a hustings in the run-up to the election and being unable to respond.

> We were asked what we should be doing about climate change and it was extremely apparent from his answers that he didn't have the faintest idea. Not a clue. Afterwards, I heard one of his aides saying to him, 'You're going to have to get better at answering questions on climate change.'

Soon after, Liz Reason, a local green campaigner, took it upon herself to offer him a tutorial.

I got myself an appointment with him at one of his surgeries. I said, 'I've come to find out how much you know about climate change.' And he said, 'Not as much as I probably should.' I said, 'Well, I've come to give you a private tutorial, if you want it?' He said, 'Thanks very much!' So that's what we did.

Now it was paying dividends and he was making the issue his own. The message was clear: under Cameron, the Tories, long seen by voters as hopelessly out of touch, were re-joining the human race.

It was the most eye-catching of a series of changes. Dispensing with a number of formalities usually associated with his job, Cameron was often seen without a tie. He continued to travel to work by bike, allowing himself to be photographed in his cycling helmet looking flushed.

Morning meetings would not start until he had finished the school run. He would pitch up around 9 a.m., slightly out of breath, and conduct the meeting in his cycling kit. In an effort to connect with voters beyond the M25, he began holding shadow Cabinet meetings outside London, prompting some good-humoured grumbling from frontbenchers who didn't relish the trek.

The opening weeks of his leadership were filled with announcements designed to take people by surprise, including a declaration that the party was ready to jettison its traditional fixation with tax cuts. Most of the initiatives were Steve Hilton's.

Tim Chatwin, then Cameron's head of strategic communications, recalls:

We were really focused on saying surprising things in very surprising places, and Steve drove that incredibly hard. Steve was very much the energy, making sure we had interesting things to say and had interesting people involved. It was all about communicating freshness and change. There was a huge amount of energy.

Addressing his party on the future of Conservatism, Cameron warned that they would face 'irrelevance, defeat and failure' if they did not reclaim the centre ground. To demonstrate that there would be no sacred cows, Cameron appointed a team of outside experts, including the multi-millionaire environmentalist Zac Goldsmith, to lead six wide-ranging policy reviews, urging them to think the unthinkable on social justice, the economy, public services, the environment, national security and international development.

James O'Shaughnessy recalls:

> I was at Policy Exchange and we went to see Oliver Letwin and Steve Hilton about the reviews – we had a bit of input in the design, helping them think through the issues. They thought that a really thorough policy renewal process was a prerequisite for winning. They looked at what Thatcher did in the 1980s and what [John] Smith, then Blair did in the 1990s. You really do need to go right back, not quite to basics, but to have a jolly good think. They were tremendously excited – I mean, it was Oliver's wet dream! That is what he was born to do, with his colossal brain.

Cameron made it clear he would not be bound by the findings, which in any case were not due for eighteen months. The time lag, coupled with the absence of any commitment to sign up to what was proposed, led to criticism during this period that he was 'policy light'. However, O'Shaughnessy says the process was designed to take time and feature false starts.

> With these policies, you've really got to put them out in one form; let them get ripped to pieces; then you put them out in another form; let them get ripped to pieces again; and so on. Each time you refine them, it gets marginally better, until you get it right.

At just thirty-nine, Cameron was more than a decade younger than Blair, fifteen years younger than Gordon Brown, and a quarter of a century younger than Liberal Democrat leader Menzies Campbell. He relished his status as a youthful leader. On the day Campbell replaced Charles Kennedy, in January 2006, the new Tory leader was looking round Liz Reason's home and did not attempt to disguise his glee when he heard that a pensioner would be leading the third main party.

'I have a low-energy house, and he came to visit because he was interested in doing the same at his house. When he heard that Menzies Campbell had been elected leader, he punched his fist in the air and said: "How wonderful! Two old fogeys…and me!"' she recalls.

This happy situation wouldn't last long, however. Little over a year later, Campbell resigned. His replacement, Nick Clegg, was quite a different beast: the same age as Cameron, and a public school boy (he went to Westminster School in London), the attractive new Lib Dem leader was cut from a strikingly similar cloth to his Tory counterpart. Cameron would now have to compete with a new kid on the block. Perhaps with a view to keeping the enemy close, he went out of his way to strike up a rapport with the new leader, inviting him and his wife to dinner. Clegg, who could see no advantage in it, politely declined.

In the early days, the commentariat was overwhelmingly enthusiastic about the Cameron regime.

After a decade of reporting Tory travails, the media was hungry for a different story. The new leader seemed to be reaching groups of voters who would not previously have given the party a hearing.

Dylan Jones, editor of the glossy magazine for men *GQ*, says, 'I was enormously impressed by him from the off, actually...the whole process was methodical, almost mathematical.'

Assessing the new leader's first hundred days, Max Hastings was particularly positive.

'For everyone who wants to see the back of New Labour rule, Cameron's is the only game in town. Single-handed, he has made British politics interesting again,' he wrote.[229]

Ground down by the endless war of attrition between Blair and Brown, Labour MPs could only watch in awe.

'Between 2005 and 2007, Cameron was a man on fire,' recalls one Labour MP admiringly. 'He had the bit between his teeth. He'd left the fireplace behind; he'd forgotten the swagger – he was out there, doing an amazing job, dragging the party into the twenty-first century. He was stealing a march, with all that green stuff – it was absolutely real.'

Encouraged by Hilton, the Tory leader was exploring new ways of getting his message across, such as Web Cameron – a regular podcast, unscripted and filmed with a shaky handheld video camera – and Cameron Direct, question-and-answer sessions open to the public up and down the country.

For those in the inner sanctum – Osborne, Hilton and Hague; press aides

---

229 Quoted at: http://news.bbc.co.uk/1/hi/uk_politics/4810212.stm. Oddly, the date at the top of the BBC webpage is incorrect.

Gabby Bertin, George Eustice and Henry Macrory; Ed Llewellyn, Kate Fall and events organiser Liz Sugg – it was an exhilarating time. The new leader was a pleasure to work with: energetic, self-deprecating and fun.

A senior aide recalls:

> I often saw the really human side of him, particularly at our early morning meeting, when he was always on great form. He is very much a morning person. He's a big James Bond fan, and one day he mentioned he'd been watching *From Russia with Love*. The next day, he walked into the morning meeting with his jacket off, flung it across the room, and it landed on the coat stand. Then he looked at Gabby and said: 'Good morning, Miss Moneypenny.'

Little fazed him. Returning to his chauffeur-driven vehicle after a Cameron Direct one day, his trousers ripped from top to bottom. He barely missed a beat. A senior aide recalls: 'His trousers tore from the crotch down, and he had another engagement to go to. He quickly swapped suits with the driver.'

His sense of humour sometimes landed him in hot water, however. On one occasion he got into trouble with both the Samaritans and the British Stammering Association within the space of two days.

An aide recalls:

> At party conference, he talked about the horrific possibility of Gordon Brown becoming Prime Minister. Then he looked up at the balconies and said words to the effect of: 'Don't all throw yourselves off.' Afterwards, he told us he knew it would cause trouble, and sure enough, the next morning, we soon had the Samaritans on the phone.

At a private reception at the same conference, Cameron was overheard impersonating the distinctive sing-song delivery of the BBC's then business editor Robert Peston. A disapproving letter from the British Stammering Association soon winged its way to him. Luckily, nobody found out.

'We kept that one quiet too,' grins a former aide, adding that working with the new leader was 'so much fun'.

'There was always a laugh going on, and he was very happy to take the piss out of himself,' he recalls.

In an attempt to avoid the bitter divisions that had plagued previous leaders, Cameron initially went out of his way to accommodate those who had opposed his candidacy, appointing several of Davis's key supporters to the front bench. Davis himself was confirmed shadow Home Secretary. Among those who had backed other leadership candidates but were nonetheless given jobs or retained their old posts were Graham Brady, appointed shadow Minister for Europe; Dominic Grieve (shadow Attorney General); David Lidington (shadow Northern Ireland Secretary); Cheryl Gillan (shadow Welsh Secretary); and Desmond Swayne, who was made Cameron's new Principal Private Secretary (PPS).

Brady says:

> Given that I had been a fairly vocal campaigner for Davis, it would have been the easiest thing in the world to drop me at that point, so I thought it was somewhat to his credit that he didn't. It was a sensible piece of leadership not to be seen to cull the other candidate's supporters.

Unfortunately, in the longer term, this willingness to overlook past differences did not turn out to be characteristic.

As early as January 2006, there was evidence the rebranding was paying off: in one poll for BPIX, 40 per cent of respondents agreed that Cameron was a 'genuinely different, more sympathetic kind of Conservative'. A YouGov poll for the *Sunday Times* just days out from the May 2006 local elections gave Cameron a higher rating than either Blair or Campbell. It was 'streets ahead of what any of his predecessors since 1997 had managed to achieve'.[230] In the event, the Tories gained over 300 council seats.

Yet there was growing disquiet within the party. Party grandees like former party chairman Michael Ancram were bemused by the new regime. An excruciating piece in the *Mirror* in April 2006 revealed that while Cameron flaunted his green credentials by cycling to work, a 'flunky' in a 'gas-guzzling motor' carrying his shoes and briefcase followed behind, giving rise to a narrative that the modernisation programme was largely cosmetic. Among

230   Tim Bale, p. 300.

critics both inside and outside the party, there was confusion over where it was all heading.

Ancram says now:

> The whole thing with huskies was all froth, to me. At the time, I thought we should be saying: 'Why have we done so badly since 1997?' With Margaret Thatcher, whether you loved her or hated her, you had a feeling of what she stood for. Since she left, we didn't know what we stood for.

The following year, he would pen a pamphlet, 'Still a Conservative', lamenting that after eighteen months of Cameron's leadership, his ideology was still unclear.

Another Tory peer, an early supporter of Cameron's leadership campaign, says: 'I never understood what being a moderniser meant. I still don't, to this day. As far as I was concerned, it meant, "Let's have somebody new and young." All the political crap which went with it meant nothing to me, quite frankly.'

Rumbling discontent found a focus in Cameron's high-profile reforms to the candidate selection process. In an initiative that became known as the 'A-list', he vowed to 'change the face of the Conservative Party by changing the faces of the Conservative Party'. For too long, he argued, local Tory associations had shown a propensity to select middle-aged, white male candidates from professional backgrounds to stand in winnable seats. This was true: many exceptional female candidates bore the scars. Now associations would be forced to choose from a list of 150 approved individuals – whittled down from a long list of 500 applicants – a 'significant proportion' of whom would be women, ethnic minorities or disabled.

Cameron took credit – and considerable flak – for the scheme. However, it was not actually his initiative. Like a number of his reforms, it might well have been adopted by another leader. It was in fact the brainchild of senior Tory women, including Anne Jenkin, Theresa May and the late Shireen Ritchie, who had been working on a campaign with objectives remarkably similar to the A-list throughout the summer of 2005. Their project was launched at Millbank Tower a fortnight before Cameron became leader. Jenkin recalls Steve Hilton attending and commenting wryly that it was the first party event he had attended that was 'full of normal people'.

Jenkin confirms that to an extent Cameron 'piggy-backed' on the cause, though she gives him credit for embracing it, reflecting that without a leader willing to stick his neck out for it there would have been a long, possibly bitter struggle to get the party on board.

The former MP Andrew MacKay, then one of Cameron's senior aides, agrees that he put his heart into the scheme.

'He pushed really hard. He didn't think everybody was trying enough. Every week, he'd want to know which seats were selecting that week; what could be done; whether we had enough women,' MacKay recalls.

Another former aide remembers the new party leader getting 'really shit-faced' after a long day campaigning in Yorkshire, and talking openly about his frustration over the lack of diversity on his front bench.

'He got quite drunk. I remember him saying: "I need more northern accents in the shadow Cabinet."'

For aspiring MPs who ticked the right boxes, particularly younger women, the A-list brought new hope of representing a party that had previously seemed impenetrable.

'I remember being very excited and then deciding to do it,' says one woman who made the grade. 'I remember someone said it was like wanting to go to space, and then suddenly there's a rocket outside your front door. You can't not get in.'

But while the media lapped up pictures of photogenic young female applicants, the A-list outraged many in the party, from a phalanx of well-qualified men whose dreams of becoming an MP were suddenly shattered, to constituency chairmen who refused to take orders from CCHQ.

Ann Widdecombe, the former shadow Home Secretary, says: 'I was completely against the A-list. Cameron was totally image obsessed – he wanted more women, more gays, more ethnics, more this, more that. It was all image.'

The policy resulted in a bitter row over the selection for Widdecombe's successor in Maidstone and the Weald, after Central Office threw out the local association's shortlist of one woman and two men.

'They said we couldn't do that – we had to have two men and two women,' Widdecombe recalls.

One of my committee said to the Central Office guy: 'Does that mean you're telling us we can't select on merit?' And he said, 'Yes, that's exactly what I'm telling you.' He was very honest. But that sort of manipulation doesn't produce the best results. I said: 'What happens if we just tell you to go to hell?' And he said, 'Central Office will just overrule the selection.' We were absolutely being told how we must do it. It had nothing to do with merit.

Among those who lost out as a result of the new system was Davis's former chief of staff Iain Dale, who wrote, on learning he had not made the approved list, that it had 'given him a lot to think about with regard to my future in politics'. He subsequently abandoned his ambition to become an MP for a career in publishing and radio. Another was Boris Johnson's father Stanley. By the time Johnson senior was searching for a seat, his son had quit Westminster to become Mayor of London, but was widely expected to return one day. Such was the meddling by CCHQ over the selection for not one but two winnable seats for which Johnson senior applied that he strongly suspected Cameron was trying to keep him out. The truth is more complicated, but Cameron's strenuous efforts to persuade a female local councillor to stand in Henley after Boris quit the seat (he personally rang the reluctant woman three times, also instructing Theresa May to call) suggest he was unenthusiastic about an American-style Johnson dynasty.

In the end, however, Cameron quietly scrapped the 'A-list'. By 2008, the voluntary party was up in arms across the country about the scheme, and Don Porter, then deputy chairman of the Conservative Party board, found himself receiving daily complaints from frustrated members who didn't fit the bill. Eventually he decided to discuss the issue with Cameron personally.

I gathered together a small working group of about three to four people, did the research, and presented him with ten slides (given his PR background). One of my last slides was: 'How would you like 550 white, heterosexual males on the parliamentary list at the next election, not committed to winning the election? Are you aware of all the talented, white heterosexuals that feel you don't want them in the party?'

This did take him by surprise. People around him made it obvious they were more interested in minority groups, or perceived minority groups. Nothing wrong with that at all, I'd be totally committed to that, but the fact was that real, talented people were missing out…So at the end he turned to me and said, 'OK, you've convinced me. Find a way [to ditch it] in which it doesn't come out that the A-list is scrapped.' I think he was concerned about a headline in the *Mirror* or *The Sun* that said, 'Cameron's beloved A-list scheme scrapped'.

The result was a compromise: the A-list would continue, but local associations would be free to ignore it – so long as there was an equal number of men and women at each stage of the selection process. Porter was happy with the deal.

'If the Association wanted a particular man, they could still get him if he wasn't on the A-list,' Porter explains.

He would be given an equal opportunity till the end. When I told the voluntary party – that they could now go to anyone when they were selecting – they were over the moon. The fact is that from that day onwards there was never a selection that only went to the A-list. Technically the A-list is still not scrapped; in reality it is scrapped.

Nonetheless, in their determination to shed the vestiges of its image as the 'nasty party', as Theresa May had provocatively put it, the new leadership took few prisoners. An early victim was Cameron's shadow Homeland Security Minister Patrick Mercer, who was ruthlessly culled for telling a journalist he had met 'a lot' of 'idle and useless' ethnic minority soldiers who used racism as a 'cover'. The former army colonel also told *The Times* that being called a 'black bastard' was a normal part of army life. Mercer was not condoning the use of such language, and his remark about workshy ethnic minorities sounded far less offensive in the context of the wider interview. However, Cameron threw him to the wolves, telling Mercer in an exchange that lasted less than sixty seconds, 'You're relieved of your command, Colonel.'

Many felt it was hasty and unjust. The following day, the Tory leader bumped into the man he had just sacked in a Commons corridor.

'Sorry about that. Thanks for being so decent. Let's catch up,' he said, leaving Mercer with the impression that, after a period of penance, he would be brought back into the fold. It did not happen.

Mercer recalls: 'I waited and waited. It took nine months for him to see me, by which time I was not so easily reconciled.'

During a stormy one-to-one meeting in Cameron's Commons office, Mercer voiced his anger over Cameron's handling of the episode.

'I've sacked men myself, and there are good and bad ways of doing it,' he told Cameron. 'You've risked turning me from a lukewarm but uncritical follower into an enemy. You don't need to alienate people. We all understand that difficult decisions have to be made.'

Looking back on it now, Mercer accepts that if he had been 'less angry and more ambitious', he and Cameron might have found some accommodation. As it was, he became a backbench critic. It was the first of a number of serious misjudgements Cameron was to make over personnel.

To some, the episode showed that Cameron was ready to sacrifice those who threatened to undermine the rebranding exercise, but it would be unfair to suggest that optics were all that mattered to the new leadership. Nobody in a position to observe what was really driving the reform agenda doubted Hilton's sincerity, at least.

Danny Kruger, Cameron's speechwriter at the time, says:

> On Steve's part, it was sincere. I remember texting him when Web Cameron was first issued, saying, 'Great gimmick.' He rang me straight back and gave me a huge bollocking, saying it wasn't a gimmick – this is how we do politics, and this is our identity; this is the politics of the future and how we speak to people. It was all part of his big view about how politics should be done in a modern democracy.

Hilton himself would argue that for Cameron, too, it was about more than appearances. Either way, many in the party were beginning to feel alienated by the process.

One of Cameron's former ministers says:

> Gradually, an attitude crept in, which seemed to be that we could not be effective as a Conservative Party unless we offended our own natural supporters. It was a fatal sentiment. Instead of saying, 'Come and be our army,' it was as if he were saying, 'You are the problem, and I am going down a different route.' That was a

mistake, because you can carve out a position for yourself without offending your own base. I also think it prompted a new left/right factionalism in the party, which otherwise could have been smothered and kept at bay.

A much parodied speech calling on society to show more love to anti-social youths alarmed those who believed a strong stance on law and order was central to the party's identity. After a barrage of 'hug a hoodie' headlines, even Cameron privately feared they might have gone too far.

A source involved in the post mortem recalls:

> That speech generated a very good conversation internally, about whether we had slightly overdone the repositioning. That was Gove's view. I remember Oliver Letwin thinking it was marvellous. I agreed. We should be hugging hoodies, frankly. It was a really Conservative speech, about moral values and doing the right thing. But Cameron regretted it.

The scale of the unease was reflected in growing tensions between Cameron and the wider party machine, which found an outlet in hostility to the party chairman, Francis Maude. James McGrath, who worked for Maude at the time, said: 'Francis was David Cameron's bad cop. People couldn't attack David because they'd just elected him, but they could attack Francis. People didn't want this; they didn't want change. The view on the ground was that we'd won elections for the past twenty-five years – we didn't need to change!'

On one occasion, a meeting of the Conservative Party board in Yorkshire became so heated that Maude was forced to leave the room. In the privacy of the corridor, the shell-shocked party chair rang Cameron to impart the bad news.

'It's dreadful in there. The board's in revolt,' he told the leader.

Back in the meeting room, with Maude out of earshot, the board erupted. Observing from the sidelines, McGrath couldn't believe what he was hearing. He dashed out to update his boss.

'They've gone feral, mate!' he hissed.

'Er, my chief of staff has just told me that the board has gone feral,' Maude informed Cameron.

A backlash was also underway in Brussels, where Cameron had decided to withdraw Tory MEPs from the European People's Party (EPP), a grouping of centre-right parties in the European Parliament. He had made the pledge in haste during the leadership contest in a bid to woo Eurosceptic right-wingers, who regarded the EPP with suspicion because it contained federalists. It soon transpired that credible alternative partners were thin on the ground. Caroline Jackson, Tory MEP for the South West of England, would later publicly describe Cameron's decision as 'dotty'.

'It will sow the seeds of endless trouble…leave bad blood…it is a stupid, stupid policy,' she said.[231]

In July 2006, in his capacity as Cameron's 'eyes and ears', Desmond Swayne fired off an email to the leader warning that moderate Tory MEPs were 'furious' about Cameron's handling of the situation. Unfortunately, he forgot to log off the Commons computer he used, and his missive was leaked to the *Sunday Times*, along with another, sent two months later, which warned of 'depression' and 'dismay' over the leadership's low-key approach to issues relating to Europe.

'The feeling of frustration and impotence is compounded by our perceived silence on things European. It is also a prime source of grumbles in our mail bags,' Swayne wrote.

For all Cameron's desire to start afresh, the batch of leaked emails revealed that backbiting was still rife in the party. Swayne, regarded by his peers as an amiable figure, privately labelled one colleague a 'mincehead', another (the MP Roger Gale) 'Mr Angry', and Maude 'a likeable fellow but…not yet trusted'. Theresa May came off worse, described as 'neither liked nor trusted across the party'. For good measure, Swayne added that she would require 'a tight rein'. He praised Cameron's decision not to bother going to a dinner being thrown by the Industry and Parliament Trust, saying: 'They are a bunch of boring colleagues with nothing better to do…'

Observing these tensions, commentators were prone to asking when it would culminate in a showdown between different elements of the party, like Blair's 'Clause Four moment' when he faced down trade unions. The question irritated Hilton, who says he saw no need for a symbolic showdown over a single issue. However, an early battle between the leadership and the wider party over grammar schools suggested Cameron was prepared for a fight – even if he did not pick it.

---

231   *The Guardian*, 5 May 2009.

The row was triggered when the shadow Education Secretary David Willetts gave an interview on the *Today* programme during which he suggested grammar schools were inimical to social mobility. Later the same day, he repeated the claim in a speech which had been cleared by the party leadership. For Conservatives who believed selective education could transform the opportunities of bright children from less well-off backgrounds, grammar schools were a touchstone issue. Willetts's claim sparked a furious backlash. Among those who were particularly exercised was his frontbench colleague, shadow Europe Minister and former grammar school boy Graham Brady. A passionate advocate for selective education, Brady rang Willetts, urging him to retract the comment.

'This is crazy!' he told the shadow Education Secretary. 'We can't do this. It's very bad politics.' Willetts stood firm.

By chance, Brady had recently received some new data which showed that every ethnic minority group in the country performed better in areas with selective schools. Determined to blow Willetts's argument out of the water, he forwarded the information to *The Times*, accompanied by some off-message quotes. When the article appeared the following day, the shadow Chief Whip, Patrick McLoughlin, was furious.

'Graham, I thought you were the fucking Europe Minister. Stop fucking talking about fucking grammar schools!' he yelled.

Shortly after, Brady quit the front bench. Looking back, he says Cameron was 'an innocent party' in the affair, having been absent from the meeting during which Willetts's speech was cleared. (At least three members of the shadow Cabinet, including Cheryl Gillan and David Davis, had warned of the ructions it would cause. Their concerns were dismissed by Hague, who signed off the speech.) Indeed, details of a private conversation that took place between Cameron and Don Porter shortly after the furore, suggest the party leader actually disagreed with Willetts. According to Porter:

> I went to see him just after the David Willetts speech. I said to him, 'David: grammar schools.' He said, 'Yeah?'
>
> I said, 'Three points. Why did we start the discussion in the first place? We didn't need to?' He said, 'Don, I totally agree with you.'
>
> I said, 'Second point: tell me how a bright guy or girl from a socially deprived background can actually make the transition

through the education system at the moment, unless they get a scholarship or go to a grammar school?' He said, 'I agree with you.'

I said, 'Third point. David – what are you going to do if a bunch of parents come into your surgery and say they want to set up a grammar school in your constituency – given that one of the big themes of your administration so far has been localism? The party really likes it. Are you going to say to parents, "No, your children can't have a grammar school"?' He seemed uncomfortable about the third point.

This is curious: if Porter's account is true – and he has no reason to misrepresent events – Cameron was happy to jettison a hugely respected and effective frontbencher to avoid muddling the message from the party leadership when he was at best equivocal about the arguments. In this case, the principle came second to the cosmetics.

As far as many party activists were concerned, the new leader was betraying their roots. For now, the friction between Cameron and rank-and-file Conservatives was only skin deep. Many were willing to bite their tongues in the hope that all the upheaval would bring electoral success. But it was not the last time Cameron's mission to change the Conservative Party would meet fearsome resistance within his own ranks.

22

SECOND MUM

'I'll need all the prayers I can get.'

– Cameron, on his electoral prospects

They may have been unconvinced by hugging huskies and hoodies, but one priority Conservatives shared with their new leader was paring back the state. It was Cameron's scheme for filling the gap when government retreated that left many bemused.

His idea was born in a red-light district in Birmingham, where violent drug dealers and pimps ruled the streets. Everyone in positions of authority had given up on Balsall Heath, abandoning it to the local mafia who controlled the crack cocaine business and prostitution rings. Then desperate local residents took matters into their own hands and began reclaiming the streets.

It started with just one pensioner with a placard on a street corner. Soon he was joined by dozens of others, who spread across the neighbourhood. It was the beginning of a community movement that would prove far more powerful than the police and local council. Slowly but surely, the vice girls and criminals were driven out, and Balsall Heath became a pleasant place to live.

Cameron heard about the neighbourhood when proud residents sent him a book about their achievements. It described how ordinary people were able to do more than local authorities to tackle socio-economic problems on their doorstep. Inspired, Cameron went to Balsall Heath to learn more. The result was to become his flagship policy: the Big Society.

The Big Society matters because Cameron made so much of it. Beyond the obvious ideal of a sound economy, it was his recipe for a better Britain. The idea was to devolve a significant slice of responsibility for running society to volunteers and community groups. He has described it as his 'passion' and his 'mission'. Though it took a while to give it a name, it was effectively launched when he first became party leader, and it was a plank of the party's 2010 campaign. He continued to refer to it for the first half of the coalition before it was, in the words of a former No. 10 aide: 'taken out the back and quietly strangled' – though the asphyxiation did not prove fatal.

His faith in the idea was sincere. He began talking about the philosophy that underpinned it during his leadership campaign, calling for a 'step change' in the way government deals with the voluntary sector. 'On occasions the government needs to get out of the way altogether, recognising that the state is failing where the voluntary sector could succeed,' he said.[232]

Over the next seven years, he repeatedly argued that profound problems required 'shared responsibility' and that the state should 'treat its citizens as adults, to be trusted and respected; not as children, to be controlled and directed. That means...not expecting government to take care of everything.'[233]

The ideology was thoroughly Conservative: that the state is too big and interfering, discouraging people from looking after themselves and each other. When he went to Balsall Heath in May 2007, Cameron immersed himself in the community, staying overnight with a local Muslim family, the Rehmans, who were involved in the regeneration project.

At the time, the Rehmans, who run a grocery on the estate, refused to talk about their special guest. Now they describe him as a great listener who 'really wanted to know what made Balsall Heath tick, and how it was transformed through people power'.

Abdullah Rehman, a father of three and a community capacity builder for the Balsall Heath Neighbourhood Forum at the time, says:

> We decided at the Forum that if David really wanted to see how we felt, he should come and stay with one of us, so I volunteered. A couple of days later, my colleagues and I went to pick him up from the station. He was asking a lot of questions and we went to the house for him to meet the family. I wanted to take him into the hub of the community, so we spent the day going round the shops. In one place, I said, 'Why don't you become a shopkeeper?' So he

232 'In Good Nick', David Cameron, *The Guardian*, 17 August 2005.
233 'I was right about Dyke', David Cameron, *The Guardian*, 23 April 2007.

served a couple of customers and was brilliant. He's very adaptable to any situation. He joked about dodgy bank notes and had people laughing. From there, we had a stroll around. People were coming over to him and complaining about their rubbish. I tried to usher him on but he wanted to listen. He had a meeting with some activists in our office and then we popped down to the local mosque and talked to some people there. We went back to my house in the evening and had a curry, with some other friends and relatives – about a dozen people. We chatted about anything and everything, like why people find it hard to integrate. David was really interested. I didn't expect that. For two days there was no press – he didn't want them there.

Cameron was in the Rehmans' house when Blair took Westminster by surprise by announcing the date of his resignation.

Abdullah Rehman recalls:

We were sitting there watching TV. David said 'Now the Blair fest will begin.' It was a surreal moment sitting with the Leader of the Opposition when the PM resigned. Everything went silent; he was obviously really interested in what Tony was saying because he had to respond. Then my mum walked in and started talking about the garden she loved, so that broke his concentration…I thought, 'Oh, Mum, this really isn't the moment.' David stopped watching TV and talked to her about pruning the flowers.

Cameron struck up a bond with Abdullah's mother and light-heartedly began referring to her as his 'second mum'. She told him she would pray for him to win the 2010 election.

'He said, "I need all the prayers I can get,"' Rehman recalls.

After spending the night with the Rehmans, Cameron took their children to school and gave an assembly.

Rehman says:

He was amazed that I was a Muslim sending my children to a Jewish school. I think it confirmed to him that faith schools really do work. He was really impressed. After school, we went down to a football pitch on some council land, which our volunteers take care of. He picked up a rake and started helping clear the football pitch. He also put on his gloves and helped us clear up a car park. He got really stuck in.

That evening, the Rehmans gave him various presents, including some Asian robes and shoes, which they hoped might come in useful when he travelled to Pakistan. Then they took him to the station, where he hugged them all and left. Later they received a warm letter of thanks. He kept in touch by post and telephoned the family when he heard, in 2014, that Mrs Rehman had died.

During his stay, Cameron also met Dr Dick Atkinson, author of *Urban Renaissance*, the book about Balsall Heath. Atkinson was one of the founding members of what became the Balsall Heath Forum. When Atkinson retired in 2013, after forty-five years of community work in Balsall Heath, Cameron sent a long letter to be read at his farewell party. The letter highlights the role the Birmingham project played in the development of the Big Society policy.

Cameron wrote:

> Spurred on by Dick's enthusiasm and by what he and the local community have managed to achieve in Balsall Heath, I was inspired to try and make it easier for grassroots organisations and social enterprises to work together and tackle problems like juvenile crime, drug abuse, and anti-social behaviour...the passion and commitment demonstrated over so many years by Dick and others in the Forum show off the Big Society at its very best.

Throughout Cameron's years as opposition leader, the Big Society continued to be a source of criticism and bemusement, but the more he learned about the long arm of the state, the more convinced he became that it had to be curtailed.

A former aide says, 'I remember having a conversation with him in opposition, about getting rid of the Downing Street Delivery Unit. We discovered it had 135 "Public Service Agreements", one of which was literally "Make Old People Happy". We all thought it was crazy.'

He believed it was naïve to imagine a better alternative would 'just spring to life' without help.

'We need strong and concerted government action to make it happen. We need to use the state to remake society,' he explained.[234]

His own contribution was the National Citizen Service, through which young people aged fifteen to seventeen could volunteer for two- or three-week residential courses at an outdoor adventure centre during school holidays. Bankrolled in its early days by former Tory donor Peter Cruddas, it was a quiet success, with tens of thousands of teenagers taking part every year.

However, the wider concept of the Big Society proved a harder sell. Focus groups repeatedly showed people just didn't get it. The more Cameron pushed it, both in the run-up to the 2010 election and later, in government, the more it was ridiculed: by Tories who thought it sounded gimmicky, by opposition politicians who wilfully misunderstood and misrepresented it, and by media commentators who attacked him for failing to explain it better. Coined by Hilton, the phrase was the snappiest anyone could come up with to convey the idea, but it simply did not resonate.

'It seemed like one of those things thought up by two kids in a think tank one night,' sighs one Tory peer now.

Others believe the mistake was giving it a name in the first place. 'Some things are better without a brand. Nobody mocked our ambitions to work with charities and encourage social enterprise when we were just doing it. It was when it became the Big Society with capital letters that it was too much,' according to a loyalist.

The journalist Daniel Finkelstein believes the leadership overlooked a fundamental flaw in the whole concept: it involved asking voters to do something for nothing.

'If you think about what the Conservative Party was offering people, it was to increase what they put in without necessarily getting more out. But people thought they were already putting in and not getting much out. I think that's what went wrong with the Big Society,' he says.

Undeterred, Cameron ploughed on.

'Have no doubt, the Big Society is on its way!' he declared defiantly, nine months after he became Prime Minister.

---

234 Hugo Young Lecture, 10 November 2009.

Naturally I would prefer to see more positive headlines…but I am very upbeat about the torrent of newsprint expended on the subject…unlike so many other political ideas which are dropped or forgotten within days of being suggested, I believe all the interest and debate means we're on to something.[235]

However, as austerity bit and money dried up for many voluntary groups and charities, the Big Society came under fire from some of the very organisations it was designed to help. With the departure of Hilton from Downing Street in May 2012, it was in effect quietly dropped (at least as a campaign theme: the 2015 Conservative manifesto included a policy section on 'Helping you build the Big Society').

'Quite frankly, that was probably the right thing to do,' says a former No. 10 aide who was initially keen on the agenda. 'It just stopped being mentioned. I distinctly remember being with a civil servant, who started talking about the Big Society. A more senior civil servant turned to him and said, "Let me make this quite clear. We don't use those words any more."'

Nonetheless, Cameron continued to believe in it – passionately so. There can be no other explanation for its sudden revival in the 2015 manifesto. A recurrent criticism from his own party and more widely is that he lacks vision. The Big Society may well be his best defence.

235 'Have no doubt, the Big Society is on its way', David Cameron, *The Guardian*, 12 February 2011.

23

LIGHTS OUT

'It's to keep the aid agencies off my back.'
    – George Osborne, on foreign aid

Surveying a half-empty auditorium, David Cameron smiled, took a deep breath and launched into a passionate defence of one of his most controversial policies.

It was July 2007, and he was in Africa making the case for protecting the overseas aid budget, a pledge despised by many in his party. From the start, his trip had been so controversial there had been speculation he would pull out. Now hardly anyone had turned up for his keynote speech, and spin doctors were panicking about embarrassing TV footage of empty seats. While aides scuttled around, languid ceiling fans, no match for the stifling heat, wafted little ripples of hot air over the smattering of Rwandan politicians in the audience. Then the lights went out.

As a symbol of the dramatic downturn in Cameron's fortunes, the scene in the Rwandan Parliament in Kigali could hardly have been more apt. Back home, his constituency was underwater following weeks of heavy rain. Hundreds of homes had to be evacuated (according to his local newspaper, the *Witney Gazette*, more than 1,600 were left uninhabitable) and there was anger that he was 4,000 miles away pontificating about global poverty.[236] A week earlier, the Tories had come a dismal third in by-elections in Ealing Southall and Sedgefield, fuelling unease over his strategy. Among Conservative MPs and activists who had never understood or supported the so-called 'modernisation agenda', the trip to Rwanda was perceived as yet another empty PR stunt. Reflecting the tempestuous mood, one anonymous

236 *Witney Gazette*, 8 January 2014.

backbencher grumbled: 'There's a hole at the heart of the Cameron project. There is a feeling that Cameronism is exhausted. MPs want to know what is at the heart of all this rebranding. The fear is that there is nothing at the heart of it.'[237]

It was the lowest point yet in Cameron's leadership. The halcyon days of his early reign, when commentators gushed about his fresh approach, and the party rank and file, weary of political defeat, were happy to give him the benefit of the doubt, were a distant memory. Now malcontents were calling for his head.

By contrast, Gordon Brown was enjoying a political honeymoon. Just three days after he took over from Blair at the end of June, a failed terror attack on Glasgow Airport gave the new premier an opportunity to demonstrate his leadership credentials. He was widely praised for his robust response. An outbreak of foot-and-mouth disease the following month was another political gift. He earned plaudits for abandoning his summer holiday and racing back to London to take control. Meanwhile Cameron just seemed irritated that his summer holiday plans were being interrupted.[238] In this febrile atmosphere, disappearing to Rwanda was a dangerous move, but he was defiant.

'There are some people in Britain who told me not to come,' he told the Rwandan Parliament when the lights flickered back on.

> They said I should stay at home and worry about domestic concerns. Well, let me tell them and let me tell you, that in the twenty-first century, a century of global trade, global migration and, yes, of global terrorism, there is no 'domestic' and 'foreign' any more. In this world, we are all in it together.

His spirited defence did nothing to blunt the dreadful headlines. As well as predictable jibes about the 'lights going down' on his leadership, a cheeky photograph of him emerging from a toilet was seized upon by tabloid editors who captioned it 'Loo-ser'.

It is a measure of the strength of his commitment to international development that he was willing to put himself through it. Other policy features

---

237 'Tories call on David Cameron to quit', *Sunday Telegraph*, 22 July 2007.
238 Damian McBride, *Power Trip: A Decade of Policy, Plots and Spin* (Biteback Publishing, 2014), pp. 292–3.

of his early leadership came and went, but the evidence is that he took a genuine interest in overseas aid, and stuck with it even when it caused him a great deal of grief.

When it came to the cause, a number of senior colleagues were ambivalent at best. During the leadership contest, Cameron and Davis had both been asked on BBC *Question Time* whether they would give each other jobs in their shadow Cabinets.

'Yes, and I'd give him a better job than overseas aid,' Davis had sniffed.

Privately, Osborne also seems to have been equivocal, though he fully appreciated the presentational advantages of embracing the cause. To the dismay of many in the party, he and Cameron adopted a UN target – set in the '70s but never met in the UK – to spend 0.7 per cent of GDP on foreign aid. It became the centrepiece of their policy on international aid, and the focus of much discontent among both Tory MPs and the wider party.

When a family friend confronted Osborne about it over lunch in 2008, she was taken aback by his reaction.

'It's to keep the aid agencies off my back,' he shrugged – hardly a ringing endorsement of the cause (though he may just have been placating a critic at a social gathering).

One who *was* evangelical about it was Andrew Mitchell, who had been given the international development brief by Michael Howard, and pushed to continue in the role under Cameron.

He recalls:

> I went to see Cameron the day his triumph was announced, and he said, 'Mitch, I'd like to promote you.' 'To what?' I replied. 'Work and pensions,' he said. I said, 'I don't really regard that as a promotion. I'm doing international development; it's a job I'm really interested in, and I think it matters to you. I'd like to stay with it.' Cameron said, 'Well, that's excellent. I'm really glad. What I'll do is make the announcement and I'll make it clear that the fact that you're staying in the portfolio is a symbol of the importance I attach to it. So the portfolio will be promoted.'

Mitchell's view was that under Labour, the department for international development had become a 'well-upholstered NGO moored off the coast of Whitehall' and needed to be converted into a smooth-functioning arm of the state which responded to ministerial priorities. Like Cameron and Osborne, he was also keenly aware of the role international development could play in the party's rebranding exercise.

'Labour had dominated this area completely. It was not only that Tories were not trusted on international development – we weren't even on the pitch!' he recalls.

> The first thing I did when I took over the brief was to go to Edinburgh for the Make Poverty History meeting. As a Tory, people would sort of come up and poke me, to see if I was real.
>
> Cameron understood that international development is very popular with people under thirty-five, and also with women. It's an area which gives 'permission' for voters of other parties to entertain the idea of voting Conservative. There are people in this country who believe this is the most important political issue.

Yet it was not all about positioning. As a constituency MP, Cameron had significant dealings with overseas aid charities, a number of which are based in Oxford, and he had proven supportive.

Liz Leffman exchanged various letters with him on development issues when he first became an MP, and says he was always helpful and receptive.

'It was definitely something that came up in the 2005 election, because we have a lot of people in the area who work for Oxfam and so on,' she remembers.

> He always took these sorts of questions very seriously. In the early days he would be quite inclined to write a letter back to me saying he agreed with what I was saying. I think his staunch defence of the aid budget now is partly due to his experience as a local MP.

With Cameron's support, Mitchell set about a total overhaul of the party's approach to international aid. The shadow Development Secretary travelled to some thirty-eight countries to see how British aid was being spent.

He recalls:

We began to see that Labour had thrown money at the problem, but actually there was a coherent centre-right case, that said development is about stopping conflict, which makes us safer; it's about boosting prosperity, which is good for us as well as them. It's not just the moral point – that it's right to do something about children dying of dirty water – it's the practical point, which is that it's in our interests as well as theirs.

That international aid was in Britain's own interests became Cameron's central argument to a sceptical Tory Party. However, many remained unconvinced. In the hope that it would help more colleagues 'get it', Mitchell asked if he could set up a project in Rwanda, through which MPs and activists could see for themselves how overseas aid transforms lives. He proposed that it be called Project Umubano, meaning 'partnership', a reference to the way in which he hoped the Conservatives would work with Rwandans.

I went to see Cameron and I said, this will do a little bit of good, in a country that's been to hell and back. It will involve members of our party going out to Rwanda. It will ensure that within the Conservative Party, there's a caucus of people who really understand, because they've been to a poor country, and seen at first hand what works and what doesn't work. These people will be supportive of development, will want to speak at party conference; hold meetings; engage with NGOs; and so on. We will have a team of Tories who really get it. And it will speak for the values of the party.

'Fine,' Cameron responded. 'But why Rwanda?'

'Because Ghana is too advanced, Kenya is too big, Uganda is too big. Rwanda is small enough for us to have an impact and know everybody there, and so on,' Mitchell replied.

'Great. Right, get on with it,' Cameron told him.

Over the next three years, waves of Tory MPs and activists took part in Project Umubano, helping to rebuild homes ravaged by war, working with local doctors and lawyers on medical and legal projects, giving English lessons, and other tasks. Photographs of eager young Tory candidates and older

MPs rolling up their sleeves to clean lavatories and build walls projected the energetic, compassionate image the leadership sought.

It was an invitation to visit Project Umubano, and to meet Rwandan President Paul Kagame, that gave rise to Cameron's controversial trip in summer 2007. He was accompanied by Hilton, Mitchell, four other MPs and some forty-five Tory volunteers. Fearing a media backlash if they stayed in a luxurious hotel, Mitchell booked the party into the Christian Mission in the Rwandan capital. The Tory leader's speech to the Kigali Parliament, grandly entitled 'The Conservative Party's Kigali Declaration on International Development', was written by Cameron, Mitchell and Steve Hilton in the kitchen of the Mission on the day the Tory leader arrived.

Later, Cameron sat down to dinner with Mitchell and the late Christopher Shale, the Tory leader's then constituency chairman, who was also on the trip. That night, Mitchell and Shale sat up into the small hours at the Mission, drinking and telling jokes, while Cameron tried to get some sleep. Mitchell recalls the opposition leader appearing in his pyjamas and jovially shouting at them to 'shut up and go to bed' because their raucous laughter was keeping him awake.

Mitchell and Hilton got on well, and Mitchell credits him with immense intellectual energy and support for the party's new focus on international development. In the pressure-cooker atmosphere of the Rwandan trip, however, the pair had a dispute that almost came to fisticuffs. The row started on the day of Cameron's speech, when Hilton, backed by Cameron's press secretary George Eustice, tried to prevent the four other MPs on the trip – Brooks Newmark, David Mundell, Mark Simmonds and Alistair Burt – from meeting the President and taking part in a photocall. Hilton argued that the pictures would not look as good with so many people, while Mitchell was adamant they should all be included. When Cameron and the President appeared on the steps of the presidential compound, Eustice tried to stop the MPs accompanying the pair. Mitchell, who felt strongly about the issue, physically prevented him from barring the way, and in the end, all four appeared in the shots.

The incident caused serious friction between Mitchell and Hilton. After a day of frayed nerves, tensions boiled over when Mitchell complained to Cameron in front of Hilton about what had happened. In an extraordinary scene in Cameron's bedroom, Hilton squared up to Mitchell.

'There were too many people. It was ridiculous!' Hilton shouted, looking as if he was about to punch the shadow International Development Secretary.

Alarmed, Cameron appealed to Hilton to back off.

'He's trying to help me, Steve – let it go,' the Tory leader soothed.

'I think we should sort this out elsewhere – this is not the place,' Mitchell said to Hilton, a steely look in his eye. The pair left the Tory leader's room and went into Mitchell's room across the corridor, closing the door. Such was Hilton's temper, and so threatening was his body language, that Mitchell genuinely thought they might come to blows. A former soldier and the taller of the two, he was confident that if push came to shove, he could fight his corner. Out of Cameron's earshot however, Hilton quickly calmed down. After a short exchange, he apologised profusely for his behaviour and the pair were quickly reconciled, later appearing in front of a nervous Cameron, with a beaming Mitchell saying, 'Look, best friends now.'

The following day, as the shadow International Development Secretary accompanied the Tory leader to the airport to see him onto his plane and back to waterlogged Witney, he apologised for his part in the Hilton incident.

'Oh, don't worry about that,' Cameron replied breezily. 'Steve frequently explodes with fury. I saw him and Rachel once nearly kill each other when an argument broke out between them. You will probably become good friends' – which they did.

By this point, international development had become emblematic of Cameron's regime. Time was set aside for the issue at party conferences, which began to attract increasing numbers of delegates from charities and NGOs. Mitchell felt they were 'winning' on the issue. When Cameron suggested a catalogue of changes to his draft Green Paper on overseas aid, the shadow International Development Secretary took it as evidence of the leader's keen personal interest in the subject.

Speaking about the Green Paper, he says:

> I spent months doing it. It was a real labour of love. I gave it to Ed Llewellyn, who thought it was fabulous, and Francis Maude, who loved it. But when we gave it to David, he said, 'Well, this bit needs to go; that bit needs to be changed; we need to do this; and that.' I was rather hurt, because I thought it was perfect. But the point was he'd read it in a way a lot of others hadn't, because he

knows so much about it, and cares. His changes were very sensible. It showed he was on the ball, really interested.

When the financial crash struck in late 2007, opponents of the 0.7 per cent pledge became far more vocal. As the scale of the crisis and the necessary cuts to public spending became apparent, Cameron came under intense pressure from colleagues, including shadow Defence Secretary Liam Fox, to abandon the ring-fence. Meanwhile Brown raised the stakes. Fearing Cameron was getting too much kudos for his stance on the 0.7 per cent target after 'stealing' the issue from Labour, the Labour Prime Minister pledged to go one better and enshrine the commitment in law. It prompted a panicked meeting between Cameron, Osborne and Mitchell, during which the shadow International Development Secretary argued that they should not try to match Brown's pledge.

'Listen, we have said we will spend 0.7 per cent. That is good enough. We don't need to pass a law. We are proper politicians, and will do what we say. Parliament shouldn't pass this kind of legislation – it's ridiculous,' Mitchell argued, pointing out that Labour had passed a law abolishing child poverty, 'since when it has gone up'.

However, the party leader and shadow Chancellor feared Brown's move would open up a damaging 'dividing line' on overseas aid, undermining their hard work.

'We need to close it down. We'll have to offer the same,' Osborne said. Cameron agreed.

It was a decision the party leader had cause to regret. As Prime Minister in a coalition whose *raison d'être* was economic recovery he could not see how to honour the pledge.

Mitchell recalls: 'It became clear this was pretty toxic on the Tory backbenches. There was a lot of sucking of teeth in the political and Whitehall machine.'

Early in the coalition, Cameron called Mitchell to No. 10 to discuss their options.

'I said, "We've got to do what we said. We've got to pass the law,"' Mitchell recalls.

Cameron demurred.

'Uh, well, it's all very difficult,' he said. 'I can't see how we can do it.'

Nonetheless, in 2013, the 0.7 per cent target was finally hit. A backbench Bill sponsored by the Liberal Democrat MP Michael Moore enshrining it in law passed through Parliament.

Cameron's robust stance on this issue in the bleakest economic circumstances was a long-running sore in the Tory Party, denting his popularity among some traditionalists. Amid austerity measures, it would have been relatively easy to drop the 0.7 per cent pledge. He deserves credit for the courage of his convictions in this case. The policy had the dual attraction of showcasing 'modern, compassionate Conservatism' and fitting comfortably with the Prime Minister's patrician view of his role in Britain and the world. He has no difficulty with the concept of *noblesse oblige*. To his critics, it was another illustration of a *de haut en bas* attitude. He would simply say it was 'the right thing to do'.

24

FLAGS AND FIREPLACES

'Totally the wrong profile.'
 – Cameron, on whether Boris Johnson should run for Mayor

In any normal year, Westminster is deserted over the summer recess. Save for a few interns sitting around aimlessly sipping coffee, the leafy atrium in Portcullis House is silent as the sun streams through the enormous glass roof. Restaurants and bars are empty, some closed altogether, and for lobby hacks with the misfortune to be working, it is torture by foreign ringtone. There is little to do but wait for autumn, when the political calendar starts again.

By the time Cameron returned from Rwanda, however, speculation was mounting that there would be a snap election. Gordon Brown's arrival at No. 10 in June had transformed the political scene. Labour's share in the polls climbed throughout the summer, along with the new PM's personal ratings. As the Tories struggled to articulate a message, voters who had grown weary after ten years of Tony Blair were eager to give his successor a chance to show what he could do. Having led consistently in the polls for more than a year, Cameron's Conservatives found themselves up to ten points behind. Westminster was buzzing with the expectation that Brown would make the most of his honeymoon and call an early election.

As the party machines cranked up, MPs in marginal seats scurried back to their constituencies. Across beaches and back gardens, holiday sun loungers were being abandoned by party workers and volunteers determined to spend every spare minute preparing for the big test.

Despite the growing excitement, Cameron spent half of August on holiday in Brittany. It was his second foreign break in three months: the family had been in Crete over half term. At Conservative headquarters, it was left to James O'Shaughnessy to cobble together a manifesto and prepare for party conference, the last hurrah before the country went to the polls. The atmosphere in the office was grim.

O'Shaughnessy says:

> I had to get a chunk of policies in place for party conference, and work on the manifesto, with the expectation that we'd get to the other side of conference and Brown would call an election. I was trying to amalgamate what crumbs of thought had come together and turn them into something half decent.

He recalls frantically sifting through the recommendations in the policy reviews – which had yet to be properly examined – for eye-catching proposals. He also remembers a sinking feeling that efforts to haul the party into the twenty-first century might come to a juddering halt, or even go into reverse.

'There was a sense that the whole modernisation process could be still-born – that if David lost, there would be a temptation to go in the other direction,' he recalls.

In local branches of the party, too, there was mounting alarm.

Don Porter, then deputy chairman of the party board, recalls receiving a gloomy phone call from Michael Spicer, then chairman of the 1922 Committee of backbenchers, as he drove home from a local constituency function in Sussex.

'What's the feeling among the volunteers?' Spicer asked.

'Pretty grim,' Porter replied. 'We all feel Labour's going to win. What's the feeling in the parliamentary party?'

'Exactly the same,' Spicer answered. 'What should we do about it, Don?'

'Well, somebody needs to go in and tell David how serious it is,' Porter replied.

'Yes, I agree. The executive has met and thought you were the best person to do it,' Spicer said.

A few days later, Porter arranged to see the party leader. His message was blunt.

'Look, the feeling is Labour is going to win,' he told Cameron. 'We are well behind; we've lost any initiative – or we never had any initiative. Morale is very poor. There's got to be something at party conference that actually changes everything.'

Cameron nodded gravely.

Porter says now: 'I think he was very worried and knew they had to come up with something big. He reassured me. I think his exact words were: "Don, rest assured – something is going to happen." I got the feeling that something was going to happen of significance.'

In front of MPs, however, Cameron was characteristically upbeat. Desmond Swayne, who was his parliamentary aide at the time, recalls:

> This was the darkest time – it looked very bleak for us. Labour was well ahead in the polls. We thought Brown would call an October election, or even a September election, and we would have been toast. And yet I remember Cameron's attitude being, 'Hey, we're riding the dip.' He was not downbeat or grumpy. He wasn't prepared to be beaten at that stage. It had a huge effect on steadying the ship.

Cameron also had a new weapon for the media offensive that lay ahead: Andy Coulson. The former newspaper man arrived at CCHQ a few months after resigning from the editorship of the *News of the World* and hit the ground running as Cameron's director of communications, impressing colleagues at every level.

'Coulson was brilliant – *is* brilliant. Incredibly effective; very popular with his team; ran a brilliant operation,' says James O'Shaughnessy. 'Everyone liked and admired him.'

Before taking up his new post, Coulson had assured Cameron he knew nothing about phone hacking in his newsroom. When he quit the paper following the conviction of its royal editor, Clive Goodman, for tapping into voicemails left by members of the royal family, he had declared that he was simply taking responsibility for what had happened on his watch.

Though there was some criticism of Cameron's decision to appoint him, the Tory leader brushed it off, first claiming that he believed Coulson was innocent of any wrongdoing, then later, as he became less certain, declaring people 'deserved a second chance'.

The job offer had been encouraged by Osborne, who had had dealings with Coulson in 2005 when the *News of the World* obtained an embarrassing photograph of him in the company of a prostitute and a substance that looked like cocaine.[239] Though Coulson did not spare Osborne's blushes – he splashed

239 Osborne later denied that it was.

the story under the headline 'Top Tory, Coke and the Hooker' – the shadow Chancellor admired the way it was handled and was grateful the editor didn't go harder (the leader column stopped short of calling for Osborne's resignation and acknowledged that he was young at the time of the indiscretion). The pair subsequently met at various editorial lunches and got on well.[240]

To Cameron, hiring Coulson seemed to make sense. During the first eighteen months of his leadership, he had tried to keep a healthy distance from newspaper barons, a strategy encouraged by Hilton and by Cameron's then press adviser George Eustice. They argued that print media was losing its influence and that there was no longer any need to 'suck up' to editors and proprietors. Rattled by the prospect of a snap election in 2007, however, the Tory leader did a volte face and began actively cultivating powerful media figures including Paul Dacre, editor of the *Daily Mail*, and Rupert Murdoch. Coulson, who was held in high esteem by Murdoch despite the phone-hacking debacle, offered a bridge between the Conservatives and four hugely influential newspaper titles: the *News of the World*, *The Sun*, *The Times* and the *Sunday Times*.

The former tabloid editor soon became an invaluable member of Cameron's inner circle. An Essex-boy-done-good, his council house background and state education gave him a very different perspective to others. He had an ear for the language of *Daily Mail* and *Sun* readers and an instinctive grasp of what would appeal to them.

'Morning after morning, in the meetings, the person who was speaking the most sense after George was Coulson. Coulson was brilliant,' says Andrew MacKay.[241]

The word that comes up most often when former colleagues talk about his qualities is 'professionalism'.

'In a way, it wasn't the big things he did: it was a collection of little things,' O'Shaughnessy says.

> He was very focused, very single-minded, always thinking, we need to get either stories attacking the other lot, or we need to have positive stuff that we can talk about that reflects well on us – always with this view of the *Sun* reader, and how those people see us. And

---

240   Janan Ganesh, p. 174.
241   Private information.

he would always think about how we could take the story on to
the next day.[242]

Coulson's job was to give what one Tory insider called a bit of 'working-class
grit in the oyster',[243] and he began with a tabloid-style campaign to put crime
at the heart of the party's message in summer 2007. Right-wing newspapers
applauded as Cameron began warning of Britain's 'broken society' and a
national 'crime crisis'. 'At last!' roared the *Daily Mail* at the end of August.
'Mr Cameron is talking like a Tory.'[244]

Coulson also devised a strategy to present Cameron as more mature and
statesmanlike. Colleagues christened it 'flags and fireplaces'.

An insider recalls:

> There was always this anxiety about David being too young – that
> he wouldn't look ready for the responsibility. Andy had this thing
> about flags and fireplaces – it was taking pictures of David shak-
> ing hands with world leaders in front of fireplaces with flags. For
> those pictures, David would adopt a 'Prime Minister in waiting'
> look. That was his flags and fireplaces look.

When colleagues suggested policies or initiatives Coulson considered flimsy,
he would send them back to the drawing board, saying, 'Needs more grit.'
As time went by, coverage of Cameron's leadership in previously sceptical
right-leaning newspapers became more favourable, and the party leader
secured more face-time with those he needed to win over. In August 2008, he
took a private jet laid on by Murdoch's son-in-law Matthew Freud to dine
on the media mogul's yacht, an important breakthrough. A year earlier, the
tycoon had dismissed him as a 'PR guy' and 'totally inexperienced'. There
would be no sudden conversion, but at least Cameron was getting face-time.

('I don't think he was ever particularly fond of him,' says a News Corp
insider today of Murdoch's attitude to the PM. 'I mean, his view of trusta-
farians is not a million miles off his view of welfare claimants.')[245]

---

242 Ibid.
243 Tim Bale, p. 335.
244 *Daily Mail*, 29 August 2007.
245 Private information.

A year after Coulson's arrival at CCHQ, Cameron's campaign to woo News International received an unexpected boost, when Rebekah Wade, then editor of *The Sun* (and shortly to become chief executive of News International) began dating racehorse trainer Charlie Brooks. Though few people knew of the connection, Brooks just happened to be exceptionally close to Cameron's brother Alex. The pair had been at Eton together. Now the link between the Tory leader and the *Sun* editor, whom he did not yet know well, was personal as well as professional. When Wade and Brooks married in 2009 and settled on Brooks's farm in Sarsden, three miles from Cameron's constituency home in Dean, the circle was complete. It was now easy and natural for them all to socialise: Alex and Sarah Cameron; David and Samantha Cameron; and Rebekah and Charlie Brooks, in any combination; with or without the company of some of the other rich and successful types living in the area. Around this time, gossip columnists began referring to the 'Chipping Norton set'. If Cameron was a little 'square' for some of its loucher members, his power, and his beautiful hippy-chick wife, gave him an obvious entrée.

With what looked like just weeks to make his case to voters, Cameron hoped to use the 2007 Conservative Party conference to blindside Brown with a series of populist policy proposals. The trump card was to be a huge rise in the threshold for paying inheritance tax.

O'Shaughnessy recalls:

> George had done some polling on the taxes that people hated most, and that was the one that got people most energised. There were two parts to our announcement, one bit of which was [that there would be] no stamp duty for first-time buyers. I remember having an argument with George on the phone, saying that the stamp duty thing was a bad policy, because it is difficult to define a first-time buyer. Somebody getting divorced, for example – are they a first-time buyer? Why should they be disadvantaged compared to somebody who's a City banker, buying a little pied-à-terre? I argued that we should just scrap stamp duty for properties under £250,000. I remember him saying, 'Yes, but that way, we can't make the inheritance tax threshold £1 million – it will have to be £750,000, and £1 million is really important because nobody will

remember £750,000. It's got to be a round number!' Which was perfectly true, and that is why he's the politician...

Everyone was sworn to secrecy about the inheritance tax proposal. Then, disaster struck. Just two days before conference opened, an aide called Chris Skidmore (now an MP) accidentally emailed a huge batch of confidential documents detailing the scheme to a Lib Dem backbencher. The papers, which were not encrypted and could be opened without a password, also contained information about some fifteen other new policy proposals.

News of the blunder sparked panic at campaign headquarters. An appalled O'Shaughnessy, who was at his desk on the 'pod' in the middle of the office, feared their entire strategy for the coming weeks would be derailed.

'Fuck! Fuck! Fuck! Fuck!' he yelled.

The documents had been sent to the then Portsmouth South MP Mike Hancock, whose parliamentary email address was similar to that of Osborne's aide, Matthew Hancock.

'It was a real *Thick of It* moment,' says one who was there.[246] 'I had actually never heard James swearing before. I heard him shouting "fuck, fuck, fuck". I asked him what had happened, and he just replied: "Fuck!" There was a massive panic. It was the whole lot – everything we planned.'

A frantic Skidmore hot-footed it to Hancock's office in the House of Commons, but it was shut. There was no sign of the MP's secretary.

The insider recalls:

> Of course, we couldn't tell them of the magnitude of it anyway. We were going to have to play it cool, say, 'Uh, I'm sorry, an email's gone missing – would you mind just deleting it or forwarding it, or whatever?' Andy and George were running around, trying to make a plan for what would happen if it got leaked en masse. Chris was sort of hanging himself somewhere...

Led by Coulson, a nervous delegation went to break the news to Cameron.

'OK, let's all calm down,' Cameron said evenly. 'Either it will be in the Sunday papers, in which case, we'll have a rapid briefing, or it won't, in which case, we'll carry on as normal.'

---

246   Referring to the satirical TV programme about the world of Whitehall.

Colleagues were impressed by his sangfroid.

'He just calmed the whole situation down. Everyone suddenly thought, "Ah, OK, that's quite sensible,"' says one, who well remembers the relief at CCHQ when the boss did not hit the roof.

O'Shaughnessy still shudders when he remembers the drama. 'Very occasionally it wakes me in the middle of the night still,' he says.

The episode also held back Skidmore's political career. He secured a parliamentary seat in 2010, but remained firmly on the backbenches, with any suggestion of advancement blackballed by Osborne.

An insider says, 'When George heard Chris was running for a seat a couple of years later, he was appalled. He said, "What the fuck is that guy doing as one of our candidates? I thought we'd killed him after the email thing."'

It took eight years, but it seems that Osborne eventually forgave Skidmore, who became MP for Kingswood. After languishing on the backbenches throughout Cameron's first term in office, he was finally given a role as the Chancellor's PPS in 2015.

In the event, Hancock never noticed the bombshell email. After a nervous forty-eight hours, Osborne was able to unveil his flagship new inheritance tax policy at conference as planned. The media reaction was rapturous. Suddenly, Brown became nervous about calling the election.

In fact, Labour's comfortable lead over the Tories had begun to ebb before the Conservative conference. Towards the end of September, the party's private polling in marginal seats began showing a shift towards the Tories. Now the gap was narrowing further, sending Brown into a tailspin.

On Saturday 6 October, in an interview with the BBC's Andrew Marr, the Prime Minister dramatically ruled out an early election, claiming he wanted more time to show the country his 'vision for change'. To widespread derision, he insisted his decision had nothing to do with the polls.

At home in Dean, Cameron was glued to the television, amazed by what he was hearing.

'My mobile phone doesn't work that well in Oxfordshire so I had to keep running between the garden and the television,' he recalled.

> So it was rather farcical. I'd actually found out the day before, but still it was fascinating to watch…We saw this incredible surge in the polls during the week before…we started to do better and he

then bottled it...when he said that not calling an election had nothing to do with the polls [it] was quite a big moment for me because
I just thought that was such rubbish.[247]

Once again the polls reversed. The Conservatives took the lead the weekend
of Brown's announcement, and by the autumn had extended their advantage
into double figures. Having seen Brown as strong, competent and straightforward, voters began to regard him as weak, dishonest and a ditherer. It was
now clear there would be no election until the last possible date in 2010. It
meant the Tory leadership could focus on longer-term strategy.

The first big test was the upcoming London Mayoral election, scheduled
for May 2008. It was a serious challenge: Labour was generally at least ten
points ahead of the Tories in the capital. Overturning such a lead would
be a huge deal, signalling loud and clear that Cameron's Conservatives
were on the warpath. To pull it off, Cameron needed a big hitter to take on
the controversial but popular incumbent, Ken Livingstone. Finding a suitable candidate proved onerous. The frontrunner, Nick Boles, a Cameroon
with impeccable modernising credentials, fell ill early in summer 2007 and
pulled out. Cameron was left frantically searching for a replacement. At one
point, he approached the former BBC director-general Greg Dyke, a former
Labour Party supporter.

Dyke recalls:

> I was first contacted by Steve Hilton, who I liked a lot because he
> was not like a traditional Tory at all. I had just left the BBC and
> they obviously thought this would be clever. I said to them, 'I am
> not a Tory.' To which they basically said, 'It doesn't matter.'

After meeting Cameron to discuss it further, the former BBC man concluded
he could not run on a Conservative ticket.

'I went back to him and said I thought the jump was too far. I said I quite
fancied the job, but I can't do it,' he recalls.

Dyke then had another idea: he would run on a joint ticket with the Lib
Dems. Cameron approved the plan – the only proviso being that Dyke should
publicly endorse him at the general election, a condition he was happy to

247   David Cameron and Dylan Jones, pp. 129–31.

meet. Dyke says now that he considered Cameron 'quite a Liberal Tory'. However, the scheme leaked and the Lib Dems, who had been making the right noises, took fright.

Day by day, Cameron found himself striking names off the list of possible Tory contenders. The situation was getting desperate. He needed someone who could inject fireworks into the race – and fast. Right up until the last moment, he refused to consider the man who seemed to many observers the obvious choice: Boris Johnson. A Tory MP recalls discussing the problem with him at a fundraising dinner. He remembers Cameron bandying around various 'random' names like Richard Branson, people who 'weren't even Tories'.

'The ideal candidate is right in front of you,' the MP told Cameron, speaking metaphorically.

'Who?' Cameron asked.

'Boris,' came the reply.

Cameron puffed out his chest.

'Totally the wrong profile,' he said, with a dismissive wave of his hand. When Johnson heard of the exchange, he took it in good part.

'Did he really say that? The fucker!' he exclaimed cheerfully.[248]

The Mayor concedes he was literally bottom of Cameron's list of desired candidates. 'He didn't want me to run,' he admits now.

Cameron's reticence was understandable: as a shadow minister under Howard, Johnson had proven something of a loose cannon. In October 2004, he was forced to go on an 'apology tour' to Liverpool after accusing the city of wallowing in 'victim status' following the beheading of Liverpudlian engineer Ken Bigley in Iraq, a remark that caused huge offence to families affected by the Hillsborough disaster. A month later, he was sacked from the front bench after lying to Howard about his notoriously complicated private life. His track record suggested he would be a liability. Additionally, Cameron may have seen him as a threat. Though the tension between the two men has been significantly overstated, their relationship has always been tinged with rivalry. For years, Johnson, the older of the two, regarded Cameron as his junior, in more ways than one.

'Boris does think he's cleverer than Cameron, and certainly a lot more thoughtful,' says one of Johnson's former advisers. 'He genuinely thinks that he has the bigger brain. He likes people who are very thoughtful and

---

248 Private information.

have a depth and intensity and profundity of understanding, whereas to him Cameron is more of a technocrat.'[249]

When they both entered Parliament in 2001, Johnson was the star, as he had always been, at school and at university. He was the editor of *The Spectator*; the *Telegraph*'s most popular columnist; and a star turn on the TV show *Have I Got News for You*. By contrast, Cameron was a nobody.

When Cameron became party leader in 2005, the tables turned. In a provocative move, the new Tory leader denied his fellow Old Etonian a place in the shadow Cabinet, despite the fact that Johnson was one of his earliest backers. The blond one was instead offered the position of shadow spokesman for higher education, which he grudgingly accepted. Two years later, when Cameron carried out a reshuffle, Johnson was passed over once again. So it was with some satisfaction that, in early summer 2007, Johnson made Cameron sweat it out for a while before eventually agreeing to run for the Mayoralty.

Initially, Cameron's misgivings seemed justified. The MP for Henley did not appear to be taking the task particularly seriously, and in the media, his candidacy was widely regarded as something of a joke.

'Leading up to Christmas 2007, it was all looking a bit dodgy,' Johnson admits now. 'It all seemed so fantastical. I really wanted to do it, but I had no idea about how to go about it. It was like telling me to climb Everest in six weeks' time. I didn't know anything about emergency planning, housing budgets...'

Amid mounting panic at party headquarters over the prospect of an ignominious defeat, Cameron stepped in, persuading Lynton Crosby to come to London and knock the Tory candidate into shape. On arrival, the Australian made it clear that he had no truck with time wasters. According to Johnson's biographer, he and the Tory peer Lord Marland took the candidate to dinner at the popular Westminster eaterie Quirinale, where they warned him – in typically fruity language – not to let them down 'or we'll cut your fucking knees off!'[250]

The result, on 1 May 2008, was a triumph for both Johnson and Cameron. A Tory now ran London – a massive coup. It heralded the start of a new

249   Private information.
250   Sonia Purnell, *Just Boris: A Tale of Blond Ambition* (Aurum Press, 2012), p. 324.

chapter in their relationship. The schoolboy rivalry would have to be put on ice.

Over in Parliament's Norman Shaw building, where the Tory leadership was based, the focus was firmly back on the party's long-term electoral strategy. Keen to avoid yet another election on the defensive over claims that they would cut public services, Cameron and Osborne had always hoped to take the wind out of Brown's sails by matching his spending plans. A party strategist describes the move as 'a way of neutralising the issue'. Then the financial crisis struck.

An insider says: 'It changed the whole tone. All of a sudden, the thing we hadn't been talking about became the most important thing in the room. It was all bound up with tax and spend, which David and George had been desperate to get away from.'

As the banking system hung in the balance and the country plunged into the deepest downturn since the Great Depression, there could be no way of ducking the economic debate. Bankers bore the brunt of public anger, putting them in the firing line of all three party leaders, who lashed out at the culture of risk taking in the City and vowed to curb excessive bonuses. A senior party adviser says Cameron, whose social circle is not stuffed with bankers, was taken aback when he realised the scale of profligacy in the City.

> David came to my room one Monday morning, which he didn't often do – because he didn't wander around the broader office very much – and he came to the desk. We had a mutual banker friend and David had been to lunch with him at the weekend…and he was genuinely shocked by the building work that had gone on in this guy's house and the lavishness of it all. And he specifically wanted to come and seek me out to tell me how even this civilised, Old Etonian friend of his was behaving in this way. And, you know, it clearly brought out in David something that resonated in terms of how much the bankers were making. Occasionally this sort of thing would come out which was more from the heart than the head.[251]

Though the Brown government's reputation for economic management and all-round competence had suffered since the cancelled election, the

---

251 Private information.

seriousness of the economic situation put pressure on the Conservatives as well as Labour. Brown was back on home territory on the economy, and voters could see him playing a leading role in international efforts to contain the crisis. Polls found that most people thought that he and the Chancellor, Alistair Darling, were making a better job of handling things than Cameron and Osborne would probably manage, and Brown's declaration in his 2008 conference speech that this was 'no time for a novice' found some resonance with the public. The Tories could not simply rely on events: when it came to being trusted to run the economy, they would have to establish real credibility of their own.

As Britain's borrowing continued to grow, questions of tax and spending took centre stage, where they would stay for the remainder of the parliament.

The insider says:

> All of a sudden, the main plank of our political strategy, which was to put that to bed and talk about other stuff…that was gone. We were back where the last Tory Party had been, which was talking about spending less than Labour, which is not where we wanted to be.

Osborne made an early decision to put tackling the deficit at the heart of the party's response to the crash. Daniel Finkelstein remembers him sketching 'a load of boxes' on a piece of scrap paper and singling out the huge gap between government spending and income as his main target.

> It was different things like VAT, tax and so on. He said, 'Look, they all move round. If you move one, another one moves. So you have to pick one fixed point, and let the others move around it.' Then he took his pencil, and said it was the deficit.

Surveying the desperate state of the public finances, the shadow Chancellor was convinced that there was no alternative to years of austerity. The big question was how much to tell voters.

'It was a massive judgement call,' says one who was involved in the debate.

> The argument went back and forth. Everybody would have preferred us not to say anything – obviously it was risky to do so.

But if we didn't, people might think we had a completely disingenuous economic policy. If we were saying that the key distinction
between us and Labour was that the country faced a massive economic problem, and we would deal with it and they wouldn't, didn't
we have to say, to some extent, how?

For the remainder of 2007 and the first half of 2008, the heat was off Cameron
and Osborne in any case, as attention focused on Brown's efforts to save
the economy and his own increasingly vulnerable position. That spring, the
Tories won two by-elections, in Crewe and Nantwich, and Henley, increasing
jitters in the Labour camp. Privately, many Labour MPs were deeply pessimistic about their party's prospects under Brown and were casting around
for an alternative leader to take them into the 2010 election. Though the
Prime Minister had clawed back some authority by showing firm leadership
during the banking crisis, he was tired, damaged and a drag on the Labour
vote. Throughout 2008 and 2009, rumours swirled of plots against him,
and there were a number of failed coups. Cameron's main concern was that
Brown stay put.

While the Tory leader considered the popular Labour Health Secretary
Alan Johnson by far the most dangerous of the potential contenders, he also
worried about David Miliband. The Foreign Secretary had disappointed
many in the Labour Party by failing to challenge Brown for the leadership
when Blair quit in 2007, but by summer 2008, there was speculation that
he might be ready to strike.

On holiday in Cornwall with Samantha and the children, Cameron was
sufficiently nervous to email his inner circle suggesting they briefed journalists that a leadership contest would be bad for the country.

Weather is so bad that I have borrowed [a] computer to browse all
the Brown/Miliband stuff. Two completely obvious points:
    We must use this opportunity to paint Miliband in the right
light. He bottled the chance last time and is behaving in a totally
weak way again. Our line should be 'either have the bottle to challenge the Prime Minister, or demonstrate the steel to back him
and show some loyalty. This sort of positioning exercise is weak
and pathetic.' The best outcome for us is that, under pressure, he

bottles it again. A sort of double Portillo without even ringing BT and ordering the phone lines.

The only good reason for not getting rid of Brown is that a 12-week leadership contest when the country is suffering from credit crunch/cost of living would be truly ghastly.

Warming to his theme, he scripted some 'lines to take'.

'Rudderless, leaderless Britain when people need strong leadership. All we have got is the prospect of a lame duck Prime Minister and Harriet Harman preening herself as being in charge when people need a strong united government.' We should start setting this up…We need to hammer away at this (it may put them off challenging Brown).

He signed off by saying he was going to the beach.

'OK, enough, back to surfing, Frisbee (sorry, didn't see the long lens)…'

While Cameron relaxed, Osborne was fretting about his conference speech. He was still agonising over how bleak a picture to paint, fearing voters would be turned off by his real assessment of the country's dire economic prospects. Some colleagues believed he could avoid spelling out the scale of the misery ahead by arguing that he did not yet have access to the books. With no clear consensus emerging at headquarters, focus groups were commissioned to test public appetite for the truth.

A No. 10 insider recalls:

We literally took a focus group through his draft conference speech, line by line. I can't remember what bizarre explanation we gave for what we were showing them. But we had a PowerPoint presentation, with a paragraph at a time, asking them: 'What if we said this? Is this enough? What fears would it provoke?' And so on. George was very unnerved by it all. I remember him saying: 'This is doing my head in.' It struck me at the time, because it was a very un-George thing to say.

The feedback from the focus group was unambiguous: the party would not be taken seriously if Cameron and Osborne were not frank.

> All the research we did showed that people just didn't buy the argu-
> ment that we couldn't decide anything until we got into government
> and saw the books. They thought it was just politician crap. They
> accepted we couldn't know everything, but said that we must know
> at least what kind of direction we'd go in – and if we said we didn't,
> then that would probably mean we weren't up to the job. Getting
> the balance right was incredibly difficult.

Nonetheless, with Brown on the rack, blamed for failing to curb the reckless-
ness and greed of the banking industry and allowing consumer debt to spiral
out of control, the momentum was with the Conservatives. At Westminster
and in the media, there was now a general consensus that the Tories would
win the next election. In mid-September 2008, one poll gave the party a
28-point lead. Cameron began to worry about appearing complacent.

'I remember George grinning all over his face, and David saying, very
quietly, "Hmm, I think this calls for a celebratory cup of tea." And then
he went back to his office, by himself, to have his celebratory cup of tea,'
recalls a CCHQ staffer. To set a suitably sober scene at party conference,
Tory ministers and staffers were banned from drinking champagne.

That autumn, Osborne's set piece to the party faithful was the big-ticket
event. After weeks of agonising over the tone, the shadow Chancellor went
all out with what one newspaper called a 'terrifically stern and remarkably
old-fashioned…sermon on prudence'.[252] While some commentators praised
his cojones, others questioned whether his dire warning about the long, hard
road ahead was a recipe for electoral success.

Any lingering anxiety the shadow Chancellor might have felt about
whether he had struck the right note was soon blown out of the water by a
far bigger drama, however. The episode, which became known as Yachtgate,
almost cost him his career. It involved a surprising figure: Peter Mandelson.

That October, Brown had stunned Westminster by announcing Mandelson's
return to frontline politics. By giving him a peerage, the Prime Minister was
able to parachute him into Cabinet as Business Secretary. The appointment
was all the more surprising given the Labour grandee's well-known antipathy
to the Prime Minister.

---

252   *The Guardian*, 29 September 2008.

Just a few weeks earlier – presumably before he knew he was about to be welcomed back into the fold – Mandelson had been deliciously indiscreet about what he really thought of Brown. The setting was the Greek island of Corfu, where he and Osborne were both guests of the financier Nat Rothschild. They had partied together on board a £70 million yacht belonging to Russian aluminium tycoon Oleg Deripaska, and had shared confidences about the political scene. During their conversation, Mandelson 'dripped pure poison' about Brown.

In the context of his shock return to government, this information was dynamite. In a move he would come to bitterly regret, Osborne leaked details of the exchange to a newspaper, sparking a media furore. Mandelson was angry enough, but Rothschild – who expected total discretion from those to whom he extended hospitality – was incandescent. In a highly unusual step, he retaliated by writing a letter to *The Times*, accusing Osborne of trying to solicit donations to the Tory Party from the Russian oligarch, a potential breach of UK election law. Writing from Klosters, Switzerland, Rothschild described Mandelson's indiscretions as 'trivial' relative to Osborne's actions, concluding archly that in future 'perhaps' it would be better 'if all involved accepted the age-old adage that private parties are just that'.

The letter unleashed a firestorm that threatened to engulf the shadow Chancellor. Initially, Cameron thought it would quickly blow over.

'It's a storm in a teacup,' he told colleagues blithely.

He was wrong.

For several days, Osborne's career hung in the balance. It was the first serious test of his bond with Cameron, who came under intense pressure to sack him. In private conversations with close confidants, the Tory leader hinted that he would be willing – if absolutely necessary – to jettison his closest ally. It did not come to that, but friends say Osborne was deeply shaken.

'It was very touch and go for him. You could tell he was worried – it was in his eyes,' says one.

For some time afterwards, Osborne was uncharacteristically subdued.

'I am in humble mode,' he told Hague, shortly after the drama had died down.

'God should take advantage of this rare moment,' came the retort.

Today, the episode is largely forgotten outside Westminster, but some Tories believe it had a profound effect on the party's fortunes.

'I've always said that was the beginning of our problems,' says one senior strategist.

> Up to that point, we were seen as entirely fresh. We were the new boys in town, and David hadn't put a foot wrong. The Deripaska thing suddenly showed that we were lunching with billionaires; going on yachts; going abroad. Suddenly, our 22-point lead started dropping down to about ten points.

Cameron's determination to hang on to Osborne was partly loyalty, but it was also driven by his dependence on the shadow Chancellor's economic expertise. In the wake of the crash in 2008, he and Osborne set up various advisory committees, including one comprising four former Chancellors – Geoffrey Howe, Nigel Lawson, Norman Lamont and Ken Clarke – to offer guidance on the party's long-term economic policy and to advise on the most effective short-term response to the financial crisis.

What surprised some of those who gave their expertise was how disengaged Cameron seemed in these discussions.

One of the party's high-profile advisers at the time says:

> I saw very little evidence that David was very interested in it...I think he was genuinely interested in what was broadly going on and wanting to sound intelligent on what the concerns were, but I didn't see him wanting to get into an intellectual debate about public spending and so on. It doesn't really interest him, the economy, does it?

Cameron's detached attitude to the raging debate about tax and spend seems all the more remarkable given that he subsequently made 'sorting out the economic mess' his defining mission. The same adviser, an extremely distinguished figure who has nothing against the Tory leader, cannot recall him asking detailed questions of the various businessmen and economists on the advisory panels, nor discussing ideology on levels of taxation.

> There were interesting things on the tax agenda – for example, George was using arguments about maximising the 'take' to justify

suggesting a cut in capital gains – but Cameron wasn't interested in debating any of that. Did he have private debates about it with George, late at night? I don't think so. If he was having troubled conversations about the big questions we faced, he was having them in a very, very narrow circle. There was no evidence that any of this exercised him.

He was bemused by Cameron's attitude.

> In no sense did this seem like a man who'd got a First in PPE. George wanted to talk to economists to get some intellectual underpinning to the way we were going to go on the deficit. He really wanted to get an understanding of the way deficits are a drag on the economy. David didn't. George, of course, was a historian [at university] and David was the man who read PPE. And this was always going to be a very big theme! I just suppose it is the way that David is, and was.

A fellow senior economic adviser said much the same thing: 'David Cameron, certainly on the economic side, doesn't get into the detail. It was clear that George Osborne was the person who was really getting involved with the details.'[253]

It's not as if he didn't receive proper economics training. Brasenose had a particularly strong reputation for the subject in the 1980s. One of his former tutors says, 'Cameron came out of this college with a great level of knowledge about the British economy.'

In any case, Cameron's detachment from economic minutiae set the scene for what would become to all intents and purposes a dual premiership. Though he would very occasionally challenge and even veto Osborne's policy proposals when they took power, the Tory leader was far happier to let his friend 'get on with it' than previous prime ministers have been with their chancellors. Unlike Blair with Brown, he never felt threatened by Osborne's power and influence and never sought to clip his wings. As a result, instead of the fluctuating balance of power between premiers and their chancellors of recent history, the relationship between Cameron and Osborne has been a steady and level partnership of equals.

---

253 Private information.

25
TIN HATS

'Fucking Douglas Hogg and his fucking moat!'

– Tory party aide

Having settled on a strategy for the nation's finances, Cameron suddenly found the spotlight turning to his own – and those of his colleagues. In May 2009, the *Telegraph* newspaper obtained confidential details of expenses claims submitted by every MP between 2004 and 2008. In excruciating detail, the paper exposed the greed and parsimony of politicians from every party at every level, from those in the highest office to the lowest-profile backbenchers, who suddenly found themselves thrust into the uncomfortable glare of the national media as their attempts to charge the taxpayer for everything from Jaffa Cakes to loo seats and silk-covered cushions were laid bare.

The revelations triggered a political earthquake, culminating in the imprisonment of a number of MPs for fraud. Few escaped unscathed, and though only a handful ended up behind bars, many were forced to repay substantial sums, or lost their careers. The reputation and status of the political class were permanently damaged. Such was the misery at Westminster at the height of the scandal that there was a real fear of suicides.

The crisis was the biggest test yet of Cameron's leadership. He had to strike the right note with an electorate baying for blood; but he also had to navigate the diplomatic minefield presented by questionable expenses claims submitted by his own friends. Even his own were a source of embarrassment: he had been reimbursed for renovation work on his cottage in Dean, including clearing wisteria and vines from the chimney, and resealing his conservatory roof.

Though the scandal presented an opportunity – he would later claim that he was the first of the three party leaders to demonstrate leadership on the issue – he would also lose friends. His handling of the crisis, in which he was accused of protecting his closest allies no matter how egregious their expenses while ruthlessly jettisoning older 'dead wood' MPs whose offences were no worse, had a deeply corrosive effect on his relationship with the parliamentary party. Though it got him through the furore, to this day, he has not been forgiven by some of his own people.

The parliamentary expenses system was ripe for abuse. The most controversial feature was a £24,000 allowance to cover the cost of running a second home.

In theory, the system was designed to compensate MPs for essential outlays. In practice, almost all MPs regarded it as a form of 'top-up salary', resulting in a very flexible interpretation of what constituted a justifiable 'expense'.

The *Telegraph* began its exposé with big-name Labour targets, splashing the receipts of, among others, Hazel Blears, the Communities Secretary; Jack Straw, the Justice Secretary; and even Gordon Brown himself, who was revealed to have paid his brother Andrew more than £6,500 for the use of a cleaner at his private flat in Westminster, as well as claiming twice for a decorating bill. However, it soon became clear that nobody would be spared scrutiny.

Cameron quickly grasped the scale of the crisis and attempted to wrest some control over events by setting up his own internal inquiry into the expenses claims of Tory MPs. On 12 May, he declared that he was 'sorry for the actions of some Conservative MPs – people are right to be angry'.[254] He then told the backbench 1922 Committee he would be setting up a 'Star Chamber' led by his chief of staff Ed Llewellyn and Patrick McLoughlin, the opposition Chief Whip, to decide if MPs had overstepped the mark. There would be no right of appeal and any Tory MP who refused to submit to a panel hearing would be thrown out. By contrast, Brown was left looking as if he was being buffeted by events. Cameron later reflected proudly that 'in terms of leadership, I got there first'.[255]

Pressure for a robust response was not coming from the media alone: those who worked tirelessly for the party at their own expense were appalled by what they were hearing. They asked Don Porter to take their views to the top.

254   *Daily Telegraph*, 12 May 2009.
255   David Cameron and Dylan Jones, p. 391.

'I have been approached by many volunteers to express our disgust,' he wrote to Cameron on 11 May. 'It is of no interest or relevance that MPs, including some of your shadow Cabinet colleagues, try to hide their behaviour behind the existing rules. What about their moral compass and their own conscience?'

He urged the party leader not to spare senior colleagues.

'I believe you have to sack all those front-bench colleagues who have exploited the system. Anything less than this will…leave our party tainted with the aura of sleaze once again. We have not worked tirelessly over the last twelve years to see our progress wasted on self-seeking colleagues,' he wrote.

At CCHQ, it fell to Henry Macrory, the genial former political editor of the *Star* and the party's head of press, to take the nightly call from Robert Winnett, the *Telegraph's* deputy political editor, detailing the next day's revelations. A former CCHQ staffer recalls how Macrory, with gallows humour, would pick up the phone and ask Winnett jovially, 'Is it a tin hat day or a steel jock strap day?'[256]

Members of the shadow Cabinet were no better than the lower ranks when it came to spurious claims. Gove found himself in trouble for claiming thousands on home furnishings from Oka and a cot mattress from Toys 'R' Us, despite children's items being banned. That he survived the Star Chamber experience continues to rankle those condemned for what they consider less serious infringements. Iain Duncan Smith was caught trying to claim nearly £40 for a single breakfast, while Alan Duncan – who had claimed more than £4,000 on gardening – was later secretly filmed declaring that MPs 'live on rations and are treated like shit'. In a reshuffle that September, Cameron demoted him from his role as shadow Leader of the House to the more junior post of shadow Minister for Prisons. By contrast, Osborne escaped lightly: receipts revealing that he had claimed for a £440.62 chauffeur-driven car to transport him from his constituency home in Cheshire to London were a relatively minor embarrassment.

For weeks, Cameron found himself summoning an endless stream of MPs to his office in Norman Shaw South, and holding crisis meetings with colleagues to decide who should be expelled and who should be forgiven.

'I used to sit outside in the corridor of the headmaster's office, as it were,' recalls a former adviser who witnessed the miserable troupe of MPs heading

---

256 Private information.

into the leader's office. 'Seeing copies of the *Telegraph* laid out there as if people hadn't seen it already, and people coming and going, looking ashen-faced…it was awful.'

Two specific cases caused Tories particular damage. Douglas Hogg, who claimed thousands of pounds to have his country estate's moat cleared, and Sir Peter Viggers, who tried to claim reimbursement for the cost of an eye-catching 'Stockholm' duck house in his garden pond, fulfilled all the Tory stereotypes Cameron was desperate to eradicate. Viggers's claim so caught the public imagination that it became the subject of a play, *The Duck House*, which ran at the Vaudeville Theatre in London. Neither of the veteran MPs showed remorse – or any real grasp of why voters were so angry – and were defensive under questioning. Their insouciance infuriated the press, and the two men quickly came to be seen as emblems of an 'out-of-touch' political class and an unreformed Conservative Party. Cameron came down hard.

'David was genuinely appalled by the duck house,' says a former aide who had the unpleasant task of acting as a go-between with miscreants.

> Peter couldn't see it initially. I had to ring him up and he said, 'But I didn't get the duck house, why is it a story?' And I replied, 'I'm afraid you're going to have to show some regret,' to which he responded, 'But I didn't even get the bloody thing!' I reported back that he didn't get the point, and David was so angry that he rang Viggers himself.[257]

Cameron threw down an ultimatum, ordering the MP of thirty-five years to quit or face expulsion.

'The decision was made for Viggers,' recalls a CCHQ staff member. 'That's one thing about David, he does sometimes just say, "Right I'm doing this. I'm doing it, it's the right thing to do." David was determined that he had to make an example, to show that we were serious about it.'[258]

'Then there was Douglas Hogg and the moat,' the aide continues.

> I just remember someone coming to see us in CCHQ saying, 'Would you fucking believe it – it's a fucking moat! Fucking Douglas Hogg and his fucking moat!'

---

257 Private information.
258 Private information.

I remember seeing him being interviewed and he'd broken the three basic rules of giving an interview. Rule One, he was wearing a hat – never wear a hat. Second, he was running away from the camera, running down the street breathless. The third one was that he refused to answer the questions properly anyway. It was absolutely awful, so David had no sympathy for him.

Oddly enough, he had a bit of sympathy for Anthony Steen, who pruned about 500 trees on his estate at taxpayers' expense – and tried to claim it was for the public benefit. David had a bit of sympathy for him, because he respected him a lot: he was a bumbling old twit but he'd done a lot of stuff on slavery – a lot of Labour MPs admired him too.[259]

Both Viggers and Hogg, having been hauled in front of the scrutiny panel, reluctantly announced they would quit before the election – although Cameron, in a surprise footnote, later put Hogg's name forward for a life barony in the 2011 New Year's honours list. The House of Lords Appointments Commission advised against it.

Throughout this traumatic period, Cameron tried to take his party with him, with mixed success. His authoritarian treatment of respected older colleagues raised suspicions that he was using the crisis to purge the party of an older generation of 'bed-blocker' MPs. Yet allies insist he had no choice. 'He had to get rid of Viggers, he had no alternative,' a former CCHQ official argues. 'Just imagine if David had done nothing, imagine what the comment would have been. His own wisteria was not a hanging offence, but some of them were hanging offences and David had to do the hanging.'[260]

The month-long *Telegraph* exposé revealed a variety of 'scams', the most notorious of which became known as 'flipping'. Under this ruse, MPs would designate a particular property as their second home, in order to claim expenses against it; then state that this was now their main home in order to claim again on the other one. 'Flippers' – among them Gove and Lansley – were therefore able to claim for refurbishment or mortgage interest on more than one home, and in some cases avoid capital gains tax when they sold the property. Then there were the 'double flippers': MPs married to other MPs

259 Private information.
260 Private information.

and claiming second-home allowances on two different properties. Andrew MacKay, Cameron's parliamentary adviser, and his wife Julie Kirkbride – also a Tory MP – were among those found guilty of this sin, and MacKay would become the first loss from Cameron's inner circle.

'Andrew used to go to the morning meeting,' recalls a member of Cameron's team.

> So when expenses started up, he was there giving good advice. Then somebody said to me at a meeting, 'I think next on the agenda for expenses is double dipping', and Andrew went terribly quiet. The next day it all came out…I think David was upset from a personal point of view. Andrew just fell on his sword straight away.

As the weeks went by, there was growing anger towards Cameron in the parliamentary party.

'It was quite shocking really, the way colleagues were treated,' says a senior backbencher.

> I was in Washington with Peter Viggers and the Treasury Select Committee on the day that the duck house story broke. Peter's office had received the dreaded call from the *Telegraph* and knew the paper wanted to talk to him. Over coffee, we chatted to him and I remember him saying, 'I think I'm going to be done for the same thing that [David] Heathcoat-Amory was done for – claiming for manure. Later, during a lunch break, he said he'd just taken a call from David Cameron's office. 'He's said I've got to decide whether I'm going to contest the next election or not!'…Then, two hours later, he said, 'I've just had another call. Apparently I've decided.' I think it had been announced [that he was stepping down] without him deciding it. It was very sad, I thought. Peter was not a particular friend but had given up a much better-paid career to come here, and given thirty-five years of public service, and was just cast out.[261]

Some backbenchers couldn't help feeling that for all the lip service Cameron paid to consensus and fairness in responding to the crisis, he formulated

261　Private information.

his response without consulting with the wider party, and gave preferential treatment to friends. A meeting of the 1922 Committee shortly after the scandal broke was simply 'brief, advance notice' of what he intended to tell the parliamentary party a few hours later. 'We had no say,' says a member of the executive.

In Cameron's defence, the scandal called for a fast and decisive response: seeming to prevaricate, let alone defend practices that had horrified and infuriated the public, would have been disastrous for a leader seeking to prove he could bring change.

However, a former adviser closely involved in the crisis management process agrees that Cameron was inconsistent in the way he dealt with colleagues: 'You could say that some people were forced to resign for not having done much really, and there were some people who didn't have to but should have. The whole thing was so horrendous. You either sack all of the party or none at all.'[262]

The discredited expenses system was replaced by a new scheme under which MPs can no longer claim for maintenance of second-home furnishings, for utility bills or for gardening, and instead receive a much more modest rental allowance – the equivalent of a one-bedroom flat. The system is monitored by an independent organisation called IPSA. It is widely hated. Some Tory MPs still feel Cameron, being personally wealthy, was too quick to sign up to it. His executive decision to bar Tory MPs from claiming a proposed £25-a-day allowance was a particular source of resentment.

'What Cameron decided to do was to have a more hair-shirt approach than the House had just announced,' one MP recalls.

> There was a sort of bidding war, in which Conservative MPs would take a worse hit than anyone else. One MP asked what would happen if the boiler in your second property broke down and you couldn't claim for it any more – could you at least claim the £25 to help offset those kinds of costs? He pointed out that the Commons authorities had said that it was right that we should be able to claim it. And Cameron said, very tersely and abruptly, 'Well, you

---

262   Private information.

can't. I've decided. That's the rule that my MPs are going to have.' I remember the MP asking him what would happen if they claimed it anyway – would they be disciplined? To which his response was, 'Yeah. It's bye-bye whip.'

In other words, those who claimed the £25 to which they were entitled would be summarily thrown out of the party.

Cameron probably did as well as could be expected under the circumstances. It is easy to forget the atmosphere of hysteria that gripped Westminster at the time. Day by day, reputations were being ruined. It is no exaggeration to say that lives – and livelihoods – were being shattered. The way the *Telegraph* strung out its revelations left many feeling as if they were on a kind of reputational death row. In this incredibly strained atmosphere, the Tory leader was under huge pressure. By throwing colleagues to the wolves, he appeased a public baying for blood, but his apparently arbitrary decisions left a legacy of resentment.

26

LOVE POD

'Christ, what have I done?'

– Cameron

While Cameron was preoccupied with the expenses scandal, the party machine was gearing up for the big battle in 2010. The Tory 'war room' was at 30 Millbank, where the architects of New Labour had plotted the path to a landslide in 1997. Built from recycled material and equipped with a state-of-the-art green energy system, the sweeping open-plan office housed some 150 staff, including the press and research operation, the treasurer and the fundraisers, as well as a burgeoning army of policy wonks and strategists. Cameron and Osborne's power base was to the end of the long, open-plan room, in a shared office called the Thatcher Room. Adjacent was a small, segregated office for the party chairman. At the opposite end was a team of party agents and pollsters overseeing 'field operations'. They were responsible for distributing up to £20,000 cash to candidates in marginal constituencies as part of a 'target seat' strategy aimed at focusing resources on parts of the map that had to turn blue to return the party to power.

One high-profile operative who had not been given a desk was Lynton Crosby. Though the Australian could not turn the tide on Labour in 2005, he had come up trumps in the London Mayoral elections of 2008, when he overturned a nineteen-point Labour lead to propel Boris Johnson to City Hall. Impressed, Cameron had hoped to re-engage him for the 2010 campaign, but not everybody shared the party leader's esteem for the strategist, and he was not hired.

Thus the most powerful figures in the camp were Cameron, Osborne, Hilton – responsible for overseeing advertising, messaging and branding – and

Coulson, whose job was to liaise with newspaper editors and broadcast chiefs, and to take charge of strategic communication. On the policy side, Oliver Letwin and James O'Shaughnessy, who were writing the manifesto, were the key players, though Letwin's propensity for getting into scrapes was a source of anxiety. In an episode that typified the sort of trouble he would get himself into, while working on the manifesto at Rachel Whetstone and Steve Hilton's house in Oxfordshire, he managed to lock himself in the loo and had to make an ungainly exit through a very small window, much to the mirth of those present.

After more than a decade in power, marked by a long war of attrition between the PM and his predecessor, the Labour Party was exhausted and demoralised. Yet the Tory mission was daunting. Though Howard had slightly narrowed the chasm between the two main parties in 2005, securing thirty-three additional seats, there was a mountain to climb: to win a one-seat majority, the Tories had to gain 117 seats. Nothing like it had been achieved in one step since 1931.

Throughout 2008 and much of 2009, however, there was reason for optimism. Polls generally gave the Tories a comfortable lead. Though Brown sought to present the financial crash as the work of global forces, the desperate state of the economy was seen by many as incontrovertible proof that Labour could not be trusted with the nation's finances. Brown's party was exhausted and divided, riven by plots against the leader. There was an overwhelming sense among voters that it was 'time for change'. At Westminster and in much of the media, it was received wisdom that the Tories would win. When the *Sun* newspaper dramatically turned its back on Labour after twelve years of support, splashing with the devastating headline 'Labour's Lost It' in the middle of Brown's last party conference, it seemed to many observers that the die was cast.

Yet the mood at 30 Millbank was cautious. The intelligence from private polling was worrying: Cameron had not (as Coulson liked to put it) 'sealed the deal'.

'[CCHQ] was doing all these tracking polls across the battleground seats, and all the results were showing we were not going to make it,' says one who was involved.

To ensure nobody at CCHQ was under any illusions, in autumn 2009, a team was assembled to put together a document for staffers called 'The

Uphill Struggle', underlining the sheer scale of the challenge to win an overall majority.[263] To many, the bleakness of the message came as a shock.

An insider recalls: 'After we presented it there was a sort of stunned silence. Some of the professionals were almost in tears.'

Some feared Cameron's eternal optimism was clouding his own judgement about the true position. Among those concerned about his attitude was Don Porter, a key figure on the party board and head of the umbrella group of Tory Party association chairmen. After nearly four decades working for the voluntary wing of the party, Porter was tapped into the mood on the ground in constituencies the length and breadth of the country, and better placed than most to detect ominous signs. As a conduit between the voluntary party and the leadership, he had regular one-to-one meetings with Cameron. These were always cordial – as an ultra-loyalist, Porter's overriding objective was to help Cameron become Prime Minister. However, on occasion, he felt it was his duty to deliver tough messages.

At the end of November 2009, he penned a frank memo to the leader warning that the party was heading for a hung parliament. He was particularly concerned about morale among activists.

'The oxygen pipeline between volunteers and the parliamentary party has been polluted … This saddens me greatly,' he wrote. 'Volunteers like strong, empathetic and clear leadership. Without this, they drift in all directions.'

In a wide-ranging analysis, he highlighted the rise of UKIP and other small parties; the nature of the Labour vote; and the 'patchy' performance of the party in the north as worrying portents. He questioned whether the party's bleak message about the economic hardship ahead was being sufficiently counterbalanced by hope.

'You have started to articulate to the electorate the size of the problem facing the country,' he wrote.

> This is morally right. You will win respect for this integrity and transparency. My concern is not about your honesty. It is about balancing this with a vision of the sunlit uplands which lie beyond the initial and possibly prolonged period of pain that will follow the election of a Conservative government. I sense that floating voters

---

263   Private information.

will respect your honesty but some of them will not vote for us without a message of hope and optimism.

Turning to policy, he argued that some initiatives appeared inconsistent with the overall vision, 'while others appear to be a case of don't upset anyone'.

In a final broadside, he took aim at the shadow Cabinet, questioning whether the team had an appropriate balance of skills and talent.

> With a handful of exceptions, I still do not sense a feeling of urgency, which existed in 1979. I have mentioned before in our conversations that the early Cabinets of Prime Minister Thatcher had a classic cocktail. Margaret provided the direction and determination; Willie Whitelaw diplomatically readjusted the flight plan from time to time; Cecil [Parkinson] appealed to traditional voters and charmed his way out of difficult situations for the party; Norman [Tebbit] connected with aspirant voters with a directness of message. Your equivalent cocktail lacks certain key elements. Of course you have William [Hague], who is indispensable. Eric [Pickles] reminds voters that not every member of the shadow Cabinet comes from a privileged background or has millionaire status. He also speaks with a genuine northern accent, which is a real asset. Beyond that, we struggle to appear 'normal'.

It was a serious message that Cameron could not ignore.

'Bloody good letter – thanks very much,' he said gamely when they next bumped into each other.

'Thanks – we should get together,' Porter replied.

'Yes, we must,' said Cameron. He was hurrying out of the building.

'When?' Porter pressed.

'Oooh, have a word with Ed [Llewellyn],' the party leader replied, dashing out of the door.

The following week, their paths crossed again at Baroness Thatcher's Christmas drinks party in Belgravia. Cameron reiterated how seriously he took Porter's missive.

'Really good letter, Don. I agree with virtually every word,' he said.

'Which is the word you don't agree with?' Porter enquired.

'Women,' Cameron replied, referring to a section of Porter's letter questioning the wisdom of all-women shortlists. 'We've got to have more women in there.'

They were not at odds on this – Porter's point was that women had to be appointed on merit, or it would come back to bite.

'David, I would be happy if the whole Cabinet were women, if they were there on merit,' he said.

He continued to press for a private meeting, but it never happened.

Of the many concerns he had listed, it was Cameron's perceived attitude to volunteers about which he was most troubled. Raising some £28 million a year for the Conservatives, the voluntary wing is the backbone of the party, responsible for selecting candidates and councillors, dropping leaflets and sticking up posters, liaising with local media, and generally keeping the party alive outside Westminster. It had been cultivated assiduously by previous party leaders, particularly Thatcher.

Porter says:

> Thatcher would come to party conference every year and probably give up two and a half hours of her time, not just to meet with the treasurers of the Association, but the people who were presenting a cheque to the party on behalf of their Association. She would personally receive them. She'd be on the platform and she orchestrated the whole procedure: no matter how small the cheque, no matter how big the cheque, she made you feel the most important person in the party. I presented a cheque to her three years running, from the Woking constituency. There would be a queue of probably 150 treasurers wanting to present cheques. She stood there, she had her photograph taken with every single one, she announced to the whole gathering, 'Here's a cheque from Woking for £10,000', and she had a story for every Association – something like 'Woking has got that first-class Member of Parliament...'
>
> I remember being followed by someone who was chairman of Ebbw Vale, who was presenting a cheque for £50 from the strongest Labour constituency in the country. She would spend as much time with that person as she would with me. If people had started to talk, she would say, 'Ladies and gentlemen, shhh – I have got a

cheque here for £50 from Ebbw Vale. Does anybody here know
who the Member of Parliament for Ebbw Vale is? It's Michael Foot
and this £50 is very eagerly received.' That person went away feeling 10ft tall. She knew how the system worked.

Many volunteers felt they were a low priority. This was not all Cameron's
fault: Porter believes those in charge of his diary bear the heaviest responsibility. Either way, he feared Cameron's perceived indifference could hamper
the party's prospects, and urged the party leader to make a symbolic gesture
to boost morale.

I told him he should 'top up his savings account' with the voluntary
party. His reply was 'What do you mean?' He seemed bemused. I
knew it was a difficult message and I tried to give it politely – but it
was what I was picking up from volunteers. He said he'd spent virtually all his time with the voluntary party. I said, 'No – that's your
current account, David. I mean your savings account.' My objective
was to get him to be Prime Minister. I wasn't trying to trip him up. I
didn't think there were enough people around telling him the truth.

Matters came to a head early in 2010, when Porter discovered plans were
afoot to axe the only salaried member of staff responsible for liaising with
volunteers. Cameron was probably unaware of the proposal, but it confirmed
Porter's suspicions that some around the leader did not care about the wider
party. Furious, he got straight on the phone to Caroline Spelman and threw
down the gauntlet.

He recalls:

She started talking about how the party had to save money. I said,
'Caroline, let me tell you three things that I am going to do unless
this job is reinstated. First of all, I will call an emergency meeting of
the Convention, which includes every [local party] chairman in the
country. They will all come to London – they will know that this is
something important. I will offer my resignation as national chairman and ask them to consider it. I will tell them the reasons why.
Then I will ask every Association in the country to stop sending

money to the centre, until this job is reinstated. Thirdly, I will ring up every Association in the country with loans at CCHQ – which was about £4.5 million – and tell them to withdraw it by Tuesday.' There was silence down the phone.

Within hours, the job had been reinstated.

The sorry state of relations between Central Office and the wider party was bad enough so close to the election, but the state of affairs at the heart of the Millbank operation was equally dysfunctional. Insiders say Cameron's propensity to give an ear to numerous conflicting viewpoints before making decisions was undermining any sense of direction, while a clash of personalities between Hilton and Coulson was an ongoing source of tension.

'There were too many cooks in the kitchen,' says a senior aide.

> In December and January, when we were trying to decide what our final message was – the four- or five-word thing we needed to get into every single voter's head – it took us a very long time to agree anything. It's because there were too many voices. Some were very radical, or interested in being very surprising and winning hearts and minds; whereas others were very risk averse and just wanted a safe and steady election. It was a symptom of David's desire to listen to everybody's point of view, and his immense loyalty to people who work for him. He wanted to hear everybody out, but there were rather a lot of people: Steve, Andy, George, Ed Llewellyn, Kate Fall…the list goes on. Nobody held sway.

In the absence of an alternative approach, Cameron and Osborne focused on attacking Brown – a strategy Cameron had been planning since 2005, when he talked about having to 'push Brown's face…in the shit'.[264]

Some felt it was misconceived.

'They thought the answer was to "keep the foot on Brown's throat" – that's how they described it. My argument was, "Look, he's completely fucked, and we're still not in a position to win the election. It's not about him, it's about us,"' recalls an aide.

---

264   Lesley White, *Sunday Times*, 22 April 2007.

The attacks were hitting home, however. According to Brown's friends, it would get to him.

'Cameron had this unnerving ability to find exactly the right place to stick his spear into Gordon,' says a former Labour Cabinet minister.

> One of his big lines of attack on Gordon as Prime Minister was to do with the funding of kit for troops in Afghanistan. He pushed it very hard. Effectively, he was accusing Gordon of sending our boys to their deaths. I would see Gordon afterwards and the impact on him personally was really troubling. He would just be saying afterwards, 'How could he really believe that about me? Does he really think I would do that?' We would say to him, 'Look, Gordon, unfortunately that's the kind of guy he is; and he's gone for the jugular.' And Gordon would say, 'But I'm not that person!' You know, the trouble is that Cameron could smell blood. There is that bullying dimension to him.

As British fatalities mounted in Afghanistan, Brown could hardly have expected tea and sympathy. Yet hardened operators in the Labour camp felt Cameron's attacks were 'more than below the belt', and reflected poorly on the Tory leader.

Meanwhile the rift between Coulson and Hilton was deepening. At the heart of the schism was Hilton's determination to talk about the Big Society while Coulson and Osborne wanted eye-catching policies.

'There were moments when it got very tasty,' O'Shaughnessy recalls. He remembers a particular blow-up between Hilton and Osborne over advertising plans, with Osborne questioning whether Hilton's suggestions 'would mean anything to people'.

'Have you polled any of this?' the shadow Chancellor asked sourly.

'No! You know I don't do that,' Hilton fired back. He had never set any store by focus groups. When his ideas were subjected to focus groups and he didn't like the results, he would dismiss voters' responses as 'too literal'.

As the row escalated, Cameron stepped in.

'Enough! We aren't going to resolve this now,' he said firmly.

It never was resolved. One very senior colleague, whom Cameron later took into Downing Street, claims Hilton was 'a complete nightmare' to deal with and blames him for the fractured campaign.

He says:

> It was largely down to him that nobody could be in charge of the campaign, because he would not cooperate with anybody else [except Cameron]; did not turn up at meetings when decisions were made – he wasn't part of them. In opposition, he was critical, but in the campaign, he caused quite a lot of damage.

In an attempt to improve interpersonal relations, Hilton and Coulson were given desks next to each other in a small, glass-walled meeting room at the heart of the office. With considerable irony, colleagues dubbed it the 'love pod'.

A colleague says:

> The idea was that by sitting them together, it would all work out, but of course it didn't. Steve's maverick way of conducting himself was in total contrast to Andy's professionalism. Steve would interfere. I don't think Andy resented Steve having a view, just the sort of random and destructive way in which he did it. It did get quite bad.

The ongoing debate about key messages came to a head in the New Year, when slogans were needed for billboards. A senior strategist recalls the panic at CCHQ at the dawning realisation that they still had a blank sheet.

'We were going to put posters all over the country and, oh my God, we had no idea what we were going to say!' he says.

They eventually settled on a huge presidential-style image of Cameron with the strapline: 'We can't go on like this. I'll cut the deficit, not the NHS.' Unveiled on 4 January 2010, it was widely lampooned, with Cameron's unnaturally smooth forehead raising suspicions that he'd been airbrushed.[265]

An insider says:

> It was David's idea. It didn't work. I remember driving back from
> a candidate's away day in early January. I was in Andy [Coulson]'s

---

265   He denied this, saying he simply has a 'baby face'. *Trevor McDonald Meets David Cameron.*

car and the posters had only been up for a day or two. He was like: 'I'm not sure they are going down very well. I have to say he looks a bit weird and they don't make any sense.' From then on, it just got worse. Every single day, they would have the same annoying arguments about messaging, with no resolution; George on one side, and Steve against Andy, and David and Andrew Feldman sort of in the middle. It drove them all mental.

Two areas gave less cause for concern: the manifesto and the target seat strategy. A decent draft manifesto had existed since the 'election that never was' in autumn 2007. Since then, it had been rewritten at least twice by O'Shaughnessy and Letwin under Cameron's direction. It meant there had been plenty time to 'stress test' policies and weed out or refine initiatives that turned out to be flawed.

Nonetheless, there were many who remained deeply unimpressed by the final version – including, according to a well-placed source, Margaret Thatcher, who took issue with its title: 'Invitation to Join the Government of Britain'.

'"What is this? What is this?" she spluttered on being shown a copy. "Invitation to join the government of Britain? People don't want to join the government of Britain! They want to elect the government of Britain, for it to govern!"'[266]

The party's private polling gave little cause for comfort. Though the public desire for change was overwhelming, enthusiasm for the Conservative Party was rather less so. Many wavering voters were unclear what kind of alternative a Cameron government would bring, and remained unconvinced that the Tories had their interests at heart. One of Osborne's friends remembers bumping into him about six weeks before polling day and being taken aback by the shadow Chancellor's mood.

'Are you enjoying the campaign?' the friend asked.

'No, I'm hating every minute of it,' came the sharp reply.

On 6 April 2010, Brown went to Buckingham Palace to ask the Queen to dissolve Parliament. It marked the start of the official 'short' election campaign. In the Tory war room, Cameron summoned the whole campaign team. Some 200 staff congregated to hear his battle cry.

---

266   Private information.

One who was there remembers:

> He walked in with the opposition Chief Whip [Patrick McLough-lin] and he made a twenty-minute speech about the fight that was about to start. It was absolutely brilliant. It was a rallying call. It was a bit like Henry at Agincourt – some of the young people there were almost in tears. They were terribly moved. He has this ability to speak off the cuff in the most amazing way.

Cameron was itching to get out on the stump. To his frustration, however, his energy was increasingly diverted to preparations for a series of televised debates between the three main party leaders. Unprecedented in British elections (Blair had always refused to take part), the programmes were a source of huge media anticipation and excitement. Though some at CCHQ had misgivings about whether the shows would be advantageous, Coulson was adamant they presented the big opportunity to 'seal the deal'. As the pressure mounted, Cameron became increasingly frustrated by all the rehearsals.

Following advice from New York Mayor Michael Bloomberg, Osborne had (at vast expense) drafted in two American political consultants, Bill Knapp and Anita Dunn, to coach the party leader. The pair played a key part in preparations.

A former Cameron aide recalls:

> They spent God knows how many hundreds of hours preparing, with Jeremy Hunt as Nick Clegg. Anita used to sit in these sessions and say, 'I'm voting for the Clegg guy.' The point she was making was that the Lib Dem position in the debate was actually very attractive – 'the more they argue, the more they sound the same' and so on. At first we found the preparation interesting, because we were learning cool stuff about how Americans prepare for TV, but it's very forced, very unnatural, and, like most politicians, David is at his most comfortable when he's able to sort of riff, and debates are not about riffing. You really have to concentrate on your key phrases and lines, not the politics. It went on and on and on, and he hated it.

What happened next set the scene for the Tory leader's dogged refusal to participate in 'three-way' televised debates in 2015. His instinctive misgivings proved entirely founded during the first debate, which saw Clegg emerge as the runaway winner. By contrast, Cameron was widely seen to have flunked it. For once, he suffered a sleepless night, devastated at the damage he might have inflicted on the party's prospects and beating himself up for signing up to the shows in the first place. Friends say there were 'tears' in the Cameron household that night as it became apparent that his exhaustive preparation had been in vain.

'He says he literally didn't sleep that night,' recalls a friend.

> He was lying there thinking of all the colleagues and friends who'd supported him whose seats he'd just lost. He says he was thinking of Oliver Letwin in particular, who'd given up everything for him and was up against the Lib Dems in a tight marginal, and he was thinking: 'I've just literally cost Oliver his seat.' David is very loyal to his core people, but that made the stakes even higher. From then on, it was even more stressful and less enjoyable preparing for the second one. He just *had* to win.

To another confidant, Cameron admitted that as he looked at the TV studio audience seconds before the cameras rolled, he suddenly thought: 'Christ, what have I done?' The friend testifies to the Tory leader's distress.

> I think he felt responsible for everybody's fate. It was obvious when you watched the first debate that he was nervous, and he is normally nerveless. It was interesting to know that he had the capacity to have those nerves. He phoned me up, and it seemed he was slightly looking for reassurance. It was a very odd thing for him, because he doesn't normally do that. He was upset.

Cameron's second performance was better – he thought he drew – and his third his best: he thought he won.

It would not be enough.

PART FIVE –
SHOW TIME

27

SHOTGUN WEDDING

'We've got our fingertips on the levers of power.'
— George Osborne to David Davis

Cameron was chopping logs in Dean. It was polling day and, by convention, electioneering was over. There was nothing he could do but wait.

As voters across the country made their way to the polls, he was savouring a brief moment of respite before his constituency count. He had spent the morning at Hilton's house in the nearby village of Asthall Leigh, swinging by with Samantha after casting his own vote in Witney. A minor ruckus had set him back a couple of hours – protestors on the roof of the polling station had unfurled a banner reading: 'Britons know your place. Vote Eton – vote Tory' – but there had been no other drama.

At Hilton's place, they had discussed how to play things if they fell just short of a majority. Those present – Osborne, Llewellyn, Coulson, Patrick McLoughlin, Stephen Gilbert (the party's head of field operations) and Kate Fall – agreed that Cameron could claim victory the following day if the Conservatives won a minimum of 300 to 310 seats. It would be less than the 326 required, but would be enough to patch something together. In a sign of their quiet optimism that they would scrape together more seats than Labour, they also touched up a provisional list of Cabinet appointments.[267] Cameron then went home. As Samantha prepared a chilli con carne for dinner, he began tackling the stack of wood in the garden.

Bored commentators wasted little time trying to interpret his choice of activity. Some suggested it was a last-ditch attempt to appear ordinary. Others thought he was simply taking out pent-up frustration on a chunk of tree.

---

267   Matthew d'Ancona, p. 3.

Cameron had previously spoken of how splitting logs helped him relax, so many concluded he was nervous.

Legend has it that William Gladstone was felling a tree when he first heard the news that he was to become Prime Minister in 1868. He reportedly leaned back on his axe and declared, 'My mission is to pacify Ireland', before returning to his labours. When the election results started coming in, Cameron would have no time for such calm reflection. The party's private polling had been right: Britain was heading for a hung parliament, and he was facing the fight of his political life. By the early hours of Friday morning he was on the M40, tearing back to London, his eyes glued to his BlackBerry as results from across the country flashed up on the tiny screen.

The dramatic five days in May that led to the formation of the first coalition government since the Second World War have been pored over by journalists, politicians and historians, resulting in a number of well-informed books. These offer meticulous hour-by-hour accounts of negotiations between the parties. What they fail to highlight, though, is the impressive leadership Cameron showed in this instance. When the final numbers became clear on the morning after the election, his most trusted aides pressed him to form a minority government. Instead, he decided to stake everything on coalition.

One of Cameron's inner circle says:

> Dave was the only one who wanted to do the coalition thing…Honestly, I know this sounds pompous, but it was a really quite inspiring moment of leadership. Everyone else, including George, was like, 'Well, we basically won, didn't we? Maybe not quite enough but, morally, we won and they lost. OK, the electoral system means we didn't get enough seats, but our vote share was the same as what Blair got last time and he got a majority. We've earned the right to form a government.' There was a very strong view among everyone that we'd earned the right to form a government. And a slightly sort of grumpy view, you know, like, 'Oh hang on, why should we even talk to them? We basically won. We should press on.' And Dave was incredibly clear about it. Incredibly clear about what he wanted. And he was the only one saying that.

Unusually, Cameron did not seek dozens of opinions before settling on a strategy. Nor did he fail to appreciate what was at stake. When (as a friend put it) his 'bollocks were on the line', he proved he had the energy, focus and commitment to pull off an unprecedented diplomatic feat. In terms of personal leadership setting the direction of the country, it was probably his finest hour.

Shortly before heading to London following his constituency count, Cameron had received a surprise call from Arnold Schwarzenegger. 'Even though results aren't in, we know the Conservatives had a great day,' the then Californian governor tweeted enthusiastically shortly afterwards. Thanking him politely, Cameron was forced to issue a correction: despite some unexpected victories, the Tories had failed to capture crucial target seats. As he would tell constituents at the formal declaration in the Windrush Leisure Centre, the rosiness of an increased personal majority belied a national picture that, at 3 a.m. on Friday morning, simply did not point to a Tory triumph. In marked contrast to Osborne's earlier speech at the Macclesfield Leisure Centre, in which the shadow Chancellor had told Brown to 'get real' and come to terms with a crushing Labour defeat, Cameron struck a cautious note, refraining from calling for the Prime Minister's immediate resignation and suggesting instead that a new government might take a while to be formed.

The first flecks of sunrise had yet to appear over the Thames as his chauffeur-driven car pulled into the driveway at Millbank. Cameron's mood was grim but focused. 'He had to think very quickly how he and George were going to get out of this alive,' according to a friend.[268] Walking briskly through the building into the heart of the party's campaign operation, he conferred rapidly with aides. Some observers recall him appearing 'dazed'[269] – most likely a mixture of fatigue and disappointment – but his mind was sharp. Standing in front of a large display board marking the seats won and lost as the results came in, he fired questions at party workers. 'He knew exactly what it meant,' said one of his team, while another observed that it was apparent from his expression that he knew it would not be enough.[270]

---

268   Francis Elliott and James Hanning, p. 391.

269   *Sunday Times*, 16 May 2010.

270   Dennis Kavanagh and Philip Cowley, *The British General Election of 2010* (Palgrave Macmillan, 2010), p. 197.

'You could see him realise that we weren't going to make it.'[271] The key question was whether the party would get at least 300 seats, putting it in a sufficiently strong position for a coalition to be a realistic prospect. Andrew Cooper told him it would.

The atmosphere at CCHQ was tense as he moved through the building, totting up numbers in his head. A few hours earlier, the place had been awash with glamour and excitement as celebrities including designer Anya Hindmarch and TV presenters Carol Vorderman and Kirstie Allsopp mingled with staff and party members for an election night party in the River Room of the adjacent Millbank Tower. By now, however, fatigue and nerves were kicking in. Waiters circulated with trays of mini croissants and pastries, handing out much needed coffees to the throng of aides and supporters wearily watching the TV screens, but the caffeine and calories failed to lift spirits.[272]

By early Friday morning, it was clear that Labour had lost, having secured just 29 per cent of the vote (their lowest share since Michael Foot in 1983). However, at twenty seats short of the magic 326 they needed for a majority, the Conservatives had not clearly won. Swings across the country were varied and unexpected, with many Labour MPs in tight contests with Tories managing to hold on to their seats. Surprise victories in seats like Cannock Chase in Staffordshire were matched by a series of defeats in metropolitan London constituencies like Hammersmith, where the Tories had been tipped to do better. Shaun Bailey, a 38-year-old black former youth worker who had epitomised the new wave of candidates and had been tipped as a star of the 2010 intake, lost by a disappointingly substantial margin. While the map turned blue across England – and particularly in the south – Labour put in a remarkably strong performance in Scotland, with an overall swing towards the party. The overhyped predictions of a 'Portillo moment' for the Schools Secretary, Ed Balls, were well wide of the mark. Most significantly, however, 'Cleggmania' had failed to translate into extra Lib Dem seats. The Liberal Democrats lost more seats than they won, reinforcing Clegg's conviction that the voting system left them at a hopeless disadvantage.

Bitter recriminations quickly spread through the Tory office. Some were heard blaming Hilton, while others had Coulson in their sights for pushing

---

271 *The Times*, 8 May 2010.
272 *Independent on Sunday*, 9 May 2010.

for the TV debates.[273] Cameron wasted no time dwelling on the past. He headed off to snatch a couple of hours' sleep in a hotel by Westminster Bridge, before regrouping with Osborne, Hilton, Llewellyn, Coulson, Patrick McLoughlin, Gabby Bertin and Liz Sugg to plot their next move.

At 10 a.m., the team met in Cameron's room at the Westminster Bridge Park Plaza Hotel.

In a rare example of strategic discord, he and Osborne were briefly at odds over how to react to the results. A few hours earlier, as he raced down the M40 from Witney, Cameron had made a crucial phone call. From the car, he had ordered Ed Llewellyn to contact Danny Alexander, Nick Clegg's chief of staff. Thinking a second election (the anticipated response to a hung parliament) would be unwinnable, the Tory leader's plan was to make immediate overtures to the Lib Dems. Alexander responded positively, if somewhat cautiously, to Llewellyn's text. A meeting had already been scheduled for a few hours later. It was not a strategy Osborne favoured. Though he had been involved in contingency planning for a hung parliament, the shadow Chancellor now believed their primary focus should be on ejecting Brown from No. 10. He was opposed to early approaches to the Lib Dems, arguing instead for forming a minority administration in order to get the Tories into government as quickly as possible.[274] According to one present, all of those in the hotel room except Cameron agreed.

> I remember it so clearly. It was just really striking. We'd agreed to meet in Dave's room and we all got there together, all feeling a bit groggy and tired and grumpy, and it was amazing, you know – he was totally fresh and perky and incredibly clear that he wanted to do it as a proper big coalition. It was really striking and it was entirely him. I think he really needs to be given credit for that leadership moment. Because no one else was saying that. It was not advice he got... Yet he arrived that morning with this incredibly clear conviction that this was the right thing to do. It was really

273 Rob Wilson, *5 Days to Power: The Journey to Coalition Britain* (Biteback Publishing, 2010), p. 88.
274 Ibid.

amazing, actually. It was 100 per cent personal leadership. People in that room argued against it, and he just said, 'No, this is what I want to do. I'm sure this is right.'

This is not quite the full story. Earlier that morning, Cameron had telephoned David Davis seeking advice. That the Tory leader should have turned to the former Home Secretary, whom he knew to be no fan, suggests he was anxious about his own position.

'He hadn't won the election and I think he feared a *coup d'état*,' an insider reflects. 'David [Davis] told him: "You've got no choice but to go for full coalition, but you mustn't give them PR. The party will not forgive you for trading one period in government for us being in opposition for the rest of our lives."'[275]

Perhaps Cameron was not the only one with an eye on his longer-term position. Some have suggested that Osborne's initial dissent may have been motivated by self-interest. According to this thesis, in arguing for a minority government, the ambitious shadow Chancellor might have been attempting to lay the ground for his own ascent to the party leadership, in the expectation that the arrangement would be unstable and short-lived. This does not seem credible. Osborne would have been fully aware of the minimal prospects of seizing the crown for himself under such circumstances. More likely his judgement simply wavered as tiredness and disappointment overwhelmed him.[276] In any case, on Friday morning, he very quickly converted to Cameron's agenda.

'After a bit of sleep, George was back as the old George. He said we needed to make a generous offer, we needed to offer "the top price for the Turkish carpet",' says a friend.[277]

Later, Cameron would claim that his decision to aim for a coalition with the Lib Dems was the result of a 'fairly epiphanous moment'[278] when he woke from his nap. For all the credit he deserves for fleet-footedness and laser focus that Friday morning, this is somewhat disingenuous. In truth, plans for approaching the Lib Dems with an offer of 'full coalition' had been

---

275 Private information.

276 Francis Elliott and James Hanning, p. 392.

277 Rob Wilson, p. 91.

278 Adam Boulton and Joey Jones, *Hung Together: The 2010 Election and the Coalition Government* (Simon & Schuster, 2012), p. 129.

in the mix for months.[279] Indeed, Osborne himself had been the key player in war-gaming the various options likely to be available in the event of a hung parliament, privately confiding to Cameron that full coalition with the Lib Dems would be preferable to a minority government backed up by the votes of Ulster Unionists, a solution that seemed natural to many Tory MPs. Cameron had agreed.

Privately, both knew outright victory was unlikely (Hague had been telling them so for at least two years). A few weeks before polling day they had carried out a comprehensive audit of every constituency in the country in an attempt to come up with their own numbers, and reached the dispiriting conclusion that all the naysayers were right. 'To win, everything had to go right,' remembers a close aide. 'I mean, *everything*. And as we got closer to the election, it just became clear that that was too much to ask.'[280]

The Tory leadership's contingency planning was carried out amid utmost secrecy. In the run-up to the election, Cameron doggedly stuck to the line that he was entirely focused on winning an outright majority. As late as 3 May, the *Daily Telegraph* reported that he was ruling out a coalition with the Lib Dems. Behind closed doors, however, he had assembled a special unit – Osborne, Hague, Letwin and Llewellyn – tasked with preparing the ground for negotiations. Foreshadowing the way in which the coalition negotiations themselves would later be conducted, the discussions were kept extremely tight (Hilton tells friends that even he was out of the loop). Twice – first on 18 April and then again on 2 May – the team met for Sunday night dinner at Osborne's house. There, Letwin presented the others with a line-by-line study of the Lib Dem manifesto, highlighting areas of potential agreement and those of possible discord. This formed the basis for what would later become the coalition agreement. Cameron signed it off shortly before election day.[281] Later, the coalition would be hailed a 'shotgun wedding'. But as the journalist Matthew d'Ancona has observed, 'the true plot twist was that Dave had been planning to settle down with Nick all along'.[282]

The essence of what Osborne and the team concluded ahead of polling day was simple: the scope for working with the Lib Dems was far greater

---

279   Dennis Kavanagh and Philip Cowley, p. 206.
280   Matthew d'Ancona, p. 15.
281   Adam Boulton and Joey Jones, p. 152.
282   Matthew d'Ancona, p. 21.

than they had previously appreciated. Cameron's 'Liberal Conservatives' were not that dissimilar to Clegg's 'Orange Bookers', particularly the younger generation of Lib Dem MPs close to the leader, like Danny Alexander and David Laws.[283]

'We hadn't quite seen that the more socially liberal Conservative Party had a lot of overlap with the fiscally conservative Liberal Democrat party,' observes one who was involved in the negotiations.[284] Once they twigged, pitching for a full-bodied coalition became an appealing option. They concluded that unless they were generous, offering Clegg Cabinet posts as well as policies, any ad hoc deal or post-election pact (like a so-called 'confidence and supply' arrangement) would be a marriage of convenience that would soon hit the rocks. They also calculated that if the Lib Dems rejected the offer (which they expected to be the case), it would be Clegg who was left looking churlish.

'Either they'll reject it, in which case we'll be on the high ground, or it might work and we'll have a much better majority,' Cameron remarked to Osborne over a private dinner a couple of days before the second TV debate.[285] It was up to the shadow Chancellor, Letwin and co. to work out the minutiae ahead of polling day.

To stand a realistic chance of wooing Clegg, they knew they would have to make some concession on electoral reform. As the election approached, a number of Tory shadow Cabinet ministers started to talk publicly about their opposition to 'proportional representation' as opposed to electoral reform per se. This subtle shift in language pointed to the space being carved out for future policy concessions in this area.[286] As would later become apparent, ruling out PR did not mean total inflexibility when it came to the Lib Dems' second-best proposal: the Alternative Vote (AV). Furthermore, Osborne – again with Cameron's approval – had decided long before election day that any coalition with the Lib Dems would require a system of fixed-term parliaments, a future component of the coalition agreement that most

---

283   *The Orange Book: Reclaiming Liberalism*, published in 2004, had become the unofficial manifesto of the Liberal Democrats' right wing. It included essays by Clegg, Laws, Vince Cable, Chris Huhne and Ed Davey, and it emphasised 'small state' liberalism.

284   Adam Boulton and Joey Jones, p. 152.

285   Francis Elliott and James Hanning, p. 386.

286   Matthew d'Ancona, p. 21.

observers took to be a Lib Dem initiative, not a preconceived Tory proposal. 'We have to find a way of stopping Clegg from dumping us,' Osborne is said to have observed to the inner circle, explaining that a fixed-term arrangement would make it far more difficult for the smaller party to pull the plug on the coalition.[287] Thus at least two key planks of the eventual coalition agreement were already settled – at least as far as the Tory leadership was concerned – well before polling day.

At 10.30 a.m. on Friday 7 May, after the full English breakfast that had become a feature of Cameron's lifestyle on the campaign trail, the Tory leader and his team gathered around a TV in the Westminster Plaza Hotel to watch Clegg make the first move.

Despite a net fall in the number of Lib Dem seats, the absence of a clear victor in the election transformed him into kingmaker. In line with the hints he had given in the run-up to the election, the Lib Dem leader was firm: the party with the largest number of seats and votes had a right to enter negotiations first. That this was an inversion of constitutional convention (in the past, the sitting Prime Minister in a hung parliament has made the first attempt to form a government) mattered little: Clegg's speech set the wheels in motion. The Tory leader ordered Hilton to get to work drafting a public response, a task he found easy, because Cameron was very clear about the tone he wished to strike.

At this point, the Tory leader made what could have been a fatal mistake: he waited another four hours before delivering the speech, giving Labour vital time to establish a foothold in negotiations. Brown pre-empted claims that he was 'squatting' in No. 10 by publicising his own offer to the Lib Dems before the Tories made theirs.[288] Milking the gravitas that only incumbency could afford, Brown made his speech at 1.40 p.m. – almost an hour ahead of Cameron's – clearly stating his willingness to enter discussions with Clegg, while re-affirming his party's manifesto commitment to voting reform. It was a naked bid to seduce the third party.

Cameron was now on the back foot. He knew he would have to surprise the Lib Dems to reclaim the initiative. His speech – delivered at 2.30 p.m.

287   Ibid., p. 16.
288   *Sunday Times*, 16 May 2010.

on the steps of the St Stephen's Club in Westminster – did the trick. Although it did not contain the word 'coalition' – it was deleted during one of the five drafts prepared by Hilton on the grounds that too stark an offer would leave them looking desperate[289] – Cameron's statement was dramatic enough. The key passage, with its 'big, open and comprehensive offer to the Liberal Democrats', caught Clegg's party off guard. They had expected the Tories to seek a minority administration, with at best lip service paid to the idea of coalition. Cameron's offer of partnership government appeared both more generous and more genuine than anyone had predicted. David Laws remembers being thrown by the enthusiasm with which Cameron spoke of 'going further' than a simple confidence and supply arrangement, and noted that the Tory leader seemed to have spotted the political capital to be had from making a virtue out of necessity. 'This was a bold, almost Blairite, attempt to seize the initiative and to capture the public mood,' he reflected later. 'The enthusiastic offer of a "new politics" is undoubtedly what Tony Blair would have made in 1997.'[290]

Inside Brown's bunker, the view was that Cameron had sold himself short. Although the Leader of the Opposition had outlined red lines in future negotiations – Europe, immigration, Trident and, of course, spending cuts – the Labour leader felt Cameron was underestimating his own strength.[291] That Cameron had been rather coy on what he knew would become the key issue in the upcoming negotiations – promising only a 'committee of inquiry' to address the question of voting reform – mattered less to the Labour side than what they took to be the excessively generous list of areas in which the Tories claimed to be able to deliver key Lib Dem manifesto commitments (a list including civil liberties, the environment, and schools funding).

Only one figure in Downing Street disagreed: Mandelson. In his memoir, *The Third Man*, the former Business Secretary recalls being 'almost alone in our ranks in being impressed' by Cameron.[292] He too identified the Blairite qualities of Cameron's declaration.

---

289   Rob Wilson, p. 92.
290   David Laws, 22 *Days in May: The Birth of the Lib Dem–Conservative Coalition* (Biteback Publishing, 2010), p. 51.
291   Andrew Adonis, 5 *Days in May: The Coalition and Beyond* (Biteback Publishing, 2013), p. 29.
292   Peter Mandelson, *The Third Man: Life at the Heart of New Labour* (Harper Press, 2010), pp. 544–5, quoted in David Laws, pp. 50–51.

'I thought this guy knows what he's doing, and he's going to motor.'[293]

And motor he did. At four o'clock on Friday afternoon, Cameron spoke to Clegg on the phone for the first time since their first flirty overtures. In what would become a running theme over the next few days, the Tory leader was candid about his desire for a coalition. He emphasised that he felt they could work well together. Conscious that many of Clegg's colleagues had spent their whole political lives fighting Tories, he stressed that he was not one of the 'old guard'.

'I favour doing things differently,' he said.[294]

Clegg was grateful, agreeing to a meeting between their respective negotiation teams that evening. 'I knew I could do business with him,' he affirmed later.[295]

Formal talks between the two parties began in earnest that evening. They took place in the Cabinet Office at No. 70 Whitehall, a location chosen by Osborne on the grounds that it would drive Brown 'wild' knowing they were physically inside government.[296] Those outside the negotiating teams waited impatiently next door, tantalised by the proximity of power. Looking out the window, James O'Shaughnessy could see the garden of No. 10, 'which seemed an exotic place we'd never been to. It was amazing; this is what we had worked for.'

Over the next four days, the two teams would meet a further three times. To the surprise of all the participants – Osborne, Hague, Letwin and Llewellyn on the Tory side; Laws, Alexander, Chris Huhne and Andrew Stunell on the Lib Dem bench – there was immediate chemistry. In marked contrast to the tense meetings between the Lib Dems and their Labour counterparts – the first of which took place on Saturday afternoon – the atmosphere surrounding the Lib–Con negotiations was relaxed. Letwin was a particular revelation to Lib Dem negotiators, who were wowed by his liberal instincts and encyclopaedic grasp of their manifesto – prompting Osborne and Hague to tease that he was a fifth column.[297] The Lib Dems also warmed to Llewellyn, the only unelected official in the meetings. It helped that Cameron's chief of

293 Nick Robinson, *Five Days That Changed Britain*, BBC 2, 29 July 2010.
294 David Laws, p. 52.
295 Rob Wilson, p. 103.
296 Ibid., p. 104; Dennis Kavanagh and Philip Cowley.
297 David Laws, p. 66.

staff was a friend of Clegg's wife and a one-time colleague of former Lib Dem leader Paddy Ashdown.

A shared policy agenda also proved surprisingly easy to thrash out. The pre-prepared document the Tory team presented to the Lib Dems at the Sunday morning meeting took Clegg's aides by surprise. 'It was startling; they were conceding a whole range of issues from the off,' one of the team later confided.[298] Aside from the expected consensus on civil liberties and the environment, there was also broad ideological agreement on the most pressing issue of the day: deficit reduction. Throughout the election campaign, Clegg had opposed Tory plans to make £6 billion in spending cuts, but by the time they sat down at the negotiating table, the much hyped threat of Greek-style market panic provided a convenient excuse for a volte face. They signed up to the Osborne plan with little fuss.

'It was amazing how willing they were to make it work,' O'Shaughnessy recalls. 'I was really taken aback by how much they were all up for it – hilarious in retrospect.'

The Conservatives too found themselves shedding manifesto commitments with relaxed abandon, offering immediate concessions on, among other areas, the personal income tax allowance and Osborne's much vaunted inheritance tax cut. The shadow Chancellor told a friend later that he was 'quite relieved' not to have to honour his death duty pledge.[299]

The main hurdle was voting reform, a subject so sensitive for both sides that it was set aside for the two party leaders to thrash out themselves.

Since his first call to Clegg on the Friday afternoon, Cameron had been lying low. On Saturday morning, he made a brief public appearance, along with the other two party leaders, at the VE Day ceremony beside the Cenotaph. The event provided a valuable opportunity for a few words with Clegg as they emerged from the Foreign Office. The two men, easy in each other's company, shared their frustration that Brown was still clinging on to power.[300] The following evening, they attempted to reach an agreement over voting reform, initially by phone, and then in person. During three tense discussions,

298 Rob Wilson, p. 147.
299 Private information.
300 Adam Boulton and Joey Jones, p. 169.

Cameron desperately tried to convince Clegg to sign up to a Tory offer that did not include a referendum on voting reform. To his frustration, the Lib Dem leader hard-balled, making it clear he would accept nothing less than a plebiscite on AV.

To add to Cameron's woes, he had a sneaking suspicion – correct, as it turned out – that Clegg was talking to Brown behind his back, playing the two parties off against each other to secure the best deal on voting reform.[301]

Heading home that night, the Tory leader was still confident a pact was within reach. His position was in more peril than he realised. Unbeknown to him, Brown was about to remove the single biggest barrier to a Lib–Lab coalition: himself. Clegg had long made it clear he could not work with the Labour leader.

'Gordon is just impossible to deal with,' he told his team on Sunday night.[302] Personal animosity, combined with a strong sense that dealing with a discredited Prime Minister would be a public relations disaster, ensured that no Lib–Lab deal could be reached while Brown remained in office. By the middle of Monday, however, word came that Brown was ready to sacrifice the premiership. Labour was back in play.

Panicked, Cameron made a crucial phone call. At 4 p.m., he and Clegg exchanged what was their most bad-tempered conversation of the negotiation period. After an explosion of recriminations about double-dealing, Cameron hung up, convinced the Lib Dem leader was on the cusp of a deal with Brown.

At the heart of this conviction lay the belief that an increasingly desperate Brown had resorted to offering Clegg AV without a referendum, a gesture Cameron believed spelled the end of Lib–Con negotiations. He knew he could not match it. Although the exact content of his final phone call with Clegg is unclear, he is said to have rounded on the Lib Dem leader for contemplating introducing AV without a mandate from the people.

'It wasn't in your manifesto, it wasn't in Labour's, it would be indefensible,' he declared.[303] Having slammed down the phone, he fell into a gloom.[304]

'I think we're fucked,' O'Shaughnessy remembers telling Coulson. 'Somehow Labour have rescued it and they are going to go with the Liberals.'

---

301 Ibid., p. 190.
302 David Laws, p. 122.
303 Rob Wilson, p. 207.
304 Adam Boulton and Joey Jones, p. 197.

In hindsight, the call was a turning point. Armed with what he regarded as proof that a Lib–Lab agreement was imminent, Cameron rushed off to consult his party. At around this time, David Davis received a call from Osborne.

'We've had to concede a referendum on AV,' the shadow Chancellor told him.

'I specifically said you shouldn't do that!' Davis retorted angrily.

'I know, I know. But we've got our fingertips on the levers of power!' Osborne replied.

'Yes, but for how long? On what basis? You mustn't do this,' Davis shot back.

'Well, we absolutely have to. We've already done the deal,' Osborne responded.

'Well, what are you asking me to do?' Davis asked.

'I'm asking you to support it,' Osborne replied.

'Don't be ridiculous. People would view that as incredible, me supporting this thing,' Davis answered.

'Well, really, that's what we absolutely need,' Osborne urged.

Grudgingly, Davis agreed to hold his tongue.

'I will give you twenty-four hours of silence,' he told the shadow Chancellor. At 4.45 p.m., Cameron met the rest of his shadow Cabinet at Norman Shaw. Their discussions were briefly interrupted by the dramatic spectacle of Brown appearing in Downing Street to announce his resignation. With his departure from No. 10 no longer in question, Cameron set out the state of play: Labour was offering Clegg AV without a referendum, and unless the Conservatives hit back hard and fast with their own offer of a referendum, the game was up.

Galvanised, colleagues quickly agreed. Only Chris Grayling dissented. Cameron then took the plan to his backbenchers, reiterating his warning that Labour was offering legislation on AV without a referendum. Though the process was rushed and informal, he secured their acquiescence, and was reportedly cheered loudly when he explained that they would have to compromise on AV if they did not want to spend the next five years on the opposition benches.

'The sense of relief was palpable,' one Tory strategist said. 'For a minute it had looked like we were out of the game and there was panic at the top.'[305]

Having moved swiftly and decisively to head off a rearguard action from Brown and his team, the Tories were able to announce on Monday

---

305 'The path to Con–Dem nation', James Macintyre, *New Statesman*, 24 May 2010.

evening that they would now 'go the extra mile'. With Lib–Lab discussions now disintegrating over other issues, Cameron's work was effectively done. Although he later spoke of his despair on Monday evening – returning home to tell Samantha that he would most likely be in opposition for several more years[306] – the pendulum had by now swung decisively in his favour. The following day he would be on his way to Buckingham Palace, to be asked to form a government.

Samantha was at home in north Kensington doing homework with Nancy when the call finally came.

'You'd better get a dress on because we're about to go and see the Queen,' Cameron told her.

Her first reaction was panic about what to wear. She was five months pregnant, that awkward stage where ordinary clothes are too tight but maternity clothes can look baggy. Pulling a suitable-looking frock from her closet, she gave herself a quick once-over, checking to make sure the tattoo on her ankle couldn't be seen through her tights. Then they zoomed off to the palace. After years of waiting for this moment, it was, in her own words, 'so surreal'.[307] Her husband was about to be become the youngest Prime Minister in 198 years.

'Cameron completely outmanoeuvred Gordon Brown during that period,' the former Tory minister Tim Yeo later reflected. 'And he drove it through the parliamentary party, which was also a big achievement.' For Gove, the coalition deal was proof that Cameron is 'just a natural born politician. He can read the currents and eddies in politics supremely well.'[308] Yet Cameron's conduct during the negotiation period is not without its critics. Many on the Conservative benches felt cheated when it later emerged that, contrary to the Tory leader's claims, Labour had not in fact made any offer of AV without a referendum. Even if, as Cameron maintains, Brown was making wild offers that effectively amounted to the same thing, the fact remains that no formal offer could have been made, for the simple reason that formal Lib–Lab negotiations had not started by the time Cameron notified his party

306   Rob Wilson, p. 224.
307   Geordie Greig interview, op. cit.
308   Adam Boulton and Joey Jones, p. 129.

of the proposition. Any discussions between the two parties were unofficial and taking place through back channels. Additionally, it remains highly unlikely that Brown – or whoever followed him – could have pushed such an agreement through the Labour Party.

For some, this amounts to saying that the coalition was built on a lie. The certainty with which Cameron informed MPs and shadow ministers of the specifics of a Labour offer that never actually existed suggests a degree of flexibility with the truth. Cameron and Osborne both emphatically deny that they knowingly deceived their MPs, suggesting instead that the 'fog of war' contributed to a firm belief in Tory circles that Brown was chucking everything onto the table in order to make a Lib–Lab deal stick.[309] Indeed, after the event Cameron continued to insist that he still believed Brown would have gone for it. 'I was absolutely certain in my own mind that that was the case. I think I had good reason to be certain.'[310]

Unless conclusive evidence incriminating Cameron and his lieutenant emerges, the most that can be said today is that Cameron – willingly or unwillingly – did not get to the bottom of what Labour was offering. It is possible he deliberately avoided seeking clarity in order to retain plausible deniability should his MPs later realise what had happened. Ultimately, however, this ruse was probably unnecessary. Ashdown, who pushed for a Lib–Lab deal throughout this period, points out that parliamentary arithmetic always pushed his party towards the Conservatives. The Labour offer – if it ever existed – may not have been the game-changer Cameron and Osborne thought. 'If I'd been a Conservative, I think I would have seen through it straight away,' Ashdown reflected later. 'I would have said, "Go ahead, do a deal with Labour."'[311] According to this line of thinking, Cameron should have called Clegg's bluff.

Yet Cameron had made the decision early on to go all-out for full coalition with the Lib Dems, so it is hardly surprising that he went to such lengths to ensure that it happened. This contributed to the feeling on the part of many Tory MPs that they had been steamrollered into an agreement that the leadership had decided to pursue well before the rest of the party had been properly consulted. Although Cameron met the parliamentary party

309   Ibid., pp. 229–30.
310   Francis Elliott and James Hanning, p. 400.
311   Ibid., p. 401.

and the shadow Cabinet on a number of occasions during the five days of negotiations, these discussions were infrequent (certainly compared to those of their Lib Dem counterparts), and brief: on the Tuesday night meeting, after Cameron had been to the palace, MPs were not even shown a copy of the coalition agreement.

A former Cabinet minister says:

> At the time he was doing it he really didn't consult with anybody. I remember sitting in a room, at the very end of the negotiation, with someone who is now a very senior minister in the government, who was equally out of the loop. Absolutely out of the loop. Eventually he rang up the leader's office and said, 'I believe a deal has been done – shouldn't there be a meeting of the shadow Cabinet?' I was in the room when he was told: 'There's no more shadow Cabinet.' So there was no meeting with the shadow Cabinet to discuss the terms on which we had concluded our agreement.[312]

While the extensive internal democracy of the Lib Dems ensured the participation and consultation of a far wider circle throughout this period, many on their side also felt aggrieved. Some MPs and activists in both parties still regard the coalition agreement as a conspiracy foisted on unwitting followers by a small elite that had always looked kindly on an alliance. The chumminess of Cameron and Clegg, combined with their striking similarities – in age, outlook, social background and career trajectories – led many to conclude it was all a stitch-up by a few individuals who were more than happy to work together, regardless of what their party members thought.

'I think there were people in his inner circle who were dead keen to see coalition,' says Michael Ancram, the former shadow Defence Secretary under Michael Howard.

> I'm sure that Ed Llewellyn, with his background, feels very comfortable with the idea of coalition. It's rather like the Roy Jenkins idea: he had this great vision of the liberal democracy of the nineteenth century, of recreating that with Harold Wilson. I think there were people in David Cameron's coterie who felt the same: that

---

312   Private information.

you could readjust British politics by creating a liberal, right-wing centre which is then going to dominate for the next generation.

Matthew d'Ancona would later reveal a confidential email from Nick Boles to the party leadership on the night of the election. It forcefully made the case for forming a coalition and holding a referendum on electoral reform in order to signal 'our openness to a new way of doing politics'. According to d'Ancona, among those permitted to read the note, few dissented from its basic conclusions.[313] This casts Cameron's 'big leadership moment' on Friday 7 May in a slightly different light. The view among his inner circle that they should go for a minority government appears to have been an about-turn prompted by the party's relative success in securing more than 300 seats. Cameron's position was more illustrative of a determination to stick with an original plan than a call for a radical change of direction.

---

313 Matthew d'Ancona, p. 21.

28

GRAPESHOT

'I would never have gone into coalition with the Lib Dems.'
— Margaret Thatcher

A ll eyes were on David Cameron's silver Jaguar as it sped away from Buckingham Palace, ferrying the new Prime Minister to Downing Street. Outside, the media pack waited expectantly. Inside, a quiet revolution was underway.

Led by Liz Sugg, the new guard was filing into Brown's old stronghold, preparing for the arrival of the boss. A little before 8.45 p.m. the team emerged from the building for the cameras, blinking in the late evening light.

Unlike Blair, who had arrived on the steps of No. 10 in 1997 amid US-style fanfare – cheered by flag-waving crowds as he proclaimed the advent of a 'new dawn' – Cameron could not play the jubilant deliverer. He had not won the election and his power would be limited.

The coalition's *raison d'être* was tackling the economic crisis, hardly an uplifting message.

Reflecting the sombre mood, he declared:

'Our country has a hung parliament where no party has an overall majority and we have some deep and pressing problems: a huge deficit, deep social problems, a political system in need of reform.'

There was little time for extended reflection. Having turned to enter No. 10 with Samantha – pausing briefly for the cameras on the doorstep – he was immediately ushered off for civil service briefings. Congratulatory phone calls from Obama, Merkel and the Canadian premier Stephen Harper were followed by a short but triumphant appearance in the House of Commons to greet the parliamentary party, during which he and Samantha were treated to a standing ovation. Samantha then returned to the family home in north Kensington (it would be several weeks until she and the children actually moved into the flat above No. 11), while Cameron set to work forming his Cabinet late into the night.

He had already made one critical appointment: that of Deputy Prime Minister. In return for securing this constitutionally vague role for Nick Clegg, the Lib Dems had relinquished any claim on the great offices of state. It meant there would be a Conservative Chancellor and Conservative secretaries of state in the Foreign Office, Home Office, Ministry of Defence, and education and welfare departments. The four other Lib Dems in Cabinet – Danny Alexander, Chris Huhne, Vince Cable and David Laws – were made Scottish Secretary, Energy Secretary, Business Secretary, and Chief Secretary to the Treasury, respectively.

As expected, Osborne was anointed Chancellor of the Exchequer. Next in was Hague as Foreign Secretary. Though not yet fifty, the former party leader was regarded as the 'elder statesman' of Cameron's inner circle. While his influence would decline over the course of the next five years, he was initially seen as one-third of the most powerful triumvirate in the coalition.[314]

Theresa May, previously shadow Secretary of Work and Pensions, was handed the Home Secretary brief. It meant the demotion of Chris Grayling, who had served as shadow Home Secretary since January 2009, to the position of Minister of State for Employment. The move was presentationally important: it represented the continuity of 'modernisation' from opposition into government. Grayling had set Cameroon alarm bells ringing during the campaign with an outspoken defence of the right of Christians running bed-and-breakfast accommodation to turn away gay couples. By contrast, as far back as 2002, May had identified herself as part of the modernising wing in her conference speech admonishing the party to escape its harsh, out-of-touch image. Furthermore, installing a woman in one of the great offices of state was a symbolic step towards fulfilling his pledge to have at least one third of the jobs in his first government occupied by women. Meanwhile Cameron appointed Gove as Education Secretary, further embedding the Tories' reach across Whitehall. In a nod to his right flank, Liam Fox was made Defence Secretary while Owen Paterson headed to Northern Ireland. Cameron's old boss at CRD, Andrew Lansley, was confirmed as Health Secretary.

314   Matthew d'Ancona, p. 3.

There was one surprise in store for Westminster pundits – and the appointee himself. While his colleagues were getting ready to move into their new offices, or return to their constituencies, Iain Duncan Smith was unpacking his bags after a weekend city break in Florence with his wife Betsy. Early on the Tuesday morning, as the negotiating teams were sewing up the agreement, he had received a call from Cameron. Duncan Smith insists he had no idea a job offer was coming. 'I want you to do a job for me,' Cameron said. 'At the Department of Work and Pensions.'

'Oh,' came the reply.

'Do you want to do it?' asked Cameron.

'The thing is,' Duncan Smith explained, 'I need to speak to Betsy, so I can't really say until I have done so.'

'What do you mean you can't say?' Cameron responded irritably.

'Well, I'll have to talk to my wife. She's been ill and this will take me away from home quite a lot.'

'Well, how long's that going to take?'

Duncan Smith asked for an hour.

'What?' bellowed Cameron down the line, his tone incredulous.

'Well, if you want an instantaneous answer, the answer would be no,' Duncan Smith replied testily. 'I do need to see her. It's only fair.'

'Can you be quick?' Cameron persisted. 'You're holding everything up!'

In the end, having received the go-ahead from his wife, Duncan Smith agreed. Within minutes of accepting the offer he was on his way down to London, listening to the news of his appointment on the radio. 'It was quite funny,' he reflected later. 'Because it had never once clicked that I'd be walking into that building to do this job. And as I walked in, I thought, "Oh God, this is the beginning of the end!"'

Less than forty-eight hours after becoming Prime Minister, Cameron chaired the first coalition Cabinet to be convened for sixty-five years. He immediately made it clear he wished to restore formal Cabinet government, a symbolic move designed to suggest the end of the informal so-called 'sofa government' of the Blair/Brown years. Cabinet ministers were told they would be expected to attend a meeting lasting an hour and a half to two hours every Tuesday.[315]

He and Osborne also emphasised that the relationship between No. 10 and

---

315   Anthony Seldon, *Independent on Sunday*, 3 April 2011.

No. 11 was to be re-set. This was crucial. Both had seen the corrosive effect of a bitter war of attrition between Blair and Brown, and both were determined to do things differently. It took a day or so for this message to filter down to mandarins. One new member of the team in No. 10 recalls telephoning No. 11 to request some information on behalf of the Prime Minister's office.

> I called this civil servant up, and said, 'Can you send over this note?' And he froze and sort of croaked: 'I – will – call – you – back,' and hung up. About three hours later nothing had come back, and I called George's office again and said, 'What's going on?' And they said, 'I don't know, we'll look into it.' And they looked into it and they found that there was a piece of advice from the Treasury intranet dating from Gordon Brown's time, stating that 'any request from No. 10 for information has to be routed through the Chancellor's political office'. So one of the first things that the government changed was that. David and George are a single team, they're one team, in a very deep way.[316]

Sweeping away the remnants of the old regime also meant a full-scale overhaul of Brown's working environment. The former Labour leader's famous open-plan 'war room' was replaced with a more traditional layout, of study, private office and den.[317] The new team also removed a number of wall-hanging televisions: Osborne felt they made the place feel too much like a newsroom.[318] Cameron felt similarly. He likes to tell people that running the country is not like running a 24-hour news channel.

Despite all the groundwork they had done in opposition, there was no disguising the fact that this was a team with very little collective experience of government. With the exception of veterans such as Ken Clarke, who took over as Justice Secretary, and Oliver Letwin, who became Cameron's Minister of State for Government Policy, most of the Cabinet was too young to have served in previous Tory administrations under either Major or Thatcher. 'No one really knew what they were doing,' O'Shaughnessy admits. 'We slightly sauntered in – this sounds ridiculous – thinking, "But am I turning up here

---

316 Private information.
317 Francis Elliott and James Hanning, p. 404.
318 Matthew d'Ancona, p. 2.

tomorrow?" Oliver [Letwin]'s advice to me was to find an office, bring your stuff in and sit down, and then they won't move you.'

Cameron quickly laid down his daily routine. He would rise at 5.30 a.m. to exercise and spend two hours working through his red box of papers, which was sent up to his flat in physical form (for the first time since the Major years) by Downing Street officials the night before.[319] At 8.30 a.m., he would chair the first formal meeting of the day. Throughout his premiership, the core attendees were Osborne (who would take over in Cameron's absence), McLoughlin (the Chief Whip), Llewellyn, Fall, Bertin, Coulson (later replaced by Craig Oliver) and occasionally Hague or, when required, other Cabinet ministers – all under the steady gaze of Jeremy Heywood, the new Downing Street Permanent Secretary, whom Cameron had known since his Treasury days. The morning meeting was to be a tactical, news agenda-driven discussion, carried out away from prying Lib Dem eyes, in contrast with the afternoon meeting – 4 p.m. – which aimed for a more strategic and long-term horizon.[320]

Beneath a grand portrait of Winston Churchill, who surveyed the scene from the walls of the No. 10 office, the new Prime Minister settled into his job with relish. The flat above No. 11 was expensively refurbished – at a cost of £30,000 to the taxpayer – and he soon made himself comfortable at Chequers. Among the first guests at his official country retreat in Buckinghamshire was his father, by then in a wheelchair. Cameron delighted in pushing him round the property, showing off its many treasures, which include the sword of Oliver Cromwell. (Reaching it involved going up a steep flight of stairs. In a touching scene, the son helped his father slowly pull himself up by the rope on the side.)[321]

Though he could no longer meet his father in White's, the private members' club to which they had once both belonged and where they would dine together when Cameron was in opposition, they continued to talk regularly. These were precious moments: just a few months later, Ian suffered a devastating stroke while on holiday with Mary and family friends in the south of France. Cameron and his brother took the first available commercial flight to Nice to be at his bedside. With Ian's condition rapidly deteriorating, the then French President Nicolas Sarkozy arranged a helicopter to rush them

319   Anthony Seldon, *Independent on Sunday*, 3 April 2011.

320   Matthew d'Ancona, p. 32.

321   Francis Elliott and James Hanning, p. 438.

from Nice to the hospital in Toulon where he had been taken. They made it just in time to say goodbye. The following day, the Prime Minister returned to work and talked openly to colleagues about his loss.

A senior Conservative aide says:

> He gave an account of what happened in the morning meeting the next day. It was quite moving. He was incredibly close to him and admired him immensely. He talked about it for ten minutes, saying how brilliant Sarkozy had been, laying on transport and so on, which made it all so much easier.

A member of his inner circle in Downing Street says Cameron still misses his father intensely.

> When his dad died he was really seriously moved, and I think he still thinks about him a lot, actually. Talks about him occasionally. His close family are very, very dear to him. He'll see things in his kids that remind him of his dad and will say, 'That's just like my dad. He takes after my dad.'

Despite his personal loss, Cameron was keen to savour his political honeymoon. He knew it would not last long. Nicholas Soames, who discussed his own political future with Cameron before the general election, recalls him anticipating trouble 'within a week'.

'They knew they were walking into a maelstrom,' he says now.

> David asked me to go and see him one day. At the end of our conversation he said to me, 'Are you going to stay on [as an MP]?' To which I replied, 'Yes, I am. I want to see you in power.' 'That's good,' he replied. 'Because, you know, within a week people will be running away at the first whiff of grapeshot.'

Nonetheless, with the luxury (and protection) of a five-year fixed-term parliament – a measure which would be enshrined in law, in accordance with the coalition agreement, on 15 September 2011 – Cameron could feel confident that, whatever the future turbulence, he would most likely be in it for the long haul.

But not everyone was happy. Though Cameron did not know it, he had upset no less a figure than Margaret Thatcher.

'I would never have gone into coalition with the Lib Dems,' she told a small group of newly elected Tory MPs invited to her house soon after the election.

'What would you have done?' asked one of the new backbenchers innocently.

'I would have done what I always did,' Thatcher replied. 'Win the election.'

29

THE NICK AND DAVE SHOW

'Trust has almost entirely broken down.'

– Andrew Cooper to Cameron, 2012

Less than three weeks into the life of the coalition, Downing Street's most powerful mandarin was in despair. Cameron and Clegg had barely pledged their political troth in Downing Street's sun-drenched rose garden, yet one of the key players was already out, victim of a scandal relating to his expenses and his gay partner.

As far as Cameron and Osborne were concerned, the quietly efficient and cerebral Liberal Democrat MP David Laws, Chief Secretary to the Treasury, was a pivotal figure. A self-made millionaire and free marketer, in 2004 he had been behind the highly controversial series of essays *The Orange Book*, an attempt to drag his party towards the centre. It even proposed an insurance scheme for the NHS. In short, he spoke their language. Now he was gone, making history as the shortest-serving Cabinet minister in modern times.

One who was in the room at the time says:

> I just remember Jeremy Heywood, slumped against a wall in Andy Coulson's office, with his head in his hands. It's the only time I've ever seen him lose control. Generally he's very calm. There was this weird sense that everything was veering out of control. It was so early…The PM and Deputy PM didn't want David to go. They didn't want to lose him. But David had decided. He made the decision himself.

It had all started with such optimism. The bonhomie in the Downing Street garden when Cameron and Clegg gushed about each other's qualities, declaring the new government would last, 'because we are united with a common purpose', set the tone for the atmosphere inside Downing Street, where everybody was determined to get on.

A former Clegg aide says:

> We were all new, and there was this feeling that it just wouldn't work if we all just kicked lumps out of each other. Between David and Nick, it was never going to be a really pally relationship – it couldn't be – but there was a sense we really could work together.

Each side was willing to cut the other some slack, turning a blind eye to the odd strategic leak or synthetic row to reassure backbenchers that relations weren't too cosy.

Underpinning the partnership was the coalition agreement – a 35-page document published on 20 May, based on the policies agreed during negotiations. At its heart was the shared fiscal priority: eliminating the 'structural deficit' by 2015 (though the original text only referred to 'significantly accelerating the pace of deficit reduction') – a pledge that went far further than Cameron's election promise to remove 'a large part' of the deficit in the first parliament. An 'emergency Budget' delivered by Osborne and Laws spelled out what this meant: £6 billion in public spending reductions and a deeply unpopular VAT hike. By the end of its first year, the coalition had devised a fiscal programme that amounted to the tightest squeeze on public spending since at least the end of the Second World War.[322]

Armed with a joint vision for the public finances and a raft of other agreed policies on banking, welfare, political reform, the environment, higher education and many other areas, the two parties set to work with an intensity and energy that took many by surprise. Cameron was convinced that legislative activity should be frontloaded – he had not forgotten Blair's advice that a successful government delivered quickly and decisively.[323]

Moreover, his speed wrong-footed the Labour Party, which was in any case hopelessly distracted by a leadership contest. Ed Miliband's decision to run against his older brother David, long considered the favourite, turned the battle into a soap opera that captivated Westminster for weeks. The

322 'The IFS Green Budget: February 2011', Institute for Fiscal Studies.
323 Francis Elliott and James Hanning, p. 408.

dramatic denouement saw the younger Miliband steal his older brother's crown after securing heavy backing from the trade unions, shattering the relationship between the siblings and their wives. The result was greeted with glee by the Tories, who believed 'Red Ed' would be far easier to beat than his suave Blairite sibling, a smooth international operator and friend of Hillary Clinton.

For the coalition, however, the harmony outlasted the summer, and the first bumps in the road were not between its partners but between the party leaders and their own MPs. By entering into government, Clegg achieved his ambition of ending the old two-party hegemony, but his determination to be the kind of politician who stuck to his word soon fell victim to realpolitik. The VAT increase – not mentioned in the party's manifesto[324] – was an early sacrifice which ruffled feathers on his backbenches, but there was far worse to come. The issue that proved the biggest test of his mettle blew up less than six months into the life of the coalition and struck at the very heart of his own and his party's integrity: university tuition fees. For Liberal Democrats, the subject could not have been more contentious: they had campaigned on a platform of no increase in tuition fees, and relied heavily on the student vote. Many Lib Dem MPs had been photographed brandishing 'No Tuition Fee Increase' placards. (Although the views of senior party members were more ambiguous in private: according to the former BBC director-general Greg Dyke, Vince Cable confided to him that he never agreed with the party's official position on tuition fees, always believing that students should pay.)[325]

Now a government-commissioned review was proposing that universities be allowed to charge up to £9,000 per year. The dilemma this presented plunged Clegg's party into an existential crisis from which it never recovered.

The hole in which the Lib Dem leader found himself was entirely of his own digging. The coalition did not have to accept the recommendations of the review. Over the summer, Osborne had looked into the possibility of a graduate tax as an alternative to increased fees. Though he rejected the idea, it suggested the Tory leadership was willing to think outside the box.[326] Clegg could have simply refused to back the £9,000-a-year scheme.

---

324 The party had also launched a poster campaign in the run-up to the election warning about the Tories increasing VAT.

325 Private information.

326 Matthew d'Ancona, p. 62.

The coalition agreement explicitly provided for Lib Dems to abstain in a vote on higher fees, and Cameron and Osborne were willing to let Clegg take this escape route.

'I remember meeting Nick [Clegg] and Danny [Alexander] and them saying, "We are going to go for it. We are going to vote for it. We have to,"' recalls O'Shaughnessy. 'David and George were saying: "Are you sure? You don't have to." But Clegg was keen – probably because it was a good policy.'

If Clegg had been in any doubt about the consequences of such a flagrant breach of voters' trust, he need only have surveyed the violent scenes when 50,000 student protestors marched on Parliament, culminating in a riot outside CCHQ. He ploughed on regardless. 'We just sort of accepted this slow-motion train crash,' recalls Sean Kemp, one of Clegg's former No. 10 aides and the party's then deputy head of press. 'It was all about trying to get through it as best we could.'

Rubbing salt into the wound, the Deputy Prime Minister even whipped his party. It prompted twenty-one Lib Dem MPs to rebel and a further eight to abstain. The majority of the remaining twenty-eight were on the government payroll. Privately, Cameron and his team were amazed.

'I wouldn't sign up to it,' Osborne reportedly told the Lib Dem leader.[327]

For Clegg personally, and for the future of his party, the repercussions were disastrous. For the remainder of the coalition, Lib Dem poll ratings never recovered. From the giddy heights of the pre-election TV debates, when Clegg hit 43 per cent in one poll, the party's popularity plunged to lows of six or seven points, rarely making it much above eleven. Public hatred of Clegg was visceral and personal: effigies were burned and excrement thrown at his door. The only upside was the strengthening of coalition relations: the Tory leadership had to respect his balls.

'I think Nick Clegg's done well – he's got real guts,' says Cameron's old ally Nicholas Soames. 'I'd kill myself rather than take all that grief.'

It was not an isolated example of self-sacrifice. A former No. 10 insider remembers the Lib Dem leader willingly taking the hit for the cancellation of an £80 million loan to Sheffield Forgemasters, a large engineering firm in his own constituency, in the name of 'austerity'. As with tuition fees, he was offered the chance to duck the pain, but declined to take the easy option.

The source recalls:

327   Ibid., p. 63.

He was told, 'Look, it's only £80 million – we can take that out.'
To which he replied firmly, 'No, no, no – we're all in it together.'
It was a real error of political judgement but in a sense I think he
did it for the right sort of reason, which was, 'If we don't seem to
be backing cuts, then the legitimacy of the deficit reduction strategy falls apart.'[328]

Meanwhile the Tories had their own troubles, located firmly in their Achilles
heel: the NHS. Cameron's style had always been to delegate, letting ministers
he rated get on with their jobs. It was a deliberate departure from Brown's
obsessive micro-management. In Andrew Lansley he had a Health Secretary
who not only had six years of experience on the brief but was also his former
boss. (At a drinks reception held in CRD in 1995, Lansley told Cameron and
Osborne: 'When you two are running the country, please make me Governor
of Bermuda.')[329] Cameron trusted him and was content to leave him be as
he put the finishing touches on a series of what were widely assumed to be
relatively innocuous structural changes to the health service.

'There was this sense of "Andrew Lansley has thought about this for years
and years so it will all be fine. He's been on top of this for ages,"' recalls an
aide.[330] Busy drawing up the spending review and distracted by the Vickers
Commission on banking reform, Osborne too paid Lansley little attention.

In fact, the Health Secretary was plotting what amounted to root-and-
branch reform of the health service. Blatantly breaching pledges in both
the Tory manifesto and the coalition agreement to put an end to 'top-down
re-organisations of the NHS', Lansley's 'NHS Reform Bill' transformed the
set-up, promising commissioning powers for GPs, the abolition of Primary Care
Trusts, and a massive expansion of market competition. In the words of the NHS
chief David Nicholson, the reorganisation was 'so big you can see it from
outer space'. Cameron's hard-won trust on the NHS (slowly accrued since
2005 via the symbolic ditching of Howard's 'patient passport' proposal,
the Tory leader's deeply personal accounts of his times in hospitals with
Ivan, and the ring-fencing of the health budget prior to the 2010 election)
was being shot away.

---

328 Private information.
329 Janan Ganesh, p. 58.
330 Private information.

Few, if any, in Downing Street noticed, not least because Lansley's proposals were so mystifying. It didn't help that Lansley himself – in the words of one weary colleague – 'spoke exclusively in jargon and health service verbiage'.

When the full implications of his proposals became apparent, there was a firestorm. Cameron found himself pitted against the massed ranks of the medical profession, while Labour whipped up old fears about Tory motives. It was a gift to Ed Miliband.

Alarmed, Cameron summoned Lansley to Downing Street in October to explain his plans. Unfortunately, the Health Secretary's presentation was, in the words of one who heard it, 'impenetrable guff'.

'Everyone looked to Oliver Letwin, who had looked at it all himself. David and George asked him what he thought. He said: "I'm completely sure about this."'

Few shared his confidence, but nobody suggested a re-think.

'George, looking back on it, feels that was the meeting where he should have said he was putting the brakes on it,' according to a confidant. 'But he didn't – and it rolled on.'[331]

By March 2011, the government seemed to be at open war with the healthcare profession. Andrew Cooper, the No. 10 strategy director, Stephen Gilbert, the PM's political secretary, and Cameron's new director of communications Craig Oliver, delivered Cameron a blunt message: the NHS had become a 'political disaster'. Damage limitation was paramount. 'I think we need to find some sort of way to reset the argument,' Cooper told Cameron diplomatically. 'And the only way we can do that is to put the brakes on the legislative process to buy ourselves a bit of time.'

In a highly unusual move, Cameron agreed to announce a two-month 'pause' on the Health Bill in spring 2011, presenting what was clearly an embarrassing retreat as a democratic 'listening exercise'.

'It caused huge internal problems,' Cooper recalls.

> Andrew was absolutely furious. He thought it was completely unnec-essary and was a sign of surrender. He thought it showed the lack of courage of our convictions and that we should go out and defend our reforms. He felt that I was pandering to left-wing health unions and their agenda. I don't think it achieved much.

---

331 Private information.

By this point, Clegg was also ratcheting up the pressure. Though he told Lansley privately that he supported the policy[332] (the decentralising, free market principles behind the reforms were quite acceptable to 'Orange Bookers'), his bruised left-wingers did not share his enthusiasm. In late May, he was overheard berating the Tory leader while they waited for Barack Obama's speech to MPs in Westminster Hall.[333] During one particularly tense meeting inside No. 10, he interrupted Lansley in full flow, coldly despatching the Health Secretary's excuses. 'Andrew, the reason why this "pause" is necessary is because YOU put the legislative cart before the political horse,' he said. According to one who witnessed the exchange, Lansley's face 'went puce'.[334] At one point Clegg threatened to pull the plug on the entire process.

The Bill returned to Parliament in June, and Lib Dems soon began to chip away at it. By the time it received royal assent in March 2012, after more than nineteen months of legislative wrangling, some 2,000 amendments had made their way onto the statute book.[335] Much of this watering down was a concession to Clegg, who was in dire need of something to present as a Lib Dem victory.

In opposition, Cameron's sustained campaigning on the NHS had gone some way to neutralising Labour's traditional advantage on the subject. The reform programme undid that progress. Research by Lord Ashcroft Polls, echoed by Downing Street's private polling, found that voters knew health professionals were largely opposed to the plans, but that most people had no idea what benefits the changes were supposed to bring for patients. In the absence of any clear alternative explanation, many assumed the reforms were simply intended to save money, or were part of a Tory scheme to privatise the NHS.

For the remainder of the coalition, Labour would exploit the fiasco, declaring it was 'the end of the NHS as we know it'. The residual hostility of the medical profession was an ongoing problem. At one point, Cooper warned Cameron: 'Trust has almost entirely broken down.'

Having been tasked by Cameron with digesting Lansley's proposals, Letwin took some of the heat.

---

332 Matthew d'Ancona, p. 113.
333 Francis Elliott and James Hanning, p. 421.
334 Private information.
335 Matthew d'Ancona, p. 116.

'I think Letwin should be locked in a darkened room and everyone just walk away,' says one adviser who still can't quite believe they got into such a mess. 'Great guy, but what has his influence on modern politics been? If there was ever a case of political misjudgement, this was it.'

Yet Cameron himself had been caught sleeping at the wheel. His remote leadership style had backfired and he looked incompetent. Critics piled in, depicting him as a complacent part-timer unable to sell his own agenda. Writing in the *Financial Times* later, Anthony King would label him 'Britain's first dilettante Prime Minister since Herbert Asquith'.[336] In a Cabinet reshuffle in September 2012, Cameron threw Lansley to the wolves, but the damage had long been done.

With his kamikaze U-turn on tuition fees, Clegg had demonstrated the scale of political and personal sacrifice he was prepared to make to keep the coalition show on the road. Whether Cameron would be willing to take such a hit was another question. Many Lib Dems feared he would dump on them as soon as it was politically advantageous. Just such an opportunity came in the form of the planned referendum on an Alternative Vote system, scheduled for May 2011.

Under the AV model, voters rank candidates in order of preference, so that no MP can be elected without the support of at least half the electorate. To most Lib Dems, it was, in Clegg's words, 'a miserable little compromise',[337] stopping far short of their dream of full proportional representation, but it was a start. Moreover, with his stock in the party at an all-time low, the Deputy Prime Minister desperately needed victory. By contrast, Cameron regarded the referendum as a bore. Conceded in the frantic final stages of the negotiations, it meant a campaign for which he had little appetite on a subject that did not interest him. A conversation with Daniel Finkelstein at a party hosted by Rupert Murdoch as the Miliband brothers slugged it out for the Labour Party leadership in September 2010 underlined his disengagement. He had not felt the need to examine how AV worked.

'I watched the *Newsnight* debate the other night,' Cameron told Finkelstein.

---

336 *Financial Times*, 9 April 2012.
337 *The Independent*, 22 April 2010.

'I thought we wanted David [Miliband], but we don't want David, we want Ed. But we are going to get David.'

'Well, not necessarily,' Finkelstein replied. 'Labour has an AV electoral system.'

'Yes, I probably ought to study more about how that system will work…' Cameron replied.

'Yes, you should – we've got a referendum on it coming up,' Finkelstein chided.

Other Tories did not share Cameron's insouciance. As early as June 2010, *The Spectator* reported grumblings on the backbenches, revealing that some MPs suspected the party leadership was plotting to let the Lib Dems win.[338] This wasn't complete pie in the sky: a number of Cameron's close allies had some sympathy with the AV system, including Letwin and potentially Gove.[339] Illustrating the leadership's relaxed attitude, Cameron had privately assured Clegg he would not spearhead the No campaign. Additionally, Clegg had been given the distinct impression that in the interests of coalition harmony, the Prime Minister would restrict Tory firepower.

Matthew Elliott, the roving right-wing campaign organiser drafted in to lead the No campaign, recalls that at least until the start of 2011 there was little interest in the subject in No. 10. Seeing it as an irritating leftover from the coalition agreement, the leadership was visibly reluctant to commit substantial money or manpower.

'The message coming out of the leadership was that this was essentially a free vote for Tory MPs. It wasn't an issue for the party machines, and the plan was that Cameron himself would only make a single speech on it before the referendum, to make his position known,' Elliott says.

Cameron's problem was that his backbenchers *did* care. Writing on Conservative Home, an online forum for the Tory grassroots, former MP Paul Goodman summed up Cameron's predicament: 'In short, the cry will be: "First he messes up the election. Now he's messed up the referendum. We'll never govern again on our own – and I'm going to lose my seat."'

Repeatedly warned that he was 'sleepwalking into disaster' unless he armed the No campaign with funding and personal support, Cameron slowly began to accept coasting was not an option.

---

338   *The Spectator*, 12 June 2010.
339   Matthew d'Ancona, p. 76.

'He knew that his neck was on the block,' Elliott confirms. In a dramatic meeting, the executive of the 1922 Committee inside No. 10 spelled out what was at stake: his party would crucify him if the referendum was lost. Yet still he appeared unruffled.

According to an insider account, 'Cameron walked into George Osborne's office to tell him that he'd just been told that he'd lose the leadership if AV passed. Cameron thought it funny that MPs could be so melodramatic. Osborne's face didn't move. "We can't rule it out," he said.'[340]

When the message finally got through, Cameron was resolute, swiftly putting party before coalition. Turning to Stephen Gilbert, he issued a simple command: 'Do whatever it takes to win.'[341]

The first thing they needed was money. They turned to Peter Cruddas, who had always proved generous when the party needed funds fast. In opposition, the philanthropist had helped bankroll a string of Cameron's Big Society initiatives, many relating to youth employment. For some time, Andrew Feldman had been dangling the prospect of rewarding him by making him party treasurer, a role he knew Cruddas would like. Now he summoned him to Central Office and asked for an urgent donation for the No to AV campaign, setting out the quid pro quo:

> Peter – the No to AV campaign – we need to ramp it up. I'd like you to be treasurer of the campaign. It's important to the party. If you take the treasurer's role, and it goes well, after that, we would then like you to be co-treasurer of the Conservative Party. You have to inject £500,000.

It was a big ask, but it was only the start. When Cruddas queried how much he would have to pay if he wanted the prestigious party treasurer role, Feldman replied bluntly: 'Probably about £750,000 a year.'

Unfazed (he says, 'If you're going to play with the big boys, you've got to be prepared to write big cheques'), Cruddas threw himself into it.

'I wanted to nail it. I knew that if I failed, they'd withdraw the treasurer offer. By the end of March I'd put in £600,000 and we'd raised about £2 million more.'

---

340 'The story of the AV campaign', Tim Montgomerie, ConservativeHome.com, 5 July 2011.

341 Private information.

Instructing his team to schedule an anti-AV event for him at least once a week, Cameron now embraced the cause, canvassing editors and delivering set-piece anti-AV speeches, including a joint platform address with John Reid, the former Labour Home Secretary.

As the referendum became a bitter partisan battle, the consequences for coalition relations were bloody and predictable. Having taken off the gloves, the No campaign turned on Clegg, personalising the issue on the question of his integrity. A batch of No leaflets featured an image of Clegg and his tuition fee pledge, complete with the words 'AV Leads to Broken Promises'. For the Lib Dem leadership, it crossed a line. In retrospect, Cameron's team concede they went too far.

'I think with hindsight we probably could have eased up a bit,' Cooper admits.

> It was over the top...a mistake. The Tories pumped a lot of money and seconded a lot of people to the campaign. Labour argued that if we were going to get reasonably uninterested voters to vote against AV, kicking Clegg [was] quite a good way to do it. But I think we should have stopped it and we didn't. Clegg felt that there was a breach of spirit of the agreement.

Clegg was hurt, but it did the job. On 5 May, the No campaign stormed to victory, with nearly 70 per cent of those who turned up to vote rejecting AV. For the Lib Dems, it was a double blow: that same day, they lost 748 councillors in the local elections, while the Tories gained 86.

The result gave Cameron a brief boost.

'In saving first past the post, the Tory leader put the long-term electoral interests of the Conservative Party before the short-term interests of his coalition...Conservative MPs, more than at any time in a year, now see him as on their side and as a winner,' one right-wing journalist wrote.[342]

Elliott was more circumspect, saying Cameron's delayed transition to full engagement was indicative of his 'somewhat short-term horizons as Prime Minister'. However, he concedes that, until his fatal miscalculations over the EU referendum, the Tory leader had an uncanny ability to deliver when it mattered.

---

342 'The story of the AV campaign', op. cit.

I was really impressed, particularly by his command of the issue, and his ability to be able to enthuse people. And, remember, this period in February overlapped with the situation in Libya, and, obviously, the Arab Spring more generally. You'd be seeing on BBC News huge events happening in Libya, but at the same time he would just walk into a meeting and be able to really command a room and be on top of his subject, and exude to people how important the subject was for him and the party and the future of the country. He'd be really on top of it and then of course leave an hour later and be back doing foreign affairs again. That massively impressed me.

The AV campaign was a turning point for the coalition. For Clegg, it meant the final loss of political innocence. 'Nick realised what we're like, what Tories are capable of,' one Downing Street official admits.[343] Though it was always business-like, Clegg and Cameron's personal relationship never fully recovered, and the Lib Dem party emerged from the battering with toughened resolve. Next time, on an issue close to their hearts, they were ready to play hard ball. It was over another potential constitutional reform.

Overhauling the House of Lords had appeared in both parties' manifestos. It also featured in the coalition agreement, which spoke of creating a 'wholly or mainly elected upper chamber' through proportional representation. The spirit was clear, but the precise wording fell well short of a commitment to legislate: the relevant passage talked only of 'bringing forward proposals'.

Under Labour, the issue had proved intractable. Endless cross-party talks had failed to produce any agreement, and there was little reason to believe that yet another attempt to change the system would be anything other than a colossal waste of time. Privately, the Tory leader had little to no appetite for change, as he had made clear in an address to the Association of Conservative Peers ahead of the 2010 election. 'Lords reform is a very important issue,' he declared, pausing for dramatic effect, 'for the start of a third term.'

For Lib Dems, however, it was a last-ditch opportunity to secure a historic piece of constitutional reform. In summer 2012, Cameron obliged Clegg by

343   Matthew d'Ancona, p. 84.

bringing forward a House of Lords Reform Bill. On the table were plans for a 50 per cent reduction in the number of peers, with 80 per cent of the remainder to be elected. All peers would be restricted to fifteen-year terms. Once again, Cameron was slow to detect how much the issue mattered to a tranche of his own MPs. Some were genuinely passionate about the historic role of the Lords and unwilling to stand by as centuries of tradition were overturned. Others simply resented Cameron for proposing constitutional upheaval just to keep the Lib Dems on side.

'It was an appalling proposition!' says Graham Brady.

> I think one of the most repellent things of that whole episode was the appearance that the government was prepared to make very profound constitutional changes for very short-term political advantage. The thing that sunk it really wasn't the radicals, but old-fashioned 'Shire Tories', who saw it as the most frightful constitutional abuse. It was a very odd mistake for David Cameron to make, given that that is far more his kind of Conservatism. In a sense, it was very odd for him not to see the problem it was going to cause with the most conservative elements of the Conservative Party.

Thatcher, by this time in very poor health, was reportedly incensed when a close friend informed her of Cameron's proposal.

'This is terrible!' she exclaimed. 'We must stop them. Who is behind it?'

'Well, the Lib Dems are behind it,' the friend explained.

'We should abolish the Lib Dems!' came the typically uncompromising reply.

As the vote approached, a showdown loomed. To Cameron's surprise and indignation, the rebellion was being orchestrated not by the 'usual suspects' but by a number of respected figures from the 2010 intake. In the lead was Jesse Norman, a cerebral Old Etonian who was the author of pamphlets on 'Compassionate Conservatism' and 'The Big Society' as well as being a former adviser to Osborne. Yet, as Norman was co-ordinating a revolt against the expected three-line whip, Cameron looked the other way. Brooks Newmark, the Tory whip in charge of the Bill, appealed for a meeting with the party leader to warn him that the numbers did not stack up. Oddly, the Prime Minister would not make time. He was equally dismissive when Clegg privately raised concerns, shrugging that Mark Harper, the minister in charge of the Bill, was 'handling it'.[344] Such was his apathy that Clegg suspected the Prime Minister didn't particularly care.

'We felt they weren't whipping it as hard as they could have done,' Sean Kemp says.

> The PM would just say, 'Look, I can't. It's not whippable.' I had some sympathy and that might have been true, but I still don't think they were trying as hard as they could have done. There was a lot of frustration on our side; we felt that was a bad-faith moment. It was like: 'You agreed to this, it was a big part of our agreement. We are keeping you in power by going into a coalition: are you just going to turn around and say no?'

Ninety-one Conservative MPs voted against the Bill on 10 July 2012, including forty-seven from the class of 2010. It was just four short of being the largest Tory rebellion in the post-war era. Cameron was furious. In a rowdy Commons lobby immediately after the vote, he turned on Norman, jabbing his finger at him while lambasting him for behaving 'dishonourably'. In a separate incident later that night, a group of Conservative whips approached Norman in a Commons bar, warning him to leave the parliamentary estate before a fight broke out.

Cameron's anger had nothing to do with the reforms themselves. It related to the longer-term consequences for the party of yet another blow to Clegg. In the run-up to the vote, the Lib Dem leader had privately made clear that if Tory MPs scuppered House of Lords reform, Lib Dems would retaliate by kiboshing plans to redraw constituency boundaries.

In the coalition agreement, boundary reform had featured without any link to Lords reform. The proposed changes to the map reduced the number of MPs by fifty, but were potentially hugely advantageous for the Tories, creating, according to some experts, as many as twenty extra Tory-leaning seats. The assumption at the time was that it could be pivotal to the Tories' fortunes in 2015. Fed up of being a passive whipping boy, Clegg decided to make it a quid pro quo.

According to one of Cameron's advisers: '[Clegg] basically said, "You've crushed my first bit of constitutional reform – AV – if I don't get my other

---

344   Ibid., p. 287.

one, I'm in an impossible position." So he couldn't let us off the hook on the Lords.'[345]

The extent to which Clegg's warning was explicit is a matter of dispute. Lib Dems insist the Prime Minister was under no illusion about what would happen if he failed to push his MPs through the Yes lobby.

'It was made clear and it was increasingly clear as the process went on,' Kemp insists. 'The night before the vote, I believe Cameron said to MPs, "If we don't vote this through, boundary reform will not happen."'

Yet Cooper says Cameron never accepted Clegg's logic.

> The coalition agreement didn't even talk about voting on Lords reform. David essentially thought, 'Well, we've brought forward proposals, which you [Lib Dems] couldn't get enough people to vote for; and we whipped our side through to get you your referendum, which you couldn't get up enough of an argument to win; there was never any link with boundary changes, and now you're suddenly retrospectively linking them? That's totally outrageous.'

To his backbench critics, however, it was yet another Cameron blunder. Many felt he had casually jettisoned an outright majority in 2015.

'There was nobody there saying the boundary changes are more important than anything else we're doing,' laments Cameron's former senior political adviser Andrew MacKay. 'I would have been saying at every meeting, *don't have the AV referendum until the boundary changes are through*, because otherwise you've lost your only leverage. There was no other policy that would affect twenty seats.'

Prior to the 2015 election, many Westminster observers regarded Cameron's failure to deliver boundary reform as one of his gravest political errors as Prime Minister. As it turned out, Cameron got away with it. However, there were other implications. The collapse of Lords reform further damaged Clegg, undermining the prospect of more radical reform in other policy areas. It also did nothing to improve Cameron's relationship with his parliamentary party. Instead of putting the episode behind him, he and Osborne demonstrated an unattractive ability to hold grudges, punishing rebels like

---

345 Private information.

Rory Stewart, the MP for Penrith and the Border, and Norman by refusing to give them ministerial jobs throughout the remainder of the coalition. The quality of their government was the poorer for it.

30

The Big Dip

'Why should we be the only saint in the brothel?'
— Cameron, on the environment

W hat was the point of David Cameron? That was the question many were asking a year into the life of the coalition. The Tory leader had made tackling the economy the defining purpose of his administration. By summer 2011, however, the public finances were deteriorating and speculation was mounting of a double-dip recession. In the absence of green shoots, voters needed to know what else the Prime Minister was about.

'When's the economy going to start growing?' Cameron asked Bruce Anderson anxiously one day.

'It will,' his old friend replied reassuringly.

'I know, but *when*?' the Prime Minister asked plaintively.

It would be a long wait.

In the increasingly desperate quest for growth, some policy priorities manufactured in the good times began to fade from the agenda. Environmental campaigners accused Cameron of abandoning his green crusade, particularly when he installed Owen Paterson, a right-winger who believes the effects of climate change have been 'consistently and widely exaggerated' in scientific forecasts, as Secretary of State at DEFRA in 2012.[346] Cameron instructed him to make the department 'pro-growth'. Osborne was loath to adopt any green measures that could frustrate business, and Cameron did not appear to have the stomach for a fight.

'Why should we be the only saint in the brothel?' he protested, during a debate over whether farmers should be forced to do more conservation

---

346   *Daily Telegraph*, 15 October 2014.

work in return for EU subsidies.[347] There was no place for husky hugging now.

The party's private research was worrying. Poll after poll revealed deepening pessimism about the state of the nation, and mounting hostility to the government. The feeling that the country was on the skids was deep-seated and widespread, and there was little optimism that things would improve any time soon.

'The public mood is turning against us,' Andrew Cooper warned.

Now based in Downing Street, Cooper was responsible for the party's polling and focus group research. Every so often, he would summarise his depressing findings in memos to the Prime Minister. Osborne, Gilbert, Llewellyn, Fall and Coulson were copied in. The director of strategy would deposit his periodic reports in Cameron's red box of an evening, and by the time he returned to his desk the following morning, the papers would be back, marked up with the Prime Minister's observations.

Taken together, Cooper's memos from summer to Christmas 2011 painted a picture of an administration and a Prime Minister in anxious search of a defining purpose.

'Most people still don't know what the government is trying to do beyond making cuts. They don't know what your vision is,' Cooper told the Prime Minister.

In early June, Osborne convened a meeting of senior Downing Street colleagues to discuss what message they should be trying to convey. Cameron was not present. The team failed to reach a conclusion. It was a damning reflection of a long-running problem: a lack of clarity on why they all wanted to be in power. For all the talk of tackling the deficit and creating a 'Big Society', voters remained confused about Cameron's purpose. Such was the uncertainty that Cooper actually carried out a survey on what people thought 'the ideal government' would aim to do. Meanwhile Labour's rhetoric about the cuts going 'too far and too fast' was gaining ground.

'People think we just don't get it,' Cooper told Downing Street colleagues. 'The single most important factor in whether someone votes for us or not is our values. We're losing that battle. Before the election, people were hopeful we'd turn out to be on their side. Now they're beginning to conclude we're not.'

Cameron and Osborne's old mantra – 'we're all in it together' – a sound bite that used to poll positively, was rapidly becoming a source of public scorn.

347 Private information.

'People just laugh when we use that phrase now,' Cooper reported. His research suggested that less than a third of voters felt the burden really was being shared. In both No. 10 and No. 11, there was growing concern that if the leadership continued to focus narrowly on deficit reduction, it was setting itself up for a fall. They needed to talk about something else.

The great Westminster exodus for summer provided some respite, and Cameron headed off to Tuscany. But the let-up proved brief: on 9 August he was forced to cut short his holiday and return to London as riots swept the capital following a fatal shooting by police. Thousands of youths rampaged through streets, looting shops and setting fire to buildings, and copycat violence broke out in other cities.[348]

The ugly scenes prompted a fierce debate about law and order, but there were subtler concerns about Cameron's leadership. September brought an unwelcome return of nagging questions about his vision – or lack of it. Writing in the *Telegraph*, the political commentator Ben Brogan lamented the paucity of people who 'seem to have any idea what Mr Cameron is for, or what he believes'. Though the Prime Minister's robust response to the London riots won plaudits from right-wingers, it re-opened questions about his political philosophy. Some commentators asked whether the 'nasty party' was back. What had happened to so-called 'compassionate Conservatism', his original leadership ticket? Had he given up 'detoxifying' the brand? There were signs that Cameron himself was unsure. Asked on the *Today* programme whether he was still a 'modern, compassionate Conservative', he demurred.

'I'm a common-sense Conservative,' he replied uncertainly.

It was so anodyne as to be meaningless. Cooper's polling was unambiguous: the detoxification strategy had been crucial in making the Conservatives the largest party in 2010. Equally, fears that Cameron and those around him never really 'meant it' were a significant factor in the failure to achieve a majority. Any backsliding could be fatal. Summarising his findings that autumn, Cooper was blunt, warning Cameron that if the party was seen to be reverting to type, millions of voters would feel 'duped' and 'millions more' would resolve not to vote Tory in 2015. He continued to push Cameron to define himself better.

---

348   Between 6 and 11 August 2011, thousands of people rioted in several London boroughs and in cities and towns across England. Looting, arson and mass deployment of police resulted. Five people died.

'The question of what kind of Conservative you are is not going away,' he warned.

Party conference was the perfect opportunity for the Prime Minister to make a new pitch. In September, he began drafting a keynote speech he hoped would help him reconnect with voters. It contained a long passage about the travails of his job.

'You've got to take that out,' Cooper advised. 'People aren't going to have much sympathy.'

Another section of Cameron's draft appeared to blame ordinary people for the state of the economy. 'Who's to blame? All of us...not just Labour, not just politicians,' he wrote. Colleagues could see it would backfire and he was persuaded to scrap it. Various other inflammatory phrases pledging 'all-out war' on 'enemies of change', and vows to be more 'ruthless' and 'radical' were also deleted, as was a line advising householders to pay off their credit cards, which leaked to the press on the eve of the speech.

To add to the already tense atmosphere, there was another anxiety: the prospect of Boris Johnson making mischief. In 2009, the Mayor had lobbed a grenade into party conference by demanding a referendum on the EU Lisbon Treaty. This time, Cameron and Osborne were taking no chances.

Osborne had particular reason to be concerned: his keynote speech was scheduled for the Monday, the same day Boris's regular *Telegraph* column appeared. Fearing his speech would be overshadowed, the Chancellor rang Johnson three days before conference opened to appeal to him to behave.

'We just want a quiet conference. Nothing unexpected,' the Chancellor told him.

'Hmm, funny you should say that,' Johnson replied mischievously. 'I'm just about to write my column for the *Telegraph* and I'm staring at a blank page.'

'Very funny,' retorted the Chancellor.

'No, seriously,' Johnson countered, sensing an opportunity. 'What price no mischief?'

'What do you want?' Osborne asked, scarcely able to believe the position the Mayor was putting him in.

Without hesitation, Johnson answered: 'Ninety million extra for policing in London.'

Before the conversation was out, the Chancellor had agreed to a package worth £93 million, allowing Johnson to make lavish pledges on policing when he ran for re-election to the London Mayoralty in 2012.

'That was the best-paid column ever,' a delighted Johnson joked to aides.

But the speech Cameron eventually delivered failed to dispel a deepening suspicion among some that, having made it to Downing Street, he lacked a burning desire to do anything else. Within his own party, a narrative was emerging that, having got the top job, he had achieved all he wanted.

'Seventy-five per cent of him wanted to be PM, and 25 per cent of him wanted to change the world. With Thatcher and Brown, it was the other way round,' sighs a Tory grandee. It is a familiar refrain among his critics. Thatcher, no less, sensed the same thing.

'She thought he was shallow, really. She'd say, "If you're leader, you've got to *believe* in something,"' said one of her former confidants. The same source, who liked Cameron, nonetheless believed he was 'in politics to be in politics'.

'It's a stimulating hobby for him. The phrase that Osborne uses, which I really dislike, is, "Oh look, it's all a game." He's said that to me lots of times. I don't think it is a game. It's a serious endeavour for the future of the country,' he says.

As Cameron bedded in to Downing Street, there was a growing perception among backbenchers that he was simply 'focused on his own position'. A former Cabinet minister says he became increasingly confused about the leader's ideals.

> My admiration for him as a tactician is almost boundless, but it's often been a case of scratching one's head and saying, 'What's the big picture? What's the intention? How does all this fit together?' He is a blank sheet and it remains unclear to me now what he really wants, or what motivates him to be Prime Minister, almost as much as it did right at the beginning…I just don't know what makes this man tick. With the one exception that his family is really important to him – that really shines through everything. But it's almost as if anything outside his family is just an exercise yard for political skills. It's as if it's just a game of chess, and he just wants to come top.

One strategist close to the leadership wonders what Cameron would have done if 'fate hadn't happened to hand him the task of dealing with the deficit'.

'I don't know, and I suspect he doesn't either,' he says. 'They were always wrestling with the question – and there was never any internal agreement – about what David Cameron's Conservative Party believed in, and what its positive proposition would be to voters.'

Cameron's perceived lack of reforming zeal in office angered those who expected more.

'There's nothing there!' says a well-known think-tank type who worked with Cameron when he first became leader, and was bitterly disappointed by his approach when he reached No. 10.

> He's just a decent guy who's on his back, floating. Not struggling. Not going anywhere. Just floating, looking at the ambient world. You have to respect his talents – he's good in public, good at the repartee; he's got a good memory for detail. But there's no guiding philosophy. You have to be able to build a philosophy. That's why Blairism succeeded. That's why Thatcherism succeeded. What is Cameronism? Fuck all!

The same source was disappointed by what he saw as the leader's failure to 'operationalise the response' to problems he had fully grasped.

> He's like an MRI scanner who can see the tumours, but doesn't know how to get them out. Just goes, 'Where's the PlayStation?' It's really sad. It's rare to find somebody who can grasp big narrative issues and problems as he does. Yet he's asleep at the wheel when he knows the road is dangerous. It's not like he's stupid or anything. It's almost as if there's a piece of equipment missing that any leader should have.

The impression that Cameron did not 'stand for anything' was fuelled by the pragmatism that enabled him to lead a coalition with a rival party in the first place. Even behind closed doors, he rarely seemed exercised by any single issue. (A confidant of Cameron's says the most animated he ever saw the Tory leader was 'in his dislike for John Bercow'.)

Andrew Mitchell says he 'travels pretty light' and 'goes with what works', which can be a political asset. The most damning assessment came from

Michael Gove's former special adviser Dominic Cummings, who publicly labelled him a 'sphinx without a riddle'.

'Cameron requires no psychological analysis,' Cummings wrote.

> He's one of the most straightforward people one will meet in politics. Pundits have wasted millions of words on what they regard as his 'mystery' but he is exactly what he seems…He's cleverer than most MPs and can hold his own in conversations with senior officials…
>
> Why is he there? Because 1) Cameron's 2005 rival was David Davis, who over a long campaign scared too many MPs about his temperament, 2) Blair blew up over the Middle East, making Cameron's rival Brown, 3) Cameron is superficially suitable for the job in the way that 'experts' often judge such things – i.e. basic chimp politics skills, height, glibness etc., so we can 'shove him out to give a statement on X'. That's it. In a dysfunctional institutional structure, someone without the skills we need in a Prime Minister can easily get the job with a few breaks like that.[349]

All this was unfair, in so far as it rested on a misunderstanding of how Cameron saw his job. He did not believe he was there to execute 'grand plans'. He also knew what kind of Britain he *didn't* want and was happy to reach a better destination step by step. He was content to rely on passionate reformers like Gove and Duncan Smith to make big things happen.

Finkelstein says:

> When asked how he'd sculpted his bust of Ernest Bevin, Jacob Epstein said he'd taken a block of marble, and chipped away anything that didn't look like Bevin. That's Conservative methodology really. Cameron knows quite strongly what he's up against; he knows which bits of Epstein's statue do not look like Bevin. But he's not an ideologue with some sort of plan.

---

349 'The Hollow Men II: Some reflections on Westminster and Whitehall dysfunction', Dominic Cummings's Blog, 30 October 2014: http://dominiccummings.wordpress.com/2014/10/30/the-hollow-men-ii-some-reflections-on-westminster-and-whitehall-dysfunction.

It was a leadership style to which some colleagues struggled to adapt, particularly those used to Thatcher's more exacting approach. Increasingly, ministers were coming to realise that Cameron didn't 'do policy detail'. In the run-up to the 2010 election, he had made much of his plans for welfare and education reform. In office, he showed little personal interest in either – though he fully understood the political importance of delivering both. According to a Whitehall source, Duncan Smith had just a single one-to-one meeting with Cameron about the welfare reform agenda during the coalition years. It was the same story with Gove.

Cummings says:

> No. 10 did not take school reform seriously and could not be engaged in any serious way on policy. Between Gove getting the job in January 2007 and January 2014, how many meetings do you think happened between a) Cameron and his senior policy advisers, and b) Gove and his senior policy advisers to discuss schools policy? If quarterly, then about twenty-five to thirty? Answer: two. One in 2009, one in 2011.[350]

Gove's former adviser argues that this was 'a *good* thing. It meant No. 10 largely left us alone for long periods. Whenever No. 10 sent word that "the PM is thinking of making an intervention", it guaranteed 100 per cent that the horror, the horror, would descend.' However, he would not argue that it made Cameron a 'good Prime Minister'.

The most generous interpretation of Cameron's apparent lack of reforming zeal is that it was a deliberate guise to enable those around him to implement radical change. According to this thesis, put forward by one of his most thoughtful friends, the Tory leader deliberately stood above the fray, adopting a consensual demeanour to give inflammatory figures like Gove, Duncan Smith and Hilton 'cover' to achieve radical reform. It is worth noting that all three figures would turn on him when the time came.

For his part, Duncan Smith respected the Prime Minister's laissez-faire approach. It reminded him of the American Civil War hero Robert E. Lee, who was famed for being laid-back.

'Lee's orders to his generals and commanders were always quite general,

---

350 Ibid.

always stressed the achievement of the overall objective. He assumed they would then act in accordance with their orders, but he gave them massive leeway in the way they did this,' Duncan Smith says.

It was an approach that relied on generals (or Cabinet ministers) being energetic and skilled.

'Lee never lost a battle while the general Stonewall Jackson was with him,' Duncan Smith says.

> But after Stonewall Jackson died of gangrene, Lee never won a battle again.[351] Jackson telepathically knew what Lee meant, and drove his men to achieve that. He was that perfect deputy, able to translate the requirements of his leader with flexibility in application. The others never quite had the same ability to maintain the overall objective. In other words, you can do it like that, providing everyone understands and sticks to the overall plan. The PM wants to look at things and understand that we are moving on a broad front. Which is fine. It's one way of doing it.

The problem was that Cameron was not dealing with soldiers – he was dealing with civil servants.

And with their jobs for life and comfy Whitehall offices, these mandarins did not necessarily share his aims. Not everyone in No. 10 could live with institutional inertia. Soon, it would blow a hole in Cameron's team – and expose the limitations of his ambitions in No. 10.

---

351 In fact, Jackson survived the amputation of his arm, but died of complications from pneumonia eight days later.

31

HALF BUDDHA, HALF PEST

'The bureaucracy masters the politicians…It's just a fact.'
– Steve Hilton

Within an hour of starting his new job as a special adviser in the education department, Dominic Cummings received a brutal lesson in the sorry state of the Whitehall machine. From the moment he sat down at his desk till he left after dark, he received a steady stream of visits from officials bearing bad news. The cock-ups were unremitting and wide ranging: procurement processes casually ballsed up, costing taxpayers millions; institutions accidentally closed, because somebody forgot to renew a contract; inaccurate figures briefed to the media; letters sent out with the wrong information.

'It seemed extraordinary at the time but soon it was normal,' he says.

Around 11 a.m. on his first day, Cummings walked into Gove's office to discuss some of the 'horrors' that had emerged that morning. While they talked, a controversial education announcement flashed up on a television screen in the room.

'Michael, we just agreed we weren't going to announce anything else. We're going dark until we get a grip of this madhouse. What the…?' Cummings spluttered.

Gove swivelled in his chair, eyeing the newsflash with bemusement.

'I haven't authorised any new announcement and certainly not that. I haven't a clue what they're on about,' he replied.

Cummings stood with his head in his hands. The organisation was in meltdown.[352]

---

352   Ibid.

If Cameron wanted to use his premiership to make radical reforms, this was what he was up against. He needed Whitehall to implement change, but it soon became apparent that the civil service was completely ill-suited to the task. To those around the Prime Minister, the intractability of the government machine came as a huge shock.

'The two feelings that overwhelmed me when I first arrived in Downing Street were a) it's impossible to get anything done, and b) it's impossible to stop anything from happening!' recalls Andrew Cooper.

> I'd always thought and assumed that if you had a strong team in No. 10 and clear priorities, your ministers and their advisers would want to tell you what was going on, and be helpful, but no! Government is so big and disconnected, and No. 10 is so small, that each department just remorselessly grinds on doing the things it does. It's got thousands of people who have been doing that for years. That's what they do, and you need an extremely good Secretary of State with a very good idea of what they're trying to achieve and a lot of confidence to mess with the system, and you need a strong team in No. 10, who are connecting it, to change anything.

In Gove and Duncan Smith, Cameron had strong Cabinet ministers willing to go to war with recalcitrant mandarins on the two areas of policy Cameron considered most important after the economy: education and welfare. Yet even they struggled to get beyond the daily firefight. To make matters worse, in what everybody around Cameron now acknowledges was a 'colossal mistake', the Prime Minister had axed the political unit in No. 10 responsible for 'getting things done'.

In the absence of anyone banging heads together, Oliver Letwin found himself picking up much of the slack. Soon Cameron's 'Stonewall Jackson' was working seventeen-hour days. By Christmas 2011, he had driven himself into the ground, and fell seriously ill. He protested that he didn't have time to be sick, but was eventually carted off to a doctor, who signed him off work for some time.

It seemed clear that root-and-branch reform of the civil service was required before big-picture priorities could be achieved, at least in departments without the benefit of ministers and senior mandarins with what

Cummings calls 'demented focus'. However, Cameron showed little interest in this challenge. A former No. 10 aide recalls trying to raise the subject and being rebuffed.

'He has no interest at all in the machinery of government. I once fleetingly tried to get him to have a conversation about it ... but I think he thought it was just a blind alley.'

In his entertaining blog, Cummings writes that the Prime Minister treated the endemic dysfunction in Whitehall 'like the weather'.

For example, when a minor and entirely resolvable problem arose in the Northern Ireland Office, he simply shrugged and let it go. He had appointed the backbencher Conor Burns as a parliamentary private secretary to Northern Ireland Minister Hugo Swire, instructing him to 'get out there; get on the ground' to ensure his old friend did a good job. Burns, who was keen to get stuck in, was dismayed to be told by mandarins that there was 'no budget' for him to travel there. Some weeks later, he bumped into Cameron in the Members' Lobby.

'How's it going in Northern Ireland?' Cameron asked.

'It's going fine, except the officials say there's no means of me going there,' Burns replied gloomily. He expected a robust reaction from Cameron: it was only a matter of the occasional cheap flight. (There seemed to be plenty of money for officials to travel to and from Stormont House and Thames House for Northern Ireland Questions, despite the fact that these sessions could easily be observed remotely.)

Instead, Cameron replied: 'Oh well, never mind. Do what you can from here.'

Cummings says scathingly:

> Everyone knows that Cameron hasn't the faintest interest in fighting over such issues, not least because he doesn't grasp the connection between such systems and why things he wants to happen don't happen, and without his support there are strict limits on what secretaries of state can do ... major changes are impossible when senior officials know that the Prime Minister's heart [is] with them.[353]

---

353   Ibid.

Despairingly, Gove's special adviser took to warning every new member of staff at the education department that with very few exceptions, it was 'safest to assume…every process will be mismanaged…every set of figures will be wrong. Every financial model will be wrong. Every bit of legal advice will be wrong. Every procurement will blow up. Every contract process will have been mismanaged.'

Cameron's approach was to do the best he could with the tools available. But not everyone in Downing Street was willing to accept the inadequacies of the system with a shrug. Hilton, who was by this time Downing Street's director of strategy, was stunned by the bureaucratic forces that militated against achieving significant policy change. It was not just the civil service, but also the overbearing weight of the EU and its endless rules and regulations.

'The bureaucracy masters the politicians…It's just a fact,' he would later remark wearily.[354]

He calculated that some 40 per cent of government business was about implementing EU regulations and a further 30 per cent was about 'random things…which were not anything to do with the coalition agreement'. The dawning realisation that just 30 per cent of time and energy could be devoted to what the coalition really wanted to do, was, he says, 'pretty horrific'.

His reaction was to push harder and louder, demanding civil servants deliver more, and faster. In meetings, he would exclaim that it *must* be possible to make things happen rapidly. When he clashed with mandarins, he would not mince his words. A Cabinet minister who witnessed one of his outbursts declared he'd 'never met anyone ruder in his life'.

'Some people did need a kick up the backside, but he did it in such an over-the-top form,' says another source.

Peter Riddell, director of the Institute for Government, says:

> In civil servants' eyes, Steve Hilton flouted the normal rules of Whitehall behaviour. It wasn't just what he said, which many regarded as wholly unrealistic, but how he said it. Officials would say, 'We don't do things like that,' and Steve would say, 'Well, why not?' – often very aggressively. Only a few, very senior, officials could handle him, so there was obvious relief when he departed for California.

---

354 *Sunday Times*, 13 January 2013.

In the early years of Cameron's leadership, Hilton had been the energy and originality in the top team, injecting a constant stream of fresh, zany ideas designed to wow voters.

James O'Shaughnessy says:

> He is a genuinely brilliant man. He would be the person who, when you thought you'd done something good, would come along, tell you it was shit, rip it up and make you do better. Then he'd sort of leave you alone for a bit because he'd go off and worry about something else. Working with him was endlessly frustrating in many ways, but he'd absolutely push you to do more and be better, which was terrific. He would do this across everything, whether it was campaigns, posters or the media.

In opposition, colleagues were prepared to overlook his foibles in deference to his creative genius. He was stimulating company, always full of surprises – right down to his shock wedding in 2008.

A friend recalls:

> Rachel and Steve organised to have their son Ben, who was about nine months old, christened down in Oxfordshire. They told their parents and [the] godparents, so they all turned up at this little church at 9.30 a.m. It didn't feel like anything unusual was about to happen...Then the vicar came in and said: 'This is a rather unusual day – we are going to marry the parents and then christen the child.' The family had no idea that this was going to happen, so then there was a wedding! Rachel turned round and asked her mother to hold Ben. Then they proceeded to get married! It was really good fun.

Later that day, Hilton was sitting upstairs in the Whetstones' home, feeding Ben with a bottle, when the phone rang. It was Cameron, calling to catch up.

'Did you see me on the Andrew Marr show this morning?' he asked.

'No, I didn't,' Hilton replied. 'I was getting married.'

Apparently Cameron had long been pressing the couple to tie the knot. As the Tory leader berated his old friend for not letting him in on the secret,

Hilton retorted, 'You shouted at us for years for not getting married – don't shout now I've got married!'

Until 2010, being around Hilton was an exhilarating ride for colleagues. During the election campaign and in government, it was different. His impatience, fiery temper and unconventional style upset old-school Tories, while his refusal to compromise or 'work within the system' alienated civil servants.

According to Bruce Anderson: 'He was impossible and couldn't adapt to government. He had ten brilliant ideas at breakfast and wanted them all implemented by lunchtime. He did some very bad things in No. 10.'

For Lib Dems, he was a particular source of bemusement.

Sean Kemp recalls:

> He was difficult: he could be really nice, funny and charming, or he would just completely lose his rag. He'd often come up with bizarre ideas, which we leaked. There was one about reducing the civil service to a size that could fit into Somerset House. We didn't leak that one because we thought it would be too popular.

Most colleagues accepted his casual sartorial style, which once prompted Obama to ask, 'Who's the beach bum?' But one Tory minister took exception to him 'lounging' in the Downing Street garden.

He recalls:

> I went over to No. 10 to talk about something…He was sitting in the garden with [his No. 10 colleague] Rohan Silva, with a beer and their feet up on the chairs. I'm not pompous, but I am a minister and this is Downing Street, and I just thought, you are being fucking rude. I found it so offensive – they were acting as if they owned the place.

There could be no doubting Hilton's determination to change Britain for the better; his readiness to confront those who cared less; and his willingness to stick his neck out for a cause. So passionate was he about his work that according to one source he was occasionally reduced to tears of frustration by the impossibility of bending the machine to his will.

His problem was that he struggled to work in such a constricted environment: his style was simply not suited to high office. Colleagues began to resent the way he used his closeness to Cameron to play by a different set of rules, failing to turn up to team meetings and appealing to the Prime Minister directly in an attempt to get his way.

'He drove other members of the team nuts,' says one No. 10 insider, who confides that Andrew Feldman once described Hilton as 'the person I hate most in the world'.

The source says:

> He always knew he could send David a text message, or have a drink with him at Chequers, and sort it all out. It frustrated people, because you'd go along in good faith, put a lot of work into planning something, and then Steve would just unplug it. All senior advisers were meant to go to the 8.30 a.m. and the 4 p.m. meetings, and he was never there. He very rarely engaged with any meetings at all. There was a constant process of trying to re-design Steve's role and job in a way that would make him happy, but it never worked. Because government is very frustrating, he basically tried to work around the system, and the system won't let you do that. So it made it even harder for him to get done the things he wanted to do, and he became more and more frustrated.

For Hilton, Ed Llewellyn was a particular source of angst. Cameron's quiet *consigliere* was his most trusted aide and was highly respected by most colleagues.

'Impossibly decent…very diligent… [with] extremely good political judgement' is how Chris Patten, with whom Llewellyn worked for half a decade, describes him. He was also multi-lingual, had dazzling diplomatic connections, and worked like a dog.

But Hilton felt Cameron's chief of staff pandered to the civil service, and should have been more robust and political. For his part, Cameron's chief of staff wryly observed that Hilton was behaving 'as if everybody else was gate-crashing his and Dave's party'.[355]

Hilton was also competing with Osborne for influence, leading to further tensions.

---

355 Private information.

One of Hilton's admirers, who worked with him in opposition and shared his impatience with the system, describes it as a 'war for the PM's ear'.

'I would get emails from Steve saying, "George is blocking everything we're doing,"' he says.

To some, he gave the impression he believed he was the only 'true moderniser', and that the others had sold out.

An insider says:

> He often behaved as if he and Dave had always had this shared agenda of radical change, and now Dave wasn't living up to it – in a sense, letting Steve down. I had a couple of conversations with George about Steve. He said: 'It's all flim-flam. Steve will go round, throwing his toys out of the pram, and asserting his obsession of the moment, but I don't care, because it's not in my way. As long as he doesn't try putting tanks on my lawn…' You sometimes got the sense that George didn't quite get why David felt he needed him. George didn't have any time for his point of view. With George it's all about realpolitik; with Steve, it's the opposite.

Hilton's refusal to work within the system left him increasingly isolated in No. 10.

'Basically, he was out on a limb,' says a former member of the inner circle. 'He was quite perceptive about realising after a while that his enormous power was all based on the fact that he spoke for Dave. The moment some of the top civil servants realised that Dave didn't necessarily agree with him, they just started ignoring him.'

By spring 2012, Cameron's old friend had had enough. For some in Downing Street, the feeling was mutual. His departure – ostensibly for a year-long 'sabbatical' in California, where his wife and sons were now based – was greeted with relief by mandarins. Others felt let down.

'He's supposed to be one of us, the last in the bunker, shooting the dogs and giving the children sleeping pills. Instead he's left us,' Feldman complained.[356]

He is rumoured to have left Downing Street prodding a senior civil servant in his ribs and accusing him of being a liar.

All that was forgotten when colleagues gathered for his big send-off, at a

---

356 Private information.

venue by the Royal Albert Hall in Kensington. The leaving do was a joyful affair, with dinner and dancing, and Gove gave a speech.

'Steve's been true to his Hungarian roots,' the Education Secretary quipped. 'Half Buddha, half pest.'

One third of the triumvirate that had taken over the party in December 2005 was now out of the game. Hilton's refusal to accept the limitations of 'the system' highlighted the contrast between him and the Prime Minister. His departure exposed Cameron's personal lack of reforming zeal and sucked the spirit out of his administration. But Hilton would return at the very end to deliver a devastating blow shortly before the EU referendum vote.

A restless revolutionary, Hilton was desperate to change the world. Cameron was content just to run Britain, improving the state of the nation in small steps. But he and Osborne were heading into choppy waters.

32

PASTIES

'Holidays are very important to me.'

– Cameron

For a close friend's 50th birthday, George Osborne offered an unusual gift: one of his Budgets. It was the original version, signed, of the third and most notorious he delivered: the so-called Omnishambles of 2012. Inside, the Chancellor had written: 'One or two brilliant phrases in this are yours. All the mistakes are mine.' The recipient was delighted.

'My wife thought it was the most idiotic present,' he says. 'She couldn't believe he'd given me it. But I was thrilled – I've almost forgotten what anyone else gave me.'

The 2012 Budget plunged the party into despair. Although some Tories now take a more generous view, at the time it was almost universally derided as a political disaster. It contained a catalogue of howlers, variously labelled the 'pasty tax', the 'granny tax', the 'charity tax', the 'caravan tax' and the 'church tax' – most of which were hastily reversed or diluted.

Both Chancellor and PM came under heavy fire. At the height of the outcry there were farcical scenes both inside and outside Downing Street, as protestors made their case, particularly over moves to raise the price of hot food from bakeries.

'I remember sitting in Downing Street and everywhere you looked there was some kind of warm, pastry-based snack. Greggs were literally delivering sausage rolls and pasties,' says Sean Kemp, a Lib Dem special adviser based in No. 10 at the time.

As a queue of supplicants lined up to lobby Osborne, a surprising aspect of the Chancellor's personality emerged: a reluctance to disappoint. According to a Treasury insider, he hated saying no to those who begged him to reverse measures.

'Intellectually, George knows and likes the case for austerity, but when it comes down to it, he's not that tough a man when he has to implement it,' said the former aide at the time.

> He absolutely tried to avoid seeing any of the aggrieved parties, some of whom were big Tory donors and philanthropists. There was complete outrage from people like John Sainsbury, and it was all done through intermediaries, because George couldn't quite face saying to them, 'Look, I had to do it for these reasons.' On the other hand, for some reason he felt he couldn't avoid seeing the Bishop of London, Richard Chartres, about the VAT on church repairs…He felt he couldn't get out of it…So Richard came in and George immediately gave him some fund to compensate for the church VAT.[357]

The fuss over most measures came and went, but a decision to slash the top rate of income tax from 50p to 45p caused long-term political grief. It was opposed by the Lib Dems (who leaked it, along with almost all the other key measures in the Budget) and was preceded by bitter coalition wrangling. Though the Chancellor argued strongly that the 50p band was harming the economy and raising 'next to nothing' in revenue – and that other Budget measures would in fact dramatically increase the contribution made by the wealthiest in society – the decision seemed to many to confirm the longstanding belief that the Tories were less interested in helping those who were striving and struggling than in rewarding the already rich. Against a backdrop of austerity and the Tory mantra about everyone being 'in it together', it triggered a furore. Miliband immediately labelled it a 'tax cut for millionaires'. 'Omnishambles' became the *Oxford English Dictionary*'s 'word of the year' for 2012.

Since taking office, the Conservatives had steadily built a reputation for prudence and sensible economic management. If they seemed too narrowly focused on the deficit, they did at least appear willing to take tough decisions for the long term. But coming as it did after a series of policy U-turns, each relatively minor in itself, the 'Omnishambles Budget' was a serious blow to the

357   Private information.

government's claim to competence. Having shown the parties neck-and-neck at the turn of the year, by April the polls gave Labour a double-digit lead, which they sustained for twelve months. By summer, Osborne had become such a pantomime villain that he was booed during a medal ceremony at the Paralympic Games.

How had it happened, and who was to blame? Osborne had certainly taken his eye off the ball. Ever the networker, in the run-up to Budget Day he had been reluctant to forgo an opportunity to hang out with the leader of the free world and had disappeared to America when he should have been fine-tuning his proposals. He and Cameron attended a glitzy dinner at the White House, the Chancellor returning excitably with a framed photograph.[358]

His biographer Janan Ganesh concludes he'd become complacent:

> He is usually meticulous in preparing the political ground for any controversial policy by commissioning third-party research, making the case via newspaper columns and organising supportive letters from business figures. He neglected to do the work on this occasion because he assumed that such footling tax changes would be ignored in favour of the Budget's bigger announcements. The leaks did for that assumption, but the Osborne of 2010 would have left nothing to chance.[359]

Finkelstein is more forgiving, arguing that Osborne's decision to cut the top rate was bold and politically far-sighted:

> I remember phoning him and saying to him, 'If you take it down to 45p it will be a disaster with polls, you won't be able to say "We are all in it together", it will be awful politically. I think it has a symbolic effect that's far in excess of its economic impact.' George's view was that it was the right thing to do, it doesn't raise any money, what's the point of being the Chancellor of the Exchequer if you don't do the things that you think are right? I remember pacing

358 Matthew d'Ancona, p. 232.
359 Janan Ganesh, p. 288.

around in a circle, saying, 'I really don't think you should do this,' and him saying, 'I'm going to do it anyway, you've got to do these things and you've got to hold your nerve on these occasions.' His view now is, 'Imagine if I hadn't done it? I'd be running the whole election on what I'm going to do with the top rate of tax.'

What about Cameron?

In 2011, he had intervened to stop Osborne going further on the 50p, when the Chancellor had wanted to cut it to 40p. This time, despite misgivings, he agreed. He seems to have paid little if any attention to the rest of the Budget. This lack of scrutiny illustrates the degree of trust between Nos 10 and 11 – the PM saw no need to check the Chancellor's homework. As we have seen, the party leadership was effectively a dual operation. From the start, Cameron and Osborne treated each other as equals. There were no boundaries. In opposition, their offices in Norman Shaw had been set up to reflect the parity of status.

'They compare notes continuously,' says a Tory peer who has worked closely with both men.

> They share everything with each other. That open-plan office in Norman Shaw was very cleverly constructed. Cameron's nice big room was at one end and George's was at the other, but between them was a big open-plan office for their staff, so the staff intermixed. So when something went wrong or there was a crisis, the first thing Cameron would do is say, 'Where's George?' and shout across at George's people, 'Where is George?' The moment there was a problem, he wanted George with him, helping him resolve it. George wasn't just the most important ally, aide, adviser: he was effectively the Deputy Prime Minister.

The result was amicable government, a far cry from the trench warfare of the Blair/Brown years. But Omnishambles revealed the flipside: Cameron's failure to act as a critical friend to No. 11.

'At the very least, David should have said to George, "Don't come to the US with me, stay and work your Budget out,"' a Treasury insider admits.[360]

360 Private information.

As early as October 2010, critics had begun depicting Cameron as 'the essay-crisis Prime Minister'.[361] These attacks escalated in the wake of the Omnishambles Budget. By the middle of 2012, the phrase had acquired real traction.

As his old friend James Delingpole put it at the time:

> Every time you think it's all going to come crashing on top of him, he stays up all night on his Red Bull and Pro Plus, and dashes off something just good enough to persuade the world that the moment to send him down has not arrived quite just yet.[362]

At Westminster, a damning new phrase to describe his propensity to put his feet up began circulating: 'chillaxing'.

'If there was an Olympic gold medal for "chillaxing" [Cameron] would win it,' someone told Elliott and Hanning. Friends weighed in with supporting evidence, testifying to the PM's fondness for country weekends, long games of tennis and snooker, and his taste for cooking, gardening and watching TV. He was even reported to have hosted karaoke nights at Chequers.[363]

No. 10 was furious with the allegation: it struck a nerve. Cameron is indeed fond of kicking back and watching a DVD box set with a large glass of wine. His cultural tastes are mainstream and low brow: TV shows with 'murder, mystery and suspense' (he named *Trial and Retribution*; *Midsomer Murders*; *He Kills Coppers*); American series like *The West Wing*, *Game of Thrones* and *Desperate Housewives* (which he has said he 'loved'); and, in the car, Virgin (now Absolute) Radio. According to Samantha, he likes to watch 'all three *Godfather* movies again and again and again'. He uses Sky+ so he can watch repeats on television and annoys Samantha with his endless channel flicking.[364] He went to see the crude Sacha Baron Cohen movie *Borat* and laughed throughout, and once admitted he liked playing Fruit Ninja on his iPad. He has made much of going on midweek 'date

---

361 The term was first used by Charles Moore, who is generally friendly towards Cameron, in an article in *The Spectator*.

362 *Daily Telegraph*, 11 September 2012.

363 Francis Elliott and James Hanning, pp. 436–7.

364 Michael Crick interview, *Newsnight*, BBC 2, 17 November 2005; *Trevor McDonald Meets David Cameron*.

nights' with Samantha. A friend says he takes his music 'very seriously' and has more than 27,000 tracks on his computer. He is also an enthusiastic, although not obsessive, sports fan.

'I like big sporting events. I love the rugby world cup. I find that fantastically exciting. I watch a lot of cricket…although I'm a terrible pessimist about British cricket. I always think we're about to collapse,' he has said.[365]

Yet he was insulted by the suggestion that any of this made him a slacker. Such was the concern in No. 10 that Andrew Cooper carried out private polling to see whether the 'chillax' label was sticking. The results were encouraging – most voters believed he worked hard enough – yet the term stubbornly refused to go away.

Part of the problem was his conspicuous number of holidays, a feature of his leadership. In summer 2007, he had become exasperated when his holiday plans were interrupted by an outbreak of foot-and-mouth disease, asking Gordon Brown 'almost pleadingly' when he thought things would calm down so that he could return to Brittany.

'His exact words were: "I can't go away until you do, and we won't get a holiday at this rate. But you really have to go away first,"' according to a damning account of their private conversation.[366]

Again and again, he would be holidaying when some crisis or other struck. By August 2014, when ISIS was rampaging across Iraq and a British terror suspect beheaded a US journalist, Cameron had clocked up fourteen breaks in just over three years, vacationing in Granada, Ibiza, Tuscany, Mallorca, Ibiza, Algarve, Jura, Lanzarote and Cascais and taking no fewer than five trips to Cornwall.

'At the moment it seems like the only way to ask him a question is to hire a Cornish ice-cream van and set up on the beach,' one MP lamented.[367]

Yet he was always honest about his taste for downtime. He told Dylan Jones in 2007 that it was one of 'Sam's rules' that 'we have plenty of time together, plenty of time with the children'. He believed that switching off and having 'a lovely family holiday' helped him do a better job.

'I think you need to do that in a high-pressure job…If you work so hard that you get completely fried in the head, and totally ragged, you start

---

365 Michael Crick interview, op. cit.

366 Damian McBride, pp. 292–3.

367 *The Guardian*, 22 August 2014.

making bad decisions and bad judgements,' he has said. 'So holidays are very important to me, to relax a bit, and then get the batteries charged up for what lies ahead.'[368]

He had no record of being poorly prepared or inadequately briefed. Indeed, among civil servants in Downing Street he acquired a reputation for efficiency. 'His first meeting in the morning is at 8.30 a.m., and all his [red] boxes are done by then,' according to a very senior No. 10 aide at the time. 'Those boxes must be two hours' work. He gets up at the crack of dawn and does them very early in the morning. He has his boxes done by the deadline and that means he spends time with his family.'

When he applied himself, he appeared to be so quick and able that he could get away with 'ring-fencing' significant amounts of leisure time. He was an exceptional multi-tasker and had a rare ability to compartmentalise, allowing him to move seamlessly from one subject or task to another, and switch on and off with ease. Numerous colleagues watched him flipping between red boxes and small children; making important phone calls one second, sandwiches the next.

Bruce Anderson said: 'He was quite capable of reading his papers and saying, "Nancy, leave your brother alone."'

Norman Lamont agreed. 'I have stayed in his house and he would play with a child, open a red box, do a bit of work, make a few phone calls, and then come back and watch James Bond. He seems very able at alternating between work and family duties.'

Another friend says his mind is 'like a mountain goat' – it can 'leap from intellectual crag to intellectual crag – and master it all'.

> That ability to take a call from President Obama one moment, meet the King of Jordan the next, then chair a Cabinet meeting, prepare for Prime Minister's Questions, and then talk about a speech you aren't going to make for four weeks – then be briefed on the Ebola virus and chair Cobra – he loves it. You can see it.

Many colleagues reject out of hand the notion that he was a loafer.

'Former prime ministers used to go away and spend the whole summer at Aix-les-Bains and nobody would notice,' says his former PPS Desmond Swayne.

---

368   David Cameron and Dylan Jones, p. 350.

I think he's as hard working, or more so, than any other. I certainly never came across any chillaxing. There was never a time when something he was responsible for, or something that depended on input from him, had not been delivered. He's very good at managing his diary and managing his time.

Yet his attitude frustrated some former colleagues. One who accompanied him on many public engagements remembers being struck by his reluctance to let his workload get in the way of a good time.

We were staying in the middle of nowhere in a crappy B&B, with a help-yourself booze cupboard, and he said: 'I've got lots of papers to do. Let's have a chill.' ...It was interesting to go on those trips; he'd have all these papers and yet he'd say: 'Let's have another one.'

He always used to talk about nights off and I just thought he was a bit lazy. I felt bad for the women in the office. There was all this talk about family time and how he had to get home for family time, but the women in the office weren't going home for family time. I thought that was really naughty. It was just a disingenuous way of saying, 'I'm actually bunking off home.'

The same aide was surprised and irritated when Cameron 'whipped out a novel' en route to a public engagement.

'We'd gone off to Gloucester with quite a large posse – there were about six or seven of us – and he sat among everyone reading it,' he recalls. 'Of course, everyone sat there in deferential silence but I remember thinking, "I'm really sorry, but the spin doctor in me thinks you should be reading some papers and looking like you've got work to do." Sitting with seven staff and reading a novel? I found that quite irritating.'

Another former aide has never forgotten his willingness to deliver a keynote speech he knew was not up to scratch.

'His fingernails are not bitten down,' he sighs. 'I remember him going to bed the night before one party conference speech and saying: "It's not that good, but it will do."'

There was something disquieting about Cameron's willingness to settle for second best. Literally and figuratively, he slept easily, whatever was going on in the world. ('Pillow, head, bang,' is how Bruce Anderson describes his ability to drop off.) Yet he was supremely capable in carrying out the job of Prime Minister as he understood it. Unlike Gordon Brown (once described as an 'insomniac obsessive'),[369] he saw no reason to kill himself in the process. Being Prime Minister was only one part of his life. In this respect, he resembled the former Tory PM Harold Macmillan. The languid Old Etonian was also famed for an ability to switch off: he had a habit of reading Victorian novels during periods of high political drama, and would spend the entire summer recess on the Scottish grouse moors. His successor-but-four was made of similar stuff.

---

369   Fraser Nelson, *Spectator* blog.

33
RIDING ROUGHSHOD

'There's only one thing worse than making a mistake, and that's not putting your hands up and admitting it.'

– Cameron

The graveyard by the church of St Mary Abbots is a surprisingly neglected place. Tucked away at the bottom of Kensington Church Street, an elegant strip of antique shops, patisseries and fashion boutiques, it is a piece of super-prime London real estate that appears to have been abandoned to the skeletons and weeds. The path through the tombs is spotted with moss, and dock leaves sprawl through the grubby grass. Tall plane trees cast a soft, dappled light over the garden, but the inscriptions on the headstones are thick with lichen. Scrawny pigeons peck on a patch of mud as cars and buses grind their way through the gridlocked intersection with Kensington High Street. In the cloisters, a notice pinned to the wall appeals for donations to the local food bank. In a clue as to the kind of people who worship here, the charity feel the need to point out that contributions should be simple: 'Foie gras and caviar just cause problems.'

Donations to the food bank are collected early on Thursday mornings, exactly the time Cameron sometimes visits. After dropping his daughter Nancy off at the Church of England primary school next door, he occasionally takes a pew for some quiet reflection.

Just how 'religious' a Prime Minister he was has been the subject of considerable debate. Unlike Blair, whose administration famously didn't 'do God' despite his strong personal faith, Cameron talked openly about his Christianity, with some honesty about the extent to which it expressed itself in regular church attendance. In his early days as leader, he answered questions about his faith in a circumspect, almost self-deprecatory way. In 2008, he borrowed Boris Johnson's line that his faith is 'like reception for Magic FM in the Chilterns: it sort of comes and goes'.[370] A few years later he described himself as 'a wishy-washy sort of Christian'.[371] To Dylan Jones, he said hesitantly: 'I always find this difficult. I'm a typical "Church of Englander" and I believe that there is a power greater than us and the life and work of Jesus Christ is an important guide to morality and action.' He went on to describe himself as a '"racked-with-doubt-and-scepticism" believer'.[372] So he is religious, but no 'born again'.

After becoming Prime Minister, Cameron seemed to become more relaxed about discussing his faith. He began making more frequent references to the Bible in speeches, and to the Gospels of Mark and Luke.

'The idea of a resurrection, a living God, of someone who's still with us, is fantastically important – even if you, as I do, struggle over some of the details,' he told Church leaders at an Easter reception in Downing Street in 2011. At a similar event in 2014, he went further in explaining his faith. He revealed that his 'moments of greatest peace' come 'perhaps every other Thursday morning' when he slips into the sung Eucharist at St Mary Abbots. 'I find a little bit of peace and hopefully a bit of guidance,' he said. He cited the vicar of his local church in Chadlington, Mark Abrey, as 'the person who looked after me' after Ivan's death. 'I can't think of anyone who was more loving or thoughtful or kind,' he said. Then, in an article in the *Church Times*, he called upon fellow Christians to be 'more evangelical' in their faith.[373]

To some observers, his faith is primarily cultural.

Chris Patten, himself a prominent Roman Catholic, says:

> I think he's like a lot of members of the Church of England. He likes medieval churches, singing hymns, the Church of England ritual…I wouldn't have thought God was a frequent household conversation, but I don't say that critically. I think he regards all that [Anglican ceremonial and ritual] as a great part of national life.

370   *The Guardian*, 16 July 2008.
371   *Church Times*, 6 May 2011.
372   David Cameron and Dylan Jones, p. 180.
373   *Church Times*, 16 April 2014.

Certainly, Cameron had a firmly religious upbringing. As he explained in his piece for the *Church Times*, 'My parents spent countless hours helping to support and maintain the village church that I grew up next to.'[374] Today, his mother is still on the flower-arranging rota at that church, while his brother Alex is chairman of the parish council. Speaking about his constituency, he has described churches that 'take your breath away with their beauty, simplicity and serenity. They are a vital part of Britain's living history.'

Yet despite his personal faith, Cameron's relationship with both the Church of England and the Vatican was strained as a result of his social liberalism. It left some with the impression that he was ignorant and insensitive in relation to the Church.

Adrian Hilton, an Anglican theologian controversially deselected as a Tory candidate by Michael Howard in 2005 because of 'anti-Catholic' articles he wrote in *The Spectator*,[375] remains disappointed that Cameron never apologised for his dismissal. Hilton accuses Cameron of 'complete ignorance of Church–state constitutional matters' and says his attitude towards religious leaders has been haughty and disdainful. He argues that Cameron has 'lectured' the Archbishop of Canterbury to be liberal on homosexuality[376] and told the Pope to alter Roman Catholic moral teaching to permit contraception and abortion. 'Of course these things are done for electoral expedience, but time and again he shows himself to be ignorant of Christian theology, history and tradition,' Hilton says.

Ann Widdecombe, a stalwart of the party's socially conservative flank, agrees.

> On just about every vote that there has been, on freedom of conscience for the Church, or for individuals, he has voted, from my point of view, the wrong way. My first real disagreement with him was whether to exempt Roman Catholic adoption agencies from homosexual equality legislation. Cameron voted not to exempt them. That was the first real bust-up I had, though it was with the Chief Whip at the time, not him personally. I wanted an exemption for

---

374 Ibid.
375 These were commissioned by Boris Johnson when he was vice-chairman of the party, and approved by the then opposition Chief Whip David Maclean.
376 Johann Hari, *Attitude*, February 2010.

Roman Catholic adoption agencies. If there were a Muslim adoption agency, I would have wanted a similar exemption. I remember bumping into Ken Clarke in the Commons at the time of this debate. He said to me, 'Do you imagine that if two gays want to adopt, they go to see Father O'Flaherty? It's a nonsense.' Now, that's Ken, and Ken normally takes the liberal line. He just thought it was complete nonsense. Gays could go elsewhere – they didn't have to use a Roman Catholic adoption agency. But Cameron insisted.

Nothing did more damage to Cameron's relations with elements of the Church – once known as the 'Tory Party at prayer' – than his support for gay marriage. His dogged insistence on pushing through the legislation exasperated MPs and alienated activists. By getting it over with mid-term, he hoped that it would all be forgotten come 2015, but for many in the party, the wounds never healed. His determination to implement such a radically progressive piece of legislation was curious given his general reluctance to be the figurehead for other radical change. He had, for example, let his Welfare Secretary Iain Duncan Smith do the talking on hugely controversial changes to the benefits system, and allowed his former Education Secretary Michael Gove to take the flak for schools reform. Yet he made himself the standard bearer for gay marriage, turning it into a rare personal mission.

This is all the more surprising given that his views on homosexuality as a young man and as a young MP were not especially liberal. An acquaintance from his stint as a special adviser at the Home Office remembers him being 'surprisingly squeamish about homosexuality for someone of his age',[377] and he himself has admitted that he didn't know any openly gay people as a child or at university.[378] Meanwhile his parliamentary record is confusing. His selection as parliamentary candidate for Witney in 2000 followed Shaun Woodward's dramatic defection to Labour over William Hague's refusal to ditch Section 28 (which banned the 'promotion' of homosexuality in schools). He will have made all the right noises to the local party association about his personal views on the matter. He is even on record attacking Blair for 'moving heaven and earth to allow the promotion of homosexuality in our schools', and mocking Labour for supporting the 'fringe agenda' of equality

---

377   Francis Elliott and James Hanning, p. 152.
378   Johann Hari, op. cit.

404

for gay people.[379] As an MP, he twice voted for amendments that would have excluded adoption by gay couples – and in 2002 simply abstained from, rather than actively rebelled against, Duncan Smith's notorious three-line whipped vote opposing Blair's gay adoption Bill. (In interviews he has attempted to gloss over this record, on more than one occasion denying that he ever voted against gay adoption.)[380] In 2003, he voted in favour of a Conservative motion to retain a version of Section 28.

On the flip side, he was exposed to the homosexual culture at the Conservative Research Department in his early twenties and was relaxed about the environment. One of his close political friends at the time was Derek Laud, who was openly gay. Ever since, he has been surrounded by various gay colleagues, including Nick Boles and Alan Duncan, both of whom he appointed ministers. One of his closest allies, Greg Barker, left his wife following a gay affair in 2006. Cameron was not judgemental and stood by Barker when the relationship was exposed. He made him a minister of state in his first government line-up and still regards him as a close personal friend.

His view on Section 28 specifically, and the status of homosexual relationships more generally, appears to have shifted a year or so before he became party leader. In 2004, he voted in favour of civil partnerships. In 2009, he took the bold step of apologising for Section 28, telling a Gay Pride event that his party 'got it wrong' when it introduced the measure in the late 1980s. The following year, he told a journalist: 'I think now looking back you can see the mistake of Section 28. There's only one thing worse than making a mistake, and that's not putting your hands up and admitting it.'[381]

Yet there remained signs of uncertainty. In a car-crash interview with Martin Popplewell of *Gay Times* in March 2010, he was grilled on the voting behaviour of Tory MEPs and was left floundering. It came after he gave MEPs a free vote on a motion to condemn the Lithuanian equivalent of Section 28. None of his party backed the motion, allowing the impression that the Brussels wing of the Tory Party remained homophobic. Under pressure from Popplewell, Cameron became visibly flustered and dodged

---

379   Ibid.
380   In an interview with Adam Boulton for Sky News in 2005 and again in an interview with Johann Hari for *Attitude* magazine in 2010: http://www.pinknews.co.uk/2010/02/11/david-cameron-criticised-for-airbrushing-his-memory-over-gay-adoption.
381   Johann Hari, op. cit.

questions. So desperate did the exchange become that, at one point, his press secretary stepped in to try to stop the interview, as Cameron himself appealed for time out.

'I have to say, I came out less than impressed by him,' Popplewell reflects now.

> I voted Tory historically, so I'm no lefty. But I came out of the interview less than convinced by the position we were being sold, which was that the Tories had thought this all through and had completely changed. When he asked me to switch the cameras off, I was like: 'Christ – you're supposed to be a PR man! You *never* do what you've just done in an interview.' He'd just given me a humdinger of a headline. It was a big clanger.

Cameron knew he'd screwed up. Popplewell remembers him disappearing to the loo, emerging a few minutes later looking 'very hot and flushed'.

'There was this rather awkward moment,' he recalls.

> We'd just sat down and had that rather strange intimate thing you have as a journalist when you're interviewing someone and it's just the two of you. You have this quite intimate engagement. Yet he didn't say anything to me. He didn't acknowledge me; he didn't smile and say, 'Fucking hell, that was terrible, wasn't it? I hope you're going to be kind to me.' He didn't say anything like that, which would perhaps have made it a bit more difficult for me to be frank and honest about the interview. He simply wasn't hanging around to spin it.

The blunder mattered because Cameron had made such a big thing of reaching out to the 'gay vote'. He made active attempts to recruit gay parliamentary candidates, and promised to make sure any tax cuts for married couples would apply equally to people in civil partnerships. His squirming response to Popplewell's questioning made him look equivocal at best. Against this backdrop, his campaign to introduce gay marriage is all the more interesting.

Allies insist he has been entirely consistent and are prone to claim that he flagged up his plan for gay marriage in the early days of his leadership.

'We actually announced it in our first conference speech,' says one senior aide. 'We said "gay marriage". We used the word "marriage".'

It is true that newspapers at the time did report the 2006 party conference speech as including a bold statement in support of gay marriage. However, Cameron's actual words are more ambiguous.

'Marriage really matters,' Cameron declared. 'And by the way, it means something whether you're a man and a woman, a woman and a woman, or a man and another man. That's why we were right to support civil partnerships, and I'm proud of that.'

He did not use the phrase 'gay marriage'. To some, it sounded as if it were simply a statement of support for civil partnerships, which already existed. It was not a clear call to go the extra step. As a result, Cameron's announcement in October 2011 that he was consulting on legalising gay marriage was a surprise. As Popplewell points out, 'Nowhere, not anywhere, not in my notes or in the interview that I did with him in 2010, did the issue of gay marriage come up. And the reason for that is simple: gay marriage was not on the agenda, for anybody, really.'

So where did it come from? Tory Party strategists were certainly struck by the debate over gay marriage in the campaign for the 2012 US presidential election. Obama's high-profile endorsement of equal marriage was a clear dividing line with the Republicans and was spurred on by polls showing, for the first time, a majority of US voters in favour of the policy, with significant majorities among younger people and women. Cameron and his aides believed the move would appeal to younger voters and reinforce the party leader's credentials as a 'modern, compassionate Conservative'. At the 2011 party conference, he delivered his infamous line about not supporting gay marriage 'despite' being a Conservative, but '*because* I'm a Conservative'.

Andrew Cooper was a key influence on the debate inside No. 10.

'You should own it,' the pollster told the Prime Minister.

Cooper believed it was vital that Cameron did not let his own party kill the proposal once the wheels had been set in motion.

'My view was, it's something you believe in, you've said it to your party, you think it's the right thing to do. If people alight on the fact that you've dropped it, it looks like a very weaselly, unprincipled thing to do.' This was a particularly acute concern in 2012, following a series of reversals, including over the proposed sell-off of national forests in February 2011, and a multitude of measures in the so-called Omnishambles Budget.

'By then, there was a real nervousness about anything that could be characterised as a U-turn,' Cooper admits.

Having declared his support for the principle in 2011, and personally intervened to get the consultation process off the ground in 2012, Cameron proceeded to drive gay marriage through Parliament so forcefully that it was already on the statute books by July 2013. He had made his decision and, in a rare display of unyielding conviction, he refused to back down. The Cabinet had no say, except over the mechanics.

The decision triggered an outcry in the parliamentary party. Many Tory MPs who did not feel strongly about the issue personally faced a furious backlash in their constituencies and were inundated with hostile letters and emails. They deeply resented having to go into battle over a policy that was in neither their manifesto nor the coalition agreement. Few believe there were any positive votes in it, whereas threats to resign from the party were commonplace.

'Pretty much the universal advice of any colleague who spoke to him on the subject was to drop it, whatever their personal view on the issue,' says Graham Brady. As chairman of the 1922 Committee, he came under intense pressure over a long period to warn Cameron off. Yet the leader ploughed on regardless.

Brady says now that the issue could have toppled the Prime Minister. Though the media did not detect this at the time, he believes there was a 'real danger point' for Cameron ahead of the crunch vote, when many MPs, including those on the government payroll, were coming under unbearable pressure from their local associations to take a stand.

Indeed, it came on the back of a bad stretch for Cameron and his relationship with the parliamentary party. In January 2013, he faced what is so far the only 'coup' attempt of his leadership, as the obscure Tory backbencher Adam Afriyie started sending letters to colleagues asking them to endorse him as Cameron's successor if a large-scale Commons revolt forced him to resign. Afriyie secretly dubbed his plan 'Project Submarine' and paid a top PR man £12,500 a month, for eighteen months, to further his quest. Unfortunately for Afriyie, who would later vote against the same-sex marriage Bill, changes to the Tory Party rules meant rebels can no longer employ the 'stalking horse' tactics used to topple Thatcher by getting a backbencher to strike the first blow and trigger a full contest. Today, 15 per cent of the parliamentary party must demand a vote of no confidence in the leader. Luckily for Cameron, there were few MPs willing to do something so drastic with little more than two years to go before the election, however disgruntled many of them were by this point. In any case, the PM never took the plot seriously. He and the whips simply chose not respond, ploughing on with the gay marriage plans unperturbed.[382]

Cameron's resolve was strengthened by polling, which suggested that despite the clamour of opposition from elements of the Tory Party faithful and the Church, most voters were broadly in favour of the measure. Yet there was more to it than that. He was genuinely committed to the idea. He may not have been an early flag-waver for gay rights, but once he came round, he did so wholeheartedly.

The best explanation for his latter-day conviction is his attitude to marriage more generally. He is unequivocally and unapologetically pro-marriage and pro-family. He has said on numerous occasions that for him, 'it comes absolutely first'. Before colleagues' weddings, he has penned long, handwritten letters extolling the institution.[383]

This, combined with his religious faith, puts him on the traditionalist side of the Tory Party. He is also a social liberal. In gay marriage, these apparently conflicting instincts come together: shoring up marriage as an institution by extending it to those who had previously been excluded, while simultaneously offering a liberating hand to a disenfranchised minority. It was conservative and liberal at the same time.

Ivan Massow, a Tory entrepreneur and gay activist who once shared a flat with Michael Gove and Nick Boles, has argued that for Cameron and his allies, gay marriage was 'the granddaughter of Thatcherism'.

> I genuinely get the impression that he really thought it was the right thing to do, and also that it would have been much more damaging if he'd gone back on it. Can you imagine doing a U-turn and what his Liberal partners would have made of that? The outcry; the return to the 'nasty party' – I don't think it was possible.

382 Isabel Oakeshott and Jack Grimston, *Sunday Times*, 3 February 2013.
383 James Forsyth, *The Spectator*, 19 April 2014.

> Unfortunately, [the storm] is the sort of thing you have to weather sometimes. You have to deadhead occasionally to bring your party forward. We needed to move this agenda on.

However, many took issue with the logic of Cameron's claim that he supported gay marriage 'because' he was a Conservative. It triggered a fierce intellectual debate within the party, pitting religious social conservatives against secular market liberals, and younger members against old.

'I wasn't quite sure I could understand the logic of it,' says one party grandee, now in the Lords.

> Fair enough, he wanted to back gay marriage – that's fine – but to say it's because he's a Conservative? That's actually pushing quite hard at the definition of what a Conservative is, and it did cause a lot of damage. A lot of Conservatives said, 'We've been Conservatives all our lives, and we haven't backed gay marriage – where does that leave us?'

The journalist and broadcaster Iain Dale recalls speaking to the PM after giving a talk to Cameron's local Conservative association at a patrons' club dinner chaired by Lord Chadlington. Dale had received considerable flak from members of the audience for his support for gay marriage.

'I hear there were one or two people who were a bit resistant,' Cameron said to Dale the following morning as they discussed the event.

'I would have thought you would have got these people round to your way of thinking by now, David,' Dale replied wearily.

Cameron laughed, reflecting that the audience were a 'lovely bunch', but some with views that were 'a bit nineteenth century'.

Brady believes Cameron did not grasp how serious an issue it was for many in the party until it was too late.

He says:

> An awful lot of colleagues were being driven to despair by the loss of support in their areas. A lot of colleagues are in very marginal seats, and in modern politics in any of the parties, even quite healthy constituencies with reasonable majorities, often you're dependent on

quite a small number of activists. And there were people with not very healthy associations, with small majorities, who were losing all of their activists, and there could have been funding implications as well. I think he did eventually get it, but he was too locked in at that point.

Even Cameron's own mother, Mary, is said to have counselled caution.

'I know, but David just won't be told,' she reportedly said at a lunch when asked about the upset felt among the party's natural supporters.[384]

To placate those who were worried about religious freedom, Cameron made sure the proposals were designed in such a way that there was a '100 per cent guarantee' that no church, synagogue or mosque could be forced to hold a same-sex marriage. The traditional Church definition of marriage, as a partnership between a man and a woman, remained untouched.

It was not enough to appease the party. In the end, more than half of his MPs voted against the Bill.

Despite the passage of time, the issue remains deeply painful for some Conservatives.

'No manifesto indication, no soundings in the party – he just decided he was going to introduce it,' says Ann Widdecombe.

When MPs who were getting grief in their constituencies tried to talk to him, he just brushed them aside. Didn't listen. Just said, 'Thank you very much, but I'm still going ahead. It's a free vote.' Then he'd walk off. It's this not-listening which is the problem, because of course it caused huge grief in the party; mass defection to UKIP, and the collapse of branches. But he just wouldn't listen.

Quite how many defections there were to UKIP is unclear. After the furore, Andrew Feldman told Cameron that the party had lost more members to death than over gay marriage. Yet the issue left a number of socially conservative right-wing voters looking for a new home. Even so, the election result in 2015 speaks for itself: the long-term damage was not that profound.

Whatever the facts and figures, the issue drove a wedge between Cameron and his party, prising open the cracks that had first appeared as a result of

---

384 *Daily Telegraph*, 25 January 2013.

the modernisation agenda. Some believe that if he had realised the full extent of the misery it would cause, he would never have picked the fight.

'I really believe that had he known the scale of the aggro, he wouldn't have done it,' says Nicholas Soames, who is nonetheless 'utterly convinced' it was the right thing to do.

> But it did cause absolute chaos. My constituency is thirty-five miles south of London: prosperous, good-hearted people, but I've never had a bigger constituency correspondence about anything. I'm talking about genuine, from the heart, people offended by it. It left a terrible mark, and it made life very difficult for him. I've got one man who continues to write to me. The Tory Party in the country bears the scars.

Cameron's conspicuous displays of religious conviction in 2014 may well have been partially an attempt to reassure traditionalists that he remained well and truly part of the flock and had no intention of eroding the authority and status of the Church in Britain. He wanted to make it clear that it remained safe in his hands.

Given his triumph in 2015, he can look back on this bitter battle without heavy regret.

'There is a great defence to it,' says Jacob Rees-Mogg, a staunch Catholic who voted against the Bill. 'Which is that it was actually something he believed in. And I do believe in politicians who stand up for things they believe in, even if I don't agree with the outcome. If that's what he really believes in, then I think it's admirable.'

Curiously, despite all he put himself through, Cameron has never accepted an invitation to a gay wedding. Given how desperate he was to implement the legislation, one would imagine he would be keen to witness first-hand the fruits of his labour. Having ridden roughshod over the party, perhaps he realised he should rein in.

34

REMOTE CONTROL

'The sad fact is I think he was comfortable with me because I am from the same background.'

– A former adviser

Cameron's stance on gay marriage had alienated a number of rich donors, who made their displeasure known by stopping writing cheques. One philanthropist who continued to give generously, however, was Peter Cruddas. Whether it was fancy dinners for Cabinet ministers, Big Society initiatives, or serious political campaigns, the Hackney-born businessman was always ready to dig deep to support the party, especially when it involved helping disadvantaged young people. In the early years of Cameron's leadership, he quietly propped up a string of the leader's pet projects, including his flagship National Citizenship Service and the party's favourite think tank, Policy Exchange. After a while, Andrew Feldman added Cruddas's name to a list of three or four trusted figures who could be relied upon to help if the party suddenly needed cash.

The entrepreneur's humble background and rags-to-riches tale made him an ideal ambassador for a party too often associated with privilege by birth. Having grown up on a council estate and left school at fifteen, he had started a business with £10,000 and turned it into a global enterprise worth more than £1 billion. Recognising his deep pockets and value as a poster boy, in 2011, Cameron brought him into the heart of the party machine as co-treasurer.

Yet the philanthropist was never welcomed into the leader's coterie, and the minute he attracted controversy they publicly washed their hands of him. His unhappy experience illustrates a recurring criticism of Cameron: his apparent reluctance to embrace those outside his tight inner circle.

Cruddas had bankrolled the No to AV campaign in May 2011 on a clear understanding that if it went well, he would be appointed party treasurer. Shortly after the referendum, the Prime Minister rang to thank him for his efforts, adding that he understood Cruddas would soon be 'coming on board'. When the businessman was invited to CCHQ two weeks later, he expected the appointment to be confirmed. Instead, in the first of a series of moves that suggest he was seen as little more than a useful source of funds, he was asked for another substantial donation, this time to pay for the Tories' summer party. There was no mention of making him treasurer. When Cruddas replied that he would only be happy to pay for the party once he was in the new role, the appointment was announced, in June 2011.

Being co-treasurer meant that he was now responsible for the party's finances and would personally have to make up any shortfall. At first, he enjoyed attending fundraising events and helping to persuade other rich party supporters to contribute. However, he was surprised not to be included in any discussions about how funds should be allocated.

He recalls:

> On one occasion I got an email asking me to attend a presentation by Stephen Gilbert and Andrew Feldman. All the troops from the treasurer's department were there, even the receptionist. Gilbert presented a fantastic new strategy to employ eighty constituency agents in the run-up to the election. They'd decided the 'air war' didn't win you as many votes as the 'ground war'. The agents would be employed part time and would go round all the marginal seats, knocking on doors and saying, 'Aren't we great; vote for us.' They would each cost £20,000 a year, so the total cost was £1.6 million. This was the first I'd heard of it. As treasurer, [I] had people in the room asking me how the idea had come about, and I didn't know how to answer. I knew a lot about business and how to finance the party, but nobody talked to me about anything. So what was my role as treasurer? What was my job? Ultimately, what they'd sold me was a title. They were not asking me for anything except the money – though they wanted me to turn up to events.

During this period, Cruddas acted as a co-treasurer with Stanley Fink, who had taken over from Michael Spencer. The following year, Fink stepped down and Cruddas was promoted to principal treasurer, with a new co-treasurer, City financier Mike Farmer. Both were expected personally to contribute at least £750,000 a year to the party. Cruddas says he didn't mind shelling out large sums – as he puts it, 'You have to be a big hitter. It's easier to ask other people for money if you're giving a lot yourself' – but he was disappointed not to be given the chance to make a wider contribution. All the same, he continued working hard on the party's behalf. He did this quietly, never seeking the limelight, and was little known outside the party.

Nonetheless, in March 2012 he was the target of a newspaper 'sting'. Two reporters posing as prospective donors approached him through an intermediary he trusted (who was also duped) and drew him into a detailed conversation about the potential business benefits of giving money. They had been sent to him via CCHQ, and so he assumed they had already undergone some checks. Though he repeatedly made it clear that they could only donate in their own names or through a bona fide British company and that they would have to comply with the spirit and letter of the law, some of his comments appeared to suggest they could expect special access to the party leader. He explained that in return for a sizeable donation, they would receive invitations to certain exclusive dinners with Cameron and other Cabinet ministers, where they could raise any business issue they liked. He was not aware that he was being filmed.

When he realised he had been stung, he was not initially concerned, being confident he had said nothing wrong.

'I had no inkling of how bad it was going to be,' he admits.

However, the 'cash for access' exposé, which subsequently appeared on the front page of the *Sunday Times* on 25 March 2012 and was trailed on television news the night before, looked, in his own words, 'horrible'. It suggested that the party treasurer was 'peddling' access to the Prime Minister. In the hours after the story broke, he says, 'the shit hit the fan'.

'It was 9.30 p.m. on Saturday night; I had Sky News on – and that was the first time I realised I'd been recorded,' Cruddas recalls.

> They portrayed me in a very bad light. I wasn't actually very well that day and was coughing a lot. The grainy footage made it look sinister. That's when the shock started to set in. My wife was in

Rome, watching it all on TV there. She and my two daughters were very upset.

Feldman was among the first to call him.

'It's really bad. David's very upset,' he said grimly.

'Do I have to resign?' Cruddas asked.

'Yes,' Feldman replied. Cruddas agreed without hesitation and Feldman promised to call him back. Half an hour later, he rang Cruddas again to read him a draft resignation statement written on his behalf by the party.

> He read it to me, and I said, 'Yeah, that's all right.' I had no input. I could have said no, I could have issued a statement after seeing my lawyer. But I was upset, my wife was upset, and that's when I needed the party to stand by me – or at the very least establish the facts. But they never asked my side of the story. If they'd just asked me what had happened, it might have been different. But they weren't concerned about me – just the political fallout. It was a terrible situation.

That Sunday, he recalls walking across Hyde Park in a daze and wandering into a café, where he ordered a bowl of pasta. He was extremely distressed.

> I remember feeling terrible; truly humiliated. My wife came back from Rome that night. I felt like I had to get out of London and suggested to my wife that we go away, but she told me I had to stay. I had to face up to what had happened. It was no good running away. She was very firm with me.

Meanwhile Cameron had taken to the airwaves to denounce him, describing his actions as 'completely unacceptable'. He announced plans for an internal inquiry to be led by Tory peer Lord Gold.

'This is not the way we raise money in the Conservative Party...It's quite right that Peter Cruddas has resigned,' he said.

The following week, Cruddas began legal proceedings against the *Sunday Times* for libel. He was particularly keen to view the evidence against him, but accessing the tape would take many months. For a while, he heard nothing from the party. Then he received a call from Fink.

'You've been stitched up,' Fink said, adding that somebody he knew who was involved with Lord Gold's inquiry had viewed the evidence and concluded that Cruddas had been wronged.

'Yes, I know. That's what I've always said,' Cruddas replied, pleased.

To his amazement, however, Fink was calling not to offer sympathy or support. He was calling to persuade him to drop his libel suit.

'You shouldn't sue. All it will do is cost you £1 million, and then you'll get a little apology in the corner, and that will be the end of it,' Fink said. He went on to suggest that Cruddas take advice from the Conservative Party lawyer and allow the lawyer to accompany him to view the video footage.

'You're having a fucking laugh, aren't you?' replied Cruddas, apoplectic.

> I've been dumped by the party; you lot don't care about me – all you want is for this to go away! I need to clear my name. I don't care about spending £1 million – that's what I was going to give to the Conservatives anyway. I'm going to do what's right for me and my family. They count for a lot more than anybody else.

Taken aback, Fink hung up.

Cruddas says now:

> Poor Stanley – he's a genuinely nice bloke and was caught in the middle. The Gold Inquiry was supposed to be impartial, but it was just there to criticise me and protect Cameron. They just wanted to limit the damage. They knew when they saw the tape that I was going to win my case and they knew that would look bad for Cameron, because he'd dumped me without even hearing my side of the story. They just didn't want any extra fuss.

Cruddas was on holiday in the south of France when the High Court finally ruled in his favour on 31 July 2013. He was awarded £180,000 in damages and substantially more in costs. It would not be the end of the matter – his damages were substantially reduced on appeal – but it was vindication nonetheless. Embarrassed, Cameron publicly apologised.

'Had I known at the time how badly the journalists had behaved, I might have been in the position to take a different approach,' he said. 'I am very sorry about that. I congratulate Peter Cruddas on his victory and on the verdict he has won. I think it is very deserved.'

Shortly afterwards, Feldman called.

'Peter, congratulations on your victory,' he said. 'We're really pleased for you. David would like to catch up with you.'

Still angry at the way he had been summarily ejected from his post and disowned by the party leadership, Cruddas was not keen. However, he reluctantly agreed, hoping he might be offered his old role back. On 13 September, he was invited to Cameron's private apartment in Downing Street for a drink.

He remembers seeing the Prime Minister's golf clubs stacked inside the door as he was ushered into the living room. Feldman and Ed Llewellyn were also there. Llewellyn poured Cameron a beer, while Cruddas asked for water. The businessman listened respectfully as Cameron acknowledged he'd been wrong to rush to judgement against him, but he was dismayed by the Prime Minister's tone.

'It wasn't much of an apology. He didn't say that he shouldn't have sacked me. He didn't offer to put things right. I said, "Well, what do you propose? Put it right! Do you realise I could have sued you too, for vicariously defaming me?"'

'Yes, I do realise that,' Cameron replied carefully, asking why Cruddas had not done so.

Cruddas explained that he hadn't wanted to damage the party further.

'Well, where do we go from here?' Cameron asked.

Cruddas explained that he would like to be reinstated as treasurer, but the Prime Minister indicated that this was not possible as there was no vacancy. The meeting broke up without resolution, with Feldman promising to 'be in touch'.

A fortnight later, Cruddas was summoned to CCHQ for a further discussion with Feldman. He hoped he was about to be offered his old job back. Instead, Feldman suggested various marginal roles, which Cruddas declined. A third meeting some weeks later broke up acrimoniously.

'He called me back and wanted me to reconsider the offers,' Cruddas recalled. 'I said, "No. I don't need to be reintegrated into the party, bit by bit. I have done nothing wrong." I felt I'd been fobbed off and that it was all very insincere.'

When Feldman suggested Cruddas was partly to blame for his own troubles, the businessman exploded. Earlier that year, Feldman had himself been at the centre of a media storm after he was linked to an anonymous quote describing Tory Party associations as 'swivel-eyed loons'. At the time, he had categorically denied he was responsible. Now Cruddas challenged him about it face to face.

'Who are you to talk about saying inappropriate things, when you say them yourself?' Cruddas asked.

'What do you mean?' Feldman replied angrily.

Cruddas looked him straight in the eye. 'Well, like swivel-eyed loons. That's a start, isn't it?' he said.

Stunned, Feldman said nothing. Cruddas took his silence as an admission of guilt.

He says now:

> I thought, there's no way I'm taking shit from these people any more. I've had enough. If I'm not part of it any more, so be it. The conversation more or less ended there. I said: 'Well, I'd better go now, hadn't I?' And he said: 'Yes, I think you'd better.' So I left. They'd pushed me to the limit.

It was the last Cruddas ever heard from Feldman or Cameron. In their defence, they had made several attempts to bring him back into the fold. Cameron's public apology following the original libel verdict was probably as far as he could be expected to go. In any case, some aspects of the *Sunday Times* story were later upheld by an appeal judge.

Yet it is hard to avoid the impression that Cameron and Feldman saw the philanthropist as a cash cow who could be relied upon to shell out large sums of money but was not to be trusted with real responsibility. The way they treated him was perfunctory and showed no regard for the devastating impact the controversy had on him, his family and his business.

Nor is it an isolated example of Cameron rushing to judgement, a tendency that first became apparent during the expenses crisis and has on occasion prompted reprimands from members of the judiciary, most memorably in December 2013 when he publicly backed celebrity chef Nigella Lawson in the middle of a fraud trial, angering the judge presiding over the case.

Ann Widdecombe believes that during the expenses scandal he was 'far more focused on what the headline was going to be than [on] individual justice', and accuses him of making 'very swift judgements, some quite unfairly without bothering to ascertain the full facts'.

Her sense is that he did not apply the same rules to everyone.

'He doesn't do it when it's his own pals. He does tend to hold on to his own. In some ways that is laudable, because it means he's a loyal person, but he should extend justice to others.'

An example is the generosity he showed Hugo Swire, one of his best friends at Westminster. In 2007, he was forced to sack Swire as shadow Culture Secretary after Swire suggested the Tories would scrap free museum entry. Unusually, however, he gave Swire a second chance, offering him a ministerial post in Northern Ireland in 2010. He told a colleague that Swire was 'a very good friend' and that it was 'very important' that he 'succeeds and is seen to succeed'.

As we shall see, there would be another example, towards the end of his administration, when he refused to sack his Oxford chum and former tennis partner Lord Feldman, following a bullying scandal in the party that saw a vulnerable young activist commit suicide.

His loyalty in these cases was in marked contrast to his treatment of others who ran into trouble, in particular Andrew Mitchell, who was forced to resign from government following an altercation with police officers manning the Downing Street gates in September 2012. That July, Cameron had persuaded Mitchell to become his Chief Whip, a promotion Mitchell accepted only reluctantly, because of his commitment to the international development brief. It was a reward for seven years of loyalty: despite having led David Davis's unsuccessful leadership bid, over the years Mitchell had not only proven an effective Secretary of State but had always been supportive when Cameron hit trouble. However, when he found himself fighting for his political career over toxic claims that he labelled police officers 'plebs' – which he always vehemently denied – Cameron let him swing in the wind.

Mitchell eventually lost the libel case he brought against the *Sun* newspaper, which first published the story, but the long, drawn-out saga was far from black and white. Three police officers were sacked and another went to prison for lying about what happened. At the time of writing, several others were still facing disciplinary action. While the episode put the Prime

Minister in a very difficult position (he could not have known exactly what happened and could not publicly accuse police of lying), Mitchell's friends feel he should have been far more supportive, both publicly and in private. Instead, immediately after the story broke, Downing Street not only advised him to 'lie low' and 'grovel to the press',[385] but actively discouraged friends and colleagues from defending him. When Mitchell obtained CCTV evidence which he felt cast doubt over the police version of events, one of Cameron's closest aides advised him against releasing it on the basis that he might be 'stitched up' by the media – a remark he greeted with derision. Among those who did privately support him throughout the saga, during which he became severely depressed, was former Prime Minister Tony Blair, who texted him words of encouragement. By contrast, Cameron has not spoken to Mitchell since he lost his legal case. During the early days of the 'Plebgate' scandal, Mitchell was amused to receive an email from his old boss in the City observing that the Prime Minister was 'clearly not a man to go tiger shooting with'.

What of his apparent reluctance to reach out beyond a tight clique of trusted friends and aides from a similar background to his own? As we have seen, the pattern was set at Eton and continued at Oxford. Returning to Cruddas, it seems significant that the businessman was never consulted about significant financial decisions during his brief stint as party treasurer, despite his expertise. Did the fact that he left school without any qualifications and had not been educated at public school or Oxbridge mean Cameron's circle didn't take him seriously – despite the fact that he is a self-made billionaire? Did they struggle to relate to somebody so different to themselves? His experience suggests so.

Yet many of those who worked with Cameron, even at the highest level, felt like 'outsiders'.

'Cameron doesn't let people in,' said Cheryl Gillan, who was Welsh Secretary until September 2012. 'I'd love to see him take a wider circle…I always think he goes into lockdown with a small group.'

Another MP who served in Cameron's Cabinet lamented that he 'keeps a very high measure of distance between himself and his colleagues' and only engaged closely with a chosen few.

His inner circle consisted primarily of people of a similar background and class to his own – Hilton and Coulson being the notable exceptions,

---

385   Private information.

along with Craig Oliver, who went to a comprehensive school in Scotland. It was almost impossible for anyone who was not with him at the beginning of his political journey to penetrate this exclusive group. For a long time, it was a source of frustration for those left outside what one critic derisively labelled the 'wigwam of trust'.[386] Many backbench MPs also felt he had an overly dogmatic approach to dissent.

'He seems to think that if you're not a 100 per cent Cameron supporter, then you're a dangerous bastard, whereas that's not how political parties work,' says one senior backbencher who has worked closely with him over the years.

> I think they work on a 75 per cent rule – if you have 75 per cent of your colleagues behind you 75 per cent of the time, you're probably doing quite well. You're never going to have 100 per cent of them. Understanding that you can have somebody who has the best interests of the party at heart who may not be somebody you'd identify as your No. 1 personal fan and recognising that you can still work with them – that's important. But I think he's always been uncomfortable with that.

The perceived remoteness was a significant factor in the rebellions he faced. Many of his MPs, including those who otherwise admired him, felt he viewed Parliament – and junior colleagues – as an irritant – an impression that only encouraged them to flex parliamentary muscle.

'He seems to think it gets in the way of the serious business of governing,' said one.

However, claims that he had 'a problem with women', a suggestion that began circulating in April 2011 after he told Labour's Angela Eagle to 'calm down, dear' during a session of Prime Minister's Questions, are hard to substantiate and are emphatically denied by women in his inner circle. Possibly women like the singer Charlotte Church, who in 2015 branded him 'really misogynistic',[387] are misinterpreting aloofness as sexism.

More damaging to the Tory brand was the perception that Cameron surrounded himself with his own type, who enjoyed special protection. During

386 @SteveHiltonguru.
387 *Daily Telegraph*, 4 June 2015.

the coalition, various Tory MPs went public with their unease at the number of Old Etonians in Downing Street, including Gove, who described it as 'preposterous'. Letwin, Llewellyn, Jo Johnson (head of the No. 10 Policy Unit until 2015) and Osborne's chief economic adviser Rupert Harrison all went to Eton. (According to a senior Downing Street adviser, Cameron has on more than one occasion privately indicated that he sees the charming Harrison as a future Prime Minister.) Another Old Etonian who used to work for him says, 'The sad fact is I think he was comfortable with me because I am from the same background. There's truth in the accusation that he surrounds himself with people like him.'

The black youth worker and former Tory candidate Shaun Bailey, who grew up in social housing in north Kensington, is a rare example of someone from the other end of the social spectrum who was given a job as a special adviser in Downing Street. It did not end well. Bailey, who worked closely with Steve Hilton and found himself increasingly isolated after Hilton left No. 10, is known to have been dismayed by the lack of socio-economic and cultural diversity on Cameron's team, and felt that the absence of people from different backgrounds in No. 10 weakened policy making.

Cameron seems to have recognised this tendency in himself before he became leader. According to the theologian Adrian Hilton, he once privately confided that he was prone to surrounding himself with 'yes men', a flaw he also detected in Michael Howard.

> He talked quite openly about his time working with Howard. He said there was quite a lot that Howard did which he didn't agree with, but he'd learned to bite his tongue. He said Howard had made some bad decisions but wouldn't take advice even from his closest advisers. He felt Howard surrounded himself by groups of like-minded people or those who were somehow beholden to him so wouldn't kick too forcefully – of which he admitted he was one. I said that such behaviour was probably understandable in politics, but the wisest keep opposing voices close in order to scrutinise beliefs or test the strength of one's argument. He said he saw Howard's tendency in himself – the tendency to surround himself by a clique. I'm pretty sure he didn't use the word clique, but that was my very clear inference.

Those who shared Cameron's long political journey earned his trust, respect and loyalty, but in the battle for his affections, they could not compete with his old school friends. He himself seemed to confirm this when he was asked in the run-up to the 2015 election whether he 'loved' Osborne. Failing to answer, he 'whooped with laughter', saying simply that they were 'very good friends, as well as work colleagues'. When asked if he loved any of his other friends, however, he immediately replied in the affirmative, referring to those 'from way back…eleven or twelve'. He named Tom Goff, now a bloodstock agent in Newmarket, as his closest friend after Samantha. They talk on the phone most weeks, with Goff acting as 'a sort of taxi driver' who rings him up with 'very frank…good, robust, strong, middle-of-the-road Conservative views'.[388] Others in this very elite category include 'Toppo' Todhunter, Dom Loehnis and Giles Andreae.

Along with family, these are the only people who actually call him Dave.

---

388   Jenni Russell interview, *The Times* magazine, 28 March 2015.

PART SIX –
ENCORE

35
BRO

*'In politics, war can change everything. It can be the making of pol-
iticians, like Thatcher, or the breaking of them, like Eden.'*

— Cameron

Graham Brady was on a beach in Cuba when the Prime Minister rang.
Lounging in the sun by the warm Caribbean waters, the chair of the
1922 Committee was enjoying the summer recess. It was 27 August 2013
and, like most MPs, he was on holiday – thousands of miles away, in body,
if not in mind, from the mounting foreign policy crisis at home.

'Graham, where are you?' Cameron asked, a slight note of urgency in
his voice.

'In Cuba, David.'

For a few surreal moments, Brady, in his beach shorts, and the PM, in
No. 10, exchanged pleasantries about the land of Castro and cigars. Then
Cameron got to the point.

'Listen, Graham. I need to recall Parliament.'

More than two years into the bloody civil war in Syria, the international
community, led by Britain and the US, was finally stirring into action. At
least 100,000 Syrians had already been killed. Now there were reports that
the Assad regime was using chemical weapons. In Obama's view, the dictator
had crossed a 'red line'. Cameron agreed.

'I don't believe we can let it stand,' he said. 'The world shouldn't stand
idly by.'

Brady, Cameron's direct line to his backbenches, was not convinced. He
knew colleagues would be sceptical. However, Cameron talked a good talk.
Brady remembers feeling impressed by his conviction and reassurances.

The CIA and the White House had known for some time that Cameron was keen to do something in Syria. However, the Prime Minister needed to take his country with him. In post-Iraq War Britain, that would not be easy.

Across the Atlantic, Cameron's handling of the Syrian crisis had already been the cause of considerable head scratching. To the surprise of many in Washington, the British Prime Minister was turning into something of a foreign policy 'hawk'. A leader who had entered office determined to focus on domestic concerns had become a strong advocate of military intervention in the Middle East.

For months he had been pushing Obama – a notoriously dilatory decision-maker on foreign policy questions – to take action to stop the bloodshed in Syria. In top-secret one-to-one correspondence, he had tabled proposals for action on two occasions. These ideas, one put forward in 2012, the other in 2013, 'fell into the "derring-do" category', according to a White House source. The source refused to go into detail, but it seems likely these 'audacious, commando-type' operations included high-risk attempts to 'take out' Bashar al-Assad, the Syrian President.

'It was sort of *Boys' Life* stuff,' the source says. 'And it was just implausible, in part because the efforts that he was proposing would have been too small to make a difference, and also quite likely to fail or be unsustainable and would have been getting everybody into deeper waters.'[389]

Cameron's response to the Syria crisis illustrated his conflicted approach to foreign intervention. His instincts were to 'act', but having observed Blair's travails over Iraq, he was keenly aware of the political pitfalls of haste. What American intelligence chiefs dismissed as 'World War Two SAS stuff' was the product of his desire to 'do something' but also indicated the limits to his ambitions.

In his early days as Tory leader, he had been a foreign policy novice. Conscious of his own shortcomings, he appointed a panel of Tory grandees including the former Hong Kong governor Chris Patten, the former Foreign Secretary Douglas Hurd and various former ambassadors to advise him. It was 'a sort of long tutorial for him', Patten explains. As his support for the Iraq War showed, he was receptive to the arguments of those with more experience.

389 Private information.

He followed up these sessions with a string of personal 'fact-finding missions' to Afghanistan and the Middle East. One former ambassador recalls Cameron and Hague visiting Afghanistan to meet the troops in 2006. He reveals – with a hint of disdain – that Cameron took time to pose for a photograph with a bunch of Old Etonians in military and diplomatic posts in Helmand Province. Yet the ambassador felt the new Tory leader had an open mind – a relief, given his obvious lack of expertise.

> I said to him privately, the military campaign is all very well, but it's tactics without strategy. This is essentially a political problem, we're wasting a lot of money and blood and treasure, and essentially applying local anaesthetic to a patient with cancer. And Cameron absorbed all that, much more quickly than Hague, who was much more cautious, less decisive. I remember we watched a great, fat, gross American sitting in an armchair, flying a drone, and conducting a strike and pressing a button, and there were these Taliban – you could see it in the camera – going across the desert, black and white, and then a puff! The missile went down...these two wounded people struggled out of the truck, and then the woman pressed the button again and another missile went down and these people were vaporised. And Cameron said, 'Isn't that a war crime?' And he immediately got it – because obviously it was a war crime, it showed the whole pointlessness of the campaign.[390]

Others in Afghanistan were less impressed. He rocked up twenty minutes late to a round-table event for charities involved in humanitarian work, and added insult to injury by misjudging the mood.

'These were very busy people,' recalls one who was there.

> He swaggered in and made a really lame joke, saying, 'I'm really glad to be here. Normally at this time of day on a Wednesday [before PMQs] I'm having a cup of tea with six lumps of sugar in it, a tip I picked up from William Hague. Except I don't really put the sugar in but he doesn't know that.' Might have worked with a bunch of Brits but everyone was bemused. All the charity reps

390   Private information.

gave their presentations, arguing why increasing British troops was going to be disastrous on a humanitarian front, and at the end of it all, Cameron clearly hadn't really been listening, and just said: 'Well, I think what we can all agree on is that we have to support the British troops.' Nobody was impressed.[391]

Still feeling his way on the world stage, in opposition, Cameron could sound quite like Blair.

'The best answer to the passionate intensity of those dedicated to destroying the liberal order is a passionate commitment to defend it. That is a truly noble cause at a time of trial,' he told an audience at the Foreign Policy Centre in August 2005. He simply advocated more caution than the Labour leader had shown.

'I think the problem with Blair was that he was a humanitarian interventionist without putting any kind of practical brake on these impulses,' he told Dylan Jones. 'I think you do need that sceptical, enquiring sense when it comes to foreign policy, so you think through the consequences of your actions, and Blair was just too eager to jump in anywhere.'[392]

On the fifth anniversary of 9/11, in London in 2006, he gave a controversial speech which hinted that circumspection in foreign affairs might become a feature of his leadership. It called for a rebalancing of the so-called 'special relationship' between Britain and America. He demanded that the UK be 'solid but not slavish' in its alliance with the US. Across the Atlantic, it did not go down well, but it hardly amounted to a radical change of approach. Indeed, in the same speech, Cameron stressed that he remained a 'passionate' Atlanticist.

> I and my party are instinctive friends of America, and passionate supporters of the Atlantic Alliance... The fact is that Britain just cannot achieve the things we want to achieve in the world unless we work with the world's superpower. So when it comes to the special relationship with America, Conservatives feel it, understand it and believe in it.

---

391 Private information.
392 David Cameron and Dylan Jones, p. 263.

According to Robert Tuttle, the US ambassador to London at the time, the White House was unruffled. Privately, however, Cameron feared he had gone too far. He was sufficiently worried by the reaction on both sides of the Atlantic to fix a meeting with Tuttle, to reassure him. That Cameron had Liam Fox as his shadow Defence Secretary was further comfort to the White House: Fox, who enjoyed close links with American Republicans and Washington 'neo-cons', was an ardent Atlanticist. On his trips to Capitol Hill, he reassured Bush's team that the new Tory leader would not rock the boat.

As the 2010 election approached, Cameron made clear that his foreign policy priority would be withdrawal from Afghanistan. Though he had had no hesitation in supporting the invasion in 2001 ('effectively invading and decapitating the regime…was absolutely the right thing to do, no question', he told Dylan Jones), he had seen the heavy toll it had taken on Blair's premiership.[393] Privately, he also knew the situation on the ground in Afghanistan was a mess. What he was not prepared to do was expend political capital – and risk more British lives – sorting it out. He just wanted out.

One of his first guests at Chequers was Afghan President Hamid Karzai. Two weeks later, he convened an Afghanistan 'seminar' at the same venue, inviting a number of figures whose disdain for the military operation was no secret. Among the guests was Rory Stewart, a former deputy governor of two Iraqi provinces, who had spent long periods in Afghanistan and believed the allied military effort was futile.

A month after becoming Prime Minister, Cameron announced that all British troops would be home by 2015. Later, he would boldly declare Afghanistan was a 'mission accomplished'.

'To me, the absolute driving part of the mission is the basic level of security so it doesn't become a haven for terror. That is the mission, that was the mission and I think we will have accomplished that mission,' he said.[394]

Very few of those familiar with life in Helmand Province agreed.

As British involvement in Afghanistan wound down, Cameron needed to find his own foreign policy voice. One of his early initiatives was the creation of the National Security Council (NSC), an attempt to give a formal structure to

393   Ibid., p. 259.
394   Speech at Camp Bastion, quoted in *The Guardian*, 16 December 2013.

foreign and national security policy decision making and bring an end to the so-called 'sofa government' characteristic of Blair's regime. Membership was drawn from the Cabinet, Foreign Office, military and intelligence agencies. Cameron's chairmanship of its meetings has been described by one former Cabinet member as the PM 'at his best'.[395]

Not everybody was inside the tent, however. Fox, accompanied by a self-styled 'adviser' named Adam Werritty, was paddling his own canoe. A close friend and former flatmate of the Defence Secretary, Werritty had no formal government role and no security clearance. Yet he tagged along with the Cabinet minister on eighteen official and unofficial trips, and attended forty of his official engagements. When his activities were exposed, Fox was forced to resign. His unusual modus operandi and staunch Atlanticism prompted claims he had been running a 'parallel operation'.

'Liam Fox was effective, colourful and yet sometimes slightly erratic,' says retired General Sir David Richards, former Chief of Defence Staff. 'At times it seemed like he was almost running his own foreign policy. He was a big Zionist, very pro-America, and prone to trotting off to places like Sri Lanka without telling the Foreign Office.'

Another former member of the NSC agrees:

> Liam always – throughout opposition – was doing his own thing. Conducted his own foreign policy, his own defence policy. He artic-ulated an almost Tea Party view of the world. He was deeply into the Republican Party and into the right wing of it. I mean, on issues like Iran, he belonged to the camp that just said, 'We ought to bomb them.'

Fox's ability to freelance was a symptom of Cameron's leadership style. Relations between the pair had never been warm, and so long as the Defence Secretary's competence was not in doubt, Cameron was willing to cut him slack. An NSC insider believes it would have been difficult to clip his wings in any case.

'It was like trying to rein in an eel or something. Very slithery.'

Following Fox's dramatic departure, the Ministry of Defence became much more risk averse. Defence ministers were irritated to find that they

---

395 Private information.

were suddenly being accompanied by civil service 'minders' wherever they went, however anodyne the engagement.

Meanwhile Cameron was trying to increase Britain's diplomatic clout through trade. This approach involved leading delegations of British businessmen to emerging economies. By 2013 he had been on more than fifty trade missions, including many to countries with dubious human rights records.[396]

But institutional tweaking and trade tours do not make big headlines. As he approached the end of his first year as PM, Cameron had not had a foreign policy success story to match Thatcher's Falklands or Blair's Kosovo. No Prime Minister wants war, but as Cameron himself acknowledged, it can be an opportunity.

'War…can be the making of politicians, like Thatcher, or the breaking of them, like Eden,' he had observed as a young MP.[397] The arrival of the Arab Spring at the start of 2011 offered the perfect opportunity to test what war would do for him.

When the first wave of protests broke out in the Middle East and North Africa, he was quick to seize the initiative. In February 2011, he became the first world leader to visit Egypt since the toppling of its dictator, Hosni Mubarak, though the trip was actually part of a tour of Arab states to flog British arms contracts ('democracies have a right to defend themselves', he said when questioned by journalists on the ethics of the trip).[398]

As unrest spread to neighbouring Libya, he became the second Western leader to call on the UN to impose a no-fly zone to prevent the country's unstable despot, Colonel Gaddafi, from massacring his own citizens. (The first was France's Nicolas Sarkozy, who, feeling guilty for failing to support the first wave of the Arab Spring, jumped at the opportunity to put things right.) Two days after the UN placed the country under an arms embargo, on 28 February, Cameron ordered the Ministry of Defence to draw up plans for Britain to step in.

It was his first major foreign policy test. Less than eight years after he had warily cast his vote in support of the Iraq invasion he found himself leading the charge to intervene in the Middle East.

---

396   Simon Jenkins, *The Guardian*, 2 December 2013. According to Cabinet Office records, Cameron visited forty-seven different countries between May 2010 and the end of March 2014.

397   *Guardian* blog, 1 April 2003.

398   *The Guardian*, 22 February 2011.

Although the question he asked the NSC – 'Is it in our national interest or not to get involved?' – was solidly realist, his real spur was the looming humanitarian crisis. As Gaddafi's troops closed in on the rebel stronghold of Benghazi in early March, there were mounting fears of genocide.

If Britain did not act, 'thousands of people will die who don't need to die', Cameron told a colleague who asked him to make the case for intervention.[399]

He told the BBC that getting involved was not only in Britain's national interest, but also 'in the wider moral interest of actually stopping the slaughter of civilians'. To those who feared another Iraq, he stressed that what he planned was 'very clearly not a repetition of anything from the past'.[400]

He believed a no-fly zone could protect civilians while avoiding 'boots on the ground'. A former Foreign Office minister who was involved in the planning says, 'Libya presented an easily identifiable objective, which he felt had a moral imperative behind it.' It was, in Cameron's words, simply a case of doing 'the right thing'.

Cameron's generals were dubious. Some saw his desire to get involved as symptomatic of an ill-informed 'Notting Hill instinct'.

'There was a great sort of cry, of "We can't let this happen on our watch." His instinct is to support the underdog, without analysing what that really means. It is government by Notting Hill intelligentsia,' laments one former member of the NSC.[401]

The Americans were equally sceptical. Obama feared being dragged into yet another war in the Middle East, and questioned the plan for a post-Gaddafi Libya. Faced with the prospect of a massacre in Benghazi, however, he came round.

Some have credited Cameron with persuading Obama to join Britain, France and the Arab League in committing to air strikes in Libya. Matthew d'Ancona sees similarities with Blair in 1999, when he managed to persuade Bill Clinton to follow Britain's lead in Kosovo.[402] While there is some truth to this – Cameron and Obama had a number of key telephone conversations – White House officials play down Cameron's influence.

---

399 Francis Elliott and James Hanning, p. 470.
400 BBC interview, 18 March 2011.
401 Private information.
402 Matthew d'Ancona, p. 170.

'I don't think there was any one European voice – let alone Cameron's – that had a profound influence on the President's thinking and swayed him from scepticism to activism or anything like that,' one says dismissively.

> There were a lot of things that came together on Libya, but if you were to say, 'but surely Cameron's really great relationship with Obama and his powers of moral persuasion led to the American support for European intervention?' I would have to say that doesn't really ring a bell.[403]

The US ambassador to NATO at the time, Ivo Daalder, says Obama feared Cameron and Sarkozy's plans were insufficiently thought through.

'Cameron and Sarkozy were the undisputed leaders, in terms of doing *something*,' Daalder explains.

> The problem was that it wasn't really clear *what* that something was going to be. Cameron was pushing for a no-fly zone, but in the US there was great scepticism. A no-fly zone wasn't effective in Bosnia, it wasn't effective in Iraq, and probably wasn't going to be effective in Libya. When President Obama was confronted with the argument for a no-fly zone, he asked how this was going to be effective. Gaddafi was attacking people. A no-fly zone wasn't going to stop him. Instead, to stop him we would need to bomb his forces attacking people.[404]

The UN resolution passed on 17 March went significantly further than a no-fly zone, permitting 'all necessary measures', including bombing. This was a direct result of Obama's pressure. He transformed an ineffective no-fly-zone policy into something with real teeth. 'The critical shift came from Obama,' Daalder says.

Nonetheless, Cameron played a key role in securing the UN vote – even if Britain's ambassador to the UN, Sir Mark Lyall Grant, did most of the legwork. The Tory leader personally telephoned the Crown Prince of Abu Dhabi, the Kings of Jordan and Saudi Arabia, and the Qatari Prime Minister,

---

403 Private information.
404 Private information.

to ensure key regional powers were on side.[405] He also called leaders of three Security Council nations: Jacob Zuma of South Africa, Goodluck Jonathan of Nigeria, and Germany's Angela Merkel.

In building the international coalition, the stakes could not have been higher, but there was still room for humour. The then Development Secretary Andrew Mitchell remembers travelling to an African Union meeting in Equatorial Guinea to try to get the African states on side. 'It was like a scene from Evelyn Waugh's *Black Mischief*,' Mitchell says.

> We arrived, and there was the British Honorary Consul, who was a sort of wonderful caricature of the Foreign Office, because Equatorial Guinea is not really on anyone's radar. It's where there was a failed coup involving Mark Thatcher and Simon Mann. Simon Mann is one of Cameron's constituents, and was once threatened by the President of Guinea, who said that he would eat him! Cameron used to joke that 'he said he would eat my constituent's brains!'
>
> Afterwards I wrote to Cameron saying that I'd been able to talk to eight Presidents and two VPs; one King, two Prime Ministers and one cannibal. And the civil service insisted on striking out 'cannibal' and I kept on putting it back in again! 'It will leak,' they said, 'and it will be dreadful!' To which I replied, 'Oh, it won't leak, it's just a letter, and I'm perfectly entitled to write it!' So I wrote my letter to Cameron with 'cannibal' in it.

Cameron's commitment to alliance building in the run-up to the Libya mission demonstrated the importance he attached to legalism and multilateralism in international affairs. He had seen what happened to Blair over Iraq. Reports of clashes with Dominic Grieve, the Attorney General, during NSC meetings in the run-up to the Libya intervention are misleading: he may have been frustrated with the legal restraints, but he respected them.

On 19 March 2011, the allied campaign, led by Britain, France and the US, began, with the overwhelming support of MPs. In Paris, Sarkozy hosted a coalition summit to finalise the allies' plans. In the course of the meeting it transpired that Gaddafi had already begun sending his soldiers towards

---

405   Francis Elliott and James Hanning, p. 473.

Benghazi. The Libyan dictator was now in a position to start destroying the city. Alarmed, Sarkozy urged Cameron and US Secretary of State Hillary Clinton to give the order to strike.

'We have to act today,' he told the pair, both of whom had assumed the operation would begin within days, not hours. 'Once the tanks are inside Benghazi, we won't be able to intervene without killing civilians.'

Faced with the full force of the French President's conviction, Cameron and Clinton fell into line. Turning to their generals, they gave the order.

Five months later, Gaddafi and his family fled Tripoli, drawing the curtain on his 42-year reign. A month later, the dictator was killed, bringing the international conflict to an end on 31 October.

Cameron had become a war leader. Furthermore, it looked like it had been a 'good war'. He did not hide his pride.

'Well, to those who predicted failure, look at what we have achieved,' he boasted at the Lord Mayor's Banquet in late 2011. 'We saved civilian lives as Gaddafi's tanks bore down on Benghazi. We helped the Libyan people to liberate themselves. And we now have the prospect of a new partner in the southern Mediterranean.'

In September, Cameron and Sarkozy flew into Tripoli to meet Libya's new leaders, the National Transitional Council. Though he had been offered a lift in Sarkozy's personal plane, Cameron took an RAF flight to avoid the embarrassment of hitching a lift. Much to the amusement of the French, however, once he was on Libyan soil and away from the cameras, he used their helicopters to get around.

In scenes reminiscent of Blair's triumphant arrival in Kosovo after the 1999 NATO campaign, Cameron and Sarkozy were hailed as heroes as they walked the Libyan streets. Taking to a podium, Cameron addressed the jubilant crowds massed in Liberty Square, declaring, 'People in Britain salute your courage' – to which the audience replied, 'Thank you Cam-Ron! Thank you Cam-Ron!' His moment of triumph was followed by a humbling reality check, however, when a bunch of Libyan teenagers confused him with the French President. They rushed up to him crying out, 'Merci, Monsieur Sarkozy!' Awkwardly, Cameron put them right.

'Moi, c'est Cameron,' he said.

Any triumphalism was short-lived. Just as Cameron's critics feared, Libya soon slid back into civil war. In 2012, neighbouring Mali suffered the knock-on effects of the collapse of the Libyan state, and Cameron was forced to authorise assistance to French forces sent in to contain the unrest.

'The way things are going at the moment you can't really class it as a success,' one former member of the NSC admits, with some understatement.[406] A fortnight before the 2015 election, William Hague admitted that Britain's intervention could not be defined as a triumph. 'Undoubtedly it has gone backwards very seriously,' he said. 'It's in a terrible state today...I'm not arguing it's a triumph of post-conflict planning.'[407]

Michael Ancram is even more critical, arguing that the intervention ultimately made the world more unstable, playing into the hands of terrorists:

> We now have a country which is ungovernable...with vast amounts of weapons from Gaddafi's arsenal moved south of the border, arming Boko Haram [in Nigeria]. They're actually more of a threat to us than Gaddafi was at the time. So what is success? I thought we shouldn't have done it in the first place. You've got to have a reason for doing these things in the first place. What was the strategy there? I can see no pattern of strategy within which we're operating.

He accuses Cameron of 'doing an Iraq'. 'To claim it was only about protecting citizens in Benghazi, so we're going to bomb the living daylights out of Gaddafi in the south and everyone else, just simply doesn't hold water. It makes me think that, rather like Blair, he was determined to change the regime,' he says.

It is true that Cameron was the most reluctant of all the allied leaders to end the intervention once its stated goal – protecting the people of Libya – had been accomplished. White House insiders say they had a 'really hard time' persuading him to 'turn off the mission'.

In retrospect, some of those involved say more attention should have been paid to what would happen to Libya long term.

'We never really analysed things properly,' General Sir David Richards admits. 'For example, we didn't understand the tribal dimension. I kept saying there was a large tribal element to Libya and it kept being pooh-poohed...I think our instinct is kneejerk support for the underdog, without doing the analysis that would necessarily legitimise that course of action.'

---

406 Private information.
407 *Daily Politics*, 24 April 2015.

Although he has been generally polite about Cameron's leadership, the former Chief of the Defence Staff later accused Cameron of attempting to 'micro-manage the campaign'. The two regularly met during the six months of the operation, and occasionally clashed. In one meeting, the general informed the PM that being in the Combined Cadet Force at Eton was not a qualification for running the tactical detail of a complex coalition war effort. Cameron smiled through gritted teeth.[408]

Unmoved by the criticisms, the Prime Minister himself remains convinced the Libya campaign was the right thing to do.

'Do I regret that Britain played our role in getting rid of Gaddafi and coming to the aid of that nation when Gaddafi was going to murder his own citizens in Benghazi? No, I don't,' he said, in February 2015.[409]

It must be to his credit that a massacre in Benghazi was avoided. Yet the episode left a bad taste in Obama's mouth. On the face of it, the special relationship, such as it was, was as warm as ever. (A state visit to the UK by Obama in May 2011, when the President gave Cameron a high-tech barbecue grill and the pair wrote a joint op-ed for *The Times* paying homage to the 'special relationship', was widely seen as the high point.) Yet according to White House insiders, Obama felt misled. It is claimed Cameron and Sarkozy assured the President that Britain and France would do the bulk of the heavy lifting after the first ten days of the operation, allowing the US to take a back seat. For an American President weary of his country's role as the world's international policeman, this was a vital promise. However, it quickly became apparent that they could not pull it off without substantial US support. From the US perspective, Cameron and Sarkozy had failed to appreciate the limit to their military capability, making what the White House insider calls 'extravagant and ultimately false assurances' that 'those who had been in the business a long time knew was all bullshit'.[410]

For his part, Cameron had been irritated by Obama's reluctance to assist in bringing the conflict to a swift end. 'He won't commit. It's unbelievably frustrating,' he reportedly complained.[411]

---

408 David Richards, *Taking Command* (Headline, 2014), p. 318.
409 *The Guardian*, 17 February 2015.
410 Private information.
411 Matthew d'Ancona, p. 170.

Yet it did not amount to a falling out. The reality was that the leaders had never been close anyway. In March 2012, Cameron had been treated to a lavish state dinner at the White House, prompting a disgruntled right-wing press in the US to denounce him as 'Obama's guard dog'.[412] He was the first foreign leader to accompany the Commander-in-Chief on board Air Force One. In the run-up to the 2015 election, he boasted that Obama sometimes called him 'bro', hoping that some of the President's glamour would rub off.[413] However, this was all spin: Obama simply doesn't do close personal friendships with fellow foreign leaders. He might have called Cameron 'bro', but he also called Osborne 'Jeffrey' – repeatedly confusing the Chancellor with the funk and soul legend Jeffrey Osborne. Though the President got on better with Cameron than he did with Brown, he did not see him as a trusted confidant. There was no comparison with Thatcher and Reagan, Blair and Bush, or Blair and Clinton. The President was personally closer to Merkel, and intellectually more interested in the world outside of Europe. The word White House insiders used to describe the relationship with Cameron was 'transactional'.

'Warm and fuzzy doesn't really come into it,' one explained.

As for the wider US public, they barely knew who Cameron was.

'Most people in the US still think Tony Blair is Prime Minister,' says Ted Bromund, a Washington expert on transatlantic relations. A Pentagon insider adds:

> He's not seen as someone who is, you know, super-confident, super-possessive of vision, as someone able to deliver in the ways that the US wants. From the standpoint of those in the bowels of the bureaucracy he just seemed a little bit too, you know, Eton. A guy who had sort of gotten ahead by being good at cocktail parties and stuff.[414]

Fast-forward to August 2013 and Cameron was once again trying to coax Obama into military action in the Middle East. The brutal civil war in Syria

---

412 *Washington Post*, 14 March 2012.
413 *Sunday Telegraph*, 4 January 2015.
414 Private information.

had ground to a bloody stalemate. A desperate Assad was resorting to gassing his own people. Britain had been giving the Syrian rebels non-lethal support for months, but it had not been enough. Events were now coming to a head.

Earlier, Cameron had rejected a secret plan to end the conflict drawn up by his Chief of the Defence Staff, General Sir David Richards. This scheme, outlined in a confidential memo to the Prime Minister via his national security adviser Kim Darroch, involved building an opposition army from scratch. Under the plan, rebel forces would be taken out of Syria to places like Jordan, Turkey or Saudi Arabia for a year or so until they were sufficiently well trained to be able to return and fight Assad, assisted by Western and Arab air and maritime forces. It would take at least a year.

Explaining his thinking at the time, Richards says now, 'We'd come off the fence and then, as we were obviously fully committed, there would be much less of a fight. Furthermore we'd have a year in which to train and prepare a government in waiting. We'd no longer be messing around.'

He acknowledges that it would have been 'very expensive' but says the bill would have been shared with allies. He was confident it would work. Curiously, Cameron did not reply to the memo. Richards believes the Prime Minister just wanted a quick fix. The general's own view was that a botched attempt at 'instant gratification' was worse than doing nothing at all. Increasingly, he found himself frozen out of discussions about how to deal with Syria. Relations with No. 10 deteriorated further when he questioned whether Downing Street understood that in Syria, it was not a simple question of 'good guys' versus 'bad guys'.

He recalls:

> I said, 'Are you certain we're backing the right side, Prime Minister?' You could see them all tutting, because they didn't want to debate it. But someone had to say it. It had got to the point where I felt there was a case for letting Assad win, because at least that would put the population out of their misery.

The August chemical weapons strikes seemed to change everything. Suddenly Obama was receptive to Cameron's calls for action. Both leaders were convinced that Assad was responsible. In the week following the attacks, they exchanged three critical phone calls, during which they made plans to bomb the Syrian regime. Obama made it clear that the timetable he envisaged was urgent: he wanted to strike within days.

'Cameron and Obama were in very close touch,' says a former White House official.

> On the night of Tuesday 27th they were on the phone for an hour. They went through the operation plan in minute detail…the timing, the duration of the strike, the nature of the strike package, the target deck, everything. Up to virtually the eve of the strike – because they were thinking of moving that Friday – they were really operating in a very intimate, very detail-intensive way about what was to happen.[415]

By the time Cameron picked up the phone to ring Graham Brady in Cuba, he had made his decision. 'I think that by that point, he had become very wrapped up with the conversations he'd had with Obama,' says a government source. 'While I'm not privy to the details of those, I got the distinct impression that he'd given assurances that he was very keen to deliver.'[416]

But could he deliver? Evidently he thought so.

Even before the summer recess there had been reports that the majority of Tory MPs would not back deeper involvement in Syria.[417] Yet the Prime Minister gave Obama no hint that he might struggle to get a Commons majority.

On Tuesday 27 August, he recalled Parliament. After meeting Miliband in Downing Street that afternoon, he was confident he could count on Labour votes, even if some of his own MPs wavered.

Once again, he had misjudged the mood in his own party. Many Tory MPs were sceptical, and disliked the sudden haste.

One Cabinet minister remembers receiving a phone call from the PM the weekend before the vote and urging caution. 'My observation was, "Of course I'll support you on this, but, like everyone, I have a series of reservations about what we're actually hoping to achieve. Tell me what success looks like?" They've never been able to answer that question, because nobody knew what success looked like.'

415 Private information.
416 Private information.
417 *Sunday Times*, 16 June 2013.

The minister advised Cameron to spend more time squaring it with the party.

> I said, 'Aren't we rushing this a bit?' I thought it would be better doing it later. I said, 'You've got to get round the MPs, because they're not happy and bruised a bit by a couple of things. They will use this as a vehicle to kick you if they can.

Finally, he asked Cameron about Miliband's position. 'He just said, "Oh well, Labour are OK." That's also why they rushed it, because they thought Labour was in the bag. Between Labour and the Tories, they thought they'd be able to rustle up enough.'

In fact, Miliband was about to drop a bombshell. As MPs from all parties abandoned their holidays to return to Parliament, the Labour leader suddenly told Cameron he would not now support the government. Having consulted his own MPs, Miliband had realised that he could not take his party with him. The trauma of the Iraq War had fundamentally transformed the Labour Party. Over a decade of cross-party consensus on foreign policy lay in ruins.

No. 10 was livid. Cameron shouted down the phone that Miliband was 'letting down America' and 'siding with [Sergey] Lavrov', the Russian Foreign Minister, an ally of Assad. One government source told journalists that No. 10 and the Foreign Office thought Miliband was 'a fucking cunt and a copper-bottomed shit'.[418]

Cameron's position was now desperate. As his whips warned him the numbers would not stack up, he started summoning potential rebels to Downing Street to lobby them one to one. A number of those who subsequently fell into line were distinctly underwhelmed by Cameron's pitch, nonetheless. Instead of making the moral case for intervention, he focused on what a catastrophe it would be for the government to lose the vote.

The motion that appeared before the House of Commons on Thursday 29 August no longer resembled anything like a declaration of war. Without Labour's support, and under heavy pressure from his backbenchers, Cameron had diluted it to little more than a vote on the *principle* of future action.

'It is not about taking sides in the Syrian conflict, it is not about invading, it is not about regime change, and it is not even about working more

---

418   *The Times*, 28 August 2013.

closely with the opposition,' he insisted to the House of Commons. 'It is about the large-scale use of chemical weapons and our response to a war crime – nothing else.'

But it was still too much. After a dramatic and lengthy day of passionate parliamentary debate, the government was defeated. Thirty Tories, nine Lib Dems, and the majority of Labour MPs voted against the motion.

Until his defeat in the EU referendum, the failure to win the Syria vote was the biggest humiliation of Cameron's premiership. For the first time since 1782, a government had been defeated on a matter of war. Cameron had misread public opinion, which was overwhelmingly opposed to military action, and he had failed in his task of public persuasion. His watered-down motion was resoundingly rejected, forcing him to draw a line under the affair.

'It is clear to me that the British Parliament, reflecting the views of the British people, does not want to see British military action. I get that and the government will act accordingly,' he told the Commons after the vote. From the opposition benches, there were cries of 'Resign!'

Some have subsequently accused him of complacency. Alan Duncan, then International Development Minister, had offered to return from his holiday, only to be told it was unnecessary. Graham Brady, on the beach in Cuba, had discovered that a flight back to London at such short notice would cost £6,000, of which more than £3,000 would have to come from his own pocket. He says that if the vote had been about committing British troops, he would willingly have paid; but the motion was unclear, and the whips seemed relaxed.

> The Whips Office didn't try hard to persuade me to take the £6k flight. It was clearly their view that the Labour Party would vote with the government. I think John Randall, the deputy Chief Whip, probably thought it would be ridiculous to spend £6k getting me back, when the motion was going to be passed with a majority of 400 or so. The way they did it, in terms of recalling Parliament without anyone knowing what the motion was going to be, was unhelpful. Frankly, if it had been a vote to commit troops, I would have got on a plane even if it was going to cost me £6,000 to vote

against it; but if it was going to be a vote to take note of worrying events, I wasn't going to waste the money. It was somewhere between the two, and it was a very, very odd thing to do.

Adam Holloway, a Tory backbencher with military experience in the Middle East, says he wasn't even contacted.

The problem is there's just not much communication with the backbenchers. I mean, if anyone had rung me up I'd have told them that there's no way lots of people will vote for little missile strikes. There was no real communication with us, no real understanding of what we'd have thought.

Some, including Gove, believe that Cameron's mistake was subjecting military action to a Commons vote in the first place. They fear it has set a dangerous precedent, undermining the ability of future prime ministers to take executive action.

Liam Fox says:

If there are things that you think are necessary for the maintenance of global security, you act right away and explain later. If Parliament thinks you've acted badly, they might decide to get rid of you, but part of the job of being there is to lead public opinion and sometimes to confront public opinion. I think that, such is the fear of the whole Iraq experience, there is a danger that politicians will be afraid to act even if they think it's the right thing to do.

Alan Duncan agrees:

This wasn't going to war – this was a reaction to the crossing the 'red line' with chemical weapons. My view was that he and Obama should have done it jointly on the Saturday, and then when Parliament was due to come back the following Monday, have a statement to explain why. As soon as you recall Parliament, people feel disturbed and you make a crisis out of a drama. He should have just done it.

Cameron's failure to carry his own MPs with him left the White House dumbfounded. Many inside the Obama administration saw it as ineptitude. 'It was one of those astonishing displays of incompetence that sort of leaves you wondering about how, you know, have we all got this far?' says one.[419]

Yet the debacle gave Obama the perfect excuse to back out. He had never been keen on getting involved, and a unilateral American campaign was out of the question.

'It would've been a bigger problem if Obama had really wanted to attack Syria, but that clearly was not the case,' a source confirms.

'The thing about both Libya and Syria is that neither constitutes strategic interest in any way,' the source continues. 'So you can get fucked over by your British counterpart on Libya and Syria and it's sort of not like the end of the world. At the end of the day it's going to be the Europeans who will pay the price for that, not the United States.'[420]

In November 2015, Cameron finally won another vote on going to war in Syria. Following the attacks by Islamic State in Paris, in which 130 people were killed, the Prime Minister went back to Parliament seeking a mandate to participate in coalition air strikes on ISIS bases. This time, assisted by a large number of Labour rebels, he won comfortably. The new Labour leader, Jeremy Corbyn, was fiercely opposed to any military action overseas, whatever the circumstances. However, he failed dismally to stamp his authority over his party, watching with contempt as his own shadow Foreign Secretary, Hilary Benn, humiliated him by making a rousing speech in support of the government. It restored some of the pride Cameron had lost after his first defeat.

Overall, Cameron's foreign policy was muddled – but he muddled through. War in Libya was not the making of him, but nor did the humiliation over Syria prove his undoing. Afghanistan is still a mess, but few regard this as his fault. Troops were home in time for the 2015 election, as he promised. In the twenty-first century, Britannia no longer ruled the waves. In the longest and deepest recession since the war, there was neither public appetite, nor military resources, to police the world.

What Cameron did do, in the face of fierce opposition from elements of

419 Private information.
420 Private information.

his own party, was maintain overseas aid. It may have been unpopular but it saved countless more lives than his military forays.

For some, his greatest mistake when it comes to Britain's place in the world is the scale of the defence cuts he has implemented. Some 8 per cent was shaved off the Budget between 2010 and 2015, resulting in the loss of 30,000 jobs and leaving Britain without a working aircraft carrier. By 2020, the army will have been cut to 80,000, from 102,000 when he entered Downing Street.

His old friend Nicholas Soames says he tried to warn him of the potential consequences.

> I regard it as my duty as a senior backbencher to support the Prime Minister through thick and thin. I've always done that. That's what I do. I don't make a row in public ever – but I cautioned very strongly against the scale and size of defence cuts. I know about it because I was a defence minister for four years. I believe we have gone too far in our defence cuts.

He fears for the strategic consequences.

> If we have to do a major intervention now – I mean, Christ, we've got nothing. They've stripped the navy down to nothing. The Labour Party stripped the navy, and we just carried it on. It's true that we've got all these marvellous new ships and submarines, but they're terribly small in number; and these two idiotic aircraft carriers, which were built in order to keep Gordon Brown in office and too late to cancel…and a very, very, very expensive aeroplane to go on top…

He trails off.

Obama himself also expressed concern.[421]

As Cameron began his second term in office, unease about Britain's depleted capability was deepening, set against a backdrop of the rising threat from the so-called Islamic State, and heightened tensions with an older enemy: Russia.

---

421   *Daily Telegraph*, 10 February 2015.

36

EYES TO THE EAST

'How are those posh boys?'
   – Chinese official Wang Qishan on Cameron and Osborne

Vladimir Putin's official summer retreat is a forbidding-looking place perched on a mountainside overlooking the Black Sea. With twenty bedrooms, two swimming pools, a tennis court and a helipad, the 'dacha' in Sochi may sound luxurious, but inside it is said to be curiously bleak, trapped in the Stalinist style in which it was built. Like generations of Russian presidents before him, Putin still makes a show of periodically using it as a backdrop for meetings with foreign dignitaries and PR stunts. How comfortable Western leaders feel standing shoulder to shoulder with him within the dacha's gloomy confines is another question: the atmosphere hardly lends itself to levity. Little wonder that the Russian President is rumoured to be building something far more fabulous in the same balmy part of southern Russia: a spectacular US$1 billion palace to rival the splendid residences of the Russian tsars. Pictures taken from the air and distributed by Russian opposition activists reveal an eye-popping property with stunning formal gardens, parks, fountains, helipads and even a small 'village' for staff.

When the Russian President heads to Sochi, his entire court accompanies him, taking a two-and-a-half-hour flight from Moscow to the seaside resort. While he is ensconced at the dacha, his people take up residence in a five-star hotel in central Sochi called the Rodina (meaning 'Motherland').

Late one night in May 2015, we were invited to the Rodina for a clandestine meeting with 'sources close to Putin' to discuss Cameron. It came some nine months after we first approached the Kremlin asking to talk about their perceptions of the Prime Minister. Our request prompted long and complicated negotiations. At one point, a mysterious figure who gave her name as 'Marina' made an unscheduled visit to our offices near the House of Commons. Finding neither of us available, she left a mobile number but never returned calls. It was a long, drawn-out and frustrating process, and we had almost given up when, out of the blue, we received a communication that 'they' were ready to talk on condition we would not reveal the identity of the very high-level source making himself available. Once this senior figure had agreed to cooperate, others fell into line, and we also received an invitation to the Russian Duma in Moscow, the equivalent of the House of Commons.

On the appointed date, we were summoned to the Rodina well after nightfall. Security was tight: the hotel had been sealed off, and our names were checked off a list by an armed guard at the gate. In the hotel grounds, shadowy figures lurked in the bushes, patrolling the perimeter. Inside, it was eerily quiet. One or two hotel staff stood on ceremony, but there were no guests in sight. The sleek, modern lobby, lined with glass cabinets displaying jewel-encrusted sunglasses and exquisite Fabergé eggs, was deserted.

It was 9 p.m. We sat on plush armchairs round a long, low coffee table and waited. An expressionless waitress served us mint tea and tiny macaroons and silently melted away. Suddenly there was a faint murmur of voices in the distance, then brisk footsteps heading in our direction, and our source appeared: alone, smiling broadly, reassuringly friendly in the strange, hollow space. He spoke excellent English. Did we want dinner? After a long and exhausting day, he had finally finished all his meetings and could relax. He came well briefed: Downing Street was advising against cooperating with this biography, he observed. Nonetheless he was happy to share his thoughts, as long as the terms were clear. After a few formalities and assurances, we began, though he remained guarded throughout.

His caution was no surprise: throughout Cameron's premiership, Britain's relationship with Russia was in the diplomatic deep freeze. The rift began four years earlier with the murder of Alexander Litvinenko, a fugitive officer of the Russian FSB secret service who suffered a lingering death in a London hospital in 2006 after being poisoned in what has been described as a 'miniature nuclear attack' in a Piccadilly sushi bar. When Moscow refused to extradite the prime suspect (a Russian government security agent called Andrey Lugovoi) to Britain, diplomatic relations all but collapsed.

ABOVE: Trying to get huskies to pose for pictures on a glacier in Norway. The iconic image of the new Tory leader 'hugging' the dogs, which came to symbolise his modernisation programme, came about by accident.

Admiring a special-breed pig in his constituency. According to the journalist Lesley White, he has a special way with pigs, though lurid tales of an initiation ceremony involving a dead hog's head at an Oxford University dining society could not be substantiated.

ABOVE: Cameron meets a factory worker in Rwanda, summer 2007. On the same trip, two of his colleagues, Steve Hilton and Andrew Mitchell, almost came to blows.

RIGHT: A hooded teenager makes a gun gesture behind Cameron's back as he tours a deprived estate in Manchester in 2007. Cameron's 'hug a hoodie' speech the previous year was widely mocked.

ABOVE: Playing shopkeeper with staff at Abdullah Rehman's shop in Balsall Heath, a deprived area of Birmingham, in 2007. It was the birthplace of the Big Society.

RIGHT: Reduced to tears listening to former drug addicts at the Ley Community in Witney tell how they conquered their demons. It was 2006, and a close relative had a desperate drug problem.

With one of his most powerful allies, Rebekah Wade, then editor of *The Sun*, at her fiancé's book launch, April 2009. She and Charlie Brooks married that summer. Cameron severed ties with the pair when they were arrested over phone-hacking allegations, but his brother Alex proved a steadfast friend.

Cameron's old friend and fellow Old Etonian Dom Loehnis. Cameron was best man at his wedding.

ABOVE: A tender moment with his disabled son Ivan. Cameron has said his 'world stopped' when Ivan died very suddenly in 2009.

LEFT: An unbearably poignant image of the Camerons arriving for Ivan's funeral at St Nicholas Church in Chadlington in March 2009. They asked mourners not to wear black.

LEFT: Feet up on the beach at Harlyn Bay, Cornwall, in July 2008. Boris Johnson had won the London Mayoralty; Gordon Brown's premiership was in turmoil after the 'election that never was'; Cameron was ahead in the polls and could afford to relax.

RIGHT: Doing the beach towel shuffle in Cornwall, July 2008. It was ungainly, but a picture of him looking sunburned and portly as he struggled to change out of his trunks under a Mickey Mouse towel in August 2013 was far worse.

Party donor Peter Cruddas, who quietly propped up a string of Cameron's pet projects when the Tories were in opposition. When a newspaper accused Cruddas of behaving improperly as party treasurer, Cameron did not repay his generosity. Cruddas later won a libel case.

Cameron with Tom Goff, one of his oldest and closest friends. They talk over the phone most weeks. He has said Goff (centre), a bloodstock agent, gives him 'very frank views', like 'a sort of taxi driver'.

Cameron with his discreet and dependable chief of staff Ed Llewellyn (middle) and Cabinet Secretary Jeremy Heywood. Bruce Anderson recalls Cameron being 'in awe' of Heywood when they both worked at the Treasury in the early 1990s.

Andy Coulson with Steve Hilton at the launch of the party's 2010 election manifesto. A 'dog-loyal' Cameron stuck by his 'brilliant' director of communications for a long period before Coulson was forced to quit Downing Street over allegations of phone hacking in January 2011.

Cameron's constituency home in Dean. He likes to spend as many weekends as possible there with his family.

Cameron in his kitchen in Dean. He and Samantha were dismayed by the original decor in their Downing Street flat, and spent tens of thousands of pounds modernising the accommodation.

With his fourth child, Florence Rose Endellion, who arrived three weeks early in August 2010 while the Camerons were on holiday. Her unusual third name is after a Cornish village, St Endellion.

Cameron and Clegg hold their first joint press conference in the Downing Street rose garden, 12 May 2010. Less than three weeks later, a Liberal Democrat Cabinet minister, David Laws, was forced to resign.

ABOVE: Off duty and hanging out with the Chipping Norton set in autumn 2011: Cameron with daughter Florence, former Blur bassist Alex James (right) and former *Top Gear* presenter Jeremy Clarkson, at a food and music festival in Kingham, Oxfordshire.

LEFT: Having a quick nap, red box at his feet, before the wedding of his sister-in-law Alice Sheffield in September 2013. The image, taken by Emily Sheffield, was posted on Instagram.

LEFT: Cameron battling not to come a cropper as he tackles the Great Brook Run, an annual fundraising event in his Witney constituency, with co-author Isabel Oakeshott in hot pursuit. December 2014.

Marching towards election victory – though they didn't know it.

Left to right: Cameron's old friend Andrew Feldman; election strategist Lynton Crosby; American political adviser Jim Messina; and Grant Shapps, then co-chairman of the party, at Tory conference in autumn 2014.

BELOW: Cameron, George Osborne and Steve Hilton in 2015. In Downing Street, Hilton and Osborne found themselves competing for Cameron's ear. Exasperated by the realities of government, Hilton left No. 10 in spring 2012.

Cameron with Scotland's then First Minister Alex Salmond at a ceremony for the armed forces in Edinburgh, June 2011. Three years later, Scotland appeared to be on the brink of voting for independence, a spectre that terrified Cameron.

LEFT: Cameron on the 2015 election campaign trail with Boris Johnson. Friends say Johnson privately thinks he is the cleverer of the two, while Cameron envies Johnson's popular appeal.

BELOW: A sombre image of Cameron with the two other party leaders, attending Holocaust Memorial Day in January 2015. A few months later, only Cameron would remain a party leader.

Matters deteriorated further in 2014 when Putin outraged the international community by annexing part of Ukraine. Cameron continued to be one of his most outspoken critics, accusing him of 'ripping up the international rule book', and warning of 'dreadful' consequences if the West turned a blind eye.

The Prime Minister's strong stance played well with British voters: few in this country believe Putin should be given any quarter. Naturally, it had the opposite effect in Russia: we didn't need a high-level Kremlin source to tell us he was not popular. Our source's long diatribe about Litvinenko, based on the usual disavowal of any link between the Kremlin and the agent's demise, is not worth repeating. Nor is his dubious justification for events in Ukraine. Suffice to say that Putin regarded Cameron's interventions on the matter as less constructive than those of other European leaders, who were similarly critical but who, Putin thinks, have 'brought more to the table'.

'Cameron has tried to present Britain as a country playing a role, but he has come up with no initiative; nothing,' according to the source.

His spin is that economic sanctions have been 'very good' for Russia, forcing it to develop home-grown industries. If they are lifted too quickly, he says, it will be very bad for the country, pushing these embryonic companies out of business. 'Ideal would be another couple of years,' he claims airily.

Of course, this should be taken with a heavy pinch of salt, but doubtless there is a grain of truth in it. He gave various examples of products, including helicopter components, that Russia used to import but can now make herself. What it boils down to is that Russia could not give two hoots for what Cameron said or did.

Cameron set his direction of travel with Russia early in his leadership, when he labelled it a 'dangerous bully' over military action in the disputed region of South Ossetia in Georgia. His rhetoric was far stronger than Brown's, though as opposition leader, he was less constrained. In a particularly provocative move, he accepted an invitation from the Georgian President to visit the country, further endearing himself to Georgians by calling for Russian tourists to be banned from visiting Britain. ('Russian armies can't march into other countries while Russian shoppers carry on marching into Selfridges,' he declared.[422] At the time, Max Hastings described aspects of his bold

422   *The Observer*, 17 August 2008.

approach as 'folly', while the *New Statesman* accused him of 'blustering and sabre-rattling', and casting himself as the 'heir to Blair'.[423]

'In his response to the crisis in Georgia, he has shown himself to have inherited the worst of the former Prime Minister's characteristics: a tendency to see the world simplistically, in terms of only the righteous and the wronged,' it said. No doubt Cameron calculated that most British voters took a dim view of Russia's aggressive expansionism, whatever the intelligentsia thought.

Once Cameron became Prime Minister, he attempted to re-set relations with Russia – to no avail. In the first visit by a British Prime Minister since Litvinenko's murder, in September 2011 he flew to Moscow for meetings with the then president Dmitry Medvedev as well as with Putin himself. He presented the trip primarily as an opportunity for trade, taking a planeload of British executives with him, from manufacturing, oil and pharmaceutical companies. The expedition came under fire: human rights activists complained he was putting commerce before justice, while Russia's Foreign Minister tried to warn him off raising the Litvinenko case. Under pressure from four former foreign secretaries (David Miliband, Jack Straw, Margaret Beckett and Sir Malcolm Rifkind) not to duck the issue, Cameron went ahead and mentioned it during a speech to Russian students, reversing any diplomatic gains. A top Kremlin aide swiftly briefed a Russian newspaper that there would be no thawing of relations. Looking back, the Russians believe the entire trip was counterproductive.

'There was no chemistry,' our source recalls, of the Prime Minister's interactions with Putin. He explains that this would not have mattered per se, because Putin is a highly pragmatic leader who does not feel the need to 'click' with foreign statesmen in order to do business. But the President apparently felt Cameron was slippery: he would not give a straight answer to a straight question; he appeared to be more focused on pleasing his domestic audience than on making genuine diplomatic progress; and to make matters worse, his facial expressions did not seem to match his true feelings.

'He is a charming guy! Always very polite; he has very refined manners,' the source says, choosing his words carefully. 'But it is better not to smile when you do not mean it.'

Wouldn't another British Prime Minister have handled the situation in much the same way?

---

423 Max Hastings, *The Guardian*, 18 August 2008; 'A Prime Opportunity to Pick Apart Tory Rhetoric', *New Statesman*, 8 September 2008.

'Blair was more direct with Putin when they spoke business,' the source says. 'The atmosphere was no easier at that time – it was the era of criticism over Chechnya, freedom of the press and so on. In public, Blair would make quite harsh statements, but meetings with him were constructive nonetheless.' He has little to say about Brown, dismissing him with a wave of the hand as a 'domestic' premier.

Asked how Cameron was perceived relative to other European leaders who adopted a hostile stance on Ukraine, our source says that Putin has the greatest respect for German Chancellor Angela Merkel – even though he rarely shares her point of view.

'She has a unique understanding of Russia; there is no contest with any other European leader,' he says admiringly.

More surprisingly, he adds that there was greater admiration for François Hollande than there was for Cameron, because the French President's foreign policy was considered more distinctive from that of the United States. The source says that the Kremlin now regards Britain as little more than a 'state department' of America, an impression enhanced by Cameron's handling of Syria.

'For reasons we cannot understand, Britain seems to have abandoned its sovereign foreign policy,' the source says. 'You just [follow] America. Sometimes you are not a good pupil; you try to run faster than your teacher. But essentially you go with America. At least Hollande has his own foreign policy.'

But there was something else he wanted to get off his chest: Cameron's attitude to homosexuality. In September 2013, Putin was taken aback when Cameron confronted him about a Russian law banning the promotion of homosexuality to children, similar to Britain's now defunct Section 28. The source revealed details of a bizarre exchange between Putin and the Prime Minister at 3 a.m., at a meeting of the G20 in St Petersburg, during which Cameron voiced his concerns about the abuse of gay people in Russia. His intervention was prompted by calls for an international boycott of the Winter Olympics, due to take place in Sochi in 2014, over the issue.

Putin pointed out that the legislation is backed by most Russians and told him – in terms – to mind his own business.

'We have lots of gays here,' the Russian President told Cameron gravely.

'But you ban them!' Cameron retorted. 'You violate gay rights.'

'I have got gay friends,' Putin protested.

> We have gay government ministers in this country; gay celebrities. They come to me, and I help them. But I am against their propaganda. If you polled this in Russia, you would find 85 per cent of people against it. You have to listen to what the people want, and respect it.

According to the source, Cameron's direct approach on this issue was highly unusual: he says Western leaders typically issue press releases to their domestic media claiming they have raised human rights issues during bilateral meetings with the Russian President, when they have not in fact done so. Many British voters will admire him for sticking his neck out. However, he may have underestimated the long-term diplomatic damage. When we met a high-profile political figure at the Duma the following day, it was among the first issues he raised. During a wider discussion about Cameron's foreign policy, this second source, who has an exceptional grasp of international relations as well as extensive diplomatic experience, argued that Cameron 'lacks a foreign policy personality', likening Britain to 'a Baltic state'.

'Even Hollande tries to be a bit different from the mainstream. But Cameron? Just singing in the choir,' he snorts.

> We have lost interest in Britain. At the end of the day, they just follow Washington. There is no separate relationship between Russia and Britain – there's always a third person in the bed. Britain's impact on Russia is nil. Of course we knew Britain would have a very strong reaction to events in Ukraine, but we don't care. It's like when you do something and you know your wife is going to go crazy, but you don't care any more, because you know it's over.

Should Cameron have handled relations with Russia any differently? It is hard to see what Britain would have to gain from a softer stance. As he put it himself:

> The instability we will yield if we don't stand up to Russia in the long term will be deeply damaging to all of us, because you will see further destabilisation – next it will be Moldova or one of the Baltic States. That…will be dreadful for our economies, dreadful for our stability – and that's why Britain takes such a clear view.[424]

---

424   Mail Online, 24 February 2015.

That Moscow doesn't think much of him is probably to his credit. Yet senior military figures are less sure about his positioning. Some feel that his approach to Putin was excessively confrontational, and that a more sophisticated and pragmatic stance would have had longer-term benefits.

What of his dealings with China? They were marked by less direct confrontation than with Russia, but were far from easy. He wound them up by meeting the Dalai Lama, took every opportunity to needle them about human rights, and once caused offence by refusing to do a photocall with the Chinese premier Li Keqiang in a pub. According to a government source involved in Keqiang's official visit to London in 2014:

> The Chinese premier wanted to go off to a country pub with David, but the message came from No. 10 that he wouldn't go off in the middle of the week to a country pub. The Chinese said, 'Well, let's go to a London pub' – but they refused that too. I can't believe he's never been photographed in a pub during the week. I mean, the Chinese did want him doing some softer stuff for the cameras…and he didn't…

An eminent British businessman claimed that Wang Qishan, a senior leader of the Communist Party and member of the seven-man Politburo Standing Committee, referred to the Prime Minister and the Chancellor – without hostility – as 'those posh boys'.

'He'll say, "How are those posh boys?" because Cameron went to Eton…They're rather intrigued by them, actually. They're certainly intrigued by the British. We've got enormous strength…soft power…we've got a lot going for us. And I think Cameron understands that,' he says.

The same government source who related the pub incident believes the Chinese were more impressed by Osborne.

'They like George and they don't particularly like David,' he says. 'It helps that George actually backpacked around China as a student, spoke a bit of Mandarin, and doesn't have to speak about human rights.'

Beyond such hearsay, it's anyone's guess. The Communist Party of China is virtually impenetrable to outsiders, and authoritative sources are thin on the ground. The general impression of MPs, peers and business figures who have a special interest in the People's Republic and some formal or informal access to President Xi Jinping's outer circle is that Cameron is neither particularly liked nor disliked, but – as in Russia – commands less respect than Merkel.

Tim Yeo, former MP for South Suffolk, who has business interests in China and has travelled there regularly in the last decade, says:

> Angela Merkel has definitely stolen the march in China. Germany is way ahead of us there. The Germans have made a huge effort. Merkel has been there many, many times, while David's only been there twice since he's been Prime Minister. She sends her top team out there all the time. German exports to China are nearly six times greater than the UK, yet the German economy is only about one and a half times bigger than ours. I think David Cameron could have prioritised this if he'd chosen to. It's not too late, but we are slightly behind now.

He believes Cameron's approach to China's abysmal human rights record was misguided.

> He will talk about human rights, because he genuinely believes it, but I think he should treat this on a pragmatic basis. The way to get China to change some of its repressive internal policies is to just try and liberalise the whole place, not just a lecture about human rights. He could have managed the situation in a different way. I think he allowed the idealism of some of the human rights groups here, to say, 'Oh, you must go and protest about that.' His first visit was in November 2010, and I was there. I said to the Foreign Office, 'What are going to be the main issues he raises?' And they said, 'Human rights.' For goodness sake, raise trade, liberalise the stock exchange…but that? I think he's got round to that thinking now. Business people have started to say to him, that's what you need to do.

Not everyone agreed that Cameron's tough stance with China on human rights affected trade.

'I just don't believe that the only way you can do business with China is by kow-towing whenever a difficult political issue comes up,' says Lord Patten, former Governor of Hong Kong.

I mean, do the Germans sell as much to China because Angela Merkel doesn't see the Dalai Lama? No. The Chinese buy from the Germans because they want Volkswagen cars. The Chinese have a huge surplus with us, they invest a lot here, but that's because they think they'll make a lot of money here. So I think the idea that if we said boo to a goose over, for example, Hong Kong, the Chinese would have stopped doing business with us, is madness! When I was Governor of Hong Kong, we had huge rows with China, and I think I'm right in saying exports to China doubled.

Cameron knew that while politicians posture, business rolls on, which allowed him to continue preaching from the human rights gospel, as he believed he should.

37
THE SCORPION AND THE TURTLE

'I don't know why I'm doing this. I hate journalists, I hate all journalists.'

– Oliver Letwin

In December 2014, David Cameron accepted an invitation that led to an awkward encounter.

The event was a carol service and the host was his Cotswold neighbour, multi-millionaire property tycoon Tony Gallagher, who has a private chapel attached to his stately home near Chipping Norton.

In the flickering candlelight, the Tory leader may not immediately have noticed his one-time friend and confidante Rebekah Brooks, the former CEO of News International, sitting quietly in one of the pews with her husband Charlie. Her trademark tumbling red hair was tucked under a hat, and her head was bowed.

Though virtually neighbours, Cameron and Brooks had taken pains to avoid crossing paths in the three years since her arrest for alleged corruption and phone hacking in July 2011. Now they were just a few feet apart at an intimate gathering, and their host ensured they could not pretend otherwise. Wrapping up the service, he offered an unusual benediction.

'Let us give thanks that Rebekah and Charlie are with us this evening,' he declared. He did not need to spell out where else the couple might have been: behind bars.

Neither Cameron nor Brooks knew how to react. Embarrassed, she turned and half smiled at the Prime Minister, shrugging and raising her palms heavenward.

The phone-hacking affair was the most serious crisis of Cameron's leadership, culminating in the imprisonment of his former communications chief Andy Coulson and criminal charges against two of his close friends. The decisions he made at the height of the furore triggered a year-long legal inquiry which turned former allies into enemies; exposed uncomfortable details of his dealings with the media; and was a hugely time-consuming distraction for himself and a string of senior aides and ministerial colleagues. It raised serious questions over his judgement and was a gift to Ed Miliband, providing the Labour leader with an unprecedented opportunity to grandstand about 'vested interests'. It was also a source of acute personal embarrassment, detonating a bomb under the Chipping Norton set. Though attention focused on the shattering of his relationship with Rebekah, there was another player in the drama, whose role was kept under wraps. It was Cameron's brother Alex.

Andy Coulson had never planned to go into Downing Street. News International's attempt to characterise Clive Goodman as a 'rogue reporter' had failed to kill off the phone-hacking story, and throughout 2009 and 2010, rumblings of further criminality at the *News of the World* during his editorship were becoming harder to ignore. Privately, he knew that by accepting a role at No. 10 he would be fanning the flames.

However, Cameron had come to rely on his clever director of communications. Convinced Coulson had known nothing of phone hacking (and presumably unaware that Coulson and Brooks had been lovers), the Prime Minister ignored at least three high-level warnings about bringing him into government. Among those who privately counselled against the move were *Daily Mail* boss Paul Dacre, who said it was 'storing up trouble', former *Evening Standard* editor Max Hastings, and his old family friend Nicholas Soames.

Soames says, 'I did make my views very strongly known about the employment of Coulson. I expressed it very strongly that, firstly, you can employ him as Leader of the Opposition, but you can't employ him in No. 10. I made my feelings known both verbally and in writing.'

His warnings fell on deaf ears.

'David is dog loyal! Dog loyal! And that's great. I mean, for heaven's sake, it is his decision, and I think he and George both decided that Andy Coulson would be the best person,' Soames says now.

And actually, they were absolutely right – he was the best person. It's never been as good since. He was brilliant at it. But I'm afraid – I never met him, though I'm told he was very nice; I'm sure lots of people are nice to their dogs and cats – he should not have been given that job.

In the early days of the coalition, few in No. 10 took the phone-hacking saga seriously, even after the *New York Times* published a long article in September 2010 accusing Coulson of having known about the practice.

'Coulson would occasionally make jokes about it,' a former aide reveals. 'I remember Andy, Henry [Macrory] and people joking a bit about [the article],' recalls the aide. '"Oh, it's another one of these ones and no one's going to care," they'd say.'[425]

Colleagues remained convinced that he was innocent.

'They really seemed to believe it, particularly in the earlier days of the coalition,' says Sean Kemp. 'There were conversations I had with Gabby [Bertin], in which she was utterly, utterly convinced Andy was telling the truth – and I don't think she would have been alone in that…He was very convincing when he denied it.'[426]

As further revelations of illegal activity inside the *News of the World* emerged in the second half of 2010 and in early 2011, Coulson himself remained good-humoured. When Henry Macrory asked him about a joke system he once introduced for fining aides who were accidentally caught on camera – 'When are the fines coming back in for being on the telly, Andy?' – Coulson replied, 'Can I just wait until my own difficulties are over? I don't want to bankrupt myself.'[427]

Yet the story would not go away. Just as Coulson had feared, Labour helped *The Guardian* keep the spotlight on his role. Under mounting political pressure, Coulson repeatedly offered to quit[428] but Cameron would not hear of it.

Finally, amid mounting evidence that phone hacking at the *News of the World* was widespread and that the editor 'must have known', on 21 January

---

425   Private information.
426   Private information.
427   Private information.
428   Francis Elliott and James Hanning, p. 454.

2011, Coulson left Downing Street, admitting that 'when the spokesman needs a spokesman' it was 'time to move on'. With characteristic 'dog loyalty', Cameron continued to defend him, claiming he was being 'punished twice for the same crime'.

The Guardian had got its scalp, but Coulson's departure was just the opening act in a drama that would dominate politics and the media for eighteen months. Brooks hoped to defuse the atmosphere of hysteria surrounding News International by engineering an industry-wide inquiry into standards in newspapers – a not unreasonable suggestion, given evidence that other tabloids, specifically the *Mirror*, were involved in similar practices.

A senior executive who works for a rival newspaper group recalls receiving a 'desperate' call from Brooks attempting to persuade him to sign up to the plan.

'Rebekah was desperate to have anything that would spread the *News of the World* virus into the whole of the rest of the industry,' he says. 'She said words to the effect of "Let's all get together and say we were all at it; we're going to take part in this Truth and Reconciliation Commission and we're going to put it all on the table so that we can move on."'[429]

The rest of the industry wanted nothing to do with it, but a head of steam was building. On 5 July 2011, *The Guardian* made the devastating claim that *News of the World* employees had hacked into the voicemail of murdered schoolgirl Milly Dowler. Suddenly, phone hacking was no longer about celebrities complaining about their privacy being invaded: it was about a feral media heartlessly exploiting victims of crime. The suggestion that somebody deliberately deleted the schoolgirl's messages, giving her parents false hope that she was still alive, made the charge even more grave. It did not matter that the claim subsequently turned out to be false: there was a public outcry. Terrified about what else might emerge, three days after the Dowler story broke, News International took the extraordinary decision to close the *News of the World*. The day after the paper closed, Coulson was arrested.

The demise of the famous tabloid came as a huge shock to the media and political establishment. However, secret talks about closing the paper had begun almost six months earlier, when senior executives at the company realised its troubles would not be limited to phone hacking and that it was likely to be embroiled in court cases over payments to public officials. It is

---

429   Private information.

understood that there were two serious discussions about shutting it down before the Dowler revelations.

Meanwhile Brooks, by now chief executive of News International, was still in post. To the outside world, it looked as if she was trying to cling on to her job. In fact, she had already tried to resign. She had assured Murdoch she knew nothing of the Dowler case, but nonetheless felt it would be best to step down. However, Murdoch wanted her to remain in post, arguing that the facts had yet to be established. News International still hoped to talk other newspaper titles into announcing an industry-wide investigation. Among those contacted by the company was Guy Black, executive director of the Telegraph Media Group, who was approached by Frédéric Michel, James Murdoch's chief UK lobbyist. When he resisted the proposal, Michel became aggressive.

'We've got to get the industry to agree to this tonight!' he shouted. Black saw no benefit.

As the police investigation into phone hacking gathered momentum, with 4,000 potential victims identified, calls for Brooks's resignation mounted. Amid the turmoil, she had every reason to hope that Cameron would do nothing to undermine her position. After all, they were close friends and she had gone out of the way to help him reach No. 10. Since the early days of his leadership, she had been more than generous with her contacts and advice, helping him meet the right people and be seen in the right places. In one example of the trouble she took, a colleague remembers her going to great lengths to secure him an invitation to a glittering party thrown by David and Victoria Beckham soon after he became leader. The event was their 'full-length and fabulous' pre-World Cup ball in the gardens of their mansion in Sawbridgeworth, and she was anxious that he be included.

> Rebekah decided Cameron had to be at the party because he needed
> to be seen rubbing shoulders with all the stars. She pulled out all the
> stops to persuade the Beckhams to invite him. From what I remem-
> ber, the Beckhams weren't very keen, and neither was he, but she is
> very persuasive, and so they all agreed. He later told someone that
> he only went because he didn't want to upset Rebekah.

In the run-up to 2010, Brooks had also done everything she could to throw News International's weight behind the Tory campaign. In countless ways, she had furthered Cameron's cause. Now she needed his support – or at least his silence.

Instead, he threw her to the wolves, declaring that if he were in charge of News International, he would have accepted her resignation. His betrayal left her devastated and was a turning point in the drama. On 15 July, she was bundled out of her office by security. It was a sensational and deeply humiliating fall from grace. Two days later, she was taken into police custody, marking the beginning of a long legal nightmare during which she lived with the constant threat of imprisonment and separation from her baby daughter. In the months and years that followed, she and her husband would find out who their real friends were.

Privately, Cameron would later admit that Miliband now had him 'on the run'.

Seizing the opportunity to exploit public hostility towards the Murdoch newspaper group, the then Labour leader broadened his attack to call for the withdrawal of a long-running and controversial bid by News International's parent company News Corporation to take control of British Sky Broadcasting (BSkyB.) This was a declaration of war: until then, phone hacking had not been a factor in the government's deliberations over whether the £8 billion bid should be given the go-ahead.

Day by day, Miliband was setting the agenda, while Cameron looked as if he was just responding to events. He desperately needed to regain the initiative, and Brooks's 'truth and reconciliation commission' seemed the ideal device.

On the back foot and 'still dancing to Rebekah's tune' (as one newspaper executive put it), on 13 July, he announced a turbo-charged version of her scheme. It would become known as the Leveson Inquiry. Its remit was to investigate the 'culture, practices and ethics of the press'.

'It's on my watch that the music has stopped,' Cameron admitted as he unveiled the plan, adding that the relationship between politicians and the media had become too close.

'I'm saying, loud and clear, things have got to change. The relationship needs to be different in the future.'

The inquiry, chaired by Lord Justice Leveson, was unprecedented and far more wide-ranging than anything the industry had anticipated. All newspapers and broadcasters would be dragged in, as would many senior politicians, including Cameron himself. Newspaper groups were horrified.

Guy Black remembers feeling 'physically sick' as he digested the announcement.

> I knew this was going to take two to three years, and poison the relations with government during the course of it. This was going to mean that all relations were put in the deep freeze, particularly the relationship with the centre-right press, *Daily Mail* and the *Daily Telegraph* – who were nothing to do with phone hacking. We were going to get dragged into this whole thing in a way that destroyed the good relationships that had been built up over the years with Cameron and senior people in Downing Street. I remember feeling very clearly that this was an appallingly rash and speedy decision which needn't have been taken.

Others, like former editor of *The Sun* Kelvin MacKenzie, were vocal in their disdain. In one of the most vitriolic and personal broadsides aimed at the PM at the time, he slammed the inquiry as 'ludicrous'.

'This is the way in which our Prime Minister is hopeful he can escape his own personal lack of judgement,' he raged. 'He knows, and Andy knows, that he should never have been hired into the heart of government. I don't blame Andy for taking the job. I do blame Cameron for offering it.'

The view in the media industry was that Cameron had panicked.

'It just suddenly happened, and he didn't talk to anyone else in the industry about it,' says a senior media figure involved in the inquiry.

> He didn't talk to me; he didn't talk to Paul Dacre; he didn't talk to any of the people who should have been his sort of friends, to say, 'What do I do?' He went completely into panic mode and announced this inquiry without any thought or consultation. There was certainly no attempt to speak to senior people in the industry; the basic courtesies just disappeared…There were all sorts of possibilities that were never looked at because of panic.[430]

---

430 Private information.

Sir Paul Stephenson, the Met Commissioner who stepped down at the height of the scandal, saw it as a desperate measure.

'It's that classic leadership trick, which a number of us pull when we are in deep difficulty, to say, "This is disgraceful and we must have an inquiry,"' he says. 'Have an inquiry and buy yourself time…I think they deliberately spread it wider to try and take the flak away from the decision to employ Coulson…I think there was a very strong agenda there to spread the heat around.'

Andrew Cooper concedes that Miliband had been driving the agenda. 'We felt a lot of political pressure,' he admits. 'We felt that Miliband really was ahead of the curve on all that.'

Amid all the furore, NewsCorp dropped its BSkyB bid – one less problem for the Prime Minister, at least.

※

Leveson began his inquiry on 14 November 2011. Its remit extended beyond newspapers to include broadcasters and social media, with more than fifty politicians, public figures and celebrities, including film star Hugh Grant and *Harry Potter* author J. K. Rowling, called as witnesses.

The intimacy between News International executives and politicians was laid bare in excruciating detail. In his appearance before the inquiry, Tony Blair admitted he had phoned Murdoch up to three times in one week in the run-up to the 2003 Iraq invasion, while Brooks revealed Blair was 'a constant presence' in her life 'for many years'.

Cameron's turn in the dock came on 14 June 2012, after months of pains-taking preparation with Andrew Feldman, who played the part of Robert Jay QC, the leading counsel for the inquiry. It was bound to be a humbling experience: by his own admission the previous year, Cameron had held twenty-six meetings with News International executives in fifteen months, at a time when the company had been focused on taking full ownership of BSkyB and phone-hacking allegations had been an open sore. It had recently emerged that Brooks went to his birthday party at Chequers and once lent him a horse called Raisa, which she herself had borrowed from the Metropolitan Police. In her own evidence to the inquiry, she embarrassed the Prime Minister by revealing that he occasionally signed texts to her 'LOL' until she gently informed him that the letters stood for 'laugh out loud' not 'lots of love'. All told, the list of parties, rendezvous and mutual backscratching that preceded Cameron into the courtroom was deeply unedifying.

In his five-and-a-half-hour testimony, the Tory leader was subjected to a thumbscrew interrogation by Jay. The exact number of times he had met Brooks socially; how often he had sought assurances about phone hacking from Coulson; the role he and his Culture Secretary Jeremy Hunt had played in decisions over BSkyB – all this was subject to meticulous and merciless examination. Cameron's performance was faltering and uncertain. He was visibly unsettled by the level of detail the inquiry wanted about aspects of his social life. Asked whether he saw Brooks every weekend in Oxfordshire, he replied cagily: 'I might be able to go back and check, but I don't think every weekend. I don't think most weekends. But it would depend...Charlie [Brooks] and I played tennis together and all sorts of other things.'

Far worse was a text Brooks had sent him in October 2009, on the eve of his party conference speech. It began by sympathising with the Prime Minister over an 'issue with *The Times*' – most likely a hostile article – and suggested she could placate him over 'country supper soon'. The message continued: 'As always Sam was wonderful (and I thought it was OE's that were charm personified!) I am so rooting for you tomorrow not just as proud friend but because professionally we're definitely in this together! Speech of your life? Yes, he Cam!'

It was toe-curling and raised uncomfortable questions about the nature of News International's support for the Conservatives in the run-up to 2010. Had the personal friendship between the Camerons and the Brookses influenced the editorial direction of one or more of the company's newspaper titles? And was there any understanding – explicit or implicit – about what News International might get in return for its support, specifically in relation to BSkyB?

Cameron's response to this last question was robust. Although he admitted the subject came up in conversation with Murdoch when they all had dinner together *chez* Brooks, he rubbished claims (made by Gordon Brown during his appearance before the inquiry) that anything untoward had occurred, dismissing the suggestion as 'an entirely specious and unjustified conspiracy theory', which was 'absolute nonsense from start to finish'. There were 'no overt deals, no covert deal, no nods and winks'. As Osborne had pointed out three days earlier, 'We had no idea that they wanted to bid for Sky before the general election.'

Leveson later agreed that there was no evidence of a secret deal. However, he was sharply critical of the 'particular kind of lobbying out of the public eye' between senior politicians and the press. The way Brooks talked about her relationship with Cameron fuelled suspicions of a stitch-up, even if the judge failed to uncover a paper trail. One industry insider claims she brandished a friendly text message from Cameron over dinner with colleagues from newspaper groups opposed to the bid, to illustrate the closeness of their relationship.

'The text said something like: "Looking forward to supper at the weekend. Love David xx". She then said words to the effect of: "I don't know why you are even bothering to run this campaign, because this is a done deal,"' he claims. 'That was typical of Rebekah's modus operandi and the way she conducted the whole Sky thing. As chief executive of that company, she had become chief lobbyist. Her job by that stage was entirely about lobbying. ' Brooks denies doing any such thing.

Leveson's long-awaited report, published in November 2012, put Cameron in a tight spot. The Tory leader had publicly pledged to implement the judge's recommendations unless they were 'bonkers', but it quickly became apparent that keeping his promise would set him on a collision course with an already hostile industry.

The controversy centred on the judge's call for a new press regulator with the power to fine newspapers up to £1 million. Crucially, Leveson wanted it to be 'underpinned by statute' and run by individuals with nothing to do with the press or government. To the media, it stank of state regulation, unseen in Britain since 1695. For Cameron, too, it crossed a line. It ran up against his instinctive liberalism on such matters and he knew the media would hate it. He rejected it out of hand.

'For the first time we would have crossed the Rubicon of writing elements of press regulation into the law of the land,' he told the Commons when the Leveson Report was unveiled. 'We should be wary of any legislation that has the potential to infringe free speech and a free press. In this House – which has been a bulwark of democracy for centuries – we should think very, very carefully before crossing that line.'

And so began a tortuous process of negotiation between political parties, the press, and the pressure group Hacked Off to find a middle way. In his first Downing Street meeting with editors from across the spectrum, Cameron made clear that – while accepting the bulk of Leveson's proposals – he would find a way to avoid a press law. '[But] he refused to tell anyone what it was,' Black says. 'Then he left the meeting in the hands of Oliver Letwin. It was Oliver's show…he kept everybody for half an hour or so, talking about this "source of unimpeachable integrity", which wouldn't involve statute. Everybody came away none the wiser.'

By his own admission, Letwin was an odd choice to conduct the negotiations. He had long been considered a hopeless liability in front of the media, and was effectively banned by Coulson from giving interviews. As talks with the industry dragged on, he made little secret of his frustration.

'I don't know why I'm doing this. I hate journalists, I hate all journalists,' he wailed at one point. It was a strange thing to admit to a room full of editors.

By mid-February, Letwin thought he had a solution. On the morning of 12 February 2013, Cameron convened a meeting of editors and proprietors to secure their backing for the plan: a new press watchdog established by royal charter.

'The Prime Minister seemed very pleased with the outcome, as were we,' recalls one who was at the meeting.

> He said, 'I fought hard to maintain the freedom of the press. Now I want you to get behind this document. We need to get out and make sure there's a proper consultation on it. You need to work hard on selling it.' He was challenged on what would happen if there was severe political opposition: was this really his final word, or were we going to be faced with a war of attrition? He said, 'The document – once it's published – is set in stone.' They were the words that everybody remembered. He said: 'You have my word – this is set in stone now.' We went away.[431]

Letwin's plan appeared to take the matter of press regulation out of the hands of Parliament while remaining faithful to the spirit of Leveson's proposal. It was a scheme many if not all in the industry felt they could support. So far from being 'set in stone', however, it soon transpired that it had no support from other parties. Editors had been sold a pup.

---

431 Private information.

'Letwin had insisted throughout that he was liaising with the other parties,' recalls one media figure involved in the process. 'We'd ask from time
to time, "Should we go see [deputy Labour leader Harriet] Harman? Should
we go see the Lib Dems…?" To which Letwin replied, "Don't worry, I've got
it all sorted, you would only complicate matters."'[432]

When the proposed scheme was published, it was immediately condemned
by Labour and the Lib Dems, who claimed it failed to honour the spirit
and letter of Leveson's recommendations. Once again, the process stalled.
Meanwhile Miliband and Clegg began working together to produce something
tougher. Exasperated with the whole saga, on 13 March 2013, Cameron
dramatically walked out of cross-party talks. 'This is all too important,' he
told one friend.

> Freedom of the press is in danger. I am going to go down fighting
> to protect a free press, and I want you with me over the course of
> the next few days, because this is all going to get very difficult. I
> am going to face them down and dare them to produce their own
> proposals on statutory controls.[433]

His bold words suggested he was preparing for a spectacular showdown
with Miliband and Clegg. Intrigued, editors waited for the big bust-up. It
never came. Following his theatrical announcement, Cameron suddenly went
'absolutely quiet, disappeared and we heard no more about it'.[434]

In the end, an alternative system was thrashed out under the supervision
of Hacked Off. Privately, Cameron presented the compromise reached on
18 March as a triumph for press freedom and claimed credit.

'I've just achieved a great victory for you,' he told one newspaper executive over the phone at the crack of dawn that morning. 'I've managed to get
some protection in place to ensure the code is still written by journalists.'

This was deeply misleading. What emerged on 18 March was – in the
eyes of the majority of the press – little more than a 'Hacked Off charter'.
It would involve an element of statute, or what Cameron called a 'relatively small legislative change'. Far from marking the end of the process,

---

432 Private information.
433 Private information.
434 Private information.

however, it triggered a new stand-off with editors, who threatened to boycott the new body.

After declaring – for the first time in his entire political career – that he was ready 'to go down fighting' on a principle, Cameron had given in.

Cameron's handling of the phone-hacking crisis exposed a characteristic weakness in his approach to the premiership. The decisions he made appeared to be driven by the need to 'get through the day' rather than by a consideration of long-term implications.

'I thought he got everything wrong,' says a key figure involved in the process.

> The way he set up Leveson was wrong. Frankly, putting Oliver Letwin in charge of anything is a terrible mistake. And then marching everyone to the top of the hill in March, saying it was all set in stone, was almost a disaster. And then backing this Hacked Off charter, which three days earlier he'd said he was willing to die in a ditch to avoid…[435]

The source trails off, still confused. He believes that the Tory leader's approach was always coloured by his need to offset his error of bringing Coulson into Downing Street.

'I think that embarrassment, and his obvious concern about the political downside of it all, has coloured every single decision he's made…which is, "I have to protect myself from people saying I'm too close to all these monsters." In those circumstances, rationality leaves you.'[436]

On 24 June 2014, Rebekah Brooks and her husband were dramatically cleared of all wrongdoing by a jury at the Old Bailey. It marked the end of a three-year ordeal, during which they lost their livelihoods, their reputations and some of their friends. Though they did not want for money, it was a desperate time, made all the worse because of their close social connection with the Camerons. From the moment they were arrested, the Prime Minister

---

435 Private information.
436 Private information.

deserted them, terrified of the political implications of being seen in their company. Samantha tried to soften the blow by sending conciliatory messages through intermediaries in Chipping Norton, but for a long period, Rebekah was deeply angry and upset.

By contrast, the Prime Minister's brother Alex proved steadfast. The relationship between the Prime Minister and Rebekah and Charlie Brooks attracted so much attention that nobody noticed the quiet figure between them. Of course, it was not in Alex Cameron's interests to shout about it. Free from political constraints, he refused to abandon his old friends. Risking acute embarrassment for the Prime Minister if his critics found out, the QC continued to see the couple throughout the long, drawn-out criminal proceedings against them, treating them as if nothing had changed. He and his wife even accompanied them on a foreign holiday while their trial was ongoing. Such is the closeness of the relationship that the Brookses consider him 'family'. Cameron 'Minor' is not in the same bracket.

Eventually, the Prime Minister would be back on speaking terms with Rebekah. But there would be no easy return to the cosy kitchen suppers and horse rides together. Though Samantha invited the couple to her much belated 40th birthday party at Chequers in December 2014, they did not feel it would be right to accept.

Torn apart by the phone-hacking saga and the divorce of several of its leading lights (Elisabeth Murdoch and Matthew Freud; Jeremy and Frances Clarkson) in 2014, the Chipping Norton set came up with an ironic new name for itself: the Upset. Things have never been the same, though there are signs that some rifts are healing. (From 2015, as their troubles eased, some started calling it the Re-Set.)

For all the hurt, Brooks understands why Cameron reacted as he did. She likes to tell friends a fable about a scorpion and a turtle, which she first heard from Peter Mandelson. The scorpion wants to cross a river, and asks the turtle for a ride. The turtle refuses, fearing he will be stung. The scorpion argues that stinging the turtle would not be in his interests, because they will both drown. So the turtle agrees to give him the ride. Halfway across the river, the scorpion stings the turtle. However good his intentions, he is conditioned to do so. They both go down. Politicians and scorpions have much in common, she feels.

38

BEACHY HEAD

'I'll be remembered for this till the day I die.'
– A panicked Cameron, fearing the collapse of the union

The night after David Cameron almost lost the United Kingdom, some of his oldest friends gathered for a reunion at Eton College.

Dressed in black tie, 150 old boys from the class of '84 stood on the steps of the school chapel for a formal photograph before trooping inside for a service of thanksgiving. As befits a school steeped in tradition, the choir sang in Latin and the alumni joined in prayers and hymns. The music was so beautiful and the atmosphere so nostalgic that some of those in the congregation – hedge fund millionaires, diplomats and captains of industry – struggled to contain their emotion.

It was Friday 19 September 2014, the day after the referendum on Scottish independence. In the run-up to the bash, rumours circulated that the Prime Minister would attend, at least for drinks before the sit-down dinner. His old classmate Chris Berthoud, who assumed Cameron would not show up and planned to give a speech with a few jokes at his expense, became increasingly worried it would have to be redrafted.

He need not have feared, for Cameron was in no state to attend parties – especially not at Eton. For the first time in his premiership, the Prime Minister had been so anxious about affairs of state that he had been losing sleep. In the run-up to the referendum, his usual sangfroid had deserted him as he contemplated what was at stake. If Scotland voted to break away, the removal vans would soon be trundling up Downing Street to help him move out. Worse, he would go down in history as the Prime Minister who presided over the break-up of Britain.

'Funnily enough, I think it was less "We're going to have to move out" than the fact that for the rest of his life that's what he would have done: he would be the Prime Minister who lost the United Kingdom,' says a confidant who knows his mind. 'He was saying, "I'll be remembered for this till the day I die."'[437]

Despite the calm reassurances of his pollster Andrew Cooper – who never wavered in his advice that Scots would reject independence – Cameron became so agitated in the final days before the vote that he gathered his team to make contingency plans in the event of a Yes vote. After a while they gave up: the implications were so overwhelming they did not know where to begin.

'They tried to draft a strategy for what they would do, what they would say the morning after the vote, who would come out and give a statement. They got about three paragraphs in and it was not clear it would work,' says the source.[438]

It was not just the Prime Minister who was suffering: in a sign of the extraordinary stress level in the Cameron household, in the run-up to 19 September, Samantha confided in friends that her hair was falling out.

Today, Scotland's political future remains deeply uncertain as the shock of the referendum continues to reverberate. Though the country voted to stay in the UK by a margin of 55/45 per cent, the result proved far less decisive than the figures suggest. In the aftermath of the referendum, the SNP enjoyed such a surge in support that independence was back on the agenda again. In the referendum on the European Union, Scotland voted overwhelmingly to remain, by a margin of 62/38, in contrast to the rest of the United Kingdom.[439] The SNP has argued that this will lead to Scotland being dragged out of the EU against its will. Party leader Nicola Sturgeon has made it clear that another referendum is very much on the cards. Polls that were supposed to settle the question for a generation have instead left continuing doubts over Scotland's destiny. Opinion over Cameron's role is split. Some observers regard what happened in Scotland as a symbol of his complacency. Others who are well placed to know the truth insist that he could not have done more.

How did the Tory leader come so close to presiding over the break-up of the United Kingdom, and to what extent was it his fault? Was the result a Pyrrhic victory, and if so, is he guilty of allowing the SNP to snatch victory from defeat?

---

437   Private information.
438   Private information.
439   Northern Ireland also voted to remain, albeit by a much narrower margin.

Cameron's Scotland is one of hunting lodges and grouse moors: long days stalking on Highland estates followed by long nights in candle-lit drawing rooms toasting the day's sporting successes by a roaring fire. He loves haggis and venison, trout fishing and bracing pre-breakfast dips in chilly burns or the Sound of Jura. He has been going to Scotland since he was a boy and feels deep affection for it. 'I am a believer in the union,' he told Dylan Jones in 2008. 'I wouldn't do anything to undermine it or put it at risk.' It is, after all, the home of his paternal ancestors: his great-great-great-grandfather Sir William Cameron came from Inverness-shire, and his great-grandfather had an impressive lodge in Aberdeenshire called Blairmore House.

But while he loved Scotland, the Scots did not feel the same about him. His roots might trace back to Clan Cameron, but with a 'posh' English accent and Eton and Oxford on his CV, he was never embraced north of the border. As a result, the campaign to save the union did not feature a starring role for him.

The cross-party team that was to become known as the Better Together campaign was formed in spring 2012 and held its inaugural meeting at Alistair Darling's house in Edinburgh. Over a delicious spread laid on by the former Chancellor's wife Maggie, they began attempting to thrash out a broad strategy for the long campaign ahead. The cast list included Labour's former International Development Secretary Douglas Alexander and former shadow Defence Secretary Jim Murphy, three Tories – Andrew Cooper; Andrew Dunlop, the PM's adviser on Scotland; and the director of the Scottish Conservatives Mark McInnes – and a handful of Lib Dems. But there were ominous signs from the start.

One who was there says:

> We sat round the kitchen table, with mugs of tea, and just sort of debated the lie of the land and how we thought the campaign should be pitched. Alistair chaired it, and it was my first sight of the fractiousness in Scottish Labour. Douglas kept intervening, talking at great lengths in very theoretical terms, and Jim Murphy would be sighing and rolling his eyes – and we were off![440]

---

440 Private information.

The simmering tensions between Alexander and Murphy, who had never seen eye to eye at Westminster but were flung together over Scotland because they were Labour's two most senior Scottish MPs, accounted for only a fraction of the rivalry and infighting inside the Better Together campaign. Over time, turf wars would break out between Murphy and the then Scottish Labour leader Johann Lamont, especially when Murphy embarked on a '100 towns in 100 days' tour armed with an Irn-Bru crate, on which he planned to stand to address passers-by. Then there was former Prime Minister Gordon Brown: ultimately a hero, but bad-tempered, uncooperative and harbouring a bitter grudge against Darling. During one particularly exasperating telephone exchange between Brown and Better Together campaign director Blair McDougall, the latter scrawled the word 'loon' on a piece of scrap paper and held it aloft to colleagues, who struggled to hide their mirth.[441] Throw in the Tories' toxic image in Scotland, the scope for Yes campaigners to set Labour and the Conservatives off against each other, and the fundamental challenge of selling any No campaign to voters as a positive message, and the scene was set for a turbulent ride.

Following the SNP's victory in the Holyrood elections of May 2011, it was clear that the SNP would demand a vote on the future of the union, and quickly. In fact, Cameron and Osborne had been privately toying with the idea of calling for one while they were in opposition. Both were attracted to the prospect of killing off Scottish nationalism for a generation. Osborne is said to have argued that they would always win so long as the middle-class Scots of the central belt remained opposed to independence.[442] They abandoned the idea in the face of staunch opposition from Gordon Brown and Labour. But in 2011, with Labour out of office in Westminster and the SNP sweeping into power in Holyrood, Cameron was inclined to seize the initiative.

'David Cameron, really from the off, understood that this was a question which would have to be answered,' according to a Tory source.[443]

In a fit of bravura, Cameron and Osborne initially considered taking a hard line with the SNP, which would have involved calling a referendum

---

441 Private information.
442 Severin Carrell, Nicholas Watt and Patrick Wintour, *The Guardian*, 15 December 2014.
443 Ibid.

themselves and controlling it from Westminster. The problem, as they and their advisers were all too aware, was the likelihood that it would backfire, playing into a narrative of 'English oppression' and bolstering the nationalists' sense of grievance.

And so, in January 2012, Cameron announced that he would offer Salmond the chance to stage his own referendum. It was a massive, unexpected concession, and it would not be the only one: he later allowed Salmond to choose the date of the poll, lower the voting age to sixteen, and propose the wording of the question.

He did have one big 'red line', however: it had to be a binary 'yes/no' question. He insisted that 'devo max' – an alternative just short of full independence – could not be on the ballot paper. Throughout the negotiations Cameron apparently believed Salmond would oppose this, and run the risk of allowing the talks to collapse. However, it has emerged since that the SNP had privately dropped plans for a multi-option ballot paper, but maintained otherwise for several months in order to extract concessions from Cameron. The result was a Holyrood-run referendum based on a question formulated by Salmond ('Should Scotland be an independent country?'), with a run-up of over two years, and with sixteen- to seventeen-year-olds (and EU and Commonwealth residents) entitled to vote. There were many inside the coalition unsure what Cameron could reasonably claim to have leveraged from Salmond in return.

With celebrity-backed fanfare in central Edinburgh, Salmond fired the starting gun of the Yes campaign on 25 May 2012. He delivered a rabble-rousing address in which he promised the 'biggest community-based campaign in Scotland's history', followed by speeches from actors Brian Cox and Alan Cumming and a message of support from Sir Sean Connery.

A month later, in a dreary lecture theatre at Napier University in Edinburgh, Alistair Darling launched the Better Together campaign. He was flanked by Scotland's unionist party leaders: Johann Lamont for Labour, Ruth Davidson for the Tories and the Lib Dem leader Willie Rennie. In contrast to Salmond's passionate appeal the previous month, Darling warned gloomily: 'If we decide to leave the United Kingdom there is no way back. It is like asking us to buy a one-way ticket to send our children to a deeply uncertain destination.' It was uninspiring and set the tone for months ahead.

For months, Better Together lacked momentum. Reassured by Cooper's private polling, Downing Street simply assumed Yes would win. Cameron kept in touch with what was happening but, according to insiders, he was content to let others get on with it.

His quiet confidence was misplaced. During those crucial early months, while the SNP juggernaut began gathering pace, the Better Together campaign was a mess. With polls continuing to show a steady and consistent margin opposed to independence, it was steeped in complacency.

'The campaign wasn't firing at all,' Cooper says now. 'It just drifted, and because of the personalities involved and because it was led by Labour, Downing Street hoped and assumed it would sort itself out. It was difficult for the Conservative side and for No. 10 to try to fix it.'

Cameron was sufficiently engaged – and concerned – to hold two face-to-face meetings with Darling in 2013, during which he urged the former Chancellor to make more use of Douglas Alexander behind the scenes.

'You can't do it all yourself,' he told Darling. 'You can't both front the campaign and run it.'

In a sign of the disarray, until as late as February 2014, Better Together had no 'war book' setting out the strategy that everybody should follow; nor any 'grid' in place plotting the course of the campaign. Cooper was exasperated.

Meanwhile Darling was struggling to stamp his authority on proceedings. At times the team could barely hold itself together, never mind protect the union. The former Chancellor – who privately admitted that he had never run a big campaign before and didn't know what he was doing – was persistently undermined by Brown and by an increasingly frustrated Douglas Alexander. The former International Development Secretary was among the first to grasp how vulnerable a position the campaign was in.

At a crisis meeting in January 2014, he erupted at colleagues. 'We've all been tiptoeing around this; we're all being so bloody polite to each other that at this rate we could lose this referendum!' he railed. 'We need to do something!'[444]

According to Cooper, the meeting ended in 'gridlock', with Alexander and Murphy still unable to agree an approach.

'We had an hour and a half for the meeting; Jim was twenty minutes late, and by [then] the time was up [and] we hadn't got anywhere. Alistair summed things up, saying, "That was incredibly helpful," but everyone else was thinking, "No, it wasn't!"' Cooper recalls.

---

444 Private information.

The handling of Better Together's advertising plans illustrated the dysfunction. Billboards could be powerful tools and were being used to great effect by the nationalists, but Darling's team had no idea what to put on theirs. The first agency they hired – without a proper pitch or brief – produced tens of thousands of pounds' worth of adverts that were never used. The second company, picked primarily because they were Scottish, created an advert based on the acclaimed American TV series *Breaking Bad* (about a chemistry teacher who launches a new career cooking methamphetamine), which was not only a copyright infringement but also bombed with focus groups: people either didn't get it or thought it was snide English insinuation that Scotland had a drugs problem. Another proposed advert showed a tiny figure at the edge of a giant cliff. It was junked for being bad taste: insiders pointed out that it looked like someone at Beachy Head.

Suddenly, with less than six months to go, the polls started to narrow.[445] For the first time, there was serious speculation in the media that Scotland might go its own way. Slowly, Cameron woke up to the potential for catastrophe. 'He and Osborne started to get uneasy,' says a No. 10 insider. 'When the polls started narrowing, the party leadership began taking notice.'[446] According to Cooper, the PM's 'gut instinct' remained that when it came to the crunch, Scottish voters would baulk at separation. But he recognised that there was a world of difference between a 61/39 result against independence and a 54/46 outcome. The latter would have been a damning indictment of his leadership and would be so dangerously close as to keep the issue on the agenda for another generation. As 2014 progressed, Cameron began requesting increasingly frequent updates from his pollster.

In a private note, Cooper warned him that the Better Together campaign was foundering. Nonetheless, he had a plan: his secret polling had made it clear for months that the key constituency for Better Together to win over was what he called the 'comfortable pragmatists' and 'uncommitted security seekers' – groups of undecided voters who wouldn't be persuaded by an emotional appeal to the union. What was needed, Cooper realised, was a negative campaign relentlessly warning of the dangers of separation.

---

445   http://www.bbc.co.uk/news/events/scotland-decides/poll-tracker.
446   Private information.

What followed was a co-ordinated attempt by the Treasury and the Bank of England to ramp up the economic risks of an independent Scotland by ruling out a currency union. This was arguably the single biggest Westminster intervention of the whole campaign.

First, in late January 2014, Mark Carney, the Bank's governor, delivered a speech in which he suggested, albeit ambiguously, that Scotland would not be able to share the pound. This was almost certainly prompted by an 'off-line' discussion with Osborne, who was increasingly concerned. Privately, Carney himself was beginning to worry about a run on the banks if Scotland went its own way. Though he was careful not to show it, friends say he was frustrated by Cameron's low-key approach. Insiders say he felt the Prime Minister could be more proactive in the fight to save the union. In the event, his carefully chosen words backfired, playing directly into Salmond's hands. The SNP leader spun the governor's dry, technocratic warnings to the Yes campaign's favour, interpreting them as confirmation that the Bank would cooperate with the Scots to make a currency union work. 'Salmond massively won that one,' a Better Together insider admits.[447]

The following month, Osborne travelled to Edinburgh to make his own set-piece speech. Backed by Ed Balls and Danny Alexander – ensuring it was a cross-party message as well as a Treasury statement – he warned: 'If Scotland walks away from the UK, it walks away from the pound.'

It was a huge gamble: to some it looked like London bullying Scotland, and Salmond did his best to exploit that sentiment. Polls in the following months suggested a boost for the Yes camp. With hindsight, however, it looks like it was a good call. Even Nicola Sturgeon, now Scotland's First Minister, has admitted that the SNP failed to outflank the early intervention on the currency and that ultimately the referendum was lost because the nationalists failed to allay people's fears about the economic dangers of independence.[448]

In early summer 2014, Cameron met Darling to discuss the state of the campaign. The former Chancellor expressed concern that whenever Cameron visited Scotland, he would fly in and out on the same day. 'There's a risk you'll be seen as a day tripper,' he warned. Next time Cameron went to

447 Private information.
448 Severin Carrell, Nicholas Watt and Patrick Wintour, op. cit.

Scotland, he made a point of staying the night and appearing on *Good Morning Scotland* the next day to prove it.

But it remained obvious to Better Together that most of the heavy lifting could only be done by Labour. The Tories were just too unpopular in Scotland. This meant that the TV debates, scheduled for early August 2014, would have to be between Salmond and Darling. Cameron could not take part, although he was keen to do so.

In preparation for the TV debates, Darling subjected himself to hours of torturous abuse at the hands of Paul Sinclair, Scottish Labour's communications chief, who took on the role of Alex Salmond impersonator behind the scenes. Sinclair anticipated the SNP leader's likely line of attack: ruthless putdowns and relentless personal insults. 'He could cheer up a room simply by leaving it,' Sinclair sniped at one point, leaving a temporarily shaken Darling to reply with a good-humoured shrug, 'What do I say in reply to that?!'[449]

The bruising preparation paid off: Darling won the first round. Salmond appeared uncharacteristically nervous, and his famous repartee seemed blunter than usual. By contrast, Darling was fired up and passionate, delivering a point-by-point demolition of the nationalists' economic case. In one particularly memorable moment, he turned on the SNP leader with a brilliant ad lib that skewered the currency question in a way that delighted the media.

'Any eight-year-old can tell you the flag of a country, the capital of a country and its currency,' Darling said. 'I presume the flag is the Saltire, I assume our capital will still be Edinburgh, but you can't tell us what currency we will have. What is an eight-year-old going to make of that?'

For the next week, the debate was all about the pound. Rattled, the Yes campaign hit back hard in the final weeks of August, embarking on an intense and aggressive ground war focusing relentlessly on the NHS. Buoyed by private polling suggesting Scottish fears of Tory privatisation of the NHS could turn tens of thousands of pro-UK voters into supporters of independence, Salmond declared: 'The Tories' privatisation drive will end Scotland's NHS as we know it.' The only solution, he argued, was to vote Yes. This, coupled with the SNP's strategy of portraying Darling as 'in bed with' the Tories, was toxic for the No campaign: the second TV debate, on 25 August, was a triumph for Salmond.

With polls putting the rival campaigns within a whisker of each other, in the final three weeks of the campaign, Better Together descended into panic.

---

449   Ben Riley-Smith, *Daily Telegraph*, 27 December 2014.

A *Times* poll published on 2 September had the No camp's lead shrinking from fourteen points to six in under a month. That weekend, the *Sunday Times* had something even more shocking in store. With just eleven days to go, YouGov put Yes in the lead, by 51 per cent to 49 per cent (excluding 'Don't Knows'). Spooked, the Cabinet Office secretly commissioned more than £537,000 worth of polling from Ipsos MORI. It confirmed what the other polls were now saying: it was too close to call.[450]

Cameron was with the Queen for his annual late summer weekend at Balmoral when the *Sunday Times* poll came out. The atmosphere over breakfast on Sunday morning was strained as the Queen noted the headline splashed across the paper's front page: 'Yes vote leads in Scots poll'.

For the first time in his career, Cameron's equilibrium deserted him. How would he be able to tell the Queen that he had managed to go one further than Lord North, who lost the North American colonies, and lost the United Kingdom itself? The enormity of it all overwhelmed him.

'One of his normal characteristics is the ability to stay completely calm when everyone is panicking. This is one of the few times he didn't do that,' says a friend.

Heading back from Balmoral on the Sunday night, he telephoned Cooper from his car.

'He was very worried,' Cooper admits. 'It was the first time he was seriously contemplating, "Shit, we might lose."'

In the 45-minute conversation that followed, Cooper continued to say what he had always said: it would all be fine. Cameron remained on edge. 'His question to me was, "Is there anything else that I can or should do?"' Cooper recalls.

The Queen too was deeply troubled. Inside Whitehall, talk turned to the possibility of the monarch somehow speaking out against independence while remaining within the constitutional boundaries of neutrality. Sir Jeremy Heywood, the Cabinet Secretary, and Sir Christopher Geidt, the Queen's private secretary, held secret discussions to work out how she might express her concerns in a suitably coded way. The result was a remark overheard after a Sunday service in Crathie Kirk, the small church the royals attend when staying at Balmoral.

---

450 Severin Carrell, Nicholas Watt and Patrick Wintour, *The Guardian*, 16 December 2014.

'I hope people will think very carefully about the future,' she was reported to have said, to the delight of the No camp. The carefully chosen words were no accident, Whitehall sources later admitted. It was a deliberate, last-minute, intervention – and it left no one in any doubt which side she was on.[451]

However, the decisive intervention came from Brown. While he had been involved in Better Together behind the scenes for several months, he had not proven an asset. Grumpy, aloof and divisive, he had contented himself, in the words of one insider, with 'just throwing grenades at the campaign'.[452] He was never seen in the offices of Better Together and flatly refused to work with Tories. 'He would just sit on his own and come up with his ideas without any consultation,' one senior member of the No team recalls. 'The man was just awful.'[453]

In the final fortnight, however, the man Tony Blair once dubbed a 'great clunking fist' roared into life. Throwing himself into the No campaign as its new chief spokesman, he delivered a series of barnstorming speeches across Scotland, while setting the seal on 'The Vow' – a declaration by the leaders of the three main UK parties that they would give 'extensive new powers' to the Scottish Parliament if the result was No. His final speech, the day before the vote, 'was just the most powerful fifteen-minute speech I've ever heard in my life', says a Tory member of the No team. Darling agreed: 'That's the best speech I've heard you give in thirty years,' he was heard telling his old boss. 'You should be getting all the credit for this, you're the one who's done the campaign,' Brown responded generously.[454]

As old divisions healed in the last heated moments, Brown even started to work with Cameron. In the aftermath of the *Sunday Times* poll, the two men spoke every day on the phone, and discussed the wording of The Vow in detail. In the run-up to Cameron's two final speeches in Scotland – one in Edinburgh in which he urged voters not to tick Yes just to give the 'effing Tories' a kicking, and another in Aberdeen in which he declared that No was the 'patriotic' choice – Brown was a regular adviser. Cameron's last speech was even sent to Brown for approval.[455] According to a No. 10 insider, the two spoke on the phone just before the event, Cameron

---

451   Ibid.
452   Private information.
453   Private information.
454   Ben Riley-Smith, op. cit.
455   Ibid.

biting his tongue as his predecessor lectured him on how he should have run the campaign.

'Gordon Brown couldn't resist saying I'm the saviour of the world and you take my advice,' the source revealed. 'I think the Prime Minister's view was indulgent: that is Gordon; Gordon has a role to play; there you are.'[456]

On 18 September, Scotland went to the polls. Despite the rain, turnout was extraordinary, with 85 per cent of Scots casting their vote. The early signs were auspicious for the No camp: a YouGov poll released at midnight suggested a 54/46 per cent win. But in Downing Street, nerves had reached fever pitch. Osborne hosted a curry dinner for Cameron and close aides in No. 11, and camp beds were brought in for staff to ensure the Prime Minister would have their full support if he found himself having to admit defeat the following morning.[457]

Having managed to snatch a couple of hours' sleep in the middle of night (a remarkable feat, under the circumstances), Cameron returned to the fray at 3 a.m. after receiving a text from Craig Oliver, his director of communications, suggesting the signs were promising. At 5 a.m., Sky News called it for No. With two of his children on his knees as the sun rose, Cameron watched the final results come in. At 55.3 per cent to 44.7 per cent, the union had been saved.

Cameron's first task, as dawn broke, was to call the Queen. It was 'the definition of relief', he later told New York's former Mayor Michael Bloomberg. In an excruciating breach of protocol, he was caught on camera telling Bloomberg that Her Majesty had 'purred down the line'.

Cameron's supporters say he deserved to savour the moment. A bold call made more than two years earlier appeared to have paid off. It would be a long time before the dust settled and the full implications of one of the most tumultuous periods in modern Scottish history became clear.

Labour figures involved with the Better Together campaign have criticised Cameron's role,[458] but Tory insiders insist he could not have done more.

456   Severin Carrell, Nicholas Watt and Patrick Wintour, *The Guardian*,
      16 December 2014.
457   Ibid.
458   Joe Pike, *Project Fear* (Biteback Publishing, 2015).

'David was very active in ensuring that the government side of the campaign delivered what was needed,' says Cooper.

> At any point where somebody asked him to put a call in to X, Y, Z, he just did it...I don't think it's fair to fault him, given how incredibly weak the stock of the Tory Party in Scotland is. I think it was very disciplined of him to acknowledge that – to be willing to be guided. He deferred to the advice of the Scots, he deferred to the people on the campaign, and he deferred to the Labour people. He did exactly what he was advised to do when he was advised to do it.

In particular, he is credited with making important calls to business leaders in the campaign's final stages, using the office of No. 10 to urge them to stick their heads above the parapet to warn of the economic risks of independence. Some have suggested that it was these warnings – from the likes of RBS and others just before the vote – that swung the 'undecideds' against independence more than anything else. They were difficult to secure. So febrile was the atmosphere north of the border in the run-up to polling day that few companies wished to nail their colours to the mast.

'If you could argue that Cameron almost lost the union, you could also make the argument that he did three successful things which saved it,' says Daniel Finkelstein.

> One: the money [that the Tories gave to Better Together]. Two: the PM doing whatever it was they told him to. And three – arguably the most important: contributing his own director of strategy to the No campaign. According to Douglas Alexander, Andrew Cooper saved the union. Which might be a slight exaggeration, but not far from it.

To Cameron's critics, however, Scotland was the ultimate example of 'essay crisis' leadership: a last-minute victory secured only when Downing Street panicked and started making desperate promises for ever more 'devo max'. But it is easier to accuse Cameron of complacency during the campaign than to find evidence for it. It is his handling of the aftermath of the referendum that raises questions about his judgement and may yet have the most devastating consequences for those who wish to see the union preserved. At the time of writing, Scotland's long-term future looks more uncertain than ever, and the Better Together campaign's achievements a Pyrrhic victory. On 28 April 2015, in the run-up to the general election and as Cameron and his allies loudly talked up the threat of a possible Labour–SNP alliance, *The Times* carried the headline '10 Days to Save the Union'. For many, this felt like head-swimming déjà vu. The SNP's performance in May 2015 speaks for itself.

The case for the prosecution is that Cameron blithely played directly into the hands of the SNP little over an hour after the union had been saved by launching a new campaign for 'English votes for English laws'.

Addressing the nation on the steps of No. 10 after the result was declared, he said: 'We have heard the voice of Scotland – and now the millions of voices of England must also be heard. The question of English votes for English laws – the so-called West Lothian question – requires a decisive answer.'

This intervention was against the express advice of Darling, who had pleaded with him over the phone just two hours earlier not to 'play the English card'. The former Chancellor believed such a move would be 'disastrous' – further alienating many people in Scotland and driving them into the warm embrace of the SNP.

In an attempt to outflank UKIP and appease his own backbenchers – many of whom were furious about The Vow – Cameron ignored him. He declared that English Votes for English Laws (EVEL), the process by which Scottish MPs would be banned from voting on matters unrelated to Scotland, needed to be addressed 'in tandem with, and at the same pace as, the settlement for Scotland'.

Within minutes, Brown was on the phone to Heywood, denouncing Cameron's statement as party political posturing and warning that he would let a defeated Salmond in through the back door by appearing to use the result as an excuse to advance 'English interests'. He was right: the SNP was incandescent, howling that Cameron had reneged on The Vow by suddenly making further devolution conditional upon the introduction of EVEL.[459]

Although Downing Street backtracked slightly only a few days later – insisting that Cameron had not in fact formally linked the issue of devolution with EVEL – the damage was done. Two years of cross-party cooperation

459   Severin Carrell, Nicholas Watt and Patrick Wintour, *The Guardian*,
      15 December 2014.

over Scotland collapsed as Labour sources bitterly accused Cameron of 'nakedly political' manoeuvring and of recklessly playing with fire over sensitive constitutional issues. Many senior Tories agreed:

'I thought what he said was very ill judged,' says one closely involved in the No campaign. 'The tone was completely wrong – it came across as much too hardline. And it has contributed significantly to the very widely held feeling in Scotland now that the devo max vow was a lie.'[460]

Whether Cameron's 7 a.m. statement the morning after the vote was the primary cause of the SNP's remarkable post-referendum fightback is unclear. Labour must bear significant responsibility for presiding over the haemorrhaging of its own support over the border. For years, many voters felt, Labour had treated Scotland as a 'branch office' and taken its swathe of Scottish seats entirely for granted. Ed Miliband paid the price.

As the general election approached in the early months of 2015, it certainly helped the SNP that it was able to depict Labour as Tory stooges – and this single fact was probably more important than anything Cameron did or said.

Either way, the referendum comprehensively failed to achieve what Cameron had originally intended, and had gambled his premiership on delivering. Nationalism in Scotland was strengthened, and the future of the UK continued to hang in the balance.

---

460   Private information.

39
THE E WORD

'Let me get this straight. I am no Euro obsessive.'

– Cameron, May 2003

Red-faced and spitting expletives, Cameron was having a rare and very un-prime-ministerial loss of cool. The immediate object of his fury was Zac Goldsmith, the multi-millionaire environmentalist turned MP who was now sitting in his Downing Street office. The more general source of his frustration was what he called the 'E word': Europe.

It was October 2012, and Eurosceptic Tory backbenchers were giving him yet another headache. For as long as he could remember they had been badgering him to commit himself to offering an EU referendum, a constant source of grief. Now they were kicking off about the European Union's budget, making demands he considered hopelessly unrealistic. Soon there would be a vote on the issue, and he was set to lose. The row was being pitched as a test of his authority on Europe – again.

It was all so familiar: Eurosceptic MPs had been causing trouble for Tory leaders ever since Cameron had been a young researcher. When he first became an MP, he was quite vocal on the subject himself, repeatedly arguing for a referendum on Britain's membership of the EU before Blair signed a new EU constitution. He used his *Guardian* blog to label the Prime Minister a 'Euro-maniac' and demolish arguments against a poll.[461] Now it was his turn to feel the heat. But where exactly did he actually stand?

As early as the 1990s, there was confusion over the scale of his hostility to Europe. As a special adviser at the Treasury, he would tell Lamont that he was 'Eurosceptic, but not as Eurosceptic as you'. The then Chancellor says

---

461   *Guardian* blog, 28 May 2003.

they never really discussed the subject, which is curious in itself, given how fiercely the debate raged at the time and how well they got on.

While he was searching for a parliamentary seat, Cameron was dismayed to discover he had been classified as a 'question mark' on a document categorising hundreds of Tories as 'Europhile' or 'Eurosceptic'. Compiled by an academic, the 'Candidlist' was designed to stop candidates deceiving selection panels on what the author, Dr Sean Gabb, described as 'the most important issue of our time'.

Nowhere was this more sensitive than in Witney, where the outgoing MP, Shaun Woodward, had glossed over his Europhilia to win selection in 1997 and where Cameron was seeking selection. A question mark was potentially very damaging, indicating he had avoided giving a view or would simply obey party whips. Some prospective parliamentary candidates took the list so seriously that they threatened to sue. For his part, Cameron emailed Gabb to protest about his classification. Published on a little-known website, this private correspondence, unearthed by one of our researchers, takes on a far greater significance in light of Cameron's subsequent rise to the forefront of national politics. It was a lengthy and somewhat ill-tempered exchange, in which Cameron argued that he should be designated a Eurosceptic 'on the basis that I oppose the single currency and any further transfer of sovereignty from the UK to the EU'. However, he conceded that he was not in favour of withdrawal and that he accepted EU law was supreme in some cases ('I don't like it, but it's a fact') – which further fuelled Gabb's suspicions about his status.

'Your complacent tone does you no credit whatever,' the academic told him. 'It is only because I believe you are sincere in what you say that I do not reclassify you as a Europhile.'

Alarmed, Cameron shot back a missive saying Gabb must have misunderstood his position. 'I am not a lawyer and perhaps my original email put it the wrong way,' he wrote. 'But these are my views – no to the single currency, no to further transfer of powers from Westminster to Brussels and yes to renegotiation of areas like Fish where the EU has been a disaster for the UK. If that is being a Europhile, then I'm a banana.'

Further missives followed, after which Gabb reluctantly re-classified Cameron as a sceptic, though he remained unconvinced.

The emails, sent between February and June 2000, offer an unusual insight into the extent of Cameron's hostility to the EU. It was primarily focused on antipathy to the euro, rather than the wider principle of membership. As a young MP, he frequently used his *Guardian* column to preach the dangers of monetary union, saying his experience at the Treasury on Black Wednesday had taught him that 'the right interest rate for Westphalia' would not always be the right rate for west Oxfordshire.

He made much of his disdain for the currency, writing, after using Euro notes for the first time on holiday, that they were 'dreadful tat'.

As a backbencher, he also enjoyed taking aim at the propensity of Brussels to overreach itself. In 2003, he became particularly exercised about an EU directive on 'equids' (as it called them), that required all horses, ponies and donkeys in Europe to have passports – a move Cameron said had 'all the ingredients of a proper Euro-farce'.

'Crucially for a true Euro-pudding, there is absolutely nothing we can do about it,' he wrote – though he did have a 'masterplan'.

> I will produce a clause so tough and illiberal on horses found without their passports that the government will fear it is being outflanked from the right and immediately back it. Equids across Britain will shiver in their stables and cower at the dreaded question: 'Where are your papers?'
>
> It won't be easy. There may be casualties. But sense will prevail in the end.
>
> Why? Because as well as being tough, it will be completely unworkable – and therefore subject to one of Blunkett's famous U-turns.[462]

Such mockery of Brussels did not mark him out as especially Eurosceptic, however – it was practically a national sport at the time. Indeed, to Europhile Labour MPs more used to Tory 'headbangers', he appeared so measured that he was sometimes mistaken for a kindred spirit. In early summer 2005, when speculation was mounting that he would run for the Tory leadership, the former Europe Minister Denis MacShane recalls encouraging him to pick a symbolic fight with the sceptics.

'I was in the Commons gentlemen's shower room having come in from a game of tennis, and David had just arrived after cycling in from Notting Hill,' he says.

---

462 *Guardian* blog, 21 January 2003.

We were both towelling down. I'd always found him funny, witty and approachable, so I said to him: 'Dave, you really have to go for the leadership of the party. You're the closest the Conservatives have to Tony Blair. You've made a very good impression, you haven't made enemies – you can't fail – even if you don't win, the act of running for it confers huge status on you, and will guarantee you're one of the top three or four new-generation Tories in very senior shadow Cabinet posts. So you really have to go for it.' He said, 'Oh, thanks very much!' I said, 'Look, if I may offer one piece of advice: a new leader really wants to make an impact when he comes in. You've got to kill a sacred cow your party loves. My honest judgement is that the British establishment, the business world and Whitehall won't confer full power or a clear majority to a Prime Minister who wants to isolate us and take us out of Europe.' He said: 'Oh, thanks very much, Denis, but I'm much more Eurosceptic than you imagine.' I just hadn't clocked him as a Eurosceptic.

In his own constituency, where Woodward's treachery was still raw, Cameron knew he had to sound hardline. To reassure local activists, he would occasionally invite his staunch Eurosceptic colleague John Redwood to visit and give a talk, which could be guaranteed to strike the right note.

'He said one of the reasons he wanted me to come was because my views were much prized among his voters,' Redwood recalls.

Yet as he put it himself, Cameron was no 'Euro obsessive'.[463] Fundamentally Eurosceptic, he was never stridently so.

Nicholas Soames says: 'He's Eurosceptic, no shadow of doubt. He's immensely irritated by it and frustrated by it in every way. But he's not a Get Out man.'

While courting Eurosceptic Tory MPs during his leadership bid, he was honest about where he drew the line. Conservative MEP Daniel Hannan says, 'I was impressed, after years of listening to Conservatives hinting at some inner Euroscepticism, by his frankness. He said, "I don't think we should leave the EU, I know we're going to disagree about that; but you'll have the chance to put your case."'

---

463 *Guardian* blog, 28 May 2003.

Ironically, considering later events, Iain Duncan Smith never thought that Cameron saw Europe as a 'die-in-the-ditch' issue.

'If you asked him instinctively, how much of what the EU does do you think is good, I think the answer would probably be not much. Does he think it's worth having huge bust-ups and fights over?…No.'

Unlike some colleagues, as Prime Minister, Cameron showed little appetite for a fight over the constant stream of EU rules and regulations requiring implementation. Dominic Cummings, special adviser to Gove, describes how Downing Street routinely encouraged ministers to sign off 'stupid' EU measures because they were unwilling to take issue with Brussels.

> EU papers are circulated in the red boxes. Nominally, these are 'for approval'. They have a little form attached for the Secretary of State to tick. *However, because they are EU papers, this 'approval' process is pure Potemkin village.* If a Cabinet minister replies saying, 'I do not approve, this EU rule is stupid and will cost a fortune,' then someone from the Cabinet Office calls their private office and says, 'Did your minister get pissed last night, he appears to have withheld approval on this EU regulation.' If the private office replies saying, 'No, the minister actually thinks this is barmy and he is withholding consent,' then Llewellyn calls them to say, 'Ahem, old boy, the PM would prefer it if you lie doggo on this one.' In the very rare cases where a minister is so infuriated that he ignores Llewellyn, then Heywood calls to explain to them that they have no choice but to approve, so please tick your box and send in your form, pronto. Game over.[464]

Such ambivalence was always going to set Cameron on collision course with those in the party for whom the issue is paramount. Having witnessed at close hand the devastating electoral consequences when his party 'banged on about Europe', when he became party leader, he considered the subject toxic, and approached it with extreme caution. There was tacit agreement in his inner circle that he should talk about it as little as possible, to avoid being characterised as leading the 'same old Tories'.

---

464 Dominic Cummings's Blog, 30 June 2014: https://dominiccummings. wordpress.com/2014/06.

After his symbolic gesture of withdrawing the party from the European People's Party, he made remarkably few speeches on Europe in opposition. When the issue could not be avoided, he was deliberately bland. He immediately regretted an LBC radio interview in 2006, in which he described members of the UK Independence Party as 'a bunch of fruitcakes and loonies and closet racists'. From that moment, the charismatic UKIP leader, Nigel Farage, took a personal dislike to him, vowing that they could never make any electoral pact.

In September 2007, Cameron made a 'cast-iron guarantee' that he would offer a vote on the Lisbon Treaty (a controversial agreement that enhanced the process of European integration). But this was later dropped once it became clear that, with EU states having ratified the treaty – including the UK under the Labour government – a referendum would be pointless.

According to a well-placed insider, the U-turn upset at least one former Conservative Prime Minister. A close friend of the late Margaret Thatcher explains that, in her eyes,

> if you'd said something, that was the same as doing something. So she was very critical of the promise to hold a referendum on the Lisbon Treaty and then just walking away from it, very casually. For her, words were very serious things, not very casual things. She believed in delivering promises.

Eurosceptic backbenchers and activists yearned for a leader who felt as strongly as they did. Spread-betting tycoon Stuart Wheeler, who once gave the party a £5 million donation, summed up the mood among many during Cameron's years as opposition leader when, in March 2009, he declared that he could no longer back the party in European elections.

'The Conservatives, though perhaps more Eurosceptic than Labour, just wish no one would talk about the EU so that they can win the general election in peace,' he complained.[465]

It was true. Cameron had no desire to emulate the disastrous 2001 election strategy focusing on Europe and the threat to the pound. The 2010 general election manifesto simply promised a referendum on any future European

---

465 Conservative Home, 28 March 2009: conservativehome.blogs.com/
torydiary/2009/03/stuart-wheeler-defects-to-ukip-with-100000-donation.html.

treaty 'that transferred areas of power or competences' from Britain to the EU. He had hoped the issue would go away. The low priority he gave to European matters in opposition reflected the view of the electorate, for whom the subject had always ranked well below issues like public services and the economy.

But from the moment he entered Downing Street, he found himself under relentless pressure from a significant and very vocal tranche of his back-benches to offer an 'in/out' referendum. It found expression in a series of Private Members' Bills and parliamentary motions and was a constant drag on his leadership.

In October 2011, he infuriated many of his own MPs by ordering them to vote against a parliamentary motion calling for a referendum. It triggered an almighty showdown. A total of eighty-one Tory MPs defied the whip, the biggest post-war rebellion on Europe. There had been nothing like it since 1993, when forty-one Tory MPs defied John Major over the Maastricht Treaty.

In this febrile atmosphere, Cameron did manage one spectacular PR coup. On 8 December 2011, he walked out of an EU summit after exercising his veto over proposals for fiscal union. Though the gesture changed very little in Brussels, few studied the small print. Backbenchers were ecstatic, and the party bounced in the polls. Privately, Cameron reflected that the positive reaction showed an entrenched Euroscepticism among most British voters. He was beginning to wonder whether any party – least of all his own – could enter the 2015 election without some sort of referendum pledge.

The following year, he clashed with backbenchers again, this time over the EU budget. The European Commission had outraged Eurosceptic MPs like Goldsmith – and many British voters – by proposing a 5 per cent hike, taking it to £898 billion for the period 2014–2020.[466]

With Britain in the grip of austerity measures, the Prime Minister was under intense pressure from MPs to block the deal. While he believed the best he could deliver was a freeze, backbenchers, including Goldsmith, were pushing for a real-terms cut. Once again, Cameron faced a Commons revolt. In the run-up to the vote on 31 October 2012, he lost his temper, letting rip at Goldsmith during a meeting in Downing Street. According to a Whitehall source, he began pacing around his office effing and blinding and ranting

---

466 BBC News, 30 June 2011: http://www.bbc.co.uk/news/world-
    europe-13970135.

about the 'disloyalty' of those whose careers he had helped. It was a highly unusual loss of temper which exposed his exasperation at finding himself in the same position as so many of his predecessors. For all his attempts to dodge the Europe ball, like so many other Tory leaders, he found it being kicked in his face. A total of fifty-three Tory MPs defied the whip. Rebel leaders now warned that he faced a war of attrition with his own party.

Meanwhile the UK Independence Party continued to gain ground, eating into the Tory vote (though as it turned out, the groundswell of support for Nigel Farage would not translate into Commons seats). In Downing Street, Cameron was pulled in both directions, his fundamental Euroscepticism kept in check by his Europhile chief of staff (Llewellyn remains extremely close to former EU Commissioner Chris Patten) but fuelled by the discovery that it was difficult to achieve anything in government without bumping up against an EU regulation or directive. He developed a particular distaste for EU summits, where he would become so bored he would while away time sending surreptitious text messages. 'He can't stand all those dreadful meetings, having to sit through meals and sit up all night. He makes a great virtue of mocking it,' says a colleague.

A little over a year after his veto, in a landmark speech at the London headquarters of the American financial data and media giant Bloomberg, he finally caved into the inevitable and pledged an in/out referendum on Europe before the end of 2017. The party was ecstatic. But first he promised to 'renegotiate' Britain's relationship with Brussels. The stage was set for the biggest test yet of his diplomatic skills, and the groundwork began immediately. First stop: Angela Merkel's *schloss* in Germany.

40

PILLOW FIGHT

'I have no choice.'
       – Cameron to François Hollande, on the EU referendum

In the state dining room of a magnificent eighteenth-century Prussian palace, two world leaders and a dozen or so guests were tucking into dinner. The host was German Chancellor Angela Merkel, flanked by her husband Joachim Sauer, an alarmingly highbrow professor of quantum chemistry. Around the table were three British men called David and their spouses: David McAllister, a distinguished German politician with Scottish roots, once tipped as a possible successor to Merkel; the architect Sir David Chipperfield; and David Cameron, with Samantha. Intimidating company by any standards, particularly given the presence of Sauer, who so loathes the limelight that he famously skipped his wife's historic inauguration, choosing to watch it on TV instead. (A German newspaper once described him as being 'as invisible as a molecule'.)[467]

Such occasions hold no fears for Cameron, however. Indeed, the Prime Minister was in his element, holding court with colourful tales of visiting East Berlin after the fall of the Berlin Wall and making everyone laugh with funny anecdotes.

'He was absolutely charming,' says one who was there. 'Germans love this British charm! And of course he was at an advantage because everyone was speaking English, so he could tell good jokes.'

Upstairs, in another wing of the *schloss*, Cameron's three children were supposed to be asleep. In a highly unusual move, Merkel had invited them to accompany their parents to stay at Castle Meseberg, her official country

---

467   Quoted in the *Daily Telegraph*, 18 May 2012.

retreat. By the time the grown-ups sat down to dinner, it was assumed that Nancy, Elwen and Florence were settled. The only blip of the evening came when one of Merkel's domestic staff slipped into the dining room and whispered to Samantha that the children were in fact having a pillow fight.[468] The Prime Minister's wife discreetly left the table to restore order.

That Merkel invited Cameron's children to stay at Castle Meseberg showed her fondness for him, and how anxious she was to enhance their diplomatic relationship. In a carefully choreographed welcome, the German Chancellor, who has no children of her own, even brought presents for the kids: a painting set for Nancy, a Lego set for Elwen and a teddy bear resembling the Berlin mascot for Florence. (The Camerons reciprocated with a very English gift: a Denby tea set.) No other world leader with young children has been afforded such an honour by Berlin. Cameron entered into the spirit of the trip, delighting the German press by sightseeing around Berlin aboard a scooter.

'It was one of those small scooters, and he went around Brandenburg Gate and so on. That went down well. I don't know if Angela Merkel would go on a scooter tour to Trafalgar Square!' recalls one German politician admiringly.

The visit took place in April 2013, three months after Cameron's pledge to offer an in/out referendum. Merkel knew that in the years ahead, the relationship between Britain and Germany would be vital to the future of the European Union, especially if the Tories won the next election. (Privately, her administration continued to hope that the Prime Minister would be forced into another coalition in 2015, making it impossible for him to honour the plebiscite commitment.) As for Cameron, he was painfully aware that the prospect of achieving any meaningful concessions in his much vaunted 'renegotiation' with Europe rested heavily on the extent to which Merkel would be willing to indulge him.

On the plus side, the German Chancellor genuinely liked and respected her British counterpart and recognised the pressure he was under from Eurosceptics in his own party. She never tired of saying both publicly and privately that Britain was an indispensable ally and a key member of the European Union.

'On a personal level, the chemistry works well,' said one of her closest aides at the time. He provided a detailed level of insight into the man Downing Street suggested she likened to a 'favourite nephew'. He agreed that they

---

468   Geordie Greig interview, op. cit.

had a good understanding of each other and even shared a similar sense of humour. Behind closed doors, Merkel was apparently willing to stick her neck out for Cameron and take on critics in her own party who were fed up with British Eurosceptics and thought he should have be given short shrift. However, the aide revealed that despite the warmth of their personal relationship, Merkel believes Cameron made a series of serious diplomatic errors, and paid the price in Europe for quitting the EPP.

Another German source, a close political ally of the Chancellor, believes that Britain's decision to leave the European Union can be traced directly to Cameron's decision to leave the bloc of European centre-right parties. He argues that it isolated Britain from her natural allies in the EU, beginning the process of disentanglement from Brussels. He added that 'the political reality cannot be denied': Cameron sometimes 'made it very difficult' for the Chancellor to support his stance on Europe, and at times she became extremely frustrated with him.

At their first meeting in Berlin in 2010 – Cameron chose Germany as the destination for his second foreign trip as PM, the first being Paris, the previous day – both tried to dispel the sense that the row over the EPP would cast a shadow over their future relationship, though Merkel 'did make clear' to Cameron that she thought he had blundered.

'We saw it as a big mistake,' says her aide. 'The EPP was and remains an indispensable forum where leaders of the conservative parties meet regularly to forge common policies and prepare key decisions. The future PM of Britain just cancelled his membership.'

Within Merkel's party, the Christian Democratic Union (CDU), Cameron's decision was seen as such an affront that the German Chancellor retaliated by recalling the CDU's representative at the Konrad Adenauer Foundation in London, a CDU-affiliated think tank that serves as a liaison office with political parties in Britain.

The next setback in relations came with Cameron's celebrated veto at the EU summit in December 2011, which forced Eurozone nations to resort to complex legal instruments outside the Lisbon Treaty to protect the common currency. Though British voters were impressed that Cameron had had the nerve to say no to a treaty he did not think was in Britain's interests, Germans saw it as a stab in the back: the country's leading magazine *Der Spiegel* ran an editorial headlined 'Bye Bye Britain', arguing that the UK was on its way out of the EU. In the immediate aftermath, Cameron attempted to smooth things over with Merkel, but she was unimpressed by his special pleading.

'Cameron explained his motives in great detail, he told the Chancellor about the pressure from the Eurosceptic British press and about his lack of room for manoeuvre; he spoke about the referendum, about the challenges at home,' Merkel's aide says.

> But there was very limited sympathy for his arguments. The Chancellor too needs to deal with domestic policy; with the opposition; with public opinion – this is the job of politicians, to take care of things at home before they make potentially historic moves on the international stage. It is true that British media are very aggressive, but Mrs Merkel's position is that dealing with challenges like that is part of the job of a leader. Allies will help each other when they can, but each must do their own homework before coming to the table in Brussels or elsewhere.

Cameron's behaviour at that EU summit also angered the French. An Élysée source has revealed details of a bitter row in the early hours of the morning between the Prime Minister and Nicolas Sarkozy at the 'veto' summit, during which the then French President rounded on Cameron, accusing him of betrayal. The war of words was prompted when French diplomatic sherpas discovered that Downing Street had gone behind their backs with Merkel.

One of Sarkozy's closest advisers recalls:

> We discovered that Downing Street had given the Germans a document setting out their conditions for agreeing to the new treaty. They thought we would be more reluctant to give in to their demands and were trying to corner us by getting everyone else to sign up to it. It was very poor judgement on their part to imagine that we wouldn't find out about it, given the strength of Franco-German ties, especially at such a sensitive moment with the Eurozone.

When the former French President heard about the ploy, he was furious and challenged Cameron face to face.

'David, how could you do this to me?' he exploded. 'We have just come out of the Libyan war together! You have made a mistake. Now is really not the time to play games. There is too much at stake!' The following morning, still fuming over what he regarded as underhand tactics, Sarkozy briefed journalists that Cameron had shot himself in the foot.

'He didn't play us; we played *him*, and he lost out,' the French President told reporters defiantly.

Sarkozy's people regarded Cameron's clumsy tactics on this occasion as evidence of a more general tendency on his part to woo Germany obsessively at the expense of wider diplomacy. They believe this narrow approach weakened his hand when it came to getting what he wanted from the EU. A source close to the former French President says: 'Cameron makes the wrong calculation about Germany every time. He thinks they are going to call the shots, but it's not as simple as that. He overestimates Germany's weight. He seems to bet on Germany only, and is always disappointed.'

At the same time, members of Merkel's inner circle believed that he tended to overestimate the extent of his influence with her. There is, for example, the case of his failed bid to block the appointment of Jean-Claude Juncker as president of the European Commission. One of the German Chancellor's former allies, who had strong links with the Tory Party and was generally an admirer of the Prime Minister, went so far as to suggest that he 'lost the ability to conduct European diplomacy'. This may be overstating the problem, but there is no doubt Cameron misjudged the situation with Juncker, whose appointment he opposed because of Juncker's reputation as an archfederalist. Downing Street aides wrongly told anyone who would listen that Merkel was on Cameron's side. However, because of a technicality in the way candidates for the post are selected, the German Chancellor could not help – leaving the Prime Minister isolated and humiliated.

'This was an enormous failure of judgement; it seemed like the whole diplomatic and political machinery behind Mr Cameron simply malfunctioned,' Merkel's aide says scathingly.

> The Chancellor never promised anything to Mr Cameron regarding preventing Mr Juncker, nor could she have promised any such thing. This is not how European politics work. Whatever her opinion of the nomination process, she was never going to go against her political family, the EPP, the voters, the public, the agreements she and

other leaders made. A deal was made by the conservative family [the EPP] that Mr Cameron chose to abandon years ago. We continually sent warning signals to [Cameron's] Cabinet; it was extraordinary to witness his public interventions against Juncker when it was long clear that he was on track to become president of the Commission.

Merkel's administration believes the Juncker fiasco should have served as a wake-up call for Cameron, encouraging him to review his approach to forging alliances in Europe. Yet he headed into another clash, this time over EU migration. In late 2014, still reeling from the embarrassment over the presidency, British officials, including Cameron's special advisers, spokespeople and senior diplomats, started briefing that the Prime Minister would secure restrictions on EU migration, again with Merkel's support. Once again, they were misrepresenting – or had misunderstood – her position. Her people point out that Germany has 'an entirely different demographic dynamic' to Britain – it needs and welcomes migration – and that she is deeply reluctant to 'open the Pandora's Box' on freedom of movement.

'We clearly set that as a red line, for Germany, but also for the rest of Europe. We can do a lot to combat benefits fraud, but the freedom of movement is non-negotiable,' the aide says.

When British briefing on migration turned into a public campaign, including leaked government memos about alleged plans to cap migration from Europe – a move that would be illegal under EU rules – Merkel herself decided to put an end to speculation about her alleged support for Cameron's efforts. 'Germany will not tamper with the fundamental principles of free movement in the EU,' Merkel declared.[469] According to her people, before the 2015 election, Cameron was prone to using UKIP leader Nigel Farage as a diplomatic weapon, particularly during an EU summit in October 2014, which coincided with revelations that Britain would have to pay an extra €2 billion to the EU budget. During the summit, Cameron is said to have become 'loud' and threatened other leaders that 'Nigel Farage would take his seat among them' if they refused to help him save face over the budget contribution controversy. The tactic annoyed the German Chancellor.

'This was an extraordinary thing to say; it was by no means a display of confidence or firm political strategy,' Merkel's aide says. 'Instead of

---

469   *Sunday Times* interview, 26 October 2014.

confronting Farage head-on, Mr Cameron allowed him to dictate the tone of his own political rhetoric – and then even used the alleged threat from UKIP to try to secure some concessions in Brussels. This was never going to be a successful approach.'

But it was a more subtle flaw in Cameron's diplomacy that Brussels insiders believed boded most ill for the renegotiation process. It was an apparent failure to attach much importance to filling influential administrative positions in the EU machine with individuals sympathetic to the Prime Minister's agenda. According to senior British EU officials, throughout the coalition, Cameron showed little interest in pushing for UK appointees in strategic jobs, focusing instead on headline-grabbing political posts. They believe this was a serious error.

'It is a mistake to focus on political appointments, as the senior administration jobs give a great strategic edge to nations interested in influencing decision making in Brussels,' says a veteran official.

By contrast, the Germans have been 'extremely strategic' in this respect, he says.

> Some years ago, Angela Merkel herself summoned the most senior EU civil servants to Berlin and gave them a lot of face-time to discuss ways to increase German influence in Brussels. Since then, they have filled all the top echelons in all key institutions. Sadly, the British government has been sleepwalking through all that. This is bizarre, because the PM's chief of staff Ed Llewellyn actually used to work here at the Commission and should know the importance of having people in the right places.

During the jostling for the position of the top EU official, the Secretary General of the Commission, one of Cameron's special advisers all but confirmed Cameron's lack of interest in the Brussels power game. 'It may be a powerful post within the Commission system, but how many headlines can we get out of appointing the Secretary General? This is important only to insiders,' Cameron's special adviser sniffed.[470]

Merkel's former political ally, who nonetheless respected Cameron, added that his approach to diplomacy was too blunt for German sensitivities.

---

470 Private information.

In relation to the debate on free movement of people, we completely understand that people in the UK are upset about people getting benefits before they qualify for it, and so on. But why doesn't the British debate focus on what we can do within the treaty, within the Common Market? The British approach always seems to be that we have to change the principle of freedom of movement. Once again, Germans would say, why are they talking about making such a huge step? Why don't we make lots of small steps, and we'll get the same thing?

The other thing people can't understand is the way he behaves at EU summits. Merkel will go to the press and say, 'This was a hard-working summit; we stayed up to 4 a.m.; and the positive things are this and that. There are a few things we didn't get, but it's all about compromise.' Whereas the British position is always, 'I came to Brussels and I said no to everything! I want my money back!' Germans wonder why he can't at least say a few words about what he managed to do, because it's his success too.

Perceptions of Cameron in the French administration were equally mixed. Before the referendum, at least, Sarkozy had nothing but warm words for the former Prime Minister.

'I have only praise for David,' he says. 'What he has achieved with his economy is splendid. He has been a very loyal counterpart, especially in the Libyan conflict, but he has this problem with the Eurosceptic wing of the Conservative Party. I wish he didn't make so many concessions, because they always ask for more,' he told us.

Yet Sarkozy's relationship with Cameron had its rocky moments. He had liked Gordon Brown, rather admiring his 'gruff' style, his originality and his modest social background. Whenever they spoke by phone, Sarkozy (whose English has never been great) would end the conversation by saying, 'I kiss you, Gordon!'

As it became apparent that Cameron was likely to be Brown's successor, the then French President began reaching out to the young Tory leader, discreetly taking the opportunity of a Franco-British summit in London in early 2008 to invite Cameron to the French ambassador's residence to discuss the future. During the conversation, Sarkozy tried in vain to persuade Cameron not to pull out of the EPP, according to one of his aides.

'If you stay in the EPP, we'll be the strongest group in Europe. Without you, it will be weaker. You want more influence in Brussels, but this takes you in the opposite direction,' Sarkozy urged.

'It's too late,' Cameron retorted. 'I made a pledge, and I can't get out of it.'

'Of course you can!' Sarkozy insisted. 'It's only a promise. You can argue that circumstances have changed; you're going to find another solution; some new links within the group?'

But Cameron was steadfast. After the meeting, when the Tory leader was safely out of earshot, the French President turned to his aides and sighed: 'We're going to have problems with this guy.'

The following year, the then French Prime Minister François Fillon remembers meeting Cameron at his official residence in Paris, Hôtel Matignon. They strolled round the garden, discussing the economy and defence. At the time, France had just returned to NATO's military command, reversing four decades of self-imposed exile.

'If I'm elected, my first priority will be NATO, my second will be NATO, and my third as well,' Cameron enthused, making it clear he had no interest in a European army. Fillon says now that Cameron 'was very keen on a good, bilateral, pragmatic and positive relationship. A year later I saw him in London. He is at heart a free trader. He doesn't like how Europe is making it harder to practise free trade.'

Fillon is one of a very small number of French politicians who supports the Prime Minister's decision to offer a referendum.

'He's taken great risks, but it's worthwhile because it avoids his party blowing up…I admire what he has achieved on the economy as well,' Fillon says today.

For the rest of Sarkozy's presidency, the relationship with Cameron was less difficult than he feared. Insiders say the former French President 'looked down' on the Tory leader, considering him very much the junior partner, and put far less effort into their meetings than he did with Merkel.

'Nothing compared to the meetings with Merkel. They were like two wild beasts with strong agendas!' recalls one of Sarkozy's aides.

Cameron met Sarkozy's successor, François Hollande, in July 2012, two months after the latter took office. During the discussion, Hollande emphasised that he did not want to see Britain leave the EU. According to one present at the meeting, Cameron seemed rather relieved to be dealing with a leader who appeared more flexible than Sarkozy. However, when they met at a one-day Franco-British summit at Brize Norton in January 2014, Hollande left Cameron in no doubt about his limits. Over a pub lunch at the Swan Inn in Swinbrook, near Cameron's Cotswold constituency home, the French President asked Cameron what he would really want from a revised EU treaty.

'I want a veto for national parliaments when they disagree with the European Parliament. I want to get rid of the declaration about 'ever closer union'. And I want to get rid of the European Court of Justice. But I want Britain to stay in Europe,' Cameron replied firmly.

For a moment, Hollande was quiet, taking in this information. Then he laid his cards on the table.

'I won't be able to support you. You're asking for too much, and you won't find any ally,' he replied, with an air of finality.

Their next private conversation was no easier. It took place on the TGV to Paris, following a meeting of the European Council in May 2014, against the backdrop of a massive surge in support for UKIP at the European elections. Hollande quizzed Cameron on his referendum pledge, questioning whether it had really been necessary.

'I have no choice,' Cameron replied wearily. 'There is a lot of frustration. Blair promised it, and then didn't honour it. It's the price we have to pay to contain the rise of Europhobia in England.'

'But the opposite just happened,' a bemused Hollande replied, referring to UKIP's gains.

All this was the diplomatic baggage Cameron was carrying when he committed himself to renegotiating Britain's relationship with the EU if he won the next election. He can have been under no illusion about the scale of the challenge ahead. In his heart of hearts, perhaps he thought he would never actually have to deliver on it. After all, in the long run-up to the 2015 general election, the prospects of a Tory victory looked remote. To defy these polls would be sweet, but it would mean there could be no escape from the gargantuan diplomatic task he had set himself.

41

THUNDERBOLT

'This is a career-defining election.'

– Cameron, April 2015

Tears streaming down his face, Cameron stared out of the tinted windows of his limousine and tried to comprehend what had just happened. It was 6 a.m. on 8 May, and against the odds he was heading back to Downing Street and to his job as Prime Minister. Less than twelve hours earlier, he had telephoned his friend and neighbour Lord Chadlington 'in a terrible state'.[471]

Over the years, the peer had increasingly become a father figure to the Prime Minister, offering the wise counsel and unflinching support Cameron missed so much from his own late father. In the tortured limbo of polling day, when he could do nothing more to influence the outcome and was suddenly overcome by a sense of foreboding, it was to Chadlington he turned.

'I don't think we're going to make it,' he told Chadlington miserably.

Though his campaign team's prediction on the eve of the election had been for 295 to 300 Conservative seats, published polls relentlessly showing the race was too close to call had inevitably sown doubts.

Seconds after 10 p.m. on 7 May, however, the first tremors of a political earthquake were being felt. A sensational exit poll broadcast moments after polls closed suggested the Conservatives were on course to win seventy-seven more seats than Labour – shattering Miliband's prospects of reaching Downing Street and all but wiping out the Liberal Democrat party. By the time Cameron's own agonisingly slow count in Witney was over, it was apparent that his party was on course for an overall majority: the one

---

471   Private information.

scenario for which the Tories had not prepared. Not since 1992 had pollsters and commentators been so wrong-footed, or the political establishment so rocked by an unexpected result. And Cameron himself? Exhausted, elated, disbelieving, he was struggling to adjust to the extraordinary turnaround in his party's fortunes – and his own. Before the day was out, three party leaders – Nick Clegg, Ed Miliband and Nigel Farage – would be gone, leaving him the last man standing.[472] As he sank back against the plush upholstery of his armoured Jaguar back to London, and to power, shock and emotion overwhelmed him.

As MPs and commentators surveyed the dramatic new political landscape on 8 May, and the wreckage of dozens of Labour and Liberal Democrat careers, there was only one name on their lips apart from David Cameron: Lynton Crosby. How had the so-called Wizard of Oz pulled it off? It was not even as if he was entirely convinced by his candidate: during a private conversation with a media tycoon towards the end of the election campaign, he went so far as to label Cameron as a 'tosser'. It was an extraordinarily risky indiscretion – though the Australian probably puts many others in the same category. Yet other sources have suggested he 'doesn't really rate' the Prime Minister.

An Australian friend says: 'He is a consummate professional, very dispassionate, and works with what he's given. But he is not a great admirer.'

Whatever his personal view of his product, on 7 May, his sales pitch worked. Had everybody underestimated the campaign mastermind and the Prime Minister, or were both men incredibly lucky?

For Crosby, the election result had been two and a half years in the making and was vindication against those who had questioned his abilities and huge salary. When he signed on the dotted line with the Conservative Party in November 2012 for a basic salary of £200,000 a year plus an undisclosed sum for overseeing all the party's private polling, a number of noses were put out of joint. Andrew Cooper decided, with no ill feeling, to leave

---

472   Nigel Farage would soon backtrack and perform a bizarre 'unresignation', by getting the party board to reject his offer. This caused a civil war to break out within UKIP, but Farage would go on to play a vital role in the referendum campaign soon after.

No. 10 at the end of his agreed two-year tour of duty to pursue other projects. The Prime Minister appealed to him to stay, but the pollster felt that there would not be room for both himself and the new hire.

Other senior strategists inside No. 10 also had concerns. Many disliked the Australian's 'unusually controlling modus operandi' and the way he monopolised the PM's ear.

'He doesn't like anybody else having the same level of input as him and he hates anybody testing his arguments,' says one former colleague.

> He welcomes input from other people, but once they give their input he makes the decision and that's it. If you disagree with him, he will try not to engage with you again. He shuts down all communications. He simply does not like anybody in a meeting disagreeing with him. *Anybody*.'[473]

For such a tough talker, he could also be surprisingly thin-skinned.

'He is cartoonishly Australian,' says one who worked closely with him through the campaign.

> He's very blunt. But the interesting thing is that for all his bluntness and his hard-man image, he hates personal criticism. He reads everything that's written about him, and if he's criticised he absolutely hates it. He doesn't shrug it off and say 'it's part of the game'. He takes it very personally and wants something done about it. That mantra he would apply to everybody else – 'nobody reads the fucking stuff, ignore it' – he never applies to himself.[474]

Some who had lived through the 2005 campaign were sceptical about the way he worked. His insistence on retaining total control over private polling, and tendency to keep it to himself, rankled colleagues who had not forgotten question marks over his research in 2005. Until relatively late in the day, even Cameron took the view that, while Crosby could be relied upon to 'make sure the trains run on time', his research, or at least the way the findings were presented, was suspect. There were also fears that Crosby might press for a

---

473 Private information.
474 Private information.

2005-style campaign, emphasising traditional Tory themes like immigration, to the detriment of Cameron's 'modernising' message.

Cameron reassured anxious colleagues that he would remain in overall charge of the strategy. He blamed Howard for signing up to the messages that failed in 2005, and promised a different approach.

'Even if it's true that Lynton comes with baggage, and will [want to] run that kind of campaign, I won't do it. If I assert the campaign that I want, and Lynton pushes back on it – well, I'm the leader,' he told Cooper, in late 2012.

Nonetheless, Cooper continued to worry about the appointment. When he again expressed concerns shortly before Crosby was hired, Cameron simply replied, 'Well, who else is there?' Such was the desperation to ensure there was no repeat of the failures of the 2010 campaign – with all the confused, ill-disciplined messages – that the PM had decided to risk it.

'The reason they all wanted Lynton was that they were all haunted by the 2010 campaign, with all those terrible meetings, and there was a determination that that wouldn't happen again,' Cooper explains.

Another insider says Cameron likes the way Crosby is 'unambiguously in charge'.

Once on board, Crosby ran a tight ship. He was quick to stamp his authority on the party, encouraging the PM to oust Gove, one of his closest friends and allies, from the education department. (In the summer of 2014, Crosby showed Cameron polling evidence suggesting Gove had become 'toxic' to parents and teachers.)[475] The demotion triggered a bitter rift between the Camerons and the Goves, who have long been close.

Though the former Education Secretary refrained from embarrassing the Prime Minister, his wife Sarah Vine did little to hide her anger, tweeting, without comment, a link to an article in the *Daily Mail* headlined: 'A shabby day's work which Cameron will live to regret'. Nonetheless, MPs were impressed by the discipline Crosby instilled. In the words of one senior MP at the time, 'We now have a battle-hardened commander as our chief of staff.' [476]

Crosby could be brazen in his drive for total control and authority. In a measure of his uncompromising style, he told Cameron that neither he nor Osborne should ever disagree with him or challenge him in front of anyone

---

475 *Daily Telegraph*, 16 May 2015.
476 Nicholas Watt, *The Observer*, 29 September 2013.

else – a demand which was rejected outright by the Chancellor. However, Crosby did succeed in whittling down the attendance list for meetings, barring all but the most senior figures from sensitive discussions.

From the start, he insisted the campaign should focus squarely on the economic recovery, and that nothing should be allowed to distract from the key message: an appeal to let the Tories 'finish the job'. MPs who strayed into riskier territory received swift and sharp reminders to stick to the text. One guilty party reportedly received a note from campaign headquarters saying: 'That's not fucking helpful, is it?'[477] Cameron himself would receive periodic emails from Crosby with the tag 'WTF', short for 'What the fuck'. The first time one of the messages appeared in his inbox he was not wearing his glasses, and mistakenly took it to be from the World Economic Forum.[478]

Crosby was particularly keen to steer clear of both the NHS and immigration, neither of which was considered a strong suit. The message he wanted was condensed into a four-word mantra – 'Long-Term Economic Plan' – which was dutifully repeated with monotonous regularity by Tory MPs. The narrowness of the sound bite frustrated many backbenchers and activists, but at least their instructions were clear. To every question thrown their way, the response was to be the same: unless the economic recovery is secured, nothing else will improve.

Throughout 2013 and 2014, Crosby carried out forensic private polling to identify the most important issues for voters in key seats. He was supported by another overseas election strategist: Jim Messina, President Obama's former election chief and an international expert on the role of 'big data' and social media in election campaigns. Using data from sources including Facebook, they were able to pinpoint the concerns of small groups of undecided voters in specific districts of constituencies the party needed to win.[479] They were aided by Stephen Gilbert, Cameron's political secretary, who was tasked with masterminding the ground operation in the party's marginal '40/40' seats (the forty seats the Tories needed to defend, and the forty they needed to win if Cameron was to achieve a comfortable majority). It was Gilbert, not Crosby, who in early 2014 made the stand-out tactical

---

477 *Daily Telegraph*, 16 May 2015.
478 David Cameron speech at Crosby Textor Fullbrook fifth birthday party, London, 14 July 2015.
479 *Daily Telegraph*, 16 May 2015.

call of the campaign: the decision to focus on going after Lib Dem seats. Winning, he realised, would require exterminating their coalition partners. There could be no room for sentiment.

'They didn't feel great about it, but they didn't hesitate,' says Daniel Finkelstein about the plan. 'David's view was, "We're trying to win a majority, and we can't win a majority without winning Liberal Democrat seats."'

It was not the strategy Cameron originally envisaged: he had thought the priority would be taking on Labour in swing seats and wooing voters leaning towards UKIP, the party he privately labelled 'our little purple friends'.[480] To Finkelstein, the approach suggests that, 'deep down', the campaign team always thought a majority could be achieved.

'It was quite a self-confident thing to do, if you think about it, because really what they needed to do was reduce the swing to Labour. It meant they were spending time on seats which logically might not have helped them,' he says.

Over in the Labour camp, most senior figures were under no illusion about the scale of the challenge their party faced. Ed Miliband's personal approval ratings remained poor, and Cameron and Osborne consistently polled ahead of the Labour leader and his shadow Chancellor Ed Balls on economic competence. As the Tories were fond of comforting themselves, history suggested that no party trailing behind the other on these two issues was likely to win.

Discipline remained tight: Labour MPs had not forgotten the corrosive effect of briefings against Brown in the run-up to 2010. However, a poorer than expected showing at the European and local elections in May 2014 heightened tensions. Far more worrying for Miliband's team was the desperate state of the Scottish Labour Party following the referendum. By October, the SNP had six times as many members as Scottish Labour[481] and evidence was mounting that the party, once so entrenched, was facing wipeout north of the border.

To make matters worse, Miliband's autumn conference performance in September was a car-crash. In previous keynote speeches, he had successfully emulated Cameron's celebrated 'no notes' approach, but this time the wheels

---

480 Ibid.
481 Tim Bale, *Five Year Mission: The Labour Party under Ed Miliband* (Oxford University Press, 2015), p. 248.

came off when he forgot an entire section about the deficit. Devastated by his mistake, the Labour leader locked himself alone in his hotel room, refusing to come out all evening.[482]

Two Tory defections to UKIP – Mark Reckless, MP for Rochester and Strood, and Douglas Carswell, MP for Clacton – gave Miliband's troops a minor boost, but behind closed doors the leader's office was fractious. With little over six months until polling day, rumours swirled that Miliband planned to sack Balls, and there was even speculation of a potential coup against the leader. One anonymous malcontent wailed that the Miliband operation was 'fucked from the start and still is. No one has been able to bring any semblance of order.'[483]

Nonetheless, Labour strategists still believed they could fight a more effective ground war than their opponents, boasting that they would achieve 4 million 'voter contacts' in the run-up to polling day. Senior Tories inside the campaign took it with a heavy pinch of salt.

'I always thought all that shit about their ground war was ridiculous,' one source says. 'All the boasting to the papers about their fantastic machine, their 4 million conversations… I knew that was just bollocks.'[484]

Indeed, the Conservatives were never aiming for volume. They were confident their campaign tools were superior. Messina had brought various 'toys' with him from the US, including a highly sophisticated technique for predicting how certain categories of voters would vote. The system was so finely tuned that MPs and activists canvassing in target seats found themselves being directed to specific properties to talk to a specific individual or family. It might be the only household they were asked to approach on that particular road, and the next property on the hit list could be two or three streets away. Letters and leaflets delivered to voters were so specific that a piece of direct mail might have up to 4,000 variations.

Cameron launched the Tories' unofficial 'long campaign' on 2 January 2015 in front of a billboard featuring a road to sunny uplands, and the

482   Patrick Wintour, *The Guardian*, 3 June 2015.
483   'Too Clever by Half: Inside the Troubled World of Team Ed', *The Times*, 18 October 2014.
484   Private information.

slogan: 'Let's stay on the road to a stronger economy'. The highway in question turned out to be in Germany, but it was only a brief blip. Three days later, Osborne released a Tory analysis of Treasury figures suggesting Labour had made £21 billion of extra spending pledges. Though it was swiftly challenged by independent experts, it put Labour on the defensive about its fiscal plans and pushed the debate onto the Tories' preferred ground of tax and spend.

Meanwhile pressure was mounting over plans for televised debates. Still haunted by his experience in 2010, Cameron was adamant he would not debate Miliband head to head. It led to a bitter battle with broadcasters. The Prime Minister's calculation was simple: that he had little to gain, whereas the Labour leader, who had long been lampooned in the media (culminating in the infamous photograph of him struggling to eat a bacon sandwich) could only benefit from addressing voters direct. The public struggle with the broadcasters rolled on for weeks, but Cameron's obstinacy finally paid off. On 17 March, he announced he had signed up to their latest proposals, which were remarkably similar to his own. As he had demanded, there would be no head-to-head with his Labour opponent, just a single seven-way debate, scheduled for the second day of the 'short campaign', on 2 April, as well as a grilling by Paxman, followed by a live question-and-answer session with a carefully selected audience.

As polling day approached, Tory strategists became increasingly concerned about Cameron's own hunger to win. While technically proficient, his public performances lacked fireworks. In contrast to a visibly energised and newly confident Miliband, he seemed ambivalent about victory.

Writing in the *Telegraph*, Charles Moore fretted that the PM was 'too posh to push', a phrase which was quick to catch on.

Meanwhile the polls stubbornly refused to shift. Cameron's competent if uninspiring performance in the keenly awaited seven-way debate failed to prompt the 'take-off' that Crosby assured the party would eventually arrive. If there was any stand-out winner it was Nicola Sturgeon, Salmond's successor as leader of the SNP. This provided the Tories with some encouragement – since it appeared to herald the collapse of Scottish Labour – but without a corresponding poll jump of their own there was little to celebrate. Yet Crosby remained cautiously optimistic. Finkelstein remembers telling colleagues at *The Times* that the Australian was by now predicting the Tories would get more than 300 seats. Against the backdrop of all the polls pointing to a hung parliament, Finkelstein feared they might greet this latest intelligence with derision. 'I was embarrassed, almost,' he recalls.

Secret preparations for the hung parliament that was by now universally expected continued apace. A string of policy proposals unveiled in the final weeks fuelled suspicions of Tory nerves. What Coulson used to call 'retail bullets' followed in rapid bursts: promises to double free childcare; a Thatcher-style plan to extend 'right to buy' to housing association tenants; and a cut in inheritance tax. The announcements came amid mounting frustration at the extent to which Miliband's policies were dominating TV news bulletins, particularly on the BBC. The amount of coverage given to a Labour pledge to introduce rent controls was a particular source of angst, prompting a discussion about how the Tories could get more airtime.

'I'll ring James Harding,' Osborne told colleagues, hoping that he could persuade the Corporation's director of news and current affairs to give the Conservatives more publicity.

When he got through to Harding, the Chancellor asked why Miliband's pledges were getting so much coverage.

'Well, Labour's rent story was top of the news because it's actually a story, and you repeating your economic plan isn't,' Harding replied bluntly.

Craig Oliver agreed.

'We can't just talk about our economic plan the whole time. We have to have something new to say,' he advised.

In response, Osborne cooked up a new pledge to legislate against certain tax rises – which duly captured news bulletins.

By now Cameron was showing the strain. In an excruciating Freudian slip, he told a crowd of Asda employees in Leeds that he was on the brink of a 'career-defining election'. Visibly flustered, he hastily corrected himself. 'This a *country*-defining election,' he explained.

'I don't know if there is something wrong with him, whether he's had some bad news,' a Tory MP wondered aloud at the time. 'But whatever it is – he's got to raise his game for the sake of the country.'[485] Privately, Crosby agreed. For the remainder of the campaign, Cameron tried to look hungrier for victory, rolling up his sleeves and injecting more energy into speeches. 'If you think I'm going to roll over in the next nine days, you've got another

485   'How Cameron killed his coalition', *Financial Times*, 8 May 2015.

think coming!' he bellowed to an audience of small-business leaders ten days before the polls opened.

Inside the Labour campaign, cautious optimism had taken root. The prevailing view on Miliband's team was that their man had fought a good election, whereas Cameron had been lacklustre. However, Crosby's team knew all along that this was not the case.

'Miliband's ratings weren't improving,' says one who studied the party's private polling at the time. 'There were a couple of moments during the campaign where they did improve, but they weren't sustained. On the question of preferred Prime Minister, they hardly changed at all. So, one of things the media was saying, that "Miliband was having a good campaign", to us clearly wasn't true.'[486]

Yet, reassured by the public polls, which continued to show a deadlock, and the knowledge that the quirks of the electoral map provided Labour with an in-built advantage, Miliband was preparing for government. In a surreal measure of the party's self-confidence, on the final weekend before the election the Labour leader unveiled what became derisively known as the Ed Stone: an 8-foot 6-inch slab of limestone into which had been carved his six key pledges. He planned to erect it in the garden of No. 10 if he won.

The stone was almost universally lampooned and was a massive source of embarrassment to many of the party's own activists. One Labour press officer is said to have howled in despair as he watched it being unveiled on TV. According to a report, the aide 'started screaming. He stood in the office, just screaming over and over again at the screen. It was so bad they thought he was having a breakdown.'[487] (After the election, the Ed Stone mysteriously went missing, reportedly destroyed. Its whereabouts remain unknown.) For the Conservatives, it was a total gift. One insider recalls feeling 'disbelief' the moment the stone was unveiled: 'I sort of thought that it must be some sort of joke. It was, instantly, obviously ridiculous. I'd never seen anything like it. Everybody was simply saying, "It is catastrophically bad."'[488]

But it was not this disastrous PR stunt, nor any personal failing of Miliband's, nor even Labour's unconvincing economic record, that ended

---

486   Private information.
487   'Did Ed Miliband sacrifice Ed Balls?', Dan Hodges, *The Spectator*, 16 May 2015.
488   Private information.

Labour's 2015 dream: it was the SNP. Since the morning after the referendum, when the nationalists began ruthlessly exploiting anti-English sentiment to transform themselves into an unstoppable political force, the stars had been slowly aligning in Cameron's favour. Tapping into a widespread sense of lost opportunity among not only their own supporters but also many voters who had been sorely tempted to back independence but had baulked at the last minute, the SNP was preparing to pulverise its political opponents in the battle for Westminster seats. By early April 2015, the post-referendum collapse of Scottish Labour and the meteoric rise of the SNP under Sturgeon gave the Tories a powerful new pitch: vote Conservative to stop a Miliband government propped up by Scottish Nationalists. With Labour facing wipe-out north of the border, where they could once rely on at least forty seats, Sturgeon became Cameron's saviour. Scenting blood, Crosby piled money into a billboard campaign depicting Miliband in Salmond's pocket. 'Don't let the SNP hold Britain to ransom' ran the tagline. Finally, the Tories had a message that would concentrate the minds of waverers.

Stocked with pizza and beer, Crosby's 'war room' in CCHQ was a hotbed of nerves on election night. Every so often, 'One Vision' by Queen – the hit Crosby used as a motivational soundtrack throughout the campaign – would blare out from speakers. While junior aides agitated, the Australian himself was buoyed by the stream of data he had been receiving all day. He was feeling quietly confident.

'On polling day we phoned one of our target groups, people who should vote Conservative but might vote UKIP, in our target seats, and 82 per cent voted Conservative,' says an insider.

Another encouraging sign was turnout. By lunchtime, Crosby's information was that the turnout of the Conservative vote was 50 per cent, against a general turnout of 30 per cent. Cameron would call Crosby periodically for updates, and would be told things were going better than published polls suggested. Osborne was one of the few to share Crosby's cautious optimism. According to friends, the Chancellor 'never wavered' from the belief that they would still be in government on 8 May, feeling sure that the 'economic competence' argument would get them over the line. On an intellectual level, he also felt Labour did not deserve to win.

An insider says:

> He and Cameron also believed that they had done an amazing amount of work to make themselves fit to govern while they were in opposition, and that Labour had not done any of that work, and that it would be grotesquely unfair for them to win, without having done any of that work. Lynton had that view too. George did think it would be nip and tuck though.

So much so that he pledged to give Crosby a French kiss if they won a majority. (He would later partially fulfil the promise, giving the Australian a peck on the cheek, but refusing to go the whole hog.) In the final hours of polling day, when Messina suddenly upped his personal prediction to 330 seats, the Chancellor, like most of his colleagues, was incredulous. Cooper privately remarked that this was 'either because [Messina] has got all that Obama-ish big data and predictive models, and knows more than everyone else, or, quite plausibly, because he's an American and doesn't know what he's talking about.' The received wisdom among Westminster pundits on 7 May was that while the Conservatives were likely to be the largest party, Miliband would be best placed to form a government. Such was the pessimism inside the Tory camp that as 10 p.m. approached, conversation focused on strategies for minority government. There was a discussion about potentially presenting a Conservative Queen's Speech to Parliament on 27 May even if the numbers made passing it impossible.

Waiting anxiously in Dean, Cameron had convinced himself it was all but over. At 6.30 p.m., he rehearsed a resignation address to a small circle of close friends and colleagues in his garden. Unlike Miliband, he had not prepared a speech for outright victory.[489] By contrast, Crosby was still upbeat. Nearly two and a half years of hard graft and meticulous planning had finally come to an end. 'We'll have 305 seats,' he predicted to staff, as the last minutes ticked by.

The exit poll broadcast a minute or two after Big Ben struck 10 p.m. dumbfounded the political establishment. Even Crosby had been too cautious: the Conservatives were set to be the largest party, with 316 seats against 239 for Labour. Nobody had seen it coming.

---

489 *The Spectator*, 13 June 2015.

'I was just completely amazed,' Finkelstein recalls.

Appalled, Labour spinners took to their phones to brief the media that they did not believe the exit poll could be correct. In Oxfordshire, the PM's phone rang. It was his old friend Andrew Feldman, stunned, like everyone else, by the figures flashing on TV screens.

'Three hundred and sixteen!' he shouted down the line. Physically and emotionally drained, Cameron had yet to take it in.

'But what about the Lib Dems?' the PM asked. The exit poll suggested they would lose all but ten of their seats.

'You won't need them, David, you've got 316!' roared Feldman.

'Oh my God, yes,' Cameron laughed. 'I don't care about the Lib Dems.'[490] The yelling and cheering was so loud at both ends that it was difficult for either to hear the other speak.

Cameron's next call was to Crosby.

'Do you believe it?' he enquired urgently. 'Is it right?'

'It is,' came the reply. 'It's absolutely consistent with what we've been hearing throughout the day.'

Inside his 'power pod', Crosby began to relax. Victory was in sight. Bolstered by the exit poll, his thoughts now moved to what until moments earlier had been regarded as utterly impossible: a majority.

'You looked at Lynton and you knew it was going to be all right,' says one who was present.[491]

One by one, results started coming in. Key marginals like Nuneaton and Warwickshire North, long expected to go to Labour, stayed blue with substantially increased majorities. In Scotland, the SNP tidal wave broke in full force. Labour and Lib Dem losses began to read like a *Who's Who* of the British left: Jim Murphy, Danny Alexander, Charles Kennedy and even shadow Foreign Secretary Douglas Alexander, whose 16,000 majority was crushed by a twenty-year-old nationalist yet to sit her university finals.

In England, Lib Dems fell like flies. Of Cameron's senior coalition partners, only Nick Clegg in Sheffield clung on. Around midnight, word reached CCHQ that Vince Cable would be ousted in Twickenham, prompting cheers and laughter across the war room. For the first time, Crosby started smiling and joking. But the seminal moment had yet to come: the unexpected

---

490 Anthony Seldon, *Sunday Times*, 10 May 2015.
491 *Mail on Sunday*, 10 May 2015.

defeat of shadow Chancellor Ed Balls. Now Crosby allowed himself to open a beer.[492]

Cameron spent the dramatic early hours of Friday morning in Witney, awaiting the result of his own count in the gym at the Windrush Leisure Centre, where he'd arrived at around 2.30 a.m. It took far longer than usual. According to one account, he used the time to think about what he was going to say when he was on stage, quietly writing the words 'One Nation' on a scrap of white paper as the first rays of light began trickling through the windows.[493] The phrase – which had been boldly appropriated by Miliband two and a half years earlier – would form the basis of his victory speech when his result finally came through just after 6 a.m.

'I want my party to reclaim a mantle we should never have lost,' he announced to his constituents as the sun began to rise. 'One nation, one United Kingdom.' With that, he set off for London, all the pent-up emotion of the long campaign finally spilling over.

By the time he reached CCHQ, he had pulled himself together. As his car drew up, a jubilant Crosby, Feldman and Gilbert headed to the lobby to greet him, but the first person he spoke to was the receptionist at the front desk.

'She was quite emotional so he went over to her first and thanked her. Then there were lots of group hugs. It was highly emotional,' says one of the team.

As he walked into the office, 200 activists gave him a hero's welcome, banging their desks and chanting, 'Five more years, five more years'.[494] A video, taken on a camera phone and later leaked, showed the euphoric PM, surrounded by ecstatic aides and Tory staffers, hailing 'the sweetest victory' of his life to rapturous applause. 'I am not an old man,' he joked.

> But I remember casting a vote in '87 and that was a great victory. I remember working just as you've been working in '92 and that was an amazing victory. And I remember 2010, achieving that dream of getting Labour out and getting the Tories back in and that was amazing. But I think *this* is the sweetest victory of them all.

By the time the final results came, the Tories were on 331 seats, defying all

---

492   *Daily Telegraph*, 16 May 2015.
493   Anthony Seldon, *Sunday Times*, 10 May 2015.
494   *Daily Telegraph*, 16 May 2015.

expectations and clinching a historic – albeit slim – majority. Labour had won 232, the SNP fifty-six (only three short of all fifty-nine Scottish seats), and the Lib Dems were reduced to eight. Despite winning nearly 4 million votes, UKIP won only a single seat – Carswell's – with Reckless summarily ousted from Rochester and Strood, and Farage (to Cameron's delight) failing to win in South Thanet.

Only one insider saw it coming: Cameron's old friend George Bridges, a member of the campaign team, who laid a £50 stake on the Conservatives winning 331 seats at odds of 100–1. Being rather bookish, apparently he didn't know how to lay the bet, so he asked Tom Newton Dunn, political editor of *The Sun*, to do it for him. Newton Dunn duly put the money on at Ladbrokes, and on 8 May, Bridges cashed in.

It was the beginning of a new era: the first majority Conservative government for eighteen years. Tired but exuberant, Cameron left CCHQ and headed back to Downing Street, where he was greeted by Osborne. The two men embraced before the PM went upstairs to his flat. Waiting for him were his children, awake and wide-eyed with excitement. Picking up Florence, who had greeted him with the same question for weeks – 'Have you won the 'lection yet, Daddy?' – Cameron hugged her and told her jubilantly:

'We've won the 'lection, Flo, we've won!'

'Hooray!' she shouted back.[495]

The children were getting ready for school, the household its usual clattering whirl of last-minute teeth brushing, lost shoes and tatty book bags. Cameron kissed them goodbye and left. By 8 a.m., he was back at his desk, wearing a new suit.

Sooner, and more dramatically than anyone ever imagined, it would all fall apart.

---

495 *Mail on Sunday*, 10 May 2015.

42
DOWN

'There are many lessons to learn, and I will learn them!'
– Cameron, responding to the criticism over
his handling of the Panama Papers

On the afternoon of 15 September 2015, a 21-year-old Conservative activist and blogger took a train from King's Cross to the sleepy town of Sandy in Bedfordshire. As usual, he was dressed in a sharp suit and sporting his beloved fob watch. The timepiece, a birthday gift from his parents, featured an etching of the young Tory's hero, Winston Churchill, on the front. Surveillance footage from the station showed nothing unusual about his behaviour, but he had been drinking heavily from a hip flask of vodka and orange juice. His father, describing the scene to journalist Andrew Pierce, told what happened next. 'He walked a mile parallel to the track, climbed over the fence, took out a blue towel, which he placed on the track, and lay down to die.'[496]

Elliott Johnson wanted to make an impact with his death, and he did. The end of his short life sparked an inferno in the party, revealing a toxic bullying culture that had seeped beyond the confines of various Tory youth organisations to the heart of CCHQ. The allegations of blackmail, sexual harassment and election fraud that subsequently emerged left a dark stain on what had hitherto appeared to be a highly professional operation.

The series of revelations and resignations that dominated the last year of Cameron's premiership invited comparisons with the 'Tory sleaze' scandals surrounding John Major's 'back to basics' policies in the early '90s. Cameron himself became an absentee Prime Minister, preoccupied with a diplomatic

---

496   Andrew Pierce, *Daily Mail*, 13 November 2015.

tour of Europe as part of his attempt to renegotiate Britain's relationship with the European Union. Serious questions began to emerge about the state of the party machine on his watch, including the conduct of the party chairman, Cameron's old friend and tennis partner Lord Feldman. In little more than a year, Cameron, at the peak of his powers after steering the Tories to an unexpected victory in 2015, would find it had all turned to dust.

The tragedy that came to be known as the '*Tatler* Tory scandal' began with a suicide note found by police on Johnson's bed, which he dedicated to 'bullies and betrayers'. It pointed the finger squarely at an individual named Mark Clarke.

Clarke was a former Tory election candidate turned election aide who had developed a scheme called RoadTrip, which involved bussing young activists to crucial marginal seats in the 2015 election. He also had close ties to figures in the higher echelons of CCHQ. His involvement in Tory politics dated back to 1997, and he can be seen at the side of John Major when the outgoing premier was giving his concession speech on the night of the 1997 general election.[497] He had been chair of Conservative Future, the official Conservative youth wing, in 2007, and was selected as Conservative candidate for Tooting. In 2008, he was tipped as a future Trade and Industry Secretary by *Tatler* magazine. This gave rise to his moniker as one of the '*Tatler* Tories'. The glossy magazine gushed that he was 'charming, big as life and twice as loud … a lad around London town!'[498]

Clarke had a much darker side, however. Shortly after the *Tatler* profile was published, a former girlfriend came forward to give a scathing interview to the *Daily Mail* in which she described him as a 'deceitful womaniser unfit to be an MP'. She claimed that he used prostitutes, despite the fact that he had campaigned to clean up a local red-light district. In an article about him in a local paper headlined 'Clarke Takes on Vice', he gave an early sign of the arrogance and narcissism that would threaten to tear the party apart. He told the paper: 'Most people are afraid of tackling [the pimps] …

---

497 'UK General Election 1997: Major concedes (ITV)', https://www.youtube.com/watch?v=VyobF-vy9Ps.

498 'Profile – Mark Clarke', BBC Radio 4, 29 November 2015.

but I can do this because everyone, including the police, knows who I am.'[499] Clarke's entitled tone jarred with Cameron's campaign to detoxify the Tory brand. Nonetheless, the party leader shared a platform with Clarke at an event showcasing young Tory talent at the party's annual conference the following week.[500]

To his chagrin, Clarke failed to win a seat in Tooting in 2010, losing to Labour's Sadiq Khan. His conduct during the election campaign had been controversial. He was accused of launching a cyber-attack on an opponent's website as well as a smear campaign against a community hospital, which drew a furious rebuke from the local NHS chief.[501] Party officials were said to be deeply relieved at his failure to win the seat, and he was removed from the candidates' list.

Clarke then attempted to resurrect his political fortunes in what he grandly titled 'Project Lazarus', coming up with the idea for the now infamous RoadTrip battle bus. A crisis in party membership, which had declined under Cameron from around 250,000 in 2005 to just 134,000 in 2015, was the opening he needed.[502]

The near collapse of some local associations left the party without the ground troops needed to deliver leaflets, carry out door-to-door canvassing and maintain the profile of candidates in target seats.[503] RoadTrip attempted to plug the gap by bussing ambitious young Tory activists around marginal constituencies, where they would seek to create a buzz.

Armed with a glowing reference from the respected Harlow MP Robert Halfon, Clarke approached party co-chair Grant Shapps in 2014 with the proposal, claiming he was a reformed character.

He acknowledged that he had been short-tempered in the past, but claimed

---

499   Simon Walters, *Mail on Sunday,* 28 September 2008.

500   Ibid.

501   Jason Beattie, *Daily Mirror,* 12 March 2010.

502   Labour and the Liberal Democrats were also affected by falling membership during this period, but the situation was particularly critical for the Tories.

503   Many associations resented Central Office's attempts to control candidate selection, while many were social conservatives who resented liberal attitudes to issues such as gay marriage. Anger at Lord Feldman's alleged 'swivel-eyed loons' comments still lingered. Cameron's success in wooing wealthy donors had left the party's coffers full, but campaigning organisations had deteriorated into husks.

he had now grown up. He stressed that he was now married, had a young daughter and a new job, and wanted to rehabilitate himself.

An initially sceptical Shapps rubber-stamped the plan and, along with Lord Feldman and campaign chief Lynton Crosby, signed off the budget. So began the chain of events that led to Johnson's untimely death.

A previously unseen 32-page witness statement to police by Paul Abbott, then chief of staff to Shapps, reveals damning new details about the scandal, exposing the full extent of CCHQ's failure in its duty of care to vulnerable young Tory activists. The document, passed to us by individuals involved in the case, shows that senior figures in CCHQ continued to indulge and embrace Clarke despite multiple warnings about his behaviour – even inviting him to Chequers. After Johnson's death, the document suggests, CCHQ was guilty of an extraordinary cover-up: issuing misleading public statements; briefing against those who complained about him; and leaking information which could have put a number of Clarke's female critics at risk. In his statement, Abbott accused CCHQ of 'a strategy to spread blame, muddy the waters and find people to blame who were not part of the current leadership':

> I note that the public line from CCHQ has been reported as 'We have been unable to find any written complaints of bullying, harassment or any other inappropriate behaviour during this period that were not dealt with. We have checked and rechecked our servers and paper files, and can find nothing.' I fear that at best, this is an extremely misleading statement, and at worst it is simply false. I have spoken with senior CCHQ officials including in the current chairman's office who accepted to me that it was false.[504]

CCHQ had good reason to mask the true picture. The truth was that the leopard had not changed his spots. Having trumpeted his new maturity, on return to the fold, Clarke began conducting a campaign of intimidation in the youth movement designed to shore up support for RoadTrip as soon as it was signed off by CCHQ. One of his first moves was to orchestrate a takeover by his friends of Conservative Future. He ensured the election of an ally, Alexandra Paterson, as chairwoman by running a smear campaign which forced her opponent to withdraw. The unsuccessful candidate has

504   Paul Abbott, statement to police.

described how she was 'besmirched in the most abhorrent fashion' by the 'RoadTrip slate'.[505] One figure in this campaign was Johnson, with whom Clarke had recently struck up a friendship. Clarke persuaded Johnson to use his blog to accuse the rival candidate of having a 'cruel neurosis … a narcissistic desire to be the centre of attention' and, crucially, of 'attempting to block grassroots campaigns like RoadTrip 2015'.

She and her boyfriend both complained to CCHQ about Clarke's behaviour, but nothing was done.

Our research has revealed an earlier complaint by the former President of the Oxford University Conservative Association, Jack Matthews. In May 2014, he and a group of other Oxford Tories were called into the austere surroundings of Conservative Central Office at 4 Matthew Parker Street by Clarke. The purpose was to try to get prominent university associations on board with his plan. Also present was Paul Abbott. 'Instead of persuading us of the merits of supporting the RoadTrip project, we were instead berated, shouted at, and smeared,' Matthews wrote.[506] He subsequently complained several times, and heard nothing official, though he did get a private apology from Abbott.[507]

Another activist from OUCA has shown emails and Facebook messages sent by Clarke in which he presented himself as the 'personal representative of Grant Shapps', and claimed he was a 'director' at CCHQ and that he had 'the full support of the Prime Minister'. He let it be known that, in his words, 'the patronage would flow', in the form of high-profile speakers and CCHQ internships, if they joined RoadTrip, but that if they refused, he and his allies 'could ruin them – ban all Tory speakers, blacklist the leadership … and much more personal stuff'.[508]

Clarke also drew recruits from the Young Britons' Foundation, a youth group described as a 'madrassa' for Tory activists.[509] Its founder, Donal Blaney, was a Freemason at the same lodge as Clarke, and he made Clarke YBF's 'director of outreach'. Blaney had close ties to many senior Conservatives.[510]

---

505   Private information.

506   http://www.jackjmatthews.co.uk/blog/what-next-for-conservative-future.

507   Private information.

508   Private information.

509   Robert Booth, *The Guardian*, 6 March 2010.

510   Six Cabinet ministers including Michael Gove, Sajid Javid and Michael Fallon were due to speak at the annual YBF conference in December before the bullying allegations broke. Within a week, all had pulled out citing 'diary conflicts'.

Despite all the complaints, Clarke was allowed to take his battle bus not only to three by-elections in 2014 but also on hundreds of expeditions through marginal seats in the run-up to the general election. The trips became infamous among young Tories, with one activist describing them as 'drunken shagfests'. Long campaign days would be followed by boozy curry nights where Tory activists were encouraged to pair off, and there are many anecdotal reports of class-A drugs being taken. Several young women have described how Clarke would encourage them to sleep with local MPs or candidates in an attempt to gain blackmail material. Reports would emerge that Clarke himself, by now a married father-of-two, was sexually aggressive.[511] A female activist told *Newsnight* that he once cornered her in a noisy bar and told her he could 'do great things' for her career.

'He tried making a move on me ... tried to put his hand up my skirt,' she said. She claimed that when she backed away, he told her he could 'ruin' her career in the party.

For each of these nights, the party signed off £250 for 'entertainment expenses'. On a number of occasions, Cameron himself visited the buses to encourage the activists.

Perhaps the Prime Minister's support made Clarke feel untouchable. In his witness statement, Abbott says that by the end of the 2015 election campaign, Clarke's behaviour was known about and was causing problems, and that the battle bus's activities were curtailed. Nonetheless, senior Tories continued to praise his contribution to the election victory.

The recently ennobled Baroness Emma Pidding, a former chair of the National Conservative Convention and a key organiser of RoadTrip, told a gathering, 'We all love crazy Clarke,' and suggested he had played a key role in achieving a Tory majority. In recognition of his efforts, Clarke was invited to an autumn reception at Chequers. Most gushing of all was Cameron himself, who wrote to Clarke personally, saying, 'We quite simply could not have done it without you.' He would soon bitterly regret their association.[512]

511   Catherine Rushton and Jack Doyle, *Daily Mail*, 18 November 2015.
512   Harry Cole, *The Sun*, 28 November 2015.

Conservative youth movements have long had a reputation for scandal. It's all good fodder for tabloid newspapers, but usually little more than student high jinks. This time was different.

A 38-year-old man with a history of serious allegations against him had been given free rein over a large number of vulnerable young activists. Most believed he was acting with the full authority of the Conservative Party.

'When he told us he could make or break our careers, what reason did we have to disbelieve him?' one said.[513]

After a stint on RoadTrip, Elliott Johnson got a job with Abbott as political editor of Conservative Way Forward, a small Thatcherite pressure group also founded by Blaney. Clarke began trying to pressure the young man into using his CWF blog to write negative pieces about his enemies, as he had done when trying to take over Conservative Future. This time Johnson refused. In a letter of complaint to the Conservative Party, he claimed that Clarke confronted him in the Marquis of Granby pub, grabbed him and pinned him to a chair, where he was told he would be 'squashed like an ant'. Shortly after, Johnson was made redundant from his job. Abbott claims this was nothing to do with Clarke (Conservative Way Forward had financial problems), but – presumably to big up his influence among senior Tories – Clarke nonetheless told Johnson he was behind it. During another showdown between the pair a few weeks later at another Westminster watering hole (captured on tape), Clarke claimed to have told Blaney that Johnson was a 'threat to the organisation'. His henchman weighed in, calling Johnson a 'fucking dickhead' and accusing him of being akin to a Nazi collaborator for making a complaint against Clarke.[514]

During this period, Clarke appears to have become increasingly unaccountable. According to Abbott's witness statement, 'His schemes to intimidate us became ever more elaborate and bizarre: revenge porn, extortion, blackmail, stings.' Two weeks later, Johnson was dead.

Following his tragic suicide, complaints and revelations came thick and fast. Three female activists told the *Mail on Sunday* that Clarke had sexually harassed them during RoadTrip.[515] One young member complained of being

---

513   Private information.
514   Simon Walters, Brendan Carlin and Tim Walker, *Mail on Sunday*, 4 October 2015.
515   Simon Walters, *Mail on Sunday*, 11 October 2015.

blackmailed for money after Clarke allegedly recorded him performing a sex act online.[516] It also emerged that Clarke had threatened the MP Robert Halfon over an affair with Alexandra Paterson, whom Clarke had since fallen out with.[517] Haley Hester, one of Clarke's former interns, claimed he had groped her repeatedly from her first day in the office. She claimed that when she complained, she was dismissed as a 'prudish American' who 'couldn't take British banter'.[518] In all, CCHQ received over twenty-five complaints against Clarke, who continues to deny wrongdoing. Eventually, Clarke was banned from the party for life. In a symbolic gesture, Shapps resigned from his junior ministerial post, saying the buck stopped with him. Despite serious questions about his own role in the tragedy, however, Feldman remained in post, protected, as always, by the Prime Minister.

One Tory activist remembers passing Cameron's old friend and fundraiser a dossier of claims about bullying within Conservative Future as far back as 2010.[519] Bath MP Ben Howlett told *Newsnight* that Feldman was well aware of claims about Clarke from the beginning. Meanwhile Abbott's statement reveals that shortly after the election, Feldman was told that Clarke was 'basically a bad man'.

At best, Cameron's fundraiser is guilty of a surprising lack of curiosity about the organisation he was running. This is in sharp contrast to former party chairs. Back in 1986, when the Federation of Conservative Students became known for riotous antics and members wearing 'Hang Nelson Mandela' T-shirts, Norman Tebbit had acted swiftly to close it down and punish those involved. Even Shapps has criticised Feldman for his 'tin ear and slow response'.[520]

Ultimately, as Johnson's father Ray put it, 'Lord Feldman was in charge when my son was being bullied and when my son died … responsibility lays squarely on [his] shoulders.'[521]

In August 2015, Feldman had ordered an internal inquiry after receiving complaints against Clarke from Johnson and Abbott, among others.

516　Simon Walters, *Mail on Sunday*, 22 November 2015.
517　Tamara Cohen and Andrew Levy, *Daily Mail*, 15 November 2015.
518　Andrew Levy and Tom Kelly, *Daily Mail*, 11 December 2015.
519　Laura Hughes, *Daily Telegraph*, 9 December 2015.
520　Simon Walters, *Mail on Sunday*, 24 January 2016.
521　Dan Bloom, *Daily Mirror*, 1 December 2015.

Following Johnson's death, that investigation was scrapped in favour of an independent inquiry by the law firm Clifford Chance.

The new inquiry ran into problems from the start. The Johnson family decided to boycott the investigation after it was revealed that Clifford Chance had longstanding links to the Conservatives. A number of witnesses also expressed fears over the potential leaking of private information. Abbott's statement recalls that there were particular concerns because a senior member of the party board who would scrutinise the inquiry, Robert Semple, owed his position in large part to Clarke's campaigning on his behalf, creating a potential conflict of interest.[522]

When the report was eventually released, in August 2016, it found thirteen alleged victims of Clarke's bullying, including six who claimed to have been sexually harassed. It found no evidence that Lord Feldman had known about bullying, but admitted that at least twelve 'significant' witnesses, including Clarke himself, had declined to give evidence to the inquiry. When the report's findings were announced, Johnson's father labelled it a 'whitewash'.[523]

By then Lord Feldman had stepped down following Cameron's own resignation. The party promised a review of its systems and procedures, but there were no serious consequences for anyone involved.

In private comments to a group of Oxford students shortly after the tragedy, Lynton Crosby offered some insight into why Clarke's behaviour was largely ignored by CCHQ.

He told undergraduates: 'Every second day I am told someone is an idiot or a crook, but that is no basis on which to investigate someone.' However, he acknowledged that the Tory Party can suffer from 'a student politics approach', in which 'some people treat politics as a game where they think things don't have consequences and that anything goes'.

In his statement to police, Abbott echoes this view. 'Politics is full of people being rude to each other, literally all the time, and everyone complaining

---

522   Abbott's witness statement suggests that this fear was well founded. He told police that information about an earlier CCHQ investigation was leaked to Clarke while it was still ongoing, potentially putting witnesses at risk. Abbott recalls the friend of one complainant getting a threatening phone call from Clarke, telling her, 'Deal with your friend, or I will.' He appeared to know every word of the complaint.

523   Ben Riley-Smith, *Daily Telegraph*, 17 August 2016.

about everyone else. It is an aggressive and contested world, extremely so. People fight and brawl, especially in CCHQ,' he said.

What of Cameron's role? His defenders will argue that he was at most a bit player in the drama and was never involved in day-to-day campaigning. There is no evidence that he knew about Clarke's behaviour. Others see the tragedy as symbolic of his indifference to the party grassroots: the voluntary organisations and local associations vital to the machine. Thanks at least in part to Clarke's excessive influence, there was something deeply wrong with the culture of the party's youth wing. The Prime Minister knew nothing about it. To his critics, the scandal encapsulates some of his political flaws: his lack of concern for the state of the wider party; his penchant for appointing cronies to key posts; his affinity for short-term showy tactics at the expense of longer-term strategy. His refusal to make Feldman take responsibility left him open to the charge, much repeated, of different standards for his friends than for others. As we have seen, he was swift to wield the axe when those outside his inner circle embarrassed him. (Allegations against Peter Cruddas and Patrick Mercer, for example, paled into insignificance relative to the death of a vulnerable young person on Feldman's watch.)

Abbott's statement ends with a note of bitter regret. 'I do not know what caused Elliott's death, which I will never understand. This haunts me every day. It consumes my mind at work and at night when I cannot sleep. I would give almost anything to bring Elliott Johnson back, to speak with him again.' Cameron had other things to worry about. By the time the Clifford Chance report was published, both he and Feldman would be long gone.

If the Tories were finished with Mark Clarke, he was not finished with them. Shortly after the New Year, Channel 4 political journalist Michael Crick produced a news report based on a stash of receipts and documents detailing what he described as a 'contempt for the law'. It appeared to show that the Tories had brazenly flouted election spending limits in a number of key constituencies – raising serious doubts about the legitimacy of the outcome in those seats.

Summer 2014 had been the zenith of support for UKIP, which was gaining support among disaffected socially conservative and Eurosceptic voters. The resignation of Patrick Mercer following a 'cash for questions' exposé by the BBC's *Panorama* programme in April 2014 and the defections of Tory MPs Douglas Carswell and Mark Reckless forced by-elections the Tories were determined to win.

In his first report, Crick showed that in the three by-elections in 2014 – Newark, Clacton, and Rochester and Strood – the Tories spent significantly more than the £100,000 legal limit. In Newark, Mercer's former constituency, receipts revealed that rooms at the Kelham House Hotel had been misleadingly registered to a Marion Little, a director at CCHQ (who had recently received an OBE for 'political services'). This spending was never declared. UKIP leader Nigel Farage had raised questions about overspending soon after the by-election result was announced. This was the evidence. Fortunately for Cameron, as the statute of limitations for election offences is only one year, it was too late for police to bring prosecutions in this case.

In a second report the following night, however, Crick produced evidence that suggested that in the key battleground of Thanet South, where Farage hoped to gain his first seat in Parliament at the 2015 general election, the Conservatives had spent nearly two and a half times the legal limit of just over £15,000. Once again, hotels had been booked under Little's name. Tory top brass stayed at the elegant Royal Harbour Hotel, while activists were relegated to the rather less fancy Premier Inn.

South Thanet had been an extremely high-profile battle. Tory big beasts including Boris Johnson were bussed in, as was the American campaign guru Jim Messina. Transport Minister John Hayes visited to campaign with the Tory candidate Craig Mackinlay over the future of a mothballed local airport, a key issue in the area. Election law is quite clear when it comes to this kind of activity, stating that any campaigning for a specific candidate must be filed on that candidate's local, not national, return. Yet the party registered most of its spending in Thanet South on forms relating to the party's national spending. Some expenses were not declared at all.

Further reports by Crick and Channel 4 showed that all of the estimated £60,000 spent on Clarke's battle bus initiative was declared on national returns.[524] Yet Crick was able to show that Clarke's troops consistently campaigned for local candidates. They handed out leaflets bearing the name of local candidates, and candidates referred to activists as 'our local team'.

---

524 The exact amount spent on the battle bus initiative is unknown because the party did not identify it in a category of its own.

A grainy mobile phone video of Cameron giving a pep talk on one of the buses features clear references to activists campaigning for local candidates.

Eventually, the Conservatives were forced to concede that £38,000 of hotel bills had not been declared, blaming an 'administrative error'. These revelations triggered investigations by ten different police forces. With very little time before the statute of limitations expired, officers applied to the High Court for extra time to investigate. In an unprecedented move, the Conservative Party attempted to block the extension, but only in South Thanet.

The judge threw out the request, declaring that the circumstances were 'wholly exceptional'.

Ominously for the party, he went on to state that the material presented by the police to him went 'far beyond ... a typical case where election offences are being investigated'.

In a further indication that the party felt it had something to hide, CCHQ refused to provide documents requested by the Electoral Commission, which had to resort to legal action to obtain the material required. In its submission to the authorities, the Electoral Commission claimed the inquiry had been 'delayed and hindered by the failure of the Conservative Party to provide complete and timely disclosure'.

Some Tory Party activists now say they feel misled by the party's high command in these elections. Katie Woodland, a local volunteer and former campaign manager, told Crick that 'the fact that it happened in three by-elections, one after the other – this is systematic. These people know the law – they've been running elections for years.'

Woodland told Crick she had been sent on a legal training day – so it seems likely that those responsible for form-filling knew the rules.

> I had a full day where we had it drummed into us what expenses were, how if somebody donated some stamps ... you still had to declare it. All of us in that room went away knowing, in no way can you spend more, or you'll go to prison. If I had known that they were going to not declare the hotel spend, then I would not have gone to Clacton, I would have questioned my own part in the party and I would not have been a campaign manager and I would have tried to get this investigated sooner.

The Conservative Party line remains that 'all spending has been declared in accordance with the law'. To Delyth Miles, chair of the local Clacton Conservative Association, that's 'just not good enough'. 'They need to be investigating this fully,' she told Crick.[525]

For Cameron and Feldman, it was another serious embarrassment. In the approach he has always adopted in times of trouble, Feldman refused all interview requests on the subject. Undeterred, the doughty Crick and his cameraman pursued him through the streets of Whitehall, demanding to know whether he had broken the law, and why so much spending had gone undeclared.

A flustered-looking Feldman couldn't get away fast enough. With Crick's microphone in his face, he gasped a series of stock responses about how 'everything had been followed in accordance with the rules', before fleeing to the sanctuary of Downing Street. In an excruciating interview with Channel 4 newsreader Jon Snow soon after, Cameron himself dissembled over the party's handling of the investigation, clearly uncomfortable.

At the time of writing, twenty-nine sitting MPs are under investigation over their electoral expenses returns. If found guilty, they could end up losing their seats – potentially jeopardising the Conservative majority.

The Electoral Commission has made no bones about the gravity of the situation. 'There is very significant public interest in this matter … The implications of the allegations are that individuals and/or the Conservative Party may have committed deliberate acts intended to circumvent the party and election finance rules … These allegations go to the very heart of our democracy,' the watchdog declared. It is a damning indictment on a party that prides itself on championing law and order – and casts a rather different complexion on Cameron's wafer-thin majority.

Cameron's *annus horribilis* would continue through the spring of 2016 (although he could take some comfort from the knowledge that the Labour Party under Jeremy Corbyn presented no threat).[526]

---

525   *Channel 4 News* video – Election Expenses, questions by Conservative Party workers, http://www.channel4.com/news/election-expenses-exposed.

526   From the moment the veteran backbencher was propelled to the party leadership on the back of a putsch by radical left-wing grassroots party members, he found himself attempting to lead the opposition without the support of his own MPs.

In early April, a mass leak of documents from a Panamanian law firm called Mossack Fonseca to German newspaper *Süddeutsche Zeitung* implicated an array of politicians, celebrities and businessmen from all over the world in various offshore tax avoidance schemes.

Revelations included an attempt by Vladimir Putin to hide £2 billion in personal funds, as well as several million hidden by Icelandic Prime Minister Sigmundur Gunnlaugsson, who was forced to resign after a tenth of Iceland's population took to the streets in protest.

Conspicuous among the names was Cameron's father Ian, who as a stockbroker had set up a sizeable offshore fund called Blairmore Holdings. It prompted immediate questions about the Prime Minister's own stake in the fund.

The timing could hardly have been worse. Both Cameron and Osborne had made a great song and dance of tackling tax avoidance in general, and the use of tax havens in particular. In a bitter irony, Cameron was preparing to chair an anti-corruption summit, to which representatives from fifty countries and institutions had been invited, aimed at tackling the financial secrecy offered by such jurisdictions. It was scheduled to take place in May.

Now he was facing questions over whether he himself had benefited from schemes in such places.

Downing Street's initial response was to claim such matters were private, a line which only served to fuel suspicion that the Prime Minister had something to hide. Under pressure, No. 10 later issued a statement to the effect that the PM had no shares, nor any offshore funds that his family 'would benefit from in the future'.

The careful choice of words was all the evidence journalists needed to keep pressing for detail. They were right to smell a rat. In an interview with ITV's Robert Peston, Cameron eventually admitted to having owned a stake in his father's company worth just over £30,000, which he had sold just before entering Downing Street in 2010.

In an attempt to close down the row, he released a summary of his tax returns since 2009, which revealed little more than the fact that he had received a £200,000 gift from his mother following his father's death. It was a legitimate and commonplace device to reduce inheritance tax. Even his critics acknowledged that he could not be held accountable for the financial affairs of his parents. But the affair was a glaring reminder of the scale of his family wealth, undermining the 'everyman' image he had so carefully cultivated since becoming Leader of the Opposition in 2005. On a personal level, too, it was deeply bruising: Cameron hated the tidal wave of disparaging commentary about his beloved father, who had done nothing improper at a time when the use of offshore tax havens was not politically sensitive.

Meanwhile another Cabinet minister was in trouble. John Whittingdale, whose appointment as Culture Secretary had been a source of widespread surprise,[527] found himself at the centre of a lowbrow scandal about a relationship with a prostitute with connections to criminal gangs. While such a revelation would have been terminal for politicians in the 1980s and 1990s, in 2016, it was no great shakes, especially since Whittingdale was no longer married. Most papers wouldn't touch it.

What made the story murkier was that four national newspapers had investigated the allegation before deciding not to publish. In theory, this gave them some sway over Whittingdale, whose ministerial brief included press regulation. Hostile commentators were swift to point out that Whittingdale had hung fire on some of Leveson's recommendations.

For a while, it looked as if questions over his ability to oversee press regulation might finish him (especially when it emerged that he had sent a different lover a snap of fellow Cabinet ministers chilling in the garden at Chequers), but he clung on. It was widely assumed that Cameron would seize the opportunity to axe him at the next Cabinet reshuffle, expected after the referendum.

In May, the Tories lost London.

It was expected: the capital remained a Labour stronghold, a bias Boris Johnson had been able to overcome by sheer force of personality. In any case, after eight years in power, there was a sense it was Labour's 'turn'.

Privately, the party leadership was not unduly dismayed: the victory of Sadiq Khan, formerly a second-tier Labour politician (he never reached full Cabinet during the Blair–Brown years), shored up Corbyn's leadership, which was far more important to the bigger picture.

Once again, the leadership had struggled to find a candidate. There was

---

527   It was widely suspected that he was only offered the job because Cameron's first choice for the position had declined.

nobody with Johnson's charisma and cross-party appeal. Eventually they opted for the fiercely independent backbencher Zac Goldsmith, whose relationship with Cameron had long been fractious.

As another Old Etonian, and the second richest Member of Parliament, Goldsmith was disadvantaged from the start.

Pitted against the son of an immigrant bus driver from Tooting, the trustafarian multi-millionaire (and former non-dom) was always going to struggle to connect with most Londoners. In a sign that Goldsmith was never expected to win, Lynton Crosby refused to handle his campaign, delegating it instead to his respected business partner Mark Fullbrook.

It faltered from the start. Fullbrook's earnest candidate was too diffident; his quiet, unassuming manner too easily misinterpreted as indicative of an absence of passion.

What the pugnacious Khan lacked in political experience and physical stature (at just 5 foot 4 inches tall), he made up for in chutzpah and street-fighting skills.

Characterising himself as the embodiment of the 'London dream', he remorselessly highlighted his humble origins, showing how he had overcome poverty and racism through sheer energy and determination (as well as the ability to land a punch, thanks to many hours training at an amateur boxing club). By contrast, Goldsmith looked wan. Those who know him never doubted his commitment to winning, but he struggled to show others how much it mattered to him. A campaign focused on Khan's alleged links to Islamic extremist organisations backfired spectacularly. Though his team uncovered some questionable connections, there was no smoking gun.

Ten days before the election, Fullbrook knew the game was up. His private polling was so dire he decided not to share it with the candidate, for fear the campaign would collapse.[528] Goldsmith himself knew that he was doomed when he discovered he had lost the support of worshippers at a mosque in his constituency. The Muslim community in Richmond, formerly strong supporters, had been alienated by the flavour of his campaign against Khan.

In retrospect, his performance was perfectly respectable. Andrew Cooper points out that on first preferences, Goldsmith and Khan both achieved the same result as their respective parties did nationally in 2015:

---

528   Private information.

London is for the time being a Labour city and to have any chance of winning at all is very, very difficult … It's only possible if you have a candidate who both really, really motivates the Tory vote in the London boroughs and has a bit of reach and appeal beyond the Tory base. Boris did; I don't think we had a candidate in Zac who did. The party leadership realised very early on that Zac didn't have what it would take.

However, he acknowledges that the relentless attempt to smear Khan over his record of 'platform sharing' with radical Islamic figures in the past was a mistake.

'I was surprised that they stuck with the campaign when it obviously wasn't working,' he says. 'I assumed there would be some kind of pay-off moment when it all came together – some big revelation – and there wasn't. The theme of his campaign meant he had no chance of getting second preferences from Lib Dems or anyone else.'

Crosby simply washed his hands of it. He never thought Goldsmith would win. Some five months before the Mayoral election, during a private event, he was asked how he thought Goldsmith would fare.

He snorted and replied: 'Well, what do you think? He's certainly no Boris, is he?'[529]

Still basking in the glow of his unexpected majority, Cameron could shrug off all these setbacks as the rough and tumble of frontline politics. Perhaps he was beginning to feel invincible. If so, the spring Budget exposed the fragility of his leadership.

From the moment that he accidentally admitted he would not seek a third term if elected in 2015, in a televised interview with the then BBC deputy political editor James Landale during the election campaign, his authority had been eroded.[530]

Six months before the Budget, a *Spectator* cartoon depicted Osborne

529 Private information.
530 The balance of power immediately shifted towards his likely successors – Osborne in particular. Preoccupied by his much vaunted 'renegotiation' of Britain's relationship with the EU, Cameron was content to let power flow towards the Chancellor.

with tentacles snaked around Westminster, one enveloping a helpless Boris Johnson. The Chancellor was now at the height of his powers, and it was not a great exaggeration of his image at Westminster and beyond. Indeed, *Politico* labelled him 'the most powerful man in Britain'.[531]

The Chancellor had long since recovered from his nadir following his notorious 2012 'Omnishambles' Budget and had revamped his image. His chief of staff Thea Rogers encouraged him to change his hairstyle (the new cut made him look more youthful) and lose weight. She was well rewarded with a 42 per cent pay rise on the taxpayer's bill,[532] as well as an OBE a few months later. The general election result appeared to have vindicated his economic strategy, and he was widely seen as the heir apparent.

The immediate post-referendum reshuffle highlighted his powers of patronage. Promotions were handed out to loyal 'friends of George', including Sajid Javid, Amber Rudd, Robert Halfon, Greg Hands and Matthew Hancock. Backbench MPs were known to grumble that you had no chance of making the ministerial ladder unless you were a woman, an ethnic minority or a 'friend of George'. His 2015 summer Budget, with its national living wage and crackdowns on non-domicile status and tax avoidance, was widely praised for capturing the centre ground. The unravelling of his 2016 Budget would prove his undoing.

Osborne's relationship with Welfare Secretary Iain Duncan Smith had long been strained. Conflicting political agendas created a natural tension between their departments: the Treasury was under constant pressure to find savings, and the bloated welfare budget was always the juiciest target for cuts. On a crusade to improve the lives of the poor, Duncan Smith's approach to reforming the system was always governed by the mantra that 'work must pay'. Time and again, Osborne's fiscal policy seemed neither compassionate nor consistent with Duncan Smith's drive to incentivise the work-shy to get jobs.

The Welfare Secretary became increasingly resentful at having to carry the can for unpopular austerity measures of which he did not privately approve.

There was also a personality clash. The urbane Chancellor had no time for the deeply traditional and religious former Scots Guard officer. At times, he barely concealed his contempt for Duncan Smith.

---

531   Amol Rajan, *Politico*, 29 July 2015.
532   Rajeev Syal, *The Guardian*, 17 December 2015.

'He thinks I'm stupid,' the Welfare Secretary would complain to friends, while the Chancellor's aides would brief journalists about their exasperation with the Welfare Secretary's failure to 'grasp detail'. Throughout the coalition years, tensions frequently threatened to boil over in the run-up to Budgets. On more than one occasion, Duncan Smith seriously considered walking out. The March 2016 Budget was the last straw.

The conflagration came over plans for £4 billion cuts to disability benefits and the personal independence payment. In a Budget that included a tax break for higher earners, it was toxic. A backbench rebellion loomed and, this time, Duncan Smith was not prepared to be the scapegoat.

Having initially done his best to defend the measure, he was incensed to discover that Downing Street planned to row back on the cut and blame him for the mess. It prompted one of the most dramatic Cabinet resignations of modern times. The Welfare Secretary erupted, declaring Osborne's cuts incompatible with 'compassionate Conservatism'. In a devastating letter to Cameron, he effectively accused the government of balancing the Budget on the backs of the working poor.[533]

For a party leadership that had devoted a decade to overturning the deep-rooted popular perception that the Conservatives were the party of the rich, it could hardly have been more damaging. Journalist Andrew Rawnsley described it as 'a poison dart shot into the Chancellor's flank'.[534] For the first time since Corbyn's election, Labour briefly drew level in the polls.

Cameron was in Brussels when he received the call from Duncan Smith. Under no illusion about the scale of the potential repercussions, he desperately tried to persuade him to stay. The Welfare Secretary made it clear he had made up his mind. In a furious private exchange, Cameron reportedly labelled him a 'shit'.

In the days that followed, Duncan Smith did not hold back, using a battery of media appearances to deliver a devastating critique of Osborne's Budget. He labelled it 'deeply unfair', claiming the unfairness was 'damaging to the government, it is damaging to the party and ... damaging to the public'.[535]

The Chancellor's allies tried to paint him as an embittered old-timer jumping from Cabinet before he was pushed, but it failed to convince anyone.

---

533 Rowena Mason and Anushka Asthana, *The Guardian*, 20 March 2016.
534 Andrew Rawnsley, *The Guardian*, 20 March 2016.
535 Iain Duncan Smith, interview with Andrew Marr, 20 March 2016.

The episode left Osborne near fatally wounded. Neither his reputation as a tactician nor his reputation for economic competence would recover. Meanwhile Duncan Smith – a staunch Eurosceptic – was now free to turn his mind to the referendum campaign. (In this, his knowledge of the welfare system for EU migrants would make him a formidable foe.)

Over a ten-month period, Cameron had suffered a series of heavy blows. Nonetheless, thanks to the woeful state of the Labour Party under Corbyn, the Tory Party remained four to six points ahead of Labour in the polls throughout most of this period.

Under other circumstances (particularly given his pledge not to seek a third term) there might have been rumblings of a coup. From the turn of the year, however, the normal cut and thrust of Westminster politics was effectively on hold. A much more important issue loomed: one which would not just last the lifetime of a parliament, but would have a defining impact on the United Kingdom's standing in the world for generations to come. This was Cameron's much heralded referendum on the most divisive question in post-war British politics: the relationship between the United Kingdom and the European Union.

Nobody anticipated the cataclysmic chain of events it would unleash.

43
OUT

'I will win this easily.'

– Cameron to Herman Van Rompuy

The night before Britain voted to leave the European Union, thunder and lightning split the skies over Westminster. An electric storm raged for two hours, illuminating the Houses of Parliament with dazzling white blasts against the indigo night. Cameron had never been devout, but perhaps he wondered what the gods were trying to say.

23 June dawned as humid as an Indian monsoon. So much rain had fallen overnight that great ponds emerged on the grass in central London parks. Activists deployed to get out the vote broiled under swollen skies. Shortly after 5 p.m., as commuters poured out of offices and began heading home, the heavens opened again. Such was the deluge that transport services throughout the capital were disrupted.

At the headquarters of the Remain campaign, the mood was increasingly nervous. Turnout would be crucial, and inclement weather threatened to disrupt journeys to the polling booth, potentially suppressing the pro-European vote that was so concentrated in the capital. The theory was that Brexiteers, fired up by their once-in-a-generation opportunity, were less likely than ambivalent Remainers to let the weather put them off casting their vote.

Polls showed the result was on a knife-edge. In keeping with the pattern in referendums both in the UK and worldwide, the final few days had seen a slight shift towards the status quo option – more than enough to rattle the Leave campaigns, but too slight to give great cause for confidence to Remain. Every vote would count.

Cameron had never been under any illusion about the EU's popularity among British voters. Back in January 2013, when he unveiled his pledge to hold an In/Out referendum, he had acknowledged that democratic consent for the institution was 'wafer thin'. He had spent months deliberating over whether to commit himself to a plebiscite, knowing that the move was a huge risk.

Not only was the outcome uncertain (though he was very confident Britain would vote to remain in the EU at that stage), the campaign would be bloody and would leave him little time or energy for anything else. He had not forgotten how the row over the Maastricht Treaty had crippled his old boss John Major's premiership.

By late 2012, however, he could see no way out. Under pressure from a rump of Eurosceptic Tory backbenchers on the one hand and a surging UKIP on the other, he feared that unless he volunteered to hold a referendum, sooner or later he would be forced into it.

'The question mark is already there and ignoring it won't make it go away,' he argued, in the so-called Bloomberg Speech, in which he announced his plan.

> In fact, quite the reverse. Those who refuse to contemplate consulting the British people would in my view make more likely our eventual exit. Simply asking the British people to carry on accepting a European settlement over which they have had little choice is a path to ensuring that when the question is finally put – and at some stage it will have to be – it is much more likely that the British people will reject the EU.[536]

From the outset, the Prime Minister argued that Britain's relationship with Brussels should be re-negotiated ahead of an In/Out vote, which he promised would take place before the end of 2017.

Calling for an EU 'fit for the twenty-first century', he challenged other EU leaders to help 'address the sclerotic, ineffective decision making that is

---

536   Bloomberg Speech, https://www.gov.uk/government/speeches/eu-speech-at-bloomberg.

holding us back' and create a 'leaner, less bureaucratic Union, relentlessly focused on helping its member countries to compete'. He promised reform that would be nothing short of 'full-on treaty change' and that he would 'not take no for an answer' on free movement of people.[537] His vision was for a 'flexible union of free member states who share treaties and institutions and pursue together the ideal of cooperation'. He urged his European partners to 'work with us on this'.[538]

He began the diplomatic process as soon as the Tories were re-elected. Having calculated that the referendum should be held sooner rather than later (dragging out the process risked paralysing his own administration and weakening his negotiating hand with French and German leaders, both of whom faced elections in 2017), he embarked on an urgent campaign to persuade EU leaders to give him what he needed to sell the benefits of EU membership to a sceptical electorate.

He found himself swimming against the tide. Merkel genuinely wanted to help, but on the single most controversial aspect of EU membership as far as UK voters were concerned – free movement of people – she would not budge, telling the Prime Minister bluntly that it was non-negotiable.

Downing Street had hoped that if they could not get an opt-out on free movement, it might be possible to secure an 'emergency brake' on migration. This would have allowed Britain to impose temporary suspensions on migration in exceptional circumstances and might have gone some way towards addressing public concern. Merkel and Hollande would not hear of it. For them, free movement was a fundamental principle.

So the Prime Minister shifted his sights to what he saw as more achievable aims: a ban on EU migrants claiming child benefit for offspring not living in the UK; a ban on migrants collecting work-related benefits; and a binding opt-out from the commitment to 'ever closer union'. He did not even get these. Instead, he was offered a complicated package of marginal reductions to child benefit and a temporary break on in-work tax credits, as

---

537   David Cameron speech to Conservative Party conference 2014, http://press.
      conservatives.com/post/98882674910/david-cameron-speech-to-conservative-
      party.

538   Bloomberg Speech, op. cit.

well as a symbolic opt-out from 'ever closer union' which was not expected to be backed up by legally enforceable treaty change.[539]

The geopolitical context did not help. The civil war in Syria had created a deepening humanitarian crisis, prompting a surge of refugees from the east. Terror attacks by so-called Islamic State, particularly in France, added to the intense pressure on EU leaders from their own voters to focus on domestic issues. Against such a backdrop, Cameron's counterparts saw Britain's incessant demands for repatriation of powers from Brussels as an irritating distraction.

After six months of diplomatic wrangling, the Prime Minister concluded he was unlikely to extract anything further and decided to wrap it up. An EU summit at the end of February 2016, at which the meagre concessions he had secured were signed off, marked the end of what had been a deeply frustrating process.

The Prime Minister had not hidden the challenges he had faced. Many MPs and Westminster observers believed that this was 'expectation management', and that he had something impressive up his sleeve.

When his 'deal' was finally unveiled on 2 February 2016, it was clear he did not. It was widely panned. On its front page, the *Daily Mail* accused him of a 'great delusion' while *The Sun* likened his renegotiation to 'a steaming pile of manure', describing it as a 'dismal failure worse than we ever imagined'.

'Sorry, Prime Minister, but … IT STINKS,' the paper declared.[540]

A cartoon in *The Spectator* showed a hapless Cameron dressed as a swanky waiter uncovering a huge platter only to show a barely visible slice of cake with a tiny Union Jack flag poking from it.

Why were the Europeans so apparently intractable, when an important member state was threatening to exit the bloc? It boils down to contrasting expectations.

A source close to Merkel highlighted the gulf in attitudes between Britain and Germany over the renegotiation.

---

539 What Cameron did get was a complicated emergency break whereby the UK could limit the access of new EU migrants to in-work benefits such as housing benefit for up to four years. But activation of this break would still have to be approved by the European Parliament and European Commission. The terms actually played into the hands of Leave, who claimed it showed that the EU would still ultimately call the shots.

540 Roy Greenslade, *The Guardian*, 3 February 2016.

'Let me be very frank – he asked for a lot and he got a lot,' the source says.

> I don't agree with the argument which I often hear in the UK, which
> is that Cameron asked for not enough and he got even less. If you
> have some clue how the debate was in December, January, Febru-
> ary, I can tell you they were very tough negotiations and the other
> twenty-seven member states went as far as they could.[541]

According to the source, concessions dismissed as derisory by a UK audience
were regarded as extremely generous by EU federalists.

He told us:

> The February agreement for the British included for the first time
> the ability of a country to give up the principle of ever closer union.
> Now, you can say this is purely symbolic, but ever closer union is
> something all other member states believe in ... for the people who
> believe in European unity, that was quite severe.

It was the same story with migrant benefits. Minor tweaks to qualification
criteria were ridiculed in Britain but, according to Merkel's ally, for the
Germans, they represented a major shift on a point of principle.

'Cameron *got* a concession on migration, which meant for the first time,
EU citizens did not have to be treated equally,' he exclaims.

> That was something quite difficult for the Eastern Europeans to
> accept. But the problem was that none of what we had negotiated
> in February played a role in the subsequent referendum campaign.
> We could have had much less trouble with Eastern Europe if we
> had known this. In Britain, people say he got nothing. But I can
> tell you, he got at least as much as Europeans were willing to give.

He is emphatic that there is nothing Cameron could have done to wring
further concessions on free movement out of the Europeans. 'I defend the
Prime Minister, who did the best job he possibly could have done,' he says.

---

541   Private information.

'The European Union *is* the free movement of people, that is its foundation. You cannot pick and choose what parts of the deal you want.'

Faced with such a disappointing offer (from the UK's perspective at least), should Cameron have simply walked out of the talks? He had repeatedly claimed, before his renegotiation began in earnest, that he would be willing to do so. Before the negotiations, he warned Europeans that if 'Britain's concerns were to be met with a deaf ear … then we will have to think again about whether this European Union is right for us … I rule nothing out.'[542]

The problem was that EU leaders could have called his bluff and refused to give further ground. Having declared that he could not support remaining without reform, Cameron would then have had no choice but to recommend that Britain leave, a move he still believed was not in the nation's interests. So he embarked on a campaign to persuade voters to stay in the EU, even though he had achieved little change to the relationship. It put him in a weak position from the start.

Matthew Elliott, Vote Leave's chief executive, now believes that Cameron lost the referendum at the summit.

> The deal was threadbare. He had set up the parameters of the negotiation as being that he couldn't support the deal 'unless the EU changed'. He had claimed that Britain could have a 'bright future' outside the EU. Then, when he got nothing, he had to perform a double somersault to a position whereby leaving would be an economic catastrophe; Project Fear. If the Europeans hadn't been intransigent, the debate could have been completely different.

Serious thinking about how to persuade voters to stay in the EU had begun almost a year earlier, before the 2015 election. That summer, it would evolve into an official campaign called 'Britain Stronger in Europe', a name with the unfortunate acronym 'BSE'.

Its leading lights were an array of experienced and influential Westminster figures. It featured Andrew Cooper as director of polling; Will Straw (son of former Labour Home Secretary Jack Straw) as chief executive; Lucy

---

542 Toby Helm, *The Guardian*, 7 November 2015.

Thomas as deputy director; and Ryan Coetzee as director of strategy, as well as various prominent business figures. But, from the beginning, they struggled to make the positive case for Remain. In the early days, Cooper recalls colleagues struggling to come up with positive facts about Britain's membership of the EU:

> I asked several of the key figures involved in setting up the Remain campaign to name what they regarded as the top five most powerful and persuasive facts showing the UK was better off in the EU. They struggled to come up with any. The point is that they were full of long narrative arguments and true-believer explanations about the benefits of membership, but because they themselves didn't see membership in transactional, pragmatic terms, they weren't accustomed to making the case on the basis of pragmatic benefits, which is the way floating voters saw things. They could readily come up with good 'things' about being in the EU; what they struggled with was hard 'facts' about the EU, probably because the economic case for membership just is – or was – more complicated. It comes down to the net effect of lots of things, on growth, employment, prices, economic dynamism and so on.

Eventually they devised the mantra 'Stronger, Safer, Better Off', the primary focus always being on the third of those claims.[543]

Taking what they believed were the correct lessons from the Scottish referendum and the 2015 election campaign, the team designed a campaign based almost exclusively on the perceived economic risk of Brexit. Dubbed 'Project Fear' by the press, the plan was to strike hard and fast with a succession of dire economic warnings from a variety of experts and organisations, in the hope of establishing a 'settled view' among voters, which Leave campaigners would be unable to dislodge.

The Prime Minister and Chancellor showed no compunction in harnessing the supposedly neutral civil service machine to the cause. In a highly

---

543   It was a mouthful, and each particular point required detailed explanation. By contrast, Vote Leave's slogan of 'Take Back Control' pithily encapsulated their campaign's message. For this reason, Leave campaigners repeated the slogan ad nauseam.

controversial initiative taken before the 'purdah' period limited Whitehall involvement, the pair arranged for leaflets extolling the benefits of Britain's membership of the EU to be sent to every household in the UK. The propaganda blitz cost taxpayers £9 million, prompting an outcry from Brexiteers about abuse of government resources.

It was followed by a report from the Treasury, which claimed that economic conditions after Brexit would be so bad that they would cost the average household £4,300. The back-of-the-envelope calculation was widely derided, but to Remainers the exact figures did not matter. The message was simple: Brexit would hit voters in the pocket.

Meanwhile a phalanx of Downing Street spin doctors was seconded to the Stronger In campaign, including the deputy head of No. 10's Policy Unit, Daniel Korski, and Craig Oliver himself. The team used every tool at its disposal, making it their business to ensure that influential organisations knew how grateful the Prime Minister would be if they fell into line. The tactics could be heavy-handed. In the early days of the campaign, for example, it emerged that Korski had leaned on the British Chambers of Commerce over its Brexit-supporting director-general, John Longworth. Longworth subsequently resigned so that he could speak freely.[544]

Stronger In had hoped that a state visit by Barack Obama would prove the knockout blow. The American President had already stated as early as June 2015 that he believed Britain would be better off inside the EU. Now he went much further. During a trip to London a month before polling day, he warned that the UK would find itself 'at the back of the queue' for future trade deals if it left the EU. Like Osborne's warnings of economic catastrophe, the intervention backfired. There were suspicions that the wording had been scripted by Downing Street (Americans talk about 'lines', not 'queues') and focus groups showed voters felt the President was interfering in UK affairs.

Project Fear was not proving as straightforward as it had in the past. In the Scottish referendum campaign, the Remain camp had a concrete issue – the question of which currency an independent Scotland could use – that the nationalists could never convincingly answer. Remain searched in vain for an equivalent issue.

Nonetheless, the general consensus, even among Brexit supporters, was

---

544 John Longworth, *The Guardian*, 11 April 2016.

that leaving the EU would have some negative economic impact, at least in the short term – making it a powerful argument.

On the back foot, Vote Leave switched its focus to immigration, an issue its strategists had been reluctant to put at the heart of their campaign any earlier, for fear of alienating some floating voters.

Stronger In had already scored a significant own goal when its chair, Marks and Spencer's boss Stuart Rose, admitted that lower EU migration would raise the wages of local workers, before scrambling to clarify that 'that is not necessarily a good thing'.[545] In a further boost for Brexit, updated figures from the Office for National Statistics put net migration at 333,000 per annum, the second largest total on record.[546] This coincided with the beginning of purdah, making it the perfect time for the Leave campaign to seize the initiative.

To all this, Cameron had no answer. Time and again, his old pledge to bring immigration down to the 'tens of thousands' per year came back to haunt him. While Britain remained a member of the EU, he simply had no way of delivering it. In a high-profile intervention in the last few days of the campaign, Steve Hilton (whose longstanding Euroscepticism had been hardened by his experience in government) claimed the Prime Minister had always known as much.

After flying back to Britain from his home in California to campaign for Brexit, Hilton revealed that Cameron had been warned 'directly and explicitly' four years earlier that the ambition was not deliverable, and questioned why the Prime Minister had continued to make the promise.

The Prime Minister faced other unexpected setbacks. He had always expected a number of his Cabinet to back Brexit, including Leader of the Commons Chris Grayling; Employment Minister Priti Patel; and Northern Ireland Secretary Theresa Villiers. All had longstanding Eurosceptic credentials. Michael Gove's decision to join them came as a shock.

The recently appointed Justice Secretary had long disliked Brussels, but

---

545 Evidence to the Treasury Select Committee: http://data.parliament.uk/ writtenevidence/committeeevidence.svc/evidencedocument/treasury-committee/ the-economic-and-financial-costs-and-benefits-of-uks-eu-membership/ oral/30171.pdf#page=35.

546 Office for National Statistics, 27 May 2016: https://www.ons. gov.uk/peoplepopulationandcommunity/populationandmigration/ internationalmigration/bulletins/migrationstatisticsquarterlyreport/may2016.

had allowed Cameron to believe that when the time came for the referendum, he would fall into line. Instead, he decided to put what his wife Sarah Vine described as his 'heartfelt beliefs' ahead of his 'loyalty to his old friend the PM' and throw his weight behind the Out campaign.[547]

It was a bitter personal blow for Cameron, depriving him of one of his most able and trusted allies. In time, there would be terrible repercussions for the friendship between the two men and their families. But it was Boris Johnson's eleventh hour decision to back Leave – announced just two days after Cameron returned from Brussels with his final 'deal' – that had the biggest political impact.

The then Mayor of London had kept Westminster waiting for months for his decision, which he made in the hours after Cameron concluded his renegotiation.[548] Central to his deliberation was the question of sovereignty. Having examined the results of the renegotiation with the help of his barrister wife Marina Wheeler, he concluded that the Prime Minister's deal had done nothing to alter the supremacy of Brussels law – and felt Britain was better off Out.

It was not an easy decision. Like the Prime Minister, Johnson had always been slightly more pro-EU than anti. He was fluent in several languages, was born in New York City, and had Turkish ancestry, so his view of the world was (and remains) cosmopolitan. But he was genuinely troubled by the overbearing power of European institutions. Moreover, if he wished to run for the party leadership some day, there were tactical advantages to backing Brexit, a position that would endear him to the party's Eurosceptic grassroots.

After a weekend at his secluded country pad in Oxfordshire, his mind was made up.

His sister has told how they thrashed it out over a game of tennis.

'Look,' Boris said, pointing down at his mud-encrusted shoes. 'Nike trainers. Wilson tennis balls and a Prince racket. These are American companies – they're not part of Europe, are they? Hasn't stopped us buying their products, has it?'

At that point, she realised, 'It wouldn't make any difference if the Outers were led by David Icke or the Cookie Monster. It wasn't about

547   Sarah Vine, *Daily Mail*, 24 February 2016.
548   Johnson's term as Mayor ended during the campaign, in early May.

the "personalities" but the issues – and he was already feeling the heavy hand of fate on his shoulder.'[549]

For Brexiteers, Johnson's decision was a sensational coup. The Leave campaign now had a charismatic figurehead with 'box office' appeal among sections of society other senior politicians could not reach. The headline acts of the 1975 Leave campaign had been eccentrics from the fringe wings of their parties – Tony Benn from the Labour left, Enoch Powell from the Tory right. Not so this time. Johnson gave the campaign a celebrity face and populist bluster, while Gove supplied the intellectual firepower and political heft that came from six years of senior Cabinet service. While their partnership lasted, they were more than a match for Cameron. A formidable operation to engage voters up and down the country, led by Nigel Farage, and an unofficial Out campaign called Leave.EU, broadened the movement, ensuring the case for Brexit resonated with audiences outside the Westminster 'bubble'.

Meanwhile much of Fleet Street was lining up against the Prime Minister. He had grown used to a broadly sympathetic press, the combined might of which had done much to shred Ed Miliband's chances of entering No. 10. This time, the country's two biggest-selling newspapers, the *Daily Mail* and *The Sun*, had their guns trained firmly on him. Both papers embarked on energetic campaigns for Brexit. The *Express* and the *Daily Telegraph* (and later the *Sunday Times*) also backed leaving the EU.

The Labour vote was also a serious worry. While Jeremy Corbyn was publicly supporting Remain, he had been a lifelong left-wing Eurosceptic. He had voted to leave the European Economic Community in 1975, and had walked through the lobby against Maastricht, against Lisbon and against the Single European Act. Like Tony Benn – and many traditional Labour voters – he had viewed the EU as a rich man's capitalist club that allowed lobbyists and business interests to collude against workers.

Outwardly, Labour appeared to be at one over the issue. The leadership, the entire shadow Cabinet and the major unions all backed Remain, with just ten MPs defying the party line. A vote on whether the party should officially back Remain, held at the party's annual conference, was passed overwhelmingly after a debate lasting just fifteen minutes.

The show of unity, however, was a façade. Senior Labour figures involved

---

549   Rachel Johnson, *Mail on Sunday*, 28 February 2016.

in the campaign have now confirmed the party was split over the issue from the leadership down.

Shortly before his election as leader, Corbyn was still making Eurosceptic noises. During the Greek debt crisis, for example, he accused the EU of creating a 'usurious Europe that turns its smaller nations into colonies of debt peonage'.[550]

It has now emerged that it was only when the then shadow Foreign Secretary Hilary Benn threatened him with a shadow Cabinet walkout that the Labour leader folded, accepting that he would have to go with the majority view in order to hold the party together. 'His "road to Brussels" conversion convinced no one,' says a campaign figure scornfully.

Indeed, when they thought they could get away with it, the leadership actively encouraged Eurosceptic elements in the party ranks. At the Scottish Labour Party conference in Perth in October 2015, Corbyn and shadow Chancellor John McDonnell paid a visit to an exhibition stand held by the Scottish branch of Labour Leave (then called 'Scottish Labour for Britain'). According to one who was present, the shadow Chancellor put his arm on the shoulder of former Edinburgh South MP Nigel Griffiths and told him to 'keep up the good work, mate'. Had this exchange been exposed at the time, it would have provoked a furious backlash from Labour MPs and activists and been a source of extreme embarrassment for the party leadership.

Despite the small number of MPs openly advocating Brexit, Labour Leave sources claim that if it had not been for the official party line, at least thirty-seven Labour MPs would have come on board. A number of trade unions were also deeply uneasy about petitioning their members to vote Remain. Insiders say the GMB feared there would be a revolt if they took this step. 'One quarter of our membership voted UKIP in the last election!' one leadership figure observed. They backed Remain reluctantly and only under pressure from party officials.

One of the most senior Labour MPs to back Brexit told colleagues that he frequently received words of congratulations during the campaign – including from at least five shadow ministers, including several from the shadow Cabinet. 'That was a great speech, mate,' one shadow Cabinet member told him. Another remarked: 'It is so important that Labour has a robust Out campaign.'

---

550   Jeremy Corbyn, Huffington Post, 29 June 2015.

Brendan Chilton, Labour Leave's chief executive, believes that Corbyn's lacklustre campaigning worked in Leave's favour. 'Every one of Jeremy Corbyn's interventions in the campaign we considered helpful to us,' he says.

Alarmed by the forces amassing against him, at the start of June, Cameron announced a press conference. His theme was 'Brexit lies'. The Leave campaign, he claimed, was 'resorting to total untruths to con people into taking a leap in the dark: it's irresponsible and it's wrong and it's time that the Leave campaign was called out on the nonsense that they are peddling'.[551]

Once again, it backfired, not least because his own side had peddled plenty of myths of their own. As Vote Leave ramped up claims about how '£350 million a week' sent to Brussels by British taxpayers could be spent on the NHS, Stronger In could only wheel out more experts and independent bodies to prophesy economic doom. Following the controversy over the Treasury report, the warnings would not stick.

'People have had enough of experts,' Gove declared, in a Sky television interview.[552] Events would show he was right.

It did not help Remain that many of the individuals warning of dire consequences of leaving the EU were the same people who had urged Britain to join the Euro. They had also failed to anticipate the financial crash, and in some cases had even been partly to blame for it. It was not hard for Brexiteers to portray these 'experts' as part of a status quo out of which they had all done very well.

Leave's final coup was to raise a long dormant issue, that of the possibility of Turkey joining the European Union, an alarming prospect for many voters. Matthew Elliott staunchly defends this, saying it was a legitimate debate. 'The government's official position was to facilitate Turkey's path to membership. The UK had just joined the other EU members in a deal agreeing to re-open membership talks and allow visa-free access for Turkish citizens,' he says. Publicly, Cameron could hardly explain that it was all a polite diplomatic fiction. As Cooper puts it:

> The truth is that Turkey is moving further and further away from accession and looking less and less like a democracy. The predominant Foreign Office view is that they will probably never join. But

551 Rowena Mason, *The Guardian*, 7 June 2016.
552 Sky News interview with Faisal Islam, 3 June 2016.

laying out the path to EU accession is a way to wean the Turks towards liberalising their economy, encouraging freedom of the press and keeping their democracy.

But, as he now ruefully admits:

That argument was much too subtle. We tried plenty of different ways to get it across, such as saying, 'Turkey will join in the year 3000.' We couldn't say it would be government policy to veto Turkish membership, because we were worried about destroying the EU deal with Turkey on Syrian migrants. We didn't want to totally rip up our foreign policy over this, but it takes ten minutes to explain the scenario. You only get forty seconds on the news...

He trails off.

Cameron was particularly incensed by Gove's interventions on this issue. Over the years, the Justice Secretary had been present at many Whitehall meetings in which Turkey's EU ambitions were discussed. He was fully aware of the difference between reality and diplomatic nicety.

As Cooper says: 'All these subtler points were well known and entirely understood by the Leave campaign – certainly by Messrs Gove and Johnson. That is why we in the Remain camp felt that their assertions about imminent Turkish accession were especially cynical and dishonest scaremongering.'

For most voters, however, the threat of Turkish accession – however remote – was enough. As polling day approached, it was clear that whatever the outcome, some of the most important personal relationships in Cameron's life would never be the same. Two of his dearest friends in politics, Hilton and Gove – men who had been at his side from the start of his leadership – had chosen to campaign against him on an issue that could bring him down.

Cameron had always guarded family time preciously, but a little over a fortnight before polling day, he was sufficiently twitchy to call a rare Sunday evening meeting in his Downing Street study. Gathered in the room were the usual members of his inner circle, as well as key figures from the official Stronger In campaign.

The Prime Minister came straight to the point. 'What does the research say, and what does the campaign think we should do?' he asked.

Cooper replied that they needed to keep hammering home their message on the economy. It was all they had.

Labour was still a worry. The Stronger In campaign knew it could count on, at best, 45 per cent of the Tory vote. To win, it would need votes from the left. Metropolitan New Labour supporters would overwhelmingly back In. Old Labour supporters were another matter. Blairite paeans about the wonders of multiculturalism, globalisation and a borderless world meant little to voters who had seen wages stagnate and working-class communities collapse. It was this vote that Leave campaigners had been skilfully targeting, portraying Brussels as an anti-democratic, corporatist racket backed by big business, bankers and other vested interests untouched by the wage repression and the squeeze on public services wrought by limitless low-skilled EU migration. Leave's appeal to 'Take Back Control' was resonating with this audience in a way that no political message had done for generations – and the Labour leadership didn't seem to care.

Stronger In had hoped Cameron and Corbyn would deliver a joint address to the nation warning of the danger of Brexit. But the Labour leader was uncomfortable with the prospect of standing shoulder to shoulder with Cameron on this issue while attacking the Tory leader at every other public event. Some in the Remain camp began to feel that the Labour leader was not just incompetent but actively sabotaging the campaign.

In Cameron's study that Sunday night, they batted around last-minute ideas. Among the possibilities discussed was a Scottish-style 'Vow', this time to find some way to limit the free movement of people. The suggestion was swiftly rejected on the basis that they had nothing to vow. All they could do, they concluded, was continue to make the economic case.

Time was also running out to stage a symbolic photoshoot with the four living British prime ministers, all of whom backed Remain. Downing Street was extremely keen to make it this happen.

'Everyone was obsessed with that,' Cooper recalls. His view was that the proposed stunt with John Major, Tony Blair, Gordon Brown and Cameron himself – 'hardly four very popular figures', as he puts it – was overrated.

In the end, it was scuppered by Brown. Just as in Scotland he has refused to work with Tories, now he refused to share a platform with Blair.

An expensive PR stunt involving projecting the Stronger In logo onto the Rock of Gibraltar also fell through, abandoned for fear of causing a diplomatic row with the Spanish.

Nor would there be any eleventh hour help from Brussels. At Westminster, rumours had been circulating that if polls looked alarmingly tight, either Merkel or Jean-Claude Juncker, the President of the European Commission, might make some dramatic last-minute intervention, designed to shore up support for Remain. There was never any truth in it. The Stronger In troops left Cameron's study with no new ace to play.

A week before polling day, an appalling crime threw the referendum campaign into disarray. A deranged loner shot and stabbed backbench Labour MP Jo Cox to death as she left a constituency meeting in Birstall, Leeds. As he killed her, 52-year-old Tommy Mair was heard to shout: 'Britain first.'

The assassination of any politician going about their work would always have been deeply shocking.[553] That Mair's victim was a popular 41-year-old mother of two very young children, who had devoted her whole career to helping those less fortunate than herself, made it all the more emotive.

Worse, while Cox was not a high-profile figure at Westminster, she was known as a staunch Remainer. The day before her murder, Farage had led a flotilla of Brexit-supporting fishermen up the Thames in protest against EU fishing quotas. Cox's husband Brendan and their two children had been pictured on a small boat tailing them, as part of a rival demonstration for Remain.

Coupled with her assassin's crazed words, this meant her death was always going to be seen by some in the context of the Brexit debate. Certain European newspapers now suggested the referendum was 'stained with blood'.[554] Privately, leading Leave campaigners feared the tragedy could prove fatal to Brexit, tarnishing patriotism and unnerving floating voters into backing the supposedly safer option of the status quo.

Amid an increasingly hysterical political atmosphere, both sides of the campaign immediately suspended hostilities. The moratorium lasted two full days, with politicians only returning to the fray on the morning of Sunday 19 June – and even then rather tentatively.

---

553 The last sitting MP to have been murdered was Thatcher's former aide Ian Gow, for whom Cameron did a little work during his early years in Central Office, and who was killed by the IRA.

554 See for instance the front page of *La Repubblica*, 17 June 2016.

But Matthew Elliott thinks the atrocity may have had unintended advantages for Leave, at least among those floating voters who were receptive to the economic risk message.

'In the final week, Downing Street had planned a series of events intended to ram home their message about economic risks,' he says. 'Mark Carney had been planning to give a speech outlining the Bank of England's analysis of how Leave would be highly damaging. The IMF was due to release its report suggesting something similar. George Osborne had actually suggested he would shut down the London stock market the day after Leave won. But the Jo Cox tragedy drowned these messages out.'

The final three days were dominated by preparation for a spirited debate for the BBC, held at Wembley Stadium. Staged less than forty-eight hours before the polls opened, the format pitted three campaigners from each side against each other.

Both teams scored blows, with Remainers Ruth Davidson, leader of the Scottish Conservatives, and Sadiq Khan, by now Mayor of London, having particularly good nights. Afterwards, both sides felt they could claim a narrow victory, perhaps because the BBC was so paranoid about its duty of impartiality at this most sensitive political moment that the event was designed to virtually eliminate the opportunity for either side to gain any significant advantage over the other. Audience participation was strictly limited and direct exchanges between the participants were meticulously choreographed and controlled. But, for many observers, Boris Johnson was responsible for the most memorable moment, when, in his concluding remarks, he declared that 'June 23rd could be our Independence Day'. There was rapturous applause.

The Stronger In campaign went into polling day nervous but quietly confident. Cooper exchanged emails with Cameron, telling the PM that he believed that Remain had a narrow lead.

Around 9 p.m. the pair spoke by phone:

'Go on, what's your feeling?' Cameron asked.

'I still hope we could get 53–47,' Cooper told the PM, though he was not bullish.

'Lunch on me at the Wild Rabbit if you're right!' Cameron replied cheerfully, referring to a gastropub near where they both live in Chipping Norton.

Others had assured the Prime Minister that it would all be fine.

According to Craig Oliver: 'Even right up to the last minute, most people, most pollsters, most people who'd modelled it – hedge funds, businesses – thought the Remain camp was going to win. They'd had data, polling, past experience.'[555]

That evening, Cameron's inner circle gathered in Downing Street to watch the results come in. Meanwhile Elliott headed to Manchester, accompanied by Labour MP and Vote Leave supporter Gisela Stuart, from where the official result would be declared. He was not confident. Earlier that afternoon, he had held a video conference with Gove, Johnson and various other senior figures to discuss how they would handle defeat. They spent some time drafting a concession speech.[556]

The 'bongs' of Big Ben at 10 p.m., when the polling booths closed, brought little information about how the country had voted. In the absence of exit polls, campaigners on both sides could only wait. Joe Twyman of YouGov appeared alongside BBC anchor David Dimbleby to reveal the results of a final poll which suggested the UK had voted to remain by 52–48, but how much this meant was anyone's guess.

Preliminary signs seemed encouraging for Remain, particularly when veteran pollster Peter Kellner, who was first to call it for the Tories on the night of the general election in 2015, tweeted that Britain was on course to stay in the EU by a margin of 54–46. Hopes were raised further when, around 11.30 p.m., a grim-faced Farage took to the airwaves dramatically to declare that it looked like Remain 'might just nick it'.

The UKIP leader was so pessimistic at this juncture that he abandoned a party at Millbank Tower thrown by the grassroots Brexit campaign, Leave.EU, retreating to his private office to be alone with his thoughts.

Cooper's team had created a sophisticated prediction model which extrapolated results from constituencies declaring early to the country at large. The first result saw a predictable Remain victory in Gibraltar, by the overwhelming margin of 96–4 per cent. But the second result to come in gave a much bigger win for Leave in Sunderland than had been expected by psephologists and political observers. At the Leave.EU party in Millbank, Brexiteers whooped and cheered as television screens showed images of sterling plunging. In Manchester, Gisela Stuart punched the air and the Leave campaign let out

555   Alex Spence, *Politico*, 8 August 2010.
556   Private information.

a cheer. Elliott says he knew right away that Leave would win. Remain's fears had been realised: the old Labour vote was breaking for Leave. Results in Swansea, Newcastle and Hartlepool confirmed the pattern. Remainers continued to hope that a huge London turnout would swing the result, but it was not to be.

Kellner then tweeted: 'Seems we are heading for result bad for UK, bad for pollsters and (least important) embarrassing for me'.[557]

It was almost dawn before the result was clear. Around 4 a.m., an emotional but jubilant Farage returned to the Leave.EU party, where he was mobbed by a huge press pack.

There were tears in his eyes, as, in a historic statement, he told supporters: 'Dare to dream that the dawn is breaking on an independent United Kingdom ... This will be a victory for real people, a victory for ordinary people ... Honesty, decency and belief in nation, I think now is going to win.'

At 4.40 a.m. veteran BBC newsreader David Dimbleby dramatically announced: 'The British people have spoken, and the answer is, we're out.'

The final figure would be 17.4 million votes for Leave, against 16.1 million for Remain.

By then Cameron had known for some time that voters had rejected his case. At 2 a.m., Oliver had phoned Coetzee and asked how it was looking.

'Very tight,' Coetzee replied grimly.

'What do you mean very tight?' Oliver asked anxiously.

'At the moment we're 20,000 ahead,' Coetzee replied.

They both knew it was not enough.

Around 3 a.m., Cameron was told there was no longer any hope. He knew it meant the end of his premiership.

In Downing Street, there was disbelief at the catastrophic turn of events. It was an outcome few in Cameron's inner circle had seriously contemplated. The outlook had been uncertain at best in the run-up to all the other big political tests they had faced together: Cameron's tilt at the leadership in 2005; the 2010 election; the Scottish referendum; the 2015 election. Yet they had triumphed every time. They had grown used to defying the odds.

Now they embarked on the most painful discussion of their political lives. Huddled together, they debated whether Cameron could survive.

Only a week or so earlier, most Brexit-supporting Conservative Party

557   https://twitter.com/PeterKellner1/status/746161085284290560.

MPs, including all the Cabinet 'outers', had signed a letter urging the Prime Minister to stay on regardless of the result. Throughout the campaign, he had paid lip service to this position, on the basis that encouraging the belief that he would quit if Britain voted Out might boost anti-Tory support for Brexit. In truth, his instinct had always been that he could not cling to office under such circumstances. How could he lead the unravelling of the diplomatic and trade relationships he had battled so hard to save?

Oliver agreed. 'It will be death by a thousand cuts if you try to stay,' he warned.

Liz Sugg suggested he could wait till the morning to assess the national mood and make a decision. She was a lone voice. Ed Llewellyn and Kate Fall both agreed he had to go.

A shell-shocked Cameron did not need convincing. The prospect of having to handle the tumultuous political, economic and diplomatic fallout from Brexit was more than he could bear. 'Why should I have to deal with the hard shit for someone else, just to hand it over to them on a plate?' he exclaimed.[558]

When George Osborne was told of the decision, he is said to have glumly replied, 'Well, that's that then.'[559]

Around 7 a.m., word went out to the media that Cameron was preparing to resign.

Meanwhile Farage too was struggling to comprehend the magnitude of what had just taken place. A heartfelt text message from his teenage daughter, acknowledging that the twenty-five years of his life he had spent campaigning for Britain to leave the EU had not been wasted, encapsulated the personal significance of the result.

In UKIP's dilapidated offices, a stone's throw from where the world's media was camped out on College Green, the leader of the UK Independence Party, hated and derided in equal measure by his establishment critics, sank into a swivel chair, swung his legs up onto a desk, and sat back to watch Cameron's resignation statement. Elated aides, high on adrenalin and sleep deprivation, dragged on cigarettes, high-fiving and back-slapping. Curls of tobacco smoke drifted into the makeshift office while a press officer frantically

---

558 Tom Newton Dunn, *The Sun*, 24 June 2016.
559 Private information.

tried to find a working television before Cameron's mooted appearance outside No. 10 at 8 a.m.

In Downing Street, penned behind crash barriers, throngs of reporters waited for the famous black door to swing open. Cameramen trained their lenses on the lectern from which Cameron would deliver his statement. Inside, the Prime Minister steadied himself. A distraught Samantha, immaculately made up and clad in a striking red and white geometric patterned dress, took him by the hand. The couple collected themselves, gave a nod to the doorman, and stepped across the threshold for the most difficult statement Cameron would ever have to make.

No bright coral lipstick or forced smile could mask the pain on Samantha's face as she stood a few feet from the podium, waiting for her husband to utter the words that would begin their political farewell.

Cameron paused and looked straight ahead at the press pack. Then he cast his eyes down to the script he had prepared:

> Good morning, everyone. The country has just taken part in a giant democratic exercise, perhaps the biggest in our history. Over 33 million people from England, Scotland, Wales, Northern Ireland and Gibraltar have all had their say. We should be proud of the fact that in these islands we trust the people for these big decisions.

He then turned to the inevitable.

> I fought this campaign in the only way I know how, which is to say directly and passionately what I think and feel – head, heart and soul. I held nothing back ... But the British people have made a very clear decision to take a different path and as such I think the country requires fresh leadership to take it in this direction. I will do everything I can as Prime Minister to steady the ship over the coming weeks and months but I do not think it would be right for me to try to be the captain that steers our country to its next destination.

Until this point, he had suppressed his emotions. Now his voice cracked, as he reached his final words.

'I love this country and I feel honoured to have served it and I will do everything I can in future to help this great country succeed. Thank you very much.'

For Farage, the working day that had begun when he rose at 5 a.m. some twenty-seven hours earlier was finally done. As an MEP and leader of a political party campaigning for UK independence, he had effectively just put himself out of a job. Unlike Cameron, it was a redundancy he wanted. It was time for a champagne breakfast at the Ritz.

Where did it all go wrong? Cameron had come close to disaster with plebiscites before. When the time came for the EU referendum, he would take no chances. On this occasion, nobody would be able to accuse him of complacency, but by putting himself at the forefront of the campaign, and by presenting the case in such uncompromising terms, he staked his premiership on the outcome. It cost him everything.

Cameron's approach came from the heart. His position on Britain's membership of the EU was clear: the country was better off in than out. Over the years, the Prime Minister's view had not shifted. As we have seen, as a prospective parliamentary candidate in 2000, he had depicted the EU as a necessary means to an end. In 2012, when he announced his ambition to hold a referendum 'before the end of 2017', his position was exactly the same.

It has been widely suggested that it was foolish and unnecessary to offer the referendum in the first place. Cooper says that nobody in No. 10 was 'enthusiastic' about the move but that they all agreed it had to be done.

> I don't recall anyone being enthusiastic about the idea. I don't think many people would have wanted to do it had we felt we had a choice. I think that almost everyone in the end came to the conclusion that we didn't really have a choice – that it was, realistically, a question of when, not if. George [Osborne] remained the most consistent opponent, though characteristically he totally backed it publicly and put his heart and soul into it.

Publicly, Cameron argued that the issue must be faced head-on.

'I believe in confronting this issue – shaping it, leading the debate. Not simply hoping a difficult situation will go away,' he said.[560] The pledge to stage it 'before the end of 2017' created an appealingly distant deadline. 'It was almost five years away!' recalls a senior figure on the policy team. 'It was absolutely designed to kick it into the long grass. I remember the feeling in Downing Street on the day of the announcement being "good day at the office; got that out of the way; now we don't have to think about it for years".'

With Labour more than ten points ahead of the Conservatives in the polls, it is tempting to suspect that Cameron assumed he'd never actually have to deliver the pledge.

Cooper insists that's not the case:

> I don't think it would be right to say we never thought we'd have to do it. Yes, it was a long way down the line, and yes, Labour was ahead in the polls but, at that point, there was no great expectation of a Labour win in 2015. Cameron meant what he said in the Bloomberg Speech.

But until the campaign itself, Europe had never been an issue of particular passion for Cameron. He had granted the vote as a tactical manoeuvre to ensure party unity during the 2015 election campaign and to forestall a UKIP surge. He had taken for granted that his skills as a political campaigner would ensure him victory. Shortly before the referendum in Scotland, he boasted to Herman Van Rompuy, then President of the European Council, 'I will win this easily and put to bed the Scottish question for twenty years. The same goes for Europe.'[561]

In his heart, Cameron may also have believed it was the right thing to do. As a young MP in the Blair years, he himself had pressed the Labour leader to give the electorate the same opportunity.

If he had not promised so much before the renegotiation, he could have perhaps saved his premiership, by standing back from the referendum campaign and allowing others to take the lead, as Harold Wilson had done in 1975. Instead, his commitment to this cause found expression in heavy-handed tactics that simply angered and alienated the electorate.

In Elliott's view, Stronger In was poorly led and made numerous errors.

560 Bloomberg Speech, op. cit.
561 George Parker and Alex Barker, *Financial Times,* 24 June 2016.

'It was a campaign run by committee,' he reflects. 'We had a real bulldog figure in [Leave Campaign director] Dominic Cummings. They had Will Straw, who is a very nice guy…' Lacking this ruthlessness, they failed to hit Leave where it could have hurt.

'They should have focused on the Leave campaign's weak points. They should have spent much more time trying to associate the leading Leave campaigners with UKIP or even the BNP.'

He argues that they missed a golden opportunity to frighten Old Labour voters over whether Brexiteers could be trusted with the NHS.

> They should have hammered home the message that Leave campaigners could not be trusted with the NHS. They should have made more of my background in the Taxpayers' Alliance, to Dominic and Michael [Gove] apparently slicing up the schools system. Yes, they did this a bit, but they should have been pumping out that message every night.

Considering that Leave campaigner Dan Hannan was on record claiming the NHS was a 'mistake',[562] this might indeed have resonated with some voters.

But Brendan Chilton believes that this vote was always going to break for Leave. 'Patriotic Labour voters don't have their affinity with the blue flag and yellow stars of Europe – their loyalty is to the Union Jack,' he says.

Merkel's confidant believes that this day had been coming ever since Cameron pulled out of the EPP. 'You know I'm heartbroken,' he said bitterly. 'But we Germans have one phrase we have borrowed from you English – Scheiße geschieht! – shit happens. Life goes on.'

Having overcome his initial shock, that seems to be exactly how Cameron sees it.

Nonchalant as ever, heading back through the door of No. 10 after announcing his resignation date, he was heard humming a cheerful ditty.

'Doo dee doo de doo dum dum. Right. Good!'

---

562 Andrew Sparrow, *The Guardian*, 5 April 2009.

44

Majority Verdict

'I was the future once.'
  – Cameron's quip at his last ever Prime Minister's Questions

When, in April 2015, Cameron told a BBC journalist that he would not seek a third term in office, he was giving a candid answer to a straightforward question.

At that point – a few weeks before a general election he never thought he would win – the prospect of securing another five years in power must have seemed remote enough. The notion of a further decade appeared fanciful.

It was never his plan to go on and on.

Writing about Tony Blair's leadership in his *Guardian* blog in 2004, Cameron had suggested that ten years at the top was enough for anyone in their right mind. 'The last seven years have brought four wars, no sleep, red boxes, Prime Minister's Questions and all the rest of it. Surely any normal person would think of packing it in?' he remarked.

As a young spin doctor at Conservative Central Office, he had witnessed Thatcher's tears as she was ruthlessly forced out of power and concluded that it was a wretched way to go. What was important to him after becoming Prime Minister was that he left on his own terms.

In the end, he served ten years and seven months as leader of the Conservative Party, a little over six years of this period as Prime Minister. He had planned to continue in Downing Street until 2019, after which he hoped that the reins might pass to Osborne. This would have ensured the continuity of their approach to government and the policies they had devised together since their partnership at the top of the Conservative Party began in 2005.

Instead, he was forced to make a brutally abrupt exit from office after spectacularly misjudging the referendum campaign.

His decision to announce his resignation within hours of the result stunned Westminster and plunged the Tory Party into a panicky leadership contest for which the bookmakers' favourite, Boris Johnson, was ill prepared.

It is now clear that neither the former Mayor of London nor Michael Gove, who had planned to enter the contest as his running mate, ever thought Britain would back Brexit. They were shocked by the result, and their joint campaign never got off the ground. As other contenders fell by the wayside, Theresa May became the beneficiary of the most extraordinary period of political turmoil in recent history. The former Home Secretary was installed as Britain's seventy-sixth Prime Minister on 11 July 2015, just eleven days after announcing her candidacy. The Camerons were left scrambling to pack up their belongings and forced to decamp to a friend's flat to make way for the new premier. It is hard to imagine a more dramatic or humiliating exit.

Cameron had not only lost power; he and Samantha had also lost two of their closest sets of friends: Michael and Sarah Gove, whose behaviour during the referendum led to a bitter fall-out between the couples, and Steve Hilton and his wife. The lengths to which Hilton went to make the case for Brexit at the expense of the Prime Minister's reputation was seen as a gross act of treachery by the occupants of No. 10 and proved terminal to a friendship that had begun almost three decades earlier, when, as fresh-faced graduates, Cameron and Hilton had worked together at Conservative Central Office. As he reflects on his premiership, the damage to these friendships will be a source of great sadness.

One relationship did survive the maelstrom: that with George Osborne, whose political career was also shattered by the referendum. After an ill-considered attempt to cling to office, the man with whom Cameron had effectively run a dual premiership bowed to the inevitable and returned to the backbenches.

In what appeared to be a clumsy attempt to compensate friends who suddenly found themselves out of a job, Cameron marked his departure from office by showering honours on his allies.

His dissolution list, which included gongs for an array of Remain campaigners (including the Labour Party's Will Straw), a knighthood for Craig Oliver and awards for obscure Downing Street press officers and special advisers, as well as an OBE for Samantha's stylist, prompted a furore. It threatened to undermine the honours system – and tarnish his legacy. Such was the shock of his sudden ignominious departure, perhaps he no longer cared.

And what of that legacy?

First and foremost, he will be remembered as the Prime Minister who accidentally took the United Kingdom out of Europe. If (as there is every reason to believe will happen) Brexit works for Britain, future generations may end up thanking him for it, though they will know it did not happen by his design.

He deserves some credit for his courageous decision to put the matter in the hands of voters in the first place. Looking back on his approach to the campaign, however, historians are likely to conclude that he catastrophically mishandled it, attempting to frighten the electorate with spurious claims about the risks of Brexit, and woefully misreading the public mood. His totally unrealistic pledge to bring net migration down to 'tens of thousands', as well as his failure during the coalition years to address mounting public concern over the scale of immigration, dogged his premiership and provides an object lesson in political accountability.

As a consequence of Brexit, he may also be remembered as the Prime Minister whose decisions ultimately led to the break-up of the United Kingdom. The Scottish National Party now has an excuse to stage another referendum on independence, and is determined to exploit this opportunity. There is no guarantee that voters north of the border, who are overwhelmingly in favour of remaining in the EU, will not decide to go their own way this time.

So much for the negative, which should not negate his many achievements. Perhaps the most important of these from the Conservative Party's point of view is that he made them electable again. Polling showed that he was always their biggest asset. Without him, the Tories would not have entered government in 2010, nor won outright in 2015. While his personal ratings remained high, public perception of the Conservatives changed little.

This was despite impressive efforts on his part to change the party's brand. In opposition, he put the environment and international aid at the forefront of his agenda and encouraged the selection of a more diverse range of prospective parliamentary candidates. In government, he enshrined his commitment to overseas development in law and legislated to introduce same-sex marriage. These efforts were unpopular with his own party, but hammered home the message that the Conservatives had changed, broadening their electoral appeal.

The fact that he entered public life at all is a point in his favour: he could have chosen any number of careers that would have been more lucrative and afforded a quieter life. Instead, he decided to 'give something back' and enter politics.[563]

Between 2005 and 2010, in an age when a wealthy background and an Eton education were more of a political hindrance than an advantage, he persuaded enough voters to switch back to the Conservatives for the first time since 1992 – or to vote Tory for the first time ever – to put the party back in government. It was not enough for outright victory but, in what his admirers describe as 'a true moment of leadership', he nonetheless manoeuvred himself into No. 10. There, he succeeded in leading a stable coalition against a backdrop of dire public finances. Through sheer force of personality, he was able to turn the most unlikely of political partners, the Liberal Democrats, into government colleagues. Five years later, he confounded the expectations of those who said he would never win an election, returning to Downing Street with an overall majority and ninety-eight more parliamentary seats than Labour. Over two elections, he increased the number of Conservative seats by 120 – more, even, than Margaret Thatcher.

Many have argued that luck played a huge part in his journey to the top. There is some truth in this. He was the first to acknowledge that he was blessed with immense good fortune. He was lucky in his upbringing, his family's wealth, his education, his talent, his temperament and his connections. Though he was eminently qualified for the string of desirable jobs he landed in his twenties, success came naturally to him and he did not have to try hard for advancement.

Once in Parliament, he was blessed with the circle of friends and advisers who surrounded him, and the qualities they brought to bear: the drive and creative genius of Steve Hilton; the political judgement (at least until the EU referendum) of Osborne; the financial backing and contacts of Andrew Feldman; and the intellectual and practical contributions of figures like Andrew Cooper and Daniel Finkelstein. Without them, it is unlikely he would ever have become leader in the first place. Though he did not doubt

563 Michael Crick interview, op. cit.

his ability to lead his party, he was never desperate for the job. (He is too balanced a character for that.) He was also lucky in his home life, his happy marriage, and the sunny outlook that helped him deal with personal tragedy, in the death of his son Ivan.

Furthermore, he was lucky in his opponents: Gordon Brown, a beleaguered Prime Minister at the head of a divided and exhausted administration; Ed Miliband, a hapless and unconvincing opposition leader whose party never managed or even really tried to show it had learned the lessons of its 2010 defeat. When the Tories failed to win a majority in 2010, he was lucky that the leader of the Liberal Democrats was Nick Clegg, a man with whom he could do business. He was lucky again when, in 2015, Labour elected veteran backbench socialist Jeremy Corbyn to replace Miliband, plunging the party into crisis. Cameron's own majority was tiny, but there was no effective opposition.

To his list of flukes, some would even add the financial crisis, for providing his administration with a defining purpose it might otherwise have lacked. Long after he became Prime Minister, the impression persisted that he was more interested in holding the office than in using its power to achieve anything in particular. More than once his laissez-faire approach nearly ended in political disaster. He made a virtue of being suspicious of big ideological visions, believing in an old-fashioned Conservative way that change was best achieved incrementally, but to his critics, this represented a poverty of ambition. His shrugging acceptance of the fundamental inadequacies of the civil service may have been pragmatic, but it pointed to the limits of his horizons. By contrast, Hilton refused to accept the intractability of the machine. The pity is that Cameron's restless revolutionary could not find a way to change the system from within, and became so exasperated and disillusioned that he left No. 10.

As with the fate of all gamblers, with the EU referendum, the Prime Minister's lucky streak finally came to an end. Ever the optimist, he was too confident that the country would vote to remain in the EU, come what may, to go to greater lengths to extract a better deal from Brussels. Had he secured more – or declared that he had failed to win meaningful concessions and stood above the fray when the referendum got underway – he could still be in power today.

APPENDIX: THE 2015 GENERAL ELECTION

By Michael Ashcroft

This Appendix was written in the weeks immediately following the general election of 7 May 2015. Much has changed since that time. None of the four main party leaders is still in post and, with the country having voted to leave the European Union, the British political agenda seems at first glance to be very different from that which faced David Cameron's newly re-elected government. Accordingly, I gave some thought as to whether to include these pages in this updated edition. I decided to keep them, for two reasons.

First, its conclusions are as relevant as ever. The Conservatives need to hold together their electoral coalition; Labour needs to show it can combine compassion with competence; UKIP needs to define a clear purpose for itself; and the Lib Dems must learn the right lessons from the cautionary tale of their implosion. The personnel have changed, and so have some of the immediate priorities, but those challenges remain and have in some cases intensified.

Second, the 2015 election and the parliament that preceded it are an indispensable part of the Cameron story that this book aims to tell. His relationship with the voters, and why they ended up making the choice they did after five years of coalition, remains a subject worth exploring in detail.

After each of the last two general elections I have written a detailed analysis of what happened and why. Both *Smell the Coffee* in 2005 and *Minority Verdict* in 2010 were based largely on evidence from opinion polls which had proved, from the Conservative point of view, depressingly accurate.

This time things look rather different. After all, the polls got it wrong, didn't they? All the final published surveys had Labour and the Conservatives within a point of each other; my own had the two parties tied on 33 per cent. Since the polls failed to detect that the Tories were heading for a decisive victory, what can they have to tell us that is of any use now?

I can certainly understand the schadenfreude felt towards the pollsters by those who believed all along that the Conservatives would do better than the polls were suggesting – and indeed by the Tories themselves, who probably got fed up with my lecturing them, even (or especially) when they knew I was right. But let's remember, specifically, what the polls got wrong. Voting intention surveys immediately before the election did not indicate anything like the outcome on the day. More specifically, since polls in Scotland proved very accurate despite the even more momentous shift in party allegiance north of the border, they understated the strength of the Conservatives in England and Wales and overstated that of Labour.

There are several possible reasons for this, including people making up (or changing) their minds very late, Labour voters not turning out in the numbers they told pollsters they would, interviewees not admitting to pollsters (or even themselves) which party they intended to vote for, and problems assembling truly representative polling samples in a more diverse and complex country. There must be further reasons why these things skewed the findings at the 2015 election despite not having done so in the previous four. As I noted in an article a year before the election, uncertainties as to whether methods that have worked in the past still apply 'are the questions that keep pollsters awake at night, and anyone in the business who tells you they know the answers is privately hoping for the best'.

Accordingly, I undertake this analysis with an appropriate measure of humility. But the question of who is going to tick which box is only one part – albeit rather an important part, especially given the attention paid to it and its potential to shape coverage and debate – of what opinion research tells us about the country's attitude to politics.

The central insight of *Smell the Coffee* was the critical importance of a party's brand – the overall way in which the voters see it. That remains true today. Everything parties do and say is seen and heard through the prism of what people already think of that party, and the context in which it finds itself. Campaigning techniques like the use of big data to micro-target particular kinds of voter can be very effective, but they necessarily operate at the margins: they help to mobilise existing supporters and to identify and win over those who are less sure but may be open to persuasion.

In other words, such tools allow parties to maximise their performance given the prevailing circumstances. That is not to dismiss them – when things are tight they can make the difference between one result and another. But it is the bigger picture that dictates whether the campaign professionals are aiming to realise the true value of their assets or make the best of a bad job.

Most of the work of Lord Ashcroft Polls has been devoted to understanding that bigger picture. It has concentrated on the longer-term strategic and brand questions whose horizons stretch beyond a single electoral cycle. My research has involved hundreds of thousands of telephone and online interviews with all kinds of British voters, as well as hundreds of face-to-face discussions in which groups of people all over the country talked about politics in their own words. I have looked in detail at what people thought about the parties: the attractions of each and the weaknesses they had to overcome; the qualities of the leaders; and the critical policy issues, such as the economy, crime, immigration, Europe and the NHS.

This will not be a forensic re-examination of every poll and news event. Instead, I will look back over that research to explore the challenge that faced each of the parties as the coalition agreement was signed, and how (or whether) they dealt with those challenges in the years that followed. This will help to explain the voters' verdict that surprised so many. More importantly, in describing how the bigger picture evolved over the last five years, the evidence I have amassed sets the scene for the parliament to come and the general election of 2020.

One question I have asked myself since the election is this: if we had known what we knew about people's attitudes to the parties, leaders and issues, but had no voting intention polls, what would we have expected the result to be? Or, to put it another way, would we have been as surprised by the outcome as many of us were?

At the time, the voting intention polls made sense. We knew people thought the Conservatives were more competent, but that Labour were ahead on values and should have the advantage of large numbers of anti-Tory former Lib Dems. But aside from the collected answers to the question 'Which party would you vote for in an election tomorrow?', what the research told us was consistent with the result that came to pass. Perhaps we should not have been so shocked that a party of government that seemed to know what it was doing was returned to office against an unconvincing opposition that had not noticeably changed for the better since voters kicked it out five years earlier.

It is a reminder for all of us to take a broader view, and focus less on the daily margins in the horse race. One way and another, after this election it is the pollsters and commentators, as much as parties and politicians, who need to smell the coffee.

I: THE CONSERVATIVES: JOB DONE?
In the conclusion of *Minority Verdict*, I summed up why the Conservatives fell short of outright victory in 2010. Why did the party fail to win an overall majority against a government so unpopular that it could muster no more than 29 per cent of the vote, only one point better than Michael Foot's Labour Party in 1983?

> Because we did not demonstrate that we were the change people wanted…When we asked people to vote for change we did not fully convey to them what sort of change we had in mind or how we would achieve it…We took it for granted, wrongly, that we would be the default choice for voters who deserted Labour…The fact that we did not complete the transformation of the brand meant that Labour scares about our plans, drawing on caricature folk memories of previous Conservative governments, had more resonance than they would otherwise have done…Ultimately, we did not make as much progress as we should have done in reassuring nervous former Labour voters that we had changed and we were on their side.

I went on to argue that the party had a chance

> to complete the rehabilitation of the Conservative brand that is essential if we are to achieve an overall majority at future elections…

Many of those who voted Conservative did so with varying degrees of doubt or even trepidation, and many more thought about doing so but found their reservations too strong…It is only in government, then, that the Conservative Party can show doubtful voters that it really is on the side of ordinary people, that it is competent to run the economy, that it can be trusted with the NHS, that it is a change for the better.

A year later, I published the first in my series of *Project Blueprint* research. Following the referendum in which the country decisively rejected switching to the Alternative Vote system for general elections, political comment was dominated by the state of relations between Tories and Liberal Democrats in government. I argued that what really mattered was not so much the coalition between the parties but 'how to create the coalition of voters who will elect a Conservative government with an overall majority at the next general election'.

That a Conservative majority was indeed the result of the following election was a remarkable achievement by any measure. But does that mean the doubts people had about the Tories that I described in *Minority Verdict* have been put to rest?

During the 2015 election campaign, I observed of the static polls that parties cannot change in four weeks what they have been unable to change in five years. How much, then, had voters' views of the Conservative Party changed since they had declined to give it a majority at the previous time of asking?

In my first round of *Project Blueprint* research, published on the first anniversary of the coalition, I asked people who had voted Conservative in 2010 what had been behind their decision. The single biggest reason was that the Tories 'seemed more likely to get the economy back on track'; this just pipped 'it was time for a change from Labour, and the Conservatives were the most obvious alternative'. The perception that the party seemed more willing to reform welfare and cut the deficit also scored highly, followed by the expectation that it would do more to control immigration.

Overall, Tory voters were evenly divided between those who made their decision mainly because they had a positive view of the Conservatives and those who were driven more by negative views of Gordon Brown and Labour.

Nearly two thirds of those who had voted Tory for the first time said negative reasons had been more important.

A year into the parliament, the Conservative share in the polls was similar to the 37 per cent they achieved in 2010. But this disguised a good deal of churn – some had moved away, while the party had won over others who had not voted Tory at the election. This latter group was distinguished by two things: they thought the Conservatives had the best approach to the economy, and they gave high approval ratings to David Cameron as Prime Minister. These would remain the central features of the Conservative Party's appeal.

Fixing the economy after the recession and financial crisis was the government's key mission, and was the main reason many people had voted Conservative. But a significant number of the party's existing and potential supporters were puzzled by the apparently narrow focus on the deficit. For both those who had voted Tory and those who had considered doing so but decided against, 'cutting the deficit and the debt' seemed more important to the Conservative Party than it was to them, while 'getting the economy growing and creating jobs' was a higher priority for them than it seemed to the Tories. The rising cost of living, meanwhile, was the biggest single economic concern, with petrol, energy and food prices regularly mentioned spontaneously by voters in my research. This was one area in which the Conservatives, who seemed to focus on the big picture rather than the day-to-day concerns of ordinary people, were thought less sympathetic than Labour (though whether Labour were in a position to do anything about it was, as I will explore in the next section, a different question).

While people understood that debt needed to be kept under control to save Britain from the kind of financial chaos that was engulfing Greece, they thought the government seemed to see all areas of policy as a means to the end of cutting the deficit. They were less sure about the end to which deficit reduction was the means. It seemed largely an abstract problem, so people were uncertain how they or the country would benefit when it was solved.

The cuts, meanwhile, felt rather more tangible. It was notable in my research that when people talked about them they did not just mean reductions in government spending: anything that was eroding their standard of living, from stagnant private sector wages to higher prices and problems getting bank credit, came under the heading of 'cuts'.

But at the height of the Eurozone crisis, the issues seemed so vast and complex that people found themselves in the uncomfortable position of having to trust that the government knew what it was doing. And, largely, they did: Cameron and Osborne seemed competent and ready to make tough decisions. If the complaint was that cuts were going too far and too fast, people could also see that the alternative was to cut less and more slowly, which unavoidably meant borrowing more and for longer – a potentially dangerous mistake. The government was helped by the absence of any credible alternative plan from Labour, whose opposition to cuts seemed to many to be a denial of reality. Indeed, as I found at the end of 2011 in my research for *The ChEx Factor: Economic Leadership in Hard Times*, people were more likely to think the economy would be in an even worse position had Labour still been in office than to think that things would be better.

The air of competence necessary for a party to be trusted to run the economy was undermined by the 2012 Budget. Over the previous two years the government had committed a series of U-turns on policies ranging from unannounced school inspections and the sale of state-owned forests to benefit changes and the scrapping of the post of Chief Coroner – each relatively minor in itself but building up a cumulative impression that policies were too often insufficiently thought through. The 'Omnishambles' Budget added several items to the list, including the imposition of VAT on static caravans, the capping of tax relief on charitable donations, and the notorious 'pasty tax', a new levy on warm baked goods. Opposition parties and the media claimed that this symbolised how out of touch the Tories were with the kind of ordinary people who bought pasties. According to my own research for the third phase of *Project Blueprint* in the summer of 2012, the more damaging point was the absurdity of a supposedly competent government embroiling itself in a row about such a trivial commodity. From the spring of 2012, Labour opened up double-digit leads in voting intention, and the Tories' advantage on being trusted to manage the economy narrowed and even, on some measures, disappeared altogether.

The 2012 Budget also featured the announcement that the 50p top rate of income tax, imposed on earnings over £150,000 at the end of Labour's term, would be cut to 45p. Though the Conservatives argued that the higher rate was raising little revenue and acted as a disincentive that was harming the economy – and that the best-off would actually pay more in tax overall as a result of other measures in the Budget – the decision was seized on as confirmation that the Conservatives were for the rich. In fact, this was never the most damaging charge against the party – as its history of election successes had shown, it was fine to be for the rich as long as you were for other people too. The real problem was the continuing perception that the Tories were primarily interested in those who had already made it.

It has been an abiding belief in Conservative circles that there are millions of people in Britain who are Tory in all respects except their voting habits. They work hard, they want to get on, own their own home, perhaps build a business, but inexplicably they vote for the wrong party. In my 2012 research paper *Blue Collar Tories?*, I identified a group of voters – I called them 'Suspicious Strivers' – who held what Tories like to think of as Conservative values but did not feel the party was really for them. Instead, they saw the Conservatives as being for people who had already achieved material success; less so for those who did the right thing but had little to show for it. These crucial swing voters felt their position was precarious. Even those who were reasonably comfortable felt they were one redundancy, interest rate rise or tax credit rule change away from real difficulty. In their lives, anxiety was as much a force as aspiration, and they were not sure they could rely on the Tories if they found themselves in trouble. What they wanted as much as anything was reassurance – that doing the right thing would be worth their while, and that if they needed help, deserving cases would be given priority. Another group, which I dubbed 'Entitlement Anxiety', felt that an unfair system seemed to reward others (who worked less hard than they did) but not them. Both groups leaned towards Labour.

In his biography of George Osborne, *The Austerity Chancellor*, Janan Ganesh records that the lack of emphasis on aspiration in the early stages of the Tories' modernising project was not an oversight or a consequence of the need to use unexpected themes to win attention, but a deliberate decision. Osborne and Cameron doubted their ability, given their backgrounds, to talk convincingly about improving the life chances of poorer people.

This began to change from the 2012 Conservative Party conference. Cameron said Britain found itself in a 'global race', and confronted claims that the Tories were for the wealthy few: 'They call us the party of the better-off…No: we are the party of the want-to-be-better-off, those who strive to make a better life for themselves and their families.' He also introduced the idea of the 'aspiration nation', which became the theme of the 2013 Budget.

But as the economy began to recover, and with it the Conservatives' reputation for overall economic management, the question for voters who had struggled during the recession became how the upturn would benefit them – if indeed they would feel it at all. In my research at the start of 2014, I found undecided voters saying, albeit sometimes grudgingly, that the government had not done too badly overall considering the situation it had found itself in. 'But none of this', I observed,

> changed that fact that, for many of them, life was hard and showed no signs of getting any easier despite the recovery they kept hearing so much about. As far as the Tories' hardworking people are concerned, where – to use a phrase from the archive of the party's lexicon – are the proceeds of growth?

By the final conference season before the election, I found in phase five of my *Project Blueprint* research that while nine in ten Conservative voters said they were already feeling some of the benefits of the recovery or that they expected to at some point, four in ten of the electorate as a whole (including the same proportion of 2010 Tories who now said they would vote for someone else) said they were not feeling any benefits, and nor did they expect to. UKIP supporters were the most likely group to think that any recovery would pass them by.

At the same time, while the majority of voters thought austerity was no longer necessary or had never been needed in the first place, three quarters of Tories accepted the need for further cuts. The task for Cameron and the Conservatives, then, was to create a 'coalition of the willing' – a big enough group of voters prepared to accept continued austerity because they believed the results would be worth waiting for. This presented the tricky task of explaining why cuts were still needed if things were, as they claimed, looking up.

Despite these qualms, I found 59 per cent of all voters saying they most trusted Cameron and Osborne to manage the economy in the best interests of Britain, compared to 41 per cent for Miliband and Balls. And on this measure, and others like it, the Conservatives held their lead throughout the parliament.

At different points the Tories may have seemed insufficiently in tune with concerns about the cost of living, or overly obsessed with the deficit compared to growth, and many people wondered when they would begin to experience for themselves the fruits of the rumoured recovery. For most of the parliament, I found people more likely to say they expected the economic situation to worsen in the following few years than to say it would improve. But overall, the Tories seemed to have a plan, and to be willing to make the hard decisions needed to implement it. And however slow the progress felt to many people, they knew that electing a government was not a referendum but a choice – and the alternative was not convincing.

If economic management was one pillar of the Conservatives' claim to be the party of competence, the other was David Cameron himself. Voters had seen him as the best available Prime Minister since Gordon Brown cancelled plans for an early election in October 2007, and they continued to do so throughout his first term in office.

A year after the election, I found that both those who had voted Conservative, and those who had thought about doing so but decided against, were more likely to have a positive view of him than a negative one. They also gave him higher ratings than the government as a whole, another feature of his leadership that persisted. Indeed, he remained the only leader to achieve consistently higher approval ratings than his party. Despite regular dissent on his own benches and from Tory commentators, Cameron also regularly scored higher among Conservative voters than Miliband did among Labour supporters or Nick Clegg among Lib Dems.

After his first year in No. 10, Cameron seemed to the public to be professional, human and a refreshing improvement on his predecessor as PM. He was also given credit for getting to grips with a tough job, especially on the economy and public finances. In the early days of coalition, however, some Conservatives worried that he did not seem fully in command, leading to concerns that he might not prove a sufficiently strong leader. This impression did not last long – the bigger complaint from most voters was that Nick Clegg had been eclipsed.

I looked further into these questions in my 2011 research paper *The Leadership Factor*. Crucially, and uniquely, Cameron was a net attractor of supporters to his party: the only leader who was a 'draw' rather than a 'drag'. People considering the Tories who had voted for other parties at the election had a more favourable view of him than of the Conservative Party generally. People would vote Conservative because of Cameron, while many of those who chose Labour would do so despite Miliband. Though Labour was ahead in the polls at the time, I noted that 'as the election nears the leadership factor will only grow in importance as people decide who they want in charge'.

To wavering voters, Cameron's opponents seemed weak or out of their depth, while the Tory leader appeared competent, determined, well up to the job, and focused on his agenda. Though for some this focus tipped over into ruthlessness, Labour's attempts at the time to characterise him as a right-wing leader who had abandoned the centre ground he had campaigned on missed the point. As far as most people were concerned, he was trying to sort out the mess he had inherited, even if he was overdoing it; only the most hostile thought he was personally motivated by ideology.

A less attractive side to Cameron's character, for some, was that he seemed rather arrogant or smug, and somewhat detached from the lives of ordinary people. This had been a persistent criticism of Cameron since he became the Tory leader, perhaps inevitably given his affluent upbringing and Eton education. It was even sometimes echoed on his own side: the Mid-Bedfordshire MP Nadine Dorries described Cameron and his Chancellor as 'two public school boys who don't know what it's like to go to the supermarket and have to put things back on the shelves because they can't afford it for their children's lunch boxes'.

Looking back over the research, though, Cameron's privileged background only really counted against him among those already least inclined to vote Conservative. More damaging was the impression of inauthenticity he sometimes gave. As someone remarked in my early research, 'he tries to show he's one of us, but he's not'.

That Cameron's 'poshness' has not proven more politically damaging has been a disappointment for Labour. Why did it not resonate more with voters? There are perhaps three main reasons. The first was that as far as many voters were concerned, there was nothing to choose between Cameron, Clegg and Miliband in terms of their upbringing, education and early career. No doubt to the exasperation of Labour, during the 2015 campaign people would often observe in my focus groups that all the party leaders had been to public school.

The second is that whatever the differences in social class, people related to Cameron more naturally than they did to his opponents. He seemed to lead as normal a family life as anyone could in his position, while Miliband seemed rather wonkish and strange. Nigel Farage was either a refreshing straight-talker or a dangerous rabble-rouser, according to taste, but the question of him being in a position of responsibility never really arose. For all Nick Clegg's flaws as a politician, people tended to like him personally. But Cameron was the only leader who seemed to combine relatability with the oomph needed to run the country.

This leads to the third reason: that when it came to the attributes needed to do the job, Cameron retained a commanding lead over his rivals. This included potential rivals on his own side. As concerns grew in the Conservative Party about the threat from UKIP, it was sometimes suggested that Boris Johnson could be the man to restore Tory fortunes. But my 2013 research into the Boris phenomenon, *Are You Serious? Boris, the Tories and the Voters*, put this claim into perspective.

The Mayor of London was widely popular. But set against Johnson, Miliband and Clegg, Cameron remained the most popular choice of Prime Minister, not least among Conservative voters, who preferred the thought of him in No. 10 by 81 per cent to 18 per cent. Cameron was thought more likely to do a good job when it came to representing Britain at international negotiations, making the right decisions even when they were unpopular, leading a team and doing the job of PM overall.

Indeed, Cameron held a clear lead over Miliband on all these measures, as well as having a well-defined idea of what he wanted to achieve, when I asked the question intermittently over the two years that followed. Miliband was ahead on only one measure – 'understanding ordinary people'. Voters' views of the leaders remained remarkably consistent. Throughout the parliament, YouGov asked at least twice a month which of the three would make the best Prime Minister. At the end of September 2010, 40 per cent chose Cameron and 24 per cent chose Miliband. At the end of April 2015, 40 per cent chose Cameron and 26 per cent chose Miliband. Over the five years, the proportion choosing Cameron never fell below 30 per cent (in April 2012, when he still led Miliband by eleven points) and the number choosing Miliband never rose above 28 per cent (in February 2014, when he was still nine points behind).

Why was it not obvious that the clear Conservative lead on overall management of the economy, together with the continuing preference for David Cameron as Prime Minister, would translate into a decisive victory for the Tories?

During the campaign, Andrew Cooper of the polling firm Populus surveyed people who preferred Cameron to Miliband and thought the Tories would do a better job than Labour on the economy but still said they planned to vote something other than Conservative. These 'Yes Yes Nos' represented nearly one in five of those likely to vote. Some of them said they could 'just never bring myself' to vote for the party; some cited local factors; some said that they didn't actively want Cameron, even if they preferred him to Miliband; quite a number said there were 'other issues that are more important in determining who I vote for, and on which I don't trust Cameron or the Conservatives' (and many of these planned to vote UKIP); and others thought that 'overall, I don't think people like me are likely to benefit from a recovering economy under the Conservatives'.

A large chunk of the 'Yes Yes Nos', representing some 2 per cent of all voters, conceded that they didn't want to vote Tory 'but in the end I may well end up doing so' because Labour and Miliband would be even worse. So there was room for a late swing, and even some late conversions inside the voting booth. But there was good reason to believe that, even though no party had ever lost when ahead on both leadership and the economy, the Tories might struggle to hold on to office in 2015 despite these twin advantages.

It is also worth remembering that the Conservatives had led on both factors at the last election too. By May 2010, Cameron had been seen as a better prime ministerial prospect than Gordon Brown for two and a half years, and the Tories had been thought more likely to do a good job running the economy since early 2009. Yet these things had not been enough to secure outright victory. As I discussed in *Minority Verdict*, much of this was down to the question of what the Conservative Party's priorities were and whose side it was on.

In my first round of *Project Blueprint* research, conducted in the spring of 2011, three quarters of those who had considered voting Conservative but decided against it said the NHS was a high priority for them, but only 42 per cent thought it was a high priority for the Conservative Party.

The Tories' commitment to the NHS had long been a reservation for voters sceptical of the party. By campaigning heavily on the issue in opposition, emphasising David Cameron's personal experience of the NHS, the Conservatives largely managed to neutralise it in political terms. But in office, the party was not able to sustain its newfound credibility on the issue as it had been able to do with the economy.

A year after the coalition was formed, I found Labour twelve points ahead of the Tories on health, a margin that had widened to twenty-four points in April 2015. The coalition's NHS reforms, introduced during the government's first year, did not help. As I found in the first round of *Project Blueprint*, most people were sceptical about the reforms, particularly since the changes were largely opposed by healthcare professionals. But the main problem was that in the absence of a clear explanation of how the reforms would benefit patients, people fell back on their old assumptions about Tory motivations. In my 2015 research project *The People, the Parties and the NHS*, I asked people what they thought had been the reason behind the coalition's health reforms. The single biggest response was 'to save money'. More thought they were 'part of a plan to privatise the NHS' than to cut bureaucracy or give more choice and control to patients.

Questions about the NHS and the Tories' perceived policy priorities are closely tied to how people see the overall motives and character of the Conservative Party. In the early months of the coalition, the Conservatives established a clear lead on making tough decisions for the long term, being competent and capable, and doing what they said they would do. Even those who had considered voting Conservative but decided against it were much more likely to say these things were true of the Tories than of Labour or the Lib Dems. But when it came to standing for fairness, equal opportunity and wanting to help ordinary people get on in life, these 'considerers' thought the Conservatives lagged well behind.

This question of the kind of people the Tories were, and who they were for, had been a constant theme in my research for a decade. In the opposition years, when I was in charge of the party's polling, we could consistently find undecided voters thinking the Conservatives were best represented by a picture of a posh family standing outside an enormous house. This did not change once the party was in government. During the 2015 campaign, my focus groups were asked to picture the Conservative Party as a house.

Inevitably it would be comfortably but expensively furnished, and home to a chocolate Labrador ('a posh dog'), but the most telling point was that 'you can't get to the door because there is an intercom at the gate' and 'once inside you have to wipe your feet'.

Ultimately, questions of leadership and economic competence played a decisive part in the election outcome. If, in the final judgement, the contrast between the parties on these attributes outweighed everything else, it is clear that for many people the question of motivation and values needed to be overcome before they would vote Conservative. Though they may have been trumped in the circumstances of this election by other things, these concerns have not gone away and they remain a sticking point for many voters. To put it more simply, many people will have voted Conservative despite what they regard as Tory values, not because of them.

During the mid-term doldrums of 2012, I proposed four tests that the Tories should apply to everything they planned to say or do. They were: Does it show the right priorities for the country? Does it show strong leadership? Does it show the party is on the side of the right people (and, if necessary, make the right enemies)? And does it offer some reassurance about the Conservative Party's character and motives? These tests will apply as much over the next five years as the last.

II: LABOUR: THE UNCLIMBED MOUNTAIN

After Labour's defeat in 2010, I conducted some research among voters who had supported the party at previous elections but switched their allegiance in the contest just gone. They were clear why Labour lost: Gordon Brown had not been a good Prime Minister, Labour did not seem to have the right answers to important questions, and the government had run out of steam. Three quarters of those questioned said the Labour government had been largely to blame for the country's economic problems, seven in ten said the coalition's cuts were unavoidable, and two thirds thought Labour would need to change quite fundamentally before they would consider voting for the party again. Acknowledging or even apologising for the government's mistakes would be an important first step.

A parallel exercise involving party members and Labour-supporting members of affiliated trade unions revealed that the Labour movement itself saw things rather differently. They thought they had lost because people did not appreciate what Labour had achieved; that voters had been influenced by the right-wing media; and that while Labour's policies had been right, they had not been well communicated. More than three quarters thought their party had not deserved to lose, and most rejected the idea that the Labour government had been largely to blame for the economic situation. They thought the swing voters they had lost (and needed to win back) were ignorant, credulous and selfish. More than half thought the coalition would prove so unpopular that Labour would probably win the 2015 election without having to change very much.

This explains a lot about the progress Labour made, or did not make, in the five years that followed. The Labour Party did not want to change, or to face up to the reasons voters lost confidence in it as a party of government. More importantly, it did not think it needed to do so. That autumn, I noted that Ed Miliband's victory in the leadership election was a symptom of these attitudes, and the 'collective refusal to come to terms with what has just happened'. But I did not believe, as some Conservatives did, that this meant the following election was already in the bag for the Tories. Having been elected by the unions, and being known to be well to the left of mainstream opinion, surely Miliband would go out of his way to defy people's assumptions? I argued that he must know that following the instincts of the Labour movement, rather than voters, would move his party further from victory. I did not think that the Tories could expect him 'to leap obligingly into every trap'.

Yet Labour showed no signs of penitence. Its mantra in the early years of the coalition was that cuts in public spending were going too far, too fast. This was echoed by some voters, particularly those for whom austerity had come a bit too close to home. But few thought the economy would be in a better position had Labour remained in office – indeed, my 2011 research paper *The ChEx Factor: Economic Leadership in Hard Times* found people were more likely to think things would be worse than better if Labour were still in charge. Rather than blaming the coalition for the economic situation, they were much more likely to blame the last Labour government, along with the banks, and people borrowing more than they could afford (even though they were roundly fed up with hearing that line from ministers).

In my first round of *Project Blueprint* research looking at the coalition of voters the Conservatives needed to build a majority, I noted that 'Labour's core support plus left-leaning former Lib Dems could theoretically give Ed Miliband close to 40 per cent of the vote without needing to get out of bed'. That seemed to be the case in the autumn of 2012, by which time a combination of economic gloom and the Omnishambolic Budget had handed Labour a sustained double-digit poll lead.

I investigated the scale and strength of Labour's support in *Project Red Alert*. People who had switched to Labour since 2010 were able to recite a litany of things that had changed over the previous two and a half years (though, tellingly, the Labour Party itself was never on this list). Even so, many of these 'joiners' had doubts. Apart from the complaint that the party had not made clear what they would do to improve things (the usual grumble about opposition parties), the biggest fears about another Labour government were that it would spend and borrow more than the country could afford, and that the party had not learned the right lessons since it was last in office.

At the same time, one group of joiners affected by austerity saw a Labour vote as the best means of restoring what they had lost, while another harboured doubts as to whether the party could yet be trusted with the public finances. In other words, some hoped another Labour government would bring back the days of lavish spending, and some feared that it would. I concluded that this meant Labour's vote share, and thus its lead, were soft – which made it a gamble for Miliband not to try to reach out any further or do more to reassure those for whom economic responsibility was the biggest hurdle.

All most people had heard from Labour was that it was against whatever the coalition happened to be doing. This included welfare reform, one government policy people spontaneously praised. In focus groups before the 2010 election, participants who were asked to choose an image to represent Labour would very often select a picture of a slob lying on a sofa to symbolise what they saw as the party's indulgence of people living on benefits when they could be at work. This impression lasted well beyond 2010 and was reinforced by what appeared to be Labour's wholesale opposition to benefit changes. By the same token, though many voters were disappointed with the Conservatives' failure to deliver their promise to cut immigration to the tens of thousands, Labour had done nothing to change their view that – since they had been responsible for mass immigration in government – whatever progress had been made might be reversed if they had another chance.

Concern grew in Labour circles that the leadership was pursuing what became known as the '35 per cent strategy': that with the constituency boundaries unreformed, all Labour needed to do was hold on to most of the supporters it already had. Two years before the election, a number of Blairites including John Reid and Alan Milburn spoke out about the dangers of this approach, arguing that Labour needed to do more than articulate grievance and that, as Tony Blair himself put it, the party needed to show leadership and move out of its 'comfort zone'.

But rather than confront the doubts people had, many in Labour seemed to prefer to change the subject or, as they put it, 'frame the debate' in a way that played to the party's strengths. In the early years, this included campaigning on issues like media regulation, on the basis of which Labour figures often claimed to be setting the political agenda – even moving the centre ground of politics – but which did nothing to help achieve the party's real task. Worse, the failure to address the biggest reservation people had about electing another Labour government meant their message was blunted in areas that should have worked to the party's advantage.

In economic policy, Labour's most resonant theme was the cost of living. This was undoubtedly people's biggest concern about the economic situation, as it affected them personally, with prices rising faster than incomes almost throughout the parliament. In my research, people would regularly mention unprompted the cost of food, petrol and home energy bills. Being central to the question of understanding people's everyday concerns, this was also an area in which Labour maintained a consistent poll lead.

Labour made this a major campaign theme. Soon after the 2010 election, the party began to talk about falling living standards among what it called the 'squeezed middle', a theme that continued in various forms in subsequent years. In his 2013 conference speech, Ed Miliband talked about the broken link between the wealth of the country and family finances. He suggested that while it was once the case that a rising tide would lift all boats, 'now the tide just seems to lift the yachts'.

But when it came to policy, Labour struggled to capitalise on these doubts. In the same speech, Miliband announced that a Labour government would freeze gas and electricity prices until the start of 2017. This was meant to embody the party's grasp of living costs and its support of ordinary people against corporate interests. In the fourth phase of my *Project Blueprint* research, which identified the connection between national and personal prosperity as a critical election issue, I found the proposal had some superficial appeal. Yet people could see that it was plagued with practical drawbacks – surely the energy companies would simply hike prices before the law came in, and again as soon as it expired? Though voters still put Labour comfortably ahead on 'tackling the cost of living', Tories had the edge when it came to 'practical policies that would work in the long run'. Swing voters in particular put the Conservatives ahead on overall competence and willingness to take tough decisions for the long term. Although people were more likely to be pessimistic than optimistic about the economy, they trusted Cameron and Osborne over Miliband and Balls by a fourteen-point margin.

As well as stifling its own economic theme, the fact that Labour allowed doubts about fiscal responsibility to continue meant the party struggled to make headway on the policy area it likes to think of as its own: the NHS. Though the Conservatives managed to narrow the gap during the opposition years, the coalition's handling of NHS reform allowed Labour to re-establish runaway leads on the issue within Cameron's first year as Prime Minister. Doubts about the Tories' commitment to the NHS were closely tied to perceptions of its character as a party, and Labour consequently sought to put the issue at the top of the agenda as the election approached. Indeed, when undecided voters in my campaign focus groups were asked to sum up Labour's main message, 'save the NHS' was usually the answer.

Yet this research also suggested that Labour's promise of 20,000 new nurses, 8,000 new GPs and 5,000 new home care workers did more to high-light the party's weaknesses than its strengths. A policy designed to confirm Labour's credentials as champions of public services simply raised again the question of whether it could be trusted with the money.

This suspicion became an integral part of how people saw the party. Asked in my focus groups to describe it as a house, wavering voters said it would be a property for ordinary working people but it would have a 50-inch plasma TV and that although the furniture is nice, 'it's all on HP'.

Then there was Ed Miliband himself. Tory strategists initially focused on his left-wing credentials, highlighting the role of the trade unions in his leadership victory. After branding him 'Red Ed', there was a shift towards portraying him as 'the Michael Dukakis of British politics' – part of a metropolitan elite with no understanding of mainstream concerns. In fact, the public formed its own view of the Labour leader with no help from his opponents, as they always do.

Nearly a year after he took charge, I found in my research paper *The Leadership Factor* that Miliband had yet to make much of an impression on most people. But their spontaneous verdict, usually delivered apologetically, as though they would use a kinder word if they could think of one, was very often 'weird'. Several things contributed to this assessment: that he had stood against his brother (by far the best-known thing about him); that he married the mother of his two children only after becoming Labour leader; and that he seemed to have an odd way of speaking.

The early research found that people thought he had been lucky to win since he had clearly not been the most able candidate, and that in the post, he now seemed out of his depth. These doubts about his competence persisted. Throughout the parliament I found he lagged behind David Cameron on important attributes like being able to represent Britain abroad, leading a team, taking difficult decisions even when they were unpopular, having a clear idea of what he wanted to achieve, and doing the job of Prime Minister overall.

Consequently, Miliband never came close to overtaking Cameron as people's preferred PM. My polling regularly found only just under one third of voters saying they were satisfied with Cameron's performance as PM – but a similar proportion would say they were dissatisfied but preferred him to the alternative. Only around three in ten would say they were dissatisfied and would rather see Miliband in No. 10, and no more than three quarters of Labour voters would say that (though this figure rose later in the campaign as those deciding to vote Labour reconciled themselves to the choice of Prime Minister their decision implied).

The only score on which Miliband had the advantage was on 'understanding ordinary people', but this seemed to be a reflection of his party's brand rather than his own. Indeed, as far as most voters were concerned there seemed to be little to choose between the established party leaders: all three had gone straight into the political world from Oxford or Cambridge, having all (an exasperating misconception for Labour) been to public school. The idea of Miliband as a member of a separate, prosperous political class was confirmed weeks before the election when he was photographed in what turned out to be the second kitchen of his London house.

The notion that Labour had chosen 'the wrong brother' pursued Miliband throughout his leadership. Even in final weeks of the 2015 campaign, nearly five years after he was elected, it was often one of the first things people said when his name was mentioned. In my qualitative research we regularly asked people to imagine the leaders in different situations, or even as different things, to understand better how people saw them. For example: whom would Miliband bring if you invited him to dinner? 'Two advisers.' What would he do on an unexpectedly free Friday night? Pore over the latest poll results or 'play with the train set in his loft'. What sort of car would he be? 'A Ford Focus, average. Actually no, a Ford Focus is reliable.' What sort of drink would he be? 'Crème de Menthe. The sort of thing nobody would order.'

Doubts about the idea of Ed Miliband as Prime Minister contributed to English voters' fears of a minority Labour government coming to a deal, formal or otherwise, with the Scottish National Party. It was not just that people resented the anticipated SNP demands for more money for Scotland (when their constituents already enjoyed free prescriptions, university tuition and other benefits unavailable to English taxpayers), or for a bigger say in the running of a country they did not want to be part of (though there was plenty of all that). It was that Nicola Sturgeon was a strong and canny leader who would probably get the better of Prime Minister Miliband.

The causes of Labour's predicament in Scotland could fill a book of their own – and of course Conservatives would still have won a majority had Labour held all its seats north of the border – but the SNP landslide was one of the most remarkable aspects of the 2015 campaign. In my research, I explored why so many people were ready to abandon a party that had been part of the fabric of their community for generations. Three main reasons emerged. First, compared to the SNP, Scottish Labour seemed like a 'branch office' of the London headquarters as opposed to a distinctively Scottish party. Second, many people thought that by campaigning alongside Tories and Lib Dems during the referendum – with what they saw as a very negative and scaremongering message – Labour had shown itself to be part of a complacent establishment. And third, since the Blair years Labour had become indistinguishable from the Conservatives – or, as someone memorably put it, 'it's just a different shade of shite'. The SNP now seemed to its newfound supporters to be the true party of the left. As for what a large SNP contingent could achieve at Westminster, specific expectations were hard to come by. The answer was usually some combination of 'standing up for

Scotland' and 'making sure our voice is heard'. Perhaps above all, potential supporters hoped the SNP would keep a Labour-led administration honest and make sure it got its priorities right.

In Britain as a whole, though always behind on leadership and overall economic management, Labour was sustained in the polls by the perception that it cared more about helping ordinary people and was ultimately more well-meaning than the Tories. Throughout the coalition, Labour consistently polled ahead of the Tories on fairness, sharing the concerns of ordinary people, and having its heart in the right place. During the campaign, while Conservatives emphasised the choice between Cameron and Miliband in Downing Street, Labour sought to exploit its advantage on these attributes with a party election broadcast featuring actor Martin Freeman. The star of *The Hobbit* and *The Office* declared that the election was not just a choice between two economic plans but a choice about values. Having been brought up to believe in things like 'community, compassion, decency', he was choosing Labour.

I found in my focus groups that this message was best received by those already most inclined to vote for the party. It was less effective for those who had harder questions, particularly about how all this compassion and decency would be paid for. As one of our participants put it, 'it's all well and good to say we're nicer people and we care about you more, but I want someone who can sort out the country'.

This, we can now see, was an important part of Labour's downfall. If, in Ed Miliband, the Labour Party chose 'the wrong brother', he was not just the wrong front man for an otherwise winning approach; he was the brother who led them down the wrong path. A party cannot change in a five-week campaign what it has been unable or unwilling to change in five years. Having suffered a bad defeat in 2010, Labour needed to show it understood why people were nervous about putting it back in power, and do everything it could to reassure doubters. Miliband's last conference speech, in which he forgot to mention the deficit, came to symbolise Labour's cavalier approach to the public finances. But the truth is that had he remembered, it would have been too late. The problem was not that the subject slipped his mind one afternoon in September 2014; it was that he had ignored it for the preceding four years.

During his time as leader, Miliband apologised for not sufficiently regulating the banks, for allowing financial services to become too big a part of the economy, for the proliferation of targets in public services, and for being photographed holding a copy of *The Sun*. But as for spending and borrowing too much – what many of his party's potential supporters regarded as the biggest failure of the Labour era – he not only declined to apologise, he refused to admit it had ever happened. As a result, he was unable to persuade voters to let Labour put its values into practice.

Too many in the Labour Party thought they would win the 2015 election almost by default. In fact, they had a mountain to climb. The mountain is still there, and if they want to win they will still need to reach the summit. Next time, however, they will be starting from even lower down the slope.

III: DOWNFALL: THE LIBERAL DEMOCRATS

The 2015 election was the most disastrous in the history of the Liberal Democrats or any of its predecessor parties. Indeed, it was the most catastrophic result for any party in the modern history of British politics. In 2010, fifty-seven Lib Dem MPs were elected; now there are eight. Only just over a quarter of those who voted for the party five years ago did so again in 2015. Nearly a third voted Labour, a fifth voted Conservative, and a tenth voted UKIP. Former Lib Dems accounted for two fifths of the Green vote.

In such circumstances it seems kinder simply to pay one's respects and stay away. But for a party of government to lose more than seventeen in every twenty of its seats is such an extraordinary phenomenon that it is worth examining. Why did the Lib Dems collapse so spectacularly? Was an implosion on such a scale inevitable once the coalition deal was signed? And if not, how could it have been avoided?

Before 2010, the party's biggest strength was the reputation of its MPs and councillors in their local strongholds, and that it was neither the Tories nor Labour. In my research project *What Future For The Liberal Democrats?*, conducted in 2010, I found that for just over four in ten of those who had voted Lib Dem, the main reason had been that they did a good job locally; a quarter of them voted to stop another party from winning, or as a way of voting against both the bigger parties. Qualitatively, many said it had been time for a change from Labour but they were not sure they wanted (or were quite sure they didn't want) the Tories. The characteristics they most associated with the Lib Dems were fairness and honesty.

There were also two big weaknesses: the assumption that since the party would never win an election outright it represented a wasted vote, and the feeling that although Lib Dems seemed like terribly nice people, their policies probably didn't really add up. Among those in my research who had considered voting Lib Dem but decided not to, majorities agreed with both these propositions.

At this stage, a few months into the parliament, those who had voted Lib Dem were split down the middle over whether the party had been right to enter coalition with the Tories. Half agreed that 'the Liberal Democrats have shown they don't really have any principles, they are just going along with what the Conservatives want in return for some jobs in government'; yet almost two thirds said they would still have voted for the party if they had known what it would end up doing. At the same time, nearly two thirds thought that 'overall, the government is different and better than would be the case without the Liberal Democrats'. In the focus groups, these people often said (though without being able to give specific examples) that the party had probably had a 'tempering' effect on the Tories or 'softened the blow' of spending cuts.

Like a brand-new car that loses a chunk of its value the moment it is driven off the forecourt, the hitherto untarnished Lib Dems were bound to lose sections of their varied followers as soon as they entered government. This was not simply because whichever of the two main parties they chose to support in coalition, they would automatically upset a swathe of voters who preferred the other one. It was also because so many voted Lib Dem precisely because they did not expect the party to sully itself with office. These people, the research showed, were the most displeased by the decision to enter a Conservative-led coalition, and took a more hostile view of it, and subsequently of the party, than Lib Dem voters as a whole.

More broadly, many Lib Dem supporters noted that the coalition partners, especially Cameron and Clegg, were working together harmoniously. But the harmony troubled them. For those who were uncomfortable with coalition policies, it was hard to discern whether Lib Dems were arguing vociferously behind closed doors, winning the best deal they could and presenting a united front in public, or (as they often suspected) whether they had no real influence – either because they were being ignored or because they were offering little or no resistance.

Still, most Lib Dem voters agreed that the party had shown it was 'prepared to take real responsibility, not just oppose from the sidelines', that it was 'making an important contribution to the government of Britain', and that Lib Dems 'behave more responsibly than most politicians'.

All this presented Lib Dems with a strategic choice. The most sensible option, I suggested, was to build on these perceptions and create a reputation as a grown-up party. Since it would never be able to please everyone, it should choose to address the voters who wanted it to be a serious force. (I also warned that 'it may not be possible for Lib Dems to return to pre-coalition levels of support in time for the next general election', which was, as it turned out, somewhat to understate the case.) The alternative, for which many disgruntled Lib Dem voters yearned, was for the party to show a bit more fighting spirit – and do so publicly – when it came to negotiating with the Tories.

The temptation, I warned, would be for the Lib Dems to try to have it both ways: 'to be both a responsible party of government capable of dealing with harsh realities and uncomfortable truths, and a party of opposition-in-office, always ready to disavow the difficult and the unpopular'.

This tension was played out in glorious technicolor on the question of university tuition fees. In December 2010, only twenty-one Lib Dem MPs kept their unambiguous pledge to vote against any increase; eight abstained and twenty-eight voted in favour, including Clegg, who had himself signed the NUS pledge not to do so just weeks before the election. The dilemma sent the party into turmoil, with Lib Dem ministers openly debating whether or not to support their own government's policy. The reversal dogged the party for the rest of the parliament and became, for many of their former voters, emblematic of the party's political treachery.

Clegg's 2012 apology over this episode was set to music and became one of the social media highlights of the parliament. However, he stressed that he was not saying sorry for the decision to raise the cap on fees, but for making 'a promise we were not absolutely sure we could deliver'. This goes to the heart of the party's travails. It was not that the leadership was (necessarily) making bad decisions as part of the coalition, but that there were no good decisions for it to make. Having simultaneously campaigned as the left-wing alternative to Labour, and the civilised, moderate alternative to Tories, as well as the most obvious choice for those who wanted 'none of the above', the party created contradictory expectations that it could not possibly have met. Entering office did not so much cause the Lib Dems' weakness as expose it.

However, the leadership had to play the hand it had been dealt (or dealt itself). Throughout the coalition, my research found many voters, including Conservatives, saying they were glad Clegg's party was there to keep the lid on the Tories' worst excesses. But few could remember any specific achievements. The pupil premium, for which the party liked to claim credit even though it was also in the 2010 Conservative manifesto, went largely unnoticed. Free school meals for younger primary school children, whether they needed them or not, was popular among some voters (specifically, parents of younger primary school children). Raising the income tax threshold also went down well, but few saw it as a distinctively Lib Dem initiative. The two major legislative issues on which the party spent much of its negotiating capital were a referendum on the Alternative Vote and proposals to reform the House of Lords. Not only had voters long forgotten both by the time of the 2015 election, they had barely noticed them at the time.

Having lost half their 24 per cent 2010 vote share within four months of the election, the Lib Dems began to drift more gently down in the polls, flat-lining at around 10 per cent for the next three years. By early 2014, the party seemed to have concluded that the answer was a 'differentiation strategy' aimed at distancing itself from the Tories. Nick Clegg raised the prospect of going into coalition with Labour after the election, saying he had observed Ed Miliband becoming more open to the possibility while the Conservatives had become more ideological in office. Danny Alexander warned in a newspaper article that George Osborne could cut the top rate of tax to 40p only 'over my dead body'. Schools Minister David Laws let it be known that he was furious with Michael Gove for removing Baroness Morgan as head of Ofsted. At the party's spring conference, Nick Clegg told his activists to ask on the doorsteps: 'Do you really think the Tories will make Britain fairer?'

Lord Oakeshott, who subsequently left the party after a botched coup attempt against the leader, described this as the 'enemy within' strategy. Rather than agitate from within government, he advised the Lib Dems to leave the coalition six months to a year before the election to allow the party to reassert its independence.

In the event, and in defiance of many people's expectations on both sides, the coalition lasted its full term and (at least as far as the outside world was concerned) with very little further discord. We will never know, but I strongly doubted that provoking public rows with government colleagues, let alone flouncing out altogether, would bring much of an upturn in the Lib Dems' fortunes. My 2013 research into the party's predicament, provocatively but not entirely facetiously titled *What Are the Liberal Democrats For?*, asked how Clegg should set about reassembling his fragmented coalition of support. I concluded that the differentiation and divorce strategies would be unlikely to do the trick with the two groups of defectors it would be intended to impress.

For 'none of the above' voters, the Lib Dems had made themselves very much 'one of the above' as soon as they entered government. These supporters had gone and were not coming back. But what about former supporters who would rather have seen the party in coalition with Labour? This group of voters identified with the Lib Dems and thought they had the luxury of voting against Gordon Brown without helping to elect a Conservative government. Imagine their surprise and delight when Clegg walked into Downing Street with Cameron. By 2015, as far as they were concerned, the Lib Dems were the party that had propped up a Tory PM and nodded through austerity. Whether they had taken the edge off an administration that would have been even worse but for their presence was neither here nor there. They did not intend to make the same mistake twice. They would prefer to hear that in a future hung parliament the Lib Dems would only be prepared to deal with Labour – something the party could surely not promise without alienating other existing and potential supporters, and which was certainly impossible for Clegg.

As their dwindling national poll share showed no signs of recovery, Lib Dems pinned ever more hope on local factors. The party's victory in the 2013 Eastleigh by-election had given it reason to believe that where it was strong on the ground, particularly with an established local government presence, it could defy the national trend. The Lib Dems' private polling confirmed this view. In early 2015 they released a series of constituency surveys, on the basis of which they claimed to be on course to hold enough seats to play a part in another coalition. I had my doubts about this research. Not only did the surveys name local candidates – a controversial if defensible practice –

they began by asking the interviewee whether they had a favourable view of the local MP and his or her opponents, before moving on to voting intention. I thought this approach put too much emphasis on the local MP's reputation, which, I argued, was just one of the many things people consider when deciding where to place their cross.

In my own constituency polls, I asked two questions: the standard 'Which party would you vote for in an election tomorrow?', plus a further question asking the respondent to think particularly about 'your own constituency and the candidates likely to stand there'. The idea was to find out whether these local factors, including the identity of the MP, were having a real impact, but without skewing the result. The Lib Dems always did better in the second question than the first, in many cases taking the lead in seats where the standard question alone would have had them behind. Indeed, my polls found Lib Dems doing much better in their own seats than national polls would imply. Of the forty-five Lib Dem seats I surveyed in the year before the election, on the basis of the localised voting intention question I found them behind in just twenty-six. Yet on the day, they held on to just two of this selection. Of course, the polls were snapshots not predictions, but the consistency of the pattern suggests that even the reminder of local circumstances may have been enough to over-egg the incumbency factor on which Lib Dems so heavily relied. This time, local hero status was trumped by views of the Lib Dems as a whole, its place in the bigger picture and the choice at hand.

At his 2015 manifesto launch, Clegg declared that his party would 'add a heart to a Conservative government and a brain to a Labour one'. But by then, even those who took a benign view of the party did not think it had what it took to be a big influence at national level. (When undecided voters in my focus groups were asked what animal Clegg reminded them of, the answer was 'the Chihuahua in David Cameron's handbag'.) The voters delivered their verdict accordingly, and what remains of the party is left to wonder where it all went wrong. The Lib Dems could probably have used their brief slice of power to greater effect. Possibly, they could have tempted back some on their disaffected left, albeit by destroying such reputation as they had for being a responsible party of government.

Ultimately, however, the party's problems did not stem from its decision to join the coalition, or from what it did in office, but from what it did to get there. In opposition, it had been all things to all voters: an impossible trick to sustain in government. The story of the party's fate is a parable that shows political opportunism will catch up with you in the end.

Clegg did the right thing by joining the coalition. He knew the decision would take a toll on his party, but also that turning down power would prove that a vote for the Lib Dems would be a vote wasted – as well as denying the country the stable government it needed. He conducted himself with dignity and fortitude through what must have been a trying five years. For what it's worth, if I lived in Sheffield Hallam I would probably have voted to keep him in the House of Commons. Whether he is glad still to be there is another question.

IV: UKIP: WHOSE ARMY?

At the 2010 general election, the United Kingdom Independence Party won 3.1 per cent of the vote. Within two years it had pulled level in the polls with the Liberal Democrats, and by the autumn of 2012 was regularly scoring into double figures, with four or even five times the share it had won at the ballot box. UKIP came second in two parliamentary by-elections, in Rotherham and Middlesbrough, prompting Nigel Farage to declare that his party was 'the new third force in British politics'.

Polls showed UKIP's support was coming disproportionately from former Tories. More than one in ten of those who voted Conservative at the election now said they would back UKIP. The data behind my research paper *They're Thinking What We're Thinking: Understanding the UKIP Temptation*, based on a poll of 20,000 people, showed that half of all those saying they would consider voting UKIP had backed the Tories in 2010.

The 'UKIP threat' and how to counter it became something of an obsession for many Conservatives. It was clear that it would not simply be a question of taking a tougher stance on immigration and Europe, not least because lurching to the right would come at a cost. As my *Project Blueprint* research had found, there were as many potential Conservatives who had voted Lib Dem at the general election as there were 2010 Tories who now said they would vote UKIP. Equally, putting more emphasis on these issues risked playing into UKIP's hands by shifting the debate onto their chosen territory.

More importantly, UKIP's appeal related more to its general outlook than any specific policy. It was true that those who were drawn to the party were more preoccupied than most with immigration, and would complain about issues such as Britain's contribution to the EU or the international aid budget. But their overarching view was that Britain was changing for the worse. They were pessimistic, even fearful, and did not think mainstream politicians were willing or able to keep their promises or change things for the better. As I noted in my paper:

> [Their complaints] are often part of a greater dissatisfaction with the way they see things going in Britain: schools, they say, can't hold nativity plays or harvest festivals any more; you can't fly a flag of St George any more; you can't call Christmas Christmas any more; you won't be promoted in the police force unless you're from a minority; you can't wear an England shirt on the bus; you won't get social housing unless you're an immigrant; you can't speak up about these things because you'll be called a racist; you can't even smack your children. All of these examples, real and imagined, were mentioned in focus groups by UKIP voters and considerers to make the point that the mainstream political parties are so in thrall to the prevailing culture of political correctness that they have ceased to represent the silent majority.

Despite the party's founding purpose, and indeed its name, little more than a quarter of those saying they were considering voting UKIP put resolving Britain's future relations with the EU among the top three issues facing the country. Only 7 per cent said it was the single most important issue. Economic growth and jobs, welfare reform, immigration and the deficit were all more important to them.

That being the case, I argued, whatever the merits of a referendum on Britain's membership of the EU, which many Conservatives were demanding, nobody should expect such a move to scupper UKIP. And so it didn't. David Cameron's speech promising an in/out referendum took place in January 2013. At this time, UKIP was battling with the Lib Dems for third place in the polls, with both scoring around 10 per cent. By the spring, UKIP had moved ahead, regularly recording poll shares in the mid- or even high teens. In the 2013 local elections, UKIP won 23 per cent of the vote, nine points ahead of the Lib Dems and just two points behind the Conservatives.

One hundred and forty-seven UKIP councillors were elected, 139 of them gains. Four months after Cameron's referendum promise, Nigel Farage declared that UKIP had taken the 'first substantial step to being a party that can credibly win seats at Westminster'.

For its potential supporters, the biggest attraction to UKIP was that the party would 'say things that need to be said but others are scared to say'. Analysis of my large-scale poll found that the biggest predictor of whether a voter would consider UKIP was agreement that the party is 'on the side of people like me'. This set the context for their views about immigration, which they often expounded at length.

Many complained that migrants from within the EU and outside had changed the character of their local area beyond recognition. Recession and austerity brought their complaints into sharper focus and heightened their resentment: they themselves worked long hours for stagnant incomes as the cost of living rose, and had in many cases lost out on tax credits or other benefits; immigrants, meanwhile, seemed to them to be entitled to extra financial help and priority access to public services, as well as depressing wages for people like themselves.

My 2013 paper *Small Island: Public Opinion and the Politics of Immigration* found that more than nine in ten of those who said they would vote UKIP in an election tomorrow thought that immigration had brought more disadvantages than advantages to Britain. By far their biggest concern was the idea of immigrants 'claiming benefits and using public services when they have contributed nothing in return'. More than half said they or someone in their family had found it harder to get work or were paid less because of competition from immigrants, and that the character of their local area had changed for the worse in recent years because of the scale of immigration. More than one third claimed someone in their family had been 'denied access to housing or other public services because priority seems to be given to immigrants'. In each case these proportions were higher than they were among other parties' supporters.

Few thought things would get any better with undiluted majority Tory government. Only one in three UKIP supporters thought Britain 'would have a firmer policy on immigration, with smaller numbers entering the country than is the case today' if the Conservatives were in government alone; most thought the policy would be much the same. However, this did not reflect discontent with the Conservative Party specifically so much as politics generally, and the ability of governments to achieve what they want. The controversial Home Office ad vans bearing the legend 'In the UK illegally? Go home or face arrest' were a case in point. My research found that of all voters, UKIP supporters were the most strongly in favour of this initiative. They were also the least likely to think it would work.

UKIP supporters' views on immigration were part of a wider pattern of pessimism and insecurity, and often a feeling of exclusion. They were generally less likely than most to be optimistic about the economy over the next few years and, crucially, less inclined to think they would gain personally if things did improve. At the end of 2013, in my research for the fourth phase of *Project Blueprint*, I found most voters saying either that they were feeling some of the benefits of an economic recovery or, more often, that they were not feeling them yet but expected to do so at some point. However, UKIP voters were more pessimistic. The majority said they were not experiencing the benefit of any recovery and did not expect to do so.

If these things mattered more than Europe to potential UKIP supporters, that is not to say they regarded the EU with anything other than hostility. The European Parliament elections of 2014 provided the ideal opportunity to 'give Europe a slap', as someone who took part in my research put it. Indeed, many voters regarded this event as something closer to the Eurovision Song Contest than a proper election (to quote another focus group participant), and took the chance to give the government *nul points* at the same time. UKIP triumphed with 27 per cent of the vote and twenty-four MEPs – the first time for more than a century that neither Labour nor the Conservatives had won a national election.

Westminster by-elections also provided a string of opportunities for UKIP to capitalise on mid-term discontent with politics in general and the government in particular. The party equalled its performances in Rotherham and Middlesbrough with second places in Eastleigh, South Shields, Wythenshawe and Sale East, Newark and Heywood and Middleton, before breaking through with victories in Clacton in October 2014 and Rochester and Strood the following month.

The question for UKIP therefore became one of converting mid-term local, Euro and by-election support into general election votes. My research suggested this would not be easy. After the Eastleigh by-election I found

83 per cent of those who had voted UKIP saying they had done so to 'send a message that I'm unhappy with the party I usually support nationally', and three quarters wanting to register that they were 'unhappy with all the main parties at the moment'. In a poll of 4,000 people who had voted in the European elections, I found eight in ten of those who had backed UKIP saying the party had the best policies on Europe, but six in ten also saying they were expressing discontent with their usual party or making a general protest. Only half said they expected to stay with the party at the general election; one in five said they would probably vote Conservative; most of the rest said they did not know what they would do. In Clacton and Rochester, the single biggest reasons for voting UKIP were that they thought the party had the best local candidate – the sitting MPs Douglas Carswell and Mark Reckless respectively – but a majority of UKIP supporters in both seats also said they were recording their dissatisfaction with established parties. In the Rochester poll, I also asked people how they expected to vote in the general election; even then, the Conservatives had the edge, and duly won the seat back on 7 May 2015.

In early 2015, it started to become clear that UKIP was going to struggle to match its successes of the previous year. In my campaign focus groups, people usually said they were glad UKIP was around to ensure a hearing for issues that the other parties might prefer to ignore. But the downside, which we heard again and again from January until the election, was that the party seemed to have nothing to say about anything other than Europe and, especially, immigration. This alone put them outside consideration in an election to choose a government, even for most of those who liked much of what they had to say.

The fact that a series of UKIP candidates and councillors were recorded making what were sometimes quite breathtakingly offensive remarks led some to suspect that the party's common-sense exterior hid a more sinister underlying agenda, or at least some rather unsavoury individuals. Most did not think this applied to Nigel Farage himself, who was generally regarded as entertaining and straight-talking, even if he did seem to thrive in the limelight and to enjoy generating the controversy that intensified it. But some were not so sure about his good intentions, often citing his remarks that he had felt uncomfortable when foreign languages had been more prevalent than English on trains from London to Kent, and that someone would be right to be concerned if a group of Romanian men moved in next door. The question of whether Farage was benign or belligerent was illustrated further in the groups when people were asked to think of the leaders in different ways. If he were an animal he would be a peacock or a weasel; if a car, a Ford Capri with tinted windows or a four-by-four with illegal bull-bars; if a cartoon character, Andy Capp or Cruella de Vil.

My campaign focus groups were also revealing on how voters saw the party more generally. If UKIP were a house, it would have 'a wrought-iron fence all round to keep everyone out'. The ageing residents would spend their time 'talking about how things were in their day' and would not get on with their neighbours 'because they are a different colour'. The timer on the stereo would be set to play the national anthem every day at noon.

In the Ashcroft National Poll at the beginning of the campaign proper, I found UKIP in the lead when it came to articulating 'things that need to be said that other parties are scared to say'. However, doubts remained over whether the party was 'reasonable and sensible'. Fewer than one in five thought UKIP was 'competent and capable'. In my final pre-election survey, I found 33 per cent saying they would like to see the party have a major say in the event of a hung parliament, compared to 48 per cent for the Greens and 54 per cent for the Lib Dems.

Between the autumn of its by-election victories and the general election, UKIP's poll share drifted down from the high teens to an average of 13 per cent, which is exactly the vote share the party received at the general election. Others can decide whether this merits Nigel Farage's description of his party as the 'People's Army', but my post-vote poll at least tells us what, on the day, the army looked like. Thirty-seven per cent of those who voted UKIP in 2015 had voted Conservative in 2010; 12 per cent had voted Labour and 16 per cent had voted Lib Dem. More than half said they had not felt any benefits from an economic recovery and did not expect to, compared to 36 per cent of voters overall and just 11 per cent of Tories. Fifty-five per cent of UKIP voters were men, a higher proportion than in any other party's coalition of voters. Twenty-seven per cent were in social group DE, compared to 24 per cent of Labour voters and 19 per cent of voters as a whole. More than six in ten had ended their formal education at secondary school, more than was the case for any other party.

Unlike Labour voters, most of those who voted UKIP agreed that 'if you work hard, it is possible to be successful in Britain today no matter what your background'. But seven in ten said that for most children growing up in Britain today, life would be worse than it was for their parents; nine in ten said changes in society over the last few years had been mostly for the worse; and seven in ten said that overall, life in Britain was worse today than it was thirty years ago (their rate of agreement with these last two statements was higher than in any other political or demographic group).

Nigel Farage and his party made themselves part of the story of the 2015 election. But the established parties know they were partially responsible for UKIP's rise. Many Labour voters felt abandoned by their party's apparent refusal, over an extended period, to take seriously the issues about which they were concerned, including immigration. When some Conservative voters looked to UKIP because they felt left behind by the Tories' (necessary) modernisation, they felt their old party's response was to abuse rather than reassure them. And the Lib Dems provided large numbers of recruits by virtue of joining the government and ruling themselves out as the premier party of perpetual opposition.

Ultimately, UKIP was unable to convince a sufficient number of voters that it represented a worthwhile vote when the government of the country was at stake. It seemed to have little to say outside its preoccupation with Europe and immigration – a point which mattered particularly now that voters had become used to the idea that a smaller party could end up in government. My research consistently found that potential Tory–UKIP defectors overwhelmingly preferred David Cameron to Ed Miliband as Prime Minister, and that their preferred election result was a Conservative government. The question was whether they would believe it mattered if they got one or not. On the day, many of them decided it did.

It would be wrong, though, to say that UKIP's 3.9 million voters wanted only to make an empty protest. As one of our focus group participants put it, it was not just about getting UKIP into government, but about 'getting them seats and a voice. They can build on that.' They certainly have an opportunity to do so. Though the party won only one seat, it came second in 120. It won more than a quarter of the vote in thirteen, and more than 30 per cent in six. Having become the third party in England and Wales, UKIP could learn the secret of the Lib Dems' (albeit abruptly terminated) success by establishing themselves as a local force. This is a matter of consistent campaigning and, above all, organisation, which Farage himself would admit has never been the party's strongest suit.

Labour's identity crisis and the near extinction of the Lib Dems present UKIP with an opportunity. To prosper, the party needs to be disciplined and professional, and to be known more for what it is for than for what it is against. To that extent, UKIP's future is in its own hands.

V – 2020 VISION

On the day of the general election, I surveyed over 12,000 people after they had voted. Their answers reveal stark differences between the respective coalitions of voters assembled by the Conservatives and Labour.

Thirty-eight per cent of men voted Conservative, as did 37 per cent of women. One third of Conservative voters were aged 65 or over, and more than half were aged 55 or above. Nearly half of Tory voters were from social group AB, compared to 40 per cent of voters overall. More than eight in ten owned their own home, and more than half owned it outright without a mortgage. Two thirds of those still employed worked in the private sector.

Three in ten men voted Labour, as did one third of women. Nearly a quarter of Labour voters were from social group DE, and just over six in ten owned their own home. Of those still in employment, nearly four in ten Labour voters worked in the public sector. David Cameron's much vaunted 'gender problem' turned out to be that he was more popular among men than Ed Miliband – or, at worst, that Miliband was less unpopular among women than among men.

The Conservatives won 30 per cent of the vote or less among voters in social groups C2DE; those aged 18 to 44; those in Scotland, Wales and the north of England; and members of ethnic minorities. Labour won fewer than three in ten votes among ABC1s, those aged 45 and above, white voters, and voters in Scotland and the south of England.

More telling than the demographics and voting histories of each party's supporters are their differences in attitude. For Conservatives, the three most important issues facing the country were getting the economy growing and creating jobs, cutting the deficit and the debt, and controlling immigration; for Labour voters they were improving the NHS, creating jobs and growth, and tackling the cost of living. When it came to issues for 'you and your family', both chose the NHS and jobs and growth, but Tories, unlike Labour voters, were as likely to mention the deficit as they were to choose living costs.

Nearly nine in ten Conservative voters, compared to less than half of Labour voters, said either that they were already feeling some of the benefits of economic recovery, or that they were expecting to at some point. Eighty-four per cent of Tories agreed that austerity and cuts to government spending would need to continue over the next five years; fewer than one in five Labour voters accepted the need for further public spending restraint.

Voters who said that trusting their party's motives and values had been the most important factor in their voting decision were evenly divided between the Tories and Labour. But those who said they had voted because their party's leader would make the best Prime Minister, and those who said they were choosing the most competent government, went for the Conservatives by margins of more than fifty points.

Conservative and Labour voters had very different attitudes to the role of the state, or what they expected from government. Three quarters of Conservatives thought that 'if some people earn a great deal of money through their own ability and hard work, that is a good thing and they should be allowed to enjoy it', while three quarters of Labour voters thought 'the government should do more to ensure that wealth in Britain is shared out more equally by imposing much higher taxes on those with the highest incomes'. More than seven in ten Labour voters thought 'people have a right to things like decent housing, healthcare, education and enough to live on, and the government should make sure everyone has them', but more than three quarters of Conservatives thought 'people are too ready to talk about their rights – they have a responsibility to provide for themselves and should not expect the government to do so for them'.

Conservatives tended to think life in Britain was good, and characterised by opportunity; Labour voters disagreed. Seven in ten Tories thought that 'overall, life in Britain today is better than it was thirty years ago'. Most Labour voters thought life in Britain today was worse. While a majority of Conservative voters agreed that 'if you work hard it is possible to be very successful in Britain no matter what your background', most Labour voters thought that 'in Britain today, people from some backgrounds will never have a chance to be successful no matter how hard they work'.

Moreover, Conservatives were optimistic about the future, both for themselves and for the country; again, Labour voters were not. Two thirds of Tories thought that 'the way society and the economy are changing will bring more opportunities for me to improve my standard of living than threats to it'. Three quarters of Labour voters thought these changes meant 'there will be more threats to my standard of living in future than opportunities to improve it'. Most Conservatives thought that 'for most children growing up in Britain today, life will be better than it was for their parents'. Two thirds of Labour voters thought it would be worse.

Not surprisingly, Conservative voters were more likely than Labour to have a positive view of globalisation and, especially, capitalism, which fewer than three in ten Labour voters thought had been a force for good. But while most Labour voters had a favourable view of multiculturalism, social liberalism, feminism and the green movement, only a minority of Tories agreed in each case – indeed, the Tories won less than a third of the vote among people who believed these things to have been a force for good. Nearly half of Labour voters thought immigration had on balance been a good thing; fewer than three in ten Conservatives said the same.

These portraits of the kinds of people each party did or did not attract, and what they thought, offer a good starting point for thinking about where the parties are at the beginning of the new parliament, and where they need to be at the end.

First, Labour. In *Project Red Alert*, my 2012 analysis of Labour's electoral challenge, I concluded that unless Ed Miliband managed to reassure wavering potential supporters that he would be responsible with the economy and the public finances, he would risk relying on 'a precarious coalition of the disaffected and the dependent' who wanted austerity ended or even reversed.

As the details above show, this is more or less what happened. In some respects Labour ended the parliament as little more than a party of protest; unfortunately, they were not the only one. The outlook of Labour voters was in some respects strikingly similar to that of UKIP supporters. In both groups, just over half said they did not expect to benefit from any economic recovery. They were equally likely to agree that for most children growing up in Britain today life would be worse than it was for their parents, and that the way the economy and society were changing would bring more threats than opportunities. Indeed, Labour voters were notably less likely than UKIP voters to think that people who work hard can be successful in Britain whatever their background. It is not surprising, or at all discreditable, that the Labour Party should have won the votes of people who were finding life hard and feared for the future; the problem was its failure to attract very many others. Optimists voted Conservative.

Analysis by Labour MPs Gloria de Piero and Jon Ashworth found that the party lost support among suburban professionals and families with young children, and did no better among people on modest incomes in small towns and housing estates. My own post-vote poll showed that Labour won only 31 per cent of C2 skilled manual workers, four points behind the Tories and down from 50 per cent in 1997. Overall, Labour's vote fell for an unprecedented fourth general election in a row.

As so often, the party could have learned something from Tony Blair, the only Labour leader to win a general election since 1974. He observed in his memoir, *A Journey*, that progressive parties needed to understand that once people were 'on the ladder of opportunity, they didn't want more state help; they wanted choice, freedom to earn more and spend it…I wanted Labour people to be ambitious and compassionate at the same time, and feel neither guilty about the first nor anxious about the second'. The 2015 Labour campaign, with its heavy focus on the minimum wage, zero-hour contracts and the NHS, lacked that balance. Labour spoke proudly of the 4 million conversations its activists would hold on the doorsteps of Britain, but all the conversations were about the same thing.

The other mistake that Blair would not have made was to risk losing an election because people feared a Labour government would be profligate with the public finances. Indeed, he went out of his way to reassure people every day on Labour's perennial weaknesses, even when he was twenty points ahead in the polls. The same applies to the doubts people had in recent years about Labour's tepid enthusiasm for (or outright opposition to) welfare reform and firmer immigration controls, however overzealous the Tories might sometimes have appeared on the former or how disappointing their delivery on the latter.

Labour succeeds when it combines its traditional virtues of compassion and fairness with competence and responsibility, and when it not only understands but supports and encourages the desire of ordinary people – including those who are already comfortable – to maintain and improve their standard of living. Convincingly redefining itself in such a way will be a huge task for the Labour Party. In doing so, it needs to start from scratch. After its 2010 defeat, Labour thought it needed to win an argument about the past in order to establish credibility for the present and the future. But trying to 'nail the lie' that the previous government had been in any way responsible for Britain's deficit, let alone the wider economic situation, was as ineffective as the Tories' post-1997 reminders of the 'golden economic legacy' bequeathed by the Major government to New Labour. In both cases, the vanquished party was telling the voters they had made a mistake. It is not an argument that can ever be won: the electorate does not hold out the right of appeal against its verdict. It is extremely hard for a party to concede and move on, but that is what Labour must do now. Harder still, it must do so with sincerity.

The mammoth task facing Labour will no doubt bring extra comfort and joy to a victorious Conservative Party. The Tories have good reason to be pleased with themselves. Having gained ninety-seven seats in 2010, they picked up a further twenty-four, as well as half a million extra voters, in 2015. They have won an election against the odds, and feel, with some justification, that their campaign and their record in office have been vindicated. But just as I have been keen in the past to help ensure the wrong lessons are not learned from disappointment, it is just as important not to draw the wrong conclusions from success.

Having been a senior figure in the Conservative campaign team of 1992, Cameron himself recalls more clearly than most the sweetness of unexpected triumph. He also knows what happened next. Having amassed 14 million votes in defiance of the polls, many Tories came to believe that there was a formidable and enduring (if taciturn) bloc of Conservative voters who shared their values. This conviction persisted despite the evident withering of support during that parliament; it even remained an article of faith for some that the Tories were somehow more in tune with the people after the people had elected New Labour.

Though the Conservatives have been liberated from coalition with the Liberal Democrats, they have not been altogether liberated from coalition politics. Avoiding a re-run of the mid-1990s will require them to understand the coalition of voters that has elected this administration, and just as crucially, to remember that this coalition of voters cannot be taken for granted. The same groups will not necessarily come together in the same way again. The evidence from my post-vote poll is that Conservative voters in 2015 valued competence and leadership. The economy was their priority but they were by no means indifferent to public services. They wanted the government to continue with its economic plan, from which they expected to benefit if they had not done so already. They accepted the need for further austerity (or, perhaps, were in a position where they could afford to be sanguine about it). They were positive and optimistic about Britain and their own prospects. At the same time, they did not share some of the social attitudes that most non-Tories took for granted.

Keeping this coalition together means that the government must first and foremost do the job it was elected to do: to deliver, as the Conservative manifesto put it, 'strong leadership; a clear economic plan; a brighter, more secure future'. That is the job the Conservatives have the mandate to finish. Naturally, the economy will not be the only item on the agenda. The EU referendum, to choose only the most obvious example, could easily dominate proceedings. It is a vital question and the debate will be vigorous; negotiations with other member states will inevitably absorb much government energy, and much of the Prime Minister's own time. But perceived priorities matter. Tories must bear in mind that the whole issue of Europe fascinates them to a much greater degree than it does the voters. While the referendum will inevitably divide the party, they must at all costs keep it civil. What did wavering 1992 voters who plumped for John Major's promise of opportunity for all and feared Labour's 'double whammy' think when, a year later, the Conservative Party tore itself to shreds over the Maastricht Treaty? And what would happen if the coalition of voters that elected the Tories in 2015, expecting competence and leadership and steady progress on the economy, were treated to a repeat performance?

The Conservatives also need to consider that at the next election the electorate will be different, and in 2025 it will be different still. According to my post-vote poll, nearly three in ten ethnic minority voters supported the Tories, compared to just 16 per cent in 2010. This development is not irreversible and further progress is certainly not guaranteed. As I found in my major 2012 research paper *Degrees of Separation: Ethnic Minority Voters and the Conservative Party*, suspicions about the Tories in minority communities run deep, and those who gave the party the benefit of the doubt in 2015 could easily think again if their reservations are realised or if they judge that Labour has earned back their allegiance.

Similarly, the Tories should build on the parts of their voting coalition that go with the grain of modern Britain. For them to win in the future, that coalition will need to expand, not just consolidate. Growing by seeking out those who are, for example, suspicious of multiculturalism, feminism and social liberalism (as are a disproportionately large share of current Conservative voters) would be misconceived, since it would simply mean taking a larger share of a shrinking market.

The biggest mistake the Conservative Party could make about the 2015 result would be to conclude that its old brand problem – the long-running perception that Tories are more concerned about the rich than they are about ordinary people – has disappeared. *Minority Verdict*, my account of the 2010 election, explained how these perceptions were at the heart of the party's failure to win an outright majority, and, as I found in *Project Blueprint*, the Tories were no more regarded as standing for fairness or being 'on the side of people like me' at the end of the parliament than they were at the beginning.

But if the Conservatives won, does that matter? Yes, it does, for two reasons. First, an election is a choice, not a referendum. In 2015, the contrast between the parties in competence and leadership, and perhaps the possibility of a minority Miliband government beholden to the SNP, outweighed questions of character and motive. But the Tories cannot rely on that being the case next time, let alone every time. Labour will not always be as hopeless as it seems right now, and people still think the party's heart is in the right place. As the 1992 saga reminds us, a complacent Conservative Party will always be vulnerable to a Labour leader who knows what he or she is doing.

Secondly, it is clear that these doubts about values are a barrier many people still have to overcome before they will vote Conservative. It may be that people were shy about admitting that they planned to do so, or that they avoided taking part in surveys so they wouldn't have to. If that is the case, rather than making the dangerous assumption that Conservative support is always higher than it looks in the polls, the Tories should ask what these people thought they had to be shy about.

The Conservative majority gives the party an unexpected opportunity to connect with those who still think the Tories are not for people like them. There will be plenty of tests, too, like remaining focused on voters' priorities, conducting the EU referendum debate in a civilised manner, and going about welfare reform and further spending cuts in a way that does not seem gratuitous. Cameron began on the right note the morning after the election, promising on the steps of No. 10 to govern 'as a party of one nation, one United Kingdom', and to ensure the recovery 'reaches all parts of our country, from north to south, east to west'.

This, then, is the race to 2020. Can the Labour Party reach beyond its core support into the moderate, comfortable, quietly ambitious mainstream that propelled it into office less than twenty years ago? And can the Conservative Party stay focused on what matters, hold together its winning coalition and become an appealing proposition for the voters of the future?

To put it another way, can Labour embrace aspiration, competence and responsibility faster than the Conservatives can come to terms with the twenty-first century?

ABOUT THE AUTHORS

LORD ASHCROFT KCMG PC is an international businessman, philanthropist, author and pollster. He was deputy chairman of the Conservative Party and is treasurer of the International Democratic Union. He is founder and chairman of the board of trustees of Crimestoppers, vice-patron of the Intelligence Corps Museum, chairman of the trustees of Ashcroft Technology Academy, chancellor of Anglia Ruskin University and a trustee of Imperial War Museums.

ISABEL OAKESHOTT is an award-winning political journalist and commentator. She is political editor at large on the *Daily Mail*. She was political editor of the *Sunday Times* and co-wrote *Farmageddon* with Philip Lymbery and *Inside Out* with Peter Watt.

www.lordashcroft.com / www.lordashcroftpolls.com
www.lordashcroftmedals.com / @LordAshcroft

LIST OF ILLUSTRATIONS

P. 6
Top left: Rob McMillan / Rex
Top right: Desmond O'Neill Features
Middle: Daily Mail / Rex Shutterstock
Bottom: Matthew Lloyd / Getty Images

P. 7
Top: Barry Clack
Bottom: Barry Clack

P. 8
Top: Barry Clack
Bottom left: Dafydd Jones
Bottom right: Rex Shutterstock

PLATE SECTION 2

P. I
Top left: Andrew Parsons / Press Association
Top right: David Hartley
Bottom left: Andrew Parsons / Press Association
Bottom right: Martin Rickett / Press Association

P. 2
Top: Abdullah Rehman
Middle left (with Rebekah Brooks): Dafydd Jones
Middle right: Barry Clack
Bottom: National Pictures

P. 3
Top: Roger Taylor / Rex Shutterstock
Middle: AFP / Getty Images
Bottom left: Mark Sutherland / SWNS
Bottom right: Tillen / Dove

P. 4
Top: Rex Shutterstock
Middle left: Rex Shutterstock
Middle right: Racingfotos.com / Rex Shutterstock
Bottom: Steve Back / Rex Shutterstock

LIST OF ILLUSTRATIONS

P. 5
Top: Postlethwaite / Rex Shutterstock
Middle left: Rex Shutterstock
Middle right: Stefan Rousseau / Press Association
Bottom: Christopher Furlong / Getty Images

P. 6
Top: PR handout
Middle: Emily Sheffield
Bottom: David Parker

P. 7
Top: David Hartley
Bottom: Dafydd Jones

P. 8
Top: Andrew Milligan / Getty Images
Middle: Toby Melville / Press Association
Bottom: Chris Jackson / Getty Images

INDEX